JAVA^{TM} PROGRAMMING

SEVENTH EDITION

JAVA^{TM} PROGRAMMING

JOYCE FARRELL

COURSE TECHNOLOGY
CENGAGE Learning®

Australia • Brazil • Japan • Korea • Mexico • Singapore • Spain • United Kingdom • United States

COURSE TECHNOLOGY
CENGAGE Learning·

Java Programming,
Seventh Edition
Joyce Farrell

Executive Editor:
Kathleen McMahon

Senior Product Manager:
Alyssa Pratt

Development Editor: Dan Seiter

Editorial Assistant: Sarah Ryan

Brand Manager: Kay Stefanski

Print Buyer: Julio Esperas

Art and Design Direction,
Production Management, and
Composition: Integra Software
Services Pvt. Ltd.

Cover Designer: Lisa Kuhn/Curio
Press, LLC www.curiopress.com

Cover Photo: © Leigh Prather/Veer

Copyeditor: Mark Goodin

Proofreader: Pamela Hunt

Indexer: Alexandra Nickerson

For product information and technology assistance, contact us at
Cengage Learning Customer & Sales Support, 1-800-354-9706

For permission to use material from this text or product,
submit all requests online at **www.cengage.com/permissions.**
Further permissions questions can be emailed to
permissionrequest@cengage.com.

Library of Congress Control Number: 2012953690

Student Edition:

ISBN-13: 978-1-285-08195-3
ISBN-10: 1-285-08195-1

Course Technology
20 Channel Center Street
Boston, MA 02210
USA

Cengage Learning is a leading provider of customized learning solutions with office locations around the globe, including Singapore, the United Kingdom, Australia, Mexico, Brazil and Japan. Locate your local office at **international.cengage.com/region**

Cengage Learning products are represented in Canada by Nelson Education, Ltd.

For your course and learning solutions, visit
www.cengage.com.

Purchase any of our products at your local college store
or at our preferred online store: **www.CengageBrain.com.**

Instructors: Please visit **login.cengage.com** and log in to access instructor-specific resources.

Printed in the United States of America
1 2 3 4 5 6 18 17 16 15 14 13

Brief Contents

Contents

CHAPTER 2   **Using Data** **51**

x

CHAPTER 10

Introduction to Inheritance 499

CHAPTER 13 **File Input and Output** **675**

Preface

Java Programming, Seventh Edition, provides the beginning programmer with a guide to developing applications using the Java programming language. Java is popular among professional programmers because it can be used to build visually interesting graphical user interface (GUI) and Web-based applications. Java also provides an excellent environment for the beginning programmer—a student can quickly build useful programs while learning the basics of structured and object-oriented programming techniques.

This textbook assumes that you have little or no programming experience. This book provides a solid background in good object-oriented programming techniques and introduces terminology using clear, familiar language. The writing is nontechnical and emphasizes good programming practices. The programming examples are business examples; they do not assume a mathematical background beyond high-school business math. In addition, the examples illustrate only one or two major points; they do not contain so many features that you become lost following irrelevant and extraneous details. The explanations in this textbook are written clearly in straightforward sentences, making it easier for native and non-native English speakers alike to master the programming concepts. Complete, working programs appear frequently in each chapter; these examples help students make the transition from the theoretical to the practical. The code presented in each chapter can also be downloaded from the publisher's Web site, so students can easily run the programs and experiment with changes to them.

The student using *Java Programming, Seventh Edition,* builds applications from the bottom up rather than starting with existing objects. This facilitates a deeper understanding of the concepts used in object-oriented programming and engenders appreciation for the existing objects students use as their knowledge of the language advances. When students complete this book, they will know how to modify and create simple Java programs, and they will have the tools to create more complex examples. They also will have a fundamental knowledge of object-oriented programming, which will serve them well in advanced Java courses or in studying other object-oriented languages such as C++, C#, and Visual Basic.

Organization and Coverage

Java Programming, Seventh Edition, presents Java programming concepts, enforcing good style, logical thinking, and the object-oriented paradigm. Objects are covered right from the beginning, earlier than in many other textbooks. You create your first Java program in Chapter 1. Chapters 2, 3, and 4 increase your understanding of how data, classes, objects, and methods interact in an object-oriented environment.

Chapters 5 and 6 explore input and repetition structures, which are the backbone of programming logic and essential to creating useful programs in any language. You learn the special considerations of string and array manipulation in Chapters 7, 8, and 9.

Chapters 10, 11, and 12 thoroughly cover inheritance and exception handling. Inheritance is the object-oriented concept that allows you to develop new objects quickly by adapting the features of existing objects; exception handling is the object-oriented approach to handling errors. Both are important concepts in object-oriented design. Chapter 13 provides information on handling files so you can permanently store and retrieve program output.

Chapters 14 and 15 introduce GUI Swing components—Java's visually pleasing, user-friendly widgets—and their layout managers. Chapters 16 and 17 show you ways to provide interactive excitement using graphics, applets, images, and sound.

Features

The following features are new for the Seventh Edition:

- **YOU DO IT:** In each chapter, step-by-step exercises help students create multiple working programs that emphasize the logic a programmer uses in choosing statements to include. These sections provide a means for students to achieve success on their own—even those in online or distance learning classes. Previous editions of the book contained a long, multipart "You Do It" section at the end of each chapter, but in this edition, more and shorter sections follow important chapter topics so the student can focus on one new concept at a time.

- **CASES:** Each chapter contains two running case problems. These cases represent projects that continue to grow throughout a semester using concepts learned in each new chapter. Two cases allow instructors to assign different cases in alternate semesters or to divide students in a class into two case teams.

- **PROGRAMMING EXERCISES:** Each chapter concludes with meaningful programming exercises that provide additional practice of the skills and concepts learned in the chapter. These exercises vary in difficulty and are designed to allow exploration of logical programming concepts. Each chapter contains several new programming exercises not seen in previous editions.

- **INCREASED EMPHASIS ON STUDENT RESEARCH:** In this edition, the student frequently is directed to the Java Web site to investigate classes and methods. Computer languages evolve, and programming professionals must understand how to find the latest language improvements. This book encourages independent research.

Additionally, *Java Programming, Seventh Edition,* includes the following features:

- **OBJECTIVES:** Each chapter begins with a list of objectives so you know the topics that will be presented in the chapter. In addition to providing a quick reference to topics covered, this feature provides a useful study aid.

- **NOTES:** These highlighted tips provide additional information—for example, an alternative method of performing a procedure, another term for a concept, background information on a technique, or a common error to avoid.

- **FIGURES:** Each chapter contains many figures. Code figures are most frequently 25 lines or fewer, illustrating one concept at a time. Frequent screen shots show exactly how program output appears. Callouts appear where needed to emphasize a point.

- **COLOR:** The code figures in each chapter contain all Java keywords in blue. This helps students identify keywords more easily, distinguishing them from programmer-selected names.

- **FILES:** More than 200 student files can be downloaded from the publisher's Web site. Most files contain the code presented in the figures in each chapter; students can run the code for themselves, view the output, and make changes to the code to observe the effects. Other files include debugging exercises that help students improve their programming skills.

- **TWO TRUTHS AND A LIE:** A short quiz reviews each chapter section, with answers provided. This quiz contains three statements based on the preceding section of text—two statements are true and one is false. Over the years, students have requested answers to problems, but we have hesitated to distribute them in case instructors want to use problems as assignments or test questions. These true-false quizzes provide students with immediate feedback as they read, without "giving away" answers to the multiple-choice questions and programming exercises.

- **DON'T DO IT:** This section at the end of each chapter summarizes common mistakes and pitfalls that plague new programmers while learning the current topic.

- **KEY TERMS:** Each chapter includes a list of newly introduced vocabulary, shown in the order of appearance in the text. The list of key terms provides a short review of the major concepts in the chapter.

- **SUMMARIES:** Following each chapter is a summary that recaps the programming concepts and techniques covered in the chapter. This feature provides a concise means for students to check their understanding of the main points in each chapter.

- **REVIEW QUESTIONS:** Each chapter includes 20 multiple-choice questions that serve as a review of chapter topics.

- **GAME ZONE:** Each chapter provides one or more exercises in which students create interactive games using the programming techniques learned up to that point; 70 game programs are suggested in the book. The games are fun to create and play; writing them motivates students to master the necessary programming techniques. Students might exchange completed game programs with each other, suggesting improvements and discovering alternate ways to accomplish tasks.

- **GLOSSARY:** A glossary contains definitions for all key terms in the book, presented in alphabetical order.

- **APPENDICES:** This edition includes useful appendices on working with the Java platform, data representation, formatting output, generating random numbers, and creating Javadoc comments.

- **QUALITY:** Every program example, exercise, and game solution was tested by the author and then tested again by a quality assurance team using Java Standard Edition (SE) 7, the most recent version available.

CourseMate

The more you study, the better the results. Make the most of your study time by accessing everything you need to succeed in one place. Read your textbook, take notes, review flashcards, watch videos, and take practice quizzes online. CourseMate goes beyond the book to deliver what you need! Learn more at *www.cengage.com/coursemate*.

The *Java Programming* CourseMate includes:

- **Debugging Exercises:** Four error-filled programs accompany each chapter. By debugging these programs, students can gain expertise in program logic in general and the Java programming language in particular.

- **Video Lessons:** Each chapter is accompanied by at least three video lessons that help to explain important chapter concepts. These videos were created and narrated by the author.

- **Interactive Study Aids:** An interactive eBook, quizzes, flashcards, and more!

Instructors may add CourseMate to the textbook package, or students may purchase CourseMate directly at *www.CengageBrain.com*.

Instructor Resources

The following teaching tools are available for download at our Instructor Companion Site. Simply search for this text at *login.cengage.com*. An instructor login is required.

- **Electronic Instructor's Manual:** The Instructor's Manual that accompanies this textbook includes additional instructional material to assist in class preparation, including items such as Overviews, Chapter Objectives, Teaching Tips, Quick Quizzes, Class Discussion Topics, Additional Projects, Additional Resources, and Key Terms. A sample syllabus is also available. Additional exercises in the Instructor's Manual include:

  o **Tough Questions:** Two or more fairly difficult questions that an applicant might encounter in a technical job interview accompany each chapter. These questions are often open-ended; some involve coding and others might involve research.

  o **Up for Discussion:** A few thought-provoking questions concerning programming in general or Java in particular supplement each chapter. The questions can be used to start classroom or online discussions, or to develop and encourage research, writing, and language skills.

- ○ **Programming exercises and solutions:** Each chapter is accompanied by several programming exercises to supplement those offered in the text. Instructors can use these exercises as additional or alternate assignments, or as the basis for lectures.

- **ExamView:** This textbook is accompanied by ExamView, a powerful testing software package that allows instructors to create and administer printed, computer (LAN-based), and Internet-based exams. ExamView includes hundreds of questions that correspond to the topics covered in this text, enabling students to generate detailed study guides that include page references for further review. The computer-based and Internet testing components allow students to take exams at their computers, and they save the instructor time by grading each exam automatically. These test banks are also available in Blackboard-compatible formats.

- **PowerPoint Presentations:** This text provides PowerPoint slides to accompany each chapter. Slides may be used to guide classroom presentations, to make available to students for chapter review, or to print as classroom handouts. Files are provided for every figure in the text. Instructors may use the files to customize PowerPoint slides, illustrate quizzes, or create handouts.

- **Solutions:** Solutions to "You Do It" exercises and all end-of-chapter exercises are available. Annotated solutions are provided for some of the multiple-choice Review Questions. For example, if students are likely to debate answer choices or not understand the choice deemed to be the correct one, a rationale is provided.

Acknowledgements

I would like to thank all of the people who helped to make this book a reality, including Dan Seiter, Development Editor; Alyssa Pratt, Senior Product Manager; Sreejith Govindan, Content Project Manager; and Chris Scriver and Serge Palladino, Quality Assurance Testers. I am lucky to work with these professionals who are dedicated to producing high-quality instructional materials.

I am also grateful to the reviewers who provided comments and encouragement during this book's development, including Lee Cottrell, Bradford School, Pittsburgh; Irene Edge, Kent State University; Susan Peterson, Henry Ford Community College; and Jackie Turner, Central Georgia Technical College.

Thanks, too, to my husband, Geoff, for his constant support and encouragement. Finally, this book is dedicated to Ruth LaFreniere, who brought us Stella, and Bob LaFreniere, who let her.

Joyce Farrell

Read This Before You Begin

The following information will help you as you prepare to use this textbook.

To the User of the Data Files

To complete the steps and projects in this book, you need data files that have been created specifically for this book. Your instructor will provide the data files to you. You also can obtain the files electronically from *www.CengageBrain.com*. Find the ISBN of your title on the back cover of your book, then enter the ISBN in the search box at the top of the Cengage Brain home page. You can find the data files on the product page that opens. Note that you can use a computer in your school lab or your own computer to complete the exercises in this book.

Using Your Own Computer

To use your own computer to complete the steps and exercises, you need the following:

- **Software:** Java SE 7, available from *www.oracle.com/technetwork/java/index.html*. Although almost all of the examples in this book will work with earlier versions of Java, this book was created using Java 7. The book clearly points out the few cases when an example is based on Java 7 and will not work with earlier versions of Java. You also need a text editor, such as Notepad. A few exercises ask you to use a browser, such as Internet Explorer.

- **Hardware:** If you are using Windows 7, the Java Web site suggests at least 128 MB of memory and at least 98 MB of disk space. For other operating system requirements, see *http://java.com/en/download/help*.

Features

This text focuses on helping students become better programmers and understand Java program development through a variety of key features. In addition to chapter Objectives, Summaries, and Key Terms, these useful features will help students regardless of their learning styles.

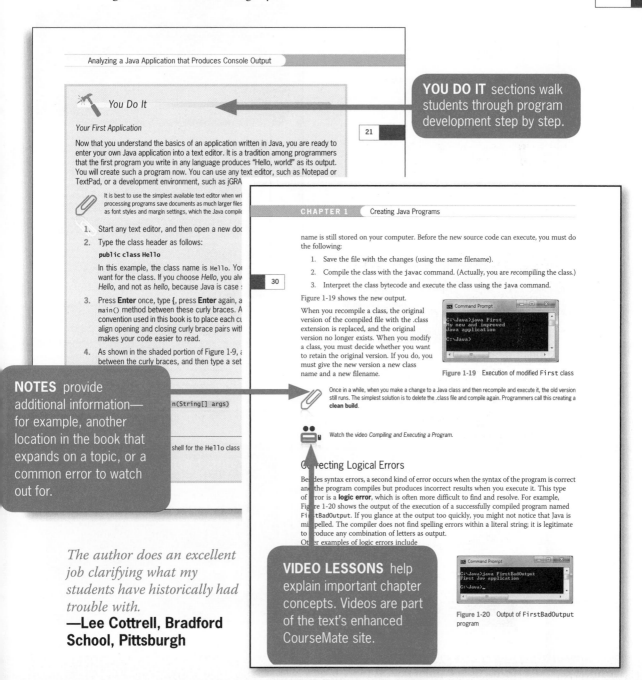

Analyzing a Java Application that Produces Console Output

You Do It

Your First Application

Now that you understand the basics of an application written in Java, you are ready to enter your own Java application into a text editor. It is a tradition among programmers that the first program you write in any language produces "Hello, world!" as its output. You will create such a program now. You can use any text editor, such as Notepad or TextPad, or a development environment, such as jGRA

It is best to use the simplest available text editor when wri processing programs save documents as much larger files as font styles and margin settings, which the Java compile

1. Start any text editor, and then open a new doc

2. Type the class header as follows:

   public class Hello

   In this example, the class name is Hello. Yo want for the class. If you choose *Hello*, you alw *Hello*, and not as *hello*, because Java is case s

3. Press **Enter** once, type {, press **Enter** again, a main() method between these curly braces. A convention used in this book is to place each cu align opening and closing curly brace pairs with makes your code easier to read.

4. As shown in the shaded portion of Figure 1-9, a between the curly braces, and then type a set

   n(String[] args)

   shell for the Hello class

YOU DO IT sections walk students through program development step by step.

21

CHAPTER 1 Creating Java Programs

name is still stored on your computer. Before the new source code can execute, you must do the following:

1. Save the file with the changes (using the same filename).

2. Compile the class with the javac command. (Actually, you are *re*compiling the class.)

3. Interpret the class bytecode and execute the class using the java command.

Figure 1-19 shows the new output.

When you recompile a class, the original version of the compiled file with the .class extension is replaced, and the original version no longer exists. When you modify a class, you must decide whether you want to retain the original version. If you do, you must give the new version a new class name and a new filename.

Figure 1-19 Execution of modified First class

Once in a while, when you make a change to a Java class and then recompile and execute it, the old version still runs. The simplest solution is to delete the .class file and compile again. Programmers call this creating a **clean build**.

Watch the video *Compiling and Executing a Program.*

Correcting Logical Errors

Besides syntax errors, a second kind of error occurs when the syntax of the program is correct and the program compiles but produces incorrect results when you execute it. This type of error is a **logic error**, which is often more difficult to find and resolve. For example, Figure 1-20 shows the output of the execution of a successfully compiled program named FirstBadOutput. If you glance at the output too quickly, you might not notice that Java is misspelled. The compiler does not find spelling errors within a literal string; it is legitimate to produce any combination of letters as output. Other examples of logic errors include

Figure 1-20 Output of FirstBadOutput program

30

NOTES provide additional information— for example, another location in the book that expands on a topic, or a common error to watch out for.

The author does an excellent job clarifying what my students have historically had trouble with.
—Lee Cottrell, Bradford School, Pittsburgh

VIDEO LESSONS help explain important chapter concepts. Videos are part of the text's enhanced CourseMate site.

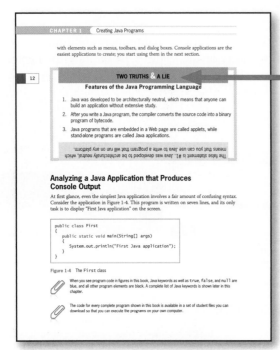

TWO TRUTHS & A LIE quizzes appear after each chapter section, with answers provided. The quiz contains three statements based on the preceding section of text—two statements are true and one is false. Answers give immediate feedback without "giving away" answers to the multiple-choice questions and programming problems later in the chapter. Students also have the option to take these quizzes electronically through the enhanced CourseMate site.

CHAPTER 1   Creating Java Programs

with elements such as menus, toolbars, and dialog boxes. Console applications are the easiest applications to create; you start using them in the next section.

12

TWO TRUTHS & A LIE

Features of the Java Programming Language

1. Java was developed to be architecturally neutral, which means that anyone can build an application without extensive study.

2. After you write a Java program, the compiler converts the source code into a binary program of bytecode.

3. Java programs that are embedded in a Web page are called applets, while stand-alone programs are called Java applications.

The false statement is #1. Java was developed to be architecturally neutral, which means that you can use Java to write a program that will run on any platform.

Analyzing a Java Application that Produces Console Output

At first glance, even the simplest Java application involves a fair amount of confusing syntax. Consider the application in Figure 1-4. This program is written on seven lines, and its only task is to display "First Java application" on the screen.

```
public class First
{
    public static void main(String[] args)
    {
        System.out.println("First Java application");
    }
}
```

Figure 1-4   The First class

When you see program code in figures in this book, Java keywords as well as true, false, and null are blue, and all other program elements are black. A complete list of Java keywords is shown later in this chapter.

The code for every complete program shown in this book is available in a set of student files you can download so that you can execute the programs on your own computer.

7. Save, compile, and execute the program. Now, the fractional portion of the result is omitted again. That's because the result of sum / 2 is calculated first, and the result is an integer. Then the whole-number result is cast to a double and assigned to a double—but the fractional part of the answer was already lost and casting is too late. Remove the newly added parentheses, save the program, compile it, and execute it again to confirm that the fractional part of the answer is reinstated.

104

8. As an alternative to the explicit cast in the division statement in the ArithmeticDemo program, you could write the average calculation as follows:

    average = sum / 2.0;

    In this calculation, when the integer sum is divided by the double constant 2.0, the result is a double. The result then does not require any cast to be assigned to the double average without loss of data. Try this in your program.

9. Go to the Java Web site (www.oracle.com/technetwork/java/index.html), select **Java APIs**, and then select **Java SE 7**. Scroll through the list of **All Classes**, and select **PrintStream**, which is the data type for the out object used with the println() method. Scroll down to view the list of methods in the Method Summary. As you did in a previous exercise, notice the many versions of the print() and println() methods, including ones that accept a String, an int, and a long. Notice, however, that no versions accept a byte or a short. That's because when a byte or short is sent to the print() or println() method, it is automatically promoted to an int, so that version of the method is used.

Don't Do It

- Don't mispronounce "integer." People who are unfamiliar with the term often say "interger," inserting an extra r.

- Don't attempt to assign a literal constant floating-point number, such as 2.5, to a float without following the constant with an uppercase or lowercase F. By default, constant floating-point values are doubles.

- Don't try to use a Java keyword as an identifier for a variable or constant. Table 1-1 in Chapter 1 contains a list of Java keywords.

- Don't attempt to assign a constant value under –2,147,483,648 or over +2,147,483,647 to a long variable without following the constant with an uppercase or lowercase L. By default, constant integers are ints, and a value under –2,147,483,648 or over 2,147,483,647 is too large to be an int.

- Don't assume that you must divide numbers as a step to determining a remainder; the remainder operator (%) is all that's needed.

DON'T DO IT sections at the end of each chapter list advice for avoiding common programming errors.

Using the Scanner Class to Accept Keyboard Input

It is legal to write a single prompt that requests multiple input values—for example, "Please enter your age, area code, and zip code." The user could then enter the three values separated with spaces, tabs, or Enter key presses. The values would then be interpreted as separate tokens and could be retrieved with three separate nextInt() method calls. However, asking a user to enter multiple values often leads to mistakes. This book will follow the practice of using a separate prompt for each input value required.

79

Pitfall: Using nextLine() Following One of the Other Scanner Input Methods

You can encounter a problem when you use one of the numeric Scanner class retrieval methods or the next() method before you use the nextLine() method. Consider the program in Figure 2-19. It is identical to the one in Figure 2-17, except that the user is asked for an age before being asked for a name. (See shading.) Figure 2-20 shows a typical execution.

```
import java.util.Scanner;
public class GetUserInfo2
{
    public static void main(String[] args)
    {
        String name;
        int age;
        Scanner inputDevice = new Scanner(System.in);
        System.out.print("Please enter your age >> ");
        age = inputDevice.nextInt();
        System.out.print("Please enter your name >> ");
        name = inputDevice.nextLine();
        System.out.println("Your name is " + name +
            " and you are " + age + " years old.");
    }
}
```

Don't Do It
If you accept numeric input prior to string input, the string input is ignored unless you take special action.

Figure 2-19   The GetUserInfo2 class

Figure 2-20   Typical execution of the GetUserInfo2 program

THE DON'T DO IT ICON illustrates how NOT to do something—for example, having a dead code path in a program. This icon provides a visual jolt to the student, emphasizing that particular figures are NOT to be emulated and making students more careful to recognize problems in existing code.

Assessment

I find the flow of information superior to [that of] other texts.

**—Susan Peterson,
Henry Ford Community College**

PROGRAMMING EXERCISES provide opportunities to practice concepts. These exercises increase in difficulty and allow students to explore each major programming concept presented in the chapter. Additional programming exercises are available in the Instructor's Resource Kit.

Review Questions

Review Questions

1. A sequence of characters enclosed within double quotation marks is a _____.
   a. symbolic string
   b. literal string
   c. prompt
   d. command

385

2. To create a `String` object, you can use the keyword _____ before the constructor call, but you are not required to use this format.
   a. object
   b. create
   c. char
   d. new

3. A `String` variable name is a _____.
   a. reference
   b. value
   c. constan
   d. literal

4. The term that programmers use to describe objects th changed is _____.
   a. irrevocable
   b. nonvolatile
   c. immuta
   d. stable

5. Suppose that you declare two `String` objects as:
   ```
   String word1 = new String("happy");
   String word2;
   ```
   When you ask a user to enter a value for word2, if the u: of word1 == word2 is _____.
   a. true
   b. false
   c. illegal
   d. unknov

6. If you declare two `String` objects as:
   ```
   String word1 = new String("happy");
   String word2 = new String("happy");
   ```
   the value of word1.equals(word2) is _____.
   a. true
   b. false
   c. illegal
   d. unknov

7. The method that determines whether two `String` obje regardless of case, is _____.
   a. equalsNoCase()
   b. toUpperCase()
   c. equals:
   d. equals

Exercises

Programming Exercises

1. Write an application containing an array of 10 `String` values, and display them in ascending order. Save the file as **SortStrings.java**.

2. a. The mean of a list of numbers is its arithmetic average. The median of a list is its middle value when the values are placed in order. For example, if a list contains 1, 4, 7, 8, and 10, then the mean is 6 and the median is 7. Write an application that allows you to enter five integers and displays the values, their mean, and their median. Save the file as **MeanMedian.java**.

   b. Revise the `MeanMedian` class so that the user can enter any number of values up to 20. If the list has an even number of values, the median is the numeric average of the values in the two middle positions. Save the file as **MeanMedian2.java**.

3. a. Radio station JAVA wants a class to keep track of recordings it plays. Create a class named `Recording` that contains fields to hold methods for setting and getting a `Recording`'s title, artist, and playing time in seconds. Save the file as **Recording.java**.

   b. Write an application that instantiates five `Recording` objects and prompts the user for values for the data fields. Then prompt the user to enter which field the `Recording`s should be sorted by—song title, artist, or playing time. Perform the requested sort procedure, and display the `Recording` objects. Save the file as **RecordingSort.java**.

4. In Chapter 8, you created a `Salesperson` class with fields for an ID number and sales values. Now, create an application that allows a user to enter values for an array of seven `Salesperson` objects. Offer the user the choice of displaying the objects in order by either ID number or sales value. Save the application as **SalespersonSort.java**.

5. In Chapter 8, you created a `Salesperson` class with fields for an ID number and sales values. Now, create an application that allows you to store an array that acts as a database of any number of `Salesperson` objects up to 20. While the user decides to continue, offer three options: to add a record to the database, to delete a record from the database, or to change a record in the database. Then proceed as follows:

   - If the user selects the add option, issue an error message if the database is full. Otherwise, prompt the user for an ID number. If the ID number already exists in the database, issue an error message. Otherwise, prompt the user for a sales value, and add the new record to the database.

492

REVIEW QUESTIONS test udent comprehension of the ajor ideas and techniques resented. Twenty questions llow each chapter.

xxx

DEBUGGING EXERCISES are included with each chapter because examining programs critically and closely is a crucial programming skill. Students can download these exercises at *www.CengageBrain.com* and through the CourseMate available for this text. These files are also available to instructors through *login.cengage.com*.

176

After reading the chapter *Making Decisions*, you will be able to have the game determine the higher card. For now, just observe how the card values change as you execute the program multiple times. Save the application as **PickTwoCards.java**.

 You use the Math.random() function to generate a random number. The function call uses only a class and method name—no object—so you know the random() method must be a static method.

2. Computer games often contain different characters or creatures. For example, you might design a game in which alien beings possess specific characteristics such as color, number of eyes, or number of lives. Design a character for a game, creating a class to hold at least three attributes for the character. Include methods to get and set each of the character's attributes. Save the file as **MyCharacter.java**. Then write an application in which you create at least two characters. In turn, pass each character to a display method that displays the character's attributes. Save the application as **TwoCharacters.java**.

 Case Problems

1. a. Carly's Catering provides meals for parties and special events. In Chapter 2, you wrote an application that prompts the user for the number of guests attending an event, displays the company motto with a border, and then displays the price of the event and whether the event is a large one. Now modify the program so that the main() method contains only three executable statements that each call a method as follows:

   • The first executable statement calls a public static int method that prompts the user for the number of guests and returns the value to the main() method.

   • The second executable statement calls a public static void displays the company motto with the border.

   • The last executable statement passes the number of guests static void method that computes the price of the event price, and displays whether the event is a large event.

   Save the file as **CarlysEventPriceWithMethods.java**.

   b. Create a class to hold Event data for Carly's Catering. The cla

   • Two public final static fields that hold the price per gue cutoff value for a large event (50 guests)

   • Three private fields that hold an event number, number of event, and the price. The event number is stored as a Strin plans to assign event numbers such as *M312*.

CASE PROBLEMS provide opportunities to build more detailed programs that continue to incorporate increasing functionality throughout the book.

---

b. Create a class named TestPainting whose main() method declares three Painting items. Create a method that prompts the user for and accepts values for two of the Painting objects, and leave the third with the default values supplied by the constructor. Then display each completed object. Finally, display a message that explains the gallery commission rate. Save the application as **TestPainting.java**.

175

 Debugging Exercises

1. Each of the following files saved in the Chapter03 folder in your downloadable student files has syntax and/or logic errors. In each case, determine and fix the problem. After you correct the errors, save each file using the same filename preceded with *Fix*. For example, DebugThree1.java will become FixDebugThree1.java.

   a. DebugThree1.java
   b. DebugThree2.java
   c. DebugThree3.java
   d. DebugThree4.java

When you change a filename, remember to change every instance of the class name within the file so that it matches the new filename. In Java, the filename and class name must always match.

 Game Zone

1. ying cards are used in many computer games, including versions of such classics solitaire, hearts, and poker. Design a Card class that contains a character data field to hold a suit (*s* for spades, *h* for hearts, *d* for diamonds, or *c* for clubs) and an integer data field for a value from 1 to 13. (When you learn more about string handling in the chapter *Characters, Strings, and the StringBuilder*, you can modify the class to hold words for the suits, such as *spades* or *hearts*, as well as words for some of the values—for example, *ace* or *king*.) Include get and set methods for each field. Save the class as **Card.java**.

Write an application that randomly selects two playing cards and displays their values. Simply assign a suit to each of the cards, but generate a random number for each card's value. Appendix D contains information on generating random numbers. To fully understand the process, you must learn more about Java classes and methods. However, for now, you can copy the following statements to generate a random number between 1 and 13 and assign it to a variable:

```
final int CARDS_IN_SUIT = 13;
myValue = ((int)(Math.random() * 100) % CARDS_IN_SUIT + 1);
```

GAME ZONE EXERCISES are included at the end of each chapter. Students can create games as an additional entertaining way to understand key programming concepts.

Creating Java Programs

In this chapter, you will:

◎ Define basic programming terminology

◎ Compare procedural and object-oriented programming

◎ Describe the features of the Java programming language

◎ Analyze a Java application that produces console output

◎ Compile a Java class and correct syntax errors

◎ Run a Java application and correct logical errors

◎ Add comments to a Java class

◎ Create a Java application that produces GUI output

◎ Find help

Learning Programming Terminology

A **computer program** is a set of instructions that you write to tell a computer what to do. Computer equipment, such as a monitor or keyboard, is **hardware**, and programs are **software**. A program that performs a task for a user (such as calculating and producing paychecks, word processing, or playing a game) is **application software**; a program that manages the computer itself (such as Windows or Linux) is **system software**. The **logic** behind any computer program, whether it is an application or system program, determines the exact order of instructions needed to produce desired results. Much of this book describes how to develop the logic to create application software.

All computer programs ultimately are converted to machine language. **Machine language**, or **machine code**, is the most basic set of instructions that a computer can execute. Each type of processor has its own set of machine language instructions. Programmers often describe machine language using 1s and 0s to represent the on-and-off circuitry of computer systems.

Machine language is a **low-level programming language**, or one that corresponds closely to a computer processor's circuitry. Low-level languages require you to use memory addresses for specific machines when you create commands. This means that low-level languages are difficult to use and must be customized for every type of machine on which a program runs.

Fortunately, programming has evolved into an easier task because of the development of high-level programming languages. A **high-level programming language** allows you to use a vocabulary of reasonable terms, such as *read*, *write*, or *add*, instead of the sequences of 1s and 0s that perform these tasks. High-level languages also allow you to assign single-word, intuitive names to areas of computer memory, such as hoursWorked or rateOfPay, rather than having to remember the memory locations. Java is a high-level programming language.

Each high-level language has its own **syntax**, or rules of the language. For example, depending on the specific high-level language, you might use the verb *print* or *write* to produce output. All languages have a specific, limited vocabulary (the language's **keywords**) and a specific set of rules for using that vocabulary. When you are learning a computer programming language, such as Java, C++, or Visual Basic, you really are learning the vocabulary and syntax rules for that language.

Using a programming language, programmers write a series of **program statements**, similar to English sentences, to carry out the tasks they want the program to perform. Program statements are also known as **commands** because they are orders to the computer, such as "output this word" or "add these two numbers."

After the program statements are written, high-level language programmers use a computer program called a **compiler** or **interpreter** to translate their language statements into machine language. A compiler translates an entire program before carrying out the statement, or **executing** it, whereas an interpreter translates one program statement at a time, executing a statement as soon as it is translated.

Whether you use a compiler or interpreter often depends on the programming language you use. For example, C++ is a compiled language, and Visual Basic is an interpreted language. Each type of translator has its supporters; programs written in compiled languages execute more quickly, whereas programs written in interpreted languages are easier to develop and debug. Java uses the best of both technologies: a compiler to translate your programming statements and an interpreter to read the compiled code line by line when the program executes (also called **at run time**).

Compilers and interpreters issue one or more error messages each time they encounter an invalid program statement—that is, a statement containing a **syntax error**, or misuse of the language. Subsequently, the programmer can correct the error and attempt another translation by compiling or interpreting the program again. Locating and repairing all syntax errors is the first part of the process of **debugging** a program—freeing the program of all errors. Figure 1-1 illustrates the steps a programmer takes while developing an executable program. You will learn more about debugging Java programs later in this chapter.

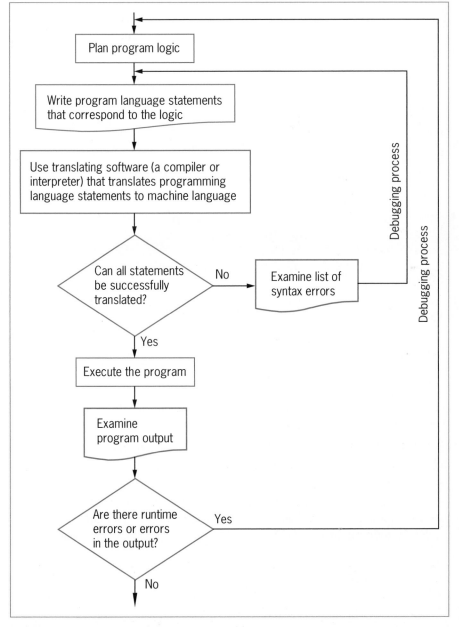

Figure 1-1 The program development process

4

As Figure 1-1 shows, you might be able to use a computer language's syntax correctly but still have errors to correct. In addition to learning the correct syntax for a particular language, a programmer must also understand computer programming logic. When you develop a program of any significant size, you should plan its logic before you write any program statements. Correct logic requires that all the right commands be issued in the appropriate order. Examples of logical errors include multiplying two values when you meant to divide them or producing output prior to obtaining the appropriate input.

Correcting logical errors is the second part of the debugging process and is much more difficult than correcting syntax errors. Syntax errors are discovered when you compile a program, but often you can identify logical errors only when you examine a program's first output. For example, if you know an employee's paycheck should contain the value $5,000, but you see that it holds $50 or $50,000 after you execute a payroll program, a logical error has occurred. Tools that help you visualize and understand logic are presented in the chapter *Making Decisions.*

Programmers call some logical errors **semantic errors**. For example, if you misspell a programming-language word, you commit a syntax error, but if you use a correct word in the wrong context, you commit a semantic error.

TWO TRUTHS & A LIE

Learning Programming Terminology

In each "Two Truths & a Lie" section, two of the numbered statements are true, and one is false. Identify the false statement and explain why it is false.

1. Unlike a low-level programming language, a high-level programming language allows you to use a vocabulary of reasonable terms instead of the sequences of on and off switches that perform the corresponding tasks.

2. A compiler executes each program statement as soon as it is translated, whereas an interpreter translates all of a program's statements before executing any.

3. A syntax error occurs when you misuse a language; locating and repairing all syntax errors is part of the process of debugging a program.

The false statement is #2. A compiler translates an entire program before carrying out any statements, whereas an interpreter translates one program statement at a time, executing a statement as soon as it is translated.

Comparing Procedural and Object-Oriented Programming Concepts

Two popular approaches to writing computer programs are procedural programming and object-oriented programming.

Procedural Programming

Procedural programming is a style of programming in which operations are executed one after another in sequence. In procedural applications, you create names for computer memory locations that can hold values—for example, numbers and text—in electronic form. The named computer memory locations are called **variables** because they hold values that might vary. For example, a payroll program written for a company might contain a variable named rateOfPay. The memory location referenced by the name rateOfPay might contain different values (a different value for every employee of the company) at different times. During the execution of the payroll program, each value stored under the name rateOfPay might have many operations performed on it—the value might be read from an input device, the value might be multiplied by another variable representing hours worked, and the value might be printed on paper. For convenience, the individual operations used in a computer program are often grouped into logical units called **procedures**. For example, a series of four or five comparisons and calculations that together determine a person's federal withholding tax value might be grouped as a procedure named calculateFederalWithholding. A procedural program defines the variable memory locations and then calls a series of procedures to input, manipulate, and output the values stored in those locations. When a program **calls a procedure**, the current logic is temporarily abandoned so that the procedure's commands can execute. A single procedural program often contains hundreds of variables and procedure calls. Procedures are also called *modules*, *methods*, *functions*, and *subroutines*. Users of different programming languages tend to use different terms. As you will learn later in this chapter, Java programmers most frequently use the term *method*.

Object-Oriented Programming

Object-oriented programming is an extension of procedural programming in which you take a slightly different approach to writing computer programs. Writing **object-oriented programs** involves creating classes, which are blueprints for objects; creating objects from those classes; and creating applications that use those objects. After creation, classes can be reused repeatedly to develop new programs. Thinking in an object-oriented manner involves envisioning program components as objects that belong to classes and that are similar to concrete objects in the real world; then, you can manipulate the objects and have them interrelate with each other to achieve a desired result.

Programmers use *OO* as an abbreviation for *object-oriented*; it is pronounced "oh oh." Object-oriented programming is abbreviated *OOP*, and pronounced to rhyme with *soup*.

Originally, object-oriented programming was used most frequently for two major types of applications:

- **Computer simulations**, which attempt to mimic real-world activities so that their processes can be improved or so that users can better understand how the real-world processes operate

- **Graphical user interfaces**, or **GUIs** (pronounced "gooeys"), which allow users to interact with a program in a graphical environment

Thinking about objects in these two types of applications makes sense. For example, a city might want to develop a program that simulates traffic patterns to help prevent traffic tie-ups. By creating a model with objects such as cars and pedestrians that contain their own data and rules for behavior, the simulation can be set in motion. For example, each car object has a specific current speed and a procedure for changing that speed. By creating a model of city traffic using objects, a computer can create a simulation of a real city at rush hour.

Creating a GUI environment for users also is a natural use for object orientation. It is easy to think of the components a user manipulates on a computer screen, such as buttons and scroll bars, as similar to real-world objects. Each GUI object contains data—for example, a button on a screen has a specific size and color. Each object also contains behaviors—for example, each button can be clicked and reacts in a specific way when clicked. Some people consider the term *object-oriented programming* to be synonymous with GUI programming, but object-oriented programming means more. Although many GUI programs are object oriented, do not assume that all object-oriented programs use GUI objects. Modern businesses use object-oriented design techniques when developing all sorts of business applications, whether they are GUI applications or not.

Understanding object-oriented programming requires grasping three basic concepts:

- Encapsulation as it applies to classes as objects

- Inheritance

- Polymorphism

Understanding Classes, Objects, and Encapsulation

In object-oriented terminology, a **class** is a term that describes a group or collection of objects with common properties. In the same way that a blueprint exists before any houses are built from it, and a recipe exists before any cookies are baked from it, so does a class definition exist before any objects are created from it. A **class definition** describes what attributes its objects will have and what those objects will be able to do. **Attributes** are the characteristics that define an object; they are **properties** of the object. When you learn a programming language such as Java, you learn to work with two types of classes: those that have already been developed by the language's creators and your own new, customized classes.

An **object** is a specific, concrete **instance** of a class. When you create an object, you **instantiate** it. You can create objects from classes that you write and from classes written by other programmers, including Java's creators. The values contained in an object's properties often differentiate instances of the same class from one another. For example, the class `Automobile` describes what `Automobile` objects are like. Some properties of the `Automobile` class are make, model, year, and color. Each `Automobile` object possesses the same attributes but not, of course, the same values for those attributes. One `Automobile` might be a 2009 white Ford Taurus and another might be a 2014 red Chevrolet Camaro. Similarly, your dog has the properties of all `Dogs`, including a breed, name, age, and whether his shots are current. The values of the properties of an object are also referred to as the object's **state**. In other words, you can think of objects as roughly equivalent to nouns, and of their attributes as similar to adjectives that describe the nouns.

When you understand an object's class, you understand the characteristics of the object. If your friend purchases an `Automobile`, you know it has a model name, and if your friend gets a `Dog`, you know the dog has a breed. Knowing what attributes exist for classes allows you to ask appropriate questions about the states or values of those attributes. For example, you might ask how many miles the car gets per gallon, but you would not ask whether the car has had shots. Similarly, in a GUI operating environment, you expect each component to have specific, consistent attributes and methods, such as a window having a title bar and a close button, because each component gains these properties as a member of the general class of GUI components. Figure 1-2 shows the relationship of some `Dog` objects to the `Dog` class.

 By convention, programmers using Java begin their class names with an uppercase letter. Thus, the class that defines the attributes and methods of an automobile would probably be named `Automobile`, and the class for dogs would probably be named `Dog`. However, following this convention is not required to produce a workable program.

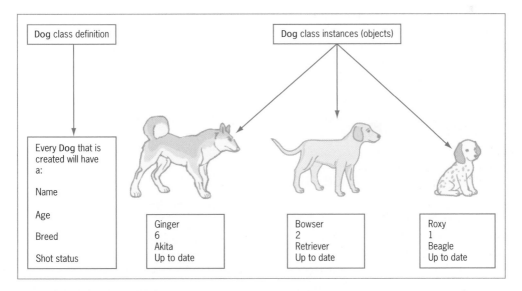

Figure 1-2 A class definition and some objects created from it

Besides defining properties, classes define methods their objects can use. A **method** is a self-contained block of program code that carries out some action, similar to a procedure in a procedural program. An Automobile, for example, might have methods for moving forward, moving backward, being filled with gasoline, and being washed. Some methods can ascertain certain attributes, such as the current speed of an Automobile and the status of its gas tank. Similarly, a Dog can walk or run, eat food, and get a bath, and there are methods to determine how hungry the Dog is or what its name is. GUI operating system components can be maximized, minimized, and dragged. In other words, if objects are similar to nouns, then methods are similar to verbs.

In object-oriented classes, attributes and methods are encapsulated into objects that are then used much like real-world objects. **Encapsulation** refers to two closely related object-oriented notions:

- Encapsulation is the enclosure of data and methods within an object. Encapsulation allows you to treat all of an object's methods and data as a single entity. Just as an actual dog contains all of its attributes and abilities, so would a program's Dog object.

- Encapsulation also refers to the concealment of an object's data and methods from outside sources. Concealing data is sometimes called *information hiding*, and concealing how methods work is *implementation hiding*; you will learn more about both terms in the chapter *Using Methods, Classes, and Objects*. Encapsulation lets you hide specific object attributes and methods from outside sources and provides the security that keeps data and methods safe from inadvertent changes.

If an object's methods are well written, the user is unaware of the low-level details of how the methods are executed, and the user must simply understand the interface or interaction between the method and the object. For example, if you can fill your Automobile with gasoline, it is because you understand the interface between the gas pump nozzle and the vehicle's gas tank opening. You don't need to understand how the pump works mechanically or where the gas tank is located inside your vehicle. If you can read your speedometer, it does not matter how the displayed figure is calculated. As a matter of fact, if someone produces a superior, more accurate speed-determining device and inserts it in your Automobile, you don't have to know or care how it operates, as long as your interface remains the same. The same principles apply to well-constructed classes used in object-oriented programs—programs that use classes only need to work with interfaces.

Understanding Inheritance and Polymorphism

An important feature of object-oriented program design is **inheritance**—the ability to create classes that share the attributes and methods of existing classes but with more specific features. For example, Automobile is a class, and all Automobile objects share many traits and abilities. Convertible is a class that inherits from the Automobile class; a Convertible is a type of Automobile that has and can do everything a "plain" Automobile does—but with an added mechanism for and an added ability to lower its top. (In turn, Automobile inherits from the Vehicle class.) Convertible is not an object—it is a class. A specific Convertible is an object—for example, my1967BlueMustangConvertible.

Inheritance helps you understand real-world objects. For example, the first time you encounter a `Convertible`, you already understand how the ignition, brakes, door locks, and other `Automobile` systems work. You need to be concerned only with the attributes and methods that are "new" with a `Convertible`. The advantages in programming are the same—you can build new classes based on existing classes and concentrate on the specialized features you are adding.

A final important concept in object-oriented terminology is **polymorphism**. Literally, polymorphism means "many forms"—it describes the feature of languages that allows the same word or symbol to be interpreted correctly in different situations based on the context. For example, although the classes `Automobile`, `Sailboat`, and `Airplane` all inherit from `Vehicle`, `turn` and `stop` methods work differently for instances of those classes. The advantages of polymorphism will become more apparent when you begin to create GUI applications containing features such as windows, buttons, and menu bars. In a GUI application, it is convenient to remember one method name, such as `setColor` or `setHeight` and have it work correctly no matter what type of object you are modifying.

When you see a plus sign (+) between two numbers, you understand they are being added. When you see it carved in a tree between two names, you understand that the names are linked romantically. Because the symbol has diverse meanings based on context, it is polymorphic. Chapters 10 and 11 provide more information about inheritance and polymorphism and how they are implemented in Java.

Watch the video *Object-Oriented Programming*.

TWO TRUTHS & A LIE

Comparing Procedural and Object-Oriented Programming Concepts

1. An instance of a class is a created object that possesses the attributes and methods described in the class definition.

2. Encapsulation protects data by hiding it within an object.

3. Polymorphism is the ability to create classes that share the attributes and methods of existing classes, but with more specific features.

The false statement is #3. Inheritance is the ability to create classes that share the attributes and methods of existing classes but with more specific features; polymorphism describes the ability to use one term to cause multiple actions.

Features of the Java Programming Language

Java was developed by Sun Microsystems as an object-oriented language for general-purpose business applications and for interactive, World Wide Web–based Internet applications. Some of the advantages that have made Java so popular in recent years are its security features and the fact that it is **architecturally neutral**: Unlike other languages, you can use Java to write a program that runs on any operating system (such as Windows, Mac OS, or Linux) or device (such as PCs, phones, and tablet computers).

Java can be run on a wide variety of computers and devices because it does not execute instructions on a computer directly. Instead, Java runs on a hypothetical computer known as the **Java Virtual Machine (JVM)**. When programmers call the JVM *hypothetical*, they don't mean it doesn't exist. Instead, they mean it is not a physical entity created from hardware but is composed only of software.

Figure 1-3 shows the Java environment. Programming statements written in a high-level programming language are **source code**. When you write a Java program, you first construct the source code using a text editor such as Notepad or a development environment and source code editor such as **jGRASP**, which you can download from the Web for free. A **development environment** is a set of tools that help you write programs by providing such features as displaying a language's keywords in color. The statements are saved in a file; then, the Java compiler converts the source code into a binary program of **bytecode**. A program called the **Java interpreter** then checks the bytecode and communicates with the operating system, executing the bytecode instructions line by line within the Java Virtual Machine. Because the Java program is isolated from the operating system, the Java program also is insulated from the particular hardware on which it is run. Because of this insulation, the JVM provides security against intruders accessing your computer's hardware through the operating system. Therefore, Java is more secure than other languages. Another advantage provided by the JVM means less work for programmers—when using other programming languages, software vendors usually have to produce multiple versions of the same product (a Windows version, Macintosh version, UNIX version, Linux version, and so on) so all users can run the program. With Java, one program version runs on all these platforms. **"Write once, run anywhere" (WORA)** is a slogan developed by Sun Microsystems to describe the ability of one Java program version to work correctly on multiple platforms.

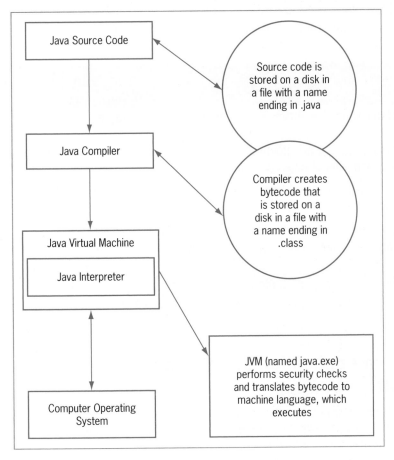

Figure 1-3 The Java environment

Java also is simpler to use than many other object-oriented languages. Java is modeled after C++. Although neither language is easy to read or understand on first exposure, Java does eliminate some of the most difficult-to-understand features in C++, such as pointers and multiple inheritance.

Java Program Types

You can write two kinds of programs using Java:

- **Applets** are programs that are embedded in a Web page. You will create applets in the chapter *Applets, Images, and Sound.*

- **Java applications** are stand-alone programs. Java applications can be further subdivided into **console applications**, which support character output to a computer screen in a DOS window, for example, and **windowed applications**, which create a GUI with elements such as menus, toolbars, and dialog boxes. Console applications are the easiest applications to create; you start using them in the next section.

TWO TRUTHS & A LIE

Features of the Java Programming Language

1. Java was developed to be architecturally neutral, which means that anyone can build an application without extensive study.

2. After you write a Java program, the compiler converts the source code into a binary program of bytecode.

3. Java programs that are embedded in a Web page are called applets, while stand-alone programs are called Java applications.

The false statement is #1. Java was developed to be architecturally neutral, which means that you can use Java to write a program that will run on any platform.

Analyzing a Java Application that Produces Console Output

At first glance, even the simplest Java application involves a fair amount of confusing syntax. Consider the application in Figure 1-4. This program is written on seven lines, and its only task is to display "First Java application" on the screen.

```java
public class First
{
    public static void main(String[] args)
    {
        System.out.println("First Java application");
    }
}
```

Figure 1-4 The First class

When you see program code in figures in this book, Java keywords as well as true, false, and null are blue, and all other program elements are black. A complete list of Java keywords is shown later in this chapter.

The code for every complete program shown in this book is available in a set of student files you can download so that you can execute the programs on your own computer.

Understanding the Statement that Produces the Output

Although the program in Figure 1-4 occupies several lines, it contains only one
Java programming statement. The statement `System.out.println("First Java
application");` does the actual work in this program. Like all Java statements, this one
ends with a semicolon. Most Java programming statements can be spread across as many
lines as you choose, as long as you place line breaks in appropriate places. For example,
in the program in Figure 1-4, you could place a line break before or after the opening
parenthesis, or before or after the closing parenthesis. However, you usually want to place
a short statement on a single line.

The text "First Java application" is a **literal string** of characters—a series of characters that
will appear in output exactly as entered. Any literal string in Java is written between double
quotation marks. In Java, a literal string cannot be broken and placed on multiple lines.
Figure 1-5 labels this string and the other parts of the statement.

Figure 1-5 Anatomy of a Java statement

The string "First Java application" appears within parentheses because the string is
an argument to a method, and arguments to methods always appear within parentheses.
Arguments are pieces of information that are sent into a method, usually because the
method requires the information to perform its task or carry out its purpose. The act of
sending arguments to a method is called **passing arguments** to the method. As an example,
consider placing a catalog order with a company that sells sporting goods. Processing a
catalog order is a method that consists of a set of standard procedures—recording the
order, checking the availability of the item, pulling the item from the warehouse, and so on.
Each catalog order also requires a set of data items, such as which item number you are
ordering and the quantity of the item desired; these data items can be considered the
order's arguments. If you order two of item 5432 from a catalog, you expect different
results than if you order 1,000 of item 9008. Likewise, if you pass the argument
"Happy Holidays" to a Java method, you expect different results than if you pass the
argument "First Java application".

Within the statement System.out.println("First Java application");, the method to which you are passing "First Java application" is named println(). The Java methods println() and print() both produce output. With println(), after the output is displayed, the insertion point moves to the following line. (The insertion point is the point at which the next output appears.) With print(), however, the insertion point does not advance to a new line; it remains on the same line as the output.

When you call a method, you always use parentheses following the method name. In this book, you will learn about many methods that require arguments between their parentheses, and many others for which you leave the parentheses empty. The println() method can be used with no arguments when you want to output a blank line. Later in this chapter, you will learn about a method named showMessageDialog() that requires two arguments. Other methods require more.

Within the statement System.out.println("First Java application");, out is an object that is a property of the System class that refers to the **standard output device** for a system, normally the monitor. The out object itself is an instance of the PrintStream class, which contains several methods, including println(). Technically, you could create the out object and write the instructions within the println()method yourself, but it would be time consuming, and the creators of Java assumed you frequently would want to display output on a screen. Therefore, the System and PrintStream classes, the out object, and the println() method were created as a convenience to the programmer.

Within the statement System.out.println("First Java application");, System is a class. Therefore, System defines attributes for System objects, just as the Dog class defines the attributes for Dog objects. One of the System attributes is out. (You can probably guess that another attribute is in and that it represents an input device.)

The dots (periods) in System.out.println() are used to separate the names of the components in the statement. You will use this format repeatedly in your Java programs.

Java is case sensitive; the class named System is a completely different class from one named system, SYSTEM, or even sYsTeM, and out is a different object from one named Out or OUT. You must pay close attention to using correct uppercase and lowercase values when you write Java programs.

So, the statement that displays the string "First Java application" contains a class, an object reference, a method call, a method argument, and a statement-ending semicolon, but the statement cannot stand alone; it is embedded within a class, as shown in Figure 1-4.

Understanding the First Class

Everything that you use within a Java program must be part of a class. When you write public class First, you are defining a class named First. You can define a Java class using any name or **identifier** you need, as long as it meets the following requirements:

- A Java identifier must begin with a letter of the English alphabet, a non-English letter (such as α or π), an underscore, or a dollar sign. A class name cannot begin with a digit.
- A Java identifier can contain only letters, digits, underscores, or dollar signs.

- A Java identifier cannot be a reserved keyword, such as `public` or `class`. (See Table 1-1 for a list of reserved keywords.)

- A Java identifier cannot be one of the following values: `true`, `false`, or `null`. These are not keywords (they are primitive values), but they are reserved and cannot be used.

Java is based on **Unicode**, which is an international system of character representation. The term *letter* indicates English-language letters as well as characters from Arabic, Greek, and other alphabets. You can learn more about Unicode in Appendix B.

abstract	continue	for	new	switch
assert	default	goto	package	synchronized
boolean	do	if	private	this
break	double	implements	protected	throw
byte	else	import	public	throws
case	enum	instanceof	return	transient
catch	extends	int	short	try
char	final	interface	static	void
class	finally	long	strictfp	volatile
const	float	native	super	while

Table 1-1   Java reserved keywords

Although they are reserved as keywords, `const` and `goto` are not used in Java programs, and they have no function. Both words are used in other languages and were reserved in case developers of future versions of Java wanted to implement them.

It is a Java standard, although not a requirement, to begin class identifiers with an uppercase letter and employ other uppercase letters as needed to improve readability. The style that joins words in which each begins with an uppercase letter is called **Pascal casing**, or sometimes **upper camel casing**. You should follow established conventions for Java so your programs will be easy for other programmers to interpret and follow. This book uses established Java programming conventions.

Table 1-2 lists some valid and conventional class names that you could use when writing programs in Java. Table 1-3 provides some examples of class names that *could* be used in Java (if you use these class names, the class will compile) but that are unconventional and not recommended. Table 1-4 provides some class name examples that are illegal.

Class Name	Description
Employee	Begins with an uppercase letter
UnderGradStudent	Begins with an uppercase letter, contains no spaces, and emphasizes each new word with an initial uppercase letter
InventoryItem	Begins with an uppercase letter, contains no spaces, and emphasizes the second word with an initial uppercase letter
Budget2014	Begins with an uppercase letter and contains no spaces

Table 1-2 Some valid class names in Java

Class Name	Description
Undergradstudent	New words are not indicated with initial uppercase letters, making this identifier difficult to read
Inventory_Item	Underscore is not commonly used to indicate new words
BUDGET2014	Using all uppercase letters for class identifiers is not conventional
budget2014	Conventionally, class names do not begin with a lowercase letter

Table 1-3 Legal but unconventional and nonrecommended class names in Java

Class Name	Description
Inventory Item	Space character is illegal in an identifier
class	class is a reserved word
2014Budget	Class names cannot begin with a digit
phone#	The number symbol (#) is illegal in an identifier

Table 1-4 Some illegal class names in Java

In Figure 1-4 (and again in Figure 1-6), the line public class First is the class header; it contains the keyword class, which identifies First as a class. The reserved word public is an access specifier. An **access specifier** defines the circumstances under which a class can be accessed and the other classes that have the right to use a class. Public access is the most liberal type of access; you will learn about public access and other types of access in the chapter *Using Methods, Classes, and Objects.*

Figure 1-6 The parts of a typical class

After the class header, you enclose the contents of a class within curly braces ({ and }); any data items and methods between the curly braces make up the **class body**. A class body can be composed of any number of data items and methods. In Figure 1-4 (and again in Figure 1-6), the class First contains only one method within its curly braces. The name of the method is main(), and the main() method, like the println() method, includes its own set of parentheses. The main() method in the First class contains only one statement—the statement that uses the println() method. The main() method does not *contain* any other methods, but it *calls* the println() method.

Indent Style

In general, whitespace is optional in Java. **Whitespace** is any combination of nonprinting characters. You use whitespace to organize your program code and make it easier to read. You can insert whitespace between words or lines in your program code by typing spaces, tabs, or blank lines because the compiler ignores these extra spaces. However, you cannot use whitespace within an identifier or keyword.

For every opening curly brace ({) in a Java program, there must be a corresponding closing curly brace (}), but the placement of the opening and closing curly braces is not important to the compiler. For example, the following class executes in exactly the same way as the one shown in Figure 1-4. The only difference is the layout of the braces—the line breaks occur in different locations.

```
public class First{
    public static void main(String[] args){
        System.out.println("First Java application");
    }
}
```

The indent style shown in the preceding example, in which opening braces are not on separate lines, is known as the **K & R style** and is named for Kernighan and Ritchie, who wrote the first book on the C programming language. The indent style shown in Figure 1-4 and used throughout this book, in which curly braces are aligned and each occupies its own line, is called the **Allman style** and is named for Eric Allman, a programmer who popularized the style. Java programmers use a variety of indent styles, and all can produce workable Java programs. When you write your own code, you should develop a consistent style. In school, your instructor might have a preferred style, and when you get a job as a Java programmer, your organization most likely will have a preferred style. With many development environments, indentations are made for you automatically as you type.

Most programmers indent a method's statements a few spaces more than its curly braces. Some programmers indent two spaces, some three, and some four. Some programmers use the Tab key to create indentations, but others are opposed to this practice because the Tab key can indicate different indentation sizes on different systems. Some programmers don't care whether tabs or spaces are used, as long as you don't mix them in the same program. The Java compiler does not care how you indent. Again, the most important rule is to develop a consistent style of which your organization approves.

Understanding the `main()` Method

The method header for the `main()` method is quite complex. Figure 1-7 shows the parts of the `main()` method.

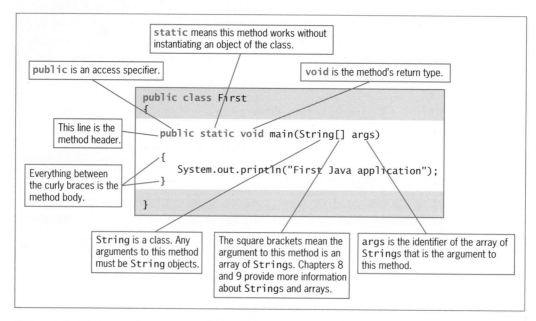

Figure 1-7   The parts of a typical `main()` method

The meaning and purpose of each of the terms used in the method header will become clearer as you complete this textbook; a brief explanation will suffice for now.

- In the method header `public static void main(String[] args)`, the word `public` is an access specifier, just as it is when you use it to define the `First` class.

- In Java, the reserved keyword **static** means that a method is accessible and usable even though no objects of the class exist.

- The keyword **void** used in the `main()` method header indicates that the `main()` method does not return any value when it is called. This doesn't mean that `main()` doesn't produce output—in fact, the method in Figure 1-4 (and in Figure 1-7) does. It only means that the `main()` method does not send any value back to any other method that might use it. You will learn more about return values in the chapter *Methods, Classes, and Objects*.

- The name of the method is `main()`. Not all classes have a `main()` method; in fact, many do not. All Java *applications*, however, must include a class containing a public method named `main()`, and most Java applications have additional classes and methods. When you execute a Java application, the JVM always executes the `main()` method first.

- In the method header `public static void main(String[] args)`, the contents between the parentheses, `String[] args`, represent the type of argument that can be passed to the `main()` method, just as the string `"First Java application"` is an argument passed to the `println()` method. `String` is a Java class that can be used to hold character strings. The identifier `args` is used to hold any `String` objects that might be sent to the `main()` method. The `main()` method could do something with those arguments, such as display them, but in Figure 1-4, the `main()` method does not actually use the `args` identifier. Nevertheless, you must place an identifier within the `main()` method's parentheses. The identifier does not need to be named `args`—it could be any legal Java identifier—but the name `args` is traditional.

You won't pass any arguments to the `main()` method in this book, but when you run a program, you could. Even though you pass no arguments, the `main()` method must contain `String[]` and a legal identifier (such as `args`) within its parentheses. When you refer to the `String` class in the `main()` method header, the square brackets indicate an array of `String` objects. You will learn more about the `String` class and arrays in Chapters 7, 8, and 9.

The simple application shown in Figure 1-4 has many pieces to remember. However, for now you can use the Java code shown in Figure 1-8 as a shell, in which you replace `AnyClassName` with a class name you choose and the line `/******/` with any statements that you want to execute.

Watch the video *A Java Program.*

```
public class AnyClassName
{
    public static void main(String[] args)
    {
        /******/
    }
}
```

20

Figure 1-8   Shell code

Saving a Java Class

When you write a Java class, you must save it using a storage medium such as a disk, DVD, or USB device. In Java, if a class is public (that is, if you use the public access specifier before the class name), you must save the class in a file with exactly the same name and a .java extension. For example, the First class must be stored in a file named First.java. The class name and filename must match exactly, including the use of uppercase and lowercase characters. If the extension is not .java, the Java compiler does not recognize the file as containing a Java class. Appendix A contains additional information on saving a Java application.

TWO TRUTHS & A LIE

Analyzing a Java Application that Produces Console Output

1. In the method header public static void main(String[] args), the word public is an access specifier.

2. In the method header public static void main(String[] args), the word static means that a method is accessible and usable, even though no objects of the class exist.

3. In the method header public static void main(String[] args), the word void means that the main() method is an empty method.

The false statement is #3. In the method header public static void main(String[] args), the word void means that the main() method does not return any value when it is called.

You Do It

Your First Application

Now that you understand the basics of an application written in Java, you are ready to enter your own Java application into a text editor. It is a tradition among programmers that the first program you write in any language produces "Hello, world!" as its output. You will create such a program now. You can use any text editor, such as Notepad or TextPad, or a development environment, such as jGRASP.

 It is best to use the simplest available text editor when writing Java programs. Multifeatured word-processing programs save documents as much larger files because of all the built-in features, such as font styles and margin settings, which the Java compiler cannot interpret.

1. Start any text editor, and then open a new document.

2. Type the class header as follows:

    public class Hello

    In this example, the class name is Hello. You can use any valid name you want for the class. If you choose *Hello*, you always must refer to the class as *Hello*, and not as *hello*, because Java is case sensitive.

3. Press **Enter** once, type {, press **Enter** again, and then type }. You will add the main() method between these curly braces. Although it is not required, the convention used in this book is to place each curly brace on its own line and to align opening and closing curly brace pairs with each other. Using this format makes your code easier to read.

4. As shown in the shaded portion of Figure 1-9, add the main() method header between the curly braces, and then type a set of curly braces for main().

```
public class Hello
{
    public static void main(String[] args)
    {
    }
}
```

Figure 1-9   The main() method shell for the Hello class

(continues)

(continued)

5. Next, add the statement within the `main()` method that will produce the output "Hello, world!". Use Figure 1-10 as a guide for adding the shaded `println()` statement to the `main()` method.

```
public class Hello
{
    public static void main(String[] args)
    {
        System.out.println("Hello, world!");
    }
}
```

Figure 1-10   Complete `Hello` class

6. Save the application as **Hello.java**. The class name and filename must match, and you must use the .java extension.

Compiling a Java Class and Correcting Syntax Errors

After you write and save an application, two steps must occur before you can view the application's output.

1. You must compile the class you wrote (called the source code) into bytecode.

2. You must use the Java interpreter to translate the bytecode into executable statements.

Compiling a Java Class

To compile your source code from the command line, your prompt should show the folder or directory where your program file is stored. Then, you type `javac` followed by the name of the file that contains the source code. For example, to compile a file named First.java, you type the following and then press Enter:

`javac First.java`

There will be one of three outcomes:

-   You receive a message such as `'javac' is not recognized as an internal or external command, operable program or batch file`.

-   You receive one or more program language error messages.

-   You receive no messages, which means that the application compiled successfully.

When compiling, if the source code file is not in the current path, you can type a full path with the filename. For example:

```
javac c:\java\MyClasses\Chapter.01\First.java
```

In a DOS environment, you can change directories using the **cd** command. For example, to change from the current directory to a subdirectory named MyClasses, you type **cd MyClasses** and press Enter. Within any directory, you can back up to the root directory by typing **cd** and pressing Enter.

If you receive an error message that the command is not recognized, it might mean one of the following:

- You misspelled the command `javac`.

- You misspelled the filename.

- You are not within the correct subfolder or subdirectory on your command line.

- Java was not installed properly. (See Appendix A for information on installation.)

If you receive a programming language error message, there are one or more syntax errors in the source code. Recall that a syntax error is a programming error that occurs when you introduce typing errors into your program or use the programming language incorrectly. For example, if your class name is `first` (with a lowercase *f*) in the source code but you saved the file as First.java (with an uppercase *F*), you will receive an error message when you compile the application. The error message will be similar to `class first is public, should be declared in a file named first.java` because *first* and *First* are not the same in a case-sensitive language. If this error occurs, you must reopen the text file that contains the source code and make the necessary corrections.

Appendix A contains information on troubleshooting, including how to change filenames in a Windows environment.

If you receive no error messages after compiling the code in a file named First.java, the application compiled successfully, and a file named First.class is created and saved in the same folder as the text file that holds the application code. After a successful compile, you can run the class file on any computer that has a Java language interpreter.

Correcting Syntax Errors

Frequently, you might make typing errors as you enter Java statements into your text editor. When you issue the command to compile the class containing errors, the Java compiler produces one or more error messages. The exact error message that appears varies depending on the compiler you are using.

The `FirstWithMissingSemicolon` class shown in Figure 1-11 contains an error—the semicolon is missing from the end of the `println()` statement. (Of course, this class has been helpfully named to alert you to the error.) When you compile this class, an error message similar to the one shown in Figure 1-12 is displayed.

```
public class FirstWithMissingSemicolon
{

  public static void main(String[] args)

  {
      System.out.println("First Java application")
  }

}
```

The statement-ending semicolon has been omitted.

Figure 1-11   The `FirstWithMissingSemicolon` class

Figure 1-12   Error message generated when the `FirstWithMissingSemicolon` class is compiled

The first line of the error message in Figure 1-12 displays the name of the file in which the error was found (FirstWithMissingSemicolon.java), the line number in which it was found (5), and the nature of the error ("';' expected"). The next line of the error message displays the statement that contains the error, including a caret that points to the exact location where the error was first discovered. As you will see when you write and compile Java programs, the place where an error is discovered is not necessarily where the error was made. Sometimes, it takes a little detective work to interpret an error message and determine its cause.

Finally, the message generated in Figure 1-12 includes a count of the number of errors found—in this case, there is just one error. This is a **compile-time error**, or one in which the compiler detects a violation of language syntax rules and is unable to translate the source code to machine code.

When you compile a class, the compiler reports as many errors as it can find so that you can fix as many errors as possible. Sometimes, one error in syntax causes multiple error messages that normally would not be errors if the first syntax error did not exist, so fixing one error might eliminate multiple error messages. Sometimes, when you fix a compile-time error and recompile a program, new error messages are generated. That's because when you fix the first error, the compiler can proceed beyond that point and possibly discover new errors. Of course, no programmer intends to type a program containing syntax errors, but when you do, the compiler finds them all for you.

25

TWO TRUTHS & A LIE

Compiling a Java Class and Correcting Syntax Errors

1. After you write and save an application, you can compile the bytecode to create source code.

2. When you compile a class, you create a new file with the same name as the original file but with a .class extension.

3. Syntax errors are compile-time errors.

The false statement is #1. After you write and save an application, you can compile the source code to create bytecode.

 You Do It

Compiling a Java Class

You are ready to compile the Hello class that you created in the previous "You Do It" section.

1. If it is not still open on your screen, open the **Hello.java** file that you saved in the previous "You Do It" section.

2. Go to the command-line prompt for the drive and folder or subdirectory in which you saved Hello.java. At the command line, type:

```
javac Hello.java
```

After a few moments, you should return to the command prompt. If you see error messages instead, reread the previous section to discover whether you can determine the source of the error.

If the error message indicates that the command was not recognized, make sure that you spelled the javac command correctly, including using the correct case. Also, make sure you are using the correct directory or folder where the Hello.java file is stored.

If the error message indicates a language error, check your file against Figure 1-10, making sure it matches exactly. Fix any errors, and compile the application again. If errors persist, read through the next section to see if you can discover the solution.

(continues)

(continued)

Correcting Syntax Errors

In this section, you examine error messages and gain firsthand experience with syntax errors.

1. If your version of the `Hello` class did not compile successfully, examine the syntax error messages. Now that you know the messages contain line numbers and carets to pinpoint mistakes, it might be easier for you to fix problems. After you determine the nature of any errors, resave the file and recompile it.

2. Even if your `Hello` class compiled successfully, you need to gain experience with error messages. Your student files contain a file named **HelloErrors.java**. Find this file and open it in your text editor. If you do not have access to the student files that accompany this book, you can type the file yourself, as shown in Figure 1-13.

```
public class HelloErrors
{
    public static void main(String[] args)
    {
        System.out.println("Hello");
        System.out.println("This is a test");
    }
}
```

Figure 1-13   The `HelloErrors` class

3. Save the file as **HelloErrors.java** in the folder in which you want to work. Then compile the class using the following command to confirm that it compiles without error:

   `javac HelloErrors.java`

4. In the first line of the file, remove the **c** from `class`, making the first line read **public lass HelloErrors**. Save the file and compile the program. Error messages are generated similar to those shown in Figure 1-14. Even though you changed only one keystroke in the file, four error messages appear. The first indicates that `class`, enum, or `interface` is expected in line 1. You haven't learned about the Java keywords enum or `interface` yet, but you know that you caused the error by altering the word `class`. The next three errors in lines 3, 6, and 7 show that the compile is continuing to look for one of the three keywords but fails to find them.

(continues)

(continued)

Figure 1-14 Error messages generated when `class` is misspelled in the `HelloErrors` program

5. Repair the program by reinserting the **c** in `class`. Save the file and compile it again. The program should compile successfully. When you fix one error, four error messages are removed.

6. Next, remove the word **void** from the third line of the program. Save the file and compile it. Figure 1-15 shows the error message, which indicates that a return type is required. The message does not indicate that `void` is missing because Java supports many return types for methods. In this case, however, `void` is the correct return type, so reinsert it into the correct place in the program, and then save and recompile the file.

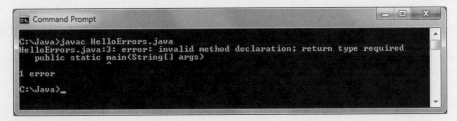

Figure 1-15 Error message generated when `void` is omitted from the `main()` method header in the `HelloErrors` program

7. Remove the final closing curly brace from the `HelloErrors` program. Save the file and recompile it. Figure 1-16 shows the generated message "reached end of file while parsing." **Parsing** is the process the compiler uses to divide your source code into meaningful portions; the message means that the compiler was in the process of analyzing the code when the end of the file was

(continues)

(continued)

encountered prematurely. If you repair the error by reinserting the closing curly brace, saving the file, and recompiling it, you remove the error message.

Figure 1-16   Error message generated when the closing curly brace is omitted from the HelloErrors program

8. Continue to introduce errors in the program by misspelling words, omitting punctuation, and adding extraneous keystrokes. Remember to save each program version before you recompile it; otherwise, you will recompile the previous version. When error messages are generated, read them carefully and try to understand their meaning in the context of the error you purposely caused. Occasionally, even though you inserted an error into the program, no error messages will be generated. That does not mean your program is correct. It only means that the program contains no syntax errors. A program can be free of syntax errors but still not be correct, as you will learn in the next section.

Running a Java Application and Correcting Logical Errors

After a program compiles with no syntax errors, you can execute it. However, just because a program compiles and executes, that does not mean the program is error free.

Running a Java Application

To run the First application in Figure 1-4 from the command line, you type the following:

```
java First
```

Figure 1-17 shows the application's output in the command window. In this example, you can see that the First class is stored in a folder named Java on the C drive. After you type the java command to execute the program, the literal string in the call is output to the println() method in the program ("First Java application"). Control then returns to the command prompt.

Figure 1-17   Output of the First application

The procedure to confirm the storage location of your First.java class varies depending on your operating system. In a Windows operating system, for example, you can open Windows Explorer, locate the icon representing the storage device you are using, find the folder in which you have saved the file, and expand the folder. You should see the First.java file.

When you run a Java application using the `java` command, do not add the .class extension to the filename. If you type `java First`, the interpreter looks for a file named *First.class*. If you type `java First.class`, the interpreter incorrectly looks for a file named *First.class.class*.

Modifying a Compiled Java Class

After viewing the application output, you might decide to modify the class to get a different result. For example, you might decide to change the `First` application's output from `First Java application` to the following:

```
My new and improved
Java application
```

To produce the new output, first you must modify the text file that contains the existing class. You need to change the existing literal string, and then add an output statement for another text string. Figure 1-18 shows the class that changes the output.

```java
public class First
{
    public static void main(String[] args)
    {
        System.out.println("My new and improved");
        System.out.println("Java application");
    }
}
```

Figure 1-18   `First` class containing output modified from the original version

The changes to the `First` class include the addition of the statement `System.out.println ("My new and improved");` and the removal of the word *First* from the string in the other `println()` statement.

If you make changes to the file, as shown in Figure 1-18, and then save the file and execute the program by typing `java First` at the command line, you will not see the new output—you will see the old output without the added line. Even though you save a text file that contains the modified source code for a class, the class in the already-compiled class file executes. After you save the file named First.java, the old compiled version of the class with the same name is still stored on your computer. Before the new source code can execute, you must do the following:

1. Save the file with the changes (using the same filename).

2. Compile the class with the javac command. (Actually, you are *re*compiling the class.)

3. Interpret the class bytecode and execute the class using the java command.

Figure 1-19 shows the new output.

When you recompile a class, the original version of the compiled file with the .class extension is replaced, and the original version no longer exists. When you modify a class, you must decide whether you want to retain the original version. If you do, you must give the new version a new class name and a new filename.

Figure 1-19   Execution of modified First class

 Once in a while, when you make a change to a Java class and then recompile and execute it, the old version still runs. The simplest solution is to delete the .class file and compile again. Programmers call this creating a **clean build**.

 Watch the video *Compiling and Executing a Program*.

Correcting Logical Errors

Besides syntax errors, a second kind of error occurs when the syntax of the program is correct and the program compiles but produces incorrect results when you execute it. This type of error is a **logic error**, which is often more difficult to find and resolve. For example, Figure 1-20 shows the output of the execution of a successfully compiled program named FirstBadOutput. If you glance at the output too quickly, you might not notice that Java is misspelled. The compiler does not find spelling errors within a literal string; it is legitimate to produce any combination of letters as output.

Other examples of logic errors include multiplying two values when you meant to add, printing one copy of a report when you meant to print five, or forgetting to produce a total at the end of a report when a user has requested one. Errors of this type must be detected by carefully examining the program output. It is the responsibility of the program author to test programs and find any logic errors.

Figure 1-20   Output of FirstBadOutput program

You have already learned that syntax errors are compile-time errors. A logic error is a type of **run-time error**—an error not detected until the program asks the computer to do something wrong, or even illegal, while executing. Not all run-time errors are the fault of the programmer. For example, a computer's hardware might fail while a program is executing. However, good programming practices can help to minimize errors.

The process of fixing computer errors has been known as debugging since a large moth was found wedged into the circuitry of a mainframe computer at Harvard University in 1947. See these Web sites for interesting details and pictures: *www.jamesshuggins.com/h/tek1/first_computer_bug.htm* and *www.history.navy.mil/photos/images/h96000/h96566kc.htm*.

TWO TRUTHS & A LIE

Running a Java Application and Correcting Logical Errors

1. In Java, if a class is `public`, you must save the class in a file with exactly the same name and a .java extension.

2. To compile a file named MyProgram.java, you type `java MyProgram`, but to execute the program you type `java MyProgram.java`.

3. When you compile a program, sometimes one error in syntax causes multiple error messages.

The false statement is #2. To compile a file named MyProgram.java, you type javac MyProgram.java, but to execute the program you type the following: java MyProgram

Adding Comments to a Java Class

As you can see, even the simplest Java class requires several lines of code and contains somewhat perplexing syntax. Large applications that perform many tasks include much more code, and as you write larger applications it becomes increasingly difficult to remember why you included steps or how you intended to use particular variables. Documenting your program code helps you remember why you wrote lines of code the way you did. **Program comments** are nonexecuting statements that you add to a program for the purpose of documentation. In other words, comments are designed for people reading the source code and not for the computer executing the program.

Programmers use comments to leave notes for themselves and for others who might read their programs in the future. At the very least, your Java class files should include comments indicating the author, the date, and the class name or function. The best practice dictates that you also include a brief comment to describe the purpose of each method you create within a class.

As you work through this book, add comments as the first lines of every file. The comments should contain the class name and purpose, your name, and the date. Your instructor might ask you to include additional comments.

Comments also can be useful when you are developing an application. If a program is not performing as expected, you can "comment out" various statements and subsequently run the program to observe the effect. When you **comment out** a statement, you turn it into a comment so the compiler does not translate it, and the JVM does not execute its command. This can help you pinpoint the location of errant statements in malfunctioning programs.

There are three types of comments in Java:

- **Line comments** start with two forward slashes (//) and continue to the end of the current line. A line comment can appear on a line by itself or at the end (and to the right) of a line following executable code. Line comments do not require an ending symbol.

- **Block comments** start with a forward slash and an asterisk (/*) and end with an asterisk and a forward slash (*/). A block comment can appear on a line by itself, on a line before executable code, or on a line after executable code. Block comments also can extend across as many lines as needed.

- **Javadoc** comments are a special case of block comments called **documentation comments** because they are used to automatically generate nicely formatted program documentation with a program named javadoc. Javadoc comments begin with a forward slash and two asterisks (/**) and end with an asterisk and a forward slash (*/). Appendix E teaches you how to create javadoc comments.

The forward slash (/) and the backslash (\ ) characters often are confused, but they are two distinct characters. You cannot use them interchangeably.

The Java Development Kit (JDK) includes the javadoc tool, which you can use when writing programs in Java. The tool produces HTML pages that describe classes and their contents.

Figure 1-21 shows how comments are used in code. In this example, the only statement that executes is the `System.out.println("Hello");` statement; everything else (all the shaded parts) is a comment.

```
// Demonstrating comments
/* This shows
   that these comments
   don't matter */
System.out.println("Hello"); // This line executes
      // up to where the comment started
/* Everything but the println()
      is a comment */
```

Figure 1-21   A program segment containing several comments

You might want to create comments simply for aesthetics. For example, you might want to use a comment that is simply a row of dashes or asterisks to use as a visual dividing line between parts of a program.

TWO TRUTHS & A LIE

Adding Comments to a Java Class

1. Line comments start with two forward slashes (//) and end with two backslashes (\\ ); they can extend across as many lines as needed.

2. Block comments start with a forward slash and an asterisk (/*) and end with an asterisk and a forward slash (*/); they can extend across as many lines as needed.

3. Javadoc comments begin with a forward slash and two asterisks (/**) and end with an asterisk and a forward slash (*/); they are used to generate documentation with a program named javadoc.

The false statement is #1. Line comments start with two forward slashes (//) and continue to the end of the current line; they do not require an ending symbol.

You Do It

Adding Comments to a Class

In this exercise, you add comments to your Hello.java application and save it as a new class named Hello2 so that you can retain copies of both the original and modified classes.

1. Open the **Hello.java** file you created earlier in this chapter. Enter the following comments at the top of the file, inserting your name and today's date where indicated.

    ```
    // Filename Hello2.java
    // Written by <your name>
    // Written on <today's date>
    ```

2. Change the class name to **Hello2**, and then type the following block comment after the class header:

    ```
    /* This class demonstrates the use of the println()
    method to print the message Hello, world! */
    ```

    (continues)

(continued)

3. Save the file as **Hello2.java**. The file must be named Hello2.java because the class name is Hello2.

4. Go to the command-line prompt for the drive and folder or subdirectory in which you saved Hello2.java, and type the following command to compile the program:

   `javac Hello2.java`

5. When the compile is successful, execute your application by typing **java Hello2** at the command line. The comments have no effect on program execution; the output should appear on the next line.

After the application compiles successfully, a file named Hello2.class is created and stored in the same folder as the Hello2.java file. If your application compiled without error but you receive an error message, such as "Exception in thread 'main' java.lang.NoClassDefFoundError," when you try to execute the application, you probably do not have your class path set correctly. See Appendix A for details.

Creating a Java Application that Produces GUI Output

Besides allowing you to use the System class to produce command window output, Java provides built-in classes that produce GUI output. For example, Java contains a class named JOptionPane that allows you to produce dialog boxes. A **dialog box** is a GUI object resembling a window in which you can place messages you want to display. Figure 1-22 shows a class named FirstDialog. The FirstDialog class contains many elements that are familiar to you; only the two shaded lines are new.

```java
import javax.swing.JOptionPane;
public class FirstDialog
{
    public static void main(String[] args)
    {
        JOptionPane.showMessageDialog(null, "First Java dialog");
    }
}
```

Figure 1-22   The FirstDialog class

In older versions of Java, any application that used a JOptionPane dialog was required to end with a System.exit(0); statement or the application would not terminate. You can add this statement to your programs, and they will work correctly, but it is not necessary.

In Figure 1-22, the first shaded line is an import statement. You use an **import statement** when you want to access a built-in Java class that is contained in a group of classes called a **package**. To use the JOptionPane class, you must import the package named javax.swing.JOptionPane. Any import statement you use must be placed outside of any class you write in a file. You will learn more about import statements in general, and the javax.swing packages in particular, as you continue to study Java.

35

You do not need to use an import statement when you use the System class (as with the System. out.println() method) because the System class is contained in the package java.lang, which is automatically imported in every Java program. You *could* include the statement import java.lang; at the top of any file in which you use the System class, but you are not required to do so.

The second shaded statement in the FirstDialog class in Figure 1-22 uses the showMessageDialog() method that is part of the JOptionPane class. Like the println() method that is used for console output, the showMessageDialog() method is followed by a set of parentheses. However, whereas the println() method requires only one argument between its parentheses to produce an output string, the showMessageDialog() method requires two arguments. (Whenever a method requires multiple arguments, they are separated by commas.) When the first argument to showMessageDialog() is null, as it is in the class in Figure 1-22, it means the output message box should be placed in the center of the screen. The second argument, after the comma, is the string that is displayed.

Earlier in this chapter, you learned that true, false, and null are all reserved words that represent values.

You will learn more about dialog boxes, including how to position them in different locations and how to add more options to them, in Chapter 2.

When a user executes the FirstDialog class, the dialog box in Figure 1-23 is displayed. The user must click the OK button or the Close button to dismiss the dialog box.

Figure 1-23 Output of the FirstDialog application

36

TWO TRUTHS & A LIE

Creating a Java Application that Produces GUI Output

1. A dialog box is a GUI object resembling a window in which you can place messages you want to display.

2. You use an append statement when you want to access a built-in Java class that is contained in a group of classes called a package.

3. Different methods can require different numbers of arguments.

The false statement is #2. You use an import statement when you want to access a built-in Java class that is contained in a group of classes called a package.

 You Do It

Creating a Dialog Box

Next, you write a Java application that produces output in a dialog box.

1. Open a new file in your text editor. Type comments similar to the following, inserting your own name and today's date where indicated.

```
// Filename HelloDialog.java
// Written by <your name>
// Written on <today's date>
```

2. Enter the import statement that allows you to use the JOptionPane class:

```
import javax.swing.JOptionPane;
```

3. Enter the HelloDialog class:

```
public class HelloDialog
{
    public static void main(String[] args)
    {
        JOptionPane.showMessageDialog(null, "Hello, world!");
    }
}
```

(continues)

(continued)

4. Save the file as **HelloDialog.java**. Compile the class using the following command:

   `javac HelloDialog.java`

   If necessary, eliminate any syntax errors, resave the file, and recompile. Then execute the program using the following command:

   `java HelloDialog`

   The output appears as shown in Figure 1-24.

5. Click **OK** to dismiss the dialog box.

Figure 1-24 Output of `HelloDialog` application

Finding Help

As you write Java programs, you can frequently consult this book as well as other Java documentation. A great wealth of helpful material exists at the Java Web site, *www.oracle.com/technetwork/java/index.html*. Of particular value is the Java application programming interface, more commonly referred to as the **Java API**. The Java API is also called the Java class library; it contains information about how to use every prewritten Java class, including lists of all the methods you can use with the classes.

Also of interest at the Java Web site are frequently asked questions (**FAQs**) that provide brief answers to many common questions about Java software and products. You can also find several versions of the Java Development Kit (**JDK**) that you can download for free. The JDK is an **SDK**—a software development kit that includes tools used by programmers. Versions are available for Windows, Linux, and Solaris operating systems. You can search and browse documentation online or you can download the documentation file for the JDK and install it on your computer. After it is installed, you can search and browse documentation locally.

A downloadable set of lessons titled "The Java Tutorial" with hundreds of complete working examples is available from *http://docs.oracle.com/javase/tutorial/*. The tutorial is organized into trails—groups of lessons on a particular subject. You can start the tutorial at the beginning and navigate sequentially to the end, or you can jump from one trail to another. As you study each chapter in this book, you are encouraged to make good use of these support materials.

38

You Do It

Exploring the Java Web Site

In this section, you explore some of the material at the Java Web site.

1. Open an Internet browser and navigate to **www.oracle.com/technetwork/java/index.html**.

2. Oracle could change the layout of its Web site after this book is published. However, you should be able to find and click a link for **Java APIs** and then another for **Java SE 7**. (If you are using an older version of Java, you can select that version instead.)

3. All the Java classes are listed in a panel labeled **All Classes**. Scroll until you can select the `System` class. The largest panel on the page should display details about the `System` class.

4. You can see that the `System` class contains three fields. You are already familiar with the `out` field, and you can see that it is an object of type `PrintStream`. Click the hypertext for the **PrintStream** type to be taken to a new page with details about that class.

5. Scroll through the methods of the `PrintStream` class. Notice that the class contains several versions of the `print()` and `println()` methods. Find the version of the `println()` method that accepts a `String` argument. Click the link to the method to read details about it, such as that it "prints a `String` and then terminates the line."

6. Many parts of the Java documentation won't mean much to you until you study data types and methods in more detail in the next few chapters of this book. For now, you can explore the Java Web site to get an idea of the wealth of classes that have been created for you.

Don't Do It

At the end of each chapter, a Don't Do It list will alert you to common mistakes made by beginning programmers.

- Don't forget that in Java, a public file's name must match the name of the class it contains. For example, if a file is named Program1.java, you can't simply rename it Program1BackUp.java and expect it to compile unless you change the class name within the file.

- Don't confuse the terms *parentheses*, *braces*, *brackets*, *curly braces*, *square brackets*, and *angle brackets*. When you are writing a program or performing some other computerized task and someone tells you, "Now, type some braces," you might want to clarify which term is meant. Table 1-5 summarizes these punctuation marks.

Punctuation	Name	Typical use in Java	Alternate names
( )	Parentheses	Follows method names as in `println()`	Parentheses can be called *round brackets*, but such usage is unusual
{ }	Curly braces	A pair surrounds a class body, a method body, and a block of code; when you learn about arrays in Chapter 8, you will find that curly braces also surround lists of array values	Curly braces might also be called *curly brackets*
[ ]	Square brackets	A pair signifies an array; arrays are covered in Chapter 8	Square brackets might be called *box brackets* or *square braces*
< >	Angle brackets	A pair of angle brackets surrounds HTML tags, as you will learn in Chapter 17; in Java, a pair also is used with generic arguments in parameterized classes	When angle brackets appear with nothing between them, they are called a *chevron*

Table 1-5   Braces and brackets used in Java

- Don't forget to end a block comment. Every /* must have a corresponding */, even if it is several lines later. It's harder to make a mistake with line comments (those that start with //), but remember that nothing on the line after the // will execute.

- Don't forget that Java is case sensitive.

- Don't forget to end every statement with a semicolon, but *not* to end class or method headers with a semicolon.

- Don't forget to recompile a program to which you have made changes. It can be very frustrating to fix an error, run a program, and not understand why you don't see evidence of your changes. The reason might be that the .class file does not contain your changes because you forgot to recompile.

- Don't panic when you see a lot of compiler error messages. Often, fixing one will fix several.

- Don't think your program is perfect when all compiler errors are eliminated. Only by running the program multiple times and carefully examining the output can you be assured that your program is logically correct.

40

Key Terms

A **computer program** is a set of instructions that you write to tell a computer what to do.

Hardware is the general term for computer equipment.

Software is the general term for computer programs.

Application software performs tasks for users.

System software manages the computer.

The **logic** behind any program involves executing the various statements and procedures in the correct order to produce the desired results.

Machine language is a circuitry-level language that represents a series of on and off switches.

Machine code is another term for machine language.

A **low-level programming language** is written to correspond closely to a computer processor's circuitry.

A **high-level programming language** allows you to use an English-like vocabulary to write programs.

Syntax refers to the rules of a language.

Keywords are the words that are part of a programming language.

Program statements are similar to English sentences; they carry out the tasks that programs perform.

Commands are program statements.

A **compiler** is a program that translates language statements into machine code; it translates an entire program at once before any part of the program can execute.

An **interpreter** is a program that translates language statements into machine code; it translates one statement at a time, allowing a program to execute partially.

Executing a statement or program means to carry it out.

At run time is a phrase that describes the period of time during which a program executes.

A **syntax error** is a programming error that occurs when you introduce typing errors into your program or use the programming language incorrectly. A program containing syntax errors will not compile.

Debugging a program is the process that frees it of all errors.

Semantic errors occur when you use a correct word in the wrong context in program code.

Procedural programming is a style of programming in which sets of operations are executed one after another in sequence.

Variables are named computer memory locations that hold values that might vary.

Procedures are sets of operations performed by a computer program.

To **call a procedure** is to temporarily abandon the current logic so that the procedure's commands can execute.

Writing **object-oriented programs** involves creating classes, creating objects from those classes, and creating applications that use those objects. Thinking in an object-oriented manner involves envisioning program components as objects that are similar to concrete objects in the real world; then, you can manipulate the objects to achieve a desired result.

Computer simulations are programs that attempt to mimic real-world activities so that their processes can be improved or so that users can better understand how the real-world processes operate.

Graphical user interfaces, or **GUIs** (pronounced "gooeys"), allow users to interact with a program in a graphical environment.

A **class** is a group or collection of objects with common properties.

A **class definition** describes what attributes its objects will have and what those objects will be able to do.

Attributes are the characteristics that define an object as part of a class.

Properties are attributes of a class.

An **object** is an instance of a class.

An **instance** of a class is an object.

To **instantiate** is to create an instance.

The **state** of an object is the set of values for its attributes.

A **method** is a self-contained block of program code, similar to a procedure.

Encapsulation refers to the enclosure of data and methods within an object.

Inheritance is the ability to create classes that share the attributes and methods of existing classes but with more specific features.

Polymorphism describes the feature of languages that allows the same word to be interpreted correctly in different situations based on the context.

Java was developed by Sun Microsystems as an object-oriented language used both for general-purpose business applications and for interactive, World Wide Web–based Internet applications.

Architecturally neutral describes the feature of Java that allows you to write programs that run on any platform (operating system).

The **Java Virtual Machine (JVM)** is a hypothetical (software-based) computer on which Java runs.

Source code consists of programming statements written in a high-level programming language.

jGRASP is a development environment and source code editor.

A **development environment** is a set of tools that help you write programs by providing such features as displaying a language's keywords in color.

Bytecode consists of programming statements that have been compiled into binary format.

The **Java interpreter** is a program that checks bytecode and communicates with the operating system, executing the bytecode instructions line by line within the Java Virtual Machine.

"Write once, run anywhere" (WORA) is a slogan developed by Sun Microsystems to describe the ability of one Java program version to work correctly on multiple platforms.

Applets are Java programs that are embedded in a Web page.

Java applications are stand-alone Java programs.

Console applications support character output to a computer screen in a DOS window.

Windowed applications create a graphical user interface (GUI) with elements such as menus, toolbars, and dialog boxes.

A **literal string** is a series of characters that appear exactly as entered. Any literal string in Java appears between double quotation marks.

Arguments are information passed to a method so it can perform its task.

Passing arguments is the act of sending them to a method.

The **standard output device** is normally the monitor.

An **identifier** is a name of a program component such as a class, object, or variable.

Unicode is an international system of character representation.

Pascal casing is a naming convention in which identifiers start with an uppercase letter and use an uppercase letter to start each new word.

Upper camel casing is Pascal casing.

An **access specifier** defines the circumstances under which a class can be accessed and the other classes that have the right to use a class.

The **class body** is the set of data items and methods between the curly braces that follow the class header.

Whitespace is any combination of nonprinting characters, such as spaces, tabs, and carriage returns (blank lines).

The **K & R style** is the indent style in which the opening brace follows the header on the same line; it is named for Kernighan and Ritchie, who wrote the first book on the C programming language.

The **Allman style** is the indent style in which curly braces are aligned and each occupies its own line; it is named for Eric Allman, a programmer who popularized the style.

The keyword `static` means that a method is accessible and usable even though no objects of the class exist.

The keyword `void`, when used in a method header, indicates that the method does not return any value when it is called.

A **compile-time error** is one in which the compiler detects a violation of language syntax rules and is unable to translate the source code to machine code.

Parsing is the process the compiler uses to divide source code into meaningful portions for analysis.

A **clean build** is created when you delete all previously compiled versions of a class before compiling again.

A **logic error** occurs when a program compiles successfully but produces an error during execution.

A **run-time error** occurs when a program compiles successfully but does not execute.

Program comments are nonexecuting statements that you add to a Java file for the purpose of documentation.

To **comment out** a statement is to turn it into a comment so the compiler will not execute its command.

Line comments start with two forward slashes (//) and continue to the end of the current line. Line comments can appear on a line by themselves or at the end of a line following executable code.

Block comments start with a forward slash and an asterisk (/*) and end with an asterisk and a forward slash (*/). Block comments can appear on a line by themselves, on a line before executable code, or on a line after executable code. Block comments also can extend across as many lines as needed.

Javadoc comments are block comments that generate documentation. They begin with a forward slash and two asterisks (/**) and end with an asterisk and a forward slash (*/).

Documentation comments are comments that automatically generate nicely formatted program documentation.

A **dialog box** is a GUI object resembling a window in which you can place messages you want to display.

An `import` **statement** accesses a built-in Java class that is contained in a package.

A **package** contains a group of built-in Java classes.

The **Java API** is the application programming interface, a collection of information about how to use every prewritten Java class.

FAQs are frequently asked questions.

The **JDK** is the Java Development Kit.

An **SDK** is a software development kit, or a set of tools useful to programmers.

Chapter Summary

- A computer program is a set of instructions that tells a computer what to do. You can write a program using a high-level programming language, which has its own syntax, or rules of the language. After you write a program, you use a compiler or interpreter to translate the language statements into machine code.

- Writing object-oriented programs involves creating classes, creating objects from those classes, and creating applications—stand-alone executable programs that use those objects. Object-oriented programming languages support encapsulation, inheritance, and polymorphism.

- A program written in Java is run on a standardized hypothetical computer called the Java Virtual Machine (JVM). When your class is compiled into bytecode, an interpreter within the JVM subsequently interprets the bytecode and communicates with your operating system to produce the program results.

- Everything within a Java program must be part of a class and contained within opening and closing curly braces. Methods within classes hold statements. All Java programming statements end with a semicolon. Periods (called dots) are used to separate classes, objects, and methods in program code. All Java applications must have a method named `main()`. Most Java applications have additional methods.

- To compile your source code from the command line, type `javac` followed by the name of the file that contains the source code. The compiler might issue syntax error messages that you must correct. When you successfully compile your source code, the compiler creates a file with a .class extension.

- You can run a compiled .class file on any computer that has a Java language interpreter by entering the `java` command followed by the name of the class file. When you modify a class, you must recompile it for the changes to take effect. After a program executes, you must examine the output for logical errors.

- Program comments are nonexecuting statements that you add to a file for the purpose of documentation. Java provides you with three types of comments: line comments, block comments, and javadoc comments.

- Java provides you with built-in classes that produce GUI output. For example, Java contains a class named `JOptionPane` that allows you to produce dialog boxes.

Review Questions

1. The most basic circuitry-level computer language, which consists of on and off switches, is _____ .

    a. a high-level language   c. Java
    b. machine language   d. C++

2. Languages that let you use a vocabulary of descriptive terms, such as *read, write,* or *add*, are known as _____ languages.

    a. high-level   c. procedural
    b. machine   d. object-oriented

3. The rules of a programming language constitute its _____ .

    a. objects   c. format
    b. logic   d. syntax

4. A _____ translates high-level language statements into machine code.

    a. programmer   c. compiler
    b. syntax detector   d. decipherer

5. Named computer memory locations are called _____ .

    a. compilers   c. addresses
    b. variables   d. appellations

6. The individual operations used in a computer program are often grouped into logical units called _____ .

    a. procedures   c. constants
    b. variables   d. logistics

7. Envisioning program components as objects that are similar to concrete objects in the real world is the hallmark of _____ .

    a. command-line operating systems   c. object-oriented programming
    b. procedural programming   d. machine languages

8. The values of an object's attributes also are known as its ——————.

    a. state   c. methods
    b. orientation   d. condition

9. An instance of a class is a(n) ——————.

    a. object   c. method
    b. procedure   d. class

10. Java is architecturally ——————.

    a. specific   c. neutral
    b. oriented   d. abstract

11. You must compile classes written in Java into ——————.

    a. bytecode   c. javadoc statements
    b. source code   d. object code

12. All Java programming statements must end with a ——————.

    a. period   c. semicolon
    b. comma   d. closing parenthesis

13. Arguments to methods always appear within ——————.

    a. parentheses   c. single quotation marks
    b. double quotation marks   d. curly braces

14. In a Java program, you must use —————— to separate classes, objects, and methods.

    a. commas   c. dots
    b. semicolons   d. forward slashes

15. All Java applications must have a method named ——————.

    a. `method()`   c. `java()`
    b. `main()`   d. `Hello()`

16. Nonexecuting program statements that provide documentation are called ——————.

    a. classes   c. comments
    b. notes   d. commands

17. Java supports three types of comments: ——————, ——————, and javadoc.

    a. line, block   c. constant, variable
    b. string, literal   d. single, multiple

18. After you write and save a Java application file, you ——————— it.

   a. interpret and then compile   c. compile and then resave
   b. interpret and then execute   d. compile and then interpret

19. The command to execute a compiled Java application is ———————.

   a. run   c. javac
   b. execute   d. java

20. You save text files containing Java source code using the file extension ———————.

   a. .java   c. .txt
   b. .class   d. .src

Exercises

 Programming Exercises

1. For each of the following Java identifiers, note whether it is legal or illegal:

   a. budgetApproval   g. ssn#
   b. German Shepherd   h. 4999
   c. static   i. 17
   d. HELLO   j. Accounts_Receivable
   e. 212AreaCode   k. 32MPG
   f. qhu6TRfg   l. rulesOfOrder

2. Name at least three attributes that might be appropriate for each of the following classes:

   a. CruiseShip
   b. InsurancePolicy
   c. StudentAcademicRecord

3. Name at least three objects that are instances of each of the following classes:

   a. Song
   b. BaseballTeam
   c. Playwright

4. Name at least three classes to which each of these objects might belong:

   a. myRedSweater
   b. londonEngland
   c. thursdaysDinner

5. Write, compile, and test a class that displays your full name on the screen. Save the class as **FullName.java**.

 As you work through the programming exercises in this book, you will create many files. To organize them, you might want to create a separate folder in which to store the files for each chapter.

6. Write, compile, and test a class that displays your full name, e-mail address, and phone number on three separate lines on the screen. Save the class as **PersonalInfo.java**.

7. Write, compile, and test a class that displays the following pattern on the screen:

```
X                               X
X                               X
X         XXXXXXXXXX             X
XXXXX   X             X   XXXXX
X    X    X             X    X    X
X    X    X             X    X    X
```

Save the class as **TableAndChairs.java**.

8. Write, compile, and test a class that displays the word "Java" on the screen. Compose each large letter using the appropriate character, as in the following example:

```
J       A       V         V       A
J         A A     V       V     A A
J        A    A    V     V     A    A
J    J   AAAAAAA     V V       AAAAAAA
JJJJJJ    A         A     V     A         A
```

Save the class as **BigJavaWord.java**.

9. Write, compile, and test a class that displays at least four lines of your favorite song. Save the class as **FavoriteSong.java**.

10. Write, compile, and test a class that uses the command window to display the following statement about comments:

"Program comments are nonexecuting statements you add to a file for the purpose of documentation."

Also include the same statement in three different comments in the class; each comment should use one of the three different methods of including comments in a Java class. Save the class as **Comments.java**.

11. Modify the Comments.java program in Exercise 10 so that the statement about comments is displayed in a dialog box. Save the class as **CommentsDialog.java**.

12. From 1925 through 1963, Burma Shave advertising signs appeared next to highways all across the United States. There were always four or five signs in a row containing pieces of a rhyme, followed by a final sign that read "Burma Shave." For example, one set of signs that has been preserved by the Smithsonian Institution reads as follows:

```
Shaving brushes
You'll soon see 'em
On a shelf
In some museum
Burma Shave
```

Find a classic Burma Shave rhyme on the Web. Write, compile, and test a class that produces a series of four dialog boxes so that each displays one line of a Burma Shave slogan in turn. Save the class as **BurmaShave.java**.

Debugging Exercises

1. Each of the following files in the Chapter01 folder in your downloadable student files has syntax and/or logic errors. In each case, determine the problem and fix the errors. After you correct the errors, save each file using the same filename preceded with *Fix*. For example, DebugOne1.java will become FixDebugOne1.java.

a. DebugOne1.java   c. DebugOne3.java

b. DebugOne2.java   d. DebugOne4.java

When you change a filename, remember to change every instance of the class name within the file so that it matches the new filename. In Java, the filename and class name must always match.

Game Zone

1. In 1952, A. S. Douglas wrote his University of Cambridge Ph.D. dissertation on human-computer interaction and created the first graphical computer game—a version of Tic-Tac-Toe. The game was programmed on an EDSAC vacuum-tube mainframe computer. The first computer game is generally assumed to be "Space-war!", developed in 1962 at MIT; the first commercially available video game was "Pong," introduced by Atari in 1973. In 1980, Atari's "Asteroids" and "Lunar Lander" became the first video games to be registered in the U. S. Copyright Office. Throughout the 1980s, players spent hours with games that now seem very simple and unglamorous; do you recall playing "Adventure," "Oregon Trail," "Where in the World Is Carmen Sandiego?," or "Myst"?

Today, commercial computer games are much more complex; they require many programmers, graphic artists, and testers to develop them, and large management and marketing staffs are needed to promote them. A game might cost many millions of dollars to develop and market, but a successful game might earn hundreds of millions of dollars. Obviously, with the brief introduction to programming you have had in this chapter, you cannot create a very sophisticated game. However, you can get started.

For games to hold your interest, they almost always include some random, unpredictable behavior. For example, a game in which you shoot asteroids loses some of its fun if the asteroids follow the same, predictable path each time you play the game. Therefore, generating random values is a key component in creating most interesting computer games.

Appendix D contains information on generating random numbers. To fully understand the process, you must learn more about Java classes and methods. However, for now, you can copy the following statement to generate and use a dialog box that displays a random number between 1 and 10:

```
JOptionPane.showMessageDialog(null,"The number is " +
    (1 + (int)(Math.random() * 10)));
```

Write a Java application that displays two dialog boxes in sequence. The first asks you to think of a number between 1 and 10. The second displays a randomly generated number; the user can see whether his or her guess was accurate. (In future chapters you will improve this game so that the user can enter a guess and the program can determine whether the user was correct. If you wish, you also can tell the user how far off the guess was, whether the guess was high or low, and provide a specific number of repeat attempts.) Save the file as **RandomGuess.java**.

 ## Case Problems

The case problems in this section introduce two fictional businesses. Throughout this book, you will create increasingly complex classes for these businesses that use the newest concepts you have mastered in each chapter.

1. Carly's Catering provides meals for parties and special events. Write a program that displays Carly's motto, which is "Carly's makes the food that makes it a party." Save the file as **CarlysMotto.java**. Create a second program that displays the motto surrounded by a border composed of asterisks. Save the file as **CarlysMotto2.java**.

2. Sammy's Seashore Supplies rents beach equipment such as kayaks, canoes, beach chairs, and umbrellas to tourists. Write a program that displays Sammy's motto, which is "Sammy's makes it fun in the sun." Save the file as **SammysMotto.java**. Create a second program that displays the motto surrounded by a border composed of repeated Ss. Save the file as **SammysMotto2.java**.

CHAPTER 2

Using Data

In this chapter, you will:

◎ Declare and use constants and variables

◎ Use integer data types

◎ Use the `boolean` data type

◎ Use floating-point data types

◎ Use the `char` data type

◎ Use the `Scanner` class to accept keyboard input

◎ Use the `JOptionPane` class to accept GUI input

◎ Perform arithmetic

◎ Understand type conversion

Declaring and Using Constants and Variables

A data item is **constant** when its value cannot be changed while a program is running. For example, when you include the following statement in a Java class, the number 459 is a constant:

```
System.out.println(459);
```

Every time an application containing the constant 459 is executed, the value 459 is displayed. Programmers refer to the number 459 as a **literal constant** because its value is taken literally at each use. The number 459 is also a **numeric constant** as opposed to a character or string constant. Additionally, it is an **unnamed constant** as opposed to a named one, because no identifier is associated with it.

Instead of using constant data, you can set up a data item to be variable. A **variable** is a named memory location that can store a value. A variable can hold only one value at a time, but the value it holds can change. For example, if you create a variable named ovenTemperature, it might hold 0 when the application starts, later be altered to hold 350, and still later be altered to hold 400.

Whether a data item is variable or constant, in Java it always has a data type. An item's **data type** describes the type of data that can be stored there, how much memory the item occupies, and what types of operations can be performed on the data. Java provides for eight primitive types of data. A **primitive type** is a simple data type. The eight types are described in Table 2-1. Later in this chapter, you will learn more specific information about several of these data types.

Keyword	Description
byte	Byte-length integer
short	Short integer
int	Integer
long	Long integer
float	Single-precision floating point
double	Double-precision floating point
char	A single character
boolean	A Boolean value (true or false)

Table 2-1   Java primitive data types

The eight data types in Table 2-1 are called *primitive* because they are simple and uncomplicated. Primitive types also serve as the building blocks for more complex data types, called **reference types**, which hold memory addresses. The classes you will begin creating in Chapter 3 are examples of reference types, as is the Scanner class you will use later in this chapter.

Declaring Variables

A **variable declaration** is a statement that reserves a named memory location and includes the following:

- A data type that identifies the type of data that the variable will store

- An identifier that is the variable's name

- An optional assignment operator and assigned value, if you want a variable to contain an initial value

- An ending semicolon

You name variables using the same naming rules as you do for legal class identifiers. Basically, variable names must start with a letter and cannot be a reserved keyword. You must declare a variable before you can use it. You can declare a variable at any point before you use it, but it is common practice to declare variables first in a method and to place executable statements after the declarations. Java is a **strongly typed language**, or one in which each variable has a well-defined data type that limits the operations you can perform with it; strong typing implies that all variables must be declared before they can be used.

Variable names conventionally begin with lowercase letters to distinguish them from class names. However, as with class names, a program can compile without error even if names are constructed unconventionally. Beginning an identifier with a lowercase letter and capitalizing subsequent words within the identifier is a style known as **camel casing**. An identifier such as lastName resembles a camel because of the uppercase "hump" in the middle.

For example, the following declaration creates a variable of type int named myAge and assigns it an initial value of 25;

```
int myAge = 25;
```

This declaration is a complete, executable statement, so it ends with a semicolon. The equal sign (=) is the **assignment operator**. Any value to the right of the equal sign is assigned to the variable on the left of the equal sign. An assignment made when you declare a variable is an **initialization**; an assignment made later is simply an **assignment**. Thus, the first statement that follows is an initialization, and the second is an assignment:

```
int myAge = 25;
myAge = 42;
```

You declare a variable just once, but you might assign new values to it any number of times.

Note that an expression with a literal to the left of the assignment operator (such as 25 = myAge) is illegal. The assignment operator has right-to-left associativity. **Associativity** refers to the order in which values are used with operators. The associativity of every operator is either right-to-left or left-to-right. An identifier that can appear on the left side of an assignment operator sometimes is referred to as an **lvalue**. A numeric constant like 25 is not an lvalue; it is only an **rvalue**, or an item that can appear only on the right side of an assignment operator. A variable can be used as an lvalue or an rvalue, but a literal number can only be an rvalue.

When you declare a variable within a method but do not assign a value to it, it is an **uninitialized variable**. For example, the following variable declaration declares a variable of type `int` named `myAge`, but no value is assigned at the time of creation:

```
int myAge;
```

An uninitialized variable contains an unknown value called a **garbage value**. Java protects you from inadvertently using the garbage value that is stored in an uninitialized variable. For example, if you attempt to display garbage or use it as part of a calculation, you receive an error message stating that the variable might not have been initialized.

When you learn about creating classes in the chapter *Using Methods, Classes, and Objects*, you will discover that variables declared in a class, but outside any method, are automatically initialized for you.

You can declare multiple variables of the same type in separate statements. You also can declare two (or more) variables of the same type in a single statement by separating the variable declarations with a comma, as shown in the following statement:

```
int myAge = 25, yourAge = 19;
```

By convention, programmers declare most variables in separate statements. You might declare multiple variables in the same statement only if they are closely related. Remember that even if a statement occupies multiple lines, the statement is not complete until the semicolon is reached.

You can declare as many variables in a statement as you want, as long as the variables are the same data type. However, if you want to declare variables of different types, you must use a separate statement for each type.

Declaring Named Constants

A variable is a named memory location for which the contents can change. If a named location's value should not change during the execution of a program, you can create it to be a **named constant**. A named constant is also known as a **symbolic constant**. A named constant is similar to a variable in that it has a data type, a name, and a value. A named constant differs from a variable in several ways:

- In its declaration statement, the data type of a named constant is preceded by the keyword **final**.

- A named constant can be assigned a value only once, and then it can never be changed. Usually you initialize a named constant when you declare it; if you do not initialize the constant at declaration, it is known as a **blank final**, and you can assign a value later. You can assign a value to a `final` constant only once, and you must assign a value before the constant is used.

- Although it is not a requirement, named constants conventionally are given identifiers using all uppercase letters, using underscores as needed to separate words.

For example, each of the following defines a conventionally named constant:

```
final int NUMBER_OF_DEPTS = 20;
final double PI = 3.14159;
final double TAX_RATE = 0.015;
final string COMPANY = "ABC Manufacturing";
```

You can use each of these named constants anywhere you can use a variable of the same type, except on the left side of an assignment statement after the first value has been assigned. In other words, after they receive their initial values, named constants are rvalues.

A constant always has the same value within a program, so you might wonder why you cannot use the actual, literal value. For example, why not use the unnamed constant *20* when you need the number of departments in a company rather than going to the trouble of creating the NUMBER_OF_DEPTS named constant? There are several good reasons to use the named constant rather than the literal one:

- The number 20 is more easily recognized as the number of departments if it is associated with an identifier. Using named constants makes your programs easier to read and understand. Some programmers refer to the use of a literal numeric constant, such as 20, as using a **magic number**—a value that does not have immediate, intuitive meaning or a number that cannot be explained without additional knowledge. For example, you might write a program that uses the value 7 for several purposes, so you might use constants such as DAYS_IN_WEEK and NUM_RETAIL_OUTLETS that both hold the value 7 but more clearly describe the purpose. Avoiding magic numbers helps provide internal documentation for your programs.

- If the number of departments in your organization changes, you would change the value of NUMBER_OF_DEPTS at one location within your program—where the constant is defined—rather than searching for every use of 20 to change it to a different number. Being able to make the change at one location saves you time and prevents you from missing a reference to the number of departments.

- Even if you are willing to search for every instance of 20 in a program to change it to the new department number value, you might inadvertently change the value of one instance of 20 that is being used for something else, such as a payroll deduction value.

- Using named constants reduces typographical errors. For example, if you must include 20 at several places within a program, you might inadvertently type 10 or 200 for one of the instances, and the compiler will not recognize the mistake. However, if you use the identifier NUMBER_OF_DEPTS, the compiler will ensure that you spell it correctly.

- When you use a named constant in an expression, it stands out as separate from a variable. For example, in the following arithmetic statement, it is easy to see which elements are variable and which are constant because the constants have been named conventionally:

```
double payAmount = hoursWorked * STD_PAY_RATE -
    numDependents * DEDUCTION;
```

Although many programmers use named constants to stand for most of the constant values in their programs, many make an exception when using 0 or 1.

The Scope of Variables and Constants

A data item's **scope** is the area in which it is visible to a program and in which you can refer to it using its simple identifier. A variable or constant is in scope from the point it is declared until the end of the block of code in which the declaration lies. A **block of code** is the code contained between a set of curly braces. So, if you declare a variable or constant within a method, it can be used from its declaration until the end of the method unless the method contains multiple sets of curly braces. Then, a data item is usable only until the end of the block that holds the declaration.

In the chapter *Using Methods, Classes, and Objects*, you will start to create classes that contain multiple sets of curly braces. In the chapter *More Object Concepts*, you will learn some techniques for using variables that are not currently in scope.

Concatenating Strings to Variables and Constants

You can display a variable or a constant in a print() or println() statement alone or in combination with a string. For example, the NumbersPrintln class shown in Figure 2-1 declares an integer billingDate, which is initialized to 5. In the first shaded statement, the value of billingDate is sent alone to the print() method; in the second shaded statement, billingDate is combined with, or **concatenated** to, a String. In Java, when a numeric variable is concatenated to a String using the plus sign, the entire expression becomes a String. In Figure 2-1, print() and println() method calls are used to display different data types, including a String, a number, and a concatenated String. The output of the application shown in Figure 2-1 appears in Figure 2-2.

```
public class NumbersPrintln
{
    public static void main(String[] args)
    {
        int billingDate = 5;
        System.out.print("Bills are sent on day ");
        System.out.print(billingDate);
        System.out.println(" of the month");
        System.out.println("Next bill: October " +
            billingDate);
    }
}
```

Figure 2-1   NumbersPrintln class

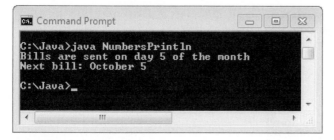

Figure 2-2   Output of NumbersPrintln application

 Later in this chapter, you will learn that a plus sign (+) between two numeric values indicates an addition operation. However, when you place a string on one or both sides of a plus sign, concatenation occurs. In Chapter 1, you learned that *polymorphism* describes the feature of languages that allows the same word or symbol to be interpreted correctly in different situations based on the context. The plus sign is polymorphic in that it indicates concatenation when used with strings but addition when used with numbers.

When you concatenate a String with numbers, the entire expression is a String. Therefore, the expression "A" + 3 + 4 results in the String "A34". If your intention is to create the String "A7", then you could add parentheses to write "A" + (3 + 4).

The program in Figure 2-1 uses the command line to display values, but you also can use a dialog box. Recall from Chapter 1 that you can use the showMessageDialog() method with two arguments: null, which indicates the box should appear in the center of the screen, and the String to be displayed in the box. Figure 2-3 shows a NumbersDialog class that uses the showMessageDialog() method twice to display an integer declared as creditDays and initialized to 30. In each shaded statement in the class, the numeric variable is concatenated to a String, making the entire second argument a String. In the first shaded statement, the concatenated String is an empty String (or **null String**), created by typing a set of quotes with nothing between them. The application produces the two dialog boxes shown in Figures 2-4 and 2-5. The first dialog box shows just the value 30; after it is dismissed by clicking OK, the second dialog box appears.

```java
import javax.swing.JOptionPane;
public class NumbersDialog
{
    public static void main(String[] args)
    {
        int creditDays = 30;
        JOptionPane.showMessageDialog(null, "" + creditDays);
        JOptionPane.showMessageDialog
            (null, "Every bill is due in " + creditDays + " days");
    }
}
```

Figure 2-3   NumbersDialog class

Figure 2-4   First dialog box created by `NumbersDialog` application

Figure 2-5   Second dialog box created by `NumbersDialog` application

Pitfall: Forgetting That a Variable Holds One Value at a Time

Each constant can hold only one value for the duration of its program; each variable can hold just one value at a time. Suppose you have two variables, x and y, and x holds 2 and y holds 10. Suppose further that you want to switch their values so that x holds 10 and y holds 2. You cannot simply make an assignment such as x = y because then both variables will hold 10, and the 2 will be lost. Similarly, if you make the assignment y = x, then both variables will hold 2, and the 10 will be lost. The solution is to declare and use a third variable, as in the following sequence of events:

```
int x = 2, y = 10, z;
z = x;
x = y;
y = z;
```

In this example, the third variable, z, is used as a temporary holding spot for one of the original values. The variable z is assigned the value of x, so z becomes 2. Then the value of y, 10, is assigned to x. Finally, the 2 held in z is assigned to y. The extra variable is used because as soon as you assign a value to a variable, any value that was previously in the memory location is gone.

 Watch the video *Declaring Variables and Constants*.

Declaring and Using Constants and Variables

1. A variable is a named memory location that you can use to store a value; it can hold only one value at a time, but the value it holds can change.

2. An item's data type determines what legal identifiers can be used to describe variables and whether the variables can occupy memory.

3. A variable declaration is a statement that reserves a named memory location and includes a data type, an identifier, an optional assignment operator and assigned value, and an ending semicolon.

The false statement is #2. An item's data type describes the type of data that can be stored, how much memory the item occupies, and what types of operations can be performed on the data. The data type does not alter the rules for a legal identifier, and the data type does not determine whether variables can occupy memory—all variables occupy memory.

 You Do It

Declaring and Using a Variable

In this section, you write an application to work with a variable and a constant.

1. Open a new document in your text editor. Create a class header and an opening and closing curly brace for a new class named `DataDemo` by typing the following:

```
public class DataDemo
{
}
```

2. Between the curly braces, indent a few spaces and type the following `main()` method header and its curly braces:

```
public static void main(String[] args)
{
}
```

(continues)

(continued)

60

3. Between the `main()` method's curly braces, type the following variable declaration:

```
int aWholeNumber = 315;
```

4. Type the following output statements. The first displays a string that includes a space before the closing quotation mark and leaves the insertion point for the next output on the same line. The second statement displays the value of `aWholeNumber` and then advances to a new line.

```
System.out.print("The number is ");
System.out.println(aWholeNumber);
```

5. Save the file as **DataDemo.java**.

6. Up to this point in the book, every `print()` and `println()` statement you have seen has used a `String` as an argument. When you added the last two statements to the `DataDemo` class, you wrote a `println()` statement that uses an `int` as an argument. As a matter of fact, there are many different versions of `print()` and `println()` that use different data types. Go to the Java Web site (***www.oracle.com/technetwork/java/index.html***), select **Java APIs**, and then select **Java SE 7**. Scroll through the list of **All Classes**, and select **PrintStream**; you will recall from Chapter 1 that `PrintStream` is the data type for the `out` object used with the `println()` method. Scroll down to view the list of methods in the **Method Summary**, and notice the many versions of the `print()` and `println()` methods, including ones that accept a `String`, an `int`, a `long`, and so on. In the last two statements you added to this program, one used a method version that accepts a `String` and the other used a method version that accepts an `int`.

7. Compile the file from the command line by typing **javac DataDemo.java**. If necessary, correct any errors, save the file, and then compile again.

8. Execute the application from the command line by typing **java DataDemo**. The command window output is shown in Figure 2-6.

Figure 2-6 Output of the `DataDemo` application

(continues)

(continued)

Trying to Use an Uninitialized Variable

In this section you see what happens when a variable is uninitialized.

1. In the `DataDemo` class, remove the assignment operator and the initialization value of the `aWholeNumber` variable so the declaration becomes:

    `int aWholeNumber;`

2. Save the class and recompile it. An error message appears as shown in Figure 2-7. Notice that the declaration statement does not generate an error because you can declare a variable without initializing it. However, the `println()` statement generates the error message because in Java, you cannot display an uninitialized variable.

```
C:\Java>javac DataDemo.java
DataDemo.java:7: error: variable aWholeNumber might not have been initialized
        System.out.println(aWholeNumber);
                           ^
1 error

C:\Java>_
```

Figure 2-7   Error message generated when a variable is not initialized

3. Modify the `aWholeNumber` declaration so that the variable is again initialized to 315. Compile the class, and execute it again.

Adding a Named Constant to a Program

In this section you add a named constant to the `DataDemo` program.

1. After the declaration of the `aWholeNumber` variable in the `DataDemo` class, insert a new line in your program and type the following constant declaration:

    `final int STATES_IN_US = 50;`

2. Following the last `println()` statement in the existing program, add a new statement to display a string and the constant. In this case, you concatenate the string and the numeric value, so the `println()` method call uses the version that accepts a `String` argument.

    ```
    System.out.println("The number of states is " +
        STATES_IN_US);
    ```

(continues)

(continued)

3. Save the program, and then compile and execute it. The output appears in Figure 2-8.

Figure 2-8   Output of DataDemo program after recent changes

Learning About Integer Data Types

In Java, you can use variables of types byte, short, int, and long to store (or hold) integers; an **integer** is a whole number without decimal places.

The **int** data type is the most commonly used integer type. A variable of type int can hold any whole number value from −2,147,483,648 to +2,147,483,647. When you assign a value to an int variable, you do not type any commas or periods; you type only digits and an optional plus or minus sign to indicate a positive or negative integer.

 The legal integer values are -2^{31} through $2^{31}-1$. These are the highest and lowest values that you can store in four bytes of memory, which is the size of an int variable.

The types **byte**, **short**, and **long** are all variations of the integer type. The byte and short types occupy less memory and can hold only smaller values; the long type occupies more memory and can hold larger values. Table 2-2 shows the upper and lower value limits for each of these types. In other programming languages, the format and size of primitive data types might depend on the platform on which a program is running. In contrast, Java consistently specifies the size and format of its primitive data types.

Type	Minimum Value	Maximum Value	Size in Bytes
byte	−128	127	1
short	−32,768	32,767	2
int	−2,147,483,648	2,147,483,647	4
long	−9,223,372,036,854,775,808	9,223,372,036,854,775,807	8

Table 2-2   Limits on integer values by type

It is important to choose appropriate types for the variables you will use in an application. If you attempt to assign a value that is too large for the data type of the variable, the compiler issues an error message, and the application does not execute. If you choose a data type that is larger than you need, you waste memory. For example, a personnel application might use a `byte` variable for number of dependents (because a limit of 127 is more than enough), a `short` for hours worked in a month (because 127 isn't enough), and an `int` for an annual salary (because even though a limit of 32,000 might be large enough for your salary, it isn't enough for the CEO's).

 Some famous glitches have occurred because programmers did not pay attention to the limits of various data types. For example, a hospital computer system in Washington, D.C., used the equivalent of a `short` to count days elapsed since January 1, 1900. The system collapsed on the 32,768th day (which was in 1989), requiring manual operations for a lengthy period.

If an application uses a literal constant integer, such as 932, the number is an `int` by default. If you need to use a constant higher than 2,147,483,647, you must follow the number with the letter *L* to indicate `long`. For example, the following statement stores a number that is greater than the maximum limit for the `int` type.

```
long mosquitosInTheNorthWoods = 2444555888L;
```

You can type either an uppercase or lowercase L after the digits to indicate the `long` type, but the uppercase *L* is preferred to avoid confusion with the number 1. You don't need any special notation to store a numeric constant in an `int`, `byte`, or a `short`.

Because integer constants, such as 18, are type `int` by default, the examples in this book almost always declare a variable as type `int` when the variable's purpose is to hold a whole number. That is, even if the expected value is less than 128, such as `hoursWorkedToday`, this book will declare the variable to be an `int`. If you are writing an application in which saving memory is important, you might choose to declare the same variable as a `byte`.

 Saving memory is seldom an issue for an application that runs on a PC. However, when you write applications for small devices with limited memory, like phones, conserving memory becomes more important.

TWO TRUTHS & A LIE

Learning About Integer Data Types

1. A variable of type `int` can hold any whole number value from approximately negative two billion to positive two billion.

2. When you assign a value to an `int` variable, you do not type any commas; you type only digits and an optional plus or minus sign to indicate a positive or negative integer.

3. You can use the data types `byte` or `short` to hold larger values than can be accommodated by an `int`.

The false statement is #3. You use a `long` if you know you will be working with very large values; you use a `byte` or a `short` if you know a variable will need to hold only small values.

You Do It

Working with Integers

In this section you work more with integer values.

1. Open a new file in your text editor, and create a shell for an `IntegerDemo` class as follows:

```
public class IntegerDemo
{
}
```

2. Between the curly braces, indent a few spaces and write the shell for a `main()` method as follows:

```
public static void main(String[] args)
{
}
```

3. Within the `main()` method, create four declarations, one each for the four integer data types.

```
int anInt = 12;
byte aByte = 12;
short aShort = 12;
long aLong = 12;
```

4. Next, add four output statements that describe and display each of the values. The spaces are included at the ends of the string literals so that the values will be aligned vertically when they are displayed.

```
System.out.println("The int is   " + anInt);
System.out.println("The byte is  " + aByte);
System.out.println("The short is " + aShort);
System.out.println("The long is  " + aLong);
```

5. Save the file as **IntegerDemo.java**. Then compile and execute it. Figure 2-9 shows the output. All the values are legal sizes for each data type, so the program compiles and executes without error.

(continues)

(continued)

Figure 2-9   Output of the `IntegerDemo` program

6. Change each assigned value in the application from 12 to **1234**, and then save and recompile the program. Figure 2-10 shows the error message generated because 1234 is too large to be placed in a `byte` variable. The message, "possible loss of precision", means that if the large number had been inserted into the small space, the accuracy of the number would have been compromised.

```
C:\Java>javac IntegerDemo.java
IntegerDemo.java:6: error: possible loss of precision
        byte aByte = 1234;
                     ^
    required: byte
    found:    int
1 error

C:\Java>
```

Figure 2-10   Error message generated when a value that is too large is assigned to a `byte` variable

7. Change the value of `aByte` back to 12. Change the value of `aShort` to **123456**. Save and recompile the program. Figure 2-11 shows the result. The error message "possible loss of precision" is the same as when the `byte` value was invalid, but the error indicates that the problem is now with the `short` variable.

(continues)

Figure 2-11   Error message generated when a value that is too large is assigned to a `short` variable

8. Change the value of the `short` variable to **12345**, and then save and compile the program. Now, the program compiles without error. Execute the program and confirm that it runs as expected.

9. At the Java Web site (*www.oracle.com/technetwork/java/index.html*), examine the list of `println()` methods in the `PrintStream` class. Although you can find versions that accept `String`, `int`, and `long` arguments, you cannot find ones that accept `byte` or `short` values. Yet, the `println()` statements in the latest version of the program work correctly. The reason has to do with *type conversion*, which you will learn about later in this chapter.

10. Replace the value of `aLong` with **1234567890987654321**. Save the program and compile it. Figure 2-12 shows the error message that indicates that the integer number is too large. The message does not say that the value is too big for a `long` type variable. Instead, it means that the literal constant was evaluated and found to be too large to be a default `int` before any attempt was made to store it in the `long` variable.

Figure 2-12   Error message generated when a value that is too large is assigned to a `long` variable

(continues)

(continued)

11. Remedy the problem by adding an **L** to the end of the `long` numeric value. Now, the constant is the correct data type that can be assigned to the `long` variable. Save, compile, and execute the program; it executes successfully.

12. Watch out for errors that occur when data values are acceptable for a data type when used alone but together might produce arithmetic results that are out of range. To demonstrate, add the following declaration at the end of the current list of variable declarations in the `IntegerDemo` program:

```
int anotherInt = anInt * 10000000;
```

13. At the end of the current list of output statements, add another output statement so that you can see the result of the arithmetic:

```
System.out.println("Another int is " + anotherInt);
```

Save, compile, and execute the program. The output appears in Figure 2-13. Although 1234 and 10000000 are both acceptable `int` values, their product is out of range for an `int`, and the resulting `int` does not appear to have been calculated correctly. Because the arithmetic result was too large, some information about the value has been lost, including the result's sign. If you see such unreasonable results in your programs, you need to consider using different data types for your values.

Figure 2-13 Output of the modified `IntegerDemo` program with an out-of-range integer

Using the boolean Data Type

Boolean logic is based on true-or-false comparisons. Whereas an `int` variable can hold millions of different values (at different times), a **boolean variable** can hold only one of two values—`true` or `false`. The following statements declare and assign appropriate values to Boolean variables:

```
boolean isItPayday = false;
boolean areYouBroke = true;
```

You also can assign values based on the result of comparisons to Boolean variables. Java supports six relational operators that are used to make comparisons. A **relational operator** compares two items; it is sometimes called a **comparison operator**. An expression that contains a relational operator has a Boolean value. Table 2-3 describes the relational operators.

When you use *Boolean* as an adjective, as in *Boolean operators*, you usually begin with an uppercase *B* because the data type is named for Sir George Boole, the founder of symbolic logic, who lived from 1815 to 1864. The Java data type `boolean`, however, begins with a lowercase *b*.

Operator	Description	True Example	False Example
<	Less than	3 < 8	8 < 3
>	Greater than	4 > 2	2 > 4
==	Equal to	7 == 7	3 == 9
<=	Less than or equal to	5 <= 5	8 <= 6
>=	Greater than or equal to	7 >= 3	1 >= 2
!=	Not equal to	5 != 6	3 != 3

Table 2-3   Relational operators

When you use any of the operators that have two symbols (==, <=, >=, or !=), you cannot place any whitespace between the two symbols. You also cannot reverse the order of the symbols. That is, =<, =>, and =! are all invalid operators.

Legal declaration statements might include the following statements, which compare two values directly:

```
boolean isSixBigger = (6 > 5);
 // Value stored would be true
boolean isSevenSmallerOrEqual = (7 <= 4);
 // Value stored would be false
```

Although you can use any legal identifier for Boolean variables, they are easily identified as Boolean if you use a form of *to be* (such as *is* or *are*) as part of the variable name, as in `isSixBigger`.

The Boolean expressions are more meaningful when variables (that have been assigned values) are used in the comparisons, as in the following examples. In the first statement, the `hours` variable is compared to a constant value of 40. If the `hours` variable is not greater than 40, the expression evaluates to `false`. In the second statement, the `income` variable must be greater than 100000 for the expression to evaluate to `true`. In the third statement, two variables are compared to determine the value of `isFirstScoreHigher`.

```
boolean isOvertimePay = (hours > 40);
boolean isTaxBracketHigh = (income > 100000);
boolean isFirstScoreHigher = (score1 > score2);
```

Boolean expressions will become far more useful to you when you learn about decision making and looping in Chapters 5 and 6.

TWO TRUTHS & A LIE

Using the boolean Data Type

1. A Boolean variable can hold only one of two values—true or false.

2. Java supports six relational operators that are used to make comparisons: =, <, >, =<, =>, and =!.

3. An expression that contains a relational operator has a Boolean value.

The false statement is #2. The six relational operators used to make comparisons are == (two equal signs), <, >, <= (the less-than sign precedes the equal sign), >= (the greater-than sign precedes the equal sign), and != (the exclamation point precedes the equal sign).

Learning About Floating-Point Data Types

A **floating-point** number contains decimal positions. Java supports two floating-point data types: float and double. A **float** data type can hold floating-point values of up to six or seven significant digits of accuracy. A **double** data type requires more memory than a float and can hold 14 or 15 significant digits of accuracy. The term **significant digits** refers to the mathematical accuracy of a value. For example, a float given the value 0.324616777 is displayed as 0.324617 because the value is accurate only to the sixth decimal position. Table 2-4 shows the minimum and maximum values for each floating-point data type. Notice that the maximum value for a double is 3.4 * 10 to the 38th power, which means 3.4 times 10 with 38 trailing zeros—a very large number.

A float given the value 324616777 is displayed as 3.24617e+008, which means approximately 3.24617 times 10 to the 8th power, or 324617000. The e in the displayed value stands for *exponent*; the +008 means the true decimal point is eight positions to the right of where it is displayed, indicating a very large number. (A negative number would indicate that the true decimal point belongs to the left, indicating a very small number.) This format is called **scientific notation**. The large value contains only six significant digits.

A programmer might choose to store a value as a float instead of a double to save memory. However, if high levels of accuracy are needed, such as in graphics-intensive software, the programmer might choose to use a double, opting for high accuracy over saved memory.

Type	Minimum	Maximum	Size in Bytes
float	$-3.4 * 10^{38}$	$3.4 * 10^{38}$	4
double	$-1.7 * 10^{308}$	$1.7 * 10^{308}$	8

70

Table 2-4   Limits on floating-point values

A value stored in a double is a **double-precision floating-point number**; a value in a float is a **single-precision floating-point number**.

Just as an integer constant, such as 18, is a value of type int by default, a floating-point constant, such as 18.23, is a double by default. To indicate that a floating-point numeric constant is a float, you can type the letter *F* after the number, as in the following:

```
float pocketChange = 4.87F;
```

You can type either a lowercase or an uppercase *F*. You also can type *D* (or *d*) after a floating-point constant to indicate it is a double, but even without the *D*, the value will be stored as a double by default. Floating-point numbers can be imprecise, as you will see later in this chapter.

TWO TRUTHS & A LIE

Learning About Floating-Point Data Types

1. Java supports two floating-point data types: float and double. The double data type requires more memory and can hold more significant digits.

2. A floating-point constant, such as 5.6, is a float by default.

3. As with integers, you can perform the mathematical operations of addition, subtraction, multiplication, and division with floating-point numbers.

The false statement is #2. A floating-point constant, such as 5.6, is a double by default.

Using the char Data Type

You use the **char** data type to hold any single character. You place constant character values within single quotation marks because the computer stores characters and integers differently. For example, the following are typical character declarations:

```
char middleInitial = 'M';
char gradeInChemistry = 'A';
char aStar = '*';
```

Some programmers prefer to pronounce *char* as *care* because it represents the first syllable in the word *character*. Others prefer to pronounce the word as *char* to rhyme with *car*. You should use the preferred pronunciation in your organization.

A character can be any letter—uppercase or lowercase. It might also be a punctuation mark or digit. A character that is a digit is represented in computer memory differently than a numeric value represented by the same digit. For example, the following two statements are legal:

```
char aCharValue = '9';
int aNumValue = 9;
```

If you display each of these values using a println() statement, you see a 9. However, only the numeric value, aNumValue, can be used to represent the value 9 in arithmetic statements.

A numeric constant can be stored in a character variable and a character that represents a number can be stored in a numeric variable. For example, the following two statements are legal, but unless you understand their meanings, they might produce undesirable results:

```
char aCharValue = 9;
int aNumValue = '9';
```

If these variables are displayed using println() statements, then the resulting output is a blank for aCharValue and the number 57 for aNumValue. The unexpected values are Unicode values. Every computer stores every character it uses as a number; every character is assigned a unique numeric code using Unicode. Table 2-5 shows some Unicode decimal values and their character equivalents. For example, the character *A* is stored using the value 65, and the character *B* is stored using the value 66. Appendix B contains more information on Unicode.

Dec	Char	Dec	Char	Dec	Char	Dec	Char
0	nul	32		64	@	96	`
1	soh^A	33	!	65	A	97	a
2	stx^B	34	"	66	B	98	b
3	etx^C	35	#	67	C	99	c
4	eot^D	36	$	68	D	100	d
5	enq^E	37	%	69	E	101	e
6	ask^F	38	&	70	F	102	f
7	bel^G	39	'	71	G	103	g
8	bs^H	40	(	72	H	104	h
9	ht^I	41	)	73	I	105	i
10	lf^J	42	*	74	J	106	j

Table 2-5   Unicode values 0 through 127 and their character equivalents (*continues*)

(continued)

Dec	Char	Dec	Char	Dec	Char	Dec	Char
11	vt^K	43	+	75	K	107	k
12	ff^L	44	,	76	L	108	l
13	cr^M	45	-	77	M	109	m
14	so^N	46	.	78	N	110	n
15	si^O	47	/	79	O	111	o
16	dle^P	48	0	80	P	112	p
17	dc1^Q	49	1	81	Q	113	q
18	dc2^R	50	2	82	R	114	r
19	dc3^S	51	3	83	S	115	s
20	dc4^T	52	4	84	T	116	t
21	nak^U	53	5	85	U	117	u
22	syn^V	54	6	86	V	118	v
23	etb^W	55	7	87	W	119	w
24	can^X	56	8	88	X	120	x
25	em^Y	57	9	89	Y	121	y
26	sub^Z	58	:	90	Z	122	z
27	esc	59	;	91	[	123	{
28	fs	60	<	92	\	124		
29	gs	61	=	93	]	125	}
30	rs	62	>	94	^	126	~
31	us	63	?	95	_	127	del

Table 2-5   Unicode values 0 through 127 and their character equivalents

A variable of type char can hold only one character. To store a string of characters, such as a person's name, you must use a data structure called a String. In Java, **String** is a built-in class that provides you with the means for storing and manipulating character strings. Unlike single characters, which use single quotation marks, string constants are written between double quotation marks. For example, the expression that stores the name *Audrey* as a string in a variable named firstName is:

```
String firstName = "Audrey";
```

You will learn more about strings and the String class in the chapter *Characters, Strings, and the StringBuilder*.

You can store any character—including nonprinting characters such as a backspace or a tab—in a char variable. To store these characters, you can use an **escape sequence**, which always begins with a backslash followed by a character—the pair represents a single character. For example, the following code stores a newline character and a tab character in the char variables aNewLine and aTabChar:

```
char aNewLine = '\n';
char aTabChar = '\t';
```

In the declarations of aNewLine and aTabChar, the backslash and character pair acts as a single character; the escape sequence serves to give a new meaning to the character. That is, the literal characters in the preceding code have different values from the "plain" characters 'n' or 't'. Table 2-6 describes some common escape sequences that you can use with command window output in Java.

Escape Sequence	Description
\b	Backspace; moves the cursor one space to the left
\t	Tab; moves the cursor to the next tab stop
\n	Newline or linefeed; moves the cursor to the beginning of the next line
\r	Carriage return; moves the cursor to the beginning of the current line
\"	Double quotation mark; displays a double quotation mark
\'	Single quotation mark; displays a single quotation mark
\\	Backslash; displays a backslash character

Table 2-6   Common escape sequences

 When you display values within JOptionPane dialog boxes rather than in a command window, the escape sequences '\n' (newline), '\"' (double quote), and '\\' (backslash) operate as expected within a JOptionPane object, but '\t', '\b', and '\r' do not work in the GUI environment.

When you want to produce console output on multiple lines in the command window, you have two options: You can use the newline escape sequence, or you can use the println() method multiple times. For example, Figures 2-14 and 2-15 both show classes that produce the same output: "Hello" on one line and "there" on another. The version you choose to use is up to you. The example in Figure 2-14 is more efficient—from a typist's point of view because the text System.out.println appears only once, and from the compiler's point of view because the println() method is called only once. The example in Figure 2-15, however, might be easier to read and understand. When programming in Java, you will find occasions when each of these approaches makes sense.

```
public class HelloThereNewLine
{
    public static void main(String[] args)
    {
        System.out.println("Hello\nthere");
    }
}
```

Figure 2-14   HelloThereNewLine class

```
public class HelloTherePrintlnTwice
{
    public static void main(String[] args)
    {
        System.out.println("Hello");
        System.out.println("there");
    }
}
```

Figure 2-15   HelloTherePrintlnTwice class

The println() method uses the local platform's line terminator character, which might or might not be the newline character \n.

TWO TRUTHS & A LIE

Using the char Data Type

1. You use the char data type to hold any single character; you place constant character values within single quotation marks.

2. To store a string of characters, you use a data structure called a Text; string constants are written between parentheses.

3. An escape sequence always begins with a backslash followed by a character; the pair represents a single character.

The false statement is #2. To store a string of characters, you use a data structure called a String; string constants are written between quotation marks.

74

You Do It

Working with the char Data Type

In the steps in this section, you create an application that demonstrates some features of the char data type.

1. Create the shells for a class named CharDemo and its main() method as follows:

```
public class CharDemo
{
    public static void main(String[] args)
    {
    }
}
```

2. Between the curly braces for the main() method, declare a char variable, and provide an initialization value:

```
char initial = 'A';
```

3. Add two statements. The first displays the variable, and the second demonstrates some escape sequence characters.

```
System.out.println(initial);
System.out.print("\t\"abc\\def\bghi\n\njkl");
```

4. Save the file as **CharDemo.java**, and then compile and execute it. Figure 2-16 shows the output. The first line of output contains the value of the char variable. The next line starts with a tab created by the escape sequence \t. The tab is followed by a quotation mark produced by the escape sequence \". Then abc is displayed, followed by the next escape sequence that produces a slash. The next series of characters to display is def, but because those letters are followed by a backspace escape sequence, the f is overridden by ghi. After ghi, two newline escape sequences provide a double-spaced effect. Finally, the last three characters jkl are displayed.

Figure 2-16   Output of the CharDemo program

5. Modify, recompile, and execute the CharDemo program as many times as you like until you can accurately predict what will be displayed when you use various combinations of characters and escape sequences.

Using the Scanner Class to Accept Keyboard Input

Although you can assign values to variables you declare, programs typically become more useful when a user can supply different values for variables each time a program executes. In Chapter 1, you learned how to display output on the monitor using the System.out property. System.out refers to the standard output device, which usually is the monitor. To create interactive programs that accept input from a user, you can use System.in, which refers to the **standard input device** (normally the keyboard).

You have learned that you can use the print() and println() methods to display many data types; for example, you can use them to display a double, int, or String. The System.in object is not as flexible; it is designed to read only bytes. That's a problem, because you often want to accept data of other types. Fortunately, the designers of Java have created a class named Scanner that makes System.in more flexible.

To create a Scanner object and connect it to the System.in object, you write a statement similar to the following:

```
Scanner inputDevice = new Scanner(System.in);
```

The portion of the statement to the left of the assignment operator, Scanner inputDevice, declares an object of type Scanner with the programmer-chosen name inputDevice, in exactly the same way that int x; declares an integer with the programmer-chosen name x.

The portion of the statement to the right of the assignment operator, new Scanner(System.in), creates a Scanner object that is connected to the System.in property. In other words, the created Scanner object is connected to the default input device. The keyword new is required by Java; you will use it whenever you create objects that are more complex than the simple data types.

In the chapter *More Object Concepts*, you will learn that the second part of the Scanner declaration calls a special method called a constructor that is part of the prewritten Scanner class. You also will learn more about the Java keyword new in the next two chapters.

The assignment operator in the Scanner declaration statement assigns the value of the new object—that is, its memory address—to the inputDevice object in the program.

The Scanner class contains methods that retrieve values from an input device. Each retrieved value is a **token**, which is a set of characters that is separated from the next set by whitespace. Most often, this means that data is accepted when a user presses the Enter key, but it could also mean that a token is accepted after a space or tab. Table 2-7 summarizes some of the most useful methods that read different data types from the default input device. Each retrieves a value from the keyboard and returns it if the next token is the correct data type.

Method	Description
nextDouble()	Retrieves input as a double
nextInt()	Retrieves input as an int
nextLine()	Retrieves the next line of data and returns it as a String
next()	Retrieves the next complete token as a String
nextShort()	Retrieves input as a short
nextByte()	Retrieves input as a byte
nextFloat()	Retrieves input as a float. Note that when you enter an input value that will be stored as a float, you do not type an F. The F is used only with constants coded within a program.
nextLong()	Retrieves input as a long. Note that when you enter an input value that will be stored as a long, you do not type an L. The L is used only with constants coded within a program.

Table 2-7   Selected Scanner class methods

The Scanner class does not contain a nextChar() method. To retrieve a single character from the keyboard, you can use the nextLine() method and then use the charAt() method. The chapter *Characters, Strings, and the StringBuilder* provides more details about the charAt() method.

Figure 2-17 contains a program that uses two of the Scanner class methods. The program reads a string and an integer from the keyboard and displays them. The Scanner class is used in the four shaded statements in the figure.

- The first shaded statement is import java.util.Scanner;. This statement imports the package necessary to use the Scanner class.

- The second shaded statement declares a Scanner object named inputDevice.

- The third shaded statement uses the nextLine() method to retrieve a line of text from the keyboard and store it in the name variable.

- The last shaded statement uses the nextInt() method to retrieve an integer from the keyboard and store it in the age variable.

Figure 2-18 shows a typical execution of the program.

Java programmers would say that the Scanner methods *return* the appropriate value. That also means that the value of the method is the appropriate value, and that you can assign the returned value to a variable, display it, or use it in other legal statements. In the chapter *Using Methods, Classes, and Objects*, you will learn how to write your own methods that return values.

```
import java.util.Scanner;
public class GetUserInfo
{
    public static void main(String[] args)
    {
        String name;
        int age;
        Scanner inputDevice = new Scanner(System.in);
        System.out.print("Please enter your name >> ");
        name = inputDevice.nextLine();
        System.out.print("Please enter your age >> ");
        age = inputDevice.nextInt();
        System.out.println("Your name is " + name +
            " and you are " + age + " years old.");
    }
}
```

Repeating as output what a user has entered as input is called **echoing the input**. Echoing input is a good programming practice; it helps eliminate misunderstandings when the user can visually confirm what was entered.

Figure 2-17   The GetUserInfo class

Figure 2-18   Typical execution of the GetUserInfo program

If you use any of the Scanner methods and the next token cannot be converted to the right data type, you receive an error message. For example, the program in Figure 2-17 uses nextInt() to retrieve age, so if the user entered a noninteger value for age, such as the double 19.5 or the String "nineteen", an error would occur. You will learn how to recover from this type of error in the chapter *Exception Handling*, but for now, you will have to trust the user to enter the correct data type.

The literal Strings contained in the print() statements that appear before each input statement in Figure 2-17 are examples of prompts. A **prompt** is a message displayed for the user that requests and describes input. Interactive programs would work without prompts, but they would not be as user-friendly. Each prompt in the GetUserInfo class ends with two greater-than signs and a space. This punctuation is not required; it just separates the words in the prompt from the user's input value on the screen, improving readability. You might prefer to use a series of periods, several dashes, or just a few spaces.

It is legal to write a single prompt that requests multiple input values—for example, "Please enter your age, area code, and zip code." The user could then enter the three values separated with spaces, tabs, or Enter key presses. The values would then be interpreted as separate tokens and could be retrieved with three separate `nextInt()` method calls. However, asking a user to enter multiple values often leads to mistakes. This book will follow the practice of using a separate prompt for each input value required.

Pitfall: Using `nextLine()` Following One of the Other Scanner Input Methods

You can encounter a problem when you use one of the numeric Scanner class retrieval methods or the `next()` method before you use the `nextLine()` method. Consider the program in Figure 2-19. It is identical to the one in Figure 2-17, except that the user is asked for an age before being asked for a name. (See shading.) Figure 2-20 shows a typical execution.

```java
import java.util.Scanner;
public class GetUserInfo2
{
    public static void main(String[] args)
    {
        String name;
        int age;
        Scanner inputDevice = new Scanner(System.in);
        System.out.print("Please enter your age >> ");
        age = inputDevice.nextInt();
        System.out.print("Please enter your name >> ");
        name = inputDevice.nextLine();
        System.out.println("Your name is " + name +
            " and you are " + age + " years old.");
    }
}
```

Don't Do It
If you accept numeric input prior to string input, the string input is ignored unless you take special action.

Figure 2-19   The GetUserInfo2 class

```
C:\Java>java GetUserInfo2
Please enter your age >> 28
Please enter your name >> Your name is  and you are 28 years old.

C:\Java>
```

Figure 2-20   Typical execution of the GetUserInfo2 program

In Figure 2-20, the user is prompted correctly for an age. However, after the user enters an age and the prompt for the name is displayed, the program does not pause to let the user enter a name. Instead, the program proceeds directly to the output statement, which does not contain a valid name, as you can see in Figure 2-20.

When you type characters using the keyboard, they are stored temporarily in a location in memory called the **keyboard buffer**. The keyboard buffer sometimes is called the **type-ahead buffer**. All keystrokes are stored in the keyboard buffer, including the Enter key. The problem occurs because of a difference in the way the nextLine() method and the other Scanner retrieval methods work:

- The Scanner methods next(), nextInt(), and nextDouble() retrieve the next token in the buffer up to the next whitespace, which might be a space, tab, or Enter key.

- The nextLine() method reads all data up to the Enter key character.

So, in the execution of the program in Figure 2-20, the user is prompted for an age, types 28, and presses Enter. The call to the nextInt() method retrieves the 28 and leaves the Enter key press in the input buffer. Then the name prompt is displayed and the call to nextLine() retrieves the waiting Enter key before the user can type a name.

The solution to the problem is simple. After any next(), nextInt(), or nextDouble() call, you can add an extra nextLine() method call that will retrieve the abandoned Enter key character. Then, no matter what type of input follows, the program will execute smoothly. Figure 2-21 shows a program that contains just one change from Figure 2-19—the addition of the shaded statement that retrieves the abandoned Enter key character from the input buffer. Although you could assign the Enter key to a character variable, there is no need to do so. When you accept an entry and discard it without using it, programmers say that the entry is **consumed**. Figure 2-21 shows that the call to nextInt() accepts the integer, the first call to nextLine() accepts the Enter key that follows the integer entry, and the second nextLine() call accepts both the entered name and the Enter key that follows it. Figure 2-22 shows that the revised program executes correctly.

```
import java.util.Scanner;
public class GetUserInfo3
{
    public static void main(String[] args)
    {
        String name;
        int age;
        Scanner inputDevice = new Scanner(System.in);
        System.out.print("Please enter your age >> ");
        age = inputDevice.nextInt();
        inputDevice.nextLine();
        System.out.print("Please enter your name >> ");
        name = inputDevice.nextLine();
        System.out.println("Your name is " + name +
            " and you are " + age + " years old.");
    }
}
```

This statement gets the integer.

This statement consumes the Enter key that follows the integer.

This statement gets the name and discards the Enter key that follows the name.

Figure 2-21   The GetUserInfo3 class

```
C:\Java>java GetUserInfo3
Please enter your age >> 28
Please enter your name >> Julie
Your name is Julie and you are 28 years old.

C:\Java>
```

Figure 2-22   Typical execution of the GetUserInfo3 program

When you write programs that accept user input, there is a risk that the user will enter the wrong type of data. For example, if you include a nextInt() method call in your program, but the user types an alphabetic character, an error will occur, and your program will stop running. You will learn to handle this type of error later in this book.

TWO TRUTHS & A LIE

Using the Scanner Class to Accept Keyboard Input

1. `System.in` refers to the standard input device, which normally is the keyboard.

2. `System.in` is more flexible than `System.out` because it can read all the basic Java data types.

3. When a user types data followed by the Enter key, the Enter key character is left in the keyboard buffer after `Scanner` class methods retrieve the other keystrokes.

The false statement is #2. System.in is not as flexible as System.out. System.out can display various data types, but System.in is designed to read only bytes.

You Do It

Accepting User Input

In the next steps you create a program that accepts user input.

1. Open the **IntegerDemo.java** file you created in a "You Do It" section earlier in this chapter. Change the class name to `IntegerDemoInteractive`, and save the file as **IntegerDemoInteractive.java**.

2. As the first line in the file, insert an `import` statement that will allow you to use the `Scanner` class:

   ```
   import java.util.Scanner;
   ```

3. Remove the assignment operator and the assigned values from each of the four numeric variable declarations.

4. Following the numeric variable declarations, insert a `Scanner` object declaration:

   ```
   Scanner input = new Scanner(System.in);
   ```

5. Following the variable declarations, insert a prompt for the integer value, and an input statement that accepts the value, as follows:

   ```
   System.out.print("Please enter an integer >> ");
   anInt = input.nextInt();
   ```

(continues)

(continued)

6. Then add similar statements for the other three variables:

```
System.out.print("Please enter a byte integer >> ");
aByte = input.nextByte();
System.out.print("Please enter a short integer >> ");
aShort = input.nextShort();
System.out.print("Please enter a long integer >> ");
aLong = input.nextLong();
```

7. Save the file, and then compile and execute it. Figure 2-23 shows a typical execution. Execute the program a few more times, using different values each time and confirming that the correct values have been accepted from the keyboard.

Figure 2-23 Typical execution of the IntegerDemoInteractive program

Adding String Input

Next, you add String input to the IntegerDemoInteractive program.

1. Change the class name of the IntegerDemoInteractive program to **IntegerDemoInteractiveWithName**, and immediately save the file as **IntegerDemoInteractiveWithName.java**.

2. Add a new variable with the other variable declarations as follows:

```
String name;
```

3. After the last input statement (that gets the value for aLong), add three statements that prompt the user for a name, accept the name, and use the name as follows:

```
System.out.print("Please enter your name >> ");
name = input.nextLine();
System.out.println("Thank you, " + name);
```

(continues)

(continued)

4. Save the file, and compile and execute it. Figure 2-24 shows a typical execution. You can enter the numbers, but when the prompt for the name appears, you are not given the opportunity to respond. Instead, the string "Thank you", including the ending comma and space, is output immediately, and the program ends. This output is incorrect because the input statement that should retrieve the name from the keyboard instead retrieves the Enter key that was still in the keyboard buffer after the last numeric entry.

Figure 2-24   Typical execution of incomplete `IntegerDemoInteractiveWithName` application that does not accept a name

5. To fix the problem, insert an extra call to the `nextLine()` method just before the statement that accepts the name. This call will consume the Enter key. You do not need an assignment operator with this statement, because there is no need to store the Enter key character.

```
input.nextLine();
```

(continues)

(continued)

6. Save, compile, and execute the program. Figure 2-25 shows a typical successful execution.

```
Command Prompt                                    _ □ X

C:\Java>java IntegerDemoInteractiveWithName
Please enter an integer >> 814
Please enter a byte integer >> 52
Please enter a short integer >> 190
Please enter a long integer >> 129654
Please enter your name >> Sarah
Thank you, Sarah
The int is    814
The byte is   52
The short is  190
The long is   129654

C:\Java>_
```

Figure 2-25 Typical successful execution of `IntegerDemoInteractiveWithName` application

Using the JOptionPane Class to Accept GUI Input

In Chapter 1, you learned how to display output at the command line and how to create GUI message boxes to display String objects. Earlier in this chapter, you learned to accept input from the keyboard at the command line. You also can accept input in a GUI dialog box using the JOptionPane class.

Two dialog boxes that can be used to accept user input are:

- InputDialog—Prompts the user for text input
- ConfirmDialog—Asks the user a question, providing buttons that the user can click for Yes, No, and Cancel responses

Using Input Dialog Boxes

An **input dialog box** asks a question and provides a text field in which the user can enter a response. You can create an input dialog box using the **showInputDialog() method**. Six versions of this method are available, but the simplest version uses a single argument that is the prompt you want to display within the dialog box. The showInputDialog() method returns a String that represents a user's response; this means that you can assign the showInputDialog() method to a String variable and the variable will hold the value that the user enters.

For example, Figure 2-26 shows an application that creates an input dialog box containing a prompt for a first name. When the user executes the application, types "William", then clicks the OK button or presses Enter on the keyboard, the response String will contain "William". In the application in Figure 2-26, the response is concatenated with a welcoming message and displayed in a message dialog box. Figure 2-27 shows the dialog box containing a user's response, and Figure 2-28 shows the resulting output message box.

```java
import javax.swing.JOptionPane;
public class HelloNameDialog
{
    public static void main(String[] args)
    {
        String result;
        result = JOptionPane.showInputDialog(null, "What is your name?");
        JOptionPane.showMessageDialog(null, "Hello, " + result + "!");
    }
}
```

Figure 2-26   The HelloNameDialog class

Figure 2-27   Input dialog box of the HelloNameDialog application

Figure 2-28   Output of the HelloNameDialog application

Within the JOptionPane class, one version of the showInputDialog() method allows the programmer flexibility in controlling the appearance of the input dialog box. The version of showInputDialog() that requires four arguments can be used to display a title in the dialog box title bar and a message that describes the type of dialog box. The four arguments to showInputDialog() include:

- The parent component, which is the screen component, such as a frame, in front of which the dialog box will appear. If this argument is null, the dialog box is centered on the screen.

- The message the user will see before entering a value. Usually this message is a String, but it actually can be any type of object.

- The title to be displayed in the title bar of the input dialog box.

- A class field describing the type of dialog box; it can be one of the following:

   ERROR_MESSAGE, INFORMATION_MESSAGE, PLAIN_MESSAGE, QUESTION_MESSAGE, or WARNING_MESSAGE.

For example, when the following statement executes, it displays the input dialog box shown in Figure 2-29.

```
JOptionPane.showInputDialog(null,
    "What is your area code?",
    "Area code information",
    JOptionPane.QUESTION_MESSAGE);
```

Note that the title bar displays "Area code information," and the dialog box shows a question mark icon.

Figure 2-29   An input dialog box with a String in the title bar and a question mark icon

The showInputDialog() method returns a String object, which makes sense when you consider that you might want a user to type any combination of keystrokes into the dialog box. However, when the value that the user enters is intended to be used as a number, as in an arithmetic statement, the returned String must be converted to the correct numeric type. Later in this chapter, you will learn how to change primitive data from one data type to another. However, the techniques you will learn work only with primitive data types— double, int, char, and so on—not with class objects (that are reference types) such as a String. To convert a String to an integer or double, you must use methods from the built-in Java classes Integer and Double. Each primitive type in Java has a corresponding class contained in the java.lang package; like most classes, the names of these classes begin with uppercase letters. These classes are called **type-wrapper classes**. They include methods that can process primitive type values.

Figure 2-30 shows a SalaryDialog application that contains two String objects—wageString and dependentsString. Two showInputDialog() methods are called, and the answers are stored in the declared Strings. The shaded statements in Figure 2-30 show how the Strings are converted to numeric values using methods from the type-wrapper classes Integer and Double. The double value is converted using the Double.parseDouble() method, and the integer is converted using the Integer.parseInt() method. Figure 2-31 shows a typical execution of the application.

Remember that in Java, the reserved keyword static means that a method is accessible and usable even though no objects of the class exist. You can tell that the method Double.parseDouble() is a static method, because the method name is used with the class name Double—no object is needed. Similarly, you can tell that Integer.parseInt() is also a static method.

The term **parse** means to break into component parts. Grammarians talk about "parsing a sentence"—deconstructing it so as to describe its grammatical components. Parsing a String converts it to its numeric equivalent.

```
import javax.swing.JOptionPane;
public class SalaryDialog
{
    public static void main(String[] args)
    {
        String wageString, dependentsString;
        double wage, weeklyPay;
        int dependents;
        final double HOURS_IN_WEEK = 37.5;
        wageString = JOptionPane.showInputDialog(null,
            "Enter employee's hourly wage", "Salary dialog 1",
            JOptionPane.INFORMATION_MESSAGE);
        weeklyPay = Double.parseDouble(wageString) *
            HOURS_IN_WEEK;
        dependentsString = JOptionPane.showInputDialog(null,
            "How many dependents?", "Salary dialog 2",
            JOptionPane.QUESTION_MESSAGE);
        dependents = Integer.parseInt(dependentsString);
        JOptionPane.showMessageDialog(null, "Weekly salary is $" +
            weeklyPay + "\nDeductions will be made for " +
            dependents + " dependents");
    }
}
```

Figure 2-30   The SalaryDialog class

Figure 2-31 Sample execution of the `SalaryDialog` application

Using Confirm Dialog Boxes

Sometimes, the input you want from a user does not have to be typed from the keyboard. When you present simple options to a user, you can offer buttons that the user can click to confirm a choice. A **confirm dialog box** displays the options Yes, No, and Cancel; you can create one using the **showConfirmDialog() method** in the JOptionPane class. Four versions of the method are available; the simplest requires a parent component (which can be null) and the String prompt that is displayed in the box. The showConfirmDialog() method returns an integer containing one of three possible values: JOptionPane.YES_OPTION, JOptionPane.NO_OPTION, or JOptionPane.CANCEL_OPTION. Figure 2-32 shows an application that asks a user a question. The shaded statement displays the dialog box shown in Figure 2-33 and stores the user's response in the integer variable named selection.

```
import javax.swing.JOptionPane;
public class AirlineDialog
{
    public static void main (String[] args)
    {
        int selection;
        boolean isYes;
        selection = JOptionPane.showConfirmDialog(null,
            "Do you want to upgrade to first class?");
        isYes = (selection == JOptionPane.YES_OPTION);
        JOptionPane.showMessageDialog(null,
            "You responded " + isYes);
    }
}
```

Figure 2-32 The AirlineDialog class

Figure 2-33   The confirm dialog box displayed by the `AirlineDialog` application

After a value is stored in `selection`, a Boolean variable named `isYes` is set to the result when `selection` and `JOptionPane.YES_OPTION` are compared. If the user has selected the Yes button in the dialog box, this variable is set to `true`; otherwise, the variable is set to `false`. Finally, the true or false result is displayed; Figure 2-34 shows the result when a user clicks the Yes button in the dialog box.

Figure 2-34   Output of `AirlineDialog` application when user clicks Yes

You can also create a confirm dialog box with five arguments, as follows:

- The parent component, which can be null

- The prompt message

- The title to be displayed in the title bar

- An integer that indicates which option button will be shown (It should be one of the class variables `YES_NO_CANCEL_OPTION` or `YES_NO_OPTION`.)

- An integer that describes the kind of dialog box (It should be one of the class variables `ERROR_MESSAGE`, `INFORMATION_MESSAGE`, `PLAIN_MESSAGE`, `QUESTION_MESSAGE`, or `WARNING_MESSAGE`.)

When the following statement is executed, it displays a confirm dialog box, as shown in Figure 2-35:

```
JOptionPane.showConfirmDialog(null,
        "A data input error has occurred. Continue?",
        "Data input error", JOptionPane.YES_NO_OPTION,
        JOptionPane.ERROR_MESSAGE);
```

Note that the title bar displays "Data input error," the Yes and No buttons appear, and the dialog box shows the error message, "A data input error has occurred. Continue?" It also displays the octagonal ERROR_MESSAGE icon.

Figure 2-35   Confirm dialog box with title, Yes and No buttons, and error icon

Confirm dialog boxes provide more practical uses when your applications can make decisions based on the users' responses. In the chapter *Making Decisions*, you will learn how to make decisions within programs.

TWO TRUTHS & A LIE

Using the JOptionPane Class to Accept GUI Input

1. You can create an input dialog box using the `showInputDialog()` method; the method returns a `String` that represents a user's response.

2. You can use methods from the Java classes `Integer` and `Double` when you want to convert a dialog box's returned values to numbers.

3. A confirm dialog box can be created using the `showConfirmDialog()` method in the `JOptionPane` class; a confirm dialog box displays the options Accept, Reject, and Escape.

The false statement is #3. A confirm dialog box displays the options Yes, No, and Cancel.

Watch the video *Getting Input*.

Performing Arithmetic

Table 2-8 describes the five **standard arithmetic operators** that you use to perform calculations with values in your programs. A value used on either side of an operator is an **operand**. For example, in the expression 45 + 2, the numbers 45 and 2 are operands. The arithmetic operators are examples of **binary operators**, so named because they require two operands.

You will learn about the Java shortcut arithmetic operators in the chapter *Looping*.

Operator	Description	Example
+	Addition	45 + 2, the result is 47
−	Subtraction	45 − 2, the result is 43
*	Multiplication	45 * 2, the result is 90
/	Division	45.0 / 2, the result is 22.5 45 / 2, the result is 22 (not 22.5)
%	Remainder (modulus)	45 % 2, the result is 1 (that is, 45 / 2 = 22 with a remainder of 1)

Table 2-8   Arithmetic operators

The operators / and % deserve special consideration. Java supports two types of division:

- **Floating-point division** occurs when either or both of the operands are floating-point values. For example, 45.0 / 2 is 22.5.

- **Integer division** occurs when both of the operands are integers. The result is an integer, and any fractional part of the result is lost. For example, the result of 45 / 2 is 22. As another example, 39 / 5 is 7 because 5 goes into 39 seven whole times; 38 / 5, 37 / 5, 36 / 5, and 35 / 5 all evaluate to 7.

The percent sign is the **remainder operator**. The remainder operator is most often used with two integers, and the result is an integer with the value of the remainder after division takes place. For example, the result of 45 % 2 is 1 because 2 "goes into" 45 twenty-two times with a remainder of 1. Other examples of remainder operations include the following:

- 39 % 5 is 4 because 5 goes into 39 seven times with a remainder of 4.

- 20 % 3 is 2 because when 20 is divided by 3, the remainder is 2. 36 % 4 is 0 because there is no remainder when 4 is divided into 36.

Note that when you perform paper-and-pencil division, you divide first to determine a remainder. In Java, you do not need to perform a division operation before you can perform a remainder operation. A remainder operation can stand alone.

Although the remainder operator is most often used with integers, it is legal but less often useful to use the operator with floating-point values. In Java, when you use the % operator with floating-point values, the result is the remainder from a rounded division.

 The remainder operator is also called the **modulus operator**, or sometimes just **mod**. Mathematicians would argue that *remainder* is the better term because in Java, the result of using the remainder operator can be negative, but in mathematics, the result of a modulus operation can never be negative.

Associativity and Precedence

When you combine mathematical operations in a single statement, you must understand both associativity and precedence. The associativity of arithmetic operators with the same precedence is left-to-right. In a statement such as answer = x + y + z;, the x and y are added first, producing a temporary result, and then z is added to the temporary sum. After the sum is computed, the result is assigned to answer.

Operator precedence refers to the rules for the order in which parts of a mathematical expression are evaluated. The multiplication, division, and remainder operators have the same precedence. Their precedence is higher than that of the addition and subtraction operators. Addition and subtraction have the same precedence, and their precedence is lower than that of the other operators. In other words, expressions are evaluated from left to right, and multiplication, division, and remainder always take place prior to addition or subtraction. Table 2-9 summarizes the precedence of the arithmetic operators.

Operators	Descriptions	Relative Precedence
* / %	Multiplication, division, remainder	Higher
+ −	Addition, subtraction	Lower

Table 2-9 Relative precedence of arithmetic operators

For example, the following statement assigns 14 to result:

```
int result = 2 + 3 * 4;
```

The multiplication operation (3 * 4) occurs before adding 2. You can override normal operator precedence by putting the operation to perform first in parentheses. The following statement assigns 20 to result:

```
int result = (2 + 3) * 4;
```

The addition within the parentheses takes place first, and then the intermediate result (5) is multiplied by 4. When multiple pairs of parentheses are used in a statement, the innermost expression surrounded by parentheses is evaluated first. For example, the value of the following expression is 46:

```
2 * (3 + (4 * 5))
```

First, 4 * 5 evaluates to 20, and then 3 is added, giving 23. Finally, the value is multiplied by 2, giving 46.

Remembering that *, /, and % have the same precedence is important in arithmetic calculations. These operations are performed from left to right, regardless of the order in which they appear. For example, the value of the following expression is 9:

```
25 / 8 * 3
```

First, 25 is divided by 8. The result is 3 because with integer division, you lose any remainder. Then 3 is multiplied by 3, giving 9. If you assumed that multiplication was performed before division, you would calculate an incorrect answer.

You will learn more about operator precedence in the chapter *Making Decisions*.

Writing Arithmetic Statements Efficiently

You can make your programs operate more efficiently if you avoid unnecessary repetition of arithmetic statements. For example, suppose you know the values for an employee's hourly pay and pay rate and you want to compute state and federal withholding tax based on known rates. You could write two statements as follows:

```
stateWithholding = hours * rate * STATE_RATE;
federalWithholding = hours * rate * FED_RATE;
```

With this approach, you perform the multiplication of hours * rate twice. It is more efficient to perform the calculation once, as follows:

```
grossPay = hours * rate;
stateWithholding = grossPay * STATE_RATE;
federalWithholding = grossPay * FED_RATE;
```

The time saved is very small, but these savings would be more important if the calculation was more complicated or if it was repeated many times in a program. As you think about the programs you write, remain on the lookout for ways to improve efficiency by avoiding duplication of operations.

Pitfall: Not Understanding Imprecision in Floating-Point Numbers

Integer values are exact, but floating-point numbers frequently are only approximations. For example, when you divide 1.0 by 3.0, the mathematical result is 0.3333333..., with the 3s continuing infinitely. No matter how many decimal places you can store, the result is only an approximation. Even values that don't repeat indefinitely in our usual numbering system, such as 0.1, cannot be represented precisely in the binary format used by computers. Imprecision leads to several problems:

Appendix B provides a more thorough explanation of numbering systems and why fractional values cannot be represented accurately.

- When you produce floating-point output, it might not look like what you expect or want.

- When you make comparisons with floating-point numbers, the comparisons might not be what you expect or want.

For example, Figure 2-36 shows a class in which an answer is computed as 2.20 − 2.00. Mathematically, the result should be 0.20. But, as the output in Figure 2-37 shows, the result

Performing Arithmetic

is calculated as a value that is slightly more than 0.20, and when answer is compared to 0.20, the result is false.

95

```java
public class ImprecisionDemo
{
    public static void main(String[] args)
    {
        double answer = 2.20 - 2.00;
        boolean isEqual = answer == 0.20;
        System.out.println("answer is " + answer);
        System.out.println("isEqual is " + isEqual);
    }
}
```

Figure 2-36   The ImprecisionDemo program

Figure 2-37   Execution of the ImprecisionDemo program

For now, you might choose to accept the slight imprecisions generated when you use floating-point numbers. However, if you want to eliminate the imprecisions, you can use one of several techniques to round values. Appendix C contains directions on how to round numbers and how to format a floating-point number so it displays the desired number of decimal positions.

Several movies have used the fact that floating-point numbers are not precise as a plot element. For example, in the movies *Superman III* and *Office Space*, thieves round currency values and divert the remaining fractions of cents to their own accounts.

Watch the video *Arithmetic*.

TWO TRUTHS & A LIE

Performing Arithmetic

1. The arithmetic operators are examples of unary operators, which are so named because they perform one operation at a time.

2. In Java, operator precedence dictates that multiplication, division, and remainder always take place prior to addition or subtraction in an expression.

3. Floating-point arithmetic might produce imprecise results.

The false statement is #1. The arithmetic operators are examples of binary operators, which are so named because they require two operands.

You Do It

Using Arithmetic Operators

In these steps, you create a program that uses arithmetic operators.

1. Open a new file in your text editor, and type the `import` statement needed for interactive input with the `Scanner` class:

    ```
    import java.util.Scanner;
    ```

2. Type the class header and its curly braces for a class named `ArithmeticDemo`. Within the class's curly braces, enter the `main()` method header and its braces.

    ```
    public class ArithmeticDemo
    {
        public static void main(String[] args)
        {
        }
    }
    ```

3. With the `main()` method, declare five `int` variables that will be used to hold two input values and their sum, difference, and average:

    ```
    int firstNumber;
    int secondNumber;
    int sum;
    int difference;
    int average;
    ```

(continues)

(continued)

4. Also declare a `Scanner` object so that keyboard input can be accepted.

```
Scanner input = new Scanner(System.in);
```

5. Prompt the user for and accept two integers:

```
System.out.print("Please enter an integer >> ");
firstNumber = input.nextInt();
System.out.print("Please enter another integer >> ");
secondNumber = input.nextInt();
```

6. Add statements to perform the necessary arithmetic operations:

```
sum = firstNumber + secondNumber;
difference = firstNumber - secondNumber;
average = sum / 2;
```

7. Display the three calculated values:

```
System.out.println(firstNumber + " + " +
    secondNumber + " is " + sum);
System.out.println(firstNumber + " - " +
    secondNumber + " is " + difference);
System.out.println("The average of " + firstNumber +
    " and " + secondNumber + " is " + average);
```

8. Save the file as **ArithmeticDemo.java**, and then compile and execute it. Enter values of your choice. Figure 2-38 shows a typical execution. Notice that because integer division was used to compute the average, the answer is an integer.

Figure 2-38 Typical execution of `ArithmeticDemo` application

9. Execute the program multiple times using various integer values and confirm that the results are accurate.

(continues)

(continued)

Performing Floating-Point Arithmetic

Next, you will modify the `ArithmeticDemo` application to work with floating-point values instead of integers.

1. Within the `ArithmeticDemo` application, change the class name to `ArithmeticDemo2`, and immediately save the file as **ArithmeticDemo2.java**. Change all the variables' data types to `double`. Change the two prompts to request `double` values, and change the two calls to the `nextInt()` method to `nextDouble()`. Save, compile, and execute the program again. Figure 2-39 shows a typical execution. Notice that the average calculation now includes decimal places.

Figure 2-39 Typical execution of the `ArithmeticDemo2` application

2. Rerun the program, experimenting with various input values. Some of your output might appear with imprecisions similar to those shown in Figure 2-40. If you are not satisfied with the slight imprecisions created when using floating-point arithmetic, you can round or change the display of the values, as discussed in Appendix C.

Figure 2-40 Another typical execution of the `ArithmeticDemo2` application

Understanding Type Conversion

When you perform arithmetic with variables or constants of the same type, the result of the operation retains the same type. For example, when you divide two `int`s, the result is an `int`, and when you subtract two `double`s, the result is a `double`. Often, however, you might want to perform mathematical operations on operands with unlike types. The process of converting one data type to another is **type conversion**. Java performs some conversions for you automatically or implicitly, but other conversions must be requested explicitly by the programmer.

Automatic Type Conversion

When you perform arithmetic operations with operands of unlike types, Java chooses a unifying type for the result. The **unifying type** is the type to which all operands in an expression are converted so that they are compatible with each other. Java performs an **implicit conversion**; that is, it automatically converts nonconforming operands to the unifying type. Implicit conversions also are called **promotions**. Figure 2-41 shows the order for establishing unifying types between values.

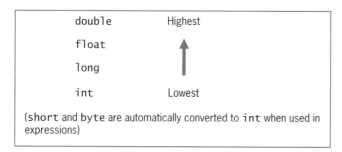

```
    double          Highest

    float

    long

    int             Lowest

(short and byte are automatically converted to int when used in
expressions)
```

Figure 2-41   Order for establishing unifying data types

When two unlike types are used in an expression, the unifying type is the one that is higher in the list in Figure 2-41. In other words, when an operand that is a type lower on the list is combined with a type that is higher, the lower-type operand is converted to the higher one. For example, the addition of a `double` and an `int` results in a `double`, and the subtraction of a `long` from a `float` results in a `float`.

Boolean values cannot be converted to another type. In some languages, such as C++, Boolean values are actually numbers. However, this is not the case in Java.

For example, assume that an `int`, hoursWorked, and a `double`, payRate, are defined and then multiplied as follows:

```
int hoursWorked = 37;
double payRate = 6.73;
double grossPay = hoursWorked * payRate;
```

The result of the multiplication is a `double` because when a `double` and an `int` are multiplied, the `int` is promoted to the higher-ranking unifying type `double`—the type that is higher in the list in Figure 2-41. Therefore, assigning the result to grossPay is legal.

The following code will not compile because hoursWorked times payRate is a `double`, and Java does not allow the loss of precision that occurs if you try to store the calculated `double` result in an `int`.

```
int hoursWorked = 37;
double payRate = 6.73;
int grossPay = hoursWorked * payRate;
```

The data types `char`, `short`, and `byte` all are promoted to `int` when used in statements with unlike types. If you perform a calculation with any combination of `char`, `short`, and `byte` values, the result is an `int` by default. For example, if you add two `bytes`, the result is an `int`, not a `byte`.

Explicit Type Conversions

You can purposely override the unifying type imposed by Java by performing a type cast. **Type casting** forces a value of one data type to be used as a value of another type. To perform a type cast, you use a **cast operator**, which is created by placing the desired result type in parentheses. Using a cast operator is an **explicit conversion**. The cast operator is followed by the variable or constant to be cast. For example, a type cast is performed in the following code:

```
double bankBalance = 189.66;
float weeklyBudget = (float) (bankBalance / 4);
  // weeklyBudget is 47.415, one-fourth of bankBalance
```

 The cast operator is more completely called the **unary cast operator**. Unlike a binary operator that requires two operands, a **unary operator** uses only one operand. The unary cast operator is followed by its operand.

In this example, the `double` value bankBalance is divided by the integer 4, and the result is a `double`. Then the `double` result is converted to a `float` before it is stored in weeklyBudget.

Without the conversion, the statement that assigns the result to weeklyBudget would not compile. Similarly, a cast from a float to an int occurs in this code segment:

```
float myMoney = 47.82f;
int dollars = (int) myMoney;
  // dollars is 47, the integer part of myMoney
```

In this example, the float value myMoney is converted to an int before it is stored in the integer variable named dollars. When the float value is converted to an int, the decimal place values are lost. The cast operator does not permanently alter any variable's data type; the alteration is only for the duration of the current operation.

The word *cast* is used in a similar fashion when referring to molding metal, as in *cast iron*. In a Java arithmetic cast, a value is "molded" into a different type.

It is easy to lose data when performing a cast. For example, the largest byte value is 127 and the largest int value is 2,147,483,647, so the following statements produce distorted results:

```
int anOkayInt = 200;

byte aBadByte = (byte)anOkayInt;
```

A byte is constructed from eight 1s and 0s, or binary digits. The first binary digit, or bit, holds a 0 or 1 to represent positive or negative. The remaining seven bits store the actual value. When the integer value 200 is stored in the byte variable, its large value consumes the eighth bit, turning it to a 1, and forcing the aBadByte variable to appear to hold the value –72, which is inaccurate and misleading.

You do not need to perform a cast when assigning a value to a higher unifying type. For example, when you write a statement such as the following, Java automatically promotes the integer constant 10 to be a double so that it can be stored in the payRate variable:

```
double payRate = 10;
```

However, for clarity, if you want to assign 10 to payRate, you might prefer to write the following:

```
double payRate = 10.0;
```

The result is identical whether you assign the literal double 10.0 or the literal int 10 to the double variable.

TWO TRUTHS & A LIE

Understanding Type Conversion

1. When you perform arithmetic operations with operands of unlike types, you must make an explicit conversion to a unifying type.

2. Summing a `double`, `int`, and `float` results in a `double`.

3. You can explicitly override the unifying type imposed by Java by performing a type cast; type casting forces a value of one data type to be used as a value of another type.

The false statement is #1. When you perform arithmetic operations with operands of unlike types, Java performs an implicit conversion to a unifying type.

You Do It

Implicit and Explicit Casting

In this section you explore the concepts of the unifying types and casting.

1. Open the **ArithmeticDemo.java** file that uses integer values to calculate a sum, difference, and average. Change the class name to `ArithmeticDemo3`, and immediately save the file as **ArithmeticDemo3.java**.

2. In the previous version of the program, the average was calculated without decimal places because when two integers are divided, the result is an integer. To compute a more accurate average, change the data type for the average variable from `int` to **double**.

3. Save, compile, and execute the program. As the sample execution in Figure 2-42 shows, the program compiles and executes, but the average is still not accurate. The average of 20 and 19 is calculated to be just 19 because the decimal portion of the arithmetic result is lost. The program executes because the result of an integer divided by an integer is an integer, and when the integer is assigned to the `double`, automatic type conversion takes place.

(continues)

(continued)

Figure 2-42 Typical execution of ArithmeticDemo3 application

4. Change the statement that computes the average to include a cast as follows:

    average = (double) sum / 2;

5. Save, compile, and execute the program. As shown in Figure 2-43, now the program displays a more accurate average. The integer sum has been cast to a double, and when the double is divided by the integer, the result is a double, which is then assigned to average.

Figure 2-43 Typical execution of ArithmeticDemo3 application after addition of a cast operation for the average

6. Change the statement that computes the average to include a second set of parentheses, as follows:

    average = (double) (sum / 2);

(continues)

(continued)

7. Save, compile, and execute the program. Now, the fractional portion of the result is omitted again. That's because the result of `sum / 2` is calculated first, and the result is an integer. Then the whole-number result is cast to a `double` and assigned to a `double`—but the fractional part of the answer was already lost and casting is too late. Remove the newly added parentheses, save the program, compile it, and execute it again to confirm that the fractional part of the answer is reinstated.

8. As an alternative to the explicit cast in the division statement in the `ArithmeticDemo` program, you could write the average calculation as follows:

    `average = sum / 2.0;`

    In this calculation, when the integer `sum` is divided by the `double` constant 2.0, the result is a `double`. The result then does not require any cast to be assigned to the `double` `average` without loss of data. Try this in your program.

9. Go to the Java Web site (***www.oracle.com/technetwork/java/index.html***), select **Java APIs**, and then select **Java SE 7**. Scroll through the list of **All Classes**, and select **PrintStream**, which is the data type for the `out` object used with the `println()` method. Scroll down to view the list of methods in the Method Summary. As you did in a previous exercise, notice the many versions of the `print()` and `println()` methods, including ones that accept a `String`, an `int`, and a `long`. Notice, however, that no versions accept a `byte` or a `short`. That's because when a `byte` or `short` is sent to the `print()` or `println()` method, it is automatically promoted to an `int`, so that version of the method is used.

Don't Do It

-   Don't mispronounce "integer." People who are unfamiliar with the term often say "interger," inserting an extra *r*.

-   Don't attempt to assign a literal constant floating-point number, such as 2.5, to a `float` without following the constant with an uppercase or lowercase *F*. By default, constant floating-point values are `double`s.

-   Don't try to use a Java keyword as an identifier for a variable or constant. Table 1-1 in Chapter 1 contains a list of Java keywords.

-   Don't attempt to assign a constant value under −2,147,483,648 or over +2,147,483,647 to a `long` variable without following the constant with an uppercase or lowercase *L*. By default, constant integers are `int`s, and a value under −2,147,483,648 or over 2,147,483,647 is too large to be an `int`.

-   Don't assume that you must divide numbers as a step to determining a remainder; the remainder operator (%) is all that's needed.

- Don't try to use a variable or named constant that has not yet been assigned a value.

- Don't forget to consume the Enter key after numeric input using the Scanner class when a nextLine() method call follows.

- Don't forget to use the appropriate import statement when using the Scanner or JOptionPane class.

- Don't forget precedence rules when you write statements that contain multiple arithmetic operations. For example, score1 + score2 / 2 does not compute the average of two scores. Instead, it adds half of score2 to score1. To compute the average, you would write (score1 + score2) / 2.

- Don't forget that integer division results in an integer, dropping any fractional part. For example, 1 / 2 is not equal to 0.5; it is equal to 0.

- Don't forget that extra parentheses can change the result of an operation that includes casting.

- Don't forget that floating-point numbers are imprecise.

- Don't attempt to assign a constant decimal value to an integer using a leading 0. For example, if you declare int num = 021; and then display num, you will see 17. The leading 0 indicates that the value is in base 8 (octal), so its value is two 8s plus one *1*. In the decimal system, 21 and 021 mean the same thing, but not in Java.

- Don't use a single equal sign (=) in a Boolean comparison for equality. The operator used for equivalency is composed of two equal signs (==).

- Don't try to store a string of characters, such as a name, in a char variable. A char variable can hold only a single character.

- Don't forget that when a String and a numeric value are concatenated, the resulting expression is a string. For example, "X" + 2 + 4 results in "X24", *not* "X6". If you want the result to be "X6", you can use the expression "X" + (2 + 4).

Key Terms

Constant describes values that cannot be changed during the execution of an application.

A **literal constant** is a value that is taken literally at each use.

A **numeric constant** is a number whose value is taken literally at each use.

An **unnamed constant** has no identifier associated with it.

A **variable** is a named memory location that you can use to store a value.

An item's **data type** describes the type of data that can be stored there, how much memory the item occupies, and what types of operations can be performed on the data.

A **primitive type** is a simple data type. Java's primitive types are byte, short, int, long, float, double, char, and boolean.

Reference types are complex data types that are constructed from primitive types.

A **variable declaration** is a statement that reserves a named memory location.

A **strongly typed language** is one in which each variable has a well-defined type that limits the operations you can perform with it; strong typing implies that variables must be declared before they can be used.

Camel casing is a style in which an identifier begins with a lowercase letter and subsequent words within the identifier are capitalized.

The **assignment operator** is the equal sign (=); any value to the right of the equal sign is assigned to the variable on the left of the equal sign.

An **initialization** is an assignment made when you declare a variable.

An **assignment** is the act of providing a value for a variable.

Associativity refers to the order in which operands are used with operators.

An **lvalue** is an expression that can appear on the left side of an assignment statement.

An **rvalue** is an expression that can appear only on the right side of an assignment statement.

An **uninitialized variable** is one that has not been assigned a value.

A **garbage value** is the unknown value stored in an uninitialized variable.

A **named constant** is a named memory location whose value cannot change after it is assigned.

A **symbolic constant** is a named constant.

The keyword **final** precedes named constant declarations.

A **blank final** is a final variable that has not yet been assigned a value.

A **magic number** is a value that does not have immediate, intuitive meaning or a number that cannot be explained without additional knowledge. Unnamed constants are magic numbers.

The **scope** of a data item is the area in which it is visible to a program and in which you can refer to it using its simple identifier.

A **block of code** is the code contained between a set of curly braces.

Concatenated describes values that are attached end to end.

A **null String** is an empty String created by typing a set of quotes with nothing between them.

An **integer** is a whole number without decimal places.

The **int** data type is used to declare variables and constants that store integers in the range of −2,147,483,648 to +2,147,483,647.

The **byte** data type holds very small integers, from −128 to 127.

The **short** data type holds small integers, from −32,768 to 32,767.

The **long** data type holds very large integers, from -9,223,372,036,854,775,808 to 9,223,372,036,854,775,807.

A **boolean variable** can hold only one of two values—true or false.

A **relational operator** compares two items; an expression that contains a relational operator has a Boolean value.

A **comparison operator** is another name for a relational operator.

A **floating-point** number contains decimal positions.

A **float** data type can hold a floating-point value of up to six or seven significant digits of accuracy.

A **double** data type can hold a floating-point value of up to 14 or 15 significant digits of accuracy.

Significant digits refers to the mathematical accuracy of a value.

Scientific notation is a display format that more conveniently expresses large or small numeric values; a multidigit number is converted to a single-digit number and multiplied by 10 to a power.

A **double-precision floating-point number** is stored in a double.

A **single-precision floating-point number** is stored in a float.

The **char** data type is used to hold any single character.

String is a built-in Java class that provides you with the means for storing and manipulating character strings.

An **escape sequence** begins with a backslash followed by a character; the pair represents a single character.

The **standard input device** normally is the keyboard.

A **token** is a unit of data separated with whitespace.

A **prompt** is a message that requests and describes user input.

Echoing the input means to repeat the user's entry as output so the user can visually confirm the entry's accuracy.

The **keyboard buffer** is a small area of memory where keystrokes are stored before they are retrieved into a program.

The **type-ahead buffer** is the keyboard buffer.

To **consume** an entry is to retrieve and discard it without using it.

An **input dialog box** asks a question and provides a text field in which the user can enter a response.

The `showInputDialog()` **method** creates an input dialog box.

Type-wrapper classes, contained in the `java.lang` package, include methods that can process primitive type values.

To **parse** means to break into component parts.

A **confirm dialog box** displays the options Yes, No, and Cancel; you can create one using the `showConfirmDialog()` **method** in the `JOptionPane` class.

Standard arithmetic operators are used to perform calculations with values.

An **operand** is a value used in an arithmetic statement.

Binary operators require two operands.

Floating-point division is the operation in which two values are divided and either or both are floating-point values.

Integer division is the operation in which two values are divided and both are integers; the result contains no fractional part.

The **remainder operator** is the percent sign; when it is used with two integers, the result is an integer with the value of the remainder after division takes place.

The **modulus operator**, sometimes abbreviated as **mod**, is an alternate name for the remainder operator.

Operator precedence is the rules for the order in which parts of a mathematical expression are evaluated.

Type conversion is the process of converting one data type to another.

A **unifying type** is a single data type to which all operands in an expression are converted.

An **implicit conversion** is the automatic transformation of one data type to another.

Promotion is an implicit conversion.

Type casting forces a value of one data type to be used as a value of another type.

A **cast operator** performs an explicit type conversion; it is created by placing the desired result type in parentheses before the expression to be converted.

An **explicit conversion** is the data type transformation caused using a cast operator.

The **unary cast operator** is a more complete name for the cast operator that performs explicit conversions.

A **unary operator** uses only one operand.

Chapter Summary

- Variables are named memory locations in which programs store values; the value of a variable can change. You must declare all variables you want to use in a program by providing a data type and a name. Java provides for eight primitive types of data: `boolean`, `byte`, `char`, `double`, `float`, `int`, `long`, and `short`. A named constant is a memory location that holds a value that can never be changed; it is preceded by the keyword `final`.

- A variable of type `int` can hold any whole number value from −2,147,483,648 to +2,147,483,647. The types `byte`, `short`, and `long` are all variations of the integer type.

- A `boolean` type variable can hold a `true` or `false` value. Java supports six relational operators: >, <, ==, >=, <=, and !=.

- A floating-point number contains decimal positions. Java supports two floating-point data types: `float` and `double`.

- You use the `char` data type to hold any single character. You type constant character values in single quotation marks. You type `String` constants that store more than one character between double quotation marks. You can store some characters using an escape sequence, which always begins with a backslash.

- You can use the `Scanner` class and the `System.in` object to accept user input from the keyboard. Several methods are available to convert input to usable data, including `nextDouble()`, `nextInt()`, and `nextLine()`.

- You can accept input using the `JOptionPane` class. The `showInputDialog()` method returns a `String`, which must be converted to a number using a type-wrapper class before you can use it as a numeric value.

- There are five standard arithmetic operators: +, −, *, /, and %. Operator precedence is the order in which parts of a mathematical expression are evaluated. Multiplication, division, and remainder always take place prior to addition or subtraction in an expression. Right and left parentheses can be added within an expression when exceptions to this rule are required. When multiple pairs of parentheses are added, the innermost expression surrounded by parentheses is evaluated first.

- When you perform mathematical operations on unlike types, Java implicitly converts the variables to a unifying type. You can explicitly override the unifying type imposed by Java by performing a type cast.

Review Questions

1. When data cannot be changed after a class is compiled, the data is _____.

    a. constant

    c. volatile

    b. variable

    d. mutable

2. Which of the following is not a primitive data type in Java?

   a. `boolean`   c. `int`

   b. `byte`   d. `sector`

3. Which of the following elements is not required in a variable declaration?

   a. a type   c. an assigned value

   b. an identifier   d. a semicolon

4. The assignment operator in Java is ———————.

   a. `=`   c. `:=`

   b. `==`   d. `::`

5. Assuming you have declared `shoeSize` to be a variable of type `int`, which of the following is a valid assignment statement in Java?

   a. `shoeSize = 9;`   c. `shoeSize = '9';`

   b. `shoeSize = 9.5;`   d. `shoeSize = "nine";`

6. Which of the following data types can store a value in the least amount of memory?

   a. `short`   c. `int`

   b. `long`   d. `byte`

7. A `boolean` variable can hold ———————.

   a. any character

   b. any whole number

   c. any decimal number

   d. the value `true` or `false`

8. The value 137.68 can be held by a variable of type ———————.

   a. `int`

   b. `float`

   c. `double`

   d. Two of the preceding answers are correct.

9. An escape sequence always begins with a(n) ———————.

   a. e   c. backslash

   b. forward slash   d. equal sign

10. Which Java statement produces the following output?

    w
    xyz

    a. `System.out.println("wxyz");`
    b. `System.out.println("w" + "xyz");`
    c. `System.out.println("w\nxyz");`
    d. `System.out.println("w\nx\ny\nz");`

11. The remainder operator ———————————.

    a. is represented by a forward slash
    b. must follow a division operation
    c. provides the quotient of integer division
    d. is none of the above

12. According to the rules of operator precedence, when division occurs in the same arithmetic statement as ———————————, the division operation always takes place first.

    a. multiplication
    b. remainder
    c. subtraction
    d. Answers a and b are correct.

13. The "equal to" relational operator is ———————————.

    a. `=`   c. `!=`
    b. `==`   d. `!!`

14. When you perform arithmetic with values of diverse types, Java ———————————.

    a. issues an error message
    b. implicitly converts the values to a unifying type
    c. requires you to explicitly convert the values to a unifying type
    d. implicitly converts the values to the type of the first operand

15. If you attempt to add a `float`, an `int`, and a `byte`, the result will be a(n) ———————————.

    a. `float`   c. `byte`
    b. `int`   d. error message

16. You use a ——————————— to explicitly override an implicit type.

    a. mistake   c. format
    b. type cast   d. type set

17. In Java, what is the value of 3 + 7 * 4 + 2?

    a. 21   c. 42

    b. 33   d. 48

18. Which assignment is correct in Java?

    a. `int value = (float) 4.5;`   c. `double value = 2.12;`

    b. `float value = 4 (double);`   d. `char value = 5c;`

19. Which assignment is correct in Java?

    a. `double money = 12;`   c. `double money = 12.0d;`

    b. `double money = 12.0;`   d. All of the above are correct.

20. Which assignment is correct in Java?

    a. `char aChar = 5.5;`

    b. `char aChar = "W";`

    c. `char aChar = '*';`

    d. Two of the preceding answers are correct.

Exercises

 Programming Exercises

1. What is the numeric value of each of the following expressions as evaluated by Java?

    a. 3 + 7 * 2   h. 15 % 2

    b. 18 / 3 + 4   i. 31 % 7

    c. 9 / 3 + 12 / 4   j. 6 % 4 + 1

    d. 15 / 2   k. (5 + 6) * 3

    e. 14 / 3   l. 25 / (3 + 2)

    f. 29 / 10   m. 13 % 15

    g. 14 % 2

2. What is the value of each of the following Boolean expressions?

    a. 5 < 8   f. 7 < 9 – 2

    b. 4 <= 9   g. 5 != 5

    c. 3 == 4   h. 15 != 3 * 5

    d. 12 >= 12   i. 9 != –9

    e. 3 + 4 == 8   j. 3 + 5 * 2 == 16

3. Choose the best data type for each of the following so that any reasonable value is accommodated but no memory storage is wasted. Give an example of a typical value that would be held by the variable, and explain why you chose the type you did.

   a. the number of siblings you have
   b. your final grade in this class
   c. the population of Earth
   d. the population of a U.S. county
   e. the number of passengers on a bus
   f. one player's score in a Scrabble game
   g. one team's score in a Major League Baseball game
   h. the year an historical event occurred
   i. the number of legs on an animal

4. a. Write a Java class that declares a named constant that holds the number of feet in a mile: 5,280. Also declare a variable to represent the distance in miles between your house and your uncle's house. Assign an appropriate value to the variable— for example, 8.5. Compute and display the distance to your uncle's house in both miles and feet. Display explanatory text with the values—for example, The distance to my uncle's house is 8.5 miles or 44880.0 feet. Save the class as **MilesToFeet.java**.

   b. Convert the MilesToFeet class to an interactive application. Instead of assigning a value to the distance, accept the value from the user as input. Save the revised class as **MilesToFeetInteractive.java**.

5. a. Write a Java class that declares a named constant that represents next year's anticipated 10 percent increase in sales for each division of a company. (You can represent 10 percent as 0.10.) Also declare variables to represent this year's sales total in dollars for the North and South divisions. Assign appropriate values to the variables—for example, 4000 and 5500. Compute and display, with explanatory text, next year's projected sales for each division. Save the class as **ProjectedSales.java**.

   b. Convert the ProjectedSales class to an interactive application. Instead of assigning values to the North and South current year sales variables, accept them from the user as input. Save the revised class as **ProjectedSalesInteractive.java**.

6. a. Write a class that declares a variable named inches that holds a length in inches, and assign a value. Display the value in feet and inches; for example, 86 inches becomes 7 feet and 2 inches. Be sure to use a named constant where appropriate. Save the class as **InchesToFeet.java**.

   b. Write an interactive version of the InchesToFeet class that accepts the inches value from a user. Save the class as **InchesToFeetInteractive.java**.

7. Write a class that declares variables to hold your three initials. Display the three initials with a period following each one, as in J.M.F. Save the class as **Initials.java**.

8. Meadowdale Dairy Farm sells organic brown eggs to local customers. They charge $3.25 for a dozen eggs, or 45 cents for individual eggs that are not part of a dozen. Write a class that prompts a user for the number of eggs in the order and then display the amount owed with a full explanation. For example, typical output might be, "You ordered 27 eggs. That's 2 dozen at $3.25 per dozen and 3 loose eggs at 45.0 cents each for a total of $7.85." Save the class as **Eggs.java**.

9. The Happy Yappy Kennel boards dogs at a cost of 50 cents per pound per day. Write a class that accepts a dog's weight and number of days to be boarded and displays the total price for boarding. Save the class as **DogBoarding.java**.

10. Write a class that calculates and displays the conversion of an entered number of dollars into currency denominations—*20*s, *10*s, *5*s, and *1*s. Save the class as **Dollars.java**.

11. Write a program that accepts a temperature in Fahrenheit from a user and converts it to Celsius by subtracting 32 from the Fahrenheit value and multiplying the result by 5/9. Display both values. Save the class as **FahrenheitToCelsius.java**.

12. Travel Tickets Company sells tickets for airlines, tours, and other travel-related services. Because ticket agents frequently mistype long ticket numbers, Travel Tickets has asked you to write an application that indicates invalid ticket number entries. The class prompts a ticket agent to enter a six-digit ticket number. Ticket numbers are designed so that if you drop the last digit of the number, then divide the number by 7, the remainder of the division will be identical to the last dropped digit. This process is illustrated in the following example:

Step 1	Enter the ticket number; for example, 123454.
Step 2	Remove the last digit, leaving 12345.
Step 3	Determine the remainder when the ticket number is divided by 7. In this case, 12345 divided by 7 leaves a remainder of 4.
Step 4	Assign the Boolean value of the comparison between the remainder and the digit dropped from the ticket number.
Step 5	Display the result—`true` or `false`—in a message box.

Accept the ticket number from the agent and verify whether it is a valid number. Test the application with the following ticket numbers:

- 123454; the comparison should evaluate to `true`
- 147103; the comparison should evaluate to `true`
- 154123; the comparison should evaluate to `false`

Save the program as **TicketNumber.java**.

e Chapter02 folder of your downloadable student files
s. In each case, determine the problem and fix the
the errors, save each file using the same filename
e, DebugTwo1.java will become FixDebugTwo1.java.

    c.   DebugTwo3.java

    d.   DebugTwo4.java

to change every instance of the class name within the file so that it
filename and class name must always match.

which the players provide a few words that are then
e game helps children understand different parts of
provide specific types of words. For example, you
other noun, an adjective, and a past-tense verb. The
vers as *table*, *book*, *silly*, and *studied*. The newly

ed

asks the user to provide at least four or five words,
rt story or nursery rhyme that uses them. Save the

hapter 1, you learned how to obtain a random
g statement generates a random number between
ve and assigns it to a variable named random:

m() * MAX);

dom number between 1 and 5 and asks the
a message that indicates the difference
the user's guess. Display another message
and the Boolean value true or false depending
s the random number. Save the file as

Case Problems

1. Carly's Catering provides meals for parties and special events. Write a program that prompts the user for the number of guests attending an event and then computes the total price, which is $35 per person. Display the company motto with the border that you created in the CarlysMotto2 class in Chapter 1, and then display the number of guests, price per guest, and total price. Also display a message that indicates true or false depending on whether the job is classified as a large event—an event with 50 or more guests. Save the file as **CarlysEventPrice.java**.

2. Sammy's Seashore Supplies rents beach equipment such as kayaks, canoes, beach chairs, and umbrellas to tourists. Write a program that prompts the user for the number of minutes he rented a piece of sports equipment. Compute the rental cost as $40 per hour plus $1 per additional minute. (You might have surmised already that this rate has a logical flaw, but for now, calculate rates as described here. You can fix the problem after you read the chapter on decision making.) Display Sammy's motto with the border that you created in the SammysMotto2 class in Chapter 1. Then display the hours, minutes, and total price. Save the file as **SammysRentalPrice.java**.

Using Methods, Classes, and Objects

In this chapter, you will:

◎ Learn about method calls and placement

◎ Identify the parts of a method

◎ Add parameters to methods

◎ Create methods that return values

◎ Learn about classes and objects

◎ Create a class

◎ Create instance methods in a class

◎ Declare objects and use their methods

◎ Create constructors

◎ Appreciate classes as data types

Understanding Method Calls and Placement

A **method** is a program module that contains a series of statements that carry out a task. You have already seen Java classes that contain a main() method, which executes automatically when you run a program. A program's main() method can execute additional methods, and those methods can execute others. Any class can contain an unlimited number of methods, and each method can be called an unlimited number of times.

To execute a method, you **invoke** or **call** it. In other words, a **calling method** makes a **method call**, and the method call invokes a **called method**. The calling method is also known as a **client method** because a called method provides a service for its client.

Consider the simple First class that you saw in Chapter 1; it displayed a single line of output, "First Java application." Suppose that you want to add three lines of output to this application to display your company's name and address. One approach would be to simply add three new println() statements, as shown in the shaded statements in Figure 3-1.

```
public class First
{
    public static void main(String[] args)
    {
        System.out.println("XYZ Company");
        System.out.println("8900 U.S. Hwy 14");
        System.out.println("Crystal Lake, IL 60014");
        System.out.println("First Java application");
    }
}
```

Figure 3-1   The First class

Instead of adding the three println() statements to the application in Figure 3-1, you might prefer to call a method that executes the three statements. Then the program would look like the one in Figure 3-2. The shaded line contains the call to the nameAndAddress() method.

```
public class First
{
    public static void main(String[] args)
    {
        nameAndAddress();
        System.out.println("First Java application");
    }
}
```

Figure 3-2   The First class with a call to the nameAndAddress() method

There are two major advantages to creating a separate method to display the three address lines. First, the main() method remains short and easy to follow because main() contains just one statement to call the method, rather than three separate println() statements to perform the work of the method. What is more important is that a method is easily reusable. After you create the name and address method, you can use it in any application that needs the company's name and address. In other words, you do the work once, and then you can use the method many times.

Besides adding a call to the method in the First class, you must actually write the method. You place a method within a class, but it must be outside of any other methods. In other words, you cannot place a method within another method. Figure 3-3 shows the two locations where you can place additional methods within the First class—within the curly braces of the class, but outside of (either before or after) any other methods. Methods can never overlap.

The order of methods in a class has no bearing on the order in which the methods are called or executed. No matter where you place it, the main() method is always executed first in any Java application, and it might call any other methods in any order and any number of times. The order in which you call methods, and not their physical placement, is what makes a difference in how an application executes.

```
public class First
{
    // You can place additional methods here, before main()
    public static void main(String[] args)
    {
        nameAndAddress();
        System.out.println("First Java application");
    }
    // You can place additional methods here, after main()
}
```

Figure 3-3   Placement of methods within a class

A main() method executes automatically when you run a program, but other methods do not execute simply because you place them within a class—they must be called. A class might contain methods that are never called from a particular application, just as some electronic devices might contain features you never use. For example, you might use a DVR to play movies but never to record TV programs, or you might use your microwave oven for popcorn but never to defrost.

Figure 3-4 shows the First class with two methods: the main() method and the nameAndAddress() method placed after main(). Figure 3-5 shows the output from the execution of the First class in Figure 3-4. When the program executes, the main() method first calls the nameAndAddress() method, which displays three lines of output. Then main() displays the phrase "First Java application".

Using a method name to contain or encapsulate a series of statements is an example of the feature that programmers call **abstraction**. Consider abstract art, in which the artist tries to capture the essence of an object without focusing on the details. Similarly, when programmers employ abstraction, they use a general method name in a module rather than list all the detailed activities that will be carried out by the method.

> The main() method in this class contains two statements. The first one is a call to the nameAndAddress() method.

```
public class First
{
    public static void main(String[] args)
    {
        nameAndAddress();
        System.out.println("First Java application");
    }

    public static void nameAndAddress()
    {
        System.out.println("XYZ Company");
        System.out.println("8900 U.S. Hwy 14");
        System.out.println("Crystal Lake, IL 60014");
    }
}
```

Figure 3-4   First class with main() calling nameAndAddress()

```
C:\Java>java First
XYZ Company
8900 U.S. Hwy 14
Crystal Lake, IL 60014
First Java application

C:\Java>
```

Figure 3-5   Output of the First application, including the nameAndAddress() method

 Watch the video *Methods*.

TWO TRUTHS & A LIE

Understanding Method Calls and Placement

1. Any class can contain an unlimited number of methods.

2. During one program execution, a method might be called any number of times.

3. A method is usually written within another method.

The false statement is #3. A method is written within a class, but not within any other methods.

Understanding Method Construction

Every method must include the two parts featured in Figure 3-6:

- A **method header**—A method's header provides information about how other methods can interact with it. A method header is also called a **declaration**.

- A **method body** between a pair of curly braces—The method body contains the statements that carry out the work of the method. A method's body is called its **implementation**. Technically, a method is not required to contain any statements in its body, but you usually would have no reason to create an empty method in a class. Sometimes, while developing a program, the programmer creates an empty method as a placeholder and fills in the implementation later. An empty method is called a **stub**.

```
public class First
{
    public static void main(String[] args)
    {
        nameAndAddress();
        System.out.println("First Java application");
    }
    public static void nameAndAddress()
    {
        System.out.println("XYZ Company");
        System.out.println("8900 U.S. Hwy 14");
        System.out.println("Crystal Lake, IL 60014");
    }
}
```

Method headers / Method bodies

Figure 3-6   The headers and bodies of the methods in the First class

The method header is the first line of a method. It contains the following:

- Optional access specifiers
- A return type
- An identifier
- Parentheses

The next few figures compare these parts of a method header for the main() method and the nameAndAddress() method in the First class.

Access Specifiers

Figure 3-7 highlights the optional access specifiers for the two methods in the First class. The access specifier for a Java method can be any of the following modifiers: public, private, protected, or, if left unspecified, package by default. Most often, methods are given public access; this book will cover the other modifiers later. Endowing a method with public access means that any other class can use it, not just the class in which the method resides.

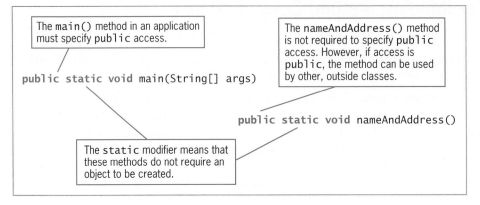

Figure 3-7   Access specifiers for two methods

 You first learned the term *access specifier* in Chapter 1. Access specifiers are sometimes called **access modifiers**.

In addition, any method that can be used without instantiating an object requires the keyword modifier static. The main() method in an application must use the keyword static, but other methods, like nameAndAddress(), can use it too. You will learn about nonstatic methods later in this chapter.

Return Type

Figure 3-8 features the return types for the main() and nameAndAddress() methods in the First class. A **return type** describes the type of data the method sends back to its calling method. Not all methods **return a value** to their calling methods; a method that returns no data has a return type of void. The main() method in an application must have a return type of void; in this example, nameAndAddress() also has a void return type. Other methods that you will see later in this chapter have different return types. The phrases *void method* and *method of type void* both refer to a method that has a void return type.

Figure 3-8   Return types for two methods

Method Name

Figure 3-9 highlights the names of the two methods in the First class. A method's name can be any legal identifier. That is, like identifiers for classes and variables, a method's identifier must be one word with no embedded spaces, and cannot be a Java keyword. The method that executes first when you run an application must be named main(), but you have a lot of leeway in naming other methods that you create within a class. Technically, you could even name another method main() as long as you did not include String[] within the parentheses, but doing so would be confusing and is not recommended.

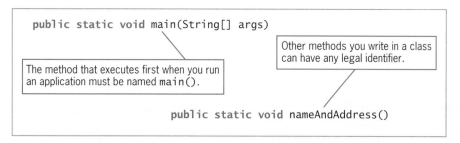

```
public static void main(String[] args)
```

Other methods you write in a class can have any legal identifier.

The method that executes first when you run an application must be named main().

```
public static void nameAndAddress()
```

Figure 3-9   Identifiers for two methods

Parentheses

As Figure 3-10 shows, every method header contains a set of parentheses that follow the identifier. The parentheses might contain data to be sent to the method. For example, when you write a main() method in a class, the parentheses in its header surround String[] args. The nameAndAddress() method in the First class requires no outside data, so its parentheses are empty. Later in this chapter, you will see several methods that accept data.

The main() method in an application must contain String[] and an identifier (args is traditional) within its parentheses.

```
public static void main(String[] args)
```

```
public static void nameAndAddress()
```

Other methods you write might accept data within their parentheses, but nameAndAddress()does not.

Figure 3-10   Parentheses and their contents for two methods

The full name of the nameAndAddress() method is First.nameAndAddress(), which includes the class name, a dot, and the method name. (The name does not include an object because nameAndAddress() is a static method.) A complete name that includes the class is a **fully qualified identifier**. When you use the nameAndAddress() method within its own class, you do not need to use the fully qualified name (although you can); the simple method name alone is enough. However, if you want to use the nameAndAddress() method in another class, the compiler does not recognize the method unless you use the full name. You have used similar syntax (including a class name, dot, and method name) when calling the JOptionPane.showMessageDialog() method.

Each of two different classes can have its own method named nameAndAddress(). Such a method in the second class would be entirely distinct from the identically named method in the first class. You could use both methods in a third class by using their fully qualified identifiers. Two classes in an application cannot have the same name.

Think of the class name as the family name. Within your own family, you might refer to an activity as "the family reunion," but outside the family people need to use a surname as well, as in "the Anderson family reunion." Similarly, within a class a method name alone is sufficient, but outside the class you need to use the fully qualified name.

TWO TRUTHS & A LIE

Understanding Method Construction

1. A method header is also called an implementation.

2. When a method is declared with public access, methods in other classes can call it.

3. Not all methods return a value, but every method requires a return type.

The false statement is #1. A method header is a declaration; a method body is its implementation.

 You Do It

Creating a static Method That Requires No Arguments and Returns No Values

Paradise Day Spa provides many personal services such as haircuts, manicures, and facials. In this section, you create a new class named ParadiseInfo, which contains a main() method that calls a displayInfo() method.

1. Open a new document in your text editor, and type the following shell for the class:

```
public class ParadiseInfo
{
}
```

(continues)

(continued)

2. Between the curly braces of the class, indent a few spaces and create the shell for the `main()` method:

```
public static void main(String[] args)
{
}
```

3. Between the braces of the `main()` method, insert a call to the `displayInfo()` method:

```
displayInfo();
```

4. Place the `displayInfo()` method outside the `main()` method, just before the closing curly brace for the `ParadiseInfo` class:

```
public static void displayInfo()
{
    System.out.println("Paradise Day Spa wants to pamper you.");
    System.out.println("We will make you look good.");
}
```

5. Save the file as **ParadiseInfo.java**.

6. Compile the class, and then execute it. The output should look like Figure 3-11.

Figure 3-11 Output of the `ParadiseInfo` application

Calling a `static` Method from Another Class

Next, you see how to call the `displayInfo()` method from a method within another class.

1. Open a new document in your text editor, and then enter the following class in which the `main()` method calls the `displayInfo()` method that resides in the `ParadiseInfo` class:

```
public class TestInfo
{
    public static void main(String[] args)
    {
        System.out.println("Calling method from another class:");
        ParadiseInfo.displayInfo();
    }
}
```

(continues)

(continued)

2. Save the file as **TestInfo.java** in the same folder as the ParadiseInfo class. If the files are not saved in the same folder and you try to compile the calling class, your compiler issues the error message "cannot find symbol"; the symbol named is the missing class you tried to call.

3. Compile the application and execute it. Your output should look like Figure 3-12. The TestInfo class does not contain the displayInfo() method; it uses the method from the ParadiseInfo class. It's important that the displayInfo() method is public. If you had omitted the keyword public from the definition of the displayInfo() method in the ParadiseInfo class, then the TestInfo class would not have been able to use it.

Figure 3-12 Output of the TestInfo application

Examining the Details of a Prewritten static Method

Recall that in Chapter 2, you used the JOptionPane class to create statements like the following:

```
JOptionPane.showMessageDialog
    (null, "Every bill is due in " + creditDays + " days");
```

In the next steps, you examine the Java API documentation for the showMessageDialog() method so that you can better understand how prewritten methods are similar to ones that you write.

1. Using a Web browser, go to the Java Web site and select **Java APIs** and **Java SE 7**.

2. In the alphabetical list of classes, find the **JOptionPane** class and select it.

3. Scroll through the class documentation until you find the **Method Summary**. Then, find the first listed version of the **showMessageDialog()** method. To the left, notice that the method is defined as a static void method, just like the main() and displayInfo() methods discussed earlier in this "You Do It" section. You can use the static showMessageDialog() method in your classes by using its class name, a dot, and the method name, in the same way that you used the ParadiseInfo static displayInfo() method in the outside class named TestInfo.

Adding Parameters to Methods

Some methods require that data be sent to them when they are called. Data items you use in a call to a method are called **arguments**. When the method receives the data items, they are called **parameters**. Methods that receive data are flexible because they can produce different results depending on what data they receive.

As a real-life example, when you make a restaurant reservation, you do not need to employ a different method for every date of the year at every possible time of day. Rather, you can supply the date and time as information to the person who carries out the method. The method, recording the reservation, is then carried out in the same manner, no matter what date and time are supplied.

In a program, if you design a method to square numeric values, it makes sense to design a square() method that you can supply with an argument that represents the value to be squared, rather than having to develop a square1() method (that squares the value 1), a square2() method (that squares the value 2), and so on. To call a square() method that takes an argument, you might write a statement like square(17); or square(86);. Similarly, any time it is called, the println() method can receive any one of an infinite number of arguments—for example, "Hello", "Goodbye", or any other String. No matter what message is sent to println(), the message is displayed correctly. If the println() method could not accept arguments, it would not be practical to use.

An important principle of object-oriented programming is **implementation hiding**, which describes the encapsulation of method details. For example, when you make a real-life restaurant reservation, you do not need to know how the reservation is actually recorded at the restaurant—perhaps it is written in a book, marked on a large chalkboard, or entered into a computerized database. The implementation details don't concern you as a client, and if the restaurant changes its methods from one year to the next, the change does not affect your use of the reservation method—you still call and provide your name, a date, and a time.

With well-written object-oriented programming methods, using implementation hiding means that a method that calls another must know the name of the called method and what type of information to send. (Usually, you also want to know about any data returned by the method; you will learn about returned data later in this chapter.) However, the client does not need to know how the method works internally. In other words, the calling method needs to understand only the **interface** to the called method. The interface is the only part of a method that the method's client sees or with which it interacts. In addition, if you substitute a new or revised method implementation, as long as the interface to the method does not change, you won't need to make any changes in any methods that call the altered method.

Hidden implementation methods are often referred to as existing in a **black box**. Many everyday devices are black boxes—that is, you can use them without understanding how they work. For example, most of us use telephones, television sets, and automobiles without understanding much about their internal mechanisms.

Creating a Method That Receives a Single Parameter

When you write the method declaration for a method that can receive a parameter, you begin by defining the same elements as you do for methods that do not accept parameters—optional access specifiers, the return type for the method, and the method name. In addition, you must include the following items within the method declaration parentheses:

- The parameter type
- A local name for the parameter

For example, the declaration for a public method named `predictRaise()` that accepts a person's annual salary and computes the value of a 10 percent raise could be written as follows:

```
public static void predictRaise(double salary)
```

You can think of the parentheses in a method declaration as a funnel into the method—parameters listed there contain data that is "dropped into" the method. A parameter accepted by a method can be any data type, including the primitive types, such as `int`, `double`, and `char`; it also can be a class type such as `String` or `PrintStream`.

In the method header for `predictRaise()`, the parameter `double salary` within the parentheses indicates that the method will receive a value of type `double`, and that within the method, the passed value will be known as `salary`. Figure 3-13 shows a complete method.

```
                    Parameter data        Parameter
                    type                  identifier

    public static void predictRaise(double salary)
    {
        double newSalary;
        final double RAISE_RATE= 1.10;
        newSalary = salary * RAISE_RATE;
        System.out.println("Current salary: " +
            salary + "     After raise: " +
            newSalary);
    }
}
```

Figure 3-13   The `predictRaise()` method

The `predictRaise()` method is a `void` method because it does not need to return a value to any other method that uses it—its only function is to receive the `salary` value, multiply it by the RAISE_RATE constant (1.10, which results in a 10 percent salary increase), and then display the result.

You can call the `predictRaise()` method by using either a constant value or a variable as an argument. Thus, both `predictRaise(472.25);` and `predictRaise(mySalary);` invoke the `predictRaise()` method correctly, assuming that `mySalary` is declared as a `double` variable and is assigned an appropriate value in the calling method. You can call the predictRaise() method any number of times, with a different constant or variable argument each time. Each of these arguments becomes known as salary within the method. The identifier salary represents a variable that holds a copy of the value of any double value passed into the method.

It is interesting to note that if the value used as an argument in the method call to predictRaise() is a variable, it might possess the same identifier as salary or a different one, such as startingWage. For example, the code in Figure 3-14 shows three calls to the predictRaise() method, and Figure 3-15 shows the output. One call uses a constant, 400.00. The other two use variables—one with the same name as salary and the other with a different name, startingWage. The identifier salary in the main() method refers to a different memory location than the one in the predictRaise() method. The parameter salary is simply a placeholder while it is being used within the predictRaise() method, no matter what name its value "goes by" in the calling method. The parameter salary is a **local variable** to the predictRaise() method; that is, it is known only within the boundaries of the method. The variable and constant declared within the method are also local to the method.

```
public class DemoRaise
{
    public static void main(String[] args)
    {
        double salary = 200.00;
        double startingWage = 800.00;
        System.out.println("Demonstrating some raises");
        predictRaise(400.00);
        predictRaise(salary);                        ──── The predictRaise() method
        predictRaise(startingWage);                       is called three times using three
    }                                                     different arguments.

    public static void predictRaise(double salary)
    {
        double newSalary;                            ──── The parameter salary
        final double RAISE_RATE= 1.10;                    receives a copy of the
        newSalary = salary * RAISE_RATE;                  value in each argument that
        System.out.println("Current salary: " +          is passed.
            salary + "    After raise: " +
            newSalary);
    }
}
```

Figure 3-14 The DemoRaise class with a main() method that uses the predictRaise() method three times

Recall that the final modifier makes RAISE_RATE constant. Because salary is not altered within the predictRaise() method in Figure 3-14, you could also make it constant by declaring the method header as public static void predictRaise(final double salary). There would be no difference in the program's execution, but declaring a parameter as final means it cannot be altered within the method. Someone reading your program would be able to see that the parameter is not intended to change.

Figure 3-15   Output of the DemoRaise application

Each time the `predictRaise()` method in Figure 3-14 executes, a `salary` variable is redeclared—that is, a new memory location large enough to hold a `double` is set up and named `salary`. Within the `predictRaise()` method, `salary` holds a copy of whatever value is passed into the method by the `main()` method. When the `predictRaise()` method ends at the closing curly brace, the local `salary` variable ceases to exist. That is, if you change the value of `salary` after you have used it in the calculation within `predictRaise()`, it affects nothing else. The memory location that holds `salary` is released at the end of the method, and any changes to its value within the method do not affect any value in the calling method. In particular, don't think there would be any change in the variable named `salary` in the `main()` method; that variable, even though it has the same name as the locally declared parameter in the method, is a different variable with its own memory address and is totally different from the one in the `predictRaise()` method. When a variable ceases to exist at the end of a method, programmers say the variable "goes out of scope." A variable's scope is the part of a program in which a variable exists and can be accessed using its unqualified name. The next chapter discusses scope in greater detail.

Creating a Method That Requires Multiple Parameters

A method can require more than one parameter. You can pass multiple arguments to a method by listing the arguments within the call to the method and separating them with commas. For example, rather than creating a `predictRaise()` method that adds a 10 percent raise to every person's salary, you might prefer to create a method to which you can pass two values—the salary to be raised as well as a percentage figure by which to raise it. Figure 3-16 shows a method that uses two such parameters.

```java
public static void predictRaiseUsingRate(double salary, double rate)
{
    double newAmount;
    newAmount = salary * (1 + rate);
    System.out.println("With raise, new salary is " + newAmount);
}
```

Figure 3-16   The `predictRaiseUsingRate()` method that accepts two parameters

In Figure 3-16, two parameters (`double salary` and `double rate`) appear within the parentheses in the method header. A comma separates each parameter, and each parameter requires its own declared type (in this case, both are `double`) as well as its own identifier. Note that a declaration for a method that receives two or more parameters must list the type for each parameter separately, even if the parameters have the same type. When values are passed to the method in a statement such as the following, the first value passed is referenced as `salary` within the method, and the second value passed is referenced as `rate`:

```
predictRaiseUsingRate(mySalary, promisedRate);
```

Therefore, arguments passed to the method must be passed in the correct order. The call `predictRaiseUsingRate(200.00, 0.10);` results in output representing a 10 percent raise based on a $200.00 salary amount (or $220.00), but `predictRaiseUsingRate(0.10, 200.00);` results in output representing a 20,000 percent raise based on a salary of 10 cents (or $20.10). If two method parameters are the same type—for example, two `double`s—passing arguments to a method in the wrong order results in a logical error; that is, the program does compile and execute, but it probably produces incorrect results. If a method expects parameters of diverse types, passing arguments in the wrong order constitutes a syntax error, and the program does not compile.

You can write a method so that it takes any number of parameters in any order. However, when you call a method, the arguments you send to a method must match in order—both in number and in type—the parameters listed in the method declaration. A method's **signature** is the combination of the method name and the number, types, and order of arguments. A method call must match the called method's signature.

Thus, a method to compute an automobile salesperson's commission amount might require arguments such as an integer dollar value of a car sold, a `double` percentage commission rate, and a character code for the vehicle type. The correct method executes only when three arguments of the correct types are sent in the correct order. Figure 3-17 shows a class containing a three-parameter method and a `main()` method that calls it twice, once using variable arguments and again using constant arguments. Figure 3-18 shows the output of the application.

```
public class ComputeCommission
{
    public static void main(String[] args)
    {
        char vType = 'S';
        int value = 23000;
        double commRate = 0.08;
        computeCommission(value, commRate, vType);
        computeCommission(40000, 0.10, 'L');
    }
```

Figure 3-17   The ComputeCommission class *(continues)*

(continued)

```java
public static void computeCommission(int value,
        double rate, char vehicle)
{
        double commission;
        commission = value * rate;
        System.out.println("\nThe " + vehicle +
            " type vehicle is worth $" + value);
        System.out.println("With " + (rate * 100) +
            "% commission rate, the commission is $" +
            commission);
}
}
```

Figure 3-17   The ComputeCommission class

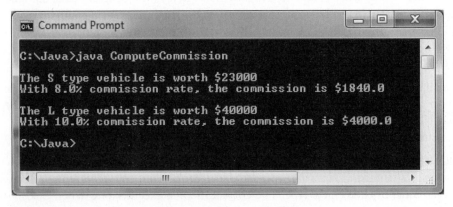

Figure 3-18   Output of the ComputeCommission application

 The arguments in a method call are often referred to as **actual parameters**. The variables in the method declaration that accept the values from the actual parameters are **formal parameters**.

 When you look at Java applications, you might see methods that appear to be callable in multiple ways. For example, you can use System.out.println() with no arguments to display a blank line, or with a String argument to display the String. You can use the method with different argument lists only because multiple versions of the method have been written, each taking a specific set of arguments. The ability to execute different method implementations by altering the argument used with the method name is known as *method overloading*, a concept you will learn about in the next chapter.

TWO TRUTHS & A LIE

Adding Parameters to Methods

1. A class can contain any number of methods, and each method can be called any number of times.

2. Arguments are used in method calls; they are passed to parameters in method headers.

3. A method header always contains a return type, an identifier, and a parameter list within parentheses.

The false statement is #3. A method header always contains a return type, an identifier, and parentheses, but the parameter list might be empty.

Creating Methods That Return Values

A method ends when any of the following events takes place:

- The method completes all of its statements. You have seen methods like this in the last section.

- The method throws an exception. Exceptions are errors; you will learn about them in the chapter *Exception Handling*.

- The method reaches a `return` statement. A **return statement** causes a method to end and the program's logic to return to the calling method. Also, a `return` statement frequently sends a value back to the calling method.

The return type for a method can be any type used in Java, which includes the primitive types `int`, `double`, `char`, and so on, as well as class types (including class types you create). Of course, a method can also return nothing, in which case the return type is `void`.

A method's return type is known more succinctly as a **method's type**. For example, the declaration for the `nameAndAddress()` method shown earlier in Figure 3-4 is written as follows:

```
public static void nameAndAddress()
```

This method returns no value, so it is type `void`.

A method that prompts a user for an age and returns the age to the calling method might be declared as:

```
public static int getAge()
```

The method returns an `int`, so it is type `int`.

As another example, a method that returns true or false, depending on whether an employee worked overtime hours, might be declared as:

public static boolean workedOvertime()

This method returns a Boolean value, so it is type boolean.

The predictRaise() method shown earlier produces output but does not return any value, so its return type is void. If you want to create a method to return the new, calculated salary value rather than display it, the header would be written as follows:

public static double predictRaise(double salary)

Figure 3-19 shows this method.

```
public static double predictRaise(double salary)
{
    double newAmount;
    final double RAISE = 1.10;
    newAmount = salary * RAISE;
    return newAmount;
}
```

Figure 3-19   The predictRaise() method returning a double

Notice the shaded return type double that precedes the method name in the predictRaise() method header in Figure 3-19. Also notice the shaded declaration of newAmount. This double variable is returned in the last shaded statement in the method. The return statement causes a value to be sent from a called method back to the calling method. In this case, the value stored in newAmount is sent back to any method that calls the predictRaise() method. A method's declared return type must match the type of the value used in the return statement; if it does not, the class does not compile. A method can return, at most, one value. The value can be a primitive data type, such as int, char, or double, or it can be a type that represents a class. (You will learn more about class types later in this chapter.) The returned value can even be a named or unnamed constant, as long as it is the correct data type or can be automatically converted to the correct data type. For example, a method with a double return type could include the statement return 1; or return 1.0;.

All methods except void methods require a return statement that returns a value of the appropriate type. You can place a return statement in a void method that is simply the word return followed by a semicolon. However, most Java programmers do not include a return statement in a method when nothing is returned.

You cannot place any statements after a method's return statement. Such statements are **unreachable statements** because the logical flow leaves the method at the return statement. An unreachable statement can never execute, and it causes a compiler error. Unreachable statements are also called **dead code**.

A method can contain multiple return clauses if they are embedded in a decision, although this practice is not recommended because it can lead to errors that are difficult to detect. However, no other statements can be placed after the last return clause in a method. You will learn about decision making in the chapter *Making Decisions*.

If a method returns a value, then when you call the method, you normally use the returned value, although you are not required to do so. For example, when you invoke the predictRaise() method, you might want to assign the returned value (also called the method's value) to a double variable named myNewSalary, as in the following statement:

myNewSalary = predictRaise(mySalary);

The predictRaise() method returns a double, so it is appropriate to assign the method's returned value to a double variable.

Alternatively, you can choose to use a method's returned value directly, without storing it in any variable. When you use a method's value, you use it in the same way you would use any variable of the same type. For example, you can display a return value in a statement such as the following:

System.out.println("New salary is " + predictRaise(mySalary));

In the preceding statement, the call to the predictRaise() method is made from within the println() method call. Because predictRaise() returns a double, you can use the method call in the same way that you would use any simple double value. As another example, you can perform arithmetic with a method's return value, as in the following statement:

double spendingMoney = predictRaise(mySalary) - expenses;

Chaining Method Calls

Any method might call any number of other methods. For example, a main() method might call a predictRaise() method, and the predictRaise() method might call a calculateBonus() method, as shown in the shaded statement in Figure 3-20.

```
public static double predictRaise(double salary)
{
    double newAmount;
    double bonusAmount;
    final double RAISE = 1.10;
    newAmount = salary * RAISE;
    bonusAmount = calculateBonus(newAmount);
    newAmount = newAmount + bonusAmount;
    return newAmount;
}
```

Figure 3-20   The predictRaise() method calling the calculateBonus() method

Looking at the call to the calculateBonus() method from the predictRaise() method, you do not know how calculateBonus() works. You only know that the calculateBonus()

method accepts a double as a parameter (because newAmount is passed into it) and that it must return either a double or a type that can automatically be promoted to a double (because the result is stored in bonusAmount). In other words, the method acts as a black box.

As examples, the calculateBonus() method might look like either of the versions shown in Figure 3-21. The first version simply adds a $50.00 bonus to a salary parameter. The second version calls another method named trickyCalculation() that returns a value added to salary. When you read the calculateBonus() method, you don't know what happens in the trickyCalculation() method, and when you read the predictRaise() method that calls calculateBonus(), you don't even necessarily know that trickyCalculation() is called.

```java
public static double calculateBonus(double salary)
{
    final double BONUS_AMT = 50.00;
    salary = salary + BONUS_AMT;
    return salary;
}

public static double calculateBonus(double salary)
{
    salary = salary + trickyCalculation();
    return salary;
}
```

Figure 3-21   Two possible versions of the calculateBonus() method

 Watch the video *Methods and Parameters*.

TWO TRUTHS & A LIE

Creating Methods That Return Values

1. The return type for a method can be any type used in Java, including int, double, and void.

2. A method's declared return type must match the type of the value used in the parameter list.

3. You cannot place a method within another method, but you can call a method from within another method.

The false statement is #2. A method's declared return type must match the type of the value used in the return statement.

You Do It

Creating static *Methods That Accept Arguments and Return a Value*

In this section, you add a method to the ParadiseInfo class you started in the last "You Do It" section. The new method receives two parameters and returns a value. The purpose of the method is to accept a minimum price for the current week's featured discount and the percentage discount, and to return the minimum amount the customer will save.

1. Open the **ParadiseInfo.java** file in your text editor, and then change the class name to **ParadiseInfo2**. Immediately save the file as **ParadiseInfo2.java**.

2. As the first line of the file, add the import statement that allows user input:

   ```
   import java.util.Scanner;
   ```

3. Add four declarations as the first statements following the opening curly brace of the main() method. One holds the minimum price for which a discount will be allowed, and another holds the discount rate. The third variable is the minimum savings, which is calculated by multiplying the minimum price for a discount and the discount rate. The fourth variable is a Scanner object to use for keyboard input.

   ```
   double price;
   double discount;
   double savings;
   Scanner keyboard = new Scanner(System.in);
   ```

 Instead of importing the Scanner class to provide console input, you could substitute JOptionPane and include program statements that provide GUI input. The input process can use other techniques too, such as getting data from a storage device—you will learn about file input in the chapter *File Input and Output*. The concept of input (getting data into memory from the outside) is the same, no matter what specific technique or type of hardware device you use.

4. Following the declarations, prompt the user for the minimum discount price, and accept a value from the keyboard:

   ```
   System.out.print("Enter cutoff price for discount >> ");
   price = keyboard.nextDouble();
   ```

5. Prompt the user for the discount rate, and accept it.

   ```
   System.out.print("Enter discount rate as a whole number >> ");
   discount = keyboard.nextDouble();
   ```

(continues)

(continued)

6. After the call to `displayInfo()`, insert a call to `computeDiscountInfo()`. You will pass the `price` and `discount` values to the method, and the method returns the minimum that a consumer will save, which is stored in `savings`:

```
savings = computeDiscountInfo(price, discount);
```

7. Just before the closing curly brace for the `main()` method, display the savings information:

```
System.out.println("Special this week on any service over " +
    price);
System.out.println("Discount of " + discount + " percent");
System.out.println("That's a savings of at least $" + savings);
```

8. After the `displayInfo()` method implementation, but before the closing curly brace for the class, add the `computeDiscountInfo()` method. It accepts two `double`s and returns a `double`.

```
public static double computeDiscountInfo(double pr, double dscnt)
{
    double savings;
    savings = pr * dscnt / 100;
    return savings;
}
```

9. Save the file, and then compile and execute it. Figure 3-22 shows a typical execution. After the user is prompted for the cutoff price for the week's sale and the discount to be applied, the program executes the `displayInfo()` method. Then the program executes the `computeDiscountInfo()` method, which returns a value to store in the `savings` variable. Finally, the discount information is displayed.

Figure 3-22   Typical execution of the `ParadiseInfo2` program

(continues)

(continued)

Understanding That Methods Can Be Used as Black Boxes

In this chapter, you have learned that methods can be used without knowing the details of their implementation. As an example of how professional programmers use implementation hiding, you can visit the Java Web site to see the interfaces for thousands of prewritten methods that reside in the Java prewritten classes. You are not allowed to see the code inside these methods; you see only their interfaces, which is all you need to be able to use the methods.

1. Open your Web browser, go to the Java Web site, and navigate to the Java APIs for Java SE 7.

2. From the alphabetical list of classes, select `PrintStream`.

3. At the `PrintStream` page, read the descriptions of several methods for the class. Note that for each method, you can see the return type, method name, and parameter list, but you do not see the implementation for any of the existing methods.

4. Examine other classes. Again, note that the Java documentation provides you with method interfaces but not implementations. When you develop your own classes in the future, you might choose to provide your users with similar documentation and compiled classes so that they cannot see, modify, or steal the code you have worked hard to develop.

Learning About Classes and Objects

When you think in an object-oriented manner, everything is an object, and every object is a member of a class. You can think of any inanimate physical item as an object—your desk, your computer, and the building in which you live are all called objects in everyday conversation. You can also think of living things as objects—your houseplant, your pet fish, and your sister are objects. Events are also objects—the stock purchase you made, the mortgage closing you attended, and a graduation party that was held in your honor are all objects.

Everything is an object, and every object is a member of a more general class. Your desk is a member of the class that includes all desks, and your pet fish is a member of the class that contains all fish. An object-oriented programmer would say that your desk is an instance of the `Desk` class and your fish is an instance of the `Fish` class. These statements represent **is-a relationships**—that is, relationships in which the object "is a" concrete example of the class. Expressing an is-a relationship is correct only when you refer to the object and the class in the proper order. You can say, "My oak desk with the scratch on top *is a* `Desk`, and my goldfish named Moby *is a* `Fish`." You don't define a `Desk` by saying, "A `Desk` *is an* oak desk with a scratch on top," or explain what a `Fish` is by saying, "A `Fish` *is a* goldfish named Moby," because both a `Desk` and a `Fish` are much more general. The difference between a class and an object parallels the difference between abstract and concrete. An object is an **instantiation** of a class, or one tangible example of a class. Your goldfish, my guppy, and the zoo's shark each constitute one instantiation of the Fish class.

Programmers also use the phrase "is-a" when talking about inheritance relationships. You will learn more about inheritance in the chapters *Introduction to Inheritance* and *Advanced Inheritance Concepts*.

The concept of a class is useful because of its reusability. Objects gain their attributes from their classes, and all objects have predictable attributes because they are members of certain classes. For example, if you are invited to a graduation party, you automatically know many things about the object (the party). You assume there will be a starting time, a certain number of guests, and some quantity of food. You understand what a party entails because of your previous knowledge of the Party class of which all parties are members. You don't know the number of guests or what food will be served at this particular party, but you understand that because all parties have guests and refreshments, this one must too. Because you understand the general characteristics of a Party, you anticipate different behaviors than if you plan to attend a TheaterPerformance object or a DentalAppointment object.

In addition to their attributes, objects have methods associated with them, and every object that is an instance of a class is assumed to possess the same methods. For example, for all Party objects, at some point you must set the date and time. In a program, you might name these methods setDate() and setTime(). Party guests need to know the date and time and might use methods named getDate() and getTime() to find out the date and time of any Party object. Method names that begin with *get* and *set* are very typical. You will learn more about get and set methods in the next section.

Your graduation party, then, might have the identifier myGraduationParty. As a member of the Party class, myGraduationParty, like all Party objects, might have data methods setDate() and setTime(). When you use them, the setDate() and setTime() methods require arguments, or information passed to them. For example, statements such as myGraduationParty.setDate("May 12") and myGraduationParty.setTime("6 P.M.") invoke methods that are available for the myGraduationParty object. When you use an object and its methods, think of being able to send a message to the object to direct it to accomplish some task—you can tell the Party object named myGraduationParty to set the date and time you request. Even though yourAnniversaryParty is also a member of the Party class, and even though it also has access to setDate() and setTime() methods, the arguments you send to yourAnniversaryParty methods will be different from those you send to myGraduationParty methods. Within any object-oriented program, you are continuously making requests to objects' methods and often including arguments as part of those requests.

In addition, some methods used in an application must return a message or value. If one of your party guests uses the getDate() method, the guest hopes that the method will respond with the desired information. Similarly, within object-oriented programs, methods are often called upon to return a piece of information to the source of the request. For example, a method within a Payroll class that calculates federal withholding tax might return a tax amount in dollars and cents, and a method within an `Inventory` class might return `true` or `false`, depending on the method's determination of whether an item is at the reorder point.

With object-oriented programming, sometimes you create classes so that you can instantiate objects from them, and other times you create classes to run as applications. Application classes frequently instantiate objects that use the objects of other classes (and their data and methods). Sometimes you write classes that do both. The same programmer does not need to write every class he or she uses. Often, you will write programs that use classes created by others; similarly, you might create a class that others will use to instantiate objects within their own applications. You can call an application or class that instantiates objects of another prewritten class a **class client** or **class user**.

The `System` class that you have used to produce output in the Command Prompt window provides an example of using a class that was written by someone else. You did not have to create it or its `println()` method; both were created for you by Java's creators.

You can identify a class that is an application because it contains a `public static void main()` method. The `main()` method is the starting point for any application. You will write and use many classes that do not contain a `main()` method—these classes can be used by other classes that are applications or applets. (You will learn about applets in the chapter *Applets, Images, and Sound*.)

A Java application can contain only one method with the header `public static void main(String[] args)`. If you write a class that imports another class, and both classes have a `public main()` method, your application will not compile.

So far, you've learned that object-oriented programming involves objects that send messages to other objects requesting they perform tasks, and that every object belongs to a class. Understanding classes and how objects are instantiated from them is the heart of object-oriented thinking.

TWO TRUTHS & A LIE

Learning About Classes and Objects

1. A class is an instantiation of many objects.

2. Objects gain their attributes and methods from their classes.

3. An application or class that instantiates objects of another prewritten class is a class client.

The false statement is #1. An object is one instantiation of a class.

Creating a Class

When you create a class, you must assign a name to the class, and you must determine what data and methods will be part of the class. Suppose you decide to create a class named Employee. One instance variable of Employee might be an employee number, and two necessary methods might be a method to set (or provide a value for) the employee number and another method to get (or retrieve) that employee number. To begin, you create a class header with three parts:

- An optional access specifier
- The keyword class
- Any legal identifier you choose for the name of your class

For example, a header for a class that represents an employee might be:

public class Employee

The most liberal form of access is public. The keyword public is a class modifier. Classes that are public are accessible by all objects. Public classes also can be **extended**, or used as a basis for any other class. Making access public means that if you develop a good Employee class, and someday you want to develop two classes that are more specific, SalariedEmployee and HourlyEmployee, then you do not have to start from scratch. Each new class can become an extension of the original Employee class, inheriting its data and methods. Although other specifiers exist, you will use the public specifier for most of your classes.

 You will learn about extended classes in the chapter *Introduction to Inheritance*.

After writing the class header public class Employee, you write the body of the Employee class between a set of curly braces. The body contains the data and methods for the class. The data components of a class are often referred to as **data fields** to help distinguish them from other variables you might use. Figure 3-23 shows an Employee class that contains one data field named empNum. Data fields are variables you declare within a class but outside of any method.

```
public class Employee
{
    private int empNum;
}
```

Figure 3-23   The Employee class with one field

In Figure 3-23, the data field empNum is not preceded by the keyword static. If the keyword static had been inserted there, only one empNum value would be shared by all Employee objects that are eventually instantiated. Because the empNum field in Figure 3-23 is not preceded by static, when you eventually create, or instantiate, objects from the class, each Employee can have its own unique empNum. Each object gets its own copy of each nonstatic data field. A nonstatic field like empNum is an **instance variable** for the class.

You have already learned that the access specifier for most Java methods is `public`. However, most fields, like empNum in the `Employee` class, are `private`, which provides the highest level of security. Assigning **private access** to a field means that no other classes can access the field's values, and only methods of the same class are allowed to set, get, or otherwise use private variables. The principle used in creating private access is sometimes called **information hiding** and is an important component of object-oriented programs. A class's private data can be changed or manipulated only by a class's own methods and not by methods that belong to other classes. In contrast to fields, most class methods are `public`, not `private`. The resulting private data/public method arrangement provides a means for you to control outside access to your data—only a class's nonprivate methods can be used to access a class's private data. The situation is similar to hiring a public receptionist to sit in front of your private office and control which messages you receive (perhaps deflecting trivial or hostile ones) and which messages you send (perhaps checking your spelling, grammar, and any legal implications). The way in which the nonprivate methods are written controls how you use the private data.

The first release of Java (1.0) supported five access levels—the four listed previously plus `private protected`. The `private protected` access level is not supported in versions of Java higher than 1.0; you should not use it in your Java programs.

In summary, a class's data fields are most often private and not static. Data fields are most frequently made public when they are both `static` and `final`—that is, when a class contains a nonchanging value that you want to use without being required to create an object. For example, the Java `Math` class contains a `public` field called `PI` that you can use without instantiating a `Math` object. You will learn about the `Math` class in the next chapter.

TWO TRUTHS & A LIE

Creating a Class

1. A class header contains an optional access specifier, the keyword `class`, and an identifier.

2. When you instantiate objects, each has its own copy of each `static` data field in the class.

3. Most fields in a class are `private`, and most methods are `public`.

The false statement is #2. When you instantiate objects, each has its own copy of each nonstatic data field in the class.

Creating Instance Methods in a Class

Besides data, classes contain methods. For example, one method you need for an `Employee` class that contains an empNum is the method to retrieve (or return) any `Employee`'s empNum for use by another class. A reasonable name for this method is getEmpNum(), and its declaration is public int getEmpNum() because it will have public access, return an integer (the employee number), and possess the identifier getEmpNum().

Similarly, you need a method with which to set the empNum field. A reasonable name for this method is setEmpNum(), and its declaration is public void setEmpNum(int emp) because it will have public access, return nothing, possess the identifier setEmpNum(), and require a parameter that represents the employee's ID number, which is type int.

Methods that set or change field values are called **mutator methods**; methods that retrieve values are called **accessor methods**. In Java, mutator methods conventionally start with the prefix *set*, and accessor methods conventionally start with the prefix *get*. Using these three-letter prefixes with your method names is not required, but it is conventional. Figure 3-24 shows the get and set methods for the empNum field for the Employee class.

```
public void setEmpNum(int emp)
{
    empNum = emp;
}

public int getEmpNum()
{
    return empNum;
}
```

Figure 3-24   The setEmpNum() and getEmpNum() methods

Notice that, unlike the methods you created earlier in this chapter, the getEmpNum() and setEmpNum() methods do not employ the static modifier. The keyword static is used for classwide methods, but not for methods that "belong" to objects. If you are creating a program with a main() method that you will execute to perform some task, many of your methods will be static so you can call them from within main() without creating objects. However, if you are creating a class from which objects will be instantiated, most methods will probably be nonstatic because you will associate the methods with individual objects. For example, the getEmpNum() method must be nonstatic because it returns a different empNum value for every Employee object you ever create. **Nonstatic methods**, those methods used with object instantiations, are called **instance methods**. You *can* use either a static or nonstatic method with an object, but only nonstatic methods behave uniquely for each object. You cannot use a nonstatic method without an object.

Understanding when to declare fields and methods as static and nonstatic is a challenge for new programmers. To help you determine whether a data field should be static or not, you can ask yourself how many times it occurs. If it occurs once per class, it is static, but if it occurs once per object, it is not static. Table 3-1 provides a summary.

Static	Nonstatic
In Java, static is a keyword. It also can be used as an adjective.	There is no keyword for nonstatic items. When you do not explicitly declare a field or method to be static, then it is nonstatic by default.
Static fields in a class are called class fields.	Nonstatic fields in a class are called instance variables.
Static methods in a class are called class methods.	Nonstatic methods in a class are called instance methods.
When you use a static field or method, you do not need to use an object; for example: JOptionPane.showDialog();	When you use a nonstatic field or method, you must use an object; for example: System.out.println();
When you create a class with a static field and instantiate 100 objects, only one copy of that field exists in memory.	When you create a class with a nonstatic field and instantiate 100 objects, then 100 copies of that field exist in memory.
When you create a static method in a class and instantiate 100 objects, only one copy of the method exists in memory and the method does not receive a this reference.	When you create a nonstatic method in a class and instantiate 100 objects, only one copy of the method exists in memory, but the method receives a this reference that contains the address of the object currently using it.
Static class variables are not instance variables. The system allocates memory to hold class variables once per class, no matter how many instances of the class you instantiate. The system allocates memory for class variables the first time it encounters a class, and every instance of a class shares the same copy of any static class variables.	Instance fields and methods are nonstatic. The system allocates a separate memory location for each nonstatic field in each instance.

Table 3-1   Comparison of static and nonstatic

Table 3-1 mentions the this reference. You will learn about the this reference in the next chapter.

Figure 3-25 also provides a summary of how public, private, static, and nonstatic class members can be used by another class. The figure shows a class named MyClass with four methods that are public static, private static, public nonstatic, and private nonstatic. The figure also shows a TestClass that instantiates a MyClass object. The TestClass contains eight method calls. The three valid calls are all to public methods. The call to the nonstatic method uses an object, and the two calls to the static method can use an object or not. The rest of the TestClass code after the comment is invalid. Private methods cannot be called from outside the class, and nonstatic methods require an object.

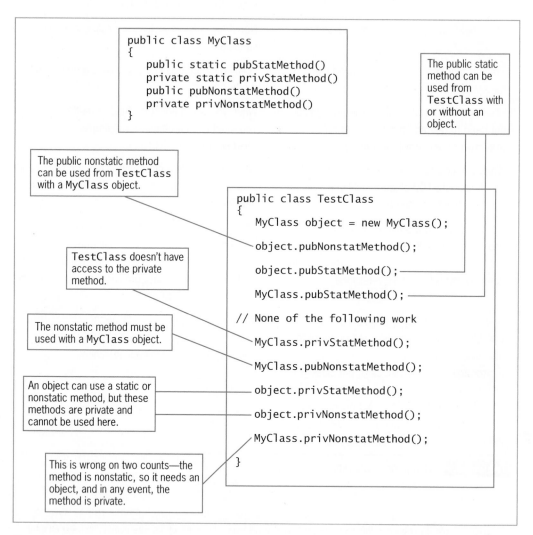

Figure 3-25   Summary of legal and illegal method calls based on combinations of method modifiers

Figure 3-26 shows the complete Employee class containing one private data field and two public methods, all of which are nonstatic. This class becomes the model for a new data type named Employee; when Employee objects eventually are created, each will have its own empNum field, and each will have access to two methods—one that provides a value for its empNum field and another that retrieves the value stored there.

```
public class Employee
{
    private int empNum;
    public int getEmpNum()
    {
        return empNum;
    }
    public void setEmpNum(int emp)
    {
        empNum = emp;
    }
}
```

Figure 3-26   The Employee class with one field and two methods

When you create a class like Employee, you can compile it, which will identify typographical errors. However, you cannot execute the class because it does not contain a main() method. A class like Employee is intended to be used as a data type for objects within other applications, as you will see in the next section.

Organizing Classes

Most classes that you create have multiple data fields and methods. For example, in addition to requiring an employee number, an Employee needs a last name, a first name, and a salary, as well as methods to set and get those fields. Figure 3-27 shows how you could code the data fields for Employee.

```
public class Employee
{
    private int empNum;
    private String empLastName;
    private String empFirstName;
    private double empSalary;
    // Methods will go here
}
```

Figure 3-27   An Employee class with several data fields

Although there is no requirement to do so, most programmers place data fields in some logical order at the beginning of a class. For example, empNum is most likely used as a unique identifier for each employee (what database users often call a **primary key**), so it makes sense to list the employee number first in the class. An employee's last name and first name "go together," so it makes sense to store these two Employee components adjacently. Despite these commonsense rules, you have a lot of flexibility in how you position your data fields within any class.

A unique identifier is one that should have no duplicates within an application. For example, an organization might have many employees with the last name Johnson or a weekly salary of $400.00, but there is only one employee with employee number 128.

Because there are two `String` components in the current `Employee` class, they might be declared within the same statement, such as the following:

```
private String empLastName, empFirstName;
```

However, it is usually easier to identify each `Employee` field at a glance if the fields are listed vertically.

You can place a class's data fields and methods in any order within a class. For example, you could place all the methods first, followed by all the data fields, or you could organize the class so that several data fields are followed by methods that use them, and then several more data fields are followed by the methods that use them. This book follows the convention of placing all data fields first so that you can see their names and data types before reading the methods that use them.

Even if the only methods in the `Employee` class started in Figure 3-27 include one `set` method and one `get` method for each instance variable, eight methods are required. When you consider an employee record for most organizations, you will realize that many more fields are often required (such as address, phone number, hire date, number of dependents, and so on), as well as many more methods. Finding your way through the list can become a formidable task. For ease in locating class methods, many programmers store them in alphabetical order. Other programmers arrange values in pairs of get and set methods, an order that also results in functional groupings. Figure 3-28 shows how the complete class definition for an `Employee` might appear.

```java
public class Employee
{
    private int empNum;
    private String empLastName;
    private String empFirstName;
    private double empSalary;
    public int getEmpNum()
    {
        return empNum;
    }
    public void setEmpNum(int emp)
    {
        empNum = emp;
    }
    public String getEmpLastName()
    {
        return empLastName;
    }
    public void setEmpLastName(String name)
    {
        empLastName = name;
    }
```

Figure 3-28   The `Employee` class with several data fields and corresponding methods *(continues)*

(continued)

```java
    public String getEmpFirstName()
    {
        return empFirstName;
    }
    public void setEmpFirstName(String name)
    {
        empFirstName = name;
    }
    public double getEmpSalary()
    {
        return empSalary;
    }
    public void setEmpSalary(double sal)
    {
        empSalary = sal;
    }
}
```

Figure 3-28   The `Employee` class with several data fields and corresponding methods

The `Employee` class is still not a particularly large class, and each of its methods is very short, but it is already becoming quite difficult to manage. It certainly can support some well-placed comments. For example, the purpose of the class and the programmer's name might appear in comments at the top of the file, and comments might be used to separate the data and method sections of the class. Your organization might have specific recommendations or requirements for placing comments within a class.

TWO TRUTHS & A LIE

Creating Instance Methods in a Class

1. The keyword `static` is used with classwide methods, but not for methods that "belong" to objects.

2. When you create a class from which objects will be instantiated, most methods are nonstatic because they are associated with individual objects.

3. Static methods are instance methods.

The false statement is #3. Nonstatic methods are instance methods; static methods are class methods.

You Do It

Creating a Class That Contains Instance Fields and Methods

Next, you create a class to store information about event services offered at Paradise Day Spa.

1. Open a new document in your text editor, and type the following class header and the curly braces to surround the class body:

    ```
    public class SpaService
    {
    }
    ```

2. Between the curly braces for the class, insert two private data fields that will hold data about a spa service:

    ```
    private String serviceDescription;
    private double price;
    ```

3. Within the class's curly braces and after the field declarations, enter the following two methods that set the field values. The `setServiceDescription()` method accepts a `String` parameter and assigns it to the `serviceDescription` field for each object that eventually will be instantiated. Similarly, the `setPrice()` method accepts a `double` parameter and assigns it to the `price` field. Note that neither of these methods is `static`.

    ```
    public void setServiceDescription(String service)
    {
        serviceDescription = service;
    }
    public void setPrice(double pr)
    {
        price = pr;
    }
    ```

4. Next, add two methods that retrieve the field values as follows:

    ```
    public String getServiceDescription()
    {
        return serviceDescription;
    }
    public double getPrice()
    {
        return price;
    }
    ```

5. Save the file as **SpaService.java**, compile it, and then correct any syntax errors. Remember, you cannot run this file as a program because it does not contain a `public static main()` method. After you read the next section, you will use this class to create objects.

Declaring Objects and Using Their Methods

Declaring a class does not create any actual objects. A class is just an abstract description of what an object will be like if any objects are ever actually instantiated. Just as you might understand all the characteristics of an item you intend to manufacture long before the first item rolls off the assembly line, you can create a class with fields and methods long before you instantiate any objects that are members of that class.

A two-step process creates an object that is an instance of a class. First, you supply a type and an identifier—just as when you declare any variable—and then you allocate computer memory for that object. For example, you might declare an integer as `int someValue;` and you might declare an `Employee` as follows:

```
Employee someEmployee;
```

In this statement, `someEmployee` stands for any legal identifier you choose to represent an `Employee`.

When you declare an integer as `int someValue;`, you notify the compiler that an integer named `someValue` will exist, and you reserve computer memory for it at the same time. When you declare the `someEmployee` instance of the `Employee` class, you are notifying the compiler that you will use the identifier `someEmployee`. However, you are not yet setting aside computer memory in which the `Employee` named `someEmployee` might be stored—that is done automatically only for primitive type variables. To allocate the needed memory for an object, you must use the **new operator**. Two statements that actually set aside enough memory to hold an `Employee` are as follows:

```
Employee someEmployee;
someEmployee = new Employee();
```

You first learned about the **new** operator when you created a `Scanner` object in Chapter 2.

Instead of using two statements, you can declare and reserve memory for `someEmployee` in one statement, as in the following:

```
Employee someEmployee = new Employee();
```

In this statement, `Employee` is the object's type (as well as its class), and `someEmployee` is the name of the object. In this statement, `someEmployee` becomes a **reference to the object**—the name for a memory address where the object is held. Every object name is also a reference—that is, a computer memory location. In Chapter 2, you learned that a class like `Employee` is a *reference type*.

The equal sign is the assignment operator, so a value is being assigned to `someEmployee` in the declaration. The `new` operator is allocating a new, unused portion of computer memory for `someEmployee`. The value that the statement is assigning to `someEmployee` is a memory address at which `someEmployee` is to be located. You do not need to be concerned with what the actual memory address is—when you refer to `someEmployee`, the compiler locates it at the appropriate address for you.

The final portion of the statement after the new operator, Employee(), with its parentheses, looks suspiciously like a method name. In fact, it is the name of a method that constructs an Employee object. The Employee() method is a **constructor**, a special type of method that creates and initializes objects. You can write your own constructor for a class, and you will learn how later in this chapter. However, when you don't write a constructor for a class, Java writes one for you. Whether you write your own constructor or use the one automatically created by Java, the name of the constructor is always the same as the name of the class whose objects it constructs.

After an object has been instantiated, its methods can be accessed using the object's identifier, a dot, and a method call. For example, Figure 3-29 shows an application that instantiates two Employee objects. The two objects, clerk and driver, each use the setEmpNum() and getEmpNum() method one time. The DeclareTwoEmployees application can use these methods because they are public, and it must use them with an Employee object because the methods are not static. Figure 3-30 shows the output of the application.

```java
public class DeclareTwoEmployees
{
    public static void main(String[] args)
    {
        Employee clerk = new Employee();
        Employee driver = new Employee();
        clerk.setEmpNum(345);
        driver.setEmpNum(567);
        System.out.println("The clerk's number is " +
            clerk.getEmpNum() + " and the driver's number is " +
            driver.getEmpNum());
    }
}
```

Figure 3-29   The DeclareTwoEmployees class

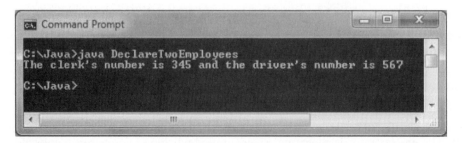

Figure 3-30   Output of the DeclareTwoEmployees application

The program in Figure 3-29 assumes that the Employee.java file is stored in the same folder as the application. If the Employee.java file was stored in a different folder, you would need an import statement at the top of the file, similar to the ones you use for the **Scanner** and **JOptionPane** classes.

Understanding Data Hiding

Within the `DeclareTwoEmployees` class, you must use the public methods `setEmpNum()` and `getEmpNum()` to be able to set and retrieve the value of the `empNum` field for each `Employee` because you cannot access the private `empNum` field directly. For example, the following statement would not be allowed:

```
clerk.empNum = 789;
```

This statement generates the error message "empNum has private access in Employee", meaning you cannot access `empNum` from the `DeclareTwoEmployees` class. If you made `empNum` `public` instead of `private`, a direct assignment statement would work, but you would violate an important principle of object-oriented programming—that of data hiding using encapsulation. Data fields should usually be private, and a client application should be able to access them only through the public interfaces—that is, through the class's public methods. However, you might reasonably ask, "When I write an application, if I *can't* set an object's data field directly, but I *can* set it using a public method, what's the difference? The field value is set either way!" Actually, the `setEmpNum()` method in the `Employee` class in Figure 3-26 *does* accept any integer value you send into it. However, you could rewrite the `setEmpNum()` method to prevent invalid data from being assigned to an object's data fields. For example, perhaps your organization has rules for valid employee ID numbers—they must be no fewer than five digits, or they must start with a 9, for instance—or perhaps you calculate a check-digit that is appended to every employee ID number. The statements that enforce these requirements would be part of the `setEmpNum()` method. Checking a value for validity requires decision making. You will learn more in the chapter *Making Decisions*.

A check-digit is a number appended to a field, typically an ID number or account number. The check-digit ensures that the number is valid. For example, an organization might use five-digit employee ID numbers in which the fifth digit is calculated by dividing the first four by 7 and taking the remainder. As an example, if the first four digits of your ID number are 7235, then the fifth digit is 4, the remainder when you divide the first four digits by 7. So the five-digit ID becomes 72354. Later, if you make a mistake and enter your ID into a company application as 82354, the application would divide the first four digits, 8235, by 7. The remainder is not 4, and the ID would be found invalid.

Similarly, a **get** method might control how a value is retrieved. Perhaps you do not want clients to have access to part of an employee's ID number, or perhaps you always want to add a company code to every ID before it is returned to the client. Even when a field has no data value requirements or restrictions, making data private and providing public **set** and **get** methods establishes a framework that makes such modifications easier in the future. You will not necessarily write **set** and **get** methods for every field in a class; there are some fields that clients will not be allowed to alter. Some fields will simply be assigned values, and some field values might be calculated from the values of others.

Watch the video *Classes and Objects*.

154

TWO TRUTHS & A LIE

Declaring Objects and Using Their Methods

1. When you declare an object, you give it a name and set aside enough memory for the object to be stored.

2. An object name is a reference; it holds a memory address.

3. When you don't write a constructor for a class, Java creates one for you; the name of the constructor is always the same as the name of its class.

The false statement is #1. When you declare an object, you are not yet setting aside computer memory in which the object is stored; to allocate the needed memory for an object, you must use the new operator.

You Do It

Declaring and Using Objects

In the previous "You Do It" section, you created a class named SpaService. Now you create an application that instantiates and uses SpaService objects.

1. Open a new file in your text editor, and type the import statement needed for an interactive program that accepts user keyboard input:

    ```
    import java.util.Scanner;
    ```

2. Create the shell for a class named CreateSpaServices:

    ```
    public class CreateSpaServices
    {
    }
    ```

3. Between the curly braces of the CreateSpaServices class, create the shell for a main() method for the application:

    ```
    public static void main(String[] args)
    {
    }
    ```

(continues)

4. Within the `main()` method, declare variables to hold a service description and price that a user can enter from the keyboard:

```
String service;
double price;
```

5. Next, declare three objects. Two are `SpaService` objects that use the class you created in the prior set of "You Do It" steps. The third object uses the built-in Java `Scanner` class. Both classes use the `new` operator to allocate memory for their objects, and both call a constructor that has the same name as the class. The difference is that the `Scanner` constructor requires an argument (`System.in`), but the `SpaService` class does not.

```
SpaService firstService = new SpaService();
SpaService secondService = new SpaService();
Scanner keyboard = new Scanner(System.in);
```

6. In the next statements, you prompt the user for a service, accept it from the keyboard, prompt the user for a price, and accept it from the keyboard.

```
System.out.print("Enter service >> ");
service = keyboard.nextLine();
System.out.print("Enter price >> ");
price = keyboard.nextDouble();
```

7. Recall that the `setServiceDescription()` method in the `SpaService` class is nonstatic, meaning it is used with an object, and that it requires a `String` argument. Write the statement that sends the service the user entered to the `setServiceDescription()` method for the `firstService` object:

```
firstService.setServiceDescription(service);
```

8. Similarly, send the price the user entered to the `setPrice()` method for the `firstService` object. Recall that this method is nonstatic and requires a `double` argument.

```
firstService.setPrice(price);
```

9. Make a call to the `nextLine()` method to remove the Enter key that remains in the input buffer after the last numeric entry. Then repeat the prompts, and accept data for the second `SpaService` object.

```
keyboard.nextLine();
System.out.print("Enter service >> ");
service = keyboard.nextLine();
System.out.print("Enter price >> ");
price = keyboard.nextDouble();
secondService.setServiceDescription(service);
secondService.setPrice(price);
```

(continued)

10. Display the details for the firstService object.

```
System.out.println("First service details:");
    System.out.println(firstService.getServiceDescription() +
"  $" + firstService.getPrice());
```

11. Display the details for the secondService object.

```
System.out.println("Second service details:");
    System.out.println(secondService.getServiceDescription() +
"  $" + secondService.getPrice());
```

12. Save the file as **CreateSpaServices.java**. Compile and execute the program. Figure 3-31 shows a typical execution. Make sure you understand how the user's entered values are assigned to and retrieved from the two SpaService objects.

Figure 3-31   Typical execution of the CreateSpaServices program

An Introduction to Using Constructors

When you create a class, such as Employee, and instantiate an object with a statement such as the following, you are actually calling the Employee class constructor that is provided by default by the Java compiler:

```
Employee chauffeur = new Employee();
```

A constructor establishes an object; a **default constructor** is one that requires no arguments. A default constructor is created automatically by the Java compiler for any class you create whenever you do not write your own constructor.

When the prewritten, default constructor for the Employee class is called, it establishes one Employee object with the identifier provided. The automatically supplied default constructor provides the following specific initial values to an object's data fields:

- Numeric fields are set to 0 (zero).

- Character fields are set to Unicode '\u0000'.

- Boolean fields are set to false.

- Fields that are object references (for example, String fields) are set to null (or empty).

If you do not want each field in an object to hold these default values, or if you want to perform additional tasks when you create an instance of a class, you can write your own constructor. Any constructor you write must have the same name as the class it constructs, and constructors cannot have a return type. You never provide a return type for a constructor—not even void. Normally, you declare constructors to be public so that other classes can instantiate objects that belong to the class. When you write a constructor for a class, you no longer have access to the automatically created version.

For example, if you want every Employee object to have a default starting salary of $300.00 per week, you could write the constructor for the Employee class that appears in Figure 3-32. Any Employee object instantiated will have an empSalary field value equal to 300.00, and the other Employee data fields will contain the automatically supplied default values. Even though you might want a field to hold the default value, you still might prefer to explicitly initialize the field for clarity.

```
public Employee()
{
    empSalary = 300.00;
}
```

Figure 3-32 The Employee class constructor

The Employee class constructor in Figure 3-32 takes no parameters. Therefore, it is a default constructor. You will learn about nondefault constructors that take parameters in the next chapter.

You can write any Java statement in a constructor. Although you usually have no reason to do so, you could display a message from within a constructor or perform any other task.

You can place the constructor anywhere inside the class, outside of any other method. Typically, a constructor is placed with the other methods. Often, programmers list the constructor first because it is the first method used when an object is created.

You never are required to write a constructor for a class; Java provides you with a default version if the class contains no explicit constructor.

A class can contain multiple constructors. You will learn how to overload constructors in the next chapter.

Watch the video *Constructors*.

158

TWO TRUTHS & A LIE

An Introduction to Using Constructors

1. In Java, you cannot write a default constructor; it must be supplied for you automatically.

2. The automatically supplied default constructor sets all numeric fields to 0, character fields to Unicode '\u0000', Boolean fields to `false`, and fields that are object references to `null`.

3. When you write a constructor, it must have the same name as the class it constructs, and it cannot have a return type.

The false statement is #1. A default constructor is one that takes no parameters. If you do not create a constructor for a class, Java creates a default constructor for you. However, you can create a default constructor that replaces the automatically supplied one.

You Do It

Adding a Constructor to a Class

1. Open the **SpaService.java** file that you created in a "You Do It" section earlier in this chapter.

2. After the field declarations, and before the method declarations, insert an explicit default constructor that sets `serviceDescription` to "XXX" and `price` to 0. Because numeric fields in objects are set to 0 by default, the last assignment is not really necessary. However, programmers sometimes code a statement like the one that sets `price` to 0 so that their intentions are clear to people reading their programs.

(continues)

(continued)

```
public SpaService()
{
    serviceDescription = "XXX";
    price = 0;
}
```

159

3. Save the class and compile it.

4. Open the **CreateSpaServices.java** file. Comment out the seven statements that prompt for, receive, and set the values for the secondService object by placing double slashes at the start of their lines, as shown below. By commenting out these lines, you change the program so that the user does not enter values for the secondService object. Instead, the values assigned by the constructor are the final values for the object.

```
//          keyboard.nextLine();
//          System.out.print("Enter service >> ");
//          service = keyboard.nextLine();
//          System.out.print("Enter price >> ");
//          price = keyboard.nextDouble();
//          secondService.setServiceDescription(service);
//          secondService.setPrice(price);
```

5. Save the file, and then compile and execute it. Figure 3-33 shows a typical execution. The firstService object contains values supplied by the user, but the secondService object shows the values assigned during the object's construction.

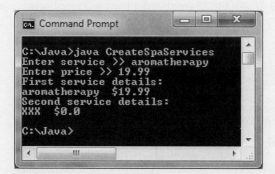

```
C:\Java>java CreateSpaServices
Enter service >> aromatherapy
Enter price >> 19.99
First service details:
aromatherapy  $19.99
Second service details:
XXX   $0.0

C:\Java>
```

Figure 3-33 Typical execution of CreateSpaServices program that uses constructor values for the second object

Understanding That Classes Are Data Types

The classes that you create become data types. Programmers sometimes refer to classes as **abstract data types**, or **ADT**s. An abstract data type is a type whose implementation is hidden and accessed through its public methods. A class can also be called a **programmer-defined data type**; in other words, it is a type that is not built into the language. A class is a composite type—that is, a class is composed from smaller parts.

Java's primitive types are not composite. Java has eight built-in primitive data types such as int and double. Primitive types can also be called *scalar* types. You do not have to define these simple types; the creators of Java have already done so. For example, when the int type was first created, the programmers who designed it had to think of the following:

Q: What shall we call it?

A: int.

Q: What are its attributes?

A: An int is stored in four bytes; it holds whole-number values.

Q: What methods are needed by int?

A: A method to assign a value to a variable (for example, num = 32;).

Q: Any other methods?

A: Some operators to perform arithmetic with variables (for example, num + 6).

Q: Any other methods?

A: Of course, there are even more attributes and methods of an int, but these are a good start.

Your job in constructing a new data type is similar. If you need a class for employees, you should ask:

Q: What shall we call it?

A: Employee.

Q: What are its attributes?

A: It has an integer ID number, a String last name, and a double salary.

Q: What methods are needed by Employee?

A: A method to assign values to a member of this class (for example, one Employee's ID number is 3232, her last name is "Walters", and her salary is 30000).

Q: Any other methods?

A: A method to display data in a member of this class (for example, display one Employee's data).

Q: Any other methods?

A: Probably, but this is enough to get started.

When you declare a primitive type object, you provide its type and an identifier. When you declare an object from one of your classes, you do the same. After each exists, you can use them in very similar ways. For example, suppose you declare an `int` named `myInt` and an `Employee` named `myEmployee`. Then each can be passed into a method, returned from a method, or assigned to another object of the same data type.

For example, Figure 3-34 shows a program in which the `main()` method uses two other methods. One method accepts an `Employee` as a parameter, and the other returns an `Employee`. (The `Employee` class is defined in Figure 3-28.) Figure 3-35 shows a typical execution. You can see in this sample program that an `Employee` is passed into and out of methods just like a primitive object would be. Classes are not mysterious; they are just new data types that you invent.

```java
import java.util.Scanner;
class MethodsThatUseAnEmployee
{
    public static void main (String args[])
    {
        Employee myEmployee;
        myEmployee = getEmployeeData();
        displayEmployee(myEmployee);
    }
    public static Employee getEmployeeData()
    {
        Employee tempEmp = new Employee();
        int id;
        double sal;
        Scanner input = new Scanner(System.in);
        System.out.print("Enter employee ID >> ");
        id = input.nextInt();
        tempEmp.setEmpNum(id);
        System.out.print("Enter employee salary >> ");
        sal = input.nextDouble();
        tempEmp.setEmpSalary(sal);
        return tempEmp;
    }
    public static void displayEmployee(Employee anEmp)
    {
        System.out.println("\nEmployee #" + anEmp.getEmpNum() +
            " Salary is " + anEmp.getEmpSalary());
    }
}
```

Figure 3-34   The MethodsThatUseAnEmployee application

162

Figure 3-35   Typical execution of the `MethodsThatUseAnEmployee`
application

Notice in the application in Figure 3-34 that the `Employee` declared in the `main()` method
is not constructed there. An `Employee` is constructed in the `getEmployeeData()` method
and passed back to the `main()` method, where it is assigned to the `myEmployee` reference.
The `Employee` constructor could have been called in `main()`, but the values assigned would
have been overwritten after the call to `getEmployeeData()`.

TWO TRUTHS & A LIE

Understanding That Classes Are Data Types

1. When you declare a primitive variable or instantiate an object from a class, you
   provide both a type and an identifier.

2. Unlike a primitive variable, an instantiated object cannot be passed into or returned
   from a method.

3. The address of an instantiated object can be assigned to a declared reference of
   the same type.

The false statement is #2. An instantiated object can be passed into or returned
from a method.

You Do It

Understanding That Classes Are Data Types

In this section, you modify the `CreateSpaServices` class to include a method for data entry. This change makes the `main()` method shorter, gives you the ability to reuse code, and shows that an object of the `SpaService` class data type can be returned from a method as easily as a primitive data type.

1. Open the **CreateSpaServices.java** file if it is not still open in your text editor.

2. Delete the declarations for `service`, `price`, and `keyboard`. Declarations for these variables will now be part of the data entry method that you will create.

3. Delete the six statements that prompt the user and get values for the `firstService` objects. Also delete the seven statements that prompt the user and retrieve data for the `secondService` object. You commented out these statements in the previous "You Do It" section.

4. In place of the statements you just deleted, insert two new statements. The first sends a copy of the `firstService` object to a method named `getData()`. The method returns a `SpaService` object that will be filled with appropriate data, and this object is assigned to `firstService`. The second statement does the same thing for `secondService`.

    ```
    firstService = getData(firstService);
    secondService = getData(secondService);
    ```

5. After the closing curly brace for the `main()` method, but before the closing curly brace for the class, start the following `public static getData()` method. The header indicates that the method both accepts and returns a `SpaService` object. Include the opening curly brace for the method, and make declarations for `service`, `price`, and `keyboard`.

    ```
    public static SpaService getData(SpaService s)
    {
        String service;
        double price;
        Scanner keyboard = new Scanner(System.in);
    ```

(continues)

(continued)

6. Continue the method by prompting the user for and accepting a service and its price. Include a final call to `nextLine()` so that the input buffer is cleared after the last numeric entry.

```
System.out.print("Enter service >> ");
service = keyboard.nextLine();
System.out.print("Enter price >> ");
price = keyboard.nextDouble();
keyboard.nextLine();
```

7. Finish the method by assigning the entered service and price to the `SpaService` object parameter using the `SpaService` class's `setServiceDescription()` and `setPrice()` methods. Then return the full object to the `main()` method, where it is assigned to the object used in the method call. Add a closing curly brace for the method.

```
    s.setServiceDescription(service);
    s.setPrice(price);
    return s;
}
```

8. Save the file, compile it, and execute it. Figure 3-36 shows a typical execution. The execution is no different from the original version of the program, but by creating a method that accepts an unfilled `SpaService` object and returns one filled with data, you have made the `main()` method shorter and reused the data entry code.

Figure 3-36   Typical execution of the `CreateSpaServices` program that uses a data entry method

Don't Do It

- Don't place a semicolon at the end of a method header. After you get used to putting semicolons at the end of every statement, it's easy to start putting them in too many places. Method headers never end in a semicolon.

- Don't think "default constructor" means only the automatically supplied constructor. Although a class's automatically supplied constructor is a default constructor, so is any constructor you create that accepts no parameters.

- Don't think that a class's methods must accept its own fields' values as parameters or return values to its own fields. When a class contains both fields and methods, each method has direct access to every field within the class.

- Don't create a class method that has a parameter with the same identifier as a class field—yet. If you do, you will only be allowed to access the local variable within the method, and you will not be able to access the field. You will be able to use the same identifier and still access both values after you read the next chapter. For now, make sure that the parameter in any class method has a different identifier from any class field.

Key Terms

A **method** is a program module that contains a series of statements that carry out a task.

When you **invoke** or **call** a method, you execute it.

The **calling method** makes a **method call** that invokes the **called method**.

A **client method** is a method that calls another.

Abstraction is the programming feature that allows you to use a method name to encapsulate a series of statements.

The **method header** is the first line of the method and contains information about how other methods can interact with it.

A **declaration** is another name for a method header.

A **method body** is the set of statements between curly braces that follow the header and that carry out the method's actions.

Implementation describes the actions that execute within a method—the method body.

A **stub** is a method that contains no statements; programmers create stubs as temporary placeholders during the program development process.

Access modifier is sometimes used as another term for *access specifier*.

A **return type** indicates the type of data that, upon completion of the method, is sent back to its calling method.

To **return a value** is to send the value from a called method back to the calling method.

A **fully qualified identifier** includes a class name and a dot before the identifier.

Arguments are data items sent to methods in a method call.

Parameters are the data items received by a method.

Implementation hiding is a principle of object-oriented programming that describes the encapsulation of method details within a class.

The **interface** to a method includes the method's return type, name, and arguments. It is the part that a client sees and uses.

A **black box** is a device you can use without understanding how it works.

A **local variable** is known only within the boundaries of a method.

A method's **signature** is the combination of the method name and the number, types, and order of arguments.

Actual parameters are the arguments in a method call.

Formal parameters are the variables in a method declaration that accept the values from actual parameters.

A **return statement** ends a method and frequently sends a value from a called method back to the calling method.

A **method's type** is its return type.

Unreachable statements are those that cannot be executed because the logical path can never encounter them; an unreachable statement causes a compiler error.

Dead code is a set of statements that are logically unreachable.

An **is-a relationship** is the relationship between an object and the class of which it is a member.

An **instantiation** of a class is an object; in other words, it is one tangible example of a class.

A **class client** or **class user** is an application or class that instantiates objects of another prewritten class.

Classes can be **extended**, or used as a basis for any other class.

Data fields are data variables declared in a class outside of any method.

The **instance variables** of a class are its data components.

Assigning **private access** to a field means that no other classes can access the field's values, and only methods of the same class are allowed to set, get, or otherwise use private variables.

Information hiding is the object-oriented programming principle used when creating private access for data fields; a class's private data can be changed or manipulated only by a class's own methods and not by methods that belong to other classes.

Mutator methods set values.

Accessor methods retrieve values.

Nonstatic methods, those methods used with object instantiations, are called **instance methods**.

A **primary key** is a unique identifier for data within a database.

The **new operator** allocates the memory needed to hold an object.

A **reference to an object** is the name for a memory address where the object is held.

A **constructor** is a method that establishes an object.

A **default constructor** is one that requires no parameters; if you do not write one, a default constructor is created for a class automatically by the Java compiler.

An **abstract data type** is a type whose implementation is hidden and accessed through its public methods.

A **programmer-defined data type** is one that is created by a programmer and not built into the language.

Chapter Summary

- A method is a series of statements that carry out a task. Any method can call, or invoke, another. You place a method within a class outside of any other methods.

- Methods must include a declaration (or header or definition), an opening curly brace, a body, and a closing curly brace. A method declaration contains optional access specifiers, the return type for the method, the method name, an opening parenthesis, an optional list of parameters, and a closing parenthesis.

- When you write the method declaration for a method that can receive a parameter, you need to include the parameter type and a local name for the parameter within the method declaration parentheses. You can pass multiple arguments to methods by listing the arguments separated by commas within the call to the method. The arguments you send to the method must match (both in number and in type) the parameters listed in the method declaration.

- The return type for a method (the method's type) can be any Java type, including `void`. You use a `return` statement to send a value back to a calling method.

- Objects are concrete instances of classes. Objects gain their attributes from their classes, and all objects have predictable attributes because they are members of certain classes. In addition to their attributes, objects have methods associated with them, and every object that is an instance of a class is assumed to possess the same methods.

- A class header contains an optional access specifier, the keyword `class`, and any legal identifier you choose for the name of your class. A class contains fields, which are frequently private, and methods, which are frequently public.

- Nonstatic instance methods operate uniquely for every object. Programmers can organize their classes in many ways. Fields can be placed before or after methods, and methods can be placed in any logical order.

- To create an object that is an instance of a class, you supply a type and an identifier, and then you allocate computer memory for that object using the new operator and the class constructor. With well-written object-oriented programming methods, using implementation hiding—or the encapsulation of method details within a class—means that the calling method needs to understand only the interface to the called method.

- A constructor establishes an object and provides specific initial values for the object's data fields. A constructor always has the same name as the class of which it is a member. By default, numeric fields are set to 0 (zero), character fields are set to Unicode '\u0000', Boolean fields are set to false, and object type fields are set to null.

- A class is an abstract, programmer-defined data type, similar to Java's built-in, primitive data types.

Review Questions

1. In Java, methods must include all of the following except ――――――――――.

    a. a declaration

    b. a call to another method

    c. curly braces

    d. a body

2. All method declarations contain ――――――――――.

    a. the keyword static

    b. one or more explicitly named access specifiers

    c. arguments

    d. parentheses

3. A public static method named computeSum() is located in classA. To call the method from within classB, use the statement ――――――――――.

    a. computeSum(classB);

    b. classB(computeSum());

    c. classA.computeSum();

    d. You cannot call computeSum() from within classB.

4. Which of the following method declarations is correct for a static method named displayFacts() if the method receives an int argument?

    a. public static int displayFacts()

    b. public void displayFacts(int data)

    c. public static void displayFacts(int data)

    d. Two of these are correct.

5. The method with the declaration `public static int aMethod(double d)` has a method type of _____.

   a. `static`

   b. `int`

   c. `double`

   d. You cannot determine the method type.

6. Which of the following is a correct call to a method declared as `public static void aMethod(char code)`?

   a. `void aMethod();`

   b. `void aMethod('V');`

   c. `aMethod(char 'M');`

   d. `aMethod('Q');`

7. A method is declared as `public static void showResults(double d, int i)`. Which of the following is a correct method call?

   a. `showResults(double d, int i);`

   b. `showResults(12.2, 67);`

   c. `showResults(4, 99.7);`

   d. Two of these are correct.

8. The method with the declaration `public static char procedure(double d)` has a method type of _____.

   a. `public`

   b. `static`

   c. `char`

   d. `double`

9. The method `public static boolean testValue(int response)` returns _____.

   a. a `boolean` value

   b. an `int` value

   c. no value

   d. You cannot determine what is returned.

10. Which of the following could be the last legally coded line of a method declared as `public static int getVal(double sum)`?

   a. `return;`

   b. `return 77;`

   c. `return 2.3;`

   d. Any of these could be the last coded line of the method.

11. The nonstatic data components of a class often are referred to as the _____ of that class.

    a. access types
    b. instance variables
    c. methods
    d. objects

12. Objects contain methods and data items, which are also known as _____.

    a. fields
    b. functions
    c. themes
    d. instances

13. You send messages or information to an object through its _____.

    a. fields
    b. methods
    c. classes
    d. type

14. A program or class that instantiates objects of another prewritten class is a(n) _____.

    a. class client
    b. superclass
    c. object
    d. patron

15. The body of a class is always written _____.

    a. in a single line, as the first statement in a class
    b. within parentheses
    c. between curly braces
    d. as a method call

16. Most class data fields are _____.

    a. `private`
    b. `public`
    c. `static`
    d. `final`

17. The concept of allowing a class's private data to be changed only by a class's own methods is known as _____.

    a. structured logic
    b. object orientation
    c. information hiding
    d. data masking

18. Suppose you declare an object as Book thisBook;. Before you store data in thisBook, you _____.

    a. also must explicitly allocate memory for it
    b. need not explicitly allocate memory for it
    c. must explicitly allocate memory for it only if it has a constructor
    d. can declare it to use no memory

19. If a class is named Student, the class constructor name is _____.

    a. any legal Java identifier
    b. any legal Java identifier that begins with *S*
    c. StudentConstructor
    d. Student

20. If you use the automatically supplied default constructor when you create an object, _____.

    a. numeric fields are set to 0 (zero)
    b. character fields are set to blank
    c. Boolean fields are set to true
    d. All of these are true.

Exercises

 Programming Exercises

1. Suppose that you have created a program with only the following variables:

```
int v = 4;
int w = 6;
double x = 2.2;
```

Suppose that you also have a method with the following header:

```
public static void calculate(int x, double y)
```

Which of the following method calls are legal?

a. calculate(v, w);   d. calculate(18, x);
b. calculate(v, x);   e. calculate(1.1, 2.2);
c. calculate(x, y);   f. calculate(5, 7);

2. Suppose that a class named ClassA contains a private nonstatic integer named b, a public nonstatic integer named c, and a public static integer named d. Which of the following are legal statements in a class named ClassB that has instantiated an object as ClassA obA = new ClassA();?

a. obA.b = 12;   d. ClassA.b = 4;
b. obA.c = 5;   e. ClassA.c = 33;
c. obA.d = 23;   f. ClassA.d = 99;

3. a. Create an application named ArithmeticMethods whose main() method holds two integer variables. Assign values to the variables. In turn, pass each value to methods named displayNumberPlus10(), displayNumberPlus100(), and displayNumberPlus1000(). Create each method to perform the task its name implies. Save the application as **ArithmeticMethods.java**.

   b. Modify the ArithmeticMethods class to accept the values of the two integers from a user at the keyboard. Save the file as **ArithmeticMethods2.java**.

4. a. Create an application named Percentages whose main() method holds two double variables. Assign values to the variables. Pass both variables to a method named computePercent() that displays the two values and the value of the first number as a percentage of the second one. For example, if the numbers are 2.0 and 5.0, the method should display a statement similar to "2.0 is 40% of 5.0." Then call the method a second time, passing the values in reverse order. Save the application as **Percentages.java**.

   b. Modify the Percentages class to accept the values of the two doubles from a user at the keyboard. Save the file as **Percentages2.java**.

5. When gasoline is $100 per barrel, then the consumer's price at the pump is between $3.50 and $4.00 per gallon. Create a class named GasPrices. Its main() method holds an integer variable named pricePerBarrel to which you will assign a value entered by a user at the keyboard. Create a method to which you pass pricePerBarrel. The method displays the range of possible prices per gallon. For example, if gas is $120 per barrel, then the price at the pump should be between $4.20 and $4.80. Save the application as **GasPrices.java**.

6. There are 2.54 centimeters in an inch, and there are 3.7854 liters in a U.S. gallon. Create a class named MetricConversion. Its main() method accepts an integer value from a user at the keyboard, and in turn passes the entered value to two methods. One converts the value from inches to centimeters and the other converts the same value from gallons to liters. Each method displays the results with appropriate explanation. Save the application as **MetricConversion.java**.

7. Assume that a gallon of paint covers about 350 square feet of wall space. Create an application with a main() method that prompts the user for the length, width, and height of a rectangular room. Pass these three values to a method that does the following:

- Calculates the wall area for a room

- Passes the calculated wall area to another method that calculates and returns the number of gallons of paint needed

- Displays the number of gallons needed

- Computes the price based on a paint price of $32 per gallon, assuming that the painter can buy any fraction of a gallon of paint at the same price as a whole gallon

- Returns the price to the main() method

The main() method displays the final price. For example, the cost to paint a 15- by-20-foot room with 10-foot ceilings is $64. Save the application as **PaintCalculator.java**.

8. The Harrison Group Life Insurance company computes annual policy premiums based on the age the customer turns in the current calendar year. The premium is computed by taking the decade of the customer's age, adding 15 to it, and multiplying by 20. For example, a 34-year-old would pay $360, which is calculated by adding the decades (3) to 15, and then multiplying by 20. Write an application that prompts a user for the current year and a birth year. Pass both to a method that calculates and returns the premium amount, and then display the returned amount. Save the application as **Insurance.java**.

9. Write an application that calculates and displays the weekly salary for an employee. The main() method prompts the user for an hourly pay rate, regular hours, and overtime hours. Create a separate method to calculate overtime pay, which is regular hours times the pay rate plus overtime hours times 1.5 times the pay rate; return the result to the main() method to be displayed. Save the program as **Salary.java**.

10. Write an application that calculates and displays the amount of money a user would have if his or her money could be invested at 5 percent interest for one year. Create a method that prompts the user for the starting value of the investment and returns it to the calling program. Call a separate method to do the calculation, and return the result to be displayed. Save the program as **Interest.java**.

11. a. Create a class named Sandwich. Data fields include a String for the main ingredient (such as "tuna"), a String for bread type (such as "wheat"), and a double for price (such as 4.99). Include methods to get and set values for each of these fields. Save the class as **Sandwich.java**.

    b. Create an application named TestSandwich that instantiates one Sandwich object and demonstrates the use of the set and get methods. Save this application as **TestSandwich.java**.

12. a. Create a class named Student. A Student has fields for an ID number, number of credit hours earned, and number of points earned. (For example, many schools compute grade point averages based on a scale of 4, so a three-credit-hour class in which a student earns an A is worth 12 points.) Include methods to assign values to all fields. A Student also has a field for grade point average. Include a method to compute the grade point average field by dividing points by credit hours earned. Write methods to display the values in each Student field. Save this class as **Student.java**.

   b. Write a class named ShowStudent that instantiates a Student object from the class you created and assign values to its fields. Compute the Student grade point average, and then display all the values associated with the Student. Save the application as **ShowStudent.java**.

   c. Create a constructor for the Student class you created. The constructor should initialize each Student's ID number to 9999, his or her points earned to 12, and credit hours to 3 (resulting in a grade point average of 4.0). Write a program that demonstrates that the constructor works by instantiating an object and displaying the initial values. Save the application as **ShowStudent2.java**.

13. a. Create a class named BankAccount with fields that hold an account number, the owner's name, and the account balance. Include a constructor that initializes each field to appropriate default values. Also include methods to get and set each of the fields. Include a method named deductMonthlyFee() that reduces the balance by $4.00. Include a static method named explainAccountPolicy() that explains that the $4 service fee will be deducted each month. Save the class as **BankAccount.java**.

   b. Create a class named TestBankAccount whose main() method declares four BankAccount objects. Call a getData() method three times. Within the method, prompt a user for values for each field for a BankAccount, and return a BankAccount object to the main() method where it is assigned to one of main()'s BankAccount objects. Do not prompt the user for values for the fourth BankAccount object, but let it continue to hold the default values. Then, in main(), pass each BankAccount object in turn to a showValues() method that displays the data, calls the method that deducts the monthly fee, and displays the balance again. The showValues() method also calls the method that explains the deduction policy. Save the application as **TestBankAccount.java**.

14. a. Create a class named Painting that contains fields for a painting's title, artist, medium (such as water color), price, and gallery commission. Create a constructor that initializes each field to an appropriate default value, and create instance methods that get and set the fields for title, artist, medium, and price. The gallery commission field cannot be set from outside the class; it is computed as 20 percent of the price each time the price is set. Save the class as **Painting.java**.

b. Create a class named `TestPainting` whose `main()` method declares three `Painting` items. Create a method that prompts the user for and accepts values for two of the `Painting` objects, and leave the third with the default values supplied by the constructor. Then display each completed object. Finally, display a message that explains the gallery commission rate. Save the application as **TestPainting.java**.

Debugging Exercises

1. Each of the following files saved in the Chapter03 folder in your downloadable student files has syntax and/or logic errors. In each case, determine and fix the problem. After you correct the errors, save each file using the same filename preceded with *Fix*. For example, DebugThree1.java will become FixDebugThree1.java.

    a. DebugThree1.java

    b. DebugThree2.java

    c. DebugThree3.java

    d. DebugThree4.java

 When you change a filename, remember to change every instance of the class name within the file so that it matches the new filename. In Java, the filename and class name must always match.

Game Zone

1. Playing cards are used in many computer games, including versions of such classics as solitaire, hearts, and poker. Design a `Card` class that contains a character data field to hold a suit (*s* for spades, *h* for hearts, *d* for diamonds, or *c* for clubs) and an integer data field for a value from 1 to 13. (When you learn more about string handling in the chapter *Characters, Strings, and the `StringBuilder`*, you can modify the class to hold words for the suits, such as *spades* or *hearts*, as well as words for some of the values—for example, *ace* or *king*.) Include get and set methods for each field. Save the class as **Card.java**.

Write an application that randomly selects two playing cards and displays their values. Simply assign a suit to each of the cards, but generate a random number for each card's value. Appendix D contains information on generating random numbers. To fully understand the process, you must learn more about Java classes and methods. However, for now, you can copy the following statements to generate a random number between 1 and 13 and assign it to a variable:

```
final int CARDS_IN_SUIT = 13;
myValue = ((int)(Math.random() * 100) % CARDS_IN_SUIT + 1);
```

After reading the chapter *Making Decisions*, you will be able to have the game determine the higher card. For now, just observe how the card values change as you execute the program multiple times. Save the application as **PickTwoCards.java**.

You use the `Math.random()` function to generate a random number. The function call uses only a class and method name—no object—so you know the `random()` method must be a static method.

2. Computer games often contain different characters or creatures. For example, you might design a game in which alien beings possess specific characteristics such as color, number of eyes, or number of lives. Design a character for a game, creating a class to hold at least three attributes for the character. Include methods to get and set each of the character's attributes. Save the file as **MyCharacter.java**. Then write an application in which you create at least two characters. In turn, pass each character to a display method that displays the character's attributes. Save the application as **TwoCharacters.java**.

Case Problems

1. a. Carly's Catering provides meals for parties and special events. In Chapter 2, you wrote an application that prompts the user for the number of guests attending an event, displays the company motto with a border, and then displays the price of the event and whether the event is a large one. Now modify the program so that the `main()` method contains only three executable statements that each call a method as follows:

   - The first executable statement calls a `public static int` method that prompts the user for the number of guests and returns the value to the `main()` method.

   - The second executable statement calls a `public static void` method that displays the company motto with the border.

   - The last executable statement passes the number of guests to a `public static void` method that computes the price of the event, displays the price, and displays whether the event is a large event.

   Save the file as **CarlysEventPriceWithMethods.java**.

   b. Create a class to hold `Event` data for Carly's Catering. The class contains:

   - Two `public final static` fields that hold the price per guest ($35) and the cutoff value for a large event (50 guests)

   - Three `private` fields that hold an event number, number of guests for the event, and the price. The event number is stored as a `String` because Carly plans to assign event numbers such as *M312*.

- Two `public` set methods that set the event number (`setEventNumber()`) and the number of guests (`setGuests()`). The price does not have a set method because the `setGuests()` method will calculate the price as the number of guests multiplied by the price per guest every time the number of guests is set.

- Three `public` get methods that return the values in the three nonstatic fields

Save the file as **Event.java**.

c. Use the `CarlysEventPriceWithMethods` class you created in Step 1a as a starting point for a program that demonstrates the `Event` class you created in Step 1b, but make the following changes:

- You already have a method that gets a number of guests from a user; now add a method that gets an event number. The `main()` method should declare an `Event` object, call the two data entry methods, and use their returned values to set the fields in the `Event` object.

- Call the method from the `CarlysEventPriceWithMethods` class that displays the company motto with the border. The method is accessible because it is public, but you must fully qualify the name because it is in another class.

- Revise the method that displays the event details so that it accepts the newly created `Event` object. The method should display the event number, and it should still display the number of guests, the price per guest, the total price, and whether the event is a large event.

Save the program as **EventDemo.java**.

2. a. Sammy's Seashore Supplies rents beach equipment such as kayaks, canoes, beach chairs, and umbrellas to tourists. In Chapter 2, you wrote an application that prompts the user for the number of minutes a piece of sports equipment was rented, displays the company motto with a border, and displays the price for the rental. Now modify the program so that the `main()` method contains only three executable statements that each call a method as follows:

- The first executable statement calls a method that prompts the user for the rental time in minutes and returns the value to the `main()` method.

- The second executable statement calls a method that displays the company motto with the border.

- The last executable statement passes the number of minutes to a method that computes the hours, extra minutes, and price for the rental, and then displays all the details.

Save the file as **SammysRentalPriceWithMethods.java**.

b. Create a class to hold `Rental` data for Sammy's Seashore Supplies. The class contains:

- Two `public final static` fields that hold the number of minutes in an hour and the hourly rental rate ($40)

- Four `private` fields that hold a contract number, number of hours for the rental, number of minutes over an hour, and the price. The contract number is stored as a `String` because Sammy plans to assign contract numbers such as *K681*.

- Two `public` set methods. One sets the contract number (`setContractNumber()`). The other is named `setHoursAndMinutes()`, and it accepts the number of minutes for the rental and then sets the hours, extra minutes over an hour, and the total price. Recall from Chapter 2 that the price is $40 per hour plus $1 for every extra minute.

- Four `public` get methods that return the values in the four nonstatic fields

Save the file as **Rental.java**.

c. Use the `SammysRentalPriceWithMethods` class you created in Step 2a as a starting point for a program that demonstrates the `Rental` class you created in Step 2b, but make the following changes:

- You already have a method that gets a number of minutes from a user; now add a method that gets a contract number. The `main()` method should declare a `Rental` object, call the two data entry methods, and use their returned values to set the fields in the `Rental` object.

- From the `SammysRentalPriceWithMethods` class, call the `RentalDemo` method that displays the company motto with the border. The method is accessible because it is public, but you must fully qualify the name because it is in another class.

- Revise the method that displays the rental details so that it accepts the newly created `Rental` object. The method should display the contract number, and it should still display the hours and minutes, the hourly rate, and the total price.

Save the program as **RentalDemo.java**.

More Object Concepts

In this chapter, you will:

◎ Understand blocks and scope

◎ Overload a method

◎ Avoid ambiguity

◎ Create and call constructors with parameters

◎ Use the `this` reference

◎ Use static fields

◎ Use automatically imported, prewritten constants and methods

◎ Use composition and nest classes

Understanding Blocks and Scope

Within any class or method, the code between a pair of curly braces is called a **block**. For example, the method shown in Figure 4-1 contains two blocks. The first block contains another, so it is an example of an **outside block** (also called an **outer block**). It begins immediately after the method declaration and ends at the end of the method. The second block is called the **inside block** or **inner block**. It is contained within the second set of curly braces and contains two executable statements: the declaration of anotherNumber and a println() statement. The inside block is **nested**, or contained entirely within, the outside block.

Figure 4-1 A method with nested blocks

A block can exist entirely within another block or entirely outside and separate from another block, but blocks can never overlap. For example, if a method contains two opening curly braces, indicating the start of two blocks, the next closing curly brace always closes the inner (second) block—it cannot close the outer block because that would make the blocks overlap. Another way to state this concept is that whenever you encounter a closing brace that ends a block, it always closes the most recently opened block.

When you declare a variable, you cannot refer to that variable outside its block. As you learned in Chapter 3, the portion of a program within which you can refer to a variable is the variable's scope. A variable comes into existence, or **comes into scope**, when you declare it. A variable ceases to exist, or **goes out of scope**, at the end of the block in which it is declared. Although you can create as many variables and blocks as you need within any program, it is not wise to do so without a reason. The use of unnecessary variables and blocks increases the likelihood of improper use of variable names and scope.

In the `methodWithNestedBlocks()` method shown in Figure 4-1, the variable `aNumber` exists from the point of its declaration until the end of the method. This means `aNumber` exists both in the outer block and in the inner block and can be used anywhere in the method. The variable `anotherNumber` comes into existence within the inner block; `anotherNumber` goes out of scope when the inner block ends and cannot be used beyond its block. Figure 4-2 shows the output when the method in Figure 4-1 is called from another method.

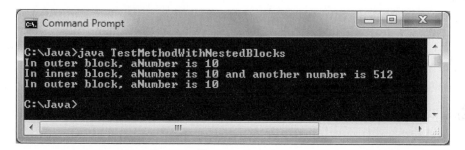

```
C:\Java>java TestMethodWithNestedBlocks
In outer block, aNumber is 10
In inner block, aNumber is 10 and another number is 512
In outer block, aNumber is 10

C:\Java>
```

Figure 4-2 Output produced by application that uses `methodWithNestedBlocks()`

The program that produces the output shown in Figure 4-2 is stored in the CodeInFigures folder in your downloadable student files.

You cannot use a data item that is not in scope. For example, Figure 4-3 shows a method that contains two blocks and some shaded, invalid statements. The opening and closing braces for each block are vertically aligned. You are not required to vertically align the opening and closing braces for a block, but your programs are much easier to read if you do.

```
public static void methodWithInvalidStatements()
{
    aNumber = 75;  ──────────── Illegal statement; this variable has not been declared yet
    int aNumber = 22;
    aNumber = 6;
    anotherNumber = 489;  ────── Illegal statement; this variable has not been declared yet
    {
        anotherNumber = 165;  ── Illegal statement; this variable still has not been declared
        int anotherNumber = 99;
        anotherNumber = 2;
    }
    aNumber = 50;           ──── Illegal statement; this variable was declared in the inner block
    anotherNumber = 34;          and has gone out of scope here
}
aNumber = 29;  ──────────────── Illegal statement; this variable has gone out of scope
```

Figure 4-3 The `methodWithInvalidStatements()` method

The first assignment statement in the first, outer block in Figure 4-3, aNumber = 75;, is invalid because aNumber has not been declared yet. Similarly, the statements that attempt to assign 489 and 165 to anotherNumber are invalid because anotherNumber has not been declared yet. After anotherNumber is declared, it can be used for the remainder of the inner block, but the statement that attempts to assign 34 to it is outside the block in which anotherNumber was declared. The last shaded statement in Figure 4-3, aNumber = 29;, does not work because it falls outside the block in which aNumber was declared; it actually falls outside the entire methodWithInvalidStatements() method.

Within a method, you can declare a variable with the same name multiple times, as long as each declaration is in its own nonoverlapping block. For example, the two declarations of variables named someVar in Figure 4-4 are valid because each variable is contained within its own block. The first instance of someVar has gone out of scope before the second instance comes into scope.

```
public static void twoDeclarations()
{
    {
        int someVar = 7;
        System.out.println(someVar);
    }
    {
        int someVar = 845;
        System.out.println(someVar);
    }
}
```

Don't declare blocks for no reason. A new block starts here only to demonstrate scope.

This variable will go out of scope at the next closing curly brace.

This variable is totally different from the one in the previous block even though their identifiers are the same.

Figure 4-4   The twoDeclarations() method

You cannot declare the same variable name more than once within a block, even if a block contains other blocks. When you declare a variable more than once in a block, you are attempting to **redeclare the variable**—an illegal action. For example, in Figure 4-5, the second declaration of aValue causes an error because you cannot declare the same variable twice within the outer block of the method. By the same reasoning, the third declaration of aValue is also invalid, even though it appears within a new block. The block that contains the third declaration is entirely within the outside block, so the first declaration of aValue has not gone out of scope.

```
public static void invalidRedeclarationMethod()
{
    int aValue = 35;
    int aValue = 44;
    {
        int anotherValue = 0;
        int aValue = 10;
    }
}
```

Invalid redeclaration of aValue because it is in same block as the first declaration

Invalid redeclaration of aValue; even though this is a new block, this block is inside the first block

Figure 4-5   The invalidRedeclarationMethod()

Although you cannot declare a variable twice within the same block, you can declare a variable within one method of a class and use the same variable name within another method of the class. In this case, the variable declared inside each method resides in its own location in computer memory. When you use the variable's name within the method in which it is declared, it takes precedence over, or **overrides**, any other variable with the same name in another method. In other words, a locally declared variable always masks or hides another variable with the same name elsewhere in the class.

For example, consider the class in Figure 4-6. In the main() method of the OverridingVariable class, aNumber is declared and assigned the value 10. When the program calls firstMethod(), a new variable is declared with the same name but with a different memory address and a new value. The new variable exists only within firstMethod(), where it is displayed holding the value 77. After firstMethod() executes and the logic returns to the main() method, the original aNumber is displayed, containing 10. When aNumber is passed to secondMethod(), a copy is made within the method. This copy has the same identifier as the original aNumber, but a different memory address. So, within secondMethod(), when the value is changed to 862 and displayed, it has no effect on the original variable in main(). When the logic returns to main() after secondMethod(), the original value is displayed again. Examine the output in Figure 4-7 to understand the sequence of events.

```
public class OverridingVariable
{
    public static void main(String[] args)          ┌─ aNumber is declared in
    {                                                └─ main().
        int aNumber = 10;
        System.out.println("In main(), aNumber is " + aNumber);       ┌─ Whenever aNumber
        firstMethod();                                                │  is used in main(), it
        System.out.println("Back in main(), aNumber is " + aNumber);  └─ retains its value of 10.
        secondMethod(aNumber);
        System.out.println("Back in main() again, aNumber is " + aNumber);
    }
    public static void firstMethod()
    {                                                   ┌─ This aNumber resides at a different
        int aNumber = 77;                               │  memory address from the one in main().
        System.out.println("In firstMethod(), aNumber is "   └─ It is declared locally in this method.
            + aNumber);
    }                                                   ┌─ This aNumber also resides at a different
    public static void secondMethod(int aNumber)        │  memory address from the one in main().
    {                                                   └─ It is declared locally in this method.
        System.out.println("In secondMethod(), at first " +
            "aNumber is " + aNumber);
        aNumber = 862;
        System.out.println("In secondMethod(), after an assignment " +
            "aNumber is " + aNumber);
    }
}
```

Figure 4-6   The OverridingVariable class

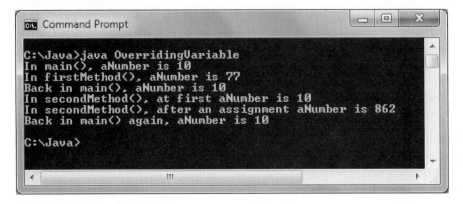

Figure 4-7   Output of the `OverridingVariable` application

 Object-oriented programmers also use the term *override* when a child class contains a field or method that has the same name as one in the parent class. You will learn more about inheritance in the chapters *Introduction to Inheritance* and *Advanced Inheritance Concepts*.

 You are familiar with local names overriding names defined elsewhere. If someone in your household is named Eric, and someone in the house next door is named Eric, members of your household who talk about Eric are referring to the local version. They would add a qualifier such as *Eric Johnson* or *Eric next door* to refer to the nonlocal version.

When they have the same name, variables within methods of a class override or hide the class's fields. Java calls this phenomenon **shadowing**; a variable that hides another shadows it. For example, Figure 4-8 shows an `Employee` class that contains two instance variables and three `void` methods. The `setValues()` method provides values for the two class instance fields. Whenever the method named `methodThatUsesInstanceAttributes()` is used with an `Employee` object, the instance values for `empNum` and `empPayRate` are used. However, when the other method, `methodThatUsesLocalVariables()`, is used with an `Employee` object, the local variable values within the method, 33333 and 555.55, shadow the class's instance variables. Figure 4-9 shows a short application that declares an `Employee` object and uses each method; Figure 4-10 shows the output.

```
public class Employee
{
    private int empNum;
    private double empPayRate;
    public void setValues()
    {
        empNum = 111;
        empPayRate = 22.22;
    }
    public void methodThatUsesInstanceAttributes()
    {
        System.out.println("Employee number is " + empNum);
        System.out.println("Pay rate is " + empPayRate);
    }
    public void methodThatUsesLocalVariables()
    {
        int empNum = 33333;
        double empPayRate = 555.55;
        System.out.println("Employee number is " + empNum);
        System.out.println("Pay rate is " + empPayRate);
    }
}
```

This method uses the class fields.

This method also uses the class fields.

This method uses the locally declared variables that happen to have the same names as the class fields.

Figure 4-8   The Employee class

```
public class TestEmployeeMethods
{
    public static void main(String[] args)
    {
        Employee aWorker = new Employee();
        aWorker.setValues();
        aWorker.methodThatUsesInstanceAttributes();
        aWorker.methodThatUsesLocalVariables();
    }
}
```

Figure 4-9   The TestEmployeeMethods application

Figure 4-10   Output of the TestEmployeeMethods application

In the `methodThatUsesLocalVariables()` method in Figure 4-8, the locally declared `empNum` and `empPayRate` are assigned 33333 and 55.55, respectively. These local variables are said to be **closer in scope** than the variables with the same name at the top of the class that are shadowed. When you write programs, you might choose to avoid confusing situations that arise when you give the same name to a class's instance field and to a local method variable. But, if you do use the same name, be aware that within the method, the method's local variable overrides the instance variable.

 Programmers frequently use the same name for an instance field and a parameter to a method in the same class simply because it is the "best name" to use; in these cases, the programmer must use the `this` reference, which you will learn about later in this chapter.

It is important to understand the impact that blocks and methods have on your variables. Variables and fields with the same names represent different memory locations when they are declared within different scopes. After you understand the scope of variables, you can avoid many potential errors in your programs.

TWO TRUTHS & A LIE

Understanding Blocks and Scope

1. A variable ceases to exist, or goes out of scope, at the end of the block in which it is declared.

2. You cannot declare the same variable name more than once within a block, even if a block contains other blocks.

3. A class's instance variables override locally declared variables with the same names that are declared within the class's methods.

The false statement is #3. When they have the same name, variables within methods of a class override a class's instance variables.

 You Do It

Demonstrating Scope

In this section, you create a method with several blocks to demonstrate block scope.

1. Start your text editor, and then open a new document, if necessary.

2. Type the first few lines for a class named `DemoBlock`:

(continues)

(continued)

```
public class DemoBlock
{
    public static void main(String[] args)
```

3. Add a statement that displays the purpose of the program:

   ```
   System.out.println("Demonstrating block scope");
   ```

4. On a new line, declare an integer named x, assign the value 1111 to it, and display its value:

   ```
   int x = 1111;
   System.out.println("In first block x is " + x);
   ```

5. Begin a new block by typing an opening curly brace on the next line. Within the new block, declare another integer named y, and display x and y. The value of x is 1111, and the value of y is 2222:

   ```
   {
       int y = 2222;
       System.out.println("In second block x is " + x);
       System.out.println("In second block y is " + y);
   }
   ```

6. On the next line, begin another new block. Within this new block, declare a new integer with the same name as the integer declared in the previous block; then display x and y. The value of y is 3333. Call a method named demoMethod(), and display x and y again. Even though you will include statements within demoMethod() that assign different values to x and y, the x and y displayed here are still 1111 and 3333:

   ```
   {
       int y = 3333;
       System.out.println("In third block x is " + x);
       System.out.println("In third block y is " + y);
       demoMethod();
       System.out.println("After method x is " + x);
       System.out.println("After method block y is " + y);
   }
   ```

7. On a new line after the end of the block, type the following:

   ```
   System.out.println("At the end x is " + x);
   ```

   This last statement in the main() method displays the value of x, which is still 1111. Type a closing curly brace.

(continues)

(continued)

8. Finally, enter the following demoMethod() that creates its own x and y variables, assigns different values, and then displays them:

```
public static void demoMethod()
{
    int x = 8888, y = 9999;
    System.out.println("In demoMethod x is " + x);
    System.out.println("In demoMethod block y is " + y);
}
```

9. Type the final closing curly brace, and then save the file as **DemoBlock.java**. At the command prompt, compile the file by typing the command **javac DemoBlock.java**. If necessary, correct any errors, and compile the program again.

10. Run the program by typing the command **java DemoBlock**. Your output should look like Figure 4-11. Make certain you understand how the values of x and y are determined in each line of output.

11. To gain a more complete understanding of blocks and scope, change the values of x and y in several locations throughout the program, and try to predict the exact output before resaving, recompiling, and rerunning the program.

Figure 4-11   Output of the DemoB1ock application

Overloading a Method

Overloading involves using one term to indicate diverse meanings. In Java, it more specifically means writing multiple methods in the same scope that have the same name but different parameter lists. The names used in the parameter lists do not matter; the lists must differ in parameter type, number of parameters, or both.

When you use the English language, you overload words all the time. When you say "open the door," "open your eyes," and "open a computer file," you are talking about three very different actions using very different methods and producing very different results. However, anyone who speaks English fluently has no trouble understanding your meaning because the verb *open* is understood in the context of the noun that follows it.

When you overload a Java method, multiple methods share a name, and the compiler understands which one to use based on the arguments in the method call. For example, suppose you create a class method to apply a simple interest rate to a bank balance. The method is named `calculateInterest()`; it receives two `double` parameters—the balance and the interest rate—and displays the multiplied result. Figure 4-12 shows the method.

```
public static void calculateInterest(double bal, double rate)
{
    double interest;
    interest = bal * rate;
    System.out.println("Simple interest on $" + bal +
        " at  " + rate + "% rate is " + interest);
}
```

Figure 4-12 The `calculateInterest()` method with two `double` parameters

When an application calls the `calculateInterest()` method and passes two `double` values, as in `calculateInterest(1000.00, 0.04)`, the interest is calculated correctly as 4% of $1000.00.

Assume, however, that different users want to calculate interest using different argument types. Some users who want to indicate an interest rate of 4% might use 0.04; others might use 4 and assume that it means 4%. When the `calculateInterest()` method is called with the arguments 1000.00 and 0.04, the interest is calculated correctly as 40.00. When the method is called using 1000.00 and 4, the method works because the integer argument is promoted to a `double`, but the interest is calculated incorrectly as 4000.00, which is 100 times too high.

A solution for the conflicting use of numbers to represent parameter values is to overload the `calculateInterest()` method. For example, in addition to the `calculateInterest()` method shown in Figure 4-12, you could add the method shown in Figure 4-13.

Notice the data type for `rate`.

```
public static void calculateInterest(double bal, int rate)
{
    double interest, rateAsPercent;
    rateAsPercent = rate / 100.0;
    interest = bal * rateAsPercent;
    System.out.println("Simple interest on $" +
        bal + " at  " + rate + "% rate is " +
        interest);
}
```

Dividing by 100.0 converts `rate` to its percent equivalent.

Figure 4-13 The `calculateInterest()` method with a `double` parameter and an `int` parameter

In Figure 4-13, note that `rateAsPercent` is calculated by dividing by 100.0 and not by 100. If two integers are divided, the result is a truncated integer; dividing by a `double` 100.0 causes the result to be a `double`. Alternatively, you could use an explicit cast such as `rateAsPercent = (double)rate / 100`.

If an application calls the method `calculateInterest()` using two `double` arguments—for example, `calculateInterest(1000.00, 0.04)`—the first version of the method, the one shown in Figure 4-12, executes. However, if an integer is used as the second argument in a call to `calculateInterest()`—as in `calculateInterest(1000.00, 4)`—the second version of the method, the one shown in Figure 4-13, executes. In this second example, the whole number rate figure is correctly divided by 100.0 before it is used to determine the interest earned.

Of course, you could use methods with different names to solve the dilemma of producing an accurate interest figure—for example, `calculateInterestUsingDouble()` and `calculateInterestUsingInt()`. However, it is easier and more convenient for programmers who use your methods to remember just one method name they can use in the form that is most appropriate for their programs. It is convenient to be able to use one reasonable name for tasks that are functionally identical except for the argument types that can be passed to them. The compiler knows which method version to call based on the passed arguments.

Automatic Type Promotion in Method Calls

In Chapter 2, you learned that Java casts variables to a unifying type when you perform arithmetic with unlike types. For example, when you multiply an `int` and a `double`, the result is a `double`. In a similar way, Java can promote one data type to another when you pass a parameter to a method. For example, if a method has a `double` parameter and you pass in an integer, the integer is promoted to a `double`. Recall that the order of promotion is `double`, `float`, `long`, and `int`. Any type in this list can be promoted to any type that precedes it.

When an application contains just one version of a method, you can call the method using a parameter of the correct data type or one that can be promoted to the correct data type. For example, consider the simple method shown in Figure 4-14.

```
public static void simpleMethod(double d)
{
    System.out.println("Method receives double parameter");
}
```

Figure 4-14   The `simpleMethod()` method with a `double` parameter

If you write an application in which you declare `doubleValue` as a `double` variable and `intValue` as an `int` variable (as shown in Figure 4-15), either of the two method calls, simpleMethod(doubleValue); or simpleMethod(intValue);, results in the output "Method receives double parameter". When you call the method with the double argument, the method works as expected, and when you call it with an integer argument, the integer is cast as (or promoted to) a double. The output of the program in Figure 4-15 is shown in Figure 4-16.

```
public class CallSimpleMethod
{
    public static void main(String[] args)
    {
        double doubleValue = 45.67;
        int intValue = 17;
        simpleMethod(doubleValue);
        simpleMethod(intValue);
    }
    public static void simpleMethod(double d)
    {
        System.out.println("Method receives double parameter");
    }
}
```

Either a double or an int can be sent to a method that accepts a double.

Figure 4-15 The CallSimpleMethod application that calls simpleMethod() with a double and an int

```
C:\Java>java CallSimpleMethod
Method receives double parameter
Method receives double parameter

C:\Java>
```

Figure 4-16 Output of the CallSimpleMethod application

Note that if the method with the declaration void simpleMethod(double d) did not exist, but the declaration void simpleMethod(int i) did exist, then the method call simpleMethod(doubleValue); would fail. Although an int can be promoted to a double, a double cannot become an int. This makes sense if you consider the potential loss of information when a double value is reduced to an integer.

Suppose that you add an overloaded version of simpleMethod() to the program in Figure 4-15. This version accepts an integer parameter, as shown in Figure 4-17. When you properly overload a method, you can call it providing different argument lists, and the appropriate version of the method executes. Now, the output changes when you call simpleMethod(intValue);. Instead of promoting an integer argument to a double, the compiler recognizes a more exact match for the method call that uses the integer argument, so it calls the version of the method that produces the output "Method receives integer parameter". Figure 4-18 shows the output.

```
public class CallSimpleMethodAgain
{
    public static void main(String[] args)
    {
        double doubleValue = 45.67;
        int intValue = 17;
        simpleMethod(doubleValue);
        simpleMethod(intValue);
    }
    public static void simpleMethod(double d)
    {
        System.out.println("Method receives double parameter");
    }
    public static void simpleMethod(int d)
    {
        System.out.println("Method receives integer parameter");
    }
}
```

The call with an int argument uses the method that is a better match when it is available.

Figure 4-17   The CallSimpleMethodAgain application that calls simpleMethod() with a double and an int

Figure 4-18   Output of the CallSimpleMethodAgain application

TWO TRUTHS & A LIE

Overloading a Method

1. When you overload Java methods, you write multiple methods with a shared name.

2. When you overload Java methods, the methods are called using different arguments.

3. Instead of overloading methods, it is preferable to write methods with unique identifiers.

The false statement is #3. Overloading methods is preferable to using unique identifiers because it is convenient for programmers to use one reasonable name for tasks that are functionally identical, except for the argument types that can be passed to them.

 You Do It

Overloading Methods

In this section, you overload methods to display dates. The date-displaying methods might be used by many different applications in an organization, such as those that schedule jobs, appointments, and employee reviews. The methods take one, two, or three integer arguments. If there is one argument, it is the month, and the date becomes the first day of the given month in the year 2014. If there are two arguments, they are the month and the day in the year 2014. Three arguments represent the month, day, and year.

 Instead of creating your own class to store dates, you can use the built-in Java class GregorianCalendar to handle dates. This exercise illustrates how some of the built-in GregorianCalendar class was constructed by Java's creators.

1. Open a new file in your text editor.

2. Begin the following DemoOverload class with three integer variables to test the method and three calls to a displayDate() method:

```
public class DemoOverload
{
    public static void main(String[] args)
```

(continues)

(continued)

```
{
    int month = 6, day = 24, year = 2015;
    displayDate(month);
    displayDate(month, day);
    displayDate(month, day, year);
}
```

3. Create the following `displayDate()` method that requires one parameter to represent the month and uses default values for the day and year:

```
public static void displayDate(int mm)
{
    System.out.println("Event date " + mm + "/1/2014");
}
```

4. Create the following `displayDate()` method that requires two parameters to represent the month and day and uses a default value for the year:

```
public static void displayDate(int mm, int dd)
{
    System.out.println("Event date " + mm + "/" + dd + "/2014");
}
```

5. Create the following `displayDate()` method that requires three parameters used as the month, day, and year:

```
public static void displayDate(int mm, int dd, int yy)
{
    System.out.println("Event date " + mm + "/" + dd + "/" + yy);
}
```

6. Type the closing curly brace for the `DemoOverload` class.

7. Save the file as **DemoOverload.java**.

8. Compile the program, correct any errors, recompile if necessary, and then execute the program. Figure 4-19 shows the output. Notice that whether you call the `displayDate()` method using one, two, or three arguments, the date is displayed correctly because you have successfully overloaded the `displayDate()` method.

Figure 4-19   Output of the DemoOverload application

Learning About Ambiguity

When you overload methods, you risk creating an **ambiguous** situation—one in which the compiler cannot determine which method to use. For example, consider the following overloaded computeBalance() method declarations:

```
public static void computeBalance(double deposit)
public static void computeBalance(double withdrawal)
```

If you declare a double variable named myDeposit and make a method call such as computeBalance(myDeposit);, you will have created an ambiguous situation. Both methods are exact matches for your call. You might argue that a call using a variable named myDeposit "seems" like it should go to the version of the method with the parameter named deposit, but Java makes no assumptions based on variable names. Each version of computeBalance() could accept a double, and Java does not presume which one you intended to use.

Sometimes, it is hard to recognize potentially ambiguous situations. For example, consider the following two method declarations:

```
public static void calculateInterest(int bal, double rate)
public static void calculateInterest(double bal, int rate)
```

These calculateInterest() methods have different types in their parameter lists. A call to calculateInterest() with an int and a double argument (in that order) executes the first version of the method, and a call to calculateInterest() with a double and an int argument executes the second version of the method. With each of these calls, the compiler can find an exact match for the arguments you send. However, if you call calculateInterest() using two integer arguments, as in calculateInterest(300, 6);, an ambiguous situation arises because there is no exact match for the method call. Because the two integers in the method call can be promoted to an integer and a double (thus matching the first version of the overloaded method), or to a double and an integer (thus matching the second version), the compiler does not know which version of the calculateInterest() method to use, and the program does not compile.

The two versions of calculateInterest() could coexist if no ambiguous calls were ever made. An overloaded method is not ambiguous on its own—it only becomes ambiguous if you create an ambiguous situation. A program containing a potentially ambiguous situation will run problem-free if you do not make any ambiguous method calls.

It is important to note that you can overload methods correctly by providing different parameter lists for methods with the same name. Methods with identical names that have identical parameter lists but different return types are not overloaded—they are illegal.

For example, the following two methods are illegal in the same class:

```
int aMethod(int x)
void aMethod(int x)
```

The compiler determines which of several versions of a method to call based on the arguments in the method call. If those two methods existed within a class, when the method call aMethod(17); was made, the compiler would not know which method to execute because both methods take an integer parameter.

The compiler determines which version of a method to call by the method's signature. In Chapter 3, you learned that a method's signature is the combination of the method name and the number, types, and order of parameters.

If the keyword final appears in a method's parameter list, it is ignored when determining ambiguity. In other words, two methods with the headers void aMethod(int x) and void aMethod(final int x) are ambiguous.

Watch the video *Overloading Methods*.

TWO TRUTHS & A LIE

Learning About Ambiguity

1. When it is part of the same program as void myMethod(int age, String name), the following method would be ambiguous:
   void myMethod(String name, int age)

2. When it is part of the same program as void myMethod(int age, String name), the following method would be ambiguous:
   String myMethod(int zipCode, String address)

3. When it is part of the same program as void myMethod(int age, String name), the following method would be ambiguous:
   void myMethod(int x, String y)

The false statement is #1. A method that accepts an int parameter followed by a String is not ambiguous with one that accepts the parameters in the reverse order.

Creating and Calling Constructors with Parameters

In Chapter 3, you learned that Java automatically provides a constructor when you create a class. You also learned that you can write your own constructor, and that you often do so when you want to ensure that fields within classes are initialized to some appropriate default value. In Chapter 3, you learned that the automatically provided constructor is a default constructor (one that does not require arguments), and you learned that you can also write a custom default constructor. However, when you write your own constructors, you can also write versions that receive parameters. Such parameters are often used to initialize data fields for an object.

For example, consider the `Employee` class with just one data field, shown in Figure 4-20. Its constructor assigns 999 to the `empNum` of each potentially instantiated `Employee` object. Anytime an `Employee` object is created using a statement such as `Employee partTimeWorker = new Employee();`, even if no other data-assigning methods are ever used, you ensure that the `partTimeWorker Employee`, like all `Employee` objects, will have an initial `empNum` of 999.

```
public class Employee
{
    private int empNum;
    Employee()
    {
        empNum = 999;
    }
}
```

Figure 4-20 The `Employee` class with a default constructor that initializes the `empNum` field

Alternatively, you might choose to create `Employee` objects with initial `empNum` values that differ for each `Employee`. To accomplish this when the object is instantiated, you can pass an employee number to the constructor. Figure 4-21 shows an `Employee` class that contains a constructor that receives a parameter. With this constructor, an argument is passed using a statement such as the following:

`Employee partTimeWorker = new Employee(881);`

When the constructor executes, the integer within the constructor call is passed to `Employee()` as the parameter `num`, which is assigned to the `empNum` field.

When you create an `Employee` class with a constructor such as the one shown in Figure 4-21, every `Employee` object you create must have an integer argument in its constructor call. In other words, with this new version of the class, the following statement no longer works:

`Employee partTimeWorker = new Employee();`

```
public class Employee
{
    private int empNum;
    Employee(int num)
    {
        empNum = num;
    }
}
```

Figure 4-21 The `Employee` class with a constructor that accepts a value

After you write a constructor for a class, you no longer receive the automatically provided default constructor. If a class's only constructor requires an argument, you must provide an argument for every object of the class that you create.

Overloading Constructors

As with any other method, you can overload constructors. Overloading constructors provides you with a way to create objects with different initializing arguments, or none, as needed. For example, in addition to using the provided constructor shown in Figure 4-21, you can create a second constructor for the `Employee` class; Figure 4-22 shows an `Employee` class that contains two constructors. When you use this class to create an `Employee` object, you have the option of creating the object either with or without an initial `empNum` value. When you create an `Employee` object with the statement `Employee aWorker = new Employee();`, the constructor with no parameters is called, and the `Employee` object receives an initial `empNum` value of 999. When you create an `Employee` object with `Employee anotherWorker = new Employee(7677);`, the constructor version that requires an integer is used, and the `anotherWorker Employee` receives an initial `empNum` of 7677.

```
public class Employee
{
    private int empNum;
    Employee(int num)
    {
        empNum = num;
    }
    Employee()
    {
        empNum = 999;
    }
}
```

Figure 4-22   The `Employee` class that contains two constructors

You can use constructor arguments to initialize field values, but you can also use arguments for any other purpose. For example, you could use the presence or absence of an argument simply to determine which of two possible constructors to call, yet not make use of the argument within the constructor. As long as the constructor parameter lists differ, the constructors are not ambiguous.

 Watch the video *Overloading Constructors.*

TWO TRUTHS & A LIE

Creating and Calling Constructors with Parameters

1. A default constructor is one that is automatically created.

2. When you write a constructor, it can be written to receive parameters or not.

3. If a class's only constructor requires an argument, you must provide an argument for every object of the class that you create.

The false statement is #1. A default constructor is one that takes no arguments. The constructor that is automatically created when you do not write your own version is a default constructor, but so is one that you write to take no arguments.

You Do It

Creating Overloaded Constructors

In this section, you create a class with overloaded constructors and demonstrate how they work.

1. Open a new file in your text editor, and start the `CarInsurancePolicy` class as follows. The class contains three fields that hold a policy number, the number of payments the policy holder will make annually, and the policy holder's city of residence.

```
public class CarInsurancePolicy
{
    private int policyNumber;
    private int numPayments;
    private String residentCity;
```

2. Create a constructor that requires parameters for all three data fields.

```
public CarInsurancePolicy(int num, int payments, String city)
{
    policyNumber = num;
    numPayments = payments;
    residentCity = city;
}
```

3. Suppose the agency that sells car insurance policies is in the city of Mayfield. Create a two-parameter constructor that requires only a policy number and number of payments. This constructor assigns *Mayfield* to `residentCity`.

```
public CarInsurancePolicy(int num, int payments)
{
    policyNumber = num;
    numPayments = payments;
    residentCity = "Mayfield";
}
```

4. Add a third constructor that requires only a policy number parameter. This constructor uses the default values of two annual payments and Mayfield as the resident city. (Later in this chapter, you will learn how to eliminate the duplicated assignments in these constructors.)

```
public CarInsurancePolicy(int num)
{
    policyNumber = num;
    numPayments = 2;
    residentCity = "Mayfield";
}
```

(continues)

(continued)

5. Add a `display()` method that outputs all the insurance policy data:

```
public void display()
{
    System.out.println("Policy #" + policyNumber + ". " +
        numPayments + " payments annually. Driver resides in " +
        residentCity + ".");
}
```

6. Add a closing curly brace for the class. Save the file as
    CarInsurancePolicy.java.

7. Open a new text file to create a short application that demonstrates the
    constructors at work. The application declares three `CarInsurancePolicy`
    objects using a different constructor version each time. Type the following code:

```
public class CreatePolicies
{
    public static void main(String[] args)
    {
        CarInsurancePolicy first = new CarInsurancePolicy(123);
        CarInsurancePolicy second = new CarInsurancePolicy(456, 4);
        CarInsurancePolicy third = new CarInsurancePolicy
            (789, 12, "Newcastle");
```

8. Display each object, and add closing curly braces for the method and the class:

```
        first.display();
        second.display();
        third.display();
    }
}
```

9. Save the file as **CreatePolicies.java**, and then compile and test the program.
    The output appears in Figure 4-23.

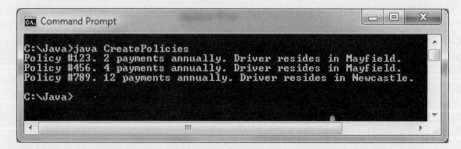

Figure 4-23   Output of the `CreatePolicies` program

(continues)

(continued)

10. Add a fourth declaration to the `CreatePolicies` class that attempts to create a `CarInsurancePolicy` object using a default constructor:

    `CarInsurancePolicy fourth = new CarInsurancePolicy();`

11. Save and compile the revised `CreatePolicies` program. The class does not compile because the `CarInsurancePolicy` class does not contain a default constructor. Change the newly added declaration to a comment, compile the class again, and observe that the class now compiles correctly.

Examining Prewritten Overloaded Methods

In this section, you examine some built-in classes and recognize their correctly overloaded methods.

1. Using a Web browser, go to the Java Web site at ***www.oracle.com/ technetwork/java/index.html***, and select **Java APIs** and **Java SE 7**.

2. Using the alphabetical list of classes, find the **`PrintStream`** class, and select it.

3. Examine the list of constructors for the class, and notice that each version has a unique parameter list.

4. Examine the list of methods named **`print()`** and **`println()`**. Notice that each overloaded version has a unique parameter list.

5. Using the alphabetical list of classes, find the **`JOptionPane`** class, and select it.

6. Examine the list of constructors for the class, and notice that each version has a unique parameter list.

7. Examine the list of methods named **`showConfirmDialog()`** and **`showInputDialog()`**. Notice that each overloaded version has a unique parameter list.

Learning About the `this` Reference

When you start creating classes, they can become large very quickly. Besides data fields, each class can have many methods, including several overloaded versions. On paper, a single class might require several pages of coded statements.

When you instantiate an object from a class, memory is reserved for each instance field in the class. For example, if a class contains 20 data fields, when you create one object from that class, enough memory is reserved to hold the 20 field values for that object. When you create 200 objects of the same class, the computer reserves enough memory for 4,000 data fields—20 fields for each of the 200 objects. In many applications, the computer memory requirements can become substantial. Fortunately, it is not necessary to store a separate copy of each variable and method for each instantiation of a class.

Usually, you want each instantiation of a class to have its own data fields. If an Employee class contains fields for employee number, name, and salary, every individual Employee object needs a unique number, name, and salary value. (When you want each object to share a value, you define the field as static; a field is not static when the value in each object can be unique.) However, when you create a method for a class, any object can use the same method. Whether the method performs a calculation, sets a field value, or constructs an object, the instructions are the same for each instantiated object. Not only would it take an enormous amount of memory to store a separate copy of each method for every object created from a class, but memory would also be wasted because you would be storing identical copies of methods—that is, each object's copy of the method would have the same contents. Luckily, in Java just one copy of each method in a class is stored, and all instantiated objects can use that copy.

When you use a nonstatic method, you use the object name, a dot, and the method name—for example, aWorker.getEmpNum() or anotherWorker.getEmpNum(). When you execute the getEmpNum() method, you are running the only copy of the method. However, within the getEmpNum() method, when you access the empNum *field*, you access a different field depending on the object. The compiler must determine *whose* copy of the empNum value should be returned by the single getEmpNum() method.

The compiler accesses the correct object's field because every time you call a nonstatic method, you implicitly pass a reference to the named object attached to the method call. A **reference** is an object's memory address. The reference is implicit because it is understood automatically without actually being written. The reference to an object that is passed to any object's nonstatic method is called the **this reference**; this is a reserved word in Java. Only nonstatic, instance methods have a this reference. For example, the two getEmpNum() methods for the Employee class shown in Figure 4-24 perform identically. The first method simply uses the this reference without your being aware of it; the second method uses the this reference explicitly. Both methods return the empNum of the object used to call the method.

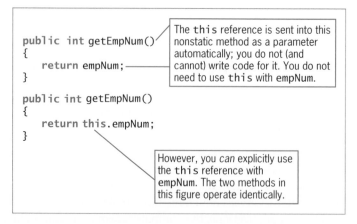

Figure 4-24   Two versions of the getEmpNum() method, with and without an explicit this reference

Frequently, you neither want nor need to refer to the **this** reference within the instance methods that you write, but the **this** reference is always there, working behind the scenes, so that the data field for the correct object can be accessed.

On a few occasions, you must use the **this** reference to make your classes work correctly; one example is shown in the **Student** class in Figure 4-25. Within the constructor for this class, the parameter names **stuNum** and **gpa** are identical to the class field names. Within the constructor, **stuNum** and **gpa** refer to the locally declared names, not the class field names. The statement **stuNum = stuNum** accomplishes nothing—it assigns the local variable value to itself. The client application in Figure 4-26 attempts to create a **Student** object with an ID number of 111 and a grade point average of 3.5, but Figure 4-27 shows the incorrect output. The values are not assigned to the fields; instead, they are just zeroes.

```
public class Student
{
    private int stuNum;
    private double gpa;
    public Student (int stuNum, double gpa)
    {
        stuNum = stuNum;
        gpa = gpa;
    }
    public void showStudent()
    {
        System.out.println("Student #" + stuNum +
            " gpa is " + gpa);
    }
}
```

> **Don't Do It**
> All four variables used in these two statements are the local versions declared in the method's parameter list. The fields are never accessed because the local variables shadow the fields. These two assignment statements accomplish nothing.

Figure 4-25   A **Student** class whose constructor does not work

```
public class TestStudent
{
    public static void main(String[] args)
    {
        Student aPsychMajor =
            new Student(111, 3.5);
        aPsychMajor.showStudent();
    }
}
```

Figure 4-26   The **TestStudent** class that instantiates a **Student** object

Figure 4-27   Output of the TestStudent application using the incorrect Student class in Figure 4-25

One way to fix the problem with the Student class is to use different identifiers for the class's fields and the parameters to the constructor. However, sometimes the identifiers you have chosen are the best and simplest identifiers for a value. If you choose to use the same identifiers, you can use the this reference explicitly to identify the fields. Figure 4-28 shows a modified Student class. The only difference between this class and the one in Figure 4-25 is the explicit use of the this reference within the constructor. When the this reference is used with a field name in a class method, the reference is to the class field instead of to the local variable declared within the method. When the TestStudent application uses this new version of the Student class, the output appears as expected, as shown in Figure 4-29.

```
public class Student
{
    private int stuNum;
    private double gpa;
    public Student(int stuNum, double gpa)
    {
        this.stuNum = stuNum;
        this.gpa = gpa;
    }
    public void showStudent()
    {
        System.out.println("Student #" +
            stuNum + " gpa is " + gpa);
    }
}
```

Figure 4-28   The Student class using the explicit this reference within the constructor

Figure 4-29   Output of the TestStudent application using the new version of the Student class

Using the this Reference to Make Overloaded Constructors More Efficient

Suppose you create a Student class with data fields for a student number and a grade point average. Further suppose you want four overloaded constructors as follows:

- A constructor that accepts an int and a double and assigns them the student number and grade point average, respectively

- A constructor that accepts a double and assigns it to the grade point average, but initializes every student number to 999

- A constructor that accepts an int and assigns it to the student number, but initializes every grade point average to 0.0

- A default constructor that assigns 999 to every student number and 0.0 to every grade point average

Figure 4-30 shows the class. Although this class works, and allows Students to be constructed in four different ways, there is a lot of repetition within the constructors.

```
public class Student
{
    private int stuNum;
    private double gpa;
    Student(int num, double avg)
    {
        stuNum = num;
        gpa = avg;
    }
    Student(double avg)
    {
        stuNum = 999;
        gpa = avg;
    }
    Student(int num)
    {
        stuNum = num;
        gpa = 0.0;
    }
    Student()
    {
        stuNum = 999;
        gpa = 0.0;
    }
}
```

Figure 4-30 Student class with four constructors

You can reduce the amount of repeated code in Figure 4-30 and make the code less error-prone by calling one constructor version from the others. To do so, you use the `this` reference from one constructor version to call another version. Figure 4-31 shows how the Student class can be rewritten.

```
public class Student
{
    private int stuNum;
    private double gpa;
    Student(int num, double avg)
    {
        stuNum = num;
        gpa = avg;
    }
    Student(double avg)
    {
        this(999, avg);
    }
    Student(int num)
    {
        this(num, 0.0);
    }
    Student()
    {
        this(999, 0.0);
    }
}
```

Figure 4-31   The Student class using `this` in three of four constructors

By writing each constructor to call one master constructor, you save coding and reduce the chance for errors. For example, if code is added later to ensure that all student ID numbers are three digits, or that no grade point average is greater than 4.0, the new code will be written only in the two-parameter version of the constructor, and all the other versions will use it. (Testing a variable to ensure it falls within the proper range of values requires decision making. The next chapter covers this topic.)

Although you can use the `this` reference with field names in any method within a class, you cannot call `this()` from other methods in a class; you can only call it from constructors. Additionally, if you call `this()` from a constructor, it must be the first statement within the constructor.

   Watch the video *The `this` Reference*.

TWO TRUTHS & A LIE

Learning About the `this` Reference

1. Usually, you want each instantiation of a class to have its own nonstatic data fields, but each object does not need its own copy of most methods.

2. When you use a nonstatic method, the compiler accesses the correct object's field because you implicitly pass an object reference to the method.

3. The `this` reference is supplied automatically in classes; you cannot use it explicitly.

The false statement is #3. Usually, you neither want nor need to refer to the `this` reference within the methods you write, but you can use it—for example, when there are conflicts between identifiers for fields and local variables.

 You Do It

Using the `this` Reference to Make Constructors More Efficient

In this section, you modify the `CarInsurancePolicy` class so that its constructors are more efficient.

1. Open the **CarInsurancePolicy.java** file. Change the class name to **CarInsurancePolicy2**, and immediately save the file as **CarInsurancePolicy2.java**.

2. Change the name of the three-parameter constructor from `CarInsurancePolicy()` to **CarInsurancePolicy2()**.

3. Replace the constructor that accepts a single parameter for the policy number with the following constructor. The name of the constructor is changed from the earlier version, and this one passes the policy number and two constant values to the three-parameter constructor:

```
public CarInsurancePolicy2(int num)
{
    this(num, 2, "Mayfield");
}
```

(continues)

(continued)

4. Replace the constructor that accepts two parameters (for the policy number and number of payments) with the following constructor. This constructor has a new name and passes the two parameters and one constant value to the three-parameter constructor:

```
public CarInsurancePolicy2(int num, int payments)
{
    this(num, payments, "Mayfield");
}
```

5. Save the file, and compile it.

6. Open the **CreatePolicies.java** file that demonstrates the use of the different constructor versions. Change the class name to `CreatePolicies2`, and save the file as **CreatePolicies2.java**.

7. Add the digit **2** in six places—three times to change the class name `CarInsurancePolicy` to **CarInsurancePolicy2** when the name is used as a data type, and in the three constructor calls.

8. Save the file, and then compile and execute it. The output is identical to that shown in Figure 4-23 in the previous "You Do It" section, but the repetitious constructor code has been eliminated.

9. You can further reduce the code in the `CarInsurancePolicy` class by changing the single-parameter constructor to the following, which removes the constant "Mayfield" from the constructor call:

```
public CarInsurancePolicy2(int num)
{
    this(num, 2);
}
```

Now, the single-parameter version calls the two-parameter version and passes the policy number and the constant 2. In turn, the two-parameter version calls the three-parameter version, adding "Mayfield" as the city.

10. Save this version of the `CarInsurancePolicy2` class, and compile it. Then recompile the **CreatePolicies2.java** file, and execute it. The output remains the same.

Using static Fields

In Chapter 3, you learned that methods you create to use without objects are static. For example, the main() method in a program and the methods that main() calls without an object reference are static. You also learned that most methods you create within a class from which objects will be instantiated are nonstatic. Static methods do not have a this reference because they have no object associated with them; therefore, they are called **class methods**.

You can also create **class variables**, which are variables that are shared by every instantiation of a class. Whereas instance variables in a class exist separately for every object you create, there is only one copy of each static class variable per class. For example, consider the BaseballPlayer class in Figure 4-32. The BaseballPlayer class contains a shaded static field named count, and two nonstatic fields named number and battingAverage. The BaseballPlayer constructor sets values for number and battingAverage and increases the count by one. In other words, every time a BaseballPlayer object is constructed, it contains individual values for number and battingAverage, and the count field contains a count of the number of existing objects and is shared by all BaseballPlayer objects.

```
public class BaseballPlayer
{
    private static int count = 0;
    private int number;
    private double battingAverage;
    public BaseballPlayer(int id, double avg)
    {
        number = id;
        battingAverage = avg;
        count = count + 1;
    }
    public void showPlayer()
    {
        System.out.println("Player #" + number +
            " batting average is " + battingAverage +
            " There are " + count + " players");
    }
}
```

Figure 4-32   The BaseballPlayer class

The showPlayer() method in the BaseballPlayer class displays a BaseballPlayer's number, batting average, and a count of all current players. This method is not static—it accesses an individual object's data. Methods declared as static cannot access instance variables, but instance methods can access both static and instance variables.

The TestPlayer class in Figure 4-33 is an application that declares two BaseballPlayer objects, displays them, and then creates a third BaseballPlayer object and displays it. When you examine the output in Figure 4-34, you can see that by the time the first two objects are declared, the count value that they share is 2. Whether count is accessed using the aCatcher object or the aShortstop object, the count is the same. After the third object is declared, its count value is 3, as is the value of count associated with the previously declared aCatcher object. In other words, because the static count variable is incremented within the class constructor, each object has access to the total number of objects that currently exist. No matter how many BaseballPlayer objects are eventually instantiated, each refers to the single count field.

```
public class TestPlayer
{
   public static void main(String[] args)
   {
      BaseballPlayer aCatcher = new BaseballPlayer(12, .218);
      BaseballPlayer aShortstop = new BaseballPlayer(31, .385);
      aCatcher.showPlayer();
      aShortstop.showPlayer();
      BaseballPlayer anOutfielder = new BaseballPlayer(44, .505);
      anOutfielder.showPlayer();
      aCatcher.showPlayer();
   }
}
```

Figure 4-33 The TestPlayer class

Figure 4-34 Output of the TestPlayer application

Using Constant Fields

In Chapter 2, you learned to create named constants by using the keyword final. Sometimes a data field in a class should be constant. For example, you might want to store a school ID value that is the same for every Student object you create, so you declare it to be static. In addition, if you want the value for the school ID to be fixed so that all Student objects use the same ID value—for example, when applying to scholarship-granting organizations or when registering for standardized tests—you might want to make the school ID unalterable. As with ordinary variables, you use the keyword final with a field to make its value unalterable after construction. For example, the class in Figure 4-35 contains the symbolic constant SCHOOL_ID. Because it is static, all objects share a single memory location for the field, and because it is final, it cannot change during program execution.

```
public class Student
{
    private static final int SCHOOL_ID = 12345;
    private int stuNum;
    private double gpa;
    public Student(int stuNum, double gpa)
    {
        this.stuNum = stuNum;
        this.gpa = gpa;
    }
    public void showStudent()
    {
        System.out.println("Student #" + stuNum +
            " gpa is " + gpa);
    }
}
```

Figure 4-35 The Student class containing a symbolic constant

A *nonstatic* final field's value can be set in the class constructor. For example, you can set it using a constant, or you can set it using a parameter passed into the constructor. However, a static final field's value must be set at declaration, as in the Student class example in Figure 4-35. This makes sense because there is only one static field stored for every object instantiated.

You can use the keyword final with methods or classes as well as with fields. When used in this manner, final indicates limitations placed on inheritance. You will learn more about inheritance in the chapters *Introduction to Inheritance* and *Advanced Inheritance Concepts*.

Fields that are final also can be initialized in a static initialization block. For more details about this technique, see the Java Web site.

Fields declared to be static are not always final. Conversely, final fields are not always static. In summary:

- If you want to create a field that all instantiations of the class can access but the field value can change, then it is static but not final. For example, in the last section you saw a nonfinal static field in the BaseballPlayer class that held a changing count of all instantiated objects.

- If you want each object created from a class to contain its own final value, you would declare the field to be final but not static. For example, you might want each BaseballPlayer object to have its own, nonchanging date of joining the team.

- If you want all objects to share a single nonchanging value, then the field is static and final.

TWO TRUTHS & A LIE

Using static Fields

1. Methods declared as static receive a this reference that contains a reference to the object associated with them.

2. Methods declared as static are called class methods.

3. A final static field's value is shared by every object of a class.

The false statement is #1. Static methods do not have a this reference because they have no object associated with them.

You Do It

Using Static and Nonstatic final Fields

In this section, you create a class for the Riverdale Kennel Club to demonstrate the use of static and nonstatic final fields. The club enters its dogs in an annual triathlon event in which each dog receives three scores in agility, conformation, and obedience.

1. Open a new file in your text editor, and enter the first few lines for a DogTriathlonParticipant class. The class contains a final field that holds the number of events in which the dog participated. Once a final field is set, it never should change. The field is not static because it is different for each dog. The class also contains a static field that holds the total cumulative score for all the participating dogs. The field is not final because its value increases as each dog participates in the triathlon, but it is static because at any moment in time, it is the same for all participants.

```
public class DogTriathlonParticipant
{
    private final int NUM_EVENTS;
    private static int totalCumulativeScore = 0;
```

2. Add six private fields that hold the participating dog's name, the dog's score in three events, the total score, and the average score:

```
private String name;
private int obedienceScore;
private int conformationScore;
private int agilityScore;
private int total;
private double avg;
```

(continues)

(continued)

3. The constructor for the class requires five parameters—the dog's name, the number of events in which the dog participated, and the dog's scores in the three events. (After you read the chapter on decision making, you will be able to ensure that the number of nonzero scores entered matches the number of events, but for now no such checks will be made.) The constructor assigns each value to the appropriate field.

```java
public DogTriathlonParticipant(String name,
    int numEvents, int score1, int score2, int score3)
{
    this.name = name;
    NUM_EVENTS = numEvents;
    obedienceScore = score1;
    conformationScore = score2;
    agilityScore = score3;
```

4. After the assignments, the constructor calculates the total score for the participant and the participant's average score. Notice the result of the division is cast to a `double` so that any fractional part of the calculated average is not lost. Also, add the participant's total score to the cumulative score for all participants. Recall that this field is `static` because it should be the same for all participants at any point in time. After these statements, add a closing curly brace for the constructor.

```java
    total = obedienceScore +
        conformationScore + agilityScore;
    avg = (double) total / NUM_EVENTS;
    totalCumulativeScore = totalCumulativeScore +
        total;
}
```

5. Start a method that displays the data for each triathlon participant.

```java
public void display()
{
    System.out.println(name + " participated in " +
        NUM_EVENTS +
        " events and has an average score of " + avg);
    System.out.println("   " + name +
        " has a total score of " + total +
        " bringing the total cumulative score to " +
        totalCumulativeScore);
}
```

6. Add a closing curly brace for the class. Then, save the file as **DogTriathlonParticipant.java**. Compile the class, and correct any errors.

(continues)

(continued)

7. Open a new file in your text editor, and then enter the header and opening and closing curly braces for a class you can use to test the `DogTriathlonParticipant` class. Also include a `main()` method header and its opening and closing braces.

```
public class TestDogs
{
    public static void main(String[] args)
    {
    }
}
```

8. Between the braces of the `main()` method, declare a `DogTriathlonParticipant` object. Provide values for the participant's name, number of events, and three scores, and then display the object.

```
DogTriathlonParticipant dog1 =
    new DogTriathlonParticipant("Bowser", 2, 85, 89, 0);
dog1.display();
```

9. Create and display two more objects within the `main()` method.

```
DogTriathlonParticipant dog2 =
    new DogTriathlonParticipant("Rush", 3, 78, 72, 80);
dog2.display();
DogTriathlonParticipant dog3 =
    new DogTriathlonParticipant("Ginger", 3, 90, 86, 72);
dog3.display();
```

10. Save the file as **TestDogs.java**. Compile and execute the program. The output looks like Figure 4-36. Visually confirm that each total, average, and cumulative total is correct.

Figure 4-36   Output of the `TestDogs` program

(continues)

(continued)

11. Experiment with the `DogTriathlonParticipant` class and its test class. For example, try the following:

   - Add a new statement at the end of the `TestDogs` class that again displays the data for any one of the participants. Note that as long as no new objects are created, the cumulative score for all participants remains the same no matter which participant uses it.

   - Try to assign a value to the `NUM_EVENTS` constant from the `display()` method, and then compile the class and read the error message generated.

   - Remove the keyword `static` from the definition of `totalCumulativeScore` in the `DogTriathlonParticipant` class, and then recompile the classes and run the program. Notice in the output that the nonstatic cumulative score no longer reflects the cumulative score for all objects but only the score for the current object using the `display()` method.

   - Use 0 as the number of events for an object. When the participant's average is calculated, the result is not numeric, and *NaN* is displayed. **NaN** is an acronym for *Not a Number*. In the next chapter, you will learn to make decisions, and then you can prevent the *NaN* output.

Using Automatically Imported, Prewritten Constants and Methods

Often, you need to create classes from which you will instantiate objects. You can create an `Employee` class with fields appropriate for describing employees in your organization and their functions, and an `Inventory` class with fields appropriate for whatever type of item you manufacture. However, many classes are commonly used by a wide variety of programmers. Rather than have each Java programmer "reinvent the wheel," the creators of Java have produced hundreds of classes for you to use in your programs.

You have already used several of these prewritten classes; for example, you have used the `System` and `JOptionPane` classes to produce output. Each of these classes is stored in a **package**, or a **library of classes**, which is simply a folder that provides a convenient grouping for classes. Many Java packages are available only if you explicitly name them within your program; for example, when you use `JOptionPane`, you must import the `javax.swing` package into your program. However, the group that contains classes such as `System` is used so frequently that it is available automatically to every program you write. The package that is implicitly imported into every Java program is named **java.lang**. The classes it contains are **fundamental classes**, or basic classes, as opposed to the **optional classes** that must be named explicitly. Some references list a few other Java classes as also being "fundamental," but the java.lang package is the only automatically imported, named package.

The class `java.lang.Math` contains constants and methods that you can use to perform common mathematical functions. All of the constants and methods in the `Math` class are `static`—they are class variables and class methods. For example, a commonly used constant is `PI`. In geometry, *pi* is an approximation of a circle's radius based on the ratio of the circumference of the circle to its diameter. Within the `Math` class, the declaration for `PI` is as follows:

```
public final static double PI = 3.14159265358979323846;
```

Notice that `PI` is:

- `public`, so any program can access it directly
- `final`, so it cannot be changed
- `static`, so only one copy exists and you can access it without declaring a `Math` object
- `double`, so it holds a floating-point value

You can use the value of `PI` within any program you write by referencing the full package path in which `PI` is defined; for example, you can calculate the area of a circle using the following statement:

```
areaOfCircle = java.lang.Math.PI * radius * radius;
```

However, the `java.lang` package is imported automatically into your programs, so if you simply reference `Math.PI`, Java recognizes this code as a shortcut to the full package path. Therefore, the preferred (and simpler) statement is the following:

```
areaOfCircle = Math.PI * radius * radius;
```

In addition to constants, many useful methods are available within the `Math` class. For example, the `Math.max()` method returns the larger of two values, and the method `Math.abs()` returns the absolute value of a number. Table 4-1 lists some common `Math` class methods.

Method	Value That the Method Returns
abs(x)	Absolute value of *x*
acos(x)	Arc cosine of *x*
asin(x)	Arc sine of *x*
atan(x)	Arc tangent of *x*
atan2(x, y)	Theta component of the polar coordinate (*r*, theta) that corresponds to the Cartesian coordinate *x*, *y*
ceil(x)	Smallest integral value not less than *x* (ceiling)
cos(x)	Cosine of *x*

Table 4-1 Common `Math` class methods *(continues)*

(continued)

Method	Value That the Method Returns
exp(x)	Exponent, where x is the base of the natural logarithms
floor(x)	Largest integral value not greater than x
log(x)	Natural logarithm of x
max(x, y)	Larger of x and y
min(x, y)	Smaller of x and y
pow(x, y)	x raised to the y power
random()	Random double number between 0.0 and 1.0
rint(x)	Closest integer to x (x is a double, and the return value is expressed as a double)
round(x)	Closest integer to x (where x is a float or double, and the return value is an int or long)
sin(x)	Sine of x
sqrt(x)	Square root of x
tan(x)	Tangent of x

Table 4-1   Common Math class methods

Because all constants and methods in the Math class are classwide (that is, static), there is no need to create an instance of the Math class. You cannot instantiate objects of type Math because the constructor for the Math class is private, and your programs cannot access the constructor.

Unless you are a mathematician, you won't use many of these Math class methods, and it is unwise to do so unless you understand their purposes. For example, because the square root of a negative number is undefined, if you display the result after the method call imaginaryNumber = Math.sqrt(-12);, you see *NaN*.

Importing Classes That Are Not Imported Automatically

Java contains hundreds of classes, only a few of which—those in the java.lang package—are included automatically in the programs you write. To use any of the other prewritten classes, you must use one of three methods:

- Use the entire path with the class name.
- Import the class.
- Import the package that contains the class you are using.

In its `java.util` package, Java includes a `GregorianCalendar` class that is useful when working with dates and time. The Gregorian calendar is used in most of the world; it was instituted on October 15, 1582, and is named for Pope Gregory XIII, who was instrumental in the calendar's adoption. (For dates that fall before the Gregorian cutover date, the `GregorianCalendar` class uses the Julian calendar, which simply uses a different leap-year rule.)

You have seen examples in this book in which the `JOptionPane` and `Scanner` classes were imported so you could use their methods. Similarly, you can import the `java.util` class package, which includes the `GregorianCalendar` class.

You can instantiate an object of type `GregorianCalendar` from this class by using the full class path, as in the following:

`java.util.GregorianCalendar myAnniversary = new java.util.GregorianCalendar();`

Alternatively, when you include `import java.util.GregorianCalendar;` as the first line in your program, you can shorten the declaration of `myAnniversary` to this:

`GregorianCalendar myAnniversary = new GregorianCalendar();`

An alternative to importing a class is to import an entire package of classes. You can use the asterisk (*) as a **wildcard symbol**, which indicates that it can be replaced by any set of characters. In a Java `import` statement, you use a wildcard symbol to represent all the classes in a package. Therefore, the following statement imports the `GregorianCalendar` class and any other `java.util` classes as well:

`import java.util.*;`

The `import` statement does not move the entire imported class or package into your program, as its name implies. Rather, it simply notifies the program that you will use the data and method names that are part of the imported class or package. There is no disadvantage to importing an entire package instead of just the classes you need, and you will commonly see the wildcard method in professionally written Java programs. However, you have the alternative of importing each class you need individually. Importing each class by name, without wildcards, can be a form of documentation; this technique specifically shows which parts of the package are being used.

You cannot use the Java-language wildcard exactly like a DOS or UNIX wildcard because you cannot import all the Java classes with `import java.*;`. The Java wildcard works only with specific packages such as `import java.util.*;` or `import java.lang.*;`. Also, note that the asterisk in an `import` statement imports all of the classes in a package, but not other packages that are within the imported package.

Your own classes are included in applications without `import` statements because of your `classpath` settings. See Appendix A for more information on `classpath`.

Using the GregorianCalendar Class

Seven constructors are available for GregorianCalendar objects. These constructors are overloaded, requiring different argument lists when they are called. The default constructor for the GregorianCalendar class creates a calendar object containing the current date and time in the default locale (time zone) that has been set for your computer. You can use other constructors to specify:

- year, month, date

- year, month, date, hour, minute

- year, month, date, hour, minute, second

- Locale

- TimeZone

- TimeZone, Locale

You can create a default GregorianCalendar object with a statement such as the following:

```
GregorianCalendar today = new
GregorianCalendar();
```

Alternatively, you can create a GregorianCalendar object using one of the overloaded constructors—for example:

```
GregorianCalendar myGraduationDate = new
GregorianCalendar(2014,5,24);
```

Specific data field values, such as the day, month, and year, can be retrieved from a GregorianCalendar object by using the get() method and specifying what you want as an argument. You could retrieve the day of the year (for example, February 1 is the 32nd day of the year) with the following statement:

```
int dayOfYear = today.get(GregorianCalendar.DAY_OF_YEAR);
```

The GregorianCalendar get() method always returns an integer. Some of the possible arguments to the get() method are shown in Table 4-2. In particular, notice that the month values in the GregorianCalendar class range from 0 through 11. Thus, January is month 0, February is month 1, and so on.

As an example of how to use a GregorianCalendar object, Figure 4-37 shows an AgeCalculator application. In this class, a default GregorianCalendar object named now is created. The user is prompted for a birth year, the current year is extracted from the now object using the get() method, and the user's age this year is calculated by subtracting the birth year from the current year. Figure 4-38 shows the output when a user born in 1986 runs the application in 2014.

Arguments	Values Returned by get()
DAY_OF_YEAR	A value from 1 to 366
DAY_OF_MONTH	A value from 1 to 31
DAY_OF_WEEK	SUNDAY, MONDAY, … SATURDAY, corresponding to values from 1 to 7
YEAR	The current year; for example, 2012
MONTH	JANUARY, FEBRUARY, … DECEMBER, corresponding to values from 0 to 11
HOUR	A value from 1 to 12; the current hour in the A.M. or P.M.
AM_PM	A.M. or P.M., which correspond to values from 0 to 1
HOUR_OF_DAY	A value from 0 to 23 based on a 24-hour clock
MINUTE	The minute in the hour, a value from 0 to 59
SECOND	The second in the minute, a value from 0 to 59
MILLISECOND	The millisecond in the second, a value from 0 to 999

Table 4-2   Some possible arguments to and returns from the GregorianCalendar get() method

```
import java.util.*;
import javax.swing.*;
public class AgeCalculator
{
    public static void main(String[] args)
    {
        GregorianCalendar now = new GregorianCalendar();
        int nowYear;
        int birthYear;
        int yearsOld;
        birthYear = Integer.parseInt
            (JOptionPane.showInputDialog(null,
            "In what year were you born?"));
        nowYear = now.get(GregorianCalendar.YEAR);
        yearsOld = nowYear - birthYear;
        JOptionPane.showMessageDialog(null,
            "This is the year you become " + yearsOld +
            " years old");
    }
}
```

Figure 4-37   The AgeCalculator application

 The parseInt() method is used in the application in Figure 4-37 to convert the user's input string to an integer. You learned about the parseInt() method in Chapter 2.

Figure 4-38 Execution of the `AgeCalculator` application

TWO TRUTHS & A LIE

Using Automatically Imported, Prewritten Constants and Methods

1. The creators of Java have produced hundreds of classes for you to use in your programs.

2. Java packages are available only if you explicitly name them within your program.

3. The implicitly imported `java.lang` package contains fundamental Java classes.

The false statement is #2. Many Java packages are available only if you explicitly name them within your program, but others are automatically imported.

 You Do It

In this section, you learn more about using the `GregorianCalendar` class.

Using the Java Web Site

1. Using a Web browser, go to the Java Web site, and select **Java APIs** and **Java SE 7**. Using the alphabetical list of classes, find the **GregorianCalendar** class and select it.

2. Notice that `java.util` is cited at the top of the description, indicating that it is the containing package.

3. Read the history and background of the `GregorianCalendar` class to get an idea of how many issues are involved in determining values like the first day of the week and a week's number in a year. Then read the rest of the documentation to get a feel for the fields and methods that are available with the class.

(continues)

(continued)

Using an Explicitly Imported, Prewritten Class

Next, you construct a program using the `GregorianCalendar` class and some of the arguments to the `GregorianCalendar get()` method.

1. Open a new file in your text editor. For the first line in the file, type the following:

    ```
    import java.util.*;
    ```

2. On the next lines, begin the class by typing the class header, the opening brace, the `main()` method header, and its opening brace, as follows:

    ```
    public class CalendarDemo
    {
        public static void main(String[] args)
        {
    ```

3. Declare a `GregorianCalendar` object named `now` that holds information about the current date and time. Then create a series of output statements that display a variety of `GregorianCalendar` fields containing information about the date:

    ```
    GregorianCalendar now = new GregorianCalendar();
    System.out.println("YEAR: " + now.get(Calendar.YEAR));
    System.out.println("MONTH: " + now.get(Calendar.MONTH));
    System.out.println("WEEK_OF_YEAR: " +
        now.get(Calendar.WEEK_OF_YEAR));
    System.out.println("WEEK_OF_MONTH: " +
        now.get(Calendar.WEEK_OF_MONTH));
    System.out.println("DATE: " + now.get(Calendar.DATE));
    System.out.println("DAY_OF_MONTH: " +
        now.get(Calendar.DAY_OF_MONTH));
    System.out.println("DAY_OF_YEAR: " +
        now.get(Calendar.DAY_OF_YEAR));
    System.out.println("DAY_OF_WEEK: " +
        now.get(Calendar.DAY_OF_WEEK));
    ```

4. Add more statements that display information about the current time, as follows:

    ```
    System.out.println("AM_PM: " +
        now.get(Calendar.AM_PM));
    System.out.println("HOUR: " + now.get(Calendar.HOUR));
    System.out.println("HOUR_OF_DAY: " +
        now.get(Calendar.HOUR_OF_DAY));
    System.out.println("MINUTE: " +
        now.get(Calendar.MINUTE));
    System.out.println("SECOND: " +
        now.get(Calendar.SECOND));
    System.out.println("MILLISECOND: " +
        now.get(Calendar.MILLISECOND));
    ```

5. Add the closing curly brace for the `main()` method and the closing curly brace for the class.

(continues)

(continued)

6. Save the file as **CalendarDemo.java**. Compile and execute the program. Figure 4-39 shows the output from the program when it is executed a little before 10 a.m. on Thursday, April 3, 2014. Notice that although people usually think of April as month 4, the month in the output is 3—the month values in the `GregorianCalendar` are 0 through 11. When you display month values in your own programs, you might choose to add 1 to a value before displaying it, so that users see month numbers to which they are accustomed.

```
C:\Java>java CalendarDemo
YEAR: 2014
MONTH: 3
WEEK_OF_YEAR: 14
WEEK_OF_MONTH: 1
DATE: 3
DAY_OF_MONTH: 3
DAY_OF_YEAR: 93
DAY_OF_WEEK: 5
AM_PM: 0
HOUR: 9
HOUR_OF_DAY: 9
MINUTE: 56
SECOND: 41
MILLISECOND: 824

C:\Java>
```

Figure 4-39   Output of the `CalendarDemo` application

Creating an Interactive Application with a Timer

Next, you use the `GregorianCalendar` class to create an application that outputs a user's response time to a question.

1. Open a new file in your text editor, and type the following two `import` statements. You need the `JOptionPane` class to use the `showConfirmDialog()` method, and you need the `java.util` package to use the `GregorianCalendar` class:

```
import javax.swing.JOptionPane;
import java.util.*;
```

2. Begin the `DialogTimer` application as follows. Declare variables named `milli1`, `milli2`, `sec1`, and `sec2`. These are used to compute `time1` and `time2` from calendar objects created at the beginning and end of the program. You then use `time1` and `time2` to compute a `timeDifference`. Also declare a constant to hold the number of milliseconds in a second.

```
public class DialogTimer
{
    public static void main(String[] args)
    {
        int time1, time2, milli1, milli2, sec1,
            sec2, timeDifference;
        final int MILLISECS_IN_SECOND = 1000;
```

(continues)

(continued)

3. Instantiate a GregorianCalendar object, and retrieve its MILLISECOND and SECOND values. Compute a time1 value by multiplying the current sec1 value by 1000 and adding it to the current milli1 value:

```
GregorianCalendar before = new GregorianCalendar();
milli1 = before.get(GregorianCalendar.MILLISECOND);
sec1 = before.get(GregorianCalendar.SECOND);
time1 = MILLISECS_IN_SECOND * sec1 + milli1;
```

4. Display a dialog box that asks the user to make a difficult choice:

```
JOptionPane.showConfirmDialog
    (null, "Is stealing ever justified?");
```

5. Next, create a new GregorianCalendar object. This statement does not execute until the user provides a response for the dialog box, so the time variables contain different values from the first GregorianCalendar object created:

```
GregorianCalendar after = new GregorianCalendar();
milli2 = after.get(GregorianCalendar.MILLISECOND);
sec2 = after.get(GregorianCalendar.SECOND);
time2 = MILLISECS_IN_SECOND * sec2 + milli2;
```

6. Compute the difference between the times, and display the result in a dialog box.

```
timeDifference = time2 - time1;
JOptionPane.showMessageDialog(null, "It took " +
    timeDifference + " milliseconds for you to answer");
```

7. Add two closing curly braces—one for the method and the other for the class—and then save the file as **DialogTimer.java**.

8. Compile and execute the program. When the question appears, choose a response. The second output looks like Figure 4-40; the actual time displayed varies depending on how long you wait before selecting an answer.

Figure 4-40 Output of the DialogTimer application

9. The output in the DialogTimer application is accurate only when the first and second GregorianCalendar objects are created during the same minute. For example, if the first object is created a few seconds before a new minute starts, and the second object is created a few seconds after the new minute starts, the second SECOND value appears to be much lower than the first one. On your own, modify the DialogTimer application to rectify this discrepancy. Save the file as **DialogTimer2.java**.

224

Understanding Composition and Nested Classes

Two of the ways that you can group classes are by using composition and by nesting classes. This section takes a brief look at both concepts.

Composition

The fields in a class can be simple data types like `int` and `double`, but they can also be class types. **Composition** describes the relationship between classes when an object of one class is a data field within another class. You have already studied many classes that contain `String` object fields. These classes employ composition.

When you use an object as a data member of another object, you must remember to supply values for the contained object if it has no default constructor. For example, you might create a class named `NameAndAddress` that stores name and address information. Such a class could be used for employees, customers, students, or anyone else who has a name and address. Figure 4-41 shows a `NameAndAddress` class. The class contains three fields, all of which are set by the constructor. A `display()` method displays the name and address information on three lines.

```
public class NameAndAddress
{
   private String name;
   private String address;
   private int zipCode;
   public NameAndAddress(String nm, String add, int zip)
   {
      name = nm;
      address = add;
      zipCode = zip;
   }
   public void display()
   {
      System.out.println(name);
      System.out.println(address);
      System.out.println(zipCode);
   }
}
```

Figure 4-41   The `NameAndAddress` class

Suppose you want to create a `School` class that holds information about a school. Instead of declaring fields for the `School`'s name and address, you could use the `NameAndAddress` class. The relationship created is sometimes called a **has-a relationship** because one class "has an" instance of another. Figure 4-42 shows a `School` class that declares and uses a `NameAndAddress` object.

```
                              public class School
This statement                {
declares a                   ┌─private NameAndAddress nameAdd;
NameAndAddress                  private int enrollment;
object.                         public School(String name, String add, int zip, int enrolled)
                                {
This statement calls the      ┌─── nameAdd = new NameAndAddress(name, add, zip);
constructor in the                  enrollment = enrolled;
NameAndAddress                  }
class.                          public void display()
                                {
                                    System.out.println("The school information:");
This statement calls the      ┌─── nameAdd.display();
display() method in                 System.out.println("Enrollment is " + enrollment);
the NameAndAddress              }
class.                        }
```

Figure 4-42   The School class

As Figure 4-42 shows, the School constructor requires four parameters. Within the constructor, three of the items—the name, address, and zip code—are passed to the NameAndAddress constructor to provide values for the appropriate fields. The fourth constructor parameter (the school's enrollment) is assigned to the School class enrollment field.

In the School class display method, the NameAndAddress object's display() method is called to display the school's name and address. The enrollment value is displayed afterward. Figure 4-43 shows a simple program that instantiates one School object. Figure 4-44 shows the execution.

```
public class SchoolDemo
{
    public static void main(String[] args)
    {
        School mySchool = new School
            ("Audubon Elementary",
            "3500 Hoyne", 60618, 350);
        mySchool.display();
    }
}
```

Figure 4-43   The SchoolDemo program

Figure 4-44 Output of the `SchoolDemo` program

Nested Classes

Every class you have studied so far has been stored in its own file, and the filename has always matched the class name. In Java, you can create a class within another class and store them together; such classes are **nested classes**. The containing class is the **top-level class**. There are four types of nested classes:

- **`static` member classes**: A `static` member class has access to all static methods of the top-level class.

- **Nonstatic member classes**, also known as **inner classes**: This type of class requires an instance; it has access to all data and methods of the top-level class.

- **Local classes**: These are local to a block of code.

- **Anonymous classes**: These are local classes that have no identifier.

The most common reason to nest a class inside another is because the inner class is used only by the top-level class; in other words, it is a "helper class" to the top-level class. Being able to package the classes together makes their connection easier to understand and their code easier to maintain.

For example, consider a `RealEstateListing` class used by a real estate company to describe houses that are available for sale. The class might contain separate fields for a listing number, the price, the street address, and the house's living area. As an alternative, you might decide that although the listing number and price "go with" the real estate listing, the street address and living area really "go with" the house. So you might create an inner class like the one in Figure 4-45.

```
public class RealEstateListing
{
    private int listingNumber;
    private double price;
    private HouseData houseData;
    public RealEstateListing(int num, double price, String address,
        int sqFt)
    {
        listingNumber = num;
        this.price = price;
        houseData = new HouseData(address, sqFt);
    }
    public void display()
    {
        System.out.println("Listing number #" + listingNumber +
            "  Selling for $" + price);
        System.out.println("Address: " + houseData.streetAddress);
        System.out.println(houseData.squareFeet + " square feet");
    }
    private class HouseData
    {
        private String streetAddress;
        private int squareFeet;
        public HouseData(String address, int sqFt)
        {
            streetAddress = address;
            squareFeet = sqFt;
        }
    }
}
```

Figure 4-45   The RealEstateListing class

Notice that the inner HouseData class in Figure 4-45 is a private class. You don't have to make an inner class private, but doing so keeps its members hidden from outside classes. If you wanted a class's members to be accessible, you would not make it an inner class. An inner class can access its top-level class's fields and methods, even if they are private, and an outer class can access its inner class's members.

You usually will not want to create inner classes. For example, if you made the HouseData class a regular class (as opposed to an inner class) and stored it in its own file, you could use it with composition in other classes—perhaps a MortgageLoan class or an Appraisal class. As it stands, it is usable only in the class in which it now resides. You probably will not create nested classes frequently, but you will see them implemented in some built-in Java classes.

TWO TRUTHS & A LIE

Understanding Composition and Nested Classes

1. Exposition describes the relationship between classes when an object of one class is a data field within another class.

2. When you use an object as a data member of another object, you must remember to supply values for the contained object if it has no default constructor.

3. A nested class resides within another class.

The false statement is #1. Composition describes the relationship between classes when an object of one class is a data field within another class.

Don't Do It

- Don't try to use a variable that is out of scope.

- Don't assume that a constant is still a constant when passed to a method's parameter. If you want a parameter to be constant within a method, you must use `final` in the parameter list.

- Don't try to overload methods by giving them different return types. If their identifiers and parameter lists are the same, then two methods are ambiguous no matter what their return types are.

- Don't think that *default constructor* means only the automatically supplied version. A constructor with no parameters is a default constructor, whether it is the one that is automatically supplied or one you write.

- Don't forget to write a default constructor for a class that has other constructors if you want to be able to instantiate objects without using arguments.

Key Terms

A **block** is the code between a pair of curly braces.

An **outside block**, or **outer block**, contains another block.

An **inside block**, or **inner block**, is contained within another block.

Nested describes the state of an inner block.

Comes into scope describes what happens to a variable when it becomes usable.

Goes out of scope describes what happens to a variable when it ceases to exist at the end of the block in which it is declared.

To **redeclare a variable** is to attempt to declare it twice—an illegal action.

A variable **overrides** another with the same name when it takes precedence over the other variable.

Shadowing is the action that occurs when a local variable hides a variable with the same name that is further away in scope.

Closer in scope describes the status of a local variable over others that it shadows.

Overloading involves using one term to indicate diverse meanings, or writing multiple methods with the same name but with different arguments.

An **ambiguous** situation is one in which the compiler cannot determine which method to use.

A **reference** is an object's memory address.

The **this reference** is a reference to an object that is passed to any object's nonstatic class method.

Class methods are static methods that do not have a `this` reference (because they have no object associated with them).

Class variables are static variables that are shared by every instantiation of a class.

NaN is an acronym for *Not a Number*.

A **package** is a library of classes.

A **library of classes** is a folder that provides a convenient grouping for classes.

The **java.lang** package is implicitly imported into every Java program.

The **fundamental classes** are basic classes contained in the `java.lang` package that are automatically imported into every program you write.

The **optional classes** reside in packages that must be explicitly imported into your programs.

A **wildcard symbol** is an asterisk—a symbol used to indicate that it can be replaced by any set of characters. In a Java `import` statement, you use a wildcard symbol to represent all the classes in a package.

Composition describes the relationship between classes when an object of one class is a data field within another class.

A **has-a relationship** is a relationship based on composition.

Nested classes are classes contained in other classes.

The **top-level class** is the containing class in nested classes.

A **static member class** is a type of nested class that has access to all static methods of its top-level class.

Nonstatic member classes, also known as **inner classes**, are nested classes that require an instance.

Local classes are a type of nested class that are local to a block of code.

Anonymous classes are nested, local classes that have no identifier.

Chapter Summary

- A variable's scope is the portion of a program within which you can reference that variable. A block is the code between a pair of curly braces. Within a method, you can declare a variable with the same name multiple times, as long as each declaration is in its own nonoverlapping block. If you declare a variable within a class and use the same variable name within a method of the class, the variable used inside the method takes precedence over (or overrides, or masks) the first variable.

- Overloading involves writing multiple methods with the same name but different parameter lists. Methods that have identical parameter lists but different return types are not overloaded; they are illegal.

- When you overload methods, you risk creating an ambiguous situation—one in which the compiler cannot determine which method to use.

- When you write your own constructors, they can receive parameters. Such parameters are often used to initialize data fields for an object. After you write a constructor for a class, you no longer receive the automatically provided default constructor. If a class's only constructor requires an argument, you must provide an argument for every object of the class that you create. You can overload constructors just as you can other methods.

- Within nonstatic methods, data fields for the correct object are accessed because a this reference is implicitly passed to nonstatic methods. Static methods do not have a this reference because they have no object associated with them; static methods are also called class methods.

- Static class fields and methods are shared by every instantiation of a class. When a field in a class is final, it cannot change after it is assigned its initial value.

- Java contains hundreds of prewritten classes that are stored in packages, which are folders that provide convenient groupings for classes. The package that is implicitly imported into every Java program is named java.lang. The classes it contains are the fundamental classes, as opposed to the optional classes, which must be explicitly named. The class java.lang.Math contains constants and methods that can be used to perform common mathematical functions. The GregorianCalendar class allows you to define and manipulate dates and time.

• Composition describes the relationship between classes when an object of one class is a data field within another class. You can create nested classes that are stored in the same file. The most common reason to nest a class inside another is because the inner class is used only by the outer or top-level class; in other words, it is a "helper class" to the top-level class.

Review Questions

1. The code between a pair of curly braces in a method is a _____.

   a. function   c. brick
   b. block   d. sector

2. When a block exists within another block, the blocks are _____.

   a. structured   c. sheltered
   b. nested   d. illegal

3. The portion of a program within which you can reference a variable is the variable's _____.

   a. range   c. domain
   b. space   d. scope

4. You can declare variables with the same name multiple times _____.

   a. within a statement
   b. within a block
   c. within a method
   d. You never can declare multiple variables with the same name.

5. If you declare a variable as an instance variable within a class, and you declare and use the same variable name within a method of the class, then within the method, _____.

   a. the variable used inside the method takes precedence
   b. the class instance variable takes precedence
   c. the two variables refer to a single memory address
   d. an error will occur

6. A method variable _____ a class variable with the same name.

   a. acquiesces to   c. overrides
   b. destroys   d. alters

7. Nonambiguous, overloaded methods must have the same _____.

    a. name

    b. number of parameters

    c. parameter names

    d. types of parameters

8. If a method is written to receive a `double` parameter, and you pass an integer to the method, then the method will _____.

    a. work correctly; the integer will be promoted to a `double`

    b. work correctly; the integer will remain an integer

    c. execute, but any output will be incorrect

    d. not work; an error message will be issued

9. A constructor _____ parameters.

    a. can receive

    b. cannot receive

    c. must receive

    d. can receive a maximum of 10

10. A constructor _____ overloaded.

    a. can be

    b. cannot be

    c. must be

    d. is always automatically

11. Usually, you want each instantiation of a class to have its own copy of _____.

    a. the data fields

    b. the class methods

    c. both of the above

    d. none of the above

12. If you create a class that contains one method and instantiate two objects, you usually store _____ for use with the objects.

    a. one copy of the method

    b. two copies of the method

    c. two different methods containing two different `this` references

    d. data only (the methods are not stored)

13. The `this` reference _____.

    a. can be used implicitly

    b. must be used implicitly

    c. must not be used implicitly

    d. must not be used

14. Methods that you reference with individual objects are _____.

    a. `private`

    b. `public`

    c. `static`

    d. `nonstatic`

15. Variables that are shared by every instantiation of a class are _____.

    a. class variables   c. `public` variables

    b. `private` variables   d. illegal

16. The keyword `final` used with a variable declaration indicates _____.

    a. the end of the program

    b. a `static` field

    c. a symbolic constant

    d. that no more variables will be declared in the program

17. Java classes are stored in a folder or _____.

    a. packet   c. bundle

    b. package   d. gaggle

18. Which of the following statements determines the square root of a number and assigns it to the variable s?

    a. `s = sqrt(number);`   c. `number = sqrt(s);`

    b. `s = Math.sqrt(number);`   d. `number = Math.sqrt(s);`

19. A `GregorianCalendar` object can be created with one of seven constructors. This means that the constructors _____.

    a. override each other   c. are overloaded

    b. are ambiguous   d. all of the above

20. The `GregorianCalendar` class `get()` method always returns a(n) _____.

    a. day of the week   c. integer

    b. date   d. `GregorianCalendar` object

Exercises

 Programming Exercises

1. Create a class named `FormLetterWriter` that includes two overloaded methods named `displaySalutation()`. The first method takes one `String` parameter that represents a customer's last name, and it displays the salutation "Dear Mr. or Ms." followed by the last name. The second method accepts two `String` parameters that represent a first and last name, and it displays the greeting "Dear" followed by the first name, a space, and the last name. After each salutation, display the rest of a short business letter: "Thank you for your recent order." Write a `main()` method that tests each overloaded method. Save the file as **FormLetterWriter.java**.

2. Create a class named `Billing` that includes three overloaded `computeBill()` methods for a photo book store.

   - When `computeBill()` receives a single parameter, it represents the price of one photo book ordered. Add 8% tax, and return the total due.

   - When `computeBill()` receives two parameters, they represent the price of a photo book and the quantity ordered. Multiply the two values, add 8% tax, and return the total due.

   - When `computeBill()` receives three parameters, they represent the price of a photo book, the quantity ordered, and a coupon value. Multiply the quantity and price, reduce the result by the coupon value, and then add 8% tax and return the total due.

   Write a `main()` method that tests all three overloaded methods. Save the application as **Billing.java**.

3. a. Create a `BirdSighting` class for the Birmingham Birdwatcher's Club that includes data fields for a bird species sighted, the number seen, and the day of the year. For example, April 1 is the 91st day of the year, assuming it is not a leap year. The class also includes methods to get each field. In addition, create a default constructor that automatically sets the species to "robin" and the number and day to 1. Save the file as **BirdSighting.java**. Create an application named `TestBirdSighting` that demonstrates that each method works correctly. Save the file as **TestBirdSighting.java**.

   b. Create an additional overloaded constructor for the `BirdSighting` class you created in Exercise 3a. This constructor receives parameters for each of the data fields and assigns them appropriately. Add any needed statements to the `TestBirdSighting` application to ensure that the overloaded constructor works correctly, save it, and then test it.

   c. Create a class with the same functionality as the `BirdSighting` class, but create the default constructor to call the three-parameter constructor. Save the class as **BirdSighting2.java**. Create an application to test the new version of the class, and name it **TestBirdSighting2.java**.

4. a. Create a class named `BloodData` that includes fields that hold a blood type (the four blood types are *O, A, B,* and *AB*) and an Rh factor (the factors are + and −). Create a default constructor that sets the fields to "O" and "+", and an overloaded constructor that requires values for both fields. Include get and set methods for each field. Save this file as **BloodData.java**. Create an application named `TestBloodData` that demonstrates that each method works correctly. Save the application as **TestBloodData.java**.

   b. Create a class named `Patient` that includes an ID number, age, and `BloodData`. Provide a default constructor that sets the ID number to "0", the age to 0, and the `BloodData` to "O" and "+". Create an overloaded constructor that provides values for each field. Also provide get methods for each field. Save the file as **Patient.java**. Create an application named `TestPatient` that demonstrates that each method works correctly, and save it as **TestPatient.java**.

5. a. Create a class for the Tip Top Bakery named Bread with data fields for bread type (such as "rye") and calories per slice. Include a constructor that takes parameters for each field, and include get methods that return the values of the fields. Also include a public final static String named MOTTO and initialize it to *The staff of life*. Write an application named TestBread to instantiate three Bread objects with different values, and then display all the data, including the motto, for each object. Save both the **Bread.java** and **TestBread.java** files.

    b. Create a class named SandwichFilling. Include a field for the filling type (such as "egg salad") and another for the calories in a serving. Include a constructor that takes parameters for each field, and include get methods that return the values of the fields. Write an application named TestSandwichFilling to instantiate three SandwichFilling objects with different values, and then display all the data for each object. Save both the **SandwichFilling.java** and **TestSandwichFilling.java** files.

    c. Create a class named Sandwich. Include a Bread field and a SandwichFilling field. Include a constructor that takes parameters for each field needed in the two objects and assigns them to each object's constructor. Write an application named TestSandwich to instantiate three Sandwich objects with different values, and then display all the data for each object, including the total calories in a Sandwich, assuming that each Sandwich is made using two slices of Bread. Save both the **Sandwich.java** and **TestSandwich.java** files.

6. a. Create a class named Circle with fields named radius, diameter, and area. Include a constructor that sets the radius to 1 and calculates the other two values. Also include methods named setRadius() and getRadius(). The setRadius() method not only sets the radius but also calculates the other two values. (The diameter of a circle is twice the radius, and the area of a circle is *pi* multiplied by the square of the radius. Use the Math class PI constant for this calculation.) Save the class as **Circle.java**.

    b. Create a class named TestCircle whose main() method declares several Circle objects. Using the setRadius() method, assign one Circle a small radius value, and assign another a larger radius value. Do not assign a value to the radius of the third circle; instead, retain the value assigned at construction. Display all the values for all the Circle objects. Save the application as **TestCircle.java**.

7. Write a Java application that uses the Math class to determine the answers for each of the following:

    a. The square root of 37

    b. The sine and cosine of 300

    c. The value of the floor, ceiling, and round of 22.8

d. The larger and the smaller of the character "D" and the integer 71

e. A random number between 0 and 20 (*Hint:* The random() method returns a value between 0 and 1; you want a number that is 20 times larger.)

Save the application as **MathTest.java**.

8. Write an application that uses methods in the GregorianCalendar class to calculate how many days are left until the first day of next month. Save the file as **NextMonth.java**.

9. Write an application that uses methods in the GregorianCalendar class to calculate the number of days from today until the end of the current year. Save the file as **YearEnd.java**.

10. a. Create a CertificateOfDeposit class. The class contains data fields that hold a certificate number, account holder's last name, balance, issue date, and maturity date, using GregorianCalendar objects for each date. Provide get and set methods for each field. Also provide a constructor that requires parameters used to set the first four fields, and sets the maturity date to exactly one year after the issue date. Save the class as **CertificateOfDeposit.java**.

    b. Create an interactive application that prompts the user for data for two CertificateOfDeposit objects. Prompt the user for certificate number, name, balance, and issue date for each CertificateOfDeposit, and then instantiate the objects. Display all the values, including the maturity dates. Save the application as **TestCertificateOfDeposit.java**.

11. Create a class named State that holds the following fields: a String for the name of the state, an integer for the population, and two City objects that hold data about the capital city and the most populous city. The State constructor requires six parameters that represent the names and populations of the state, its capital, and its most populous city. Provide get methods for each field. Create the City class to be a nonstatic, private inner class within the State class; the City class contains a city's name and population. Create a class to assign values to and display values from two State objects. Save the files as **State.java** and **TestState.java**.

 Debugging Exercises

1. Each of the following files in the Chapter04 folder of your downloadable student files has syntax and/or logic errors. In each case, determine the problem and fix the program. After you correct the errors, save each file using the same filename preceded with *Fix*. For example, save DebugFour1.java as FixDebugFour1.java.

    a. DebugFour1.java

    b. DebugFour2.java

    c. DebugFour3.java and DebugBox.java

    d. DebugFour4.java

When you change a filename, remember to change every instance of the class name within the file so that it matches the new filename. In Java, the filename and class name must always match.

Game Zone

1. Dice are used in many games. One die can be thrown to randomly show a value from 1 through 6. Design a `Die` class that can hold an integer data field for a value (from 1 to 6). Include a constructor that randomly assigns a value to a die object. Appendix D contains information on generating random numbers. To fully understand the process, you must learn more about Java classes and methods. However, for now, you can copy the following statement to generate a random number between 1 and 6 and assign it to a variable. Using this statement assumes you have assigned appropriate values to the static constants.

```
randomValue = ((int)(Math.random() * 100) % HIGHEST_DIE_VALUE +
    LOWEST_DIE_VALUE);
```

Also include a method in the class to return a die's value. Save the class as **Die.java**.

Write an application that randomly "throws" two dice and displays their values. After you read the chapter *Making Decisions*, you will be able to have the game determine the higher die. For now, just observe how the values change as you execute the program multiple times. Save the application as **TwoDice.java**.

2. Using the `Die` class, write an application that randomly "throws" five dice for the computer and five dice for the player. Display the values and then, by observing the results, decide who wins based on the following hierarchy of `Die` values. (The computer will not decide the winner; the player will determine the winner based on observation.) Any higher combination beats a lower one; for example, five of a kind beats four of a kind.

   - Five of a kind
   - Four of a kind
   - Three of a kind
   - A pair

   After you learn about decision making in the next chapter, you will be able to make the program determine whether you or the computer had the better roll, and after you read the chapter *Arrays*, you will be able to make the determination more efficient. For now, just observe how the values change as you execute the program multiple times. Save the application as **FiveDice.java**.

Case Problems

These projects build on the ones you created in Chapter 3, so they have the same filenames. If you want to retain both versions of the files, save them in different folders.

1. a. Carly's Catering provides meals for parties and special events. In Chapter 3, you created an Event class for the company. The Event class contains two public final static fields that hold the price per guest ($35) and the cutoff value for a large event (50 guests), and three private fields that hold an event number, number of guests for the event, and the price. It also contains two public set methods and three public get methods.

   Now, modify the Event class to contain two overloaded constructors.

   - One constructor accepts an event number and number of guests as parameters. Pass these values to the setEventNumber() and setGuests() methods, respectively. The setGuests() method will automatically calculate the event price.

   - The other constructor is a default constructor that passes "A000" and 0 to the two-parameter constructor.

   Save the file as **Event.java**.

   b. In Chapter 3, you also created an EventDemo class to demonstrate using two Event objects. Now, modify that class to instantiate two Event objects, and include the following new methods in the class:

   - Instantiate one object to retain the constructor default values.

   - Accept user data for the event number and guests fields, and use this data set to instantiate the second object. Display all the details for both objects.

   Save the file as **EventDemo.java**.

2. a. Sammy's Seashore Supplies rents beach equipment such as kayaks, canoes, beach chairs, and umbrellas to tourists. In Chapter 3, you created a Rental class for the company. The Rental class contains two public final static fields that hold the number of minutes in an hour and the hourly rental rate ($40), and four private fields that hold a contract number, number of hours for the rental, number of minutes over an hour, and the price. It also contains two public set methods and four public get methods.

   Now, modify the Rental class to contain two overloaded constructors.

   - One constructor accepts a contract number and number of minutes as parameters. Pass these values to the setContractNumber() and setHoursAndMinutes() methods, respectively. The setHoursAndMinutes() method will automatically calculate the hours, extra minutes, and price.

- The other constructor is a default constructor that passes "A000" and 0 to the two-parameter constructor.

Save the file as **Rental.java**.

b. In Chapter 3, you also created a RentalDemo class to demonstrate a Rental object. Now, modify that class to instantiate two Rental objects.

- Instantiate one object to retain the constructor default values.

- Accept user data for the contract number and minutes fields and use this data set to instantiate the second object. Display all the details for both objects.

Save the file as **RentalDemo.java**.

Making Decisions

In this chapter, you will:

◎ Plan decision-making logic

◎ Make decisions with the `if` and `if...else` structures

◎ Use multiple statements in `if` and `if...else` clauses

◎ Nest `if` and `if...else` statements

◎ Use AND and OR operators

◎ Make accurate and efficient decisions

◎ Use the `switch` statement

◎ Use the conditional and NOT operators

◎ Assess operator precedence

◎ Add decisions and constructors to instance methods

Planning Decision-Making Logic

When computer programmers write programs, they rarely just sit down at a keyboard and begin typing. Programmers must plan the complex portions of programs using paper and pencil. Programmers often use **pseudocode**, a tool that helps them plan a program's logic by writing plain English statements. Using pseudocode requires that you write down the steps needed to accomplish a given task. You write pseudocode in everyday language, not the syntax used in a programming language. In fact, a task you write in pseudocode does not have to be computer-related. If you have ever written a list of directions to your house—for example, (1) go west on Algonquin Road, (2) turn left on Roselle Road, (3) enter expressway heading east, and so on—you have written pseudocode. A **flowchart** is similar to pseudocode, but you write the steps in diagram form, as a series of shapes connected by arrows.

Some programmers use a variety of shapes to represent different tasks in their flowcharts, but you can draw simple flowcharts that express very complex situations using just rectangles and diamonds. You use a rectangle to represent any unconditional step and a diamond to represent any decision. For example, Figure 5-1 shows a flowchart describing driving directions to a friend's house. The logic in Figure 5-1 is an example of a logical structure called a **sequence structure**—one step follows another unconditionally. A sequence structure might contain any number of steps, but when one task follows another with no chance to branch away or skip a step, you are using a sequence.

Sometimes, logical steps do not follow in an unconditional sequence—some tasks might or might not occur based on decisions you make. To represent a decision, flowchart creators use a diamond shape to hold a question, and they draw paths to alternative courses of action emerging from the sides of the diamonds. Figure 5-2 shows a flowchart describing directions in which the execution of some steps depends on decisions.

Figure 5-1   Flowchart of a series of sequential steps

Figure 5-2 includes a **decision structure**—one that involves choosing between alternative courses of action based on some value within a program. For example, the program that produces your paycheck can make decisions about the proper amount to withhold for taxes, the program that guides a missile can alter its course, and a program that monitors your blood pressure during surgery can determine when to sound an alarm. Making decisions is what makes computer programs seem "smart."

When reduced to their most basic form, all computer decisions are yes-or-no decisions. That is, the answer to every computer question is yes or no (or true or false, or on or off). This is because computer circuitry consists of millions of tiny switches that are either on or off, and the result of every decision sets one of these switches in memory. As you learned in Chapter 2, the values `true` and `false` are **Boolean values**; every computer decision results in a Boolean value.

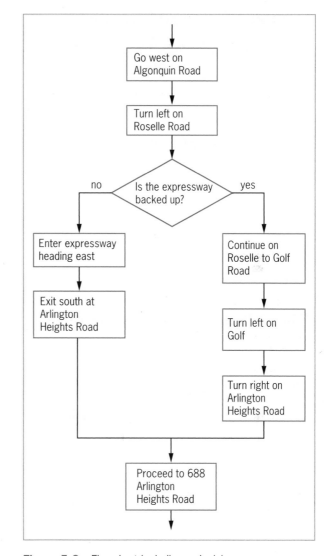

Figure 5-2 Flowchart including a decision

Thus, internally, a program never asks, for example, "What number did the user enter?" Instead, the decisions might be "Did the user enter a *1*?" "If not, did the user enter a *2*?" "If not, did the user enter a *3*?"

 Sir George Boole lived from 1815 to 1864. He developed a type of linguistic algebra, based on 0s and 1s, the three most basic operations of which were (and still are) AND, OR, and NOT. All computer logic is based on his discoveries.

TWO TRUTHS & A LIE

Planning Decision-Making Logic

1. Pseudocode and flowcharts are both tools that are used to check the syntax of computer programs.

2. In a sequence structure, one step follows another unconditionally.

3. In a decision structure, alternative courses of action are chosen based on a Boolean value.

The false statement is #1. Pseudocode and flowcharts are both tools that help programmers plan a program's logic.

The if and if...else Structures

In Java, the simplest statement you can use to make a decision is the **if statement**. For example, suppose you have declared an integer variable named quizScore, and you want to display a message when the value of quizScore is 10. The if statement in Figure 5-3 makes the decision whether to produce output. Note that the double equal sign (==) is used to determine equality; it is Java's **equivalency operator**.

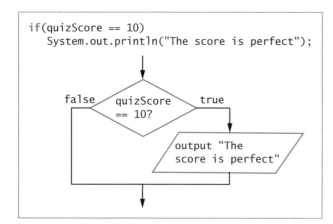

```
if(quizScore == 10)
    System.out.println("The score is perfect");
```

Figure 5-3   A Java if statement

In the example in Figure 5-3, if quizScore holds the value 10, the Boolean value of the expression quizScore == 10 is true, and the subsequent output statement executes. If the value of the expression quizScore == 10 is false, the output statement does not execute.

As the flowchart segment shows, whether the tested expression is true or false, the program continues and executes any statements that follow the `if` statement.

An `if` statement always includes parentheses. Within the parentheses, you can place any Boolean expression. Most often you use a comparison that includes one of the relational operators you learned about in Chapter 2 (==, <, >, <=, >=, or !=). However, you can use any expression that evaluates as true or false, such as a simple `boolean` variable or a call to a method that returns a `boolean` value.

Pitfall: Misplacing a Semicolon in an `if` Statement

In a Java `if` statement, the Boolean expression, such as `(quizScore == 10)`, must appear within parentheses. In Figure 5-3, there is no semicolon at the end of the first line of the `if` statement following the parentheses because the statement does not end there. The statement ends after the `println()` call, so that is where you type the semicolon. You could type the entire `if` statement on one line and it would execute correctly; however, the two-line format for the `if` statement is more conventional and easier to read, so you usually type `if` and the Boolean expression on one line, press Enter, and then indent a few spaces before coding the action that occurs if the Boolean expression evaluates as `true`. Be careful—if you use the two-line format and type a semicolon at the end of the first line, as in the example shown in Figure 5-4, the results might not be what you intended.

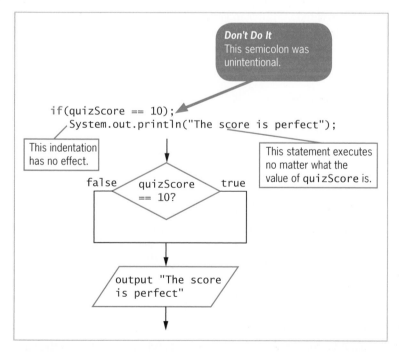

Figure 5-4   Logic that executes when an extra semicolon is inserted in an `if` statement

When the Boolean expression in Figure 5-4 is `true`, an **empty statement** that contains only a semicolon executes. Whether the tested expression evaluates as `true` or `false`, the decision is over immediately, and execution continues with the next independent statement that displays a message. In this case, because of the incorrect semicolon, the `if` statement accomplishes nothing.

Pitfall: Using the Assignment Operator Instead of the Equivalency Operator

Another common programming error occurs when a programmer uses a single equal sign rather than the double equal sign when attempting to determine equivalency. The expression `quizScore = 10` does not compare `quizScore` to 10; instead, it attempts to assign the value 10 to `quizScore`. When the expression `quizScore = 10` is used in the `if` statement, the assignment is illegal because only Boolean expressions are allowed. The confusion arises in part because the single equal sign is used within Boolean expressions in `if` statements in several older programming languages, such as COBOL, Pascal, and BASIC. Adding to the confusion, Java programmers use the word *equals* when speaking of equivalencies. For example, you might say, "If `quizScore` *equals* 10...".

 The expression `if(x = true)` will compile only if x is a `boolean` variable, because it would be legal to assign `true` to x. However, such a statement would be useless because the value of such an expression could never be `false`.

An alternative to using a Boolean expression in an `if` statement, such as `quizScore == 10`, is to store the Boolean expression's value in a Boolean variable. For example, if `isPerfectScore` is a Boolean variable, then the following statement compares `quizScore` to 10 and stores `true` or `false` in `isPerfectScore`:

```
isPerfectScore = (quizScore == 10);
```

Then, you can write the `if` statement as:

```
if(isPerfectScore)
    System.out.println("The score is perfect");
```

This adds an extra step to the program, but makes the `if` statement more similar to an English-language statement.

 When comparing a variable to a constant, some programmers prefer to place the constant to the left of the comparison operator, as in `10 == quizScore`. This practice is a holdover from other programming languages, such as C++, in which an accidental assignment might be made when the programmer types the assignment operator (a single equal sign) instead of the comparison operator (the double equal sign). In Java, the compiler does not allow you to make a mistaken assignment in a Boolean expression.

Pitfall: Attempting to Compare Objects Using the Relational Operators

You can use the standard relational operators (==, <, >, <=, >=, and !=) to compare the values of primitive data types such as `int` and `double`. However, you cannot use <, >, <=, or >= to compare objects; a program containing such comparisons does not compile. You can use the equals and not equals comparisons (== and !=) with objects, but when you use them, you compare the objects' memory addresses instead of their values. Recall that every object name is a reference; the equivalency operators compare objects' references. In other words, == only yields `true` for two objects when they refer to the same object in memory, not when they are different objects with the same value. To compare the values of objects, you should write specialized methods. Remember, `Strings` are objects, so do not use == to compare `Strings`. You will learn more about this in the chapter *Characters, Strings, and the StringBuilder*.

Although object names are references, their field names are not references if they represent simple, primitive data types. You can compare the values between objects' fields by using public accessor methods. For example, suppose you have created a class named `Student` with a `double` grade point average field and a nonstatic public method named `getGpa()`. After instantiating two objects named `student1` and `student2`, you can write a statement such as the following:

```
if(student1.getGpa() > student2.getGpa())
    System.out.println("The first student has a higher gpa");
```

The values represented by `student1.getGpa()` and `student2.getGpa()` are both `doubles`, so they can be compared using any of the relational operators.

The `if...else` Structure

Consider the following statement:

```
if(quizScore == 10)
    System.out.println("The score is perfect");
```

Such a statement is sometimes called a **single-alternative `if`** because the program only performs an action, or not, based on one alternative; in this example, a statement is displayed when `quizScore` is 10. Often, you require two options for the course of action following a decision. A **dual-alternative `if`** is the decision structure you use when you need to take one or the other of two possible courses of action. For example, you would use a dual-alternative `if` structure if you wanted to display one message when the value of `quizScore` is 10 and a different message when it is not. In Java, the **`if...else` statement** provides the mechanism to perform one action when a Boolean expression evaluates as `true` and to perform a different action when a Boolean expression evaluates as `false`.

The code in Figure 5-5 displays one of two messages. In this example, when the value of `quizScore` is 10, the **`if` clause** of the statement executes, displaying the message "The score is perfect". When `quizScore` is any other value, the **`else` clause** of the statement executes and the program displays the message "No, it's not". You can code an `if` without an `else`, but it is illegal to code an `else` without an `if` that precedes it.

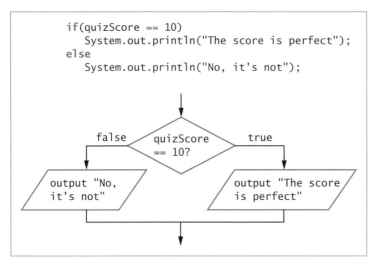

```
if(quizScore == 10)
    System.out.println("The score is perfect");
else
    System.out.println("No, it's not");
```

Figure 5-5   An if...else structure

The indentation shown in the example code in Figure 5-5 is not required but is standard usage. You vertically align the keyword if with the keyword else, and then indent the action statements that depend on the evaluation.

When you execute an if...else statement, only one of the resulting actions takes place depending on the evaluation of the Boolean expression. Each statement, the one following the if and the one following the else, is a complete statement, so each ends with a semicolon.

 Watch the video *Making Decisions*.

TWO TRUTHS & A LIE

The if and if...else Structures

1. In a Java if statement, the keyword if is followed by a Boolean expression within parentheses.

2. In a Java if statement, a semicolon follows the Boolean expression.

3. When determining equivalency in Java, you use a double equal sign.

The false statement is #2. In a Java if statement, a semicolon ends the statement. It is used following the action that should occur if the Boolean expression is true. If a semicolon follows the Boolean expression, then the body of the if statement is empty.

You Do It

Using an if...else *Statement*

In this section, you start writing a program for Sacks Fifth Avenue, a nonprofit thrift shop. The program determines which volunteer to assign to price a donated item. To begin, you prompt the user to answer a question about whether a donation is clothing or some other type, and then the program displays the name of the volunteer who handles such donations. Clothing donations are handled by Regina, and other donations are handled by Marco.

1. Open a new text file, and then enter the first lines of code to create a class named AssignVolunteer. You import the Scanner class so that you can use keyboard input. The class contains a main() method that performs all the work of the class:

```java
import java.util.Scanner;
public class AssignVolunteer
{
    public static void main(String[] args)
    {
```

2. On new lines, declare the variables and constants this application uses. The user will be prompted to enter one of the values stored in the two constants. That value will then be assigned to the integer donationType and compared to the CLOTHING_CODE constant. Then, based on the results of that comparison, the program will assign the value of one of the PRICER constants to the String variable volunteer.

```java
int donationType;
String volunteer;
final int CLOTHING_CODE = 1;
final int OTHER_CODE = 2;
final String CLOTHING_PRICER = "Regina";
final String OTHER_PRICER = "Marco";
```

3. Define the input device, and then add the code that prompts the user to enter a *1* or *2* for the donation type. Accept the response, and assign it to donationType:

```java
Scanner input = new Scanner(System.in);
System.out.println("What type of donation is this?");
System.out.print("Enter " + CLOTHING_CODE + " for clothing, " +
    OTHER_CODE + " for anything else... ");
donationType = input.nextInt();
```

(continues)

(continued)

4. Use an if…else statement to choose the name of the volunteer to be assigned to the volunteer String, as follows:

```
if(donationType == CLOTHING_CODE)
    volunteer = CLOTHING_PRICER;
else
    volunteer = OTHER_PRICER;
```

5. Display the chosen code and corresponding volunteer's name:

```
System.out.println("You entered " + donationType);
System.out.println("The volunteer who will price this item is " +
    volunteer);
```

6. Type the two closing curly braces to end the main() method and the AssignVolunteer class.

7. Save the program as **AssignVolunteer.java**, and then compile and run the program. Confirm that the program selects the correct volunteer when you choose *1* for a clothing donation or *2* for any other donation type. For example, Figure 5-6 shows a typical execution of the program when the user enters *1* for a clothing donation.

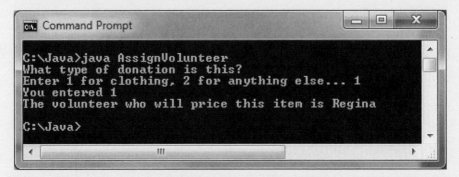

Figure 5-6   Typical execution of the AssignVolunteer application

Using Multiple Statements in if and if…else Clauses

Often, you want to take more than one action following the evaluation of a Boolean expression within an if statement. For example, you might want to display several separate lines of output or perform several mathematical calculations. To execute more than one statement that depends on the evaluation of a Boolean expression, you use a pair of curly braces to place the dependent statements within a block. For example, the program segment shown in Figure 5-7 determines whether an employee has worked more than the value of a FULL_WEEK constant; if so, the program computes regular and overtime pay.

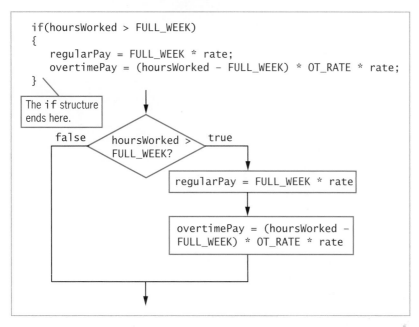

```
if(hoursWorked > FULL_WEEK)
{
    regularPay = FULL_WEEK * rate;
    overtimePay = (hoursWorked - FULL_WEEK) * OT_RATE * rate;
}
```

The if structure ends here.

false   hoursWorked > FULL_WEEK?   true

regularPay = FULL_WEEK * rate

overtimePay = (hoursWorked - FULL_WEEK) * OT_RATE * rate

Figure 5-7 An if structure that determines pay

When you place a block within an if statement, it is crucial to place the curly braces correctly. For example, in Figure 5-8, the curly braces have been omitted. Within the code segment in Figure 5-8, when hoursWorked > FULL_WEEK is true, regularPay is calculated and the if expression ends. The next statement that computes overtimePay executes every time the program runs, no matter what value is stored in hoursWorked. This last statement does not depend on the if statement; it is an independent, stand-alone statement. The indentation might be deceiving; it looks as though two statements depend on the if statement, but indentation does not cause statements following an if statement to be dependent. Rather, curly braces are required if multiple statements must be treated as a block.

When you create a block, you do not have to place multiple statements within it. It is perfectly legal to place curly braces around a single statement. For clarity, some programmers always use curly braces to surround the actions in an if statement, even when there is only one statement in the block.

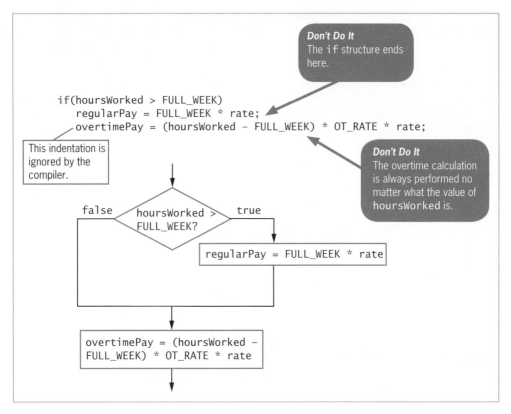

Figure 5-8 Erroneous overtime pay calculation with missing curly braces

Because the curly braces are missing, regardless of whether hoursWorked is more than FULL_WEEK, the last statement in Figure 5-8 is a new stand-alone statement that is not part of the if, and so it always executes. If hoursWorked is 30, for example, and FULL_WEEK is 40, then the program calculates the value of overtimePay as a negative number (because 30 minus 40 results in −10). Therefore, the output is incorrect. Correct blocking is crucial to achieving valid output.

When you fail to block statements that should depend on an if, and you also use an else clause, the program will not compile. For example, consider the following code:

```
if(hoursWorked > FULL_WEEK)
    regularPay = FULL_WEEK * rate;
    overtimePay = (hoursWorked - FULL_WEEK) * OT_RATE * rate;
else
    regularPay = FULL_WEEK * rate;
```

> **Don't Do It**
> These statements should be blocked.

In this case, the if statement ends after the first regularPay calculation, and the second complete stand-alone statement performs the overtimePay calculation. The third statement in this code starts with else, which is illegal. An error message will indicate that the program contains "else without if".

Just as you can block statements to depend on an if, you can also block statements to depend on an else. Figure 5-9 shows an application that contains an if structure with two dependent statements and an else with two dependent statements. The program executes the final println() statement without regard to the hoursWorked variable's value; it is not part of the if structure. Figure 5-10 shows the output from two executions of the program. In the first execution, the user entered 39 for the hoursWorked value and 20.00 for rate; in the second execution, the user entered 42 for hoursWorked and 20.00 for rate.

```java
import java.util.Scanner;
public class Payroll
{
  public static void main(String[] args)
  {
    double rate;
    double hoursWorked;
    double regularPay;
    double overtimePay;
    final int FULL_WEEK = 40;
    final double OT_RATE = 1.5;
    Scanner keyboard = new Scanner(System.in);
    System.out.print("How many hours did you work this week? ");
    hoursWorked = keyboard.nextDouble();
    System.out.print("What is your regular pay rate? ");
    rate = keyboard.nextDouble();
    if(hoursWorked > FULL_WEEK)
    {
      regularPay = FULL_WEEK * rate;
      overtimePay = (hoursWorked - FULL_WEEK) * OT_RATE * rate;
    }
    else
    {
      regularPay = hoursWorked * rate;
      overtimePay = 0.0;
    }
    System.out.println("Regular pay is " +
      regularPay + "\nOvertime pay is " + overtimePay);
  }
}
```

Figure 5-9 Payroll application containing an if and else clause with blocks

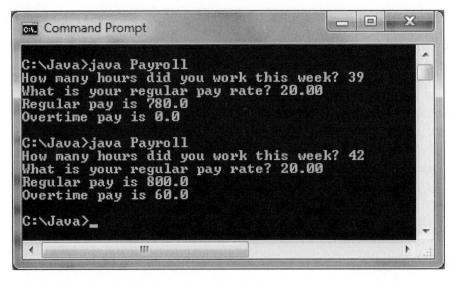

Figure 5-10   Output of the Payroll application

When you block statements, you must remember that any variable you declare within a block is local to that block. For example, the following code segment contains a variable named sum that is local to the block following the if. The last println() statement causes an error because the sum variable is not recognized:

```
if(a == b)
{
    int sum = a + b;
    System.out.println
        ("The two variables are equal");
}
System.out.println("The sum is " + sum);
```

The sum variable is declared in this block...

...so it is not recognized here.

TWO TRUTHS & A LIE

Using Multiple Statements in if and if...else Clauses

1. To execute more than one statement that depends on the evaluation of a Boolean expression, you use a pair of curly braces to place the dependent statements within a block.

2. Indentation can be used to cause statements following an if statement to depend on the evaluation of the Boolean expression.

3. When you declare a variable within a block, it is local to that block.

The false statement is #2. Indentation does not cause statements following an if statement to be dependent; curly braces are required if multiple statements must be treated as a block.

You Do It

Using Multiple Statements in `if` and `else` Clauses

In this section, you use a block of code to add multiple actions to an `if...else` statement.

1. Open the `AssignVolunteer` application from the previous "You Do It" section. Change the class name to **AssignVolunteer2**, and immediately save the file as **AssignVolunteer2.java**.

2. Add a `String` to the variables. This `String` will be assigned a message that displays the donation type:

    ```
    String message;
    ```

3. In place of the existing `if...else` statement in the program, insert the following statement that takes two blocked actions for each donation type. It assigns a volunteer and assigns a value to the `message` `String`.

    ```
    if(donationType == CLOTHING_CODE)
    {
       volunteer = CLOTHING_PRICER;
       message = "a clothing donation";
    }
    else
    {
       volunteer = OTHER_PRICER;
       message = "another donation type";
    }
    ```

4. Following the output statement that displays the donation type, add the following statement that displays the assigned message:

    ```
    System.out.println("This is " + message);
    ```

(continues)

(continued)

5. Save the file, and compile and execute the program. Figure 5-11 shows two executions.

Figure 5-11   Two executions of the `AssignVolunteer2` program

Nesting `if` and `if...else` Statements

Within an `if` or an `else` clause, you can code as many dependent statements as you need, including other `if` and `else` structures. Statements in which an `if` structure is contained inside another `if` structure are commonly called **nested `if` statements**. Nested `if` statements are particularly useful when two conditions must be met before some action is taken.

For example, suppose you want to pay a $50 bonus to a salesperson only if the salesperson sells at least three items that total at least $1,000 in value during a specified time. Figure 5-12 shows the logic and the code to solve the problem.

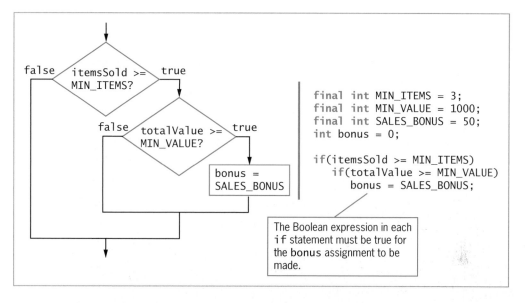

```
final int MIN_ITEMS = 3;
final int MIN_VALUE = 1000;
final int SALES_BONUS = 50;
int bonus = 0;

if(itemsSold >= MIN_ITEMS)
    if(totalValue >= MIN_VALUE)
        bonus = SALES_BONUS;
```

The Boolean expression in each if statement must be true for the bonus assignment to be made.

Figure 5-12   Determining whether to assign a bonus using nested if statements

Notice there are no semicolons in the if statement code shown in Figure 5-12 until after the bonus = SALES_BONUS; statement. The expression itemsSold >= MIN_ITEMS is evaluated first. Only if this expression is true does the program evaluate the second Boolean expression, totalValue >= MIN_VALUE. If that expression is also true, the bonus assignment statement executes, and the if structure ends.

When you use nested if statements, you must pay careful attention to placement of any else clauses. For example, suppose you want to distribute bonuses on a revised schedule. If the salesperson does not sell at least three items, you want to give a $10 bonus. If the salesperson sells at least three items whose combined value is less than $1,000, the bonus is $25. If the salesperson sells at least three items whose combined value is at least $1,000, the bonus is $50. Figure 5-13 shows the logic.

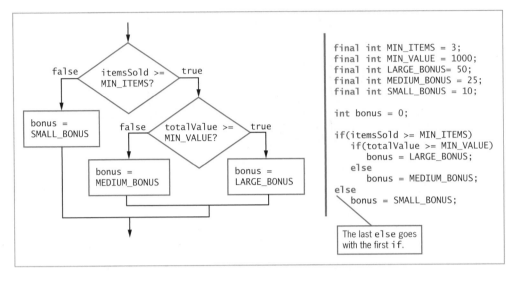

```
final int MIN_ITEMS = 3;
final int MIN_VALUE = 1000;
final int LARGE_BONUS= 50;
final int MEDIUM_BONUS = 25;
final int SMALL_BONUS = 10;

int bonus = 0;

if(itemsSold >= MIN_ITEMS)
    if(totalValue >= MIN_VALUE)
        bonus = LARGE_BONUS;
    else
        bonus = MEDIUM_BONUS;
else
    bonus = SMALL_BONUS;
```

The last else goes with the first if.

Figure 5-13 Determining one of three bonuses using nested if statements

As Figure 5-13 shows, when one if statement follows another, the first else clause encountered is paired with the most recent if encountered. In this figure, the complete nested if...else structure fits entirely within the if portion of the outer if...else statement. No matter how many levels of if...else statements are needed to produce a solution, the else statements are always associated with their ifs on a "first in-last out" basis. In Figure 5-13, the indentation of the lines of code helps to show which else statement is paired with which if statement. Remember, the compiler does not take indentation into account, but consistent indentation can help readers understand a program's logic.

TWO TRUTHS & A LIE

Nesting if and if...else Statements

1. Statements in which an if structure is contained inside another if structure commonly are called nested if statements.

2. When one if statement follows another, the first else clause encountered is paired with the first if that occurred before it.

3. A complete nested if...else structure always fits entirely within either the if portion or the else portion of its outer if...else statement.

The false statement is #2. When one if statement follows another, the first else clause encountered is paired with the most recent if encountered.

You Do It

Using a Nested `if` *Statement*

In this section, you add a nested `if` statement to the `AssignVolunteer2` application.

1. Rerun the `AssignVolunteer2` program, and enter an invalid code, such as *3*. The selected volunteer is Marco because the program tests only for an entered value of *1* or not *1*. Modify the program to display the entered code, volunteer, and donation type message only when the entered value is *1* or *2*, and to display the entered code and an error message otherwise. Rename the class **AssignVolunteer3**, and save the file as **AssignVolunteer3.java**. Figure 5-14 shows two typical executions of the program.

Figure 5-14 Two executions of the `AssignVolunteer3` program

Using Logical AND and OR Operators

In Java, you can combine two Boolean tests into a single expression using the logical AND and OR operators.

The AND Operator

For an alternative to some nested `if` statements, you can use the **logical AND operator** between two Boolean expressions to determine whether both are `true`. In Java, the AND operator is written as two ampersands (&&). For example, the two statements shown in Figure 5-15 work exactly the same way. In each case, both the itemsSold variable must be at least the minimum number of items required for a bonus and the totalValue variable must be at least the minimum required value for the bonus to be set to SALES_BONUS.

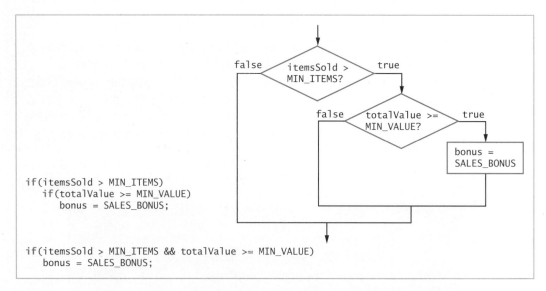

```
if(itemsSold > MIN_ITEMS)
    if(totalValue >= MIN_VALUE)
        bonus = SALES_BONUS;


if(itemsSold > MIN_ITEMS && totalValue >= MIN_VALUE)
    bonus = SALES_BONUS;
```

Figure 5-15   Code for bonus-determining decision using nested ifs and using the && operator

It is important to note that when you use the && operator, you must include a complete Boolean expression on each side. In other words, like many arithmetic operators, the && operator is a binary operator, meaning it requires an operand on each side. If you want to set a bonus to $400 when a saleAmount is both over $1,000 and under $5,000, the correct statement is:

```
if(saleAmount > 1000 && saleAmount < 5000)
    bonus = 400;
```

Even though the saleAmount variable is intended to be used in both parts of the AND expression, the following statement is incorrect and does not compile because there is not a complete expression on both sides of the binary && operator:

```
if(saleAmount > 1000 && < 5000)
    bonus = 400;
```

Don't Do It
This statement will not compile because it does not have a Boolean expression on each side of the && operator.

For clarity, many programmers prefer to surround each Boolean expression that is part of a compound Boolean expression with its own set of parentheses, as in the following example:

& (saleAmount < 5000))

doing so makes the compound expression clearer to you.

se the && operator because using nested if statements always
it using the && operator often makes your code more concise,
to understand.

n to occur even if only one of two conditions is **true**, you can
r you can use the **logical OR operator**, which is written as ||.

give a discount to any customer who satisfies at least one of two
num number of items or buying any number of items that total
write the code using either of the ways shown in Figure 5-16.

sed in the OR operator are sometimes called "pipes." The pipe appears on the same
n your keyboard.

```
MS)
IT;

VALUE)
COUNT;

MS || itemsValue >= MIN_VALUE)
IT;
```

ustomer discount when customer needs to meet only one of two criteria

As with the && operator, you are never required to use the || operator because using nested
if statements always achieves the same result. However, using the || operator often makes
your code more concise, less error-prone, and easier to understand.

Short-Circuit Evaluation

The expressions on each side of the && and || operators are evaluated only as far as necessary to determine whether the entire expression is true or false. This feature is called **short-circuit evaluation**. With the && operator, both Boolean expression operands must be true before the action in the result statement can occur. (The same is true for nested ifs, as you can see in Figure 5-15.) When you use the && operator, if the first tested expression is false, the second expression is never evaluated because its value does not matter.

The || operator also uses short-circuit evaluation. In other words, because only one of the Boolean expressions in an || expression must be true to cause the dependent statements to execute, if the expression to the left of the || is true, then there is no need to evaluate the expression to the right of the ||. (The same is true for nested ifs, as you can see in Figure 5-16.) When you use the || operator, if the first tested expression is true, the second expression is never evaluated because its value does not matter.

If you are using simple comparisons as the operands for the && or || operators, as in the examples in Figures 5-15 and 5-16, you won't notice that short-circuit evaluation is occurring. However, suppose that you have created two methods that return Boolean values and you use calls to those methods in an if statement, as in the following:

```
if(method1() && method2())
    System.out.println("OK");
```

Depending on the actions performed within the methods, it might be important to understand that in this case, if method1() is false, then method2() will not execute.

 Watch the video *Using && and ||*.

TWO TRUTHS & A LIE

Using Logical AND and OR Operators

1. The AND operator is written as two ampersands (&&), and the OR operator is written as two pipes (||).

2. When you use the && and || operators, you must include a complete Boolean expression on each side.

3. When you use an && or || operator, each Boolean expression that surrounds the operator is always tested in order from left to right.

The false statement is #3. The expressions in each part of an AND or OR expression are evaluated only as much as necessary to determine whether the entire expression is true or false. For example, in an AND expression, if the first Boolean value is false, the second expression is not tested. In an OR expression, if the first Boolean value is true, the second expression is not tested. This feature is called short-circuit evaluation.

You Do It

Using the && Operator

This section helps you create a program that demonstrates how short-circuiting works with the && operator.

1. Open a new file in your text editor, and type the header and curly braces for a class named ShortCircuitTestAnd:

```
public class ShortCircuitTestAnd
{
}
```

2. Between the curly braces for the class, type the header and braces for a main() method:

```
public static void main(String[] args)
{
}
```

3. Within the main() method, insert an if…else statement that tests the return values of two method calls. If both methods are true, then "Both are true" is displayed. Otherwise, "Both are not true" is displayed.

```
if(trueMethod() && falseMethod())
    System.out.println("Both are true");
else
    System.out.println("Both are not true");
```

4. Following the closing curly brace for the main() method, but before the closing curly brace for the class, insert a method named trueMethod(). The method displays the message "True method" and returns a true value.

```
public static boolean trueMethod()
{
    System.out.println("True method");
    return true;
}
```

5. Following the closing curly brace of trueMethod(), insert a method named falseMethod() that displays the message "False method" and returns a false value.

```
public static boolean falseMethod()
{
    System.out.println("False method");
    return false;
}
```

(continues)

(continued)

6. Save the file as **ShortCircuitTestAnd.java**, and then compile and execute it. Figure 5-17 shows the output. First, "True method" is displayed because `trueMethod()`was executed as the first half of the Boolean expression in the program's `if` statement. Then, the second half of the Boolean expression calls `falseMethod()`. Finally, "Both are not true" is displayed because both halves of the tested expression were not true.

Figure 5-17 Execution of `ShortCircuitTestAnd` program

7. Change the position of the method calls in the `if` statement so that the statement becomes the following:

```
if(falseMethod() && trueMethod())
   System.out.println("Both are true");
else
   System.out.println("Both are not true");
```

8. Save the file, compile it, and execute it. Now the output looks like Figure 5-18. The `if` statement makes a call to `falseMethod()`, and its output is displayed. Because the first half of the Boolean expression is false, there is no need to test the second half, so `trueMethod()` never executes, and the program proceeds directly to the statement that displays "Both are not true."

(continues)

(continued)

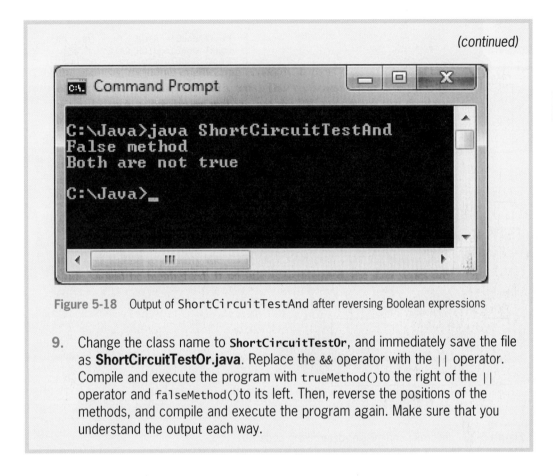

Figure 5-18   Output of ShortCircuitTestAnd after reversing Boolean expressions

9. Change the class name to **ShortCircuitTestOr**, and immediately save the file
    as **ShortCircuitTestOr.java**. Replace the && operator with the || operator.
    Compile and execute the program with trueMethod() to the right of the ||
    operator and falseMethod() to its left. Then, reverse the positions of the
    methods, and compile and execute the program again. Make sure that you
    understand the output each way.

Making Accurate and Efficient Decisions

When new programmers must make a range check, they often introduce incorrect or
inefficient code into their programs. In this section, you learn how to make accurate
and efficient range checks, and you also learn how to use the && and || operators
appropriately.

Making Accurate Range Checks

A **range check** is a series of statements that determine to which of several consecutive series
of values another value falls. Consider a situation in which salespeople can receive one of
three possible commission rates based on their sales. For example, a sale totaling $1,000 or
more earns the salesperson an 8% commission, a sale totaling $500 through $999 earns 6%
of the sale amount, and any sale totaling $499.99 or less earns 5%. Using three separate
if statements to test single Boolean expressions might result in some incorrect commission
assignments. For example, examine the code shown in Figure 5-19.

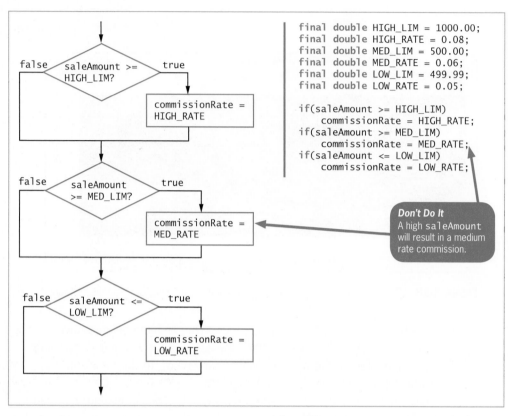

```
final double HIGH_LIM = 1000.00;
final double HIGH_RATE = 0.08;
final double MED_LIM = 500.00;
final double MED_RATE = 0.06;
final double LOW_LIM = 499.99;
final double LOW_RATE = 0.05;

if(saleAmount >= HIGH_LIM)
    commissionRate = HIGH_RATE;
if(saleAmount >= MED_LIM)
    commissionRate = MED_RATE;
if(saleAmount <= LOW_LIM)
    commissionRate = LOW_RATE;
```

Don't Do It
A high saleAmount will result in a medium rate commission.

Figure 5-19   Incorrect commission-determining code

Using the code shown in Figure 5-19, when a saleAmount is $5,000, for example, the first if statement executes, and the Boolean expression (saleAmount >= HIGH_LIM) evaluates as true, so HIGH_RATE is correctly assigned to commissionRate. However, the next if expression, (saleAmount >= MED_LIM), also evaluates as true, so the commissionRate, which was just set to HIGH_RATE, is incorrectly reset to MED_RATE.

A partial solution to this problem is to use an else statement following the first evaluation, as shown in Figure 5-20.

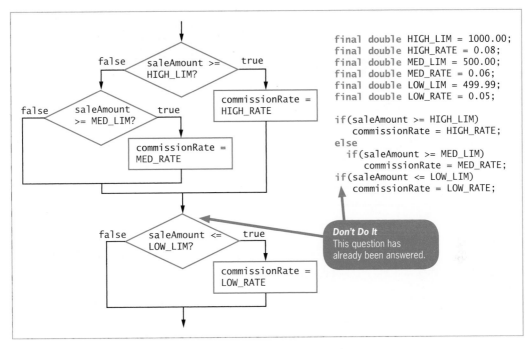

```
final double HIGH_LIM = 1000.00;
final double HIGH_RATE = 0.08;
final double MED_LIM = 500.00;
final double MED_RATE = 0.06;
final double LOW_LIM = 499.99;
final double LOW_RATE = 0.05;

if(saleAmount >= HIGH_LIM)
    commissionRate = HIGH_RATE;
else
  if(saleAmount >= MED_LIM)
      commissionRate = MED_RATE;
if(saleAmount <= LOW_LIM)
    commissionRate = LOW_RATE;
```

Don't Do It
This question has already been answered.

Figure 5-20 Improved, but inefficient, commission-determining code

With the new code in Figure 5-20, when the saleAmount is $5,000, the expression (saleAmount >= HIGH_LIM) is true and the commissionRate becomes HIGH_RATE; then the entire if structure ends. When the saleAmount is not greater than or equal to $1,000 (for example, $800), the first if expression is false, and the else statement executes and correctly sets the commissionRate to MED_RATE.

The code shown in Figure 5-20 works, but it is somewhat inefficient. When the saleAmount is any amount over LOW_RATE, either the first if sets commissionRate to HIGH_RATE for amounts that are at least $1,000, or its else sets commissionRate to MED_RATE for amounts that are at least $500. In either of these two cases, the Boolean value tested in the next statement, if(saleAmount <= LOW_LIM), is always false, so commissionRate retains its correct value. However, it was unnecessary to ask the LOW_LIM question.

After you know that saleAmount is not at least MED_LIM, rather than asking if(saleAmount <= LOW_LIM), it's easier, more efficient, and less error-prone to use an else. If the saleAmount is not at least HIGH_LIM and is also not at least MED_LIM, it must by default be less than or equal to LOW_LIM. Figure 5-21 shows this improved logic. Notice that the LOW_LIM constant is no longer declared because it is not needed anymore—if a saleAmount is not greater than or equal to MED_LIMIT, the commissionRate must receive the LOW_RATE.

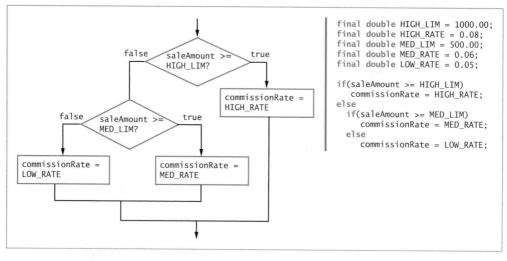

Figure 5-21   Improved and efficient commission-determining logic

Making Efficient Range Checks

Within a nested if...else, like the one shown in Figure 5-21, it is most efficient to ask the question that is most likely to be true first. In other words, if you know that most saleAmount values are high, compare saleAmount to HIGH_LIM first. That way, you most frequently avoid asking multiple questions. If, however, you know that most saleAmounts are small, you should ask if(saleAmount < LOW_LIM) first. The code shown in Figure 5-22 results in the same commission value for any given saleAmount, but this sequence of decisions is more efficient when most saleAmount values are small.

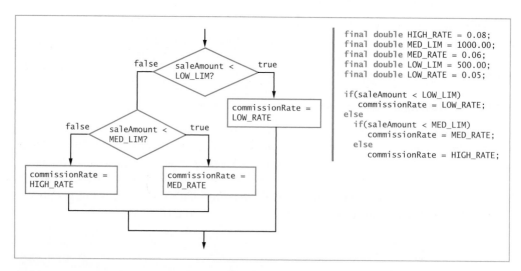

Figure 5-22   Commission-determining code asking about smallest saleAmount first

In Figure 5-22, notice that the comparisons use the < operator instead of <=. That's because a saleAmount of $1,000.00 should result in a HIGH_RATE, and a saleAmount of $500.00 should result in a MED_RATE. If you wanted to use <= comparisons, then you could change the MED_LIM and LOW_LIM cutoff values to 999.99 and 499.99, respectively.

Using && and || Appropriately

Beginning programmers often use the && operator when they mean to use ||, and often use || when they should use &&. Part of the problem lies in the way we use the English language. For example, your boss might request, "Display an error message when an employee's hourly pay rate is under $5.85 and when an employee's hourly pay rate is over $60." You define $5.85 as a named constant LOW and $60 as HIGH. However, because your boss used the word *and* in the request, you might be tempted to write a program statement like the following:

```
if(payRate < LOW && payRate > HIGH)
    System.out.println("Error in pay rate");
```

This message can never be output because the Boolean expression can never be true.

However, as a single variable, no payRate value can ever be both below 5.85 *and* over 60 at the same time, so the output statement can never execute, no matter what value the payRate has. In this case, you must write the following code that uses the || operator to display the error message under the correct circumstances:

```
if(payRate < LOW || payRate > HIGH)
    System.out.println("Error in pay rate");
```

Similarly, your boss might request, "Display the names of those employees in departments 1 and 2." Because the boss used the word *and* in the request, you might be tempted to write the following:

```
if(department == 1 && department == 2)
    System.out.println("Name is: " + name);
```

However, the variable department can never contain both a *1* and a *2* at the same time, so no employee name will ever be output, no matter what the value of department is. The correct statement chooses employees whose department is 1 or 2, as follows:

```
if(department == 1 || department == 2)
    System.out.println("Name is: " + name);
```

Another type of mistake occurs if you use a single ampersand or pipe when you try to indicate a logical AND or OR. Both & and | are valid Java operators, but they have two different functions. When you use a single & or | with integer operands, it operates on bits. When you use a single & or | with Boolean expressions, it always evaluates both expressions instead of using short-circuitry.

270

TWO TRUTHS & A LIE

Making Accurate and Efficient Decisions

1. A range check is a series of statements that determine within which of a set of ranges a value falls.

2. When you must make a series of decisions in a program, it is most efficient to first ask the question that is most likely to be true.

3. The statement `if(payRate < 6.00 && payRate > 50.00)` can be used to select `payRate` values that are higher or lower than the specified limits.

The false statement is #3. The statement `if(payRate < 6.00 && payRate > 50.00)` cannot be used to make a selection because no value for payRate can be both below 6.00 and above 50.00 at the same time.

Using the `switch` Statement

By nesting a series of `if` and `else` statements, you can choose from any number of alternatives. For example, suppose you want to display a student's class year based on a stored number. Figure 5-23 shows one possible implementation of the program.

```
if(year == 1)
   System.out.println("Freshman");
else
   if(year == 2)
      System.out.println("Sophomore");
   else
      if(year == 3)
         System.out.println("Junior");
      else
         if(year == 4)
            System.out.println("Senior");
         else
            System.out.println("Invalid year");
```

Figure 5-23   Determining class status using nested `if` statements

In program segments like the one in Figure 5-23, many programmers (particularly those familiar with the Visual Basic programming language) would code each `else` and the `if` clause that follows it on the same line, and refer to the format as an **else…if clause**. Because Java ignores whitespace, the logic is the same whether each `else` and the subsequent `if` are on the same line or different lines.

An alternative to using the series of nested `if` statements shown in Figure 5-23 is to use the `switch` statement. The **switch statement** is useful when you need to test a single variable against a series of exact integer (including `int`, `byte`, and `short` types), character, or string values. The ability to use strings as the tested values in a `switch` statement is a new feature in Java 7.

The `switch` statement uses four keywords:

- `switch` starts the structure and is followed immediately by a test expression enclosed in parentheses.

- `case` is followed by one of the possible values for the test expression and a colon.

- `break` optionally terminates a `switch` statement at the end of each case.

- `default` optionally is used prior to any action that should occur if the test variable does not match any case.

Figure 5-24 shows the `switch` statement used to display the four school years based on an integer named `year`.

```
switch(year)
{
   case 1:
      System.out.println("Freshman");
      break;
   case 2:
      System.out.println("Sophomore");
      break;
   case 3:
      System.out.println("Junior");
      break;
   case 4:
      System.out.println("Senior");
      break;
   default:
      System.out.println("Invalid year");
}
```

Figure 5-24   Determining class status using a `switch` statement

You are not required to list the `case` values in ascending order, as shown in Figure 5-24, although doing so often makes a statement easier to understand. For efficiency, you might want to list the most likely case first.

The `switch` statement shown in Figure 5-24 begins by evaluating the `year` variable shown in the first line. If `year` is equal to the first `case` value, which is 1, the statement that displays "Freshman" executes. The `break` statement bypasses the rest of the `switch` structure, and execution continues with any statement after the closing curly brace of the `switch` structure.

If the year variable is not equivalent to the first case value of 1, the next case value is compared, and so on. If the year variable does not contain the same value as any of the case statements, the default statement or statements execute.

You can leave out the break statements in a switch structure. However, if you omit the break and the program finds a match for the test variable, all the statements within the switch statement execute from that point forward. For example, if you omit each break statement in the code shown in Figure 5-24, when the year is 3, the first two cases are bypassed, but *Junior*, *Senior*, and *Invalid year* all are output. You should intentionally omit the break statements if you want all subsequent cases to execute after the test variable is matched.

You do not need to write code for each case in a switch statement. For example, suppose that the supervisor for departments 1, 2, and 3 is *Jones*, but other departments have different supervisors. In that case, you might use the code in Figure 5-25.

```java
int department;
String supervisor;
// Statements to get department go here
switch(department)
{
    case 1:
    case 2:
    case 3:
        supervisor = "Jones";
        break;
    case 4:
        supervisor = "Staples";
        break;
    case 5:
        supervisor = "Tejano";
        break:
    default:
        System.out.println("Invalid department code");
}
```

Figure 5-25   Using empty case statements so the same result occurs in multiple cases

On the other hand, you might use strings in a switch structure to determine whether a supervisor name is valid, as shown in the method in Figure 5-26.

```
public static boolean isValidSupervisor(String name)
{
    boolean isValid;
    switch(name)
    {
        case "Jones":
        case "Staples":
        case "Tejano":
            isValid = true;
            break;
        default:
            isValid = false;
    }
    return isValid;
}
```

Figure 5-26   A method that uses a switch structure with string values

When several char variables must be checked and you want to ignore whether they are uppercase or lowercase, one frequently used technique employs empty case statements, as in Figure 5-27.

```
switch(departmentCode)
{
    case 'a':
    case 'A':
        departmentName = "Accounting";
        break;
    case 'm':
    case 'M':
        departmentName = "Marketing";
        break;
    // and so on
}
```

Figure 5-27   Using a switch structure to ignore character case

You are never required to use a switch structure; you can always achieve the same results with nested if statements. The switch structure is simply convenient to use when there are several alternative courses of action that depend on a single integer, character, or string value. In addition, it makes sense to use switch only when a reasonable number of specific matching values need to be tested.

 Watch the video Using the switch Statement.

TWO TRUTHS & A LIE

Using the `switch` Statement

1. When you must make more decisions than Java can support, you use a `switch` statement instead of nested `if...else` statements.

2. The `switch` statement is useful when you need to test a single variable against a series of exact integer or character values.

3. A `break` statement bypasses the rest of its `switch` structure, and execution continues with any statement after the closing curly brace of the `switch` structure.

The false statement is #1. By nesting a series of `if` and `else` statements, you can choose from any number of alternatives. The `switch` statement is just a more convenient way of expressing nested `if...else` statements when the tested value is an integer or character.

 You Do It

Using the `switch` Statement

In this section, you alter the `AssignVolunteer3` program to add more options for donation types, and then use a `switch` statement to assign the appropriate volunteer.

1. Open the **AssignVolunteer3.java** file that you created in a "You Do It" section earlier in this chapter. Change the class name to **AssignVolunteer4**, and immediately save the file as **AssignVolunteer4.java**.

2. Keep the declaration `CLOTHING_CODE`, but replace the `OTHER_CODE` declaration with three new ones:

   ```
   final int FURNITURE_CODE = 2;
   final int ELECTRONICS_CODE = 3;
   final int OTHER_CODE = 4;
   ```

3. Retain the two pricing volunteer declarations, but add two new ones:

   ```
   final String FURNITURE_PRICER = "Walter";
   final String ELECTRONICS_PRICER = "Lydia";
   ```

(continues)

(continued)

4. Replace the output statement that asks the user to enter 1 or 2 with the following simpler statement:

```
System.out.print("Enter an integer... ");
```

In a professional program, you might want to present the user with details about all the options, but this example keeps the prompt simple to save you from excessive typing.

5. Replace the existing `if...else` structure with the following `switch` structure:

```
switch(donationType)
{
    case(CLOTHING_CODE):
        volunteer = CLOTHING_PRICER;
        message = "a clothing donation";
        break;
    case(FURNITURE_CODE):
        volunteer = FURNITURE_PRICER;
        message = "a furniture donation";
        break;
    case(ELECTRONICS_CODE):
        volunteer = ELECTRONICS_PRICER;
        message = "an electronics donation";
        break;
    case(OTHER_CODE):
        volunteer = OTHER_PRICER;
        message = "another donation type";
        break;
    default:
        volunteer = "invalid";
        message = "an invalid donation type";
}
```

6. Save the file, and then compile and execute it. Figure 5-28 shows a typical execution.

(continues)

276

(continued)

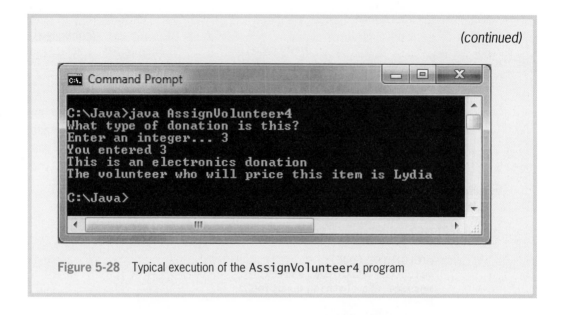

Figure 5-28   Typical execution of the `AssignVolunteer4` program

Using the Conditional and NOT Operators

Besides using `if` statements and `switch` structures, Java provides one more way to make decisions. The **conditional operator** requires three expressions separated with a question mark and a colon and is used as an abbreviated version of the `if...else` structure. As with the `switch` structure, you are never required to use the conditional operator; it is simply a convenient shortcut. The syntax of the conditional operator is:

```
testExpression ? trueResult : falseResult;
```

The first expression, `testExpression`, is a Boolean expression that is evaluated as `true` or `false`. If it is `true`, the entire conditional expression takes on the value of the expression following the question mark (`trueResult`). If the value of the `testExpression` is `false`, the entire expression takes on the value of `falseResult`.

 You have seen many examples of binary operators such as `==` and `&&`. The conditional operator is a **ternary operator**—one that needs three operands. Through Java 6, the conditional operator is the only ternary operator in Java, so it is sometimes referred to as "the" ternary operator. Java 7 introduces a collapsed version of the ternary operator that checks for `null` values assigned to objects. The new operator is called *the Elvis operator* because it uses a question mark and colon together (`?:`); if you view it sideways, it reminds you of Elvis Presley.

For example, suppose you want to assign the smallest price to a sale item. Let the variable a be the advertised price and the variable b be the discounted price on the sale tag. The expression for assigning the smallest cost is:

```
smallerNum = (a < b) ? a : b;
```

When evaluating the expression a < b, where a is less than b, the entire conditional expression takes the value to the left of the colon, a, which then is assigned to smallerNum. If a is not less than b, the expression assumes the value to the right of the colon, b, and b is assigned to smallerNum.

You could achieve the same results with the following if...else structure:

```
if(a < b)
    smallerNum = a;
else
    smallerNum = b;
```

The advantage of using the conditional operator is the conciseness of the statement.

Using the NOT Operator

You use the **NOT operator**, which is written as the exclamation point (!), to negate the result of any Boolean expression. Any expression that evaluates as true becomes false when preceded by the NOT operator, and accordingly, any false expression preceded by the NOT operator becomes true.

For example, suppose a monthly car insurance premium is $200 if the driver is age 25 or younger and $125 if the driver is age 26 or older. Each of the if...else statements in Figure 5-29 correctly assigns the premium values.

```
if(age <= 25)                     if(!(age <= 25))
    premium = 200;                    premium = 125;
else                              else
    premium = 125;                    premium = 200;


if(age >= 26)                     if(!(age >= 26))
    premium = 125;                    premium = 200;
else                              else
    premium = 200;                    premium = 125;
```

Figure 5-29 Four if...else statements that all do the same thing

In Figure 5-29, the statements with the ! operator are somewhat harder to read, particularly because they require the double set of parentheses, but the result of the decision-making process is the same in each case. Using the ! operator is clearer when the value of a Boolean variable is tested. For example, a variable initialized as boolean oldEnough = (age >= 25); can become part of the relatively easy-to-read expression if(!oldEnough)....

TWO TRUTHS & A LIE

Using the Conditional and NOT Operators

1. The conditional operator is used as an abbreviated version of the `if...else` structure and requires two expressions separated with an exclamation point.

2. The NOT operator is written as the exclamation point (!).

3. The value of any false expression becomes true when preceded by the NOT operator.

The false statement is #1. The conditional operator requires three expressions separated with a question mark and a colon.

Understanding Operator Precedence

You can combine as many **&&** or **||** operators as you need to make a decision. For example, if you want to award bonus points (defined as BONUS) to any student who receives a perfect score on any of four quizzes, you might write a statement like the following:

```
if(score1 == PERFECT || score2 == PERFECT ||
   score3 == PERFECT || score4 == PERFECT)
      bonus = BONUS;
else
   bonus = 0;
```

In this case, if at least one of the score variables is equal to the PERFECT constant, the student receives the bonus points.

Although you can combine any number of **&&** or **||** operations in an expression, special care must be taken when you mix them. You learned in Chapter 2 that arithmetic operations have higher and lower precedences, and an operator's precedence makes a difference in how an expression is evaluated. For example, within an arithmetic expression, multiplication and division are always performed prior to addition or subtraction. Table 5-1 shows the precedence of the operators you have used so far.

Precedence	Operator(s)	Symbol(s)
Highest	Logical NOT	!
Intermediate	Multiplication, division, modulus	* / %
	Addition, subtraction	+ -
	Relational	> < >= <=
	Equality	== !=
	Logical AND	&&
	Logical OR	||
	Conditional	?:
Lowest	Assignment	=

Table 5-1 Operator precedence for operators used so far

In general, the order of precedence agrees with common algebraic usage. For example, in any mathematical expression, such as x = a + b, the arithmetic is done first and the assignment is done last, as you would expect. The relationship of && and || might not be as obvious. The && operator has higher precedence than the || operator. For example, consider the program segments shown in Figure 5-30. These code segments are intended to be part of an insurance company program that determines whether an additional premium should be charged to a driver who meets both of the following criteria:

- Has more than two traffic tickets or is under 25 years old
- Is male

```
// Assigns extra premiums incorrectly
if(trafficTickets > 2 || age < 25 && gender == 'M')
   extraPremium = 200;
```
The && operator is evaluated first.

```
// Assigns extra premiums correctly
if((trafficTickets > 2 || age < 25) && gender == 'M')
extraPremium = 200;
```
The expression within the inner parentheses is evaluated first.

Figure 5-30 Two comparisons using && and ||

One way to remember the precedence of the AND and OR operators is to remember that they are evaluated in alphabetical order.

Consider a 30-year-old female driver with three traffic tickets; according to the stated criteria, she should not be assigned the extra premium because she is not male. With the first `if` statement in Figure 5-30, the `&&` operator takes precedence, so `age < 25 && gender == 'M'` is evaluated first. The value is `false` because `age` is not less than 25, so the expression is reduced to `trafficTickets > 2` or `false`. Because the value of the tickets variable is greater than 2, the entire expression is `true`, and $200 is assigned to `extraPremium`, even though it should not be.

In the second `if` statement shown in Figure 5-30, parentheses have been added so the `||` operator is evaluated first. The expression `trafficTickets > 2 || age < 25` is `true` because the value of `trafficTickets` is 3. So the expression evolves to `true && gender == 'M'`. Because gender is not 'M', the value of the entire expression is `false`, and the `extraPremium` value is not assigned 200, which is correct. Even when an expression would be evaluated as you intend without adding extra parentheses, you can always add them to help others more easily understand your programs.

The following two conventions are important to keep in mind:

- The order in which you use operators makes a difference.

- You can always use parentheses to change precedence or make your intentions clearer.

TWO TRUTHS & A LIE

Understanding Operator Precedence

1. Assume p, q, and r are all Boolean variables that have been assigned the value true. After the following statement executes, the value of p is still true.
   `p = !q || r;`

2. Assume p, q, and r are all Boolean variables that have been assigned the value true. After the following statement executes, the value of p is still true.
   `p = !(!q && !r);`

3. Assume p, q, and r are all Boolean variables that have been assigned the value true. After the following statement executes, the value of p is still true.
   `p = !(q || !r);`

The false statement is #3. If p, q, and r are all Boolean variables that have been assigned the value true, then after `p = !(q || !r);` executes, the value of p is false. First q is evaluated as true, so the entire expression within the parentheses is true. The leading NOT operator reverses that result to false and assigns it to p.

Adding Decisions and Constructors to Instance Methods

You frequently will want to use what you have learned about decision making to control the allowed values in objects' fields. Whether values are assigned to objects by constructors or by mutator methods, you often will need to use decisions to control values.

For example, suppose that you create an Employee class as shown in Figure 5-31. The class contains two fields that hold an employee ID number and pay rate. The constructor accepts values for these fields as parameters, but instead of simply assigning the parameters to the fields, the code determines whether each value is within the allowed limits for the field. Similar logic could be used in any set methods created for the class. Using decisions helps you ensure that fields have acceptable values.

```java
public class Employee
{
    private int empNum;
    private double payRate;
    public int MAX_EMP_NUM = 9999;
    public double MAX_RATE = 60.00;
    Employee(int num, double rate)
    {
        if(num <= MAX_EMP_NUM)
            empNum = num;
        else
            empNum = MAX_EMP_NUM;
        if(payRate <= MAX_RATE)
            payRate = rate;
        else
            payRate = 0;
    }
    public int getEmpNum()
    {
        return empNum;
    }
    public double getPayRate()
    {
        return payRate;
    }
}
```

Figure 5-31   The Employee class that contains a constructor that makes decisions

You Do It

Adding Decisions to Constructors and Instance Methods

In this section, you modify the `DogTriathlonParticipant` class you created in Chapter 4. Because some points are awarded for participation in each event, a score of 0 is not possible unless a dog did not participate. In the existing class, the constructor accepts the number of events in which a dog participated and the participant's score in each event. Currently, there is no way to check whether these values are in agreement. Now, you can modify the class so that the number of events matches the number of valid scores supplied to the constructor.

1. Open the **DogTriathlonParticipant.java** file that you created in Chapter 4. Change the class name to `DogTriathlonParticipant2`, and immediately save the file as **DogTriathlonParticipant2.java**.

2. Change the constructor name to `DogTriathlonParticipant2`.

3. If 0 is assigned to the number of events in the existing program, computing the average score produces a nonnumeric result. Now that you know how to use decisions, you can fix this problem. In place of the arithmetic statement that produces the average score using division, use the following `if…else` structure:

   ```
   if(NUM_EVENTS == 0)
       avg = 0;
   else
       avg = (double) total / NUM_EVENTS;
   ```

4. Add a Boolean field to the list of class fields. This field holds `true` if the number of events reported matches the number of nonzero scores. Otherwise, the field holds `false`:

   ```
   private boolean scoresAgree;
   ```

5. There are several ways to ensure that the number of events passed to the constructor matches the number of nonzero scores passed. One way is to add 1 to a total for each nonzero score and then determine whether that total equals the passed number of events. To accomplish this, first add the following code to the constructor immediately after the statements that assign values to the name and number of events. These statements declare a variable that holds the number of nonzero scores passed to the constructor, and then add 1 to the variable for each nonzero event score:

(continues)

(continued)

```
int totalNot0 = 0;
if(score1 != 0)
    totalNot0 = totalNot0 + 1;
if(score2 != 0)
    totalNot0 = totalNot0 + 1;
if(score3 != 0)
    totalNot0 = totalNot0 + 1;
```

6. Compare the number of events to the total of nonzero scores, and set the Boolean variable scores Agree:

```
if(numEvents == totalNot0)
    scoresAgree = true;
else
    scoresAgree = false;
```

7. Replace the statements that unconditionally assigned values to obedienceScore, conformationScore, and agilityScore with the following if...else structure, which assigns the constructor's parameters to the three scores only when scoresAgree is true.

```
if(scoresAgree)
{
    obedienceScore = score1;
    conformationScore = score2;
    agilityScore = score3;
}
else
{
    obedienceScore = 0;
    conformationScore = 0;
    agilityScore = 0;
}
```

8. In the display() method for the DogTriathlonParticipant2 class, add the following statement that displays a special notice if an error occurred in the number of events value.

```
if(!scoresAgree)
    System.out.println("Notice! Number of events for " +
name + " does not agree with scores reported.");
```

9. Save the file and compile it.

10. Open the **TestDogs.java** file that you created in a "You Do It" section in Chapter 4. Rename the class **TestDogs2**, and immediately save the file as **TestDogs2.java**.

(continues)

(continued)

11. Change `DogTriathlonParticipant` to **DogTriathlonParticipant2** in the six places it occurs in the three object declarations.

12. Change the object declarations so that the number of events and the number of nonzero scores used as constructor arguments agree for some objects but not for others.

13. Save the file, and then compile and execute it. Figure 5-32 shows a typical execution in which one participant's entries are valid but the other two contain errors.

Figure 5-32   Execution of `TestDogs2` program

14. Change the values in the `TestDogs2` program. Recompile and reexecute the program several times to ensure that using various combinations of number of events and event scores produces appropriate results.

15. On your own, modify the `DogTriathlonParticipant2` class and rename it **DogTriathlon3**. In this version, do not use a count of the nonzero score parameters to determine whether the number of events matches the number of valid scores used as arguments. Instead, use only decisions to ensure that the parameters are in agreement. Save the file as **DogTriathlon3.java**, and create a file named **TestDogs3.java** that you can use to test the class. Be sure to test every possible combination of constructor parameters in the `TestDogs3` class—for example, when the events parameter is 2, it is correct whether the nonzero scores are the first and second, the first and third, or the second and third.

Don't Do It

- Don't ignore subtleties in boundaries used in decision making. For example, selecting employees who make less than $20 an hour is different from selecting employees who make $20 an hour or less.

- Don't use the assignment operator instead of the comparison operator when testing for equality.

- Don't insert a semicolon after the Boolean expression in an `if` statement; insert the semicolon after the entire statement is completed.

- Don't forget to block a set of statements with curly braces when several statements depend on the `if` or the `else` statement.

- Don't forget to include a complete Boolean expression on each side of an `&&` or `||` operator.

- Don't try to use a `switch` structure to test anything other than an integer, character, or string value.

- Don't forget a `break` statement if one is required by the logic of your `switch` structure.

- Don't use the standard relational operators to compare objects; use them only with the built-in Java types. In the chapter *Characters, Strings, and the StringBuilder*, you will learn how to compare `Strings` correctly, and in the chapter *Advanced Inheritance Concepts* you will learn to compare other objects.

Key Terms

Pseudocode is a tool that helps programmers plan a program's logic by writing plain English statements.

A **flowchart** is a tool that helps programmers plan a program's logic by writing the steps in diagram form, as a series of shapes connected by arrows.

A **sequence structure** is a logical structure in which one step follows another unconditionally.

A **decision structure** is a logical structure that involves choosing between alternative courses of action based on some value within a program.

True or `false` values are **Boolean values**; every computer decision results in a Boolean value.

In Java, the simplest statement you can use to make a decision is the **if statement**; you use it to write a single-alternative decision.

The **equivalency operator** (==) compares values and returns `true` if they are equal.

An **empty statement** contains only a semicolon.

A **single-alternative if** is a decision structure that performs an action, or not, based on one alternative.

A **dual-alternative if** is a decision structure that takes one of two possible courses of action.

In Java, the **if...else statement** provides the mechanism to perform one action when a Boolean expression evaluates as `true` and to perform a different action when a Boolean expression evaluates as `false`.

The **if clause** of an if...else statement is the part that executes when the evaluated Boolean expression is true.

The **else clause** of an if...else statement is the part that executes when the evaluated Boolean expression is false.

A **nested if statement** contains an if structure within another if structure.

The **logical AND operator** uses two Boolean expressions as operands and evaluates to `true` if both operands are `true`. The AND operator is written as two ampersands (&&).

The **logical OR operator** uses two Boolean expressions as operands and evaluates to `true` if either operand is `true`. The OR operator is written as two pipes (||).

Short-circuit evaluation describes the feature of the AND and OR operators in which evaluation is performed only as far as necessary to make a final decision.

A **range check** is a series of statements that determine within which of a set of ranges a value falls.

An **else...if clause** is a format used in nested if statements in which each instance of else and its subsequent if are placed on the same line.

The **switch statement** uses up to four keywords to test a single variable against a series of exact integer or character values. The keywords are `switch`, `case`, `break`, and `default`.

The **conditional operator** requires three expressions separated with a question mark and a colon and is used as an abbreviated version of the if...else structure.

A **ternary operator** is one that needs three operands.

You use the **NOT operator**, which is written as the exclamation point (!), to negate the result of any Boolean expression.

Chapter Summary

- Making a decision involves choosing between two alternative courses of action based on some value within a program.

- You can use the `if` statement to make a decision based on a Boolean expression that evaluates as `true` or `false`. If the Boolean expression enclosed in parentheses within an `if` statement is `true`, the subsequent statement or block executes. A single-alternative `if` performs an action based on one alternative; a dual-alternative `if`, or `if...else`, provides the mechanism for performing one action when a Boolean expression is `true` and a different action when the expression is `false`.

- To execute more than one statement that depends on the evaluation of a Boolean expression, you use a pair of curly braces to place the dependent statements within a block. Within an `if` or an `else` statement, you can code as many dependent statements as you need, including other `if` and `else` statements.

- Nested `if` statements are particularly useful when two conditions must be met before some action occurs.

- You can use the AND operator (`&&`) within a Boolean expression to determine whether two expressions are both `true`. You use the OR operator (`||`) when you want to carry out some action even if only one of two conditions is `true`.

- New programmers frequently cause errors in their `if` statements when they perform a range check incorrectly or inefficiently, or when they use the wrong operator while trying to make an AND or OR decision.

- You use the `switch` statement to test a single variable against a series of exact integer, character, or string values.

- The conditional operator requires three expressions, a question mark, and a colon and is used as an abbreviated version of the `if...else` statement. The NOT operator (`!`) negates the result of any Boolean expression.

- Operator precedence makes a difference in how expressions are evaluated. You can always use parentheses to change precedence or make your intentions clearer.

- Decisions are frequently used to control field values in constructors and mutator methods.

Review Questions

1. The logical structure in which one instruction occurs after another with no branching is a ――――――――― .

   a. sequence   c. loop

   b. selection   d. case

2. Which of the following is typically used in a flowchart to indicate a decision?

    a. square

    b. rectangle

    c. diamond

    d. oval

3. Which of the following is not a type of `if` statement?

    a. single-alternative `if`

    b. dual-alternative `if`

    c. reverse `if`

    d. nested `if`

4. A decision is based on a(n) ——————— value.

    a. Boolean

    b. absolute

    c. definitive

    d. convoluted

5. In Java, the value of (4 > 7) is ———————.

    a. 4

    b. 7

    c. `true`

    d. `false`

6. Assuming the variable q has been assigned the value 3, which of the following statements displays XXX?

    a. `if(q > 0) System.out.println("XXX");`

    b. `if(q > 7); System.out.println("XXX");`

    c. Both of the above statements display XXX.

    d. Neither of the above statements displays XXX.

7. What is the output of the following code segment?

    ```
    t = 10;
    if(t > 7)
    {
        System.out.print("AAA");
        System.out.print("BBB");
    }
    ```

    a. AAA

    b. BBB

    c. AAABBB

    d. nothing

8. What is the output of the following code segment?

    ```
    t = 10;
    if(t > 7)
        System.out.print("AAA");
        System.out.print("BBB");
    ```

    a. AAA

    b. BBB

    c. AAABBB

    d. nothing

9. What is the output of the following code segment?

```
t = 7;
if(t > 7)
   System.out.print("AAA");
   System.out.print("BBB");
```

   a.   AAA   c.   AAABBB

   b.   BBB   d.   nothing

10. When you code an if statement within another if statement, as in the following, then the if statements are _____ .

```
if(a > b)
   if(c > d)x = 0;
```

   a.   notched   c.   nested

   b.   nestled   d.   sheltered

11. The operator that combines two conditions into a single Boolean value that is true only when both of the conditions are true, but is false otherwise, is _____ .

   a. $$ c. ||

   b.   !!   d.   &&

12. The operator that combines two conditions into a single Boolean value that is true when at least one of the conditions is true is _____ .

   a. $$ c. ||

   b.   !!   d.   &&

13. Assuming a variable f has been initialized to 5, which of the following statements sets g to 0?

   a.   `if(f > 6 || f == 5) g = 0;`

   b.   `if(f < 3 || f > 4) g = 0;`

   c.   `if(f >= 0 || f < 2) g = 0;`

   d.   All of the above statements set g to 0.

14. Which of the following groups has the lowest operator precedence?

   a.   relational   c.   addition

   b.   equality   d.   logical OR

15. Which of the following statements correctly outputs the names of voters who live in district 6 and all voters who live in district 7?

a. `if(district == 6 || 7)`
    `System.out.println("Name is " + name);`

b. `if(district == 6 || district == 7)`
    `System.out.println("Name is " + name);`

c. `if(district = 6 && district == 7)`
    `System.out.println("Name is " + name);`

d. two of these

16. Which of the following displays "Error" when a student ID is less than 1000 or more than 9999?

a. `if(stuId < 1000) if(stuId > 9999)`
    `System.out.println("Error");`

b. `if(stuId < 1000 && stuId > 9999)`
    `System.out.println("Error");`

c. `if(stuId < 1000)`
    `   System.out.println("Error");`
    `else`
    `  if(stuId > 9999)`
    `     System.out.println("Error");`

d. Two of these are correct.

17. You can use the ——————— statement to terminate a `switch` structure.

a. `switch`   c. `case`
b. `end`   d. `break`

18. The argument tested in a `switch` structure can be any of the following *except* a(n) ——————— .

a. `int`   c. `double`
b. `char`   d. `String`

19. Assuming a variable w has been assigned the value 15, what does the following statement do?

`w == 15 ? x = 2 : x = 0;`

a. assigns 15 to w   c. assigns 0 to x
b. assigns 2 to x   d. nothing

20. Assuming a variable y has been assigned the value 6, the value of `!(y < 7)` is —————— .

    a. 6   c. `true`
    b. 7   d. `false`

Exercises

Programming Exercises

1. Write an application that asks a user to enter an integer. Display a statement that indicates whether the integer is even or odd. Save the file as **EvenOdd.java**.

2. Write an application that prompts the user for the day's high and low temperatures. If the high is greater than or equal to 90 degrees, display the message, "Heat warning." If the low is less than 32 degrees, display the message "Freeze warning." If the difference between the high and low temperatures is more than 40 degrees, display the message, "Large temperature swing." Save the file as **Temperatures.java**.

3. a. Write an application for the Summerdale Condo Sales office; the program determines the price of a condominium. Ask the user to choose *1* for park view, *2* for golf course view, or *3* for lake view. The output is the name of the chosen view as well as the price of the condo. Park view condos are $150,000, condos with golf course views are $170,000, and condos with lake views are $210,000. If the user enters an invalid code, set the price to 0. Save the file as **CondoSales.java**.

   b. Add a prompt to the `CondoSales` application to ask the user to specify a (1) garage or a (2) parking space, but only if the condo view selection is valid. Add $5,000 to the price of any condo with a garage. If the parking value is invalid, display an appropriate message and assume that the price is for a condo with no garage. Save the file as **CondoSales2.java**.

4. a. The Williamsburg Women's Club offers scholarships to local high school students who meet any of several criteria. Write an application that prompts the user for a student's numeric high school grade point average (for example, 3.2), the student's number of extracurricular activities, and the student's number of service activities. Display the message "Scholarship candidate" if the student has any of the following:

   • A grade point average of 3.8 or above and at least one extracurricular activity and one service activity

   • A grade point average below 3.8 but at least 3.4 and a total of at least three extracurricular and service activities

   • A grade point average below 3.4 but at least 3.0 and at least two extracurricular activities and three service activities

If the student does not meet any of the qualification criteria, display "Not a candidate." Save the file as **Scholarship.java**.

b. Modify the Scholarship application so that if a user enters a grade point average under 0 or over 4.0, or a negative value for either of the activities, an error message appears. Save the file as **Scholarship2.java**.

5. Write an application that displays a menu of three items for the Jivin' Java Coffee Shop as follows:

(1) American	1.99
(2) Espresso	2.50
(3) Latte	2.15

Prompt the user to choose an item using the number (1, 2, or 3) that corresponds to the item, or to enter *0* to quit the application. After the user makes the first selection, if the choice is *0*, display a total bill of $0. Otherwise, display the menu again. The user should respond to this prompt with another item number to order or *0* to quit. If the user types *0*, display the cost of the single requested item. If the user types *1*, *2*, or *3*, add the cost of the second item to the first, and then display the menu a third time. If the user types *0* to quit, display the total cost of the two items; otherwise, display the total for all three selections. Save the file as **Coffee.java**.

6. Barnhill Fastener Company runs a small factory. The company employs workers who are paid one of three hourly rates depending on skill level:

Skill Level	Hourly Pay Rate ($)
1	17.00
2	20.00
3	22.00

Each factory worker might work any number of hours per week; any hours over 40 are paid at one and one-half times the usual rate.

In addition, workers in skill levels 2 and 3 can elect the following insurance options:

Option	Explanation	Weekly Cost to Employee ($)
1	Medical insurance	32.50
2	Dental insurance	20.00
3	Long-term disability insurance	10.00

Also, workers in skill level 3 can elect to participate in the retirement plan at 3% of their gross pay.

Write an interactive Java payroll application that calculates the net pay for a factory worker. The program prompts the user for skill level and hours worked, as well as appropriate insurance and retirement options for the employee's skill level category. The application displays: (1) the hours worked, (2) the hourly pay rate, (3) the regular pay for 40 hours, (4) the overtime pay, (5) the total of regular and overtime pay, and (6) the total itemized deductions. If the deductions exceed the gross pay, display an error message; otherwise, calculate and display (7) the net pay after all the deductions have been subtracted from the gross. Save the file as **Pay.java**.

7. Create a class for Shutterbug's Camera Store, which is having a digital camera sale. The class is named DigitalCamera, and it contains data fields for a brand, the number of megapixels in the resolution, and price. Include a constructor that takes arguments for the brand and megapixels. If the megapixel parameter is greater than 10, the constructor sets it to 10. The sale price is set based on the resolution; any camera with 6 megapixels or fewer is $99, and all other cameras are $129. Also include a method that displays DigitalCamera details. Write an application named TestDigitalCamera in which you instantiate at least four objects, prompt the user for values for the camera brand and number of megapixels, and display all the values. Save the files as **DigitalCamera.java** and **TestDigitalCamera.java**.

8. Create a class for the Parks Department in Cloverdale. The class is named Park, and it contains a String field for the name of the park, an integer field for the size in acres, and four Boolean fields that hold whether the park has each of these features: picnic facilities, a tennis court, a playground, and a swimming pool. Include get and set methods for each field. Include code in the method that sets the number of acres and does not allow a negative number or a number over 400. Save the file as **Park.java**.

Then, create a program with methods that do the following:

- Accepts a Park parameter and returns a Boolean value that indicates whether the Park has both picnic facilities and a playground.

- Accepts a Park parameter and four Boolean parameters that represent requests for the previously mentioned Park features. The method returns true if the Park has all the requested features.

- Accepts a `Park` parameter and four Boolean parameters that represent requests for the previously mentioned `Park` features. The method returns `true` if the `Park` has exactly all the requested features and no others.

- Accepts a `Park` parameter and returns the number of facilities that the `Park` features.

- Accepts two `Park` parameters and returns the larger `Park`.

Declare at least three `Park` objects, and demonstrate that all the methods work correctly. Save the program as **TestPark.java**.

9. a. Create a class named `Invoice` that holds an invoice number, balance due, and three fields representing the month, day, and year when the balance is due. Create a constructor that accepts values for all five data fields. Within the constructor, assign each argument to the appropriate field with the following exceptions:

- If an invoice number is less than 1000, force the invoice number to 0.

- If the month field is less than 1 or greater than 12, force the month field to 0.

- If the day field is less than 1 or greater than 31, force the day field to 0.

- If the year field is less than 2011 or greater than 2017, force the year field to 0.

In the `Invoice` class, include a display method that displays all the fields on an `Invoice` object. Save the file as **Invoice.java**.

b. Write an application containing a `main()` method that declares several `Invoice` objects, proving that all the statements in the constructor operate as specified. Save the file as **TestInvoice.java**.

c. Modify the constructor in the `Invoice` class so that the day is not greater than 31, 30, or 28, depending on the month. For example, if a user tries to create an invoice for April 31, force it to April 30. Also, if the month is invalid, and thus forced to 0, also force the day to 0. Save the modified `Invoice` class as **Invoice2.java**. Then modify the `TestInvoice` class to create `Invoice2` objects. Create enough objects to test every decision in the constructor. Save this file as **TestInvoice2.java**.

10. Use the Web to locate the lyrics to the traditional song "The Twelve Days of Christmas." The song contains a list of gifts received for the holiday. The list is cumulative so that as each "day" passes, a new verse contains all the words of the previous verse, plus a new item. Write an application that displays the words to the song starting with any day the user enters. (*Hint*: Use a `switch` statement with `cases` in descending day order and without any `break` statements so that the lyrics for any day repeat all the lyrics for previous days.) Save the file as **TwelveDays.java**.

Debugging Exercises

1. Each of the following files in the Chapter05 folder of your downloadable student files has syntax and/or logic errors. In each case, determine the problem and fix the program. After you correct the errors, save each file using the same filename preceded with *Fix*. For example, save DebugFive1.java as FixDebugFive1.java.

   a. DebugFive1.java

   b. DebugFive2.java

   c. DebugFive3.java

   d. DebugFive4.java

Game Zone

1. In Chapter 1, you created a class called RandomGuess. In this game, players guess a number, the application generates a random number, and players determine whether they were correct. Now that you can make decisions, modify the application so it allows a player to enter a guess before the random number is displayed and then displays a message indicating whether the player's guess was correct, too high, or too low. Save the file as **RandomGuess2.java**. (After you finish the next chapter, you will be able to modify the application so that the user can continue to guess until the correct answer is entered.)

2. Create a lottery game application. Generate three random numbers (see Appendix D for help in doing so), each between 0 and 9. Allow the user to guess three numbers. Compare each of the user's guesses to the three random numbers and display a message that includes the user's guess, the randomly determined three-digit number, and the amount of money the user has won as follows:

Matching Numbers	Award ($)
Any one matching	10
Two matching	100
Three matching, not in order	1,000
Three matching in exact order	1,000,000
No matches	0

Make certain that your application accommodates repeating digits. For example, if a user guesses 1, 2, and 3, and the randomly generated digits are 1, 1, and 1, do not give the user credit for three correct guesses—just one. Save the file as **Lottery.java**.

3. In Chapter 3, you created a Card class. Modify the Card class so the setValue() method does not allow a Card's value to be less than 1 or higher than 13. If the argument to setValue() is out of range, assign 1 to the Card's value.

    In Chapter 3, you also created a PickTwoCards application that randomly selects two playing cards and displays their values. In that application, all Card objects arbitrarily were assigned a suit represented by a single character, but they could have different values, and the player observed which of two Card objects had the higher value. Now, modify the application so the suit and the value both are chosen randomly. Using two Card objects, play a very simple version of the card game War. Deal two Cards—one for the computer and one for the player—and determine the higher card, then display a message indicating whether the cards are equal, the computer won, or the player won. (Playing cards are considered equal when they have the same value, no matter what their suit is.) For this game, assume the Ace (value 1) is low. Make sure that the two Cards dealt are not the same Card. For example, a deck cannot contain more than one Card representing the 2 of spades. If two cards are chosen to have the same value, change the suit for one of them. Save the application as **War.java**. (After you study the chapter *Arrays*, you will be able to create a more sophisticated War game in which you use an entire deck without repeating cards.)

4. In Chapter 4, you created a Die class from which you could instantiate an object containing a random value from 1 through 6. You also wrote an application that randomly "throws" two dice and displays their values. Modify the application so it determines whether the two dice are the same, the first has a higher value, or the second has a higher value. Save the application as **TwoDice2.java**.

5. In the game Rock Paper Scissors, two players simultaneously choose one of three options: rock, paper, or scissors. If both players choose the same option, then the result is a tie. However, if they choose differently, the winner is determined as follows:

    • Rock beats scissors, because a rock can break a pair of scissors.

    • Scissors beats paper, because scissors can cut paper.

    • Paper beats rock, because a piece of paper can cover a rock.

    Create a game in which the computer randomly chooses rock, paper, or scissors. Let the user enter a number 1, 2, or 3, each representing one of the three choices. Then, determine the winner. Save the application as **RockPaperScissors.java**. (In the chapter *Characters, Strings, and the* StringBuilder, you will modify the game so that the user enters a string for *rock*, *paper*, and *scissors*, rather than just entering a number.)

Case Problems

1. a. Carly's Catering provides meals for parties and special events. In Chapters 3 and 4, you created an Event class for the company. Now, make the following changes to the class:

   - Currently, the class contains a field that holds the price for an Event. Now add another field that holds the price per guest, and add a public method to return its value.

   - Currently, the class contains a constant for the price per guest. Replace that field with two fields—a lower price per guest that is $32, and a higher price per guest that is $35.

   - Add a new method named isLargeEvent() that returns true if the number of guests is 50 or greater and otherwise returns false.

   - Modify the method that sets the number of guests so that a large Event (over 50 guests) uses the lower price per guest to set the new pricePerGuest field and calculate the total Event price. A small Event uses the higher price.

   Save the file as **Event.java**.

   b. In Chapter 4, you modified the EventDemo class to demonstrate two Event objects. Now, modify that class again as follows:

   - Instantiate three Event objects, and prompt the user for values for each object.

   - Change the method that displays Event details to use the new isLargeEvent() method and the new price per guest value. Use the display method with all three objects.

   - Create a method that accepts two Event objects and returns the larger one based on number of guests. (If the Events have the same number of guests, you can return either object.) Call this method three times—once with each pair of instantiated Events—and display the event number and number of guests for each argument as well as the event number and number of guests for the larger Event.

   Save the file as **EventDemo.java**.

2. a. Sammy's Seashore Supplies rents beach equipment such as kayaks, canoes, beach chairs, and umbrellas to tourists. In Chapters 3 and 4, you created a Rental class for the company.

Now, make the following change to the class:

- Currently, a rental price is calculated as $40 per hour plus $1 for each minute over a full hour. This means that a customer who rents equipment for 41 or more minutes past an hour pays more than a customer who waits until the next hour to return the equipment. Change the price calculation so that a customer pays $40 for each full hour and $1 for each extra minute up to and including 40 minutes.

Save the file as **Rental.java**.

b. In Chapter 4, you modified the RentalDemo class to demonstrate a Rental object. Now, modify that class again as follows:

- Instantiate three Rental objects, and prompt the user for values for each object. Display the details for each object to verify that the new price calculation works correctly.

- Create a method that accepts two Rental objects and returns the one with the longer rental time. (If the Rentals have the same time, you can return either object.) Call this method three times—once with each pair of instantiated Rentals—and display the contract number and time in hours and minutes for each argument as well as the contract number of the longer Rental.

Save the file as **RentalDemo.java**.

Looping

In this chapter, you will:

◎ Learn about the loop structure

◎ Create `while` loops

◎ Use shortcut arithmetic operators

◎ Create `for` loops

◎ Create `do...while` loops

◎ Nest loops

◎ Improve loop performance

Learning About the Loop Structure

If making decisions is what makes programs seem smart, looping is what makes programs seem powerful. A **loop** is a structure that allows repeated execution of a block of statements. Within a looping structure, a Boolean expression is evaluated. If it is true, a block of statements called the **loop body** executes and the Boolean expression is evaluated again. The loop body can be a single statement or a block of statements between curly braces. As long as the expression is true, the statements in the loop body continue to execute. When the Boolean evaluation is false, the loop ends. One execution of any loop is called an **iteration**. Figure 6-1 shows a diagram of the logic of a loop.

In Java, you can use several mechanisms to create loops. In this chapter, you learn to use three types of loops:

- A while loop, in which the loop-controlling Boolean expression is the first statement in the loop

- A for loop, which is usually used as a concise format in which to execute loops

- A do...while loop, in which the loop-controlling Boolean expression is the last statement in the loop

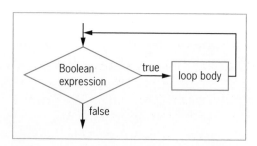

Figure 6-1 Flowchart of a loop structure

Creating while Loops

You can use a **while loop** to execute a body of statements continually as long as the Boolean expression that controls entry into the loop continues to be true. In Java, a while loop consists of the keyword while followed by a Boolean expression within parentheses, followed by the body of the loop.

You can use a while loop when you need to perform a task either a predetermined or unpredictable number of times. A loop that executes a specific number of times is a **definite loop**, or a counted loop. On the other hand, the number of times the loop executes might not be determined until the program is running. Such a loop is an **indefinite loop** because you don't know how many times it will eventually loop.

Writing a Definite while Loop

To write a definite loop, you initialize a **loop control variable**, a variable whose value determines whether loop execution continues. While the Boolean value that results from comparing the loop control variable and another value is true, the body of the while loop continues to execute. In the body of the loop, you must include a statement that alters the loop control variable. For example, the program segment shown in Figure 6-2 displays the series of integers 1 through 10. The variable val is the loop control variable—it starts the loop holding a value of 1, and while the value remains under 11, val continues to be output and increased.

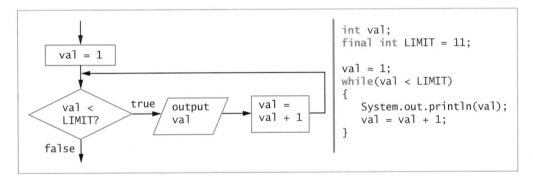

Figure 6-2   A while loop that displays the integers 1 through 10

When you write applications containing loops, it is easy to make mistakes. For example, executing the code shown in Figure 6-3 causes the message "Hello" to be displayed forever (theoretically) because there is no code to end the loop. A loop that never ends is called an **infinite loop**.

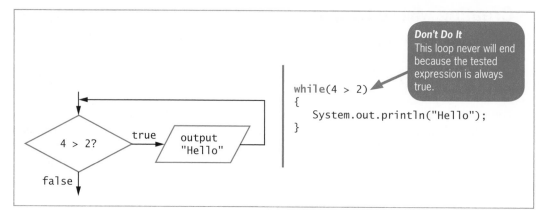

Figure 6-3 A loop that displays "Hello" infinitely

An infinite loop might not actually execute infinitely. Depending on the tasks the loop performs, eventually the computer memory might be exhausted (literally and figuratively) and execution might stop. Also, it's possible that the processor has a time-out feature that forces the loop to end. Either way, and depending on your system, quite a bit of time could pass before the loop stops running.

As an inside joke to programmers, the address of Apple Computer, Inc. is One Infinite Loop, Cupertino, California.

In Figure 6-3, the expression 4 > 2 evaluates to `true`. You obviously never need to make such an evaluation, but if you do so in this `while` loop, the body of the loop is entered and "Hello" is displayed. Next, the expression is evaluated again. The expression 4 > 2 is still `true`, so the body is entered again. "Hello" is displayed repeatedly; the loop never finishes because 4 > 2 is never `false`.

It is a bad idea to write an infinite loop intentionally. However, even experienced programmers write them by accident. So, before you start writing loops, it is good to know how to exit from an infinite loop. You might suspect an infinite loop if the same output is displayed repeatedly, or if the screen simply remains idle for an extended period of time without displaying expected output. If you think your application is in an infinite loop, you can press and hold Ctrl, and then press C or Break; the looping program should terminate. (On many keyboards, the Break key is also the Pause key.)

To prevent a `while` loop from executing infinitely, three separate actions must occur:

- A loop control variable is initialized to a starting value.
- The loop control variable is tested in the `while` statement.
- The loop control variable is altered within the body of the loop. The variable must be altered so that the test expression can eventually evaluate to `false` and the loop can end.

All of these conditions are met by the example in Figure 6-4. First, a loop control variable loopCount is named and set to a value of 1. Second, the statement while(loopCount < 3) is tested. Third, the loop body is executed because the loop control variable loopCount is less than 3. Note that the loop body shown in Figure 6-4 consists of two statements made into a block by their surrounding curly braces. The first statement displays "Hello," and then the second statement adds 1 to loopCount. The next time loopCount is evaluated, it is 2. It is still less than 3, so the loop body executes again. "Hello" is displayed a second time, and loopCount becomes 3. Finally, because the expression loopCount < 3 now evaluates to false, the loop ends. Program execution then continues with any subsequent statements.

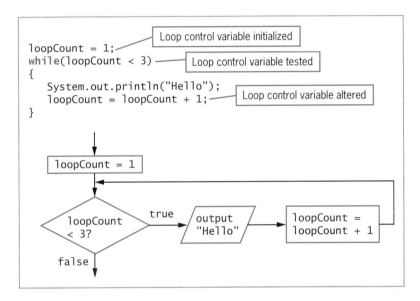

Figure 6-4 A while loop that displays "Hello" twice

Pitfall: Failing to Alter the Loop Control Variable Within the Loop Body

It is important that the loop control variable be altered within the body of the loop. Figure 6-5 shows the same code as in Figure 6-4, but the curly braces have been eliminated. In this case, the while loop body ends at the semicolon that appears at the end of the "Hello" statement. Adding 1 to the loopCount is no longer part of a block that contains the loop, so the value of loopCount never changes, and an infinite loop is created.

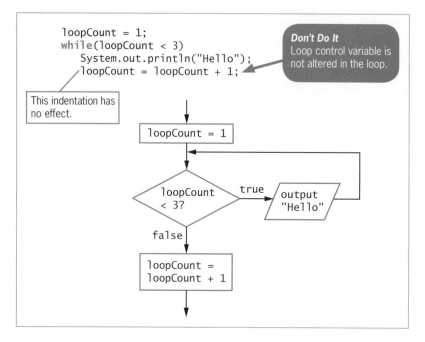

Figure 6-5   A `while` loop that displays "Hello" infinitely because `loopCount` is not altered in the loop body

Pitfall: Creating a Loop with an Empty Body

As with the decision-making `if` statement that you learned about in Chapter 5, placement of the statement-ending semicolon is important when you work with the `while` statement. If a semicolon is mistakenly placed at the end of the partial statement `while(loopCount < 3);`, as shown in Figure 6-6, the loop is also infinite. This loop has an **empty body**, or a body with no statements in it. So, the Boolean expression is evaluated, and because it is `true`, the loop body is entered. Because the loop body is empty, no action is taken, and the Boolean expression is evaluated again. Nothing has changed, so it is still `true`, the empty body is entered, and the infinite loop continues.

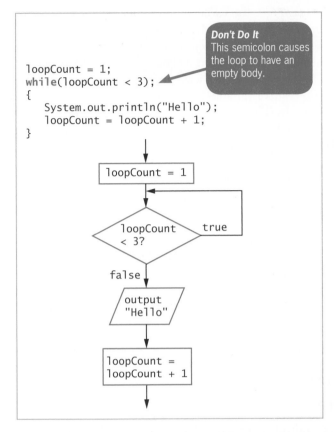

```
loopCount = 1;
while(loopCount < 3);
{
    System.out.println("Hello");
    loopCount = loopCount + 1;
}
```

Don't Do It
This semicolon causes the loop to have an empty body.

Figure 6-6 A while loop that loops infinitely with no output because the loop body is empty

Altering a Definite Loop's Control Variable

A definite loop is a **counter-controlled loop** because the loop control variable is changed by counting. It is very common to alter the value of a loop control variable by adding 1 to it, or **incrementing** the variable. However, not all loops are controlled by adding 1. The loop shown in Figure 6-7 displays "Hello" twice, just as the loop in Figure 6-4 does, but its loop is controlled by subtracting 1 from a loop control variable, or **decrementing** it.

```
loopCount = 3;
while(loopCount > 1)
{
    System.out.println("Hello");
    loopCount = loopCount - 1;
}
```

Figure 6-7 A while loop that displays "Hello" twice, decrementing the loopCount variable in the loop body

306

In the program segment shown in Figure 6-7, the variable loopCount begins with a value of 3. The loopCount is greater than 1, so the loop body displays "Hello" and decrements loopCount to 2. The Boolean expression in the while loop is tested again. Because 2 is more than 1, "Hello" is displayed again, and loopCount becomes 1. Now loopCount is not greater than 1, so the loop ends. There are many ways to execute a loop two times. For example, you can initialize a loop control variable to 10 and continue while the value is greater than 8, decreasing the value by 1 each time you pass through the loop. Similarly, you can initialize the loop control variable to 12, continue while it is greater than 2, and decrease the value by 5 each time. In general, you should not use such unusual methods to count repetitions because they simply make a program confusing. To execute a loop a specific number of times, the clearest and best method is to start the loop control variable at 0 or 1, increment by 1 each time through the loop, and stop when the loop control variable reaches the appropriate limit.

When you first start programming, it seems reasonable to initialize counter values to 1, and that is a workable approach. However, many seasoned programmers start counter values at 0 because they are used to doing so when working with arrays. When you study arrays in the chapter *Introduction to Arrays*, you will learn that their elements are numbered beginning with 0.

Watch the video *Looping*.

Writing an Indefinite while Loop

You are not required to alter a loop control variable by adding to it or subtracting from it. Often, the value of a loop control variable is not altered by arithmetic, but instead is altered by user input. Instead of being a counter-controlled loop, an indefinite loop is an **event-controlled loop**. That is, an event occurs that determines whether the loop continues. An event-controlled loop is a type of indefinite loop because you don't know how many times it will eventually repeat. For example, perhaps you want to continue performing some task as long as the user indicates a desire to continue by pressing a key. In this case, while you are writing the program, you do not know whether the loop eventually will be executed two times, 200 times, or at all.

Consider an application in which you ask the user for a bank balance and then ask whether the user wants to see the balance after interest has accumulated. Each time the user chooses to continue, an increased balance appears, reflecting one more year of accumulated interest. When the user finally chooses to exit, the program ends. The program appears in Figure 6-8.

```
import java.util.Scanner;
public class BankBalance
{
    public static void main(String[] args)
    {
        double balance;
        int response;
        int year = 1;
        final double INT_RATE = 0.03;
        Scanner keyboard = new Scanner(System.in);
        System.out.print("Enter initial bank balance > ");
        balance = keyboard.nextDouble();
        System.out.println("Do you want to see next year's balance?");
        System.out.print("Enter 1 for yes");
        System.out.print("   or any other number for no >> ");
        response = keyboard.nextInt();
        while(response == 1)
        {
            balance = balance + balance * INT_RATE;
            System.out.println("After year " + year + " at " +  INT_RATE +
                " interest rate, balance is $" + balance);
            year = year + 1;
            System.out.println("\nDo you want to see the balance " +
                "at the end of another year?");
            System.out.print("Enter 1 for yes");
            System.out.print("   or any other number for no >> ");
            response = keyboard.nextInt();
        }
    }
}
```

Figure 6-8 The BankBalance application

 In the BankBalance program, as in any interactive program, the user must enter data that has the expected data types. If not, an error occurs and the program terminates. You will learn to manage user entry errors in the chapter *Exception Handling*.

The program shown in Figure 6-8 declares needed variables and a constant for a 3 percent interest rate, and then asks the user for a balance. The application then asks the user to enter a *1* if the user wants see the next year's balance. As long as the user wants to continue, the application continues to display increasing bank balances.

The loop in the application in Figure 6-8 begins with the line that contains:

```
while(response == 1)
```

If the user enters any integer value other than *1*, the loop body never executes; instead, the program ends. However, if the user enters *1*, all the statements within the loop body execute. The application increases the balance by the interest rate value, displays the new balance, adds 1 to year, and asks whether the user wants another balance. The last statement in the loop body accepts the user's response. After the loop body executes, control returns to the top of the loop, where the Boolean expression in the while loop is tested again. If the user's response is *1*, the loop is entered and the process begins again. Figure 6-9 shows the output of the BankBalance application after the user enters a $575.00 starting balance and responds with *1* five times to the prompt for increased interest payments before responding *2*.

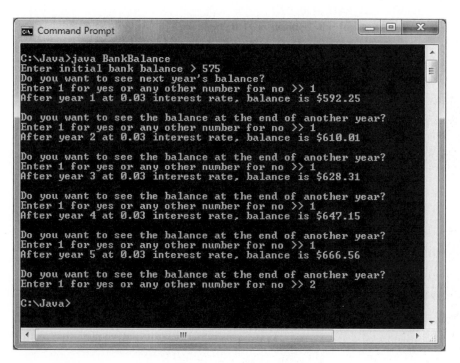

```
C:\Java>java BankBalance
Enter initial bank balance > 575
Do you want to see next year's balance?
Enter 1 for yes or any other number for no >> 1
After year 1 at 0.03 interest rate, balance is $592.25

Do you want to see the balance at the end of another year?
Enter 1 for yes or any other number for no >> 1
After year 2 at 0.03 interest rate, balance is $610.01

Do you want to see the balance at the end of another year?
Enter 1 for yes or any other number for no >> 1
After year 3 at 0.03 interest rate, balance is $628.31

Do you want to see the balance at the end of another year?
Enter 1 for yes or any other number for no >> 1
After year 4 at 0.03 interest rate, balance is $647.15

Do you want to see the balance at the end of another year?
Enter 1 for yes or any other number for no >> 1
After year 5 at 0.03 interest rate, balance is $666.56

Do you want to see the balance at the end of another year?
Enter 1 for yes or any other number for no >> 2

C:\Java>
```

Figure 6-9   Typical execution of the BankBalance application

Validating Data

Programmers commonly use indefinite loops when validating input data. **Validating data** is the process of ensuring that a value falls within a specified range. For example, suppose you require a user to enter a value no greater than 3. Figure 6-10 shows an application that does not progress past the data entry loop until the user enters a correct value. If the user enters 3 or less at the first prompt, the shaded loop never executes. However, if the user enters a number greater than 3, the shaded loop executes, providing the user with another chance to enter a correct value. While the user continues to enter incorrect data, the loop repeats. Figure 6-11 shows a typical execution.

```
import java.util.Scanner;
public class EnterSmallValue
{
    public static void main(String[] args)
    {
        int userEntry;
        final int LIMIT = 3;
        Scanner input = new Scanner(System.in);
        System.out.print("Please enter an integer no higher than " +
            LIMIT + " > ");
        userEntry = input.nextInt();
        while(userEntry > LIMIT)
        {
            System.out.println("The number you entered was too high");
            System.out.print("Please enter an integer no higher than " +
                LIMIT + " > ");
            userEntry = input.nextInt();
        }
        System.out.println("You correctly entered " + userEntry);
    }
}
```

Figure 6-10   The EnterSmallValue application

Figure 6-11   Typical execution of the EnterSmallValue program

Figure 6-10 illustrates an excellent method for validating input. Before the loop is entered, the first input is retrieved. This first input might be a value that prevents any executions of the loop. This first input statement prior to the loop is called a **priming read** or **priming input**. Within the loop, the last statement retrieves subsequent input values for the same variable that will be checked at the entrance to the loop.

Novice programmers often make the mistake of checking for invalid data using a decision instead of a loop. That is, they ask whether the data is invalid using an `if` statement; if the data is invalid, they reprompt the user. However, they forget that a user might enter incorrect data multiple times. Usually, a loop is the best structure to use when validating input data.

310

TWO TRUTHS & A LIE

Creating `while` Loops

1. A finite loop executes a specific number of times; an indefinite loop is one that never ends.

2. A well-written `while` loop contains an initialized loop control variable that is tested in the `while` expression and then altered in the loop body.

3. In an indefinite loop, you don't know how many times the loop will occur.

The false statement is #1. A loop that executes a specific number of times is a definite loop or a counted loop; a loop that never ends is an infinite loop.

 You Do It

Writing a Loop to Validate Data Entries

In Chapter 5, you created an `AssignVolunteer4` application for Sacks Fifth Avenue, a nonprofit thrift shop. The application accepts a donation code and assigns the appropriate volunteer to price the item for sale. Now you add a loop to ensure that a valid code always is entered.

1. Open the **AssignVolunteer4.java** file that you created in Chapter 5. Change the class name to `AssignVolunteer5`, and immediately save the file as **AssignVolunteer5.java**.

2. After the input statement that gets a code from the user, but before the `switch` structure that assigns a volunteer, insert the following loop. The loop continues while the input `donationType` is less than the lowest valid code or higher than the highest valid code. (Recall that the values of CLOTHING_CODE, FURNITURE_CODE, ELECTRONICS_CODE, and OTHER_CODE are 1 through 4,

(continues)

(continued)

respectively.) Within the loop body, statements explain the error to the user and then get a new value for donationType.

```
while(donationType < CLOTHING_CODE || donationType > OTHER_CODE)
{
    System.out.println("You entered " + donationType +
        " which is not a valid donation type");
    System.out.print("Please enter a value between " +
        CLOTHING_CODE + " and " + OTHER_CODE + "... ");
    System.out.print("Enter an integer... ");
    donationType = input.nextInt();
}
```

3. Save the file, and compile and execute it. Figure 6-12 shows a typical execution in which a user enters an invalid code three times before entering a valid one.

Figure 6-12 Typical execution of the AssignVolunteer5 application

4. In the current program, the default case assigns "invalid" to the volunteer. At this point, some professionals would advise that you remove the default case from the case structure because it is no longer possible for the user to enter an invalid code. Others would argue that leaving the default case in place serves two purposes. First, it provides documentation that clarifies the course of action if the entered code does not match any of the listed cases. Second, the program requirements might change in the future. For example, perhaps one of the categories will be eliminated. Then, if you remove the case instructions for that category, a default block will already be in place to handle the new error.

Using Shortcut Arithmetic Operators

Programmers commonly need to increase the value of a variable in a program. As you saw in the previous section, many loops are controlled by continually adding 1 to some variable, as in count = count + 1;. Incrementing a variable in a loop to keep track of the number of occurrences of some event is also known as **counting**. Similarly, in the looping bank balance program shown in Figure 6-8, the program not only incremented the year variable by adding 1, it also increased a bank balance by an interest amount with the statement balance = balance + balance * INT_RATE;. In other words, the bank balance became its old value *plus* a new interest amount; the process of repeatedly increasing a value by some amount is known as **accumulating**.

Because increasing a variable is so common, Java provides you with several shortcuts for incrementing and accumulating. The statement count += 1; is identical in meaning to count = count + 1. The += is the **add and assign operator**; it adds and assigns in one operation. Similarly, balance += balance * INT_RATE; increases a balance by the INT_RATE percentage. Besides using the shortcut operator +=, you can use the **subtract and assign operator** (-=), the **multiply and assign operator** (*=), the **divide and assign operator** (/=), and the **remainder and assign operator** (%=). Each of these operators is used to perform the operation and assign the result in one step. For example, balanceDue -= payment subtracts payment from balanceDue and assigns the result to balanceDue.

When you want to increase a variable's value by exactly 1, you can use two other shortcut operators—the **prefix ++**, also known as the **prefix increment operator**, and the **postfix ++**, also known as the **postfix increment operator**. To use a prefix ++, you type two plus signs before the variable name. The statement someValue = 6; followed by ++someValue; results in someValue holding 7—one more than it held before you applied the ++. To use a postfix ++, you type two plus signs just after a variable name. The statements anotherValue = 56; anotherValue++; result in anotherValue containing 57. Figure 6-13 shows four ways you can increase a value by 1; each method produces the same result. You are never required to use shortcut operators; they are merely a convenience.

```
int value;
value = 24;
++value;   // Result: value is 25
value = 24;
value++;   // Result: value is 25
value = 24;
value = value + 1;   // Result: value is 25
value = 24;
value += 1;  // Result: value is 25
```

Figure 6-13   Four ways to add 1 to a value

You can use the prefix ++ and postfix ++ with variables but not with constants. An expression such as ++84; is illegal because an 84 must always remain an 84. However, you can create a variable named val, assign 84 to it, and then write ++val; or val++; to increase the variable's value.

 The prefix and postfix increment operators are unary operators because you use them with one value. As you learned in Chapter 2, most arithmetic operators, such as those used for addition and multiplication, are binary operators—they operate on two values. Other examples of unary operators include the cast operator, as well as (+) and (–) when used to indicate positive and negative values.

When you simply want to increase a variable's value by 1, there is no difference in the outcome, whether you use the prefix or postfix increment operator. For example, when value is set to 24 in Figure 6-13, both ++value and value++ result in value becoming 25; each operator results in increasing the variable by 1. However, when a prefix or postfix operator is used as part of a larger expression, it does make a difference which operator you use because they function differently in terms of what they *return*. When a prefix operator is used in an expression, the value after the calculation is used, but when a postfix operator is used in an expression, the value used is the one before the calculation takes place.

When you use the prefix ++, the result is calculated, and then its value is used. For example, consider the following statements:

```
b = 4;
c = ++b;
```

The result is that both b and c hold the value 5 because b is increased to 5 and then the value of the expression is assigned to c.

When you use the postfix ++, the value of the expression before the increase is stored. For example, consider these statements:

```
b = 4;
c = b++;
```

The result is still that b is 5, but c is only 4. Although b is increased, its original value is assigned to c.

In other words, if b = 4, the value of b++ is also 4, but after the statement is completed, the value of b is 5.

Figure 6-14 shows an application that illustrates the difference between how the prefix and postfix increment operators work. Notice from the output in Figure 6-15 that when the prefix increment operator is used on myNumber, the value of myNumber increases from 17 to 18, and the result is stored in answer, which also becomes 18. After the value is reset to 17, the postfix increment operator is used; 17 is assigned to answer, and myNumber is incremented to 18.

```
public class IncrementDemo
{
    public static void main(String[] args)
    {
        int myNumber, answer;
        myNumber = 17;
        System.out.println("Before incrementing, myNumber is " +
            myNumber);
        answer = ++myNumber;
        System.out.println("After prefix increment, myNumber is " +
            myNumber);
        System.out.println("  and answer is " + answer);
        myNumber = 17;
        System.out.println("Before incrementing, myNumber is " +
            myNumber);
        answer = myNumber++;
        System.out.println("After postfix increment, myNumber is " +
            myNumber);
        System.out.println("  and answer is " + answer);
    }
}
```

Figure 6-14   The IncrementDemo application

Figure 6-15   Output of the IncrementDemo application

 Later in this chapter, you will learn another reason why you might want to use a prefix operator instead of a postfix operator.

Choosing whether to use a prefix or postfix operator is important when one is part of a larger expression. For example, if d is 5, then 2 * ++d is 12, but 2 * d++ is 10.

Similar logic can be applied when you use the **prefix and postfix decrement operators**. For example, if b = 4 and c = b--, 4 is assigned to c, but b is decreased and takes the value 3. If b = 4 and c = --b, b is decreased to 3 and 3 is assigned to c.

Watch the video *Using Shortcut Arithmetic Operators*.

TWO TRUTHS & A LIE

Using Shortcut Arithmetic Operators

1. Assume that x = 4 and y = 5. The value of ++y + ++x is 11.

2. Assume that x = 4 and y = 5. The value of y == x++ is true.

3. Assume that x = 4 and y = 5. The value of y += x is 9.

The false statement is #2. If x is 4 and y is 5, then the value of x++ is 4, and so y is not equal to 4.

 You Do It

Working with Prefix and Postfix Increment Operators

Next, you write an application that demonstrates how prefix and postfix operators are used to increment variables and how incrementing affects the expressions that contain these operators.

1. Open a new text file, and begin a demonstration class named DemoIncrement by typing:

   ```
   public class DemoIncrement
   {
       public static void main(String[] args)
       {
   ```

2. On a new line, add a variable v, and assign it a value of 4. Then declare a variable named plusPlusV, and assign it a value of ++v by typing:

   ```
   int v = 4;
   int plusPlusV = ++v;
   ```

3. The last statement, int plusPlusV = ++v;, increases v to 5, so before declaring a vPlusPlus variable to which you assign v++, reset v to 4 by typing:

   ```
   v = 4;
   int vPlusPlus = v++;
   ```

(continues)

(continued)

4. Add the following statements to display the three values:

```
System.out.println("v is " + v);
System.out.println("++v is " + plusPlusV);
System.out.println("v++ is " + vPlusPlus);
```

5. Add the closing curly brace for the `main()` method and the closing curly brace for the `DemoIncrement` class. Save the file as **DemoIncrement.java**, then compile and execute the program. Your output should look like Figure 6-16.

Figure 6-16   Output of the `DemoIncrement` class

6. To illustrate how comparisons are made, add a few more variables to the `DemoIncrement` program. Change the class name to **DemoIncrement2**, and immediately save the file as **DemoIncrement2.java**.

7. After the last `println()` statement, add three new integer variables and two new Boolean variables. The first Boolean variable compares `++w` to `y`; the second Boolean variable compares `x++` to `y`:

```
int w = 17, x = 17, y = 18;
boolean compare1 = (++w == y);
boolean compare2 = (x++ == y);
```

8. Add the following statements to display the values stored in the `compare` variables:

```
System.out.println("First compare is " + compare1);
System.out.println("Second compare is " + compare2);
```

9. Save, compile, and run the program. The output appears in Figure 6-17. Make certain you understand why each statement displays the values it does. Experiment by changing the values of the variables, and see if you can predict the output before recompiling and rerunning the program.

(continues)

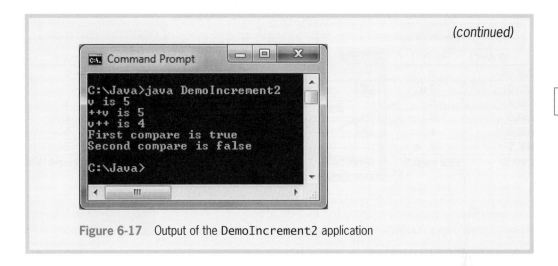

(continued)

Figure 6-17   Output of the DemoIncrement2 application

Creating a for Loop

A **for loop** is a special loop that is used when a definite number of loop iterations is required; it provides a convenient way to create a counter-controlled loop. Although a while loop can also be used to meet this requirement, the for loop provides you with a shorthand notation for this type of loop. When you use a for loop, you can indicate the starting value for the loop control variable, the test condition that controls loop entry, and the expression that alters the loop control variable—all in one convenient place.

You begin a for loop with the keyword for followed by a set of parentheses. Within the parentheses are three sections separated by exactly two semicolons. The three sections are usually used for the following:

- Initializing the loop control variable
- Testing the loop control variable
- Updating the loop control variable

The body of the for statement follows the parentheses. As with an if statement or a while loop, you can use a single statement as the body of a for loop, or you can use a block of statements enclosed in curly braces. Many programmers recommend that you always use a set of curly braces to surround the body of a for loop for clarity, even when the body contains only a single statement. You should use the conventions recommended by your organization.

Assuming that a variable named val has been declared as an integer, then the for statement shown in Figure 6-18 produces the same output as the while statement shown below it— both display the integers 1 through 10.

```
for(val = 1; val < 11; ++val)
{
    System.out.println(val);
}

val = 1;
while(val < 11)
{
    System.out.println(val);
    ++val;
}
```

Figure 6-18   A for loop and a while loop that display the integers 1 through 10

Within the parentheses of the for statement shown in Figure 6-18, the first section prior to the first semicolon initializes val to 1. The program executes this statement once, no matter how many times the body of the for loop executes.

After initialization, program control passes to the middle, or test section, of the for statement that lies between the two semicolons. If the Boolean expression found there evaluates to true, the body of the for loop is entered. In the program segment shown in Figure 6-18, val is set to 1, so when val < 11 is tested, it evaluates to true. The loop body displays val. In this example, the loop body is a single statement, so no curly braces are needed (although they could be added).

After the loop body executes, the final one-third of the for loop that follows the second semicolon executes, and val is increased to 2. Following the third section in the for statement, program control returns to the second section, where val is compared to 11 a second time. Because val is still less than 11, the body executes: val (now 2) is displayed, and then the third, altering portion of the for loop executes again. The variable val increases to 3, and the for loop continues.

Eventually, when val is not less than 11 (after 1 through 10 have been displayed), the for loop ends, and the program continues with any statements that follow the for loop. Although the three sections of the for loop are most commonly used for initializing, testing, and incrementing, you can also perform the following tasks:

- Initialization of more than one variable in the first section of the for statement by placing commas between the separate statements, as in the following:

  ```
  for(g = 0, h = 1; g < 6; ++g)
  ```

- Performance of more than one test using AND or OR operators in the second section, as in the following:

  ```
  for(g = 0; g < 3 && h > 1; ++g)
  ```

- Decrementation or performance of some other task in the third section, as in the following:

  ```
  for(g = 5; g >= 1; --g)
  ```

- Altering more than one variable in the third section, as in the following:

  ```
  for(g = 0; g < 10; ++g, ++h, sum += g)
  ```

- You can leave one or more portions of a for loop empty, although the two semicolons are still required as placeholders. For example, if x has been initialized in a previous program statement, you might write the following:

  ```
  for(; x < 10; ++x)
  ```

  However, to someone reading your program, leaving a section of a for statement empty is less clear than using all three sections.

In general, you should use the same loop control variable in all three parts of a for statement, although you might see some programs written by others in which this is not the case. You should also avoid altering the loop control variable in the body of the loop. If a variable is altered both within a for statement and within the block it controls, it can be very difficult to follow the program's logic. This technique can also produce program bugs that are hard to find. Usually, you should use the for loop for its intended purpose—as a shorthand way of programming a definite loop.

Occasionally, you will encounter a for loop that contains no body, such as the following:

```
for(x = 0; x < 100000; ++x);
```

This kind of loop exists simply to use time—that is, to occupy the central processing unit for thousands of processing cycles—when a brief pause is desired during program execution, for example. As with if and while statements, usually you do not want to place a semicolon at the end of the for statement before the body of the loop. Java also contains a built-in method to pause program execution. The sleep() method is part of the Thread class in the java.lang package, and you will learn how to use it as you continue to study Java.

You also can declare a variable within a for statement, as in the following:

```
for(int val = 1; val < 11; ++val)
```

Programmers often use this technique when the variable is not needed in any other part of the program. If you declare a variable within a for statement, the variable can be used only in the block that depends on the for statement; when the block ends, the variable goes out of scope.

Java also supports an enhanced for loop. You will learn about this loop in the chapter *Introduction to Arrays*.

Watch the video *Using the* for *Loop.*

TWO TRUTHS & A LIE

Creating a for Loop

1. A for loop always must contain two semicolons within its parentheses.

2. The body of a for loop might never execute.

3. Within the parentheses of a for loop, the last section must alter the loop control variable.

The false statement is #3. Frequently, the third section of a for loop is used to alter the loop control variable, but it is not required.

You Do It

Working with Definite Loops

Suppose you want to find all the numbers that divide evenly into 100. You want to write a definite loop—one that executes exactly 100 times. In this section, you write a for loop that sets a variable to 1 and increments it to 100. Each of the 100 times through the loop, if 100 is evenly divisible by the variable, the application displays the number.

1. Open a new text file. Begin the application named DivideEvenly by typing the following code. Use a named constant for the 100 value and a variable named var that will hold, in turn, every value from 1 through 100:

```
public class DivideEvenly
{
    public static void main(String[] args)
    {
        final int LIMIT = 100;
        int var;
```

2. Type a statement that explains the purpose of the program:

```
System.out.print(LIMIT + " is evenly divisible by ");
```

3. Write the for loop that varies var from 1 through 100. With each iteration of the loop, test whether 100 % var is 0. If you divide 100 by a number and there is no remainder, the number goes into 100 evenly.

(continues)

(continued)

```
for(var = 1; var <= LIMIT; ++var)
    if(LIMIT % var == 0)
        System.out.print(var + " ");
        // Display the number and a space
```

4. Add an empty `println()` statement to advance the insertion point to the next line by typing the following:

   ```
   System.out.println();
   ```

5. Type the closing curly braces for the `main()` method and the `DivideEvenly` class.

6. Save the program as **DivideEvenly**. Compile and run the program. Figure 6-19 shows the output.

Figure 6-19   Output of the `DivideEvenly` application

7. By definition, no value that is greater than half of `LIMIT` can possibly go into `LIMIT` evenly. Therefore, the loop in the `DivideEvenly` program could be made to execute faster if the loop executes while `var` is less than or equal to half of `LIMIT`. If you decide to make this change to the program, remember that you must include the value of `LIMIT` in the output because it is evenly divisible into itself.

Learning How and When to Use a do...while Loop

With all the loops you have written so far, the loop body might execute many times, but it is also possible that the loop will not execute at all. For example, recall the bank balance program that displays compound interest, which was shown in Figure 6-8. The program begins by asking whether the user wants to see next year's balance. If the user doesn't enter a *1* for *yes*, the loop body never executes.

Similarly, recall the `EnterSmallValue` application in Figure 6-10. The user is prompted to enter a value, and if the user enters a value that is 3 or less, the error-reporting loop body never executes.

In each of these cases, the loop control variable is evaluated at the "top" of the loop before the body has a chance to execute. Both `while` loops and `for` loops are **pretest loops**—ones in which the loop control variable is tested before the loop body executes.

Sometimes, you might need to ensure that a loop body executes at least one time. If so, you want to write a loop that checks at the "bottom" of the loop after the first iteration. The **do...while loop** is such a loop; it is a **posttest loop**—one in which the loop control variable is tested after the loop body executes.

Figure 6-20 shows the general structure of a do...while loop. Notice that the loop body executes before the loop-controlling question is asked even one time. Figure 6-21 shows a `BankBalance2` application that contains a do...while loop. The loop starts with the shaded keyword do. The body of the loop follows and is contained within curly braces. The first year's balance is output before the user has any option of responding. At the bottom of the loop, the user is prompted, "Do you want to see the balance at the end of another year?" Now the user has the option of seeing more balances, but viewing the first display was unavoidable. The user's response is checked in the shaded evaluation at the bottom of the loop; if it is *1* for *yes*, the loop repeats. Figure 6-22 shows a typical execution.

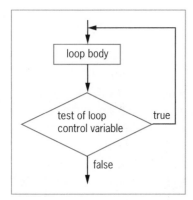

Figure 6-20   General structure of a do...while loop

```
import java.util.Scanner;
public class BankBalance2
{
    public static void main(String[] args)
    {
        double balance;
        int response;
        int year = 1;
        final double INT_RATE = 0.03;
        Scanner keyboard = new Scanner(System.in);
        System.out.print("Enter initial bank balance > ");
        balance = keyboard.nextDouble();
        keyboard.nextLine();
        do
        {
            balance = balance + balance * INT_RATE;
            System.out.println("After year " + year + " at " + INT_RATE +
                " interest rate, balance is $" + balance);
            year = year + 1;
            System.out.println("\nDo you want to see the balance " +
                " at the end of another year?");
            System.out.println("Enter 1 for yes");
            System.out.print("   or any other number for no >> ");
            response = keyboard.nextInt();
        } while(response == 1);
    }
}
```

Figure 6-21   A do...while loop for the BankBalance2 application

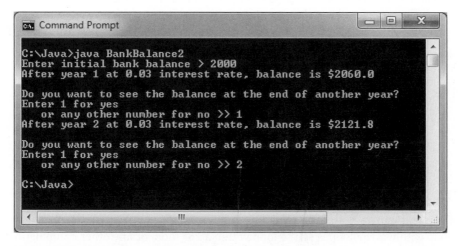

Figure 6-22   Typical execution of the BankBalance2 program

When the body of a do...while loop contains a single statement, you do not need to use curly braces to block the statement. For example, the following loop correctly adds numberValue to total while total remains less than 200:

```
do
    total += numberValue;
while(total < 200);
```

Even though curly braces are not required in this case, many programmers recommend using them. Doing so prevents the third line of code from looking like it should begin a new while loop instead of ending the previous do...while loop. Therefore, even though the result is the same, the following example that includes curly braces is less likely to be misunderstood by a reader:

```
do
{
    total += numberValue;
} while(total < 200);
```

You are never required to use a do...while loop. Within the bank balance example, you could achieve the same results as the logic shown in Figure 6-21 by unconditionally displaying the first year's bank balance once before starting the loop, prompting the user, and then starting a while loop that might not be entered. However, when you know you want to perform some task at least one time, the do...while loop is convenient.

TWO TRUTHS & A LIE

Learning How and When to Use a do...while Loop

1. The do...while loop checks the value of the loop control variable at the top of the loop prior to loop execution.

2. When the statements in a loop body must execute at least one time, it is convenient to use a do...while loop.

3. When the body of a do...while loop contains a single statement, you do not need to use curly braces to block the statement.

The false statement is #1. The do...while loop checks the value of the loop control variable at the bottom of the loop after one repetition has occurred.

Learning About Nested Loops

Just as if statements can be nested, so can loops. You can place a while loop within a while loop, a for loop within a for loop, a while loop within a for loop, or any other combination. When loops are nested, each pair contains an **inner loop** and an **outer loop**. The inner loop must be entirely contained within the outer loop; loops can never overlap. Figure 6-23 shows a diagram in which the shaded loop is nested within another loop; the shaded area is the inner loop. You can nest virtually any number of loops; however, at some point, your machine will no longer be able to store all the necessary looping information.

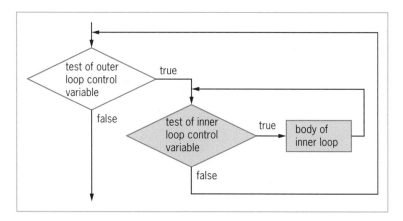

Figure 6-23   Nested loops

Suppose you want to display future bank balances while varying both years and interest rates. Figure 6-24 shows an application that contains an outer loop that varies interest rates between specified limits. At the start of the outer loop, the working balance is reset to its initial value so that calculations are correct for each revised interest rate value. The shaded inner loop varies the number of years and displays each calculated balance. Figure 6-25 shows a typical execution.

```
import java.util.Scanner;
public class BankBalanceByRateAndYear
{
    public static void main(String[] args)
    {
        double initialBalance;
        double balance;
        int year;
        double interest;
        final double LOW = 0.02;
        final double HIGH = 0.05;
        final double INCREMENT = 0.01;
        final int MAX_YEAR = 4;
        Scanner keyboard = new Scanner(System.in);
        System.out.print("Enter initial bank balance > ");
        initialBalance = keyboard.nextDouble();
        keyboard.nextLine();
```

Figure 6-24   The `BankBalanceByRateAndYear` class containing nested loops *(continues)*

(continued)

```
        for(interest = LOW; interest <= HIGH; interest += INCREMENT)
        {
            balance = initialBalance;
            System.out.println("\nWith an initial balance of $" +
                balance + " at an interest rate of " + interest);
            for(year = 1; year <= MAX_YEAR; ++ year)
            {
                balance = balance + balance * interest;
                System.out.println("After year " + year +
                    " balance is $" + balance);
            }
        }
    }
}
```

Figure 6-24   The `BankBalanceByRateAndYear` class containing nested loops

Figure 6-25   Typical execution of the `BankBalanceByRateAndYear` program

In Figure 6-25, the floating-point calculations result in balances that contain fractions of pennies. If you wrote this program for a bank, you would have to ask whether interest should be compounded on fractions of a cent as it is here, or whether the amounts should be either rounded or truncated.

When you nest loops, sometimes it doesn't make any difference which variable controls the outer loop and which variable controls the inner one, but frequently it does make a difference. When you use a loop within a loop, you should always think of the outer loop as the all-encompassing loop. The variable in the outer loop changes more infrequently. For example, suppose a method named `outputLabel()` creates customer mailing labels in three different colors to use in successive promotional mailings. The following nested loop calls the method 60 times and produces three labels for the first customer, three labels for the second customer, and so on:

```
for(customer = 1; customer <= 20; ++customer)
   for(color = 1; color <= 3; ++color)
      outputLabel();
```

The following nested loop also calls `outputLabel()` 60 times, and it ultimately produces the same 60 labels, but it creates 20 labels in the first color, 20 labels in the second color, and then 20 labels in the third color.

```
for(color = 1; color <= 3; ++color)
   for(customer = 1; customer <= 20; ++customer)
      outputLabel();
```

If changing the ink color is a time-consuming process that occurs in the method, the second nested loop might execute much faster than the first one.

 Watch the video *Nested Loops.*

TWO TRUTHS & A LIE

Learning About Nested Loops

1. You can place a `while` loop within a `while` loop or a `for` loop within a `for` loop, but you cannot mix loop types.

2. An inner nested loop must be entirely contained within its outer loop.

3. The body of the following loop executes 20 times:

   ```
   for(int x = 0; x < 4; ++x)
      for(int y = 0; y < 5; ++y)
         System.out.println("Hi");
   ```

The false statement is #1. You can place a `while` loop within a `while` loop, a `for` loop within a `for` loop, a `while` loop within a `for` loop, or any other combination.

You Do It

Working with Nested Loops

328

Suppose you want to know not just what numbers go evenly into 100 but also what numbers go evenly into every positive number, up to and including 100. You can write 99 more loops—one that shows the numbers that divide evenly into 1, another that shows the numbers that divide evenly into 2, and so on—or you can place the current loop inside a different, outer loop, as you do next.

1. If necessary, open the file **DivideEvenly.java** in your text editor, change the class name to **DivideEvenly2**, and then save the class as **DivideEvenly2.java**.

2. Add a new variable declaration at the beginning of the file with the other variable declarations:

   ```
   int number;
   ```

3. Replace the existing `for` loop with the following nested loop. The outer loop varies `number` from 1 to 100. For each number in the outer loop, the inner loop uses each positive integer from 1 up to the number and tests whether it divides evenly into the number:

   ```
   for(number = 1; number <= LIMIT; ++number)
   {
       System.out.print(number + " is evenly divisible by ");
       for(var = 1; var <= number; ++var)
           if(number % var == 0)
               System.out.print(var + " ");
               // Display the number and a space
       System.out.println();
   }
   ```

4. Make certain the file ends with three curly braces—one for the `for` outer loop that varies `number`, one for the `main()` method, and one for the class. The inner loop does not need curly braces because it contains a single output statement, although you could add a set of braces for the loop.

5. Save the file as **DivideEvenly2.java**, and then compile and execute the application. When the output stops scrolling, it should look similar to Figure 6-26.

(continues)

(continued)

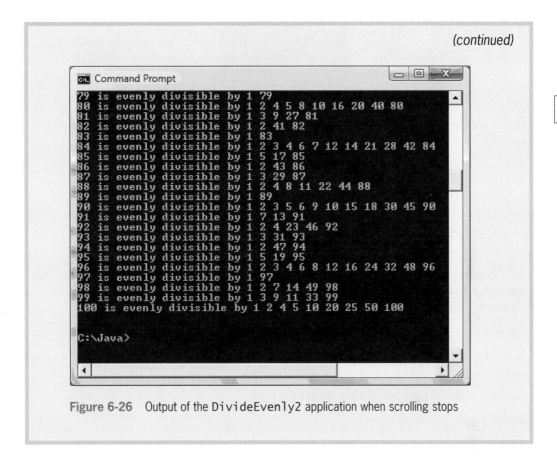

Figure 6-26 Output of the `DivideEvenly2` application when scrolling stops

Improving Loop Performance

Whether you decide to use a `while`, `for`, or `do...while` loop in an application, you can improve loop performance by doing the following:

- Making sure the loop does not include unnecessary operations or statements
- Considering the order of evaluation for short-circuit operators
- Making a comparison to 0
- Employing loop fusion
- Using prefix incrementing rather than postfix incrementing

Avoiding Unnecessary Operations

You can make loops more efficient by not using unnecessary operations or statements, either within a loop's tested expression or within the loop body. For example, suppose a loop should execute while x is less than the sum of two integers, a and b. The loop could be written as:

```
while (x < a + b)
    // loop body
```

> **Don't Do It**
> It might be inefficient to
> recalculate a + b
> for every loop iteration.

If this loop executes 1,000 times, then the expression a + b is calculated 1,000 times. Instead, if you use the following code, the results are the same, but the arithmetic is performed only once:

```
int sum = a + b;
while(x < sum)
    // loop body
```

Of course, if a or b is altered in the loop body, then a new sum must be calculated with every loop iteration. However, if the sum of a and b is fixed prior to the start of the loop, then writing the code the second way is far more efficient.

Similarly, try to avoid a method call within a loop if possible. For example, if the method getNumberOfEmployees() always returns the same value during a program's execution, then a loop that begins as follows might unnecessarily call the method many times:

```
while(count < getNumberOfEmployees())...
```

It is more efficient to call the method once, store the result in a variable, and use the variable in the repeated evaluations, as in this example:

```
numEmployees = getNumberOfEmployees();

while(count < numEmployees)...
```

Considering the Order of Evaluation of Short-Circuit Operators

In Chapter 5 you learned that the expressions in each part of an AND or an OR expression use short-circuit evaluation; that is, they are evaluated only as much as necessary to determine whether the entire expression is true or false. When a loop might execute many times, it becomes increasingly important to consider the number of evaluations that take place.

For example, suppose a user can request any number of printed copies of a report from 0 to 15, and you want to validate the user's input before proceeding. If you believe that users are far more likely to enter a value that is too high than to enter a negative one, then you want to start a loop that reprompts the user with the following expression:

```
while(requestedNum > LIMIT || requestedNum < 0)...
```

Because you believe that the first Boolean expression is more likely to be true than the second one, you can eliminate testing the second one on more occasions. The order of the expressions is not very important in a single loop, but if this loop is nested within another loop, then the difference in the number of tests increases. Similarly, the order of the evaluations in if statements is more important when the if statements are nested within a loop.

Comparing to Zero

Making a comparison to 0 is faster than making a comparison to any other value. Therefore, if your application makes comparison to 0 feasible, you can improve loop performance by structuring your loops to compare the loop control variable to 0 instead of some other value. For example, a loop that performs based on a variable that varies from 0 up to 100,000 executes the same number of times as a loop based on a variable that varies from 100,000 down to 0. However, the second loop performs slightly faster. Comparing a value to 0 instead of other values is faster because in a compiled language, condition flags for the comparison are set once, no matter how many times the loop executes. Comparing a value to 0 is faster than comparing to other values, no matter which comparison operator you use—greater than, less than, equal to, and so on.

Figure 6-27 contains a program that tests the execution times of two nested do-nothing loops. (A **do-nothing loop** is one that performs no actions other than looping.) Before each loop, the System method currentTimeMillis() is called to retrieve the current time represented in milliseconds. After each nested loop repeats 100,000 times, the current time is retrieved again. Subtracting the two times computes the interval. As the execution in Figure 6-28 shows, there is a small difference in execution time between the two loops—about 1/100 of a second. The amount of time will vary on different machines, but the loop that uses the 0 comparison will never be slower than the other one. The difference would become more pronounced with additional repetitions or further nesting levels. If the loops used the loop control variable, for example, to display a count to the user, then they might need to increment the variable. However, if the purposes of the loops are just to count iterations, you might consider making the loop comparison use 0.

```java
public class CompareLoops
{
    public static void main(String[] args)
    {
        long startTime1, startTime2, endTime1, endTime2;
        final int REPEAT = 100000;
        startTime1 = System.currentTimeMillis();
        for(int x = 0; x <= REPEAT; ++x)
            for(int y = 0; y <= REPEAT; ++y);
        endTime1 = System.currentTimeMillis();
        System.out.println("Time for loops starting from 0: " +
            (endTime1 - startTime1) + " milliseconds");
        startTime2 = System.currentTimeMillis();
        for(int x = REPEAT; x >= 0; --x)
            for(int y = REPEAT; y >= 0; --y);
        endTime2 = System.currentTimeMillis();
        System.out.println("Time for loops ending at 0: " +
            (endTime2 - startTime2) + " milliseconds");
    }
}
```

Figure 6-27 The CompareLoops application

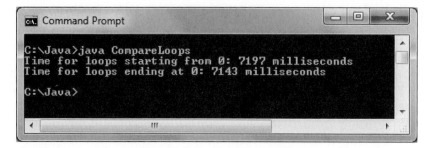

Figure 6-28   Typical execution of the CompareLoops application

 If you execute the program in Figure 6-27, you probably will see different results. With a fast operating system, you might not see the differences shown in Figure 6-28. If so, experiment with the program by increasing the value of REPEAT or by adding more nested levels to the loops.

Employing Loop Fusion

Loop fusion is the technique of combining two loops into one. For example, suppose you want to call two methods 100 times each. You can set a constant named TIMES to 100 and use the following code:

```
for(int x = 0; x < TIMES; ++x)
    method1();
for(int x = 0; x < TIMES; ++x)
    method2();
```

However, you can also use the following code:

```
for(int x = 0; x < TIMES; ++x)
{
    method1();
    method2();
}
```

Fusing loops will not work in every situation; sometimes all the activities for method1() must be finished before those in method2() can begin. However, if the two methods do not depend on each other, fusing the loops can improve performance. On the other hand, if saving a few milliseconds ends up making your code harder to understand, you almost always should err in favor of slower but more readable programs.

Using Prefix Incrementing Rather than Postfix Incrementing

Probably the most common action after the second semicolon in a for statement is to increment the loop control variable. In most textbooks and in many professional programs, the postfix increment operator is used for this purpose, as in the following:

```
for(int x = 0; x < LIMIT; x++)
```

Because incrementing x is a stand-alone statement in the for loop, the result is identical whether you use x++ or ++x. However, using the prefix increment operator produces a faster loop. Consider the program in Figure 6-29. It is similar to the CompareLoops application in Figure 6-27, but instead of comparing loops that count up and down, it compares loops that use prefix and postfix incrementing. The two timed, bodyless loops that repeat 1 billion times each are shaded in the figure.

```java
public class CompareLoops2
{
    public static void main(String[] args)
    {
        long startTime1, startTime2, endTime1, endTime2;
        final long REPEAT = 1000000000L;
        startTime1 = System.currentTimeMillis();
        for(int x = 0; x < REPEAT; x++);
        endTime1 = System.currentTimeMillis();
        System.out.println("Time with postfix increment: " +
            (endTime1 - startTime1)+ " milliseconds");
        startTime2 = System.currentTimeMillis();
        for(int x = 0; x < REPEAT; ++x);
        endTime2 = System.currentTimeMillis();
        System.out.println("Time with prefix increment: " +
            (endTime2 - startTime2)+ " milliseconds");
    }
}
```

Figure 6-29   The CompareLoops2 program

Figure 6-30 shows the output of the program. The program that uses prefix incrementing runs slightly faster than the one that uses postfix incrementing because when the compiler uses postfix incrementing, it first makes a copy of the variable it uses as the expression's value, and then it increments the variable. In other words, the operators are methods that behave as follows:

- When you use the prefix incrementing method, as in ++x, the method receives a reference to x, increases it, and returns the increased value.

- When you use the postfix incrementing method, as in x++, the method receives a reference to x, makes a copy of the value and stores it, increments the value indicated by the reference, and returns the copy. The extra time required to make the copy is what causes postfix incrementing to take longer.

As you can see in Figure 6-30, the difference in duration for the loops is very small. If you run the program multiple times, you will get different results, and sometimes the prefix operator loop will take longer because other programs are running concurrently on your computer. However, using the prefix operator typically saves a small amount of time. As a professional, you will encounter programmers who insist on using either postfix or prefix increments in their loops. You should follow the conventions established by your organization, but now you have the tools to prove that prefix incrementing is faster.

334

Figure 6-30 Typical execution of the `CompareLoops2` application

In the previous sections, you have learned to improve loop performance by eliminating unnecessary operations, considering the order of evaluation for short-circuit operators, making comparisons to 0, employing loop fusion, and using prefix incrementing rather than postfix incrementing. As you become an experienced programmer, you will discover other ways to enhance the operation of the programs you write. You should always be on the lookout for ways to improve program performance.

TWO TRUTHS & A LIE

Improving Loop Performance

1. You can improve the performance of a loop by making sure the loop does not include unnecessary operations in the tested expression.

2. You can improve loop performance by making sure the loop does not include unnecessary operations in the body of the loop.

3. You can improve loop performance when two conditions must both be true by testing for the most likely occurrence first.

The false statement is #3. You can improve loop performance when two conditions must both be true by testing for the least likely occurrence first. That way, the second test will need to be performed less frequently.

You Do It

Comparing Execution Times for Separate and Fused Loops

In this section, you compare the execution times for accomplishing the same tasks using two loops or a single one.

1. Open a new file in your text editor, and start a class named TimeFusedLoop.

    ```
    public class TimeFusedLoop
    {
        public static void main(String[] args)
        {
    ```

2. Create variables to hold starting and ending times for two operations, and create a constant that holds a number of times to repeat loops:

    ```
    long startTime1, startTime2, endTime1, endTime2;
    final int REPEAT = 10000;
    ```

3. Get a starting time. Then, in a loop that repeats 10,000 times, call a method named method1(), which accepts a parameter that controls loop repetitions within the method. When the iterations are complete, call a similar method, method2(), 10,000 times.

    ```
    startTime1 = System.currentTimeMillis();
    for(int x = REPEAT; x >= 0; --x)
        method1(REPEAT);
    for(int x = REPEAT; x >= 0; --x)
        method2(REPEAT);
    ```

4. Get the ending time, and display the difference between the starting and ending times.

    ```
    endTime1 = System.currentTimeMillis();
    System.out.println("Time for two separate loops: " +
        (endTime1 - startTime1)+ " milliseconds");
    ```

5. Get a new starting time, and call method1() and method2() 10,000 times each in a single loop. Then get the ending time, and display the difference. Add a closing curly brace for the main() method.

    ```
    startTime2 = System.currentTimeMillis();
    for(int x = REPEAT; x >= 0; --x)
    {
        method1(REPEAT);
        method2(REPEAT);
    }
    endTime2 = System.currentTimeMillis();
    System.out.println("Time for fused loops: " +
        (endTime2 - startTime2)+ " milliseconds");
    }
    ```

(continues)

(continued)

6. Create the two methods named method1() and method2(). Each simply executes a do-nothing loop the number of times indicated by its parameter. Add a closing curly brace for the class.

```
public static void method1(final int REPEAT)
{
    for(int x = REPEAT; x >= 0; --x);
}
public static void method2(final int REPEAT)
{
    for(int x = REPEAT; x >= 0; --x);
}
}
```

7. Save the file as **TimeFusedLoop.java**, and then compile and execute it. Figure 6-31 shows the execution. The times might differ on your system, but you should be able to see that using a single loop significantly improves performance over using separate loops. If your system is very fast, you might have to increase the value of the REPEAT constant (perhaps changing it from an int to a long), or change the body of each method to contain a nested loop such as the following:

```
for(int x = REPEAT; x >= 0; --x);
    for(int y = REPEAT; y >= 0; --y);
```

Figure 6-31   Execution of the TimeFusedLoop program

8. Experiment with increasing and decreasing the value of REPEAT, and observe the effects. The time values you observe might also differ when you run the program at different times, depending on what other tasks are running on your system concurrently.

Don't Do It

- Don't insert a semicolon at the end of a `while` clause before the loop body; doing so creates an empty loop body.

- Don't forget to block multiple statements that should execute in a loop.

- Don't make the mistake of checking for invalid data using a decision instead of a loop. Users might enter incorrect data multiple times, so a loop is the superior choice for input validation.

- Don't ignore subtleties in the boundaries used to stop loop performance. For example, looping while interest rates are less than 8% is different than looping while interest rates are no more than 8%.

- Don't repeat steps within a loop that could just as well be placed outside the loop; your program performance will improve.

Key Terms

A **loop** is a structure that allows repeated execution of a block of statements.

A **loop body** is the block of statements that executes when the Boolean expression that controls the loop is `true`.

An **iteration** is one loop execution.

A **`while` loop** executes a body of statements continually as long as the Boolean expression that controls entry into the loop continues to be `true`.

A loop that executes a specific number of times is a **definite loop** or a counted loop.

An **indefinite loop** is one in which the final number of loops is unknown.

A **loop control variable** is a variable whose value determines whether loop execution continues.

An **infinite loop** is a loop that never ends.

An **empty body** is a block with no statements in it.

A **counter-controlled loop** is a definite loop.

Incrementing a variable adds 1 to its value.

Decrementing a variable reduces its value by 1.

An indefinite loop is an **event-controlled loop**.

Validating data is the process of ensuring that a value falls within a specified range.

A **priming read** or **priming input** is the first input statement prior to a loop that will execute subsequent input statements for the same variable.

Counting is the process of continually incrementing a variable to keep track of the number of occurrences of some event.

Accumulating is the process of repeatedly increasing a value by some amount to produce a total.

The **add and assign operator** (+=) alters the value of the operand on the left by adding the operand on the right to it.

The **subtract and assign operator** (−=) alters the value of the operand on the left by subtracting the operand on the right from it.

The **multiply and assign operator** (*=) alters the value of the operand on the left by multiplying the operand on the right by it.

The **divide and assign operator** (/=) alters the value of the operand on the left by dividing the operand on the right into it.

The **remainder and assign operator** (%=) alters the value of the operand on the left by assigning the remainder when the left operand is divided by the right operand.

The **prefix ++**, also known as the **prefix increment operator**, adds 1 to a variable, then evaluates it.

The **postfix ++**, also known as the **postfix increment operator**, evaluates a variable, then adds 1 to it.

The **prefix and postfix decrement operators** subtract 1 from a variable.

A **for loop** is a special loop that can be used when a definite number of loop iterations is required.

A **pretest loop** is one in which the loop control variable is tested before the loop body executes.

The **do...while loop** executes a loop body at least one time; it checks the loop control variable at the bottom of the loop after one repetition has occurred.

A **posttest loop** is one in which the loop control variable is tested after the loop body executes.

An **inner loop** is contained entirely within another loop.

An **outer loop** contains another loop.

A **do-nothing loop** is one that performs no actions other than looping.

Loop fusion is the technique of combining two loops into one.

Chapter Summary

- A loop is a structure that allows repeated execution of a block of statements. Within a looping structure, a Boolean expression is evaluated, and if it is true, a block of statements called the loop body executes; then the Boolean expression is evaluated again.

- You can use a while loop to execute a body of statements continually while some condition continues to be true. To execute a while loop, you initialize a loop control variable, test it in a while statement, and then alter the loop control variable in the body of the while structure.

- The add and assign operator (+=) adds and assigns in one operation. Similar versions are available for subtraction, multiplication, and division. The prefix and postfix increment operators increase a variable's value by 1. The prefix and postfix decrement operators reduce a variable's value by 1. An expression that uses a prefix operator uses the altered value, but an expression that uses a postfix operator uses the initial value before the increase.

- A for loop initializes, tests, and increments in one statement. There are three sections within the parentheses of a for loop that are separated by exactly two semicolons.

- The do...while loop tests a Boolean expression after one repetition has taken place, at the bottom of the loop.

- Loops can be nested, creating inner and outer loops.

- You can improve loop performance by making sure the loop does not include unnecessary operations or statements and by considering factors such as short-circuit evaluation, zero comparisons, loop fusion, and prefix incrementing.

Review Questions

1. A structure that allows repeated execution of a block of statements is a _____ .

   a. cycle   c. ring

   b. loop   d. band

2. A loop that never ends is a(n) _____ loop.

   a. iterative   c. structured

   b. infinite   d. illegal

3. To construct a loop that works correctly, you should initialize a loop control _____ .

   a. variable   c. structure

   b. constant   d. condition

4. What is the output of the following code?

```
b = 1;
while(b < 4)
    System.out.print(b + " ");
```

a. 1

b. 1 2 3

c. 1 2 3 4

d. 1 1 1 1 1 1...

5. What is the output of the following code?

```
b = 1;
while(b < 4)
{
    System.out.print(b + " ");
    b = b + 1;
}
```

a. 1

b. 1 2 3

c. 1 2 3 4

d. 1 1 1 1 1...

6. What is the output of the following code?

```
e = 1;
while(e < 4);
    System.out.print(e + " ");
```

a. Nothing

b. 1 1 1 1 1 1...

c. 1 2 3 4

d. 4 4 4 4 4 4...

7. If total = 100 and amt = 200, then after the statement total +=
amt, _____ .

a. total is equal to 200

b. total is equal to 300

c. amt is equal to 100

d. amt is equal to 300

8. The prefix ++ is a _____ operator.

a. unary

b. binary

c. tertiary

d. postfix

9. If g = 5, then after h = ++g, the value of h is _____ :

a. 4

b. 5

c. 6

d. 7

10. If m = 9, then after n = m++, the value of m is _____ .

a. 8

b. 9

c. 10

d. 11

11. If m = 9, then after n = m++, the value of n is _____ .

    a. 8   c. 10
    b. 9   d. 11

12. If j = 5 and k = 6, then the value of j++ == k is _____ .

    a. 5   c. true
    b. 6   d. false

13. You must always include _____ in a for loop's parentheses.

    a. two semicolons
    b. three semicolons
    c. two commas
    d. three commas

14. What does the following statement output?

    ```
    for(a = 0; a < 5; ++a)
       System.out.print(a + " ");
    ```

    a. 0 0 0 0 0   c. 0 1 2 3 4 5
    b. 0 1 2 3 4   d. nothing

15. What does the following statement output?

    ```
    for(b = 1; b > 3; ++b)
       System.out.print(b + " ");
    ```

    a. 1 1 1   c. 1 2 3 4
    b. 1 2 3   d. nothing

16. What does the following statement output?

    ```
    for(f = 1, g = 4; f < g; ++f, --g)
       System.out.print(f + " " + g + " ");
    ```

    a. 1 4 2 5 3 6 4 7...   c. 1 4 2 3
    b. 1 4 2 3 3 2   d. nothing

17. The loop that performs its conditional check at the bottom of the loop is a _____ loop.

    a. while   c. for
    b. do...while   d. for...while

18. What does the following program segment output?

```
d = 0;
do
{
    System.out.print(d + " ");
    d++;
} while (d < 2);
```

a. 0   c. 0 1 2

b. 0 1   d. nothing

19. What does the following program segment output?

```
for(f = 0; f < 3; ++f)
    for(g = 0; g < 2; ++g)
        System.out.print(f + " " + g + " ");
```

a. 0 0 0 1 1 0 1 1 2 0 2 1   c. 0 1 0 2 1 1 1 2

b. 0 1 0 2 0 3 1 1 1 2 1 3   d. 0 0 0 1 0 2 1 0 1 1 1 2 2 0 2 1 2 2

20. What does the following program segment output?

```
for(m = 0; m < 4; ++m);
    for(n = 0; n < 2; ++n);
        System.out.print(m + " " + n + " ");
```

a. 0 0 0 1 1 0 1 1 2 0 2 1 3 0 3 1   c. 4 2

b. 0 1 0 2 1 1 1 2 2 1 2 2   d. 3 1

Exercises

Programming Exercises

1. a. Write an application that counts by five from 5 through 200 inclusive, and that starts a new line after every multiple of 50 (50, 100, 150, and 200). Save the file as **CountByFives.java**.

    b. Modify the CountByFives application so that the user enters the value to count by. Start each new line after 10 values have been displayed. Save the file as **CountByAnything.java**.

2. Write an application that asks a user to type an even number to continue or to type 999 to stop. When the user types an even number, display the message "Good job!" and then ask for another input. When the user types an odd number, display an error message and then ask for another input. When the user types 999, end the program. Save the file as **EvenEntryLoop.java**.

3. Write an application that displays the factorial for every integer value from 1 to 10. A factorial of a number is the product of that number multiplied by each positive integer lower than it. For example, 4 factorial is 4 * 3 * 2 * 1, or 24. Save the file as **Factorials.java**.

4. Write an application that prompts a user for two integers and displays every integer between them. Display a message if there are no integers between the entered values. Make sure the program works regardless of which entered value is larger. Save the file as **InBetween.java**.

5. A knot is a unit of speed equal to one nautical mile per hour. Write an application that displays every integer knot value from 15 through 30 and its kilometers per hour and miles per hour equivalents. One nautical mile is 1.852 kilometers or 1.151 miles. Save the file as **Knots.java**.

6. Write an application that shows the sum of 1 to *n* for every *n* from 1 to 50. That is, the program displays 1 (the sum of 1 alone), 3 (the sum of 1 and 2), 6 (the sum of 1, 2, and 3), 10 (the sum of 1, 2, 3, and 4), and so on. Save the file as **EverySum.java**.

7. Write an application that displays every perfect number from 1 through 1,000. A perfect number is one that equals the sum of all the numbers that divide evenly into it. For example, 6 is perfect because 1, 2, and 3 divide evenly into it, and their sum is 6; however, 12 is not a perfect number because 1, 2, 3, 4, and 6 divide evenly into it, and their sum is greater than 12. Save the file as **Perfect.java**.

8. Write an application that uses a loop to create the pattern of *X*s shown in Figure 6-32, in which each *X* is displayed one additional space to the right. Save the file as **Diagonal.java**.

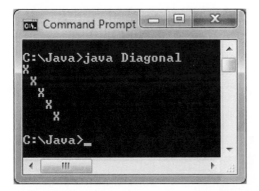

Figure 6-32 Output of the `Diagonal` application

9. Write an application that prompts a user for a child's current age and the estimated college costs for that child at age 18. Continue to reprompt a user who enters an age value greater than 18. Display the amount that the user needs to save each year until the child turns 18, assuming that no interest is earned on the money. For this application, you can assume that integer division provides a sufficient answer. Save the file as **CollegeCost.java**.

10. a. Write an application that prompts a user for the number of years the user has until retirement and the amount of money the user can save annually. If the user enters 0 or a negative number for either value, reprompt the user until valid entries are made. Assume that no interest is earned on the money. Display the amount of money the user will have at retirement. Save the file as **RetirementGoal.java**.

   b. Modify the `RetirementGoal` application to display the amount of money the user will have if the user earns 5% interest on the balance every year. Save the file as **RetirementGoal2.java**.

11. Pickering Manufacturing Company randomly selects one of its four factories to inspect each week. Write an application that determines which factory will be selected each week for the next 52 weeks. Use the `Math.random()` function explained in Appendix D to generate a factory number between 1 and 4; you use a statement similar to:

```
factory = 1 + (int) (Math.random() * 4);
```

   After each selection, display the factory to inspect, and after the 52 selections are complete, display the percentage of inspections at each factory for the year. Run the application several times until you are confident that the factory selection is random. Save the file as **Inspections.java**.

12. Assume that the population of Mexico is 114 million and that the population increases 1.01 percent annually. Assume that the population of the United States is 312 million and that the population is reduced 0.15 percent annually. Write an application that displays the populations for the two countries every year until the population of Mexico exceeds that of the United States, and display the number of years it took. Save the file as **Population.java**.

13. Friendly Hal's Used Cars has four salespeople named Pam, Leo, Kim, and Bob. Accept values for the number of cars sold by each salesperson in a month, and create a bar chart that illustrates sales, similar to the one in Figure 6-33. Save the file as **BarGraph.java**.

Figure 6-33   Typical execution of the `BarGraph` application

14. a. Create a class named `Purchase`. Each `Purchase` contains an invoice number, amount of sale, and amount of sales tax. Include set methods for the invoice number and sale amount. Within the `set()` method for the sale amount, calculate the sales tax as 5% of the sale amount. Also include a display method that displays a purchase's details. Save the file as **Purchase.java**.

   b. Create an application that declares a `Purchase` object and prompts the user for purchase details. When you prompt for an invoice number, do not let the user proceed until a number between 1,000 and 8,000 has been entered. When you prompt for a sale amount, do not proceed until the user has entered a nonnegative value. After a valid `Purchase` object has been created, display the object's invoice number, sale amount, and sales tax. Save the file as **CreatePurchase.java**.

15. Create a `BabysittingJob` class for Georgette's Babysitting Service. The class contains fields to hold the following:

   - A job number that contains six digits. The first two digits represent the year, and the last four digits represent a sequential number. For example, the first job in 2014 has a job number of 140001.

   - A code representing the employee assigned to the job. Assume that the code will always be 1, 2, or 3.

   - A name based on the babysitter code. Georgette has three babysitters: (1) Cindy, (2) Greg, and (3) Marcia.

   - The number of children to be watched. Assume that this number is always greater than zero.

   - The number of hours in the job. Assume that all hour values are whole numbers.

   - The fee for the job. Cindy is paid $7 per hour per child. Greg and Marcia are paid $9 an hour for the first child, and $4 per additional hour for each additional child. For example, if Greg watches three children for two hours, he makes $17 per hour for two hours, or $34.

   Create a constructor for the `BabysittingJob` class that accepts arguments for the job number, babysitter code, number of children, and hours. The constructor determines the babysitter name and fee for the job. Also include a method that displays every `BabysittingJob` object field. Save the file as **BabysittingJob.java**.

   Next, create an application that prompts the user for data for a babysitting job. Keep prompting the user for each of the following values until they are valid:

   - A four-digit year between 2013 and 2025 inclusive

   - A job number for the year between 1 and 9999 inclusive

   - A babysitter code of 1, 2, or 3

- A number of children for the job between 1 and 9 inclusive

- A number of hours between 1 and 12 inclusive

When all the data entries are valid, construct a job number from the last two digits of the year and a four-digit sequential number (which might require leading zeroes). Then, construct a `BabysittingJob` object, and display its values. Save the file as **CreateBabysittingJob.java**.

 Debugging Exercises

1. Each of the following files in the Chapter06 folder of your downloadable student files has syntax and/or logic errors. In each case, determine the problem and fix the program. After you correct the errors, save each file using the same filename preceded with *Fix*. For example, save DebugSix1.java as FixDebugSix1.java.

   a. DebugSix1.java
   b. DebugSix2.java
   c. DebugSix3.java
   d. DebugSix4.java

 Game Zone

1. a. Write an application that creates a quiz. The quiz should contain at least five questions about a hobby, popular music, astronomy, or any other personal interest. Each question should be a multiple-choice question with at least four answer options. When the user answers the question correctly, display a congratulatory message. If the user responds to a question incorrectly, display an appropriate message as well as the correct answer. At the end of the quiz, display the number of correct and incorrect answers and the percentage of correct answers. Save the file as **Quiz.java**.

   b. Modify the `Quiz` application so that the user is presented with each question continually until it is answered correctly. Remove the calculation for percentage of correct answers—all users will have 100 percent correct by the time they complete the application. Save the file as **Quiz2.java**.

2. In Chapter 1, you created a class called `RandomGuess`. In this game, players guess a number, the application generates a random number, and players determine whether they were correct. In Chapter 5, you improved the application to display a message indicating whether the player's guess was correct, too high, or too low. Now, add a loop that continuously prompts the user for the number, indicating whether the guess is high or low, until the user enters the correct value. After the user correctly guesses the number, display a count of the number of attempts it took. Save the file as **RandomGuess3.java**.

3. In Chapter 4, you created a `Die` class from which you could instantiate an object containing a random value from 1 through 6. Now use the class to create a simple dice game in which the user chooses a number between 2 (the lowest total possible from two dice) and 12 (the highest total possible). The user "rolls" two dice up to three times. If the number chosen by the user comes up, the user wins and the game ends. If the number does not come up within three rolls, the computer wins. Save the application as **TwoDice3.java**.

4. a. Using the `Die` class you created in Chapter 4, create a version of the dice game Pig that a user can play against the computer. The object of the game is to be the first to score 100 points. The user and computer take turns rolling a pair of dice following these rules:

   - On a turn, each player "rolls" two dice. If no *1* appears, the dice values are added to a running total, and the player can choose whether to roll again or pass the turn to the other player.

   - If a *1* appears on one of the dice, nothing more is added to the player's total, and it becomes the other player's turn.

   - If a *1* appears on both of the dice, not only is the player's turn over but the player's entire accumulated score is reset to 0.

   - In this version of the game, when the computer does not roll a *1* and can choose whether to roll again, generate a random value between 0 and 1. Have the computer continue to roll the dice when the value is 0.5 or more, and have the computer quit and pass the turn to the player when the value is not 0.5 or more.

   Save the game as **PigDiceGame.java**.

   b. Modify the `PigDiceGame` application so that if a player rolls a *1*, not only does the player's turn end but all the player's earned points during that round are eliminated. (Points from earlier rounds are not affected. That is, when either the player or computer rolls a 1, all the points accumulated since the other had a turn are subtracted.) Save the game as **PigDiceGame2.java**.

5. Two people play the game of Count 21 by taking turns entering a 1, 2, or 3, which is added to a running total. The player who adds the value that makes the total exceed 21 loses the game. Create a game of Count 21 in which a player competes against the computer, and program a strategy that always allows the computer to win. On any turn, if the player enters a value other than 1, 2, or 3, force the player to reenter the value. Save the game as **Count21.java**.

Case Problems

1. Carly's Catering provides meals for parties and special events. In previous chapters, you developed a class that holds catering event information and an application that tests the methods using four objects of the class. Now modify the EventDemo class to do the following:

   - Continuously prompt for the number of guests for each Event until the value falls between 5 and 100 inclusive.

   - For one of the Event objects, create a loop that displays "Please come to my event!" as many times as there are guests for the Event.

   Save the modified file as **EventDemo.java**.

2. Sammy's Seashore Supplies rents beach equipment to tourists. In previous chapters, you developed a class that holds equipment rental information and an application that tests the methods using four objects of the class. Now modify the RentalDemo class to do the following:

   - Continuously prompt for the number of minutes of each Rental until the value falls between 60 and 7,200 inclusive.

   - For one of the Rental objects, create a loop that displays "Coupon good for 10 percent off next rental" as many times as there are full hours in the Rental.

   Save the modified file as **RentalDemo.java**.

Characters, Strings, and the StringBuilder

In this chapter, you will:

◎ Identify string data problems

◎ Manipulate characters

◎ Declare and compare `String` objects

◎ Use other `String` methods

◎ Convert `String` objects to numbers

◎ Use the `StringBuilder` and `StringBuffer` classes

Understanding String Data Problems

Manipulating characters and strings provides some challenges for the beginning Java programmer. For example, consider the `TryToCompareStrings` application shown in Figure 7-1. The `main()` method declares a `String` named `aName` and assigns "Carmen" to it. The user is then prompted to enter a name. The application compares the two names using the equivalency operator (==) and displays one of two messages indicating whether the strings are equivalent.

```java
import java.util.Scanner;
public class TryToCompareStrings
{
    public static void main(String[] args)
    {
        String aName = "Carmen";
        String anotherName;
        Scanner input = new Scanner(System.in);
        System.out.print("Enter your name > ");
        anotherName = input.nextLine();
        if(aName == anotherName)
            System.out.println(aName + " equals " + anotherName);
        else
            System.out.println(aName + " does not equal " + anotherName);
    }
}
```

Don't Do It
Do not use == to compare Strings' contents.

Figure 7-1   The `TryToCompareStrings` application

Figure 7-2 shows the execution of the application. When the user types "Carmen" as the value for `anotherName`, the application concludes that the two names are not equal.

Figure 7-2   Execution of the `TryToCompareStrings` application

The application in Figure 7-1 seems to produce incorrect results. The problem stems from the fact that in Java, `String` is a class, and each created `String` is an object. As an object, a `String` variable name is not a simple data type—it is a **reference**; that is, a variable that holds a memory address. Therefore, when you compare two `String` objects using the == operator, you are comparing not their values but their computer memory locations.

Programmers want to compare the contents of memory locations (the values stored there) more frequently than they want to compare the locations themselves (the addresses). Fortunately, the creators of Java have provided three classes that you can use when working with text data; these classes provide you with many methods that make working with characters and strings easier:

- **Character**—A class whose instances can hold a single character value and whose methods manipulate and inspect single-character data

- **String**—A class for working with fixed-string data—that is, unchanging data composed of multiple characters

- StringBuilder and StringBuffer—Classes for storing and manipulating changeable data composed of multiple characters

---

TWO TRUTHS & A LIE

Understanding String Data Problems

1. A String is a simple data type that can hold text data.

2. Programmers want to compare the values of Strings more frequently than they want to compare their memory addresses.

3. Character, String, and StringBuilder are useful built-in classes for working with text data.

The false statement is #1. A String variable name is a reference; that is, it holds a memory address.

Manipulating Characters

You learned in Chapter 2 that the char data type is used to hold any single character—for example, a letter, digit, or punctuation mark. In addition to the primitive data type char, Java offers a Character class. The Character class contains standard methods for testing the values of characters. Table 7-1 describes many of the Character class methods. The methods that begin with "is", such as isUpperCase(), return a Boolean value that can be used in comparison statements; the methods that begin with "to", such as toUpperCase(), return a character that has been converted to the stated format.

Method	Description
isUpperCase()	Tests if character is uppercase
toUpperCase()	Returns the uppercase equivalent of the argument; no change is made if the argument is not a lowercase letter
isLowerCase()	Tests if character is lowercase
toLowerCase()	Returns the lowercase equivalent of the argument; no change is made if the argument is not an uppercase letter
isDigit()	Returns `true` if the argument is a digit (0–9) and `false` otherwise
isLetter()	Returns `true` if the argument is a letter and `false` otherwise
isLetterOrDigit()	Returns `true` if the argument is a letter or digit and `false` otherwise
isWhitespace()	Returns `true` if the argument is whitespace and `false` otherwise; this includes the space, tab, newline, carriage return, and form feed

Table 7-1   Commonly used methods of the `Character` class

The `Character` class is defined in `java.lang` and is automatically imported into every program you write. The `Character` class inherits from `java.lang.Object`. You will learn more about the `Object` class when you study inheritance concepts in the chapter *Introduction to Inheritance*.

Figure 7-3 contains an application that uses many of the methods shown in Table 7-1. The application asks a user to enter a character. A `String` is accepted and the `charAt()` method is used to extract the first character in the user-entered `String`. (The `charAt()` method belongs to the `String` class; you will learn more about this class and method later in this chapter.) The application determines the attributes of the character and displays information about it.

```
import java.util.Scanner;
public class TestCharacter
{
    public static void main(String[] args)
    {
        char aChar;
        String aString;
        Scanner keyboard = new Scanner(System.in);
        System.out.print("Enter a character… ");
        aString = keyboard.nextLine();
        aChar = aString.charAt(0);
        System.out.println("The character is " + aChar);
```

Figure 7-3   The `TestCharacter` application *(continues)*

(continued)

```
        if(Character.isUpperCase(aChar))
            System.out.println(aChar + " is uppercase");
        else
            System.out.println(aChar + " is not uppercase");
        if(Character.isLowerCase(aChar))
            System.out.println(aChar + " is lowercase");
        else
            System.out.println(aChar + " is not lowercase");
        aChar = Character.toLowerCase(aChar);
        System.out.println("After toLowerCase(), aChar is " + aChar);
        aChar = Character.toUpperCase(aChar);
        System.out.println("After toUpperCase(), aChar is " + aChar);
        if(Character.isLetterOrDigit(aChar))
            System.out.println(aChar + " is a letter or digit");
        else
            System.out.println(aChar +
                " is neither a letter nor a digit");
        if(Character.isWhitespace(aChar))
            System.out.println(aChar + " is whitespace");
        else
            System.out.println(aChar + " is not whitespace");
    }
}
```

Figure 7-3 The `TestCharacter` application

 You can tell that each of the `Character` class methods used in the `TestCharacter` application in Figure 7-3 is a static method because the method name is used without an object reference—you use only the class name, a dot, and the method name. You learned about the difference between static and instance methods in Chapter 3.

The output of three typical executions of the `TestCharacter` application is shown in Figure 7-4. For example, notice that when the character *C* is tested, you can see the following:

- The value returned by the `isUpperCase()` method is `true`.

- The value returned by the `isLowerCase()` method is `false`.

- The value returned by the `toLowerCase()` method is 'c'.

- The value returned by the `toUpperCase()` method is 'C'.

- The value returned by the `isLetterOrDigit()` method is `true`.

- The value returned by the `isWhitespace()` method is `false`.

353

354

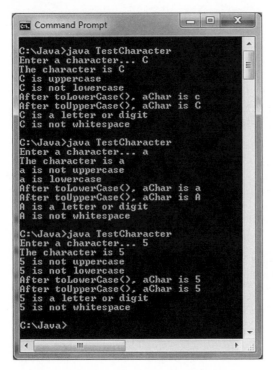

Figure 7-4   Three typical executions of the `TestCharacter` application

TWO TRUTHS & A LIE

Manipulating Characters

1. `Character` is a class, but `char` is a simple data type.

2. The `Character` class method `isLowerCase()` returns the lowercase version of any uppercase character.

3. If a `char` variable holds the Unicode value for the Tab key, `isWhitespace()` would be true and `isLetterOrDigit()` would be false.

The false statement is #2. The `Character` class method `isLowerCase()` returns true or false, as do all the `Character` class methods whose names use the `is` prefix.

You Do It

Retrieving and Testing a Character

In this section, you write a short program that extracts a character from a `String` and uses its lowercase equivalent.

1. Open a new file in your text editor, and start a program that accepts a response from a user using an input dialog box.

```java
import javax.swing.JOptionPane;
public class YLoop
{
    public static void main(String[] args)
    {
```

2. Declare a constant character that holds the value that indicates a user wants to continue. Also include the `String` the user enters, a variable to hold the contents of the first character in that `String`, and a count of the number of iterations performed.

```java
final char YES_OPTION = 'y';
String entryString;
char entryChar;
int count = 0;
```

3. Accept a `String` response from the user, and use the `charAt()` method to extract the first character in the `String`.

```java
entryString = JOptionPane.showInputDialog(null,
    "Do you want to see a greeting?");
entryChar = entryString.charAt(0);
```

4. Write a loop that is controlled by comparing the lowercase equivalent of the entry `String`'s first character to `'y'`. Within the loop, `count` is incremented and then displayed along with a greeting and a prompt that asks the user whether an additional greeting should be displayed. The first character is extracted from the new `String` the user enters.

```java
while(Character.toLowerCase(entryChar) == YES_OPTION)
{
    ++count;
    entryString = JOptionPane.showInputDialog(null,
        "Greeting #" + count +
        " Hello!\nDo you want to see another greeting?");
    entryChar = entryString.charAt(0);
}
```

(continues)

(continued)

5. Add closing curly braces for the `main()` method and for the class.

6. Save the file as **YLoop.java**, and then compile and execute it. Figure 7-5 shows the input dialog box that appears. Whether the user enters *Yes, yes, yeah, Yup, Y,* or *y,* the loop will continue. When the user enters anything that does not start with *y* or *Y,* the loop ends. (If the user clicks OK without entering anything in the dialog box, an error message is displayed and the program ends abruptly. You will learn to manage this type of error in the chapter *Exception Handling.*)

Figure 7-5   Dialog box displayed by the `YLoop` application

Examining the `Character` Class at the Java Web Site

1. Using a Web browser, go to the Java Web site at **www.oracle.com/technetwork/java/index.html**, and select **Java APIs** and **Java SE 7**. Using the alphabetical list of classes, find the `Character` class and select it.

2. Examine the extensive list of methods for the `Character` class. Find one with which you are familiar, such as `toLowerCase()`. Notice that there are two overloaded versions of the method. The one you used in the `YLoop` application accepts a `char` and returns a `char`. The other version that accepts and returns an `int` uses Unicode values. Appendix B of this book provides more information on Unicode.

Declaring and Comparing String Objects

You learned in Chapter 1 that a sequence of characters enclosed within double quotation marks is a literal string. (Programmers might also call it a "string literal.") You have used many literal strings, such as "First Java application", and you have assigned values to String objects and used them within methods, such as println() and showMessageDialog(). A literal string is an unnamed object, or **anonymous object**, of the String class, and a **String variable** is simply a named object of the same class. The class String is defined in java.lang.String, which is automatically imported into every program you write.

 You have declared a String array named args in every main() method header that you have written. You will learn about arrays in the next chapter.

When you declare a String object, the String itself—that is, the series of characters contained in the String—is distinct from the identifier you use to refer to it. You can create a String object by using the keyword new and the String constructor, just as you would create an object of any other type. For example, the following statement defines an object named aGreeting, declares it to be of type String, and assigns an initial value of "Hello" to the String:

```
String aGreeting = new String("Hello");
```

The variable aGreeting stores a reference to a String object—it keeps track of where the String object is stored in memory. When you declare and initialize aGreeting, it links to the initializing String value. Because Strings are declared so routinely in programs, Java provides a shortcut, so you can declare a String containing "Hello" with the following statement that omits the keyword new and does not explicitly call the class constructor:

```
String aGreeting = "Hello";
```

Comparing String Values

In Java, String is a class, and each created String is an object. A String variable name is a reference; that is, a String variable name refers to a location in memory, rather than to a particular value.

The distinction is subtle, but when you declare a variable of a basic, primitive type, such as int x = 10;, the memory address where x is located holds the value 10. If you later assign a new value to x, the new value replaces the old one at the assigned memory address. For example, if you code x = 45;, then 45 replaces 10 at the address of x.

In contrast, when you declare a String, such as String aGreeting = "Hello";, aGreeting does not hold the characters "Hello"; instead it holds a memory address where the characters are stored.

The left side of Figure 7-6 shows a diagram of computer memory if aGreeting happens to be stored at memory address 10876 and the String "Hello" happens to be stored at memory address 26040. You cannot choose the memory address where a value is stored. Addresses such as 10876 and 26040 are chosen by the operating system.

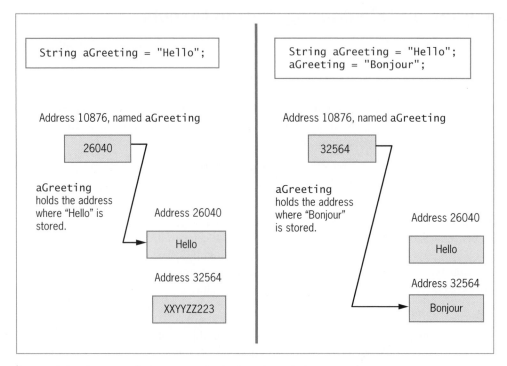

Figure 7-6   Contents of `aGreeting` at declaration and after an assignment

When you refer to `aGreeting`, you actually are accessing the address of the characters you want to use. (In the example on the left side of Figure 7-6, the memory location beginning at address 32564 has not yet been used and holds garbage values.)

If you subsequently assign a new value to `aGreeting`, such as `aGreeting = "Bonjour";`, the address held by `aGreeting` is altered; now, `aGreeting` holds a new address where the characters "Bonjour" are stored. As shown on the right side of Figure 7-6, "Bonjour" is an entirely new object created with its own location. The "Hello" `String` is still in memory, but `aGreeting` no longer holds its address. Eventually, a part of the Java system called the garbage collector discards the "Hello" characters. `String`s, therefore, are never actually changed; instead, new `String`s are created and `String` references hold the new addresses. `String`s and other objects that can't be changed are **immutable**.

The creators of Java made `String`s immutable for several reasons. For example, in environments where multiple programs (or parts of programs, called *threads of execution*) run concurrently, one logical path cannot change a `String` being used by another path. The compiler can also be made to execute more efficiently with immutable `String` objects. In simple programs, you don't care much about these features. However, immutability leads to performance problems. Later in this chapter, you will learn that if you want to use a mutable object to hold strings of characters, you can use the `StringBuilder` class.

Because String references hold memory addresses, making simple comparisons between them often produces misleading results. For example, recall the TryToCompareStrings application in Figure 7-1. In this example, Java evaluates the String variables aName and anotherName as not equal because even though the variables contain the same series of characters, one set is assigned directly and the other is entered from the keyboard and stored in a different area of memory. When you compare Strings with the == operator, you are comparing their memory addresses, not their values. Furthermore, when you try to compare Strings using the less-than (<) or greater-than (>) operator, the program will not even compile.

If you declare two String objects and initialize both to the same value, the value is stored only once in memory and the two object references hold the same memory address. Because the String is stored just once, memory is saved. Consider the following example in which the same value is assigned to two Strings (as opposed to getting one from user input). The reason for the output in the following example is misleading. When you write the following code, the output is *Strings are the same*.

```
String firstString = "abc";
String secondString = "abc";
if(firstString == secondString)
   System.out.println("Strings are the same");
```

The output is *Strings are the same* because the memory addresses held by firstString and secondString are the same, not because their contents are the same.

Fortunately, the String class provides you with a number of useful methods that compare Strings in the way you usually intend. The String class **equals() method** evaluates the contents of two String objects to determine if they are equivalent. The method returns true if the objects have identical contents, no matter how the contents were assigned. For example, Figure 7-7 shows a CompareStrings application, which is identical to the TryToCompareStrings application in Figure 7-1 except for the shaded comparison.

```
import java.util.Scanner;
public class CompareStrings
{
   public static void main(String[] args)
   {
      String aName = "Carmen";
      String anotherName;
      Scanner input = new Scanner(System.in);
      System.out.print("Enter your name > ");
      anotherName = input.nextLine();
      if(aName.equals(anotherName))
         System.out.println(aName + " equals " + anotherName);
      else
         System.out.println(aName + " does not equal " + anotherName);
   }
}
```

Figure 7-7   The CompareStrings application

When a user runs the `CompareStrings` application and enters "Carmen" for the name, the output appears as shown in Figure 7-8; the contents of the `String`s are equal. The `String` class `equals()` method returns `true` only if two `String`s are identical in content. Thus, a `String` that refers to "Carmen " (with a space after the *n*) is not equivalent to a `String` that refers to "Carmen" (with no space after the *n*).

Figure 7-8   Output of the `CompareStrings` application

 Technically, the `equals()` method does not perform an alphabetical comparison with `String`s; it performs a **lexicographical comparison**—a comparison based on the integer Unicode values of the characters.

Each `String` declared in Figure 7-7 (`aName` and `anotherName`) is an object of type `String`, so each `String` has access to the `String` class `equals()` method. If you analyze how the `equals()` method is used in the application in Figure 7-7, you can tell quite a bit about how the method was written by Java's creators:

- Because you use the `equals()` method with a `String` object and the method uses the unique contents of that object to make a comparison, you can tell that it is not a static method.

- Because the call to the `equals()` method can be used in an `if` statement, you can tell that it returns a Boolean value.

- Because you see a `String` used between the parentheses in the method call, you can tell that the `equals()` method takes a `String` argument.

So, the method header of the `equals()` method within the `String` class must be similar to the following:

```
public boolean equals(String s)
```

The only thing you do not know about the method header is the local name used for the `String` argument—it might be `s`, or it might be any other legal Java identifier. When you use a prewritten method such as `equals()`, you do not know how the code looks inside it. For example, you do not know whether the `equals()` method compares the characters in the `String`s from left to right or from right to left. All you know is that the method returns `true` if the two `String`s are completely equivalent and `false` if they are not.

Because both aName and anotherName are Strings in the application in Figure 7-7, the aName object can call equals() with aName.equals(anotherName) as shown, or the anotherName object could call equals() with anotherName.equals(aName). The equals() method can take either a variable String object or a literal string as its argument.

The String class **equalsIgnoreCase() method** is similar to the equals() method. As its name implies, this method ignores case when determining if two Strings are equivalent. Thus, if you declare a String as String aName = "Carmen";, then aName.equals("caRMen") is false, but aName.equalsIgnoreCase("caRMen") is true. This method is useful when users type responses to prompts in your programs. You cannot predict when a user might use the Shift key or the Caps Lock key during data entry.

When the String class **compareTo() method** is used to compare two Strings, it provides additional information to the user in the form of an integer value. When you use compareTo() to compare two String objects, the method returns zero only if the two Strings refer to the same value. If there is any difference between the Strings, a negative number is returned if the calling object is "less than" the argument, and a positive number is returned if the calling object is "more than" the argument. Strings are considered "less than" or "more than" each other based on their Unicode values; thus, "a" is less than "b", and "b" is less than "c". For example, if aName refers to "Roger", then aName.compareTo("Robert"); returns a 5. The number is positive, indicating that "Roger" is more than "Robert". This does not mean that "Roger" has more characters than "Robert"; it means that "Roger" is alphabetically "more" than "Robert". The comparison proceeds as follows:

- The R in "Roger" and the R in "Robert" are compared, and found to be equal.

- The o in "Roger" and the o in "Robert" are compared, and found to be equal.

- The g in "Roger" and the b in "Robert" are compared; they are different. The numeric value of g minus the numeric value of b is 5 (because g is five letters after b in the alphabet), so the compareTo() method returns the value 5.

Often, you won't care what the specific return value of compareTo() is; you simply want to determine if it is positive or negative. For example, you can use a test such as if(aWord.compareTo(anotherWord) < 0) to determine whether aWord is alphabetically less than anotherWord. If aWord is a String variable that refers to the value "hamster", and anotherWord is a String variable that refers to the value "iguana", the comparison if(aWord.compareTo(anotherWord) < 0) yields true.

Empty and null Strings

Programmers are often confused by the difference between empty Strings and null Strings. You can create an empty String named word1 and two null Strings named word2 and word3 with the following statements:

```
String word1 = "";
String word2 = null;
String word3;
```

The empty `String word1` references a memory address where no characters are stored. The **null `String`** word2 uses the Java keyword `null` so that word2 does not yet hold a memory address. The unassigned `String word3` is also a `null String` by default. A significant difference between these declarations is that word1 can be used with the `String` methods described in this chapter, but word2 and word3 cannot. For example, assuming a `String` named someOtherString has been assigned a value, then the comparison word1.equals(someOtherString) is valid, but word2.equals(someOtherString) causes an error.

Because `Strings` are set to `null` by default, some programmers think explicitly setting a `String` to `null` is redundant. Other programmers feel that explicitly using the keyword `null` makes your intentions clearer to those reading your program. You should use the style your organization recommends.

 Watch the video *Comparing Strings*.

TWO TRUTHS & A LIE

Declaring and Comparing `String` Objects

1. To create a `String` object, you must use the keyword new and explicitly call the class constructor.

2. When you compare `Strings` with the == operator, you are comparing their memory addresses, not their values.

3. When you compare `Strings` with the equals() method, you are comparing their values, not their memory addresses.

The false statement is #1. You can create a String object with or without the keyword new and without explicitly calling the String constructor.

 You Do It

Examining the `String` Class at the Java Web Site

In this section, you learn more about the `String` class.

1. Using a Web browser, go to the Java Web site, and select **Java APIs** and **Java SE 7**. Using the alphabetical list of classes, find the **String** class and select it.

(continues)

(continued)

2. Examine the equals() method. In the last section you saw this method used in expressions such as aName.equals(anotherName). Because equals() is used with the object aName, you could predict that the equals() method is not static. When you look at the documentation for the equals() method, you can see this is true. You also can see that it returns a boolean value. What you might have predicted is that the equals() method takes a String argument, because anotherName is a String. However, the documentation shows that the equals() method accepts an Object argument. You will learn more about the Object class in the chapter *Advanced Inheritance Concepts*, but for now understand that a String is a type of Object. Object is a class from which all other classes stem. In Java, every class is a type of Object.

Using Other String Methods

A wide variety of additional methods are available with the String class. The methods **toUpperCase()** and **toLowerCase()** convert any String to its uppercase or lowercase equivalent. For example, if you declare a String as String aWord = "something";, then the string "something" is created in memory and its address is assigned to aWord. The statement aWord = aWord.toUpperCase() creates "SOMETHING" in memory and assigns its address to aWord. Because aWord now refers to "SOMETHING," aWord = aWord.toLowerCase() alters aWord to refer to "something".

The **length() method** is an accessor method that returns the length of a String. For example, the following statements result in the variable len that holds the value 5.

```
String greeting = "Hello";
int len = greeting.length();
```

 In Chapter 2, you learned that your own accessor methods often start with the prefix *get*. The creators of Java did not follow this convention when naming the length() method.

When you must determine whether a String is empty, it is more efficient to compare its length to 0 than it is to use the equals() method.

The **indexOf() method** determines whether a specific character occurs within a String. If it does, the method returns the position of the character; the first position of a String is zero. The return value is –1 if the character does not exist in the String. For example, in String myName = "Stacy";, the value of myName.indexOf('S') is "0", the value of myName.indexOf('a') is "2", and the value of myName.indexOf('q') is "–1".

The **charAt() method** requires an integer argument that indicates the position of the character that the method returns, starting with 0. For example, if myName is a String that refers to "Stacy", the value of myName.charAt(0) is "S" and the value of myName.charAt(4) is "y". An error occurs if you use an argument that is negative, or greater than or equal to the length of the calling String. Instead of using a constant argument with charAt(), frequently you will want to use a variable argument to examine every character in a loop. For example, to count the number of spaces in the String mySentence, you might write a loop like the following:

```
for(int x = 0; x < myName.length(); ++x)
   if(mySentence.charAt(x) == ' ')
      ++countOfSpaces;
```

The **endsWith() method** and the **startsWith() method** each take a String argument and return true or false if a String object does or does not end or start with the specified argument. For example, if String myName = "Stacy";, then myName.startsWith("Sta") is true, and myName.endsWith("z") is false. These methods are case sensitive, so if String myName = "Stacy";, then myName.startsWith("sta") is false.

The **replace() method** allows you to replace all occurrences of some character within a String. For example, if String yourName = "Annette";, then String goofyName = yourName.replace('n', 'X'); assigns "AXXette" to goofyName. The statement goofyName = yourName.replace('p', 'X'); would assign "Annette" to goofyName without any changes because 'p' is not found in yourName. The replace() method is case sensitive, so if String yourName = "Annette";, then String goofyName = yourName.replace('N', 'X'); results in no change.

Although not part of the String class, the **toString() method** is useful when working with String objects. It converts any object to a String. In particular, it is useful when you want to convert primitive data types to Strings. So, if you declare theString and someInt = 4;, as follows, then after the following statements, theString refers to "4":

```
String theString;
int someInt = 4;
theString = Integer.toString(someInt);
```

If you declare another String and a double as follows, then after the following statements, aString refers to "8.25":

```
String aString;
double someDouble = 8.25;
aString = Double.toString(someDouble);
```

You also can use **concatenation** to convert any primitive type to a String. You can join a simple variable to a String, creating a longer String using the + operator. For example, if you declare a variable as int myAge = 25;, the following statement results in aString that refers to "My age is 25":

```
String aString = "My age is " + myAge;
```

Similarly, if you write the following, then `anotherString` refers to "12.34".

```
String anotherString;
float someFloat = 12.34f;
anotherString = "" + someFloat;
```

The Java interpreter first converts the float 12.34f to a `String` "12.34" and adds it to the empty `String` "".

The `toString()` method does not originate in the `String` class; it is a method included in Java that you can use with any type of object. In the chapter *Advanced Inheritance Concepts*, you will learn how to construct versions of the method for your own classes and that `toString()` originates in the `Object` class. You have been using `toString()` throughout this book without knowing it. When you use `print()` and `println()`, their arguments are automatically converted to `String`s if necessary. You don't need import statements to use `toString()` because it is part of `java.lang`, which is imported automatically. Because the `toString()` method you use with `println()` takes arguments of any primitive type, including `int`, `char`, `double`, and so on, it is a working example of polymorphism.

You already know that you can concatenate `String`s with other `String`s or values by using a plus sign (+); you have used this approach in methods such as `println()` and `showMessageDialog()` since Chapter 1. For example, you can display a `firstName`, a space, and a `lastName` with the following statement:

```
System.out.println(firstName + " " + lastName);
```

In addition, you can extract part of a `String` with the **substring() method** and use it alone or concatenate it with another `String`. The `substring()` method takes two integer arguments—a start position and an end position—that are both based on the fact that a `String`'s first position is position zero. The length of the extracted substring is the difference between the second integer and the first integer; if you call the method without a second integer argument, the substring extends to the end of the original string.

For example, the application in Figure 7-9 prompts the user for a customer's first and last names. The application then extracts these names so that a friendly business letter can be constructed. After the application prompts the user to enter a name, a loop control variable is initialized to 0. While the variable remains less than the length of the entered name, each character is compared to the space character. When a space is found, two new strings are created. The first, `firstName`, is the substring of the original entry from position 0 to the location where the space was found. The second, `familyName`, is the substring of the original entry from the position after the space to the end of the string. Once the first and last names have been created, the loop control variable is set to the length of the original string so the loop will exit and proceed to the display of the friendly business letter. Figure 7-10 shows the data entry screen as well as the output letter created.

```
import javax.swing.*;
public class BusinessLetter
{
    public static void main(String[] args)
    {
        String name;
        String firstName = "";
        String familyName = "";
        int x;
        char c;
        name = JOptionPane.showInputDialog(null,
            "Please enter customer's first and last name");
        x = 0;
        while(x < name.length())
        {
            if(name.charAt(x) == ' ')
            {
                firstName = name.substring(0, x);
                familyName = name.substring(x + 1, name.length());
                x = name.length();
            }
            ++x;
        }
        JOptionPane.showMessageDialog(null,
            "Dear " + firstName +
            ",\nI am so glad we are on a first name basis" +
            "\nbecause I would like the opportunity to" +
            "\ntalk to you about an affordable insurance" +
            "\nprotection plan for the entire " + familyName +
            "\nfamily. Call A-One Family Insurance today" +
            "\nat 1-800-555-9287.");
    }
}
```

Figure 7-9   The BusinessLetter application

To keep the example simple, the BusinessLetter application in Figure 7-9 displays a letter for just one customer. An actual business application would most likely allow a clerk to enter dozens or even hundreds of customer names and store them in a data file for future use. You will learn to store data permanently in files in the chapter *File Input and Output*. For now, just concentrate on the string-handling capabilities of the application.

Figure 7-10   Typical execution of the BusinessLetter application

The **regionMatches() method** can be used to test whether two String regions are the same. One version of the regionMatches() method takes four arguments—the position at which to start in the calling String, the other String being compared, the position to start in the other String, and the length of the comparison. For example, suppose that you have declared two String objects as follows:

```
String firstString = "abcde";
String secondString = "xxbcdef";
```

Then, the expression firstString.regionMatches(1, secondString, 2, 4) is true because the four-character substring starting at position 1 in firstString is "bcde" and the four-character substring starting at position 2 in secondString is also "bcde". The expression firstString.regionMatches(0, secondString, 3, 2) is false because the two-character substring starting at position 0 in firstString is "ab" and the two-character substring starting at position 3 in secondString is "cd".

A second version of the regionMatches() method takes an additional boolean argument as the first argument. This argument represents whether case should be ignored in deciding whether regions match. For example, suppose that you have declared two Strings as follows:

```
String thirdString = "123 Maple Drive";
String fourthString = "a maple tree";
```

Then the following expression is true because the substring of thirdString that starts at position 4 and continues for five characters is "Maple", the substring of fourthString that starts at position 2 and continues for five characters is "maple", and the argument that ignores case has been set to true:

```
thirdString.regionMatches(true, 4, fourthString, 2, 5)
```

368

TWO TRUTHS & A LIE

Using Other String Methods

1. Assume that `myName` is a `String` defined as "molly". The value of `myName.toUpperCase()` is "Molly".

2. Assume that `myName` is a `String` defined as "molly". The value of `myName.length()` is "5".

3. Assume that `myName` is a `String` defined as "molly". The value of `myName.indexOf('M')` is –1.

The false statement is #1. If myName is "molly", then myName.toUpperCase() is "MOLLY".

 You Do It

Using `String` Class Methods

To demonstrate the use of the `String` methods, in this section you create an application that asks a user for a name and then "fixes" the name so that the first letter of each new word is uppercase, whether or not the user entered the name that way.

1. Open a new text file in your text editor. Enter the following first few lines of a `RepairName` program. The program declares several variables, including two strings that will refer to a name: one will be "repaired" with correct capitalization; the other will be saved as the user entered it so it can be displayed in its original form at the end of the program. After declaring the variables, prompt the user for a name:

```
import javax.swing.*;
public class RepairName
{
    public static void main(String[] args)
    {
        String name, saveOriginalName;
        int stringLength;
        int i;
        char c;
        name = JOptionPane.showInputDialog(null,
            "Please enter your first and last name");
```

(continues)

(continued)

2. Store the name entered in the saveOriginalName variable. Next, calculate the length of the name the user entered, then begin a loop that will examine every character in the name. The first character of a name is always capitalized, so when the loop control variable i is 0, the character in that position in the name string is extracted and converted to its uppercase equivalent. Then the name is replaced with the uppercase character appended to the remainder of the existing name.

```
saveOriginalName = name;
stringLength = name.length();
for(i=0; i < stringLength; i++)
{
    c = name.charAt(i);
    if(i == 0)
    {
        c = Character.toUpperCase(c);
        name = c + name.substring(1, stringLength);
    }
```

3. After the first character in the name is converted, the program looks through the rest of the name, testing for spaces and capitalizing every character that follows a space. When a space is found at position i, i is increased, the next character is extracted from the name, the character is converted to its uppercase version, and a new name string is created using the old string up to the current position, the newly capitalized letter, and the remainder of the name string. The if...else ends and the for loop ends.

```
    else
        if(name.charAt(i) == ' ')
        {
            ++i;
            c = name.charAt(i);
            c = Character.toUpperCase(c);
            name = name.substring(0, i) + c +
                name.substring(i + 1, stringLength);
        }
}
```

4. After every character has been examined, display the original and repaired names, and add closing braces for the main() method and the class.

```
        JOptionPane.showMessageDialog(null, "Original name was " +
            saveOriginalName + "\nRepaired name is " + name);
    }
}
```

(continues)

(continued)

5. Save the application as **RepairName.java**, and then compile and run the program. Figure 7-11 shows a typical program execution. Make certain you understand how all the `String` methods contribute to the success of this program.

Figure 7-11   Typical execution of the `RepairName` application

Converting `String` Objects to Numbers

If a `String` contains all numbers, as in "649", you can convert it from a `String` to a number so you can use it for arithmetic or you can use it like any other number. For example, suppose you ask a user to enter a salary in an input dialog box. When you accept input using `showInputDialog()`, the accepted value is always a `String`. To be able to use the value in arithmetic statements, you must convert the `String` to a number.

When you use any of the methods described in this section to attempt to convert a `String` to a number, but the `String` does not represent a valid number (for example, if it contains letters), or the `String` represents the wrong kind of number (for example, it contains a decimal point but is being converted to an integer), an error called a `NumberFormatException` occurs. You will learn about exceptions in the chapter *Exception Handling*.

To convert a `String` to an integer, you use the **Integer class**, which is part of `java.lang` and is automatically imported into programs you write. The `Integer` class is an example of a wrapper. A **wrapper** is a class or object that is "wrapped around" a simpler element; the `Integer` wrapper class contains a simple integer and useful methods to manipulate it. You have already used the **parseInt() method**, which is part of the `Integer` class; it takes a `String` argument and returns its integer value. For example, the following statement stores the numeric value 649 in the variable `anInt`:

```
int anInt = Integer.parseInt("649");
```

You can then use the integer value just as you would any other integer. You can tell that parseInt() is a static method because you use it with the class name and not with an object.

Alternatively, you can use the Integer class valueOf() method to convert a String to an Integer class object, and then use the Integer class intValue() method to extract the simple integer from its wrapper class. The ConvertStringToInteger application in Figure 7-12 shows how you can accomplish the conversion. When the user enters a String in the showInputDialog() method, the String is stored in stringHours. The application then uses the valueOf() method to convert the String to an Integer object and uses the intValue() method to extract the integer. When the user enters "37" as the String, it is converted to a number that can be used in a mathematical statement, and the output appears as expected; this output is shown in Figure 7-13.

```java
import javax.swing.JOptionPane;
public class ConvertStringToInteger
{
    public static void main(String[] args)
    {
        String stringHours;
        int hours;
        Integer integerHours;
        final double PAY_RATE = 12.25;
        stringHours = JOptionPane.showInputDialog(null,
            "How many hours did you work this week?");
        integerHours = Integer.valueOf(stringHours);
        hours = integerHours.intValue();
        JOptionPane.showMessageDialog(null, "You worked " +
            hours + " hours at $" + PAY_RATE + " per hour" +
            "\nThat's $" + (hours * PAY_RATE));
    }
}
```

Figure 7-12   The ConvertStringToInteger application

Figure 7-13   Typical execution of the ConvertStringToInteger application

It is also easy to convert a `String` object to a `double` value. You must use the **Double class**, which, like the `Integer` class, is a wrapper class and is imported into your programs automatically. The `Double` class **parseDouble() method** takes a `String` argument and returns its `double` value. For example, the following statement stores the numeric value 147.82 in the variable `doubleValue`.

```
double doubleValue = Double.parseDouble("147.82");
```

To convert a `String` containing "147.82" to a `double`, you also can use the following code:

```
String stringValue = new String("147.82");
Double tempValue = Double.valueOf(stringValue);
double value = tempValue.doubleValue();
```

In this example, `stringValue` is passed to the `Double.valueOf()` method, which returns a `Double` object. The `doubleValue()` method is used with the `tempValue` object; this method returns a simple `double` that is stored in `value`.

The methods `parseInt()` and `parseDouble()` are newer than the `valueOf()` methods, and many programmers prefer to use them when writing new applications.

Besides `Double` and `Integer`, other wrapper classes such as `Float` and `Long` also provide `valueOf()` methods that convert `String`s to the wrapper types. Additionally, the classes provide `parseFloat()` and `parseLong()` methods, respectively.

Watch the video *String Methods*.

TWO TRUTHS & A LIE

Converting `String` Objects to Numbers

1. The `Integer` and `Double` classes are wrapper classes.

2. The value of `Integer.parseInt("22.22")` is 22.

3. The value of `Double.parseDouble("22.22")` is 22.22.

The false statement is #2. `Integer.parseInt("22.22")` does not work because the `String` argument to the `parseInt()` method cannot be converted to an integer.

You Do It

Converting a String to an Integer

In the next steps, you write a program that prompts the user for a number, reads characters from the keyboard, stores the characters in a String, and then converts the String to an integer that can be used in arithmetic statements.

1. Open a new text file in your text editor. Type the first few lines of a NumberInput class that will accept string input:

```
import javax.swing.*;
public class NumberInput
{
    public static void main(String[] args)
    {
```

2. Declare the following variables for the input String, the integer to which it is converted, and the result:

```
String inputString;
int inputNumber;
int result;
```

3. Declare a constant that holds a multiplier factor. This program will multiply the user's input by 10:

```
final int FACTOR = 10;
```

4. Enter the following input dialog box statement that stores the user keyboard input in the String variable inputString:

```
inputString = JOptionPane.showInputDialog(null,
    "Enter a number");
```

5. Use the following Integer.parseInt() method to convert the input String to an integer. Then multiply the integer by 10 and display the result:

```
inputNumber = Integer.parseInt(inputString);
result = inputNumber * FACTOR;
JOptionPane.showMessageDialog(null,
        inputNumber + " * " + FACTOR + " = " + result);
```

6. Add the final two closing curly braces for the program, then save the program as **NumberInput.java** and compile and test the program. Figure 7-14 shows a typical execution. Even though the user enters a String, it can be used successfully in an arithmetic statement because it was converted using the parseInt() method.

(continues)

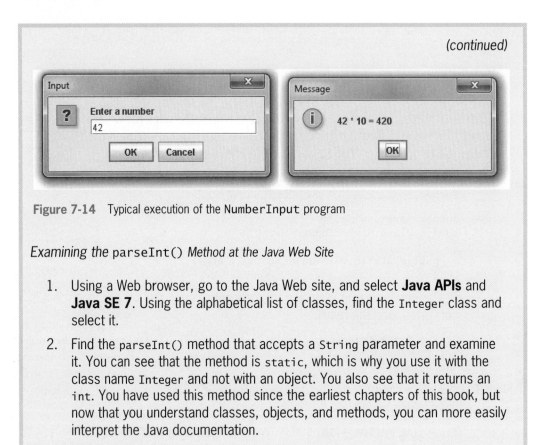

(continued)

Figure 7-14   Typical execution of the `NumberInput` program

Examining the `parseInt()` Method at the Java Web Site

1. Using a Web browser, go to the Java Web site, and select **Java APIs** and **Java SE 7**. Using the alphabetical list of classes, find the `Integer` class and select it.

2. Find the `parseInt()` method that accepts a `String` parameter and examine it. You can see that the method is `static`, which is why you use it with the class name `Integer` and not with an object. You also see that it returns an `int`. You have used this method since the earliest chapters of this book, but now that you understand classes, objects, and methods, you can more easily interpret the Java documentation.

Learning About the `StringBuilder` and `StringBuffer` Classes

In Java, the value of a `String` is fixed after the `String` is created; `String`s are immutable, or unchangeable. When you write `someString = "Hello";` and follow it with `someString = "Goodbye";`, you have neither changed the contents of computer memory at the address represented by `someString` nor eliminated the characters "Hello". Instead, you have stored "Goodbye" at a new computer memory location and stored the new address in the `someString` variable. If you want to modify `someString` from "Goodbye" to "Goodbye Everybody", you cannot add a space and "Everybody" to the `someString` that contains "Goodbye". Instead, you must create an entirely new `String`, "Goodbye Everybody", and assign it to the `someString` address. If you perform many such operations with `String`s, you end up creating many different `String` objects in memory, which takes time and resources.

To circumvent these limitations, you can use either the **StringBuilder** or **StringBuffer** class. You use one of these classes, which are alternatives to the `String` class, when you know a `String` will be modified; usually, you can use a `StringBuilder` or `StringBuffer` object anywhere you would use a `String`. Like the `String` class, these two classes are part of the `java.lang` package and are automatically imported into every program. The classes are identical except for the following:

- `StringBuilder` is more efficient.

- `StringBuffer` is thread safe. This means you should use it in applications that run multiple **threads of execution**, which are units of processing that are scheduled by an operating system and that can be used to create multiple paths of control during program execution. Because most programs you write (and all the programs you will write using this book) contain a single thread, usually you should use `StringBuilder`.

The rest of this section discusses `StringBuilder`, but every statement is also true of `StringBuffer`.

You can create a `StringBuilder` object that contains a `String` with a statement such as the following:

```
StringBuilder message = new StringBuilder("Hello there");
```

When you use the `nextLine()` method with a `Scanner` object for console input or a `JOptionPane.showInputDialog()` method for GUI input, user input almost always comes into your program as a `String`. If you want to work with the input as a `StringBuilder` object, you can convert the `String` using the `StringBuilder` constructor. For example, the following statement gets a user's input using a `Scanner` object named `keyboard` and then stores it in the `StringBuilder` name:

```
StringBuilder name = new StringBuilder(keyboard.nextLine());
```

When you create a `String`, you have the option of omitting the keyword `new`, but when you initialize a `StringBuilder` object you must use the keyword `new`, the constructor name, and an initializing value between the constructor's parentheses. You can create an empty `StringBuilder` variable using a statement such as the following:

```
StringBuilder uninitializedString = null;
```

The variable does not refer to anything until you initialize it with a defined `StringBuilder` object. Generally, when you create a `String` object, sufficient memory is allocated to accommodate the number of Unicode characters in the string. A `StringBuilder` object, however, contains a memory block called a **buffer**, which might or might not contain a string. Even if it does contain a string, the string might not occupy the entire buffer. In other words, the length of a string can be different from the length of the buffer. The actual length of the buffer is the **capacity** of the `StringBuilder` object.

You can change the length of a string in a `StringBuilder` object with the **setLength() method**. The length of a `StringBuilder` object equals the number of characters in the `String` contained in the `StringBuilder`. When you increase a `StringBuilder` object's length to be longer than the `String` it holds, the extra characters contain '\u0000'. If you use the `setLength()` method to specify a length shorter than its `String`, the string is truncated.

To find the capacity of a `StringBuilder` object, you use the **`capacity()` method**. The `StringBuilderDemo` application in Figure 7-15 demonstrates this method. The application creates a `nameString` object containing the seven characters "Barbara". The capacity of the `StringBuilder` object is obtained and stored in an integer variable named `nameStringCapacity` and displayed.

```java
import javax.swing.JOptionPane;
public class StringBuilderDemo
{
    public static void main(String[] args)
    {
        StringBuilder nameString = new StringBuilder("Barbara");
        int nameStringCapacity = nameString.capacity();
        System.out.println("Capacity of nameString is " +
            nameStringCapacity);
        StringBuilder addressString = null;
        addressString = new
            StringBuilder("6311 Hickory Nut Grove Road");
        int addStringCapacity = addressString.capacity();
        System.out.println("Capacity of addressString is " +
            addStringCapacity);
        nameString.setLength(20);
        System.out.println("The name is " + nameString + "end");
        addressString.setLength(20);
        System.out.println("The address is " + addressString);
    }
}
```

Figure 7-15   The `StringBuilderDemo` application

Figure 7-16 shows the `StringBuilder` capacity is 23, which is 16 characters more than the length of the string "Barbara". Whenever you create a `StringBuilder` object, its capacity is the length of the `String` contained in `StringBuilder`, plus 16. The "extra" 16 positions allow for reasonable modification of the `StringBuilder` object after creation without allocating any new memory locations.

Figure 7-16 Output of the StringBuilderDemo application

The creators of Java chose 16 characters as the "extra" length for a StringBuilder object because 16 characters fully occupy four bytes of memory. As you work more with computers in general and programming in particular, you will notice that storage capacities are almost always created in exponential values of 2—for example, 4, 8, 16, 32, 64, and so on.

In the application in Figure 7-15, the addressString variable is created as StringBuilder addressString = null;. The variable does not refer to anything until it is initialized with the defined StringBuilder object in the following statement:

addressString = new StringBuilder("6311 Hickory Nut Grove Road");

The capacity of this new StringBuilder object is shown in Figure 7-16 as the length of the string plus 16, or 43.

In the application shown in Figure 7-15, the length of each of the Strings is changed to 20 using the setLength() method. The application displays the expanded nameString and "end", so you can see in the output that there are 13 extra spaces at the end of the String. The application also displays the truncated addressString so that you can see the effect of reducing its length to 20.

Using StringBuilder objects provides improved computer performance over String objects because you can insert or append new contents into a StringBuilder. In other words, unlike immutable Strings, the ability of StringBuilder objects to be modified makes them more efficient when you know string contents will change.

Although the equals() method compares String object contents, when you use it with StringBuilder objects, it compares references. You can compare the contents of two StringBuilder objects named obj1 and obj2 by converting them to Strings with an expression such as the following:

obj1.toString().equals(obj2.toString())

The StringBuilder class provides you with four constructors as follows:

- public StringBuilder() constructs a StringBuilder with no characters and a default size of 16 characters.

- public StringBuilder(int capacity) constructs a StringBuilder with no characters and a capacity specified by the parameter.

377

- public StringBuilder(String s) contains the same characters as those stored in the String object s. The capacity of the StringBuilder is the length of the String argument you provide, plus 16 additional characters.

- The fourth StringBuilder constructor uses an argument of type CharSequence. CharSequence is another Java class; it is an interface that holds a sequence of char values. You will learn to create interfaces in the chapter *Advanced Inheritance Concepts*.

The **append() method** lets you add characters to the end of a StringBuilder object. For example, the following two statements together declare phrase to hold "Happy" and alter the phrase to hold "Happy birthday":

```
StringBuilder phrase = new StringBuilder("Happy");
phrase.append(" birthday");
```

The **insert() method** lets you add characters at a specific location within a StringBuilder object. For example, if phrase refers to "Happy birthday", then phrase.insert(6, "30th "); alters the StringBuilder to contain "Happy 30th birthday". The first character in the StringBuilder object occupies position zero.

To alter just one character in a StringBuilder, you can use the **setCharAt() method**, which allows you to change a character at a specified position within a StringBuilder object. This method requires two arguments: an integer position and a character. If phrase refers to "Happy 30th birthday", then phrase.setCharAt(6,'4'); changes the value into a 40th birthday greeting.

One way you can extract a character from a StringBuilder object is to use the charAt() method. The **charAt() method** accepts an argument that is the offset of the character position from the beginning of a String and returns the character at that position. The following statements assign the character 'P' to the variable letter:

```
StringBuilder text = new StringBuilder("Java Programming");
char letter = text.charAt(5);
```

If you try to use an index that is less than 0 or greater than the index of the last position in the StringBuilder object, you cause an error known as an exception and your program terminates.

When you can approximate the eventual size needed for a StringBuilder object, assigning sufficient capacity can improve program performance. For example, the program in Figure 7-17 compares the time needed to append "Java" 20,000 times to two StringBuilder objects—one that has the initial default size of 16 characters and another that has an initial size of 80,000 characters. Figure 7-18 shows the execution. The extra time needed for the loop that uses the shorter StringBuilder is the result of repeatedly assigning new memory as the object grows in size.

```java
public class CompareConcatenationTimes
{
    public static void main(String[] args)
    {
        long startTime1, startTime2,
            endTime1, endTime2;
        final int TIMES = 20000;
        int x;
        StringBuilder string1 = new StringBuilder("");
        StringBuilder string2 = new StringBuilder(TIMES * 4);
        startTime1 = System.currentTimeMillis();
        for(x = 0; x < TIMES; ++x)
            string1.append("Java");
        endTime1 = System.currentTimeMillis();
        System.out.println("Time for empty StringBuilder : "
            + (endTime1 - startTime1)+ " milliseconds");
        startTime2 = System.currentTimeMillis();
        for(x = 0; x < TIMES; ++x)
            string2.append("Java");
        endTime2 = System.currentTimeMillis();
        System.out.println("Time for large StringBuilder : "
            + (endTime2 - startTime2)+ " milliseconds");
    }
}
```

Figure 7-17   The CompareConcatenationTimes application

Figure 7-18   Output of the CompareConcatenationTimes program

You saw a demonstration of the currentTimeMillis() method in Chapter 6.

Watch the video *StringBuilder*.

TWO TRUTHS & A LIE

Learning About the StringBuilder and StringBuffer Classes

1. When you create a String, you have the option of omitting the keyword new, but when you initialize a StringBuilder object, you must use the keyword new, the constructor name, and an initializing value between the constructor's parentheses.

2. When you create a StringBuilder object with an initial value of "Juan", its capacity is 16.

3. If a StringBuilder named myAddress contains "817", then myAddress.append(" Maple Lane"); alters myAddress to contain "817 Maple Lane".

The false statement is #2. When you create a StringBuilder object with an initial value of "Juan", its capacity is the length of the String contained in StringBuilder, 4, plus 16 more, for a total of 20.

 You Do It

Using StringBuilder *Methods*

In these steps, you write a program that demonstrates the StringBuilder class.

1. Open a new text file, and type the following first lines of a DemoStringBuilder class:

```
public class DemoStringBuilder
{
    public static void main(String[] args)
    {
```

2. Use the following code to create a StringBuilder object, and then call a print() method (that you will create in Step 7) to display the StringBuilder:

(continues)

(continued)

```
StringBuilder str = new StringBuilder("singing");
print(str);
```

381

3. Enter the following `append()` method to add characters to the existing `StringBuilder` and display it again:

```
str.append(" in the dead of ");
print(str);
```

4. Enter the following `insert()` method to insert characters. Then display the `StringBuilder`, insert additional characters, and display it again:

```
str.insert(0, "Black");
print(str);
str.insert(5, "bird ");
print(str);
```

5. Add one more `append()` and `print()` combination:

```
str.append("night");
print(str);
```

6. Add a closing curly brace for the `main()` method.

7. Enter the following `print()` method that displays `StringBuilder` objects:

```
public static void print(StringBuilder s)
{
    System.out.println(s);
}
```

8. Type the closing curly brace for the class, and then save the file as **DemoStringBuilder.java**. Compile and execute, and then compare your output to Figure 7-19.

Figure 7-19 Output of the `DemoStringBuilder` application

Don't Do It

- Don't attempt to compare String objects using the standard comparison operators. The == operator will compare only the addresses of Strings, and the < and > operators will not work.

- Don't forget that startsWith(), endsWith(), and replace() are case sensitive, so you might want to convert participating Strings to the same case before using them.

- Don't forget to use the new operator and the constructor when declaring initialized StringBuilder or StringBuffer objects.

Key Terms

A **reference** is a variable that holds a memory address.

The **Character class** is one whose instances can hold a single character value. This class also defines methods that can manipulate or inspect single-character data.

The **String class** is for working with fixed-string data—that is, unchanging data composed of multiple characters.

A **String variable** is a named object of the String class.

An **anonymous object** is an unnamed object.

Immutable objects cannot be changed.

The String class **equals() method** evaluates the contents of two String objects to determine if they are equivalent.

A **lexicographical comparison** is based on the integer Unicode values of characters.

The String class **equalsIgnoreCase() method** is similar to the equals() method. As its name implies, it ignores case when determining if two Strings are equivalent.

The String class **compareTo() method** is used to compare two Strings; the method returns zero only if the two Strings refer to the same value. If there is any difference between the Strings, a negative number is returned if the calling object is "less than" the argument, and a positive number is returned if the calling object is "more than" the argument.

A **null String** does not hold a memory address.

The String class **toUpperCase() method** converts any String to its uppercase equivalent.

The String class **toLowerCase() method** converts any String to its lowercase equivalent.

The String class **length() method** returns the length of a String.

The String class **indexOf() method** determines whether a specific character occurs within a String. If it does, the method returns the position of the character; the first position of a String begins with zero. The return value is −1 if the character does not exist in the String.

The String class **charAt() method** requires an integer argument that indicates the position of the character that the method returns.

The String class **endsWith() method** takes a String argument and returns true or false if a String object does or does not end with the specified argument.

The String class **startsWith() method** takes a String argument and returns true or false if a String object does or does not start with the specified argument.

The String class **replace() method** replaces all occurrences of some character within a String.

The **toString() method** converts any object to a String.

Concatenation is the process of joining a variable to a string to create a longer string.

The **substring() method** extracts part of a String.

The **regionMatches() method** tests whether two String regions are the same.

The **Integer class** is a wrapper class that contains a simple integer and useful methods to manipulate it.

A **wrapper** is a class or object that is "wrapped around" a simpler element.

The Integer class **parseInt() method** takes a String argument and returns its integer value.

The **Double class** is a wrapper class that contains a simple double and useful methods to manipulate it.

The Double class **parseDouble() method** takes a String argument and returns its double value.

The **StringBuilder** class is used as an alternative to the String class because it is more efficient if a String's contents will change.

The **StringBuffer** class is an alternative to the String and StringBuilder classes because it is efficient and thread safe.

Threads of execution are units of processing that are scheduled by an operating system and that can be used to create multiple paths of control during program execution.

A **buffer** is a block of memory.

The **capacity** of a StringBuilder object is the actual length of the buffer, as opposed to that of the string contained in the buffer.

The `StringBuilder` class **setLength() method** changes the length of the string in a `StringBuilder` object.

The `StringBuilder` class **capacity() method** returns the actual length, or capacity, of the `StringBuilder` object.

The `StringBuilder` class **append() method** lets you add characters to the end of a `StringBuilder` object.

The `StringBuilder` class **insert() method** lets you add characters at a specific location within a `StringBuilder` object.

The `StringBuilder` class **setCharAt() method** allows you to change a character at a specified position within a `StringBuilder` object.

The `StringBuilder` class **charAt() method** accepts an argument that is the offset of the character position from the beginning of a `String` and returns the character at that position.

Chapter Summary

- `String` variables are references, so they require special techniques for making comparisons.

- The `Character` class is one whose instances can hold a single character value. This class also defines methods that can manipulate or inspect single-character data.

- A sequence of characters enclosed within double quotation marks is a literal string. You can create a `String` object by using the keyword new and the `String` constructor. Unlike other classes, you also can create a `String` object without using the keyword new or explicitly calling the class constructor. `Strings` are immutable. Useful `String` class methods include `equals()`, `equalsIgnoreCase()`, and `compareTo()`.

- Additional useful `String` methods include `toUpperCase()`, `toLowerCase()`, `length()`, `indexOf()`, `charAt()`, `endsWith()`, `startsWith()`, and `replace()`. The `toString()` method converts any object to a `String`. You can join `Strings` with other `Strings` or values by using a plus sign (+); this process is called concatenation. You can extract part of a `String` with the `substring()` method.

- If a `String` contains appropriate characters, you can convert it to a number with the help of the following methods: `Integer.parseInt()`, `Integer.valueOf()`, `intValue()`, `Double.parseDouble()`, `Double.valueOf()`, and `doubleValue()`.

- You can use the `StringBuilder` or `StringBuffer` class to improve performance when a string's contents must change.

Review Questions

1. A sequence of characters enclosed within double quotation marks is a _____.

   a. symbolic string

   b. literal string

   c. prompt

   d. command

2. To create a `String` object, you can use the keyword _____ before the constructor call, but you are not required to use this format.

   a. `object`

   b. `create`

   c. `char`

   d. `new`

3. A `String` variable name is a _____.

   a. reference

   b. value

   c. constant

   d. literal

4. The term that programmers use to describe objects that cannot be changed is _____.

   a. irrevocable

   b. nonvolatile

   c. immutable

   d. stable

5. Suppose that you declare two `String` objects as:

   ```
   String word1 = new String("happy");
   String word2;
   ```

   When you ask a user to enter a value for word2, if the user types "happy", the value of word1 == word2 is _____.

   a. `true`

   b. `false`

   c. illegal

   d. unknown

6. If you declare two `String` objects as:

   ```
   String word1 = new String("happy");
   String word2 = new String("happy");
   ```

   the value of word1.equals(word2) is _____.

   a. `true`

   b. `false`

   c. illegal

   d. unknown

7. The method that determines whether two `String` objects are equivalent, regardless of case, is _____.

   a. `equalsNoCase()`

   b. `toUpperCase()`

   c. `equalsIgnoreCase()`

   d. `equals()`

8. If a `String` is declared as:

    `String aStr = new String("lima bean");`

    then `aStr.equals("Lima Bean")` is _____.

    a. true   c. illegal
    b. false   d. unknown

9. If you create two `String` objects:

    `String name1 = new String("Jordan");`
    `String name2 = new String("Jore");`

    then `name1.compareTo(name2)` has a value of _____.

    a. true   c. −1
    b. false   d. 1

10. If `String myFriend = new String("Ginny");`, which of the following has the value 1?

    a. `myFriend.compareTo("Gabby");`
    b. `myFriend.compareTo("Gabriella");`
    c. `myFriend.compareTo("Ghazala");`
    d. `myFriend.compareTo("Hammie");`

11. If `String movie = new String("West Side Story");`, the value of `movie.indexOf('s')` is _____.

    a. true   c. 2
    b. false   d. 3

12. The `String` class `replace()` method replaces _____.

    a. a `String` with a character
    b. one `String` with another `String`
    c. one character in a `String` with another character
    d. every occurrence of a character in a `String` with another character

13. The `toString()` method converts a(n) _____ to a `String`.

    a. char   c. float
    b. int   d. all of the above

14. Joining `String`s with a plus sign is called _____.

    a. chaining   c. parsing
    b. concatenation   d. linking

15. The first position in a String _____.

    a. must be alphabetic

    b. must be uppercase

    c. is position zero

    d. is ignored by the compareTo() method

16. The method that extracts a string from within another string is _____.

    a. extract()   c. substring()

    b. parseString()   d. append()

17. The method parseInt() converts a(n) _____.

    a. integer to a String   c. Double to a String

    b. integer to a Double   d. String to an integer

18. The difference between int and Integer is _____.

    a. int is a primitive type; Integer is a class

    b. int is a class; Integer is a primitive type

    c. nonexistent; both are primitive types

    d. nonexistent; both are classes

19. For an alternative to the String class, and so that you can change a String's contents, you can use _____.

    a. char   c. StringBuilder

    b. StringHolder   d. StringMerger

20. Unlike when you create a String, when you create a StringBuilder, you must use the keyword _____.

    a. buffer   c. null

    b. new   d. class

Exercises

Programming Exercises

1. Write an application that prompts the user for three first names and concatenates them in every possible two-name combination so that new parents can easily compare them to find the most pleasing baby name. Save the file as **BabyNameComparison.java**.

2. a. Write an application that counts the total number of spaces contained in the `String` "The person who says something is impossible should not interrupt the person who is doing it." Save the file as **CountSpaces.java**.

    b. Write an application that counts the total number of spaces contained in a `String` entered by the user. Save the file as **CountSpaces2.java**.

3. Write an application that prompts the user for a `String` that contains at least five letters and at least five digits. Continuously reprompt the user until a valid `String` is entered. Display a message indicating whether the user was successful or did not enter enough digits, letters, or both. Save the file as **FiveLettersAndFiveDigits.java**.

4. Write an application that allows a user to enter two `Strings`. Output the number of characters in the first `String` that also appear in the second `String`, and output those characters. Figure 7-20 shows two typical executions. Save the file as **CountMatches.java**.

Figure 7-20   Two typical executions of the `CountMatches` application

5. Write an application that counts the words in a `String` entered by a user. Words are separated by any combination of spaces, periods, commas, semicolons, question marks, exclamation points, or dashes. Figure 7-21 shows two typical executions. Save the file as **CountWords.java**.

Figure 7-21 Two typical executions of the CountWords application

6. a. Write an application that accepts three Strings from the user and displays one of two messages depending on whether the user entered the Strings in alphabetical order without regard to case. Save the file as **Alphabetize.java**.

    b. Write an application that accepts three Strings from the user and displays them in alphabetical order without regard to case. Save the file as **Alphabetize2.java**.

7. Write an application that demonstrates each of the following methods based on the following quote:

    "You can never cross the ocean until you have the courage to lose sight of the shore." – Christopher Columbus

    - indexOf('v')
    - indexOf('x')
    - charAt(16)
    - endsWith("bus")
    - endsWith("car")
    - replace('c', 'C')

    Save the file as **DemonstratingStringMethods.java**.

8. Three-letter acronyms are common in the business world. For example, in Java you use the IDE (Integrated Development Environment) in the JDK (Java Development Kit) to write programs used by the JVM (Java Virtual Machine) that you might send over a LAN (local area network). Programmers even use the acronym TLA to stand for *three-letter acronym*. Write a program that allows a user to enter three words, and display the appropriate three-letter acronym in all uppercase letters. If the user enters more than three words, ignore the extra words. Figure 7-22 shows a typical execution. Save the file as **ThreeLetterAcronym.java**.

Figure 7-22   Typical execution of the `ThreeLetterAcronym` program

9. Prompt a user to enter a series of integers separated by spaces and accept the input as a `String`. Display the list of integers and their sum. Save the file as **SumIntegersInString.java**.

10. Write an application that determines whether a phrase entered by the user is a palindrome. A palindrome is a phrase that reads the same backward and forward without regarding capitalization or punctuation. For example, "Dot saw I was Tod", "Was it a car or a cat I saw?", and "Madam, I'm Adam" are palindromes. Save the file as **Palindrome.java**.

11. Write an application that prompts a user for a full name and street address and constructs an ID from the user's initials and numeric part of the address. For example, the user William Henry Harrison who lives at 34 Elm would have an ID of WHH34, whereas user Addison Mitchell who lives at 1778 Monroe would have an ID of AM1778. Save the file as **ConstructID.java**.

12. Write an application that accepts a user's password from the keyboard. When the entered password has fewer than six characters, more than 10 characters, or does not contain at least one letter and one digit, prompt the user again. When the user's entry meets all the password requirements, prompt the user to reenter the password, and do not let the user continue until the second password matches the first one. Save the file as **Password.java**.

13. Create a `TaxReturn` class with fields that hold a taxpayer's Social Security number, last name, first name, street address, city, state, zip code, annual income, marital status, and tax liability. Include a constructor that requires arguments that provide values for all the fields other than the tax liability. The constructor calculates the tax liability based on annual income and the percentages in the following table.

Income ($)	Marital status	
	Single	Married
0–20,000	15%	14%
20,001–50,000	22%	20%
50,001 and over	30%	28%

In the TaxReturn class, also include a display method that displays all the TaxReturn data. Save the file as **TaxReturn.java**.

Create an application that prompts a user for the data needed to create a TaxReturn. Continue to prompt the user for data as long as any of the following are true:

- The Social Security number is not in the correct format, with digits and dashes in the appropriate positions; for example, 999-99-9999.

- The zip code is not five digits.

- The marital status does not begin with one of the following: "S", "s", "M", or "m".

- The annual income is negative.

After all the input data is correct, create a TaxReturn object and then display its values. Save the file as **PrepareTax.java**.

Debugging Exercises

1. Each of the following files in the Chapter07 folder of your downloadable student files has syntax and/or logic errors. In each case, determine the problem and fix the program. After you correct the errors, save each file using the same filename preceded with *Fix*. For example, DebugSeven1.java will become FixDebugSeven1.java.

    a. DebugSeven1.java   c. DebugSeven3.java
    b. DebugSeven2.java   d. DebugSeven4.java

Game Zone

1. a. In Chapter 3, you designed a Card class. The class holds fields that contain a Card's value and suit. Currently, the suit is represented by a single character (s, h, d, or c). Modify the class so that the suit is a string ("Spades", "Hearts", "Diamonds", or "Clubs"). Also, add a new field to the class to hold the string representation of a Card's rank based on its value. Within the Card class setValue() method, besides setting the numeric value, also set the string rank value as follows.

Numeric value	String value for rank
1	"Ace"
2 through 10	"2" through "10"
11	"Jack"
12	"Queen"
13	"King"

b. In Chapter 5, you created a War `Card` game that randomly selects two cards (one for the player and one for the computer) and declares a winner (or a tie). Modify the game to set each `Card`'s suit as the appropriate string, then execute the game using the newly modified `Card` class. Figure 7-23 shows four typical executions. Recall that in this version of War, you assume that the Ace is the lowest-valued card. Save the game as **War2.java**.

Figure 7-23   Four typical executions of the `War2` game

2. In Chapter 5, you created a Rock Paper Scissors game. In the game, a player entered a number to represent one of the three choices. Make the following improvements to the game:

● Allow the user to enter a string ("rock", "paper", or "scissors") instead of a digit.

● Make sure the game works correctly whether the player enters a choice in uppercase or lowercase letters or a combination of the two.

- To allow for player misspellings, accept the player's entry as long as the first two letters are correct. (In other words, if a player types "scixxrs", you will accept it as "scissors" because at least the first two letters are correct.)

- When the player does not type at least the first two letters of the choice correctly, reprompt the player and continue to do so until the player's entry contains at least the first two letters of one of the options.

- Allow 10 complete rounds of the game. At the end, display counts of the number of times the player won, the number of times the computer won, and the number of tie games.

Save the file as **RockPaperScissors2.java**.

3. Create a simple guessing game, similar to Hangman, in which the user guesses letters and then attempts to guess a partially hidden phrase. Display a phrase in which some of the letters are replaced by asterisks; for example, "G* T***" (for "Go Team"). Each time the user guesses a letter, either place the letter in the correct spot (or spots) in the phrase and display it again, or tell the user the guessed letter is not in the phrase. Display a congratulatory message when the entire correct phrase has been deduced. Save the game as **SecretPhrase.java**. In the next chapter, you will modify this program so that instead of presenting the user with the same phrase every time the game is played, the program randomly selects the phrase from a list of phrases.

4. Eliza is a famous 1966 computer program written by Joseph Weizenbaum. It imitates a psychologist (more specifically, a Rogerian therapist) by rephrasing many of a patient's statements as questions and posing them to the patient. This type of therapy (sometimes called nondirectional) is often parodied in movies and television shows, in which the therapist does not even have to listen to the patient, but gives "canned" responses that lead the patient from statement to statement. For example, when the patient says, "I am having trouble with my brother," the therapist might say, "Tell me more about your brother." If the patient says, "I dislike school," the therapist might say, "Why do you say you dislike school?" Eliza became a milestone in the history of computers because it was the first time a computer programmer attempted to create the illusion of human-to-human interaction.

Create a simple version of Eliza by allowing the user to enter statements continually until the user quits by typing "Goodbye". After each statement, have the computer make one of the following responses:

- If the user entered the word "my" (for example, "I am having trouble with my brother"), respond with "Tell me more about your" and insert the noun in question—for example, "Tell me more about your brother". When you search for a word in the user's entry, make sure it is the entire word and not just letters within another word. For example, when searching for *my*, make sure it is not part of another word such as *dummy* or *mystic*.

- If the user entered a strong word, such as "love" or "hate", respond with, "You seem to have strong feelings about that".

- Add a few other appropriate responses of your choosing.

- In the absence of any of the preceding inputs, respond with a random phrase from the following: "Please go on", "Tell me more", or "Continue".

Save the file as **Eliza.java**.

Case Problems

1. Carly's Catering provides meals for parties and special events. In previous chapters, you have developed a class that holds catering event information and an application that tests the methods using four objects of the class. Now modify the `Event` and `EventDemo` classes as follows:

   - Modify the method that sets the event number in the `Event` class so that if the argument passed to the method is not a four-character `String` that starts with a letter followed by three digits, then the event number is forced to "A000". If the initial letter in the event number is not uppercase, force it to be so.

   - Add a contact phone number field to the `Event` class.

   - Add a set method for the contact phone number field in the `Event` class. Whether the user enters all digits or any combination of digits, spaces, dashes, dots, or parentheses for a phone number, store it as all digits. For example, if the user enters *(920) 872-9182*, store the phone number as *9208729182*. If the user enters a number with fewer or more than 10 digits, store the number as *0000000000*.

   - Add a get method for the phone number field. The get method returns the phone number as a `String` constructed as follows: parentheses surround a three-digit area code, followed by a space, followed by the three-digit phone exchange, followed by a hyphen, followed by the last four digits of the phone number.

   - Modify the `EventDemo` program so that besides the event number and guests, the program also prompts the user for and retrieves a contact phone number for each of the sample objects. Display the phone number along with the other `Event` details. Test the `EventDemo` application to make sure it works correctly with valid and invalid event and phone numbers.

   Save the files as **Event.java** and **EventDemo.java**.

2. Sammy's Seashore Supplies rents beach equipment to tourists. In previous chapters, you have developed a class that holds equipment rental information and an application that tests the methods using four objects of the class. Now modify the `Rental` and `RentalDemo` classes as follows:

   - Modify the method that sets the contract number in the `Rental` class so that if the argument passed to the method is not a four-character `String` that starts with a letter followed by three digits, then the contract number is forced to "A000". If the initial letter in the contract number is not uppercase, force it to be so.

- Add a contact phone number field to the Rental class.

- Add a set method for the contact phone number field in the Rental class. Whether the user enters all digits or any combination of digits, spaces, dashes, dots, or parentheses for a phone number, store it as all digits. For example, if the user enters *(920) 872-9182*, store the phone number as *9208729182*. If the user enters a number with fewer or more than 10 digits, store the number as *0000000000*.

- Add a get method for the phone number field. The get method returns the phone number as a String constructed as follows: parentheses surround a three-digit area code, followed by a space, followed by the three-digit phone exchange, followed by a hyphen, followed by the last four digits of the phone number.

- Modify the RentalDemo program so that besides the contract number and minutes, the program also prompts the user for and retrieves a contact phone number for each of the sample objects. Display the phone number along with the other Rental details. Test the RentalDemo application to make sure it works correctly with valid and invalid contract and phone numbers.

Save the files as **Rental.java** and **RentalDemo.java**.

Arrays

In this chapter, you will:

◎ Declare arrays

◎ Initialize an array

◎ Use variable subscripts with an array

◎ Declare and use arrays of objects

◎ Search an array and use parallel arrays

◎ Pass arrays to and return arrays from methods

Declaring Arrays

While completing the first five chapters in this book, you stored values in variables. In those early chapters, you simply stored a value and used it, usually only once, but never more than a few times. In Chapter 6, you created loops that allow you to "recycle" variables and use them many times; that is, after creating a variable, you can assign a value, use the value, and then, in successive cycles through the loop, reuse the variable as it holds different values.

At times, however, you might encounter situations in which storing just one value at a time in memory does not meet your needs. For example, a sales manager who supervises 20 employees might want to determine whether each employee has produced sales above or below the average amount. When you enter the first employee's sales value into an application, you can't determine whether it is above or below average because you don't know the average until you have all 20 values. Unfortunately, if you attempt to assign 20 sales values to the same variable, when you assign the value for the second employee, it replaces the value for the first employee.

A possible solution is to create 20 separate employee sales variables, each with a unique name, so you can store all the sales until you can determine an average. A drawback to this method is that if you have 20 different variable names to be assigned values, you need 20 separate assignment statements. For 20 different variable names, the statement that calculates total sales will be unwieldy, such as:

```
total = firstAmt + secondAmt + thirdAmt + …
```

This method might work for 20 salespeople, but what if you have 10,000 salespeople?

The best solution is to create an array. An **array** is a named list of data items that all have the same type. Each data item is an **element** of the array. You declare an array variable in the same way you declare any simple variable, but you insert a pair of square brackets after the type. For example, to declare an array of `double` values to hold sales figures for salespeople, you can write the following:

```
double[] salesFigures;
```

Similarly, to create an array of integers to hold student ID numbers, you can write the following:

```
int[] idNums;
```

 In Java, you can also declare an array variable by placing the square brackets after the array name, as in `double salesFigures[];`. This format is familiar to C and C++ programmers, but the preferred format among Java programmers is to place the brackets following the variable type and before the variable name.

You can provide any legal identifier you want for an array, but Java programmers conventionally name arrays by following the same rules they use for variables—array names start with a lowercase letter and use uppercase letters to begin subsequent words. Additionally, many programmers observe one of the following conventions to make it more obvious that the name represents a group of items:

- Arrays are often named using a plural noun such as `salesFigures`.

- Arrays are often named by adding a final word that implies a group, such as `salesList`, `salesTable`, or `salesArray`.

After you create an array variable, you still need to reserve memory space. You use the same procedure to create an array that you use to create an object. Recall that when you create a class named `Employee`, you can declare an `Employee` object with a declaration such as:

`Employee oneWorker;`

However, that declaration does not actually create the `oneWorker` object. You create the `oneWorker` object when you use the keyword `new` and the constructor method, as in:

`oneWorker = new Employee();`

Similarly, declaring an array and reserving memory space for it are two distinct processes. To reserve memory locations for 20 `salesFigures` values, you can declare the array variable and create the array with two separate statements as follows:

```
double[] salesFigures;
salesFigures = new double[20];
```

Alternatively, just as with objects, you can declare and create an array in one statement with the following:

```
double[] salesFigures = new double[20];
```

In Java, the size of an array follows the data type and is never declared immediately following the array name, as it is in some other languages such as C++. Other languages, such as Visual Basic, BASIC, and COBOL, use parentheses rather than brackets to refer to individual array elements. By using brackets, the creators of Java made it easier for you to distinguish array names from methods.

The statement `double[] salesFigures = new double[20];` reserves 20 memory locations for 20 `double` values. You can distinguish each `salesFigures` item from the others with a subscript. A **subscript** is an integer contained within square brackets that specifies one of an array's elements. In Java, any array's elements are numbered beginning with 0, so you can legally use any subscript from 0 through 19 when working with an array that has 20 elements. In other words, the first `salesFigures` array element is `salesFigures[0]` and the last `salesFigures` element is `salesFigures[19]`. Figure 8-1 shows how the first few and last few elements of an array of 20 `salesFigures` values appears in computer memory.

Figure 8-1 The first few and last few elements of an array of 20 `salesFigures` items in memory

A subscript is also called an **index**. In particular, you will see the term *index* in some error messages issued by the compiler.

It is a common mistake to forget that the first element in an array is element 0, especially if you know another programming language in which the first array element is element 1. Making this mistake means you will be "off by one" in your use of any array. It is also common to forget that the last element's subscript is one less than the array's size and not the array's size. For example, the highest allowed subscript for a 100-element array is 99. To remember that array elements begin with element 0, it might help if you think of the first array element as being "zero elements away from" the beginning of the array, the second element as being "one element away from" the beginning of the array, and so on. If you use a subscript that is too small (that is, negative) or too large for an array, the subscript is **out of bounds** and an error message is generated.

When you work with any individual array element, you treat it no differently than you would treat a single variable of the same type. For example, to assign a value to the first `salesFigures` element in an array, you use a simple assignment statement, such as the following:

```
salesFigures[0] = 2100.00;
```

To display the last `salesFigures` element in an array of 20, you can write:

```
System.out.println(salesFigures[19]);
```

When programmers talk about these statements, they typically say things like, "`salesFigures` sub zero is assigned 2100.00," and "`salesFigures` sub 19 is output." In other words, they use *sub* as shorthand for "with the subscript."

When you declare or access an array, you can use any expression to represent the size, as long as the expression is an integer. For example, to declare a `double` array named `moneyValues`, you might use any of the following:

- A literal integer constant; for example:

  ```
  double[] moneyValues = new double[10];
  ```

- A named integer constant; for example:

  ```
  double[] moneyValues = new double[NUMBER_ELS];
  ```

  In this example, the constant `NUMBER_ELS` must have been declared previously and assigned a value.

- An integer variable; for example:

  ```
  double[] moneyValues = new double[numberOfEls];
  ```

  In this example, the variable `numberOfEls` must have been declared previously and assigned a value.

- A calculation; for example:

  ```
  double[] moneyValues = new double[x + y * z];
  ```

  In this example, the variables x, y, and z must have been declared previously and assigned values, and the result of the mathematical expression must be an integer.

- A method's return value; for example:

  ```
  double[] moneyValues = new double[getElements()];
  ```

  In this example, the method getElements() must return an integer.

Some other programming languages, such as C++, allow only named or unnamed constants to be used for the size when an array is declared. Java allows variables, arithmetic expressions, and method return values, which makes array declaration more flexible.

TWO TRUTHS & A LIE

Declaring Arrays

1. The statement `int[] idNums = new int[35];` reserves enough memory for exactly 34 integers.

2. The first element in any array has a subscript of 0, no matter what data type is stored.

3. In Java, you can use a variable as well as a constant to declare an array's size.

The false statement is #1. The statement `int[] idNums = new int[35];` reserves enough memory for exactly 35 integers numbered 0 through 34.

You Do It

Declaring an Array

In this section, you create a small array to see how arrays are used. The array holds salaries for four categories of employees.

1. Open a new text file in your text editor.

2. Begin the class that demonstrates how arrays are used by typing the following class and main() headers and their corresponding opening curly braces:

(continues)

```
public class DemoArray
{
    public static void main(String[] args)
    {
```
(continued)

3. On a new line, declare and create an array that can hold four `double` values by typing the following:

```
double[] salaries = new double[4];
```

4. One by one, assign four values to the four array elements by typing the following:

```
salaries[0] = 6.25;
salaries[1] = 6.55;
salaries[2] = 10.25;
salaries[3] = 16.85;
```

5. To confirm that the four values have been assigned, display the salaries one by one using the following code:

```
System.out.println("Salaries one by one are:");
System.out.println(salaries[0]);
System.out.println(salaries[1]);
System.out.println(salaries[2]);
System.out.println(salaries[3]);
```

6. Add the two closing curly braces that end the `main()` method and the `DemoArray` class.

7. Save the program as **DemoArray.java**. Compile and run the program. The program's output appears in Figure 8-2.

Figure 8-2   Output of the DemoArray application

(continues)

(continued)

Using a Subscript that is Out of Bounds

In this section, you purposely generate an out-of-bounds error so you can familiarize yourself with the error message generated.

1. As the last executable line in the DemoArray.java file, add a new output statement that attempts to display a `salaries` value using a subscript that is beyond the range of the array:

    ```
    System.out.println(salaries[4]);
    ```

2. Save the file, and then compile and execute it. The output looks like Figure 8-3. The program runs successfully when the subscript used with the array is 0, 1, 2, or 3. However, when the subscript reaches 4, the error in Figure 8-3 is generated. The message indicates that an `ArrayIndexOutOfBoundsException` has occurred and that the offending index is 4.

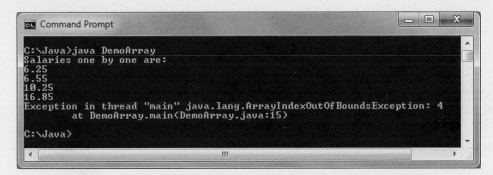

```
C:\Java>java DemoArray
Salaries one by one are:
6.25
6.55
10.25
16.85
Exception in thread "main" java.lang.ArrayIndexOutOfBoundsException: 4
        at DemoArray.main(DemoArray.java:15)

C:\Java>
```

Figure 8-3   Output of the `DemoArray` application when a subscript is out of bounds

In Chapter 12, you will learn more about the term *exception* and learn new ways to deal with exceptions.

3. Remove the offending statement from the `DemoArray` class. Save the program, and then compile and run it again to confirm that it again executes correctly.

Initializing an Array

A variable that has a primitive type, such as `int`, holds a value. A variable with a reference type, such as an array, holds a memory address where a value is stored. In other words, array names contain references, as do all Java objects.

No memory address is assigned when you declare an array using only a data type, brackets, and a name. Instead, the array variable name has the special value `null`, which means the identifier is not associated with a memory address. For example, when you define `someNums` in the following statement, the value of `someNums` is `null`:

```
int[] someNums;
```

When you use the keyword `new` to define an array, the array name acquires an actual memory address value. For example, when you define `someNums` in the following statement, a memory address is assigned:

```
int[] someNums = new int[10];
```

When you declare `int[] someNums = new int[10];`, `someNums` holds an address, but each element of `someNums` has a value of 0 because `someNums` is an integer array. Each element in a `double` or `float` array is assigned 0.0. By default, `char` array elements are assigned '\u0000', which is the Unicode value for a `null` character, and `boolean` array elements automatically are assigned the value `false`. In arrays of objects, including `Strings`, each element is assigned `null` by default.

You already know how to assign a different value to a single element of an array, as in:

```
someNums[0] = 46;
```

You can also assign nondefault values to array elements upon creation. To initialize an array, you use an **initialization list** of values separated by commas and enclosed within curly braces. Providing values for all the elements in an array also is called **populating an array**.

For example, if you want to create an array named `tenMults` and store the first six multiples of 10 within the array, you can declare `tenMults` as follows:

```
int[] tenMults = {10, 20, 30, 40, 50, 60};
```

Notice the semicolon at the end of the statement. You don't use a semicolon following a method's closing curly brace, but you do use one following the closing brace of an array initialization list.

When you populate an array upon creation by providing an initialization list, you do not give the array a size—the size is assigned based on the number of values you place in the initializing list. For example, the `tenMults` array just defined has a size of 6. Also, when you initialize an array, you do not need to use the keyword `new`; instead, new memory is assigned based on the length of the list of provided values.

In Java, you cannot directly initialize part of an array. For example, you cannot create an array of 10 elements and initialize only five; you either must initialize every element or none of them.

 Watch the video *Arrays*.

TWO TRUTHS & A LIE

Initializing an Array

1. When you declare `int[] idNums = new int[35];`, each element of the array has a value of 0.

2. When you declare `double[] salaries = new double[10];`, each element of the array has a value of 0.0.

3. When you declare `int[] scores = {100, 90, 80};`, the first three elements of the array are assigned the values listed, but all the remaining elements are assigned 0.

The false statement is #3. When you provide an initialization list for an array, the array contains exactly that many elements.

You Do It

Initializing an Array

Next, you alter your `DemoArray` program to initialize the array of `double`s, rather than declaring the array and assigning values later.

1. Open the **DemoArray.java** file in your text editor. Immediately save the file as **DemoArray2.java**. Change the class name to `DemoArray2`. Delete the statement that declares the array of four `double`s named `salaries`, and then replace it with the following initialization statement:

   ```
   double[] salaries = {6.25, 6.55, 10.25, 16.85};
   ```

2. Delete the following four statements that individually assign the values to the array:

   ```
   salaries[0] = 6.25; salaries[1] = 6.55; salaries[2] = 10.25;
       salaries[3] = 16.85;
   ```

3. Save the file (as **DemoArray2.java**), compile, and test the application. The values that are output are the same as those shown for the `DemoArray` application in Figure 8-2.

Using Variable Subscripts with an Array

If you treat each array element as an individual entity, there isn't much of an advantage to declaring an array over declaring individual primitive type variables, such as those with the type int, double, or char. The power of arrays becomes apparent when you begin to use subscripts that are variables, rather than subscripts that are constant values.

For example, suppose you declare an array of five integers that holds quiz scores, such as the following:

```
int[] scoreArray = {2, 14, 35, 67, 85};
```

You might want to perform the same operation on each array element, such as increasing each score by a constant amount. To increase each scoreArray element by three points, for example, you can write the following:

```
final int INCREASE = 3;
scoreArray[0] += INCREASE;
scoreArray[1] += INCREASE;
scoreArray[2] += INCREASE;
scoreArray[3] += INCREASE;
scoreArray[4] += INCREASE;
```

With five scoreArray elements, this task is manageable, requiring only five statements. However, you can reduce the amount of program code needed by using a variable as the subscript. Then, you can use a loop to perform arithmetic on each array element, as in the following example:

```
final int INCREASE = 3;
for(sub = 0; sub < 5; ++sub)
   scoreArray[sub] += INCREASE;
```

The variable sub is set to 0, and then it is compared to 5. Because the value of sub is less than 5, the loop executes and 3 is added to scoreArray[0]. Then, the variable sub is incremented and it becomes 1, which is still less than 5, so when the loop executes again, scoreArray[1] is increased by 3, and so on. A process that took five statements now takes only one. In addition, if the array had 100 elements, the first method of increasing the array values by 3 in separate statements would result in 95 additional statements. The only changes required using the second method would be to change the array size to 100 by inserting additional initial values for the scores, and to change the middle portion of the for statement to compare sub to 100 instead of to 5. The loop to increase 100 separate scores by 3 each is:

```
for(sub = 0; sub < 100; ++sub)
   scoreArray[sub] += INCREASE;
```

When an application contains an array and you want to use every element of the array in some task, it is common to perform loops that vary the loop control variable from 0 to one less than the size of the array. For example, if you get input values for the elements in the array, alter every value in the array, sum all the values in the array, or display every element in the array, you need to perform a loop that executes the same number of times as there are elements. When there are 10 array elements, the subscript varies from 0 through 9; when there are 800 elements, the subscript varies from 0 through 799. Therefore, in an application that includes an array, it is convenient to declare a symbolic constant equal to the size of the array and use the symbolic constant as a limiting value in every loop that processes the array. That way, if the array size changes in the future, you need to modify only the value stored in the symbolic constant, and you do not need to search for and modify the limiting value in every loop that processes the array.

For example, suppose you declare an array and a symbolic constant as follows:

```
int[] scoreArray = {2, 14, 35, 67, 85};
final int NUMBER_OF_SCORES = 5;
```

Then, the following two loops are identical:

```
for(sub = 0; sub < 5; ++sub)
    scoreArray[sub] += INCREASE;
for(sub = 0; sub < NUMBER_OF_SCORES; ++sub)
    scoreArray[sub] += INCREASE;
```

The second format has two advantages. First, by using the symbolic constant, NUMBER_OF_SCORES, the reader understands that you are processing every array element for the size of the entire array. If you use the number 5, the reader must look back to the array declaration to confirm that 5 represents the full size of the array. Second, if the array size changes because you remove or add scores, you change the symbolic constant value only once, and all loops that use the constant are automatically altered to perform the correct number of repetitions.

As another option, you can use a field (instance variable) that is automatically assigned a value for every array you create; the **length field** contains the number of elements in the array. For example, when you declare an array using either of the following statements, the field scoreArray.length is assigned the value 5:

```
int[] scoreArray = {2, 14, 35, 67, 85};
int[] scoreArray = new int[5];
```

Therefore, you can use the following loop to add 3 to every array element:

```
for(sub = 0; sub < scoreArray.length; ++sub)
    scoreArray[sub] += INCREASE;
```

Later, if you modify the size of the array and recompile the program, the value in the length field of the array changes appropriately. When you work with array elements, it is always better to use a symbolic constant or the length field when writing a loop that manipulates an array.

A frequent programmer error is to attempt to use length as an array method, referring to scoreArray.length(). However, length is not an array method; it is a field. An instance variable or object field such as length is also called a **property** of the object.

In Chapter 6, you learned to use the for loop. Java also supports an **enhanced for loop**. This loop allows you to cycle through an array without specifying the starting and ending points for the loop control variable. For example, you can use either of the following statements to display every element in an array named scoreArray:

```
for(int sub = 0; sub < scoreArray.length; ++sub)
    System.out.println(scoreArray[sub]);
for(int val : scoreArray)
    System.out.println(val);
```

In the second example, val is defined to be the same type as the array named following the colon. Within the loop, val takes on, in turn, each value in the array. You can read the second example as, "For each val in scoreArray, display val." As a matter of fact, you will see the enhanced for loop referred to as a **foreach loop**.

You also can use the enhanced for loop with more complicated Java objects, as you will see in the next section.

Using Part of an Array

Sometimes, you do not want to use every value in an array. For example, suppose that you write a program that allows a student to enter up to 10 quiz scores and then computes and displays the average. To allow for 10 quiz scores, you create an array that can hold 10 values, but because the student might enter fewer than 10 values, you might use only part of the array. Figure 8-4 shows such a program.

```java
import java.util.*;
public class FlexibleQuizAverage
{
   public static void main(String[] args)
   {
      int[] scores = new int[10];
      int score = 0;
      int count = 0;
      int total = 0;
      final int QUIT = 999;
      final int MAX = 10;
      Scanner input = new Scanner(System.in);
      System.out.print("Enter quiz score >> ");
      score = input.nextInt();
      while(count < MAX && score != QUIT)
      {
         if(score != QUIT)
         {
            scores[count] = score;
            total += scores[count];
            System.out.print("Enter next quiz score or " +
               QUIT + " to quit >> ");
            score = input.nextInt();
         }
         count++;
      }
      System.out.println("The scores entered were:");
      for(int x = 0; x < count; ++x)
         System.out.print(scores[x] + "  ");
      System.out.println("\n The average is " + (total * 1.0 / count));
   }
}
```

Figure 8-4   The FlexibleQuizAverage application

The `FlexibleQuizAverage` program declares an array that can hold 10 quiz scores. The user is prompted for a first quiz score; then, in the `while` loop that starts with the first shaded line in Figure 8-4, the score is placed in the `scores` array. Then the score is added to a running total, and the user is prompted to enter another quiz score or a `QUIT` value of 999 to stop. The `while` loop continuously checks to ensure that no more than 10 scores have been entered and that the user has not entered 999 to quit. After each score entry, the variable `count` is incremented, which serves two purposes: It indicates the element where the next score should be stored, and when the loop eventually ends, `count` holds the number of scores entered. The variable `count` then can be used to control the output loop (in the shaded `for` statement) and to help calculate the average score. Figure 8-5 shows a typical execution of the program.

```
Command Prompt                                    _  □  X

C:\Java>java FlexibleQuizAverage
Enter quiz score >> 80
Enter next quiz score or 999 to quit >> 90
Enter next quiz score or 999 to quit >> 82
Enter next quiz score or 999 to quit >> 72
Enter next quiz score or 999 to quit >> 999
The scores entered were:
80  90  82  72
 The average is 81.0

C:\Java>
```

Figure 8-5   Typical execution of the `FlexibleQuizAverage` application

TWO TRUTHS & A LIE

Using Variable Subscripts with an Array

1. When an application contains an array, it is common to perform loops that vary the loop control variable from 0 to one less than the size of the array.

2. An array's `length` field contains the highest value that can be used as the array's subscript.

3. The enhanced `for` loop allows you to cycle through an array without specifying the starting and ending points for the loop control variable.

The false statement is #2. An array's `length` field contains the number of elements in the array.

You Do It

Using a for Loop to Access Array Elements

Next, you modify the DemoArray2 program to use a for loop with the array.

1. Open the **DemoArray2.java** file in your text editor. Immediately save the file as **DemoArray3.java**. Change the class name to DemoArray3. Delete the four println() statements that display the four array values, and then replace them with the following for loop:

```
for(int x = 0; x < salaries.length; ++x)
    System.out.println(salaries[x]);
```

2. Save the program (as **DemoArray3.java**), compile, and run the program. Again, the output is the same as that shown in Figure 8-2.

Declaring and Using Arrays of Objects

Just as you can declare arrays of ints or doubles, you can declare arrays that hold elements of any type, including objects. For example, assume you create the Employee class shown in Figure 8-6. This class has two data fields (empNum and empSal), a constructor, and a get method for each field.

```
public class Employee
{
    private int empNum;
    private double empSal;
    Employee(int e, double s)
    {
        empNum = e;
        empSal = s;
    }
    public int getEmpNum()
    {
        return empNum;
    }
    public double getSalary()
    {
        return empSal;
    }
}
```

Figure 8-6   The Employee class

You can create separate `Employee` objects with unique names, such as either of the following:

```
Employee painter, electrician, plumber;
Employee firstEmployee, secondEmployee, thirdEmployee;
```

However, in many programs it is far more convenient to create an array of `Employee` objects. An array named `emps` that holds seven `Employee` objects can be defined as:

```
Employee[] emps = new Employee[7];
```

This statement reserves enough computer memory for seven `Employee` objects named `emps[0]` through `emps[6]`. However, the statement does not actually construct those `Employee` objects; instead, you must call the seven individual constructors. According to the class definition shown in Figure 8-6, the `Employee` constructor requires two arguments: an employee number and a salary. If you want to number your `Employee`s 101, 102, 103, and so on, and start each `Employee` at a salary of $6.35, the loop that constructs seven `Employee` objects is as follows:

```
final int START_NUM = 101;
final double PAYRATE = 6.35;
for(int x = 0; x < emps.length; ++x)
   emps[x] = new Employee(START_NUM + x, PAYRATE);
```

As x varies from 0 through 6, each of the seven `emps` objects is constructed with an employee number that is 101 more than x, and each of the seven `emps` objects holds the same salary of $6.35, as assigned in the constant PAYRATE.

Unlike the `Employee` class in Figure 8-6, which contains a constructor that requires arguments, some classes contain only a default constructor, which might be supplied automatically when no other constructors are created or might be written explicitly. To construct an array of objects using a default constructor, you must still call the constructor using the keyword `new` for each declared array element. For example, suppose you have created a class named `InventoryItem` but have not written a constructor. To create an array of 1,000 `InventoryItem` objects, you would write the following:

```
final int NUM_ITEMS = 1000;
InventoryItem[] items = new InventoryItem[NUM_ITEMS];
for(int x = 0; x < NUM_ITEMS; ++x)
   items[x] = new InventoryItem();
```

To use a method that belongs to an object that is part of an array, you insert the appropriate subscript notation after the array name and before the dot that precedes the method name. For example, to display data for seven `Employee`s stored in the `emps` array, you can write the following:

```
for(int x = 0; x < emps.length; ++x)
   System.out.println (emps[x].getEmpNum() + " " +
      emps[x].getSalary());
```

Pay attention to the syntax of the `Employee` objects' method calls, such as `emps[x].getEmpNum()`. Although you might be tempted to place the subscript at the end of the expression after the method name—as in `emps.getEmpNum[x]` or `emps.getEmpNum()[x]`—you cannot; the values in x (0 through 6) refer to a particular `emps` object, each of which has access to a single `getEmpNum()` method. Placement of the bracketed subscript so it follows `emps` means the method "belongs" to a particular element of `emps`.

Using the Enhanced for Loop with Objects

You can use the enhanced for loop to cycle through an array of objects. For example, to display data for seven Employees stored in the emps array, you can write the following:

```
for(Employee worker : emps)
    System.out.println(worker.getEmpNum() + " " + worker.getSalary());
```

In this loop, worker is a local variable that represents each element of emps in turn. Using the enhanced for loop eliminates the need to use a limiting value for the loop and eliminates the need for a subscript following each element.

Manipulating Arrays of Strings

As with any other object, you can create an array of String objects. For example, you can store three company department names as follows:

```
String[] deptNames = {"Accounting", "Human Resources", "Sales"};
```

You can access these department names like any other array object. For example, you can use the following code to display the list of Strings stored in the deptNames array:

```
for(int a = 0; a < deptNames.length; ++a)
    System.out.println(deptNames[a]);
```

Notice that deptNames.length; refers to the length of the array deptNames (three elements) and not to the length of any String objects stored in the deptNames array. Arrays use a length field (no parentheses follow). Each String object has access to a length() method that returns the length of a String. For example, if deptNames[0] is "Accounting", then deptNames[0].length() is 10 because "Accounting" contains 10 characters.

TWO TRUTHS & A LIE

Declaring and Using Arrays of Objects

1. The following statement declares an array named students that holds 10 Student objects:

   ```
   Student[] students = new Student[10];
   ```

2. When a class has a default constructor and you create an array of objects from the class, you do not need to call the constructor explicitly.

3. To use a method that belongs to an object that is part of an array, you insert the appropriate subscript notation after the array name and before the dot that precedes the method name.

The false statement is #2. Whether a class has a default constructor or not, when you create an array of objects from the class, you must call the constructor using the keyword new for each declared array element.

You Do It

Creating a Class That Contains an Array of Strings

In this section, you create a class named BowlingTeam that contains the name of a bowling team and an array that holds the names of the four team members.

1. Open a new file in your text editor, and type the header and curly braces for the BowlingTeam class:

```
public class BowlingTeam
{
}
```

2. Create a field for the team name and an array that holds the team members' names.

```
private String teamName;
private String[] members = new String[4];
```

3. Create get and set methods for the teamName field as follows:

```
public void setTeamName(String team)
{
    teamName = team;
}
public String getTeamName()
{
    return teamName;
}
```

4. Add a method that sets a team member's name. The method requires a position and a name, and it uses the position as a subscript to the members array.

```
public void setMember(int number, String name)
{
    members[number] = name;
}
```

5. Add a method that returns a team member's name. The method requires a value used as the subscript that determines which member's name to return.

```
public String getMember(int number)
{
    return members[number];
}
```

6. Save the file as **BowlingTeam.java**. Compile it and correct any errors.

(continues)

(continued)

Creating a Program to Demonstrate an Instance of the BowlingTeam *Class*

In this section, you write a program in which you create an instance of the BowlingTeam class and provide values for it.

1. Open a new file in your text editor, and enter the following code to begin the class.

```
public class BowlingTeamDemo
{
   public static void main(String[] args)
   {
```

2. Add five declarations. These include a String that holds user input, a BowlingTeam object, an integer to use as a subscript, a constant that represents the number of members on a bowling team, and a Scanner object for input.

```
String name;
BowlingTeam bowlTeam = new BowlingTeam();
int x;
final int NUM_TEAM_MEMBERS = 4;
Scanner input = new Scanner(System.in);
```

3. Prompt the user for a bowling team name. Accept it, and then assign it to the BowlingTeam object:

```
System.out.print("Enter team name >> ");
name = input.nextLine();
bowlTeam.setTeamName(name);
```

4. In a loop that executes four times, prompt the user for a team member's name. Accept the name and assign it to the BowlingTeam object using the subscript to indicate the team member's position in the array in the BowlingTeam class.

```
for(x = 0; x < NUM_TEAM_MEMBERS; ++x)
{
   System.out.print("Enter team member's name >> ");
   name = input.nextLine();
   bowlTeam.setMember(x, name);
}
```

5. Display the details of the BowlingTeam object using the following code:

```
System.out.println("\nMembers of team " +
   bowlTeam.getTeamName());
for(x = 0; x < NUM_TEAM_MEMBERS; ++x)
   System.out.print(bowlTeam.getMember(x) + "  ");
System.out.println();
```

(continues)

(continued)

6. Add a closing curly brace for the `main()` method and another for the class.

7. Save the file as **BowlingTeamDemo.java**, and then compile and execute it. Figure 8-7 shows a typical execution.

```
C:\Java>java BowlingTeamDemo
Enter team name >> The Lucky Strikes
Enter team member's name >> Vic
Enter team member's name >> Nick
Enter team member's name >> Stan
Enter team member's name >> Bill

Members of team The Lucky Strikes
Vic   Nick   Stan   Bill

C:\Java>_
```

Figure 8-7   Typical execution of the `BowlingTeamDemo` class

Creating a Program That Declares an Array of `BowlingTeam` *Objects*

Next, you create and use an array of `BowlingTeam` objects.

1. Open the **BowlingTeamDemo.java** file. Rename the class `BowlingTeamDemo2`, and immediately save the file as **BowlingTeamDemo2.java**.

2. Above the declaration of the `BowlingTeam` object, add a new named constant that holds a number of `BowlingTeam`s, and then replace the statement that declares the single `BowlingTeam` object with an array declaration of four `BowlingTeam` objects.

   ```
   final int NUM_TEAMS = 4;
   BowlingTeam[] teams = new BowlingTeam[NUM_TEAMS];
   ```

3. The current program declares `x`, which is used as a subscript to display team member names. Now, following the declaration of `x`, add a variable that is used as a subscript to display the teams:

   ```
   int y;
   ```

4. Following the declaration of the `Scanner` object, and before the team name prompt, insert a `for` loop that executes as many times as there

(continues)

(continued)

are BowlingTeams. Add the opening curly brace, and within the loop, allocate memory for each array element:

```
for(y = 0; y < NUM_TEAMS; ++y)
{
    teams[y] = new BowlingTeam();
```

5. Delete the statement that uses the setTeamName() method with the single bowlTeam object. In its place, insert a statement that uses the method with one of the array elements:

```
teams[y].setTeamName(name);
```

6. Within the first for loop controlled by x, delete the statement that uses the setMember() method with the single bowlTeam object. In its place, insert a statement that uses the method with one of the array elements:

```
teams[y].setMember(x, name);
```

7. Add a closing curly brace for the for loop controlled by the variable y.

8. Adjust the indentation of the program statements so that the program logic is easy to follow with the new nested loops. The nested loops that you just modified should look like the following 13 lines of code:

```
for(y = 0; y < NUM_TEAMS; ++y)
{
    teams[y] = new BowlingTeam();
    System.out.print("Enter team name >> ");
    name = input.nextLine();
    teams[y].setTeamName(name);
    for(x = 0; x < NUM_TEAM_MEMBERS; ++x)
    {
        System.out.print("Enter team member's name >> ");
        name = input.nextLine();
        teams[y].setMember(x, name);
    }
}
```

9. The for loop at the end of the current program lists four team members' names. Replace this loop with the following nested version that lists four members' names for each of four teams:

```
for(y = 0; y < NUM_TEAMS; ++y)
{
    System.out.println("\nMembers of team " +
        teams[y].getTeamName());
    for(x = 0; x < NUM_TEAM_MEMBERS; ++x)
        System.out.print(teams[y].getMember(x) + "  ");
    System.out.println();
}
```

(continues)

10. Save the file, and then compile and execute the program. Figure 8-8 shows a typical execution. The user can enter data into the array of BowlingTeam objects, including the array of Strings within each object, and then see all the entered data successfully displayed.

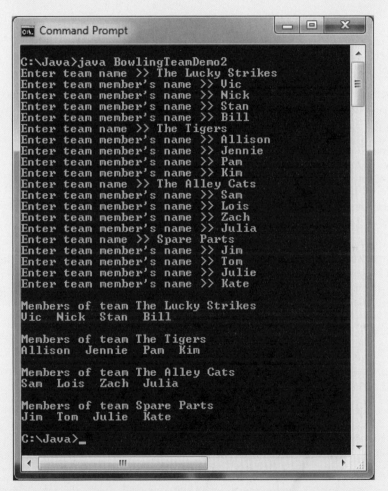

```
C:\Java>java BowlingTeamDemo2
Enter team name >> The Lucky Strikes
Enter team member's name >> Vic
Enter team member's name >> Nick
Enter team member's name >> Stan
Enter team member's name >> Bill
Enter team name >> The Tigers
Enter team member's name >> Allison
Enter team member's name >> Jennie
Enter team member's name >> Pam
Enter team member's name >> Kim
Enter team name >> The Alley Cats
Enter team member's name >> Sam
Enter team member's name >> Lois
Enter team member's name >> Zach
Enter team member's name >> Julia
Enter team name >> Spare Parts
Enter team member's name >> Jim
Enter team member's name >> Tom
Enter team member's name >> Julie
Enter team member's name >> Kate

Members of team The Lucky Strikes
Vic   Nick   Stan   Bill

Members of team The Tigers
Allison   Jennie   Pam   Kim

Members of team The Alley Cats
Sam   Lois   Zach   Julia

Members of team Spare Parts
Jim   Tom   Julie   Kate

C:\Java>_
```

Figure 8-8 Typical execution of the BowlingTeamDemo2 application

Searching an Array and Using Parallel Arrays

Suppose that a company manufactures 10 items. When a customer places an order for an item, you need to determine whether the item number on the order form is valid. When you want to determine whether a variable holds one of many valid values, one option is to use a series of `if` statements to compare the variable to a series of valid values. If valid item numbers are sequential, such as 101 through 110, the following simple `if` statement that uses a logical AND can verify the order number and set a Boolean field to `true`:

```
final int LOW = 101;
final int HIGH = 110;
boolean validItem = false;
if(itemOrdered >= LOW && itemOrdered <= HIGH)
   validItem = true;
```

If the valid item numbers are nonsequential—for example, 101, 108, 201, 213, 266, 304, and so on—you can code the following deeply nested `if` statement or a lengthy OR comparison to determine the validity of an item number:

```
if(itemOrdered == 101)
   validItem = true;
else if(itemOrdered == 108)
   validItem = true;
else if(itemOrdered == 201)
   validItem = true;
// and so on
```

Instead of a long series of `if` statements, a more elegant solution is to compare the `itemOrdered` variable to a list of values in an array, a process called **searching an array**. You can initialize the array with the valid values using the following statement, which creates exactly 10 array elements with subscripts 0 through 9:

```
int[] validValues = {101, 108, 201, 213, 266,
   304, 311, 409, 411, 412};
```

After the list of valid values is initialized, you can use a `for` statement to loop through the array, and set a Boolean variable to `true` when a match is found:

```
for(int x = 0; x < validValues.length; ++x)
{
   if(itemOrdered == validValues[x])
      validItem = true;
}
```

This simple `for` loop replaces the long series of `if` statements; it checks the `itemOrdered` value against each of the 10 array values in turn. Also, if a company carries 1,000 items instead of 10, nothing changes in the `for` statement—the value of `validValues.length` is updated automatically.

Using Parallel Arrays

As an added bonus, if you set up another array with the same number of elements and corresponding data, you can use the same subscript to access additional information.

A **parallel array** is one with the same number of elements as another and for which the values in corresponding elements are related. For example, if the 10 items your company carries have 10 different prices, you can set up an array to hold those prices as follows:

```
double[] prices = {0.29, 1.23, 3.50, 0.69…};
```

The prices must appear in the same order as their corresponding item numbers in the validValues array. Now, the same for loop that finds the valid item number also finds the price, as shown in the application in Figure 8-9. In the shaded portion of the code, notice that when the ordered item's number is found in the validValues array, the itemPrice value is "pulled" from the prices array. In other words, if the item number is found in the second position in the validValues array, you can find the correct price in the second position in the prices array. Figure 8-10 shows a typical execution of the program. A user requests item 409, which is the eighth element in the validValues array, so the price displayed is the eighth element in the prices array.

```java
import javax.swing.*;
public class FindPrice
{
    public static void main(String[] args)
    {
        final int NUMBER_OF_ITEMS = 10;
        int[] validValues = {101,  108,  201,  213,  266,
            304,  311,  409,  411,  412};
        double[] prices = {0.29,  1.23,  3.50,  0.69,  6.79,
            3.19,  0.99,  0.89,  1.26,  8.00};
        String strItem;
        int itemOrdered;
        double itemPrice = 0.0;
        boolean validItem = false;
        strItem = JOptionPane.showInputDialog(null,
            "Enter the item number you want to order");
        itemOrdered = Integer.parseInt(strItem);
        for(int x = 0; x < NUMBER_OF_ITEMS; ++x)
        {
            if(itemOrdered == validValues[x])
            {
                validItem = true;
                itemPrice = prices[x];
            }
        }
        if(validItem)
            JOptionPane.showMessageDialog(null, "The price for item " +
                itemOrdered + " is $" + itemPrice);
        else
            JOptionPane.showMessageDialog(null,
                "Sorry - invalid item entered");
    }
}
```

Figure 8-9 The FindPrice application that accesses information in parallel arrays

Figure 8-10   Typical execution of the `FindPrice` application

When you initialize parallel arrays, it is convenient to use spacing so that the values that correspond to each other visually align on the screen or printed page.

Instead of parallel arrays containing item numbers and prices, you might prefer to create a class named `Item` in which each instance contains two fields—`itemOrdered` and `itemPrice`. Then you could create a single array of objects that encapsulate item numbers and prices. There are almost always multiple ways to approach programming problems.

Within the code shown in Figure 8-9, you compare every `itemOrdered` with each of the 10 `validValues`. Even when an `itemOrdered` is equivalent to the first value in the `validValues` array (101), you always make nine additional cycles through the array. On each of these nine additional cycles, the comparison between `itemOrdered` and `validValues[x]` is always `false`. As soon as a match for an `itemOrdered` is found, it is most efficient to break out of the `for` loop early. An easy way to accomplish this is to set x to a high value within the block of statements executed when there is a match. Then, after a match, the `for` loop does not execute again because the limiting comparison (x < NUMBER_OF_ITEMS) is surpassed. Figure 8-11 shows this loop. In an array with many possible matches, it is most efficient to place the more common items first, so they are matched right away. For example, if item 311 is ordered most often, place 311 first in the `validValues` array, and place its price ($0.99) first in the `prices` array.

```
for(int x = 0; x < NUMBER_OF_ITEMS; ++x)
{
    if(itemOrdered == validValues[x])
    {
        validItem = true;
        itemPrice = prices[x];
        x = NUMBER_OF_ITEMS;
    }
}
```

Figure 8-11   A `for` loop with an early exit

In the code in Figure 8-11, the loop control variable is altered within the loop body. Some programmers object to altering a loop control variable within the body of a for loop; they feel that the loop control variable should be altered only in the third section of the for clause (where x is incremented). These programmers would prefer the loop in Figure 8-12, in which two Boolean expressions appear in the shaded section in the middle portion of the for clause. In this example, the loop control variable is not altered within the loop body. Instead, x must be within range before each iteration and validItem must not yet have been set to true.

```
for(int x = 0; x < NUMBER_OF_ITEMS && !validItem; ++x)
{
    if(itemOrdered == validValues[x])
    {
        validItem = true;
        itemPrice = prices[x];
    }
}
```

Figure 8-12   A for loop that uses a compound test for termination

Searching an Array for a Range Match

Searching an array for an exact match is not always practical. Suppose your company gives customer discounts based on the quantity of items ordered. Perhaps no discount is given for any order of fewer than a dozen items, but there are increasing discounts available for orders of increasing quantities, as shown in Table 8-1.

Total Quantity Ordered	Discount
1 to 12	None
13 to 49	10%
50 to 99	14%
100 to 199	18%
200 or more	20%

Table 8-1   Discount table

One awkward programming option is to create a single array to store the discount rates. You could use a variable named numOfItems as a subscript to the array, but the array would need hundreds of entries, as in the following example:

```
double[] discounts = {0, 0, 0, 0, 0, 0, 0, 0,
    0, 0, 0, 0, 0, 0.10, 0.10, 0.10 …};
```

Thirteen zeroes are listed in the `discounts` array. The first array element has a 0 subscript and represents a zero discount for zero items. The next 12 discounts (for items 1 through 12) are also zero. When `numOfItems` is 13, `discounts[numOfItems]`, or `discounts[13]`, is 0.10. The array would store 37 copies of 0.10 for elements 13 through 49. The `discounts` array would need to be ridiculously large to hold an exact value for each possible quantity ordered.

A better option is to create two corresponding arrays and perform a **range match**, in which you compare a value to the endpoints of numerical ranges to find the category in which a value belongs. For example, one array can hold the five discount rates, and the other array can hold five discount range limits. The Total Quantity Ordered column in Table 8-1 shows five ranges. If you use only the first figure in each range, you can create an array that holds five low limits:

```
int[] discountRangeLimits = {1, 13, 50, 100, 200};
```

A parallel array can hold the five discount rates:

```
double[] discountRates = {0, 0.10, 0.14, 0.18, 0.20};
```

Then, starting at the last `discountRangeLimits` array element, for any `numOfItems` greater than or equal to `discountRangeLimits[4]`, the appropriate discount is `discounts[4]`. In other words, for any `numOrdered` less than `discountRangeLimits[4]`, you should decrement the subscript and look in a lower range. Figure 8-13 shows an application that uses the parallel arrays, and Figure 8-14 shows a typical execution of the program.

```java
import javax.swing.*;
public class FindDiscount
{
    public static void main(String[] args)
    {
        final int NUM_RANGES = 5;
        int[] discountRangeLimits = {   1,   13,   50,  100,  200};
        double[] discountRates =    {0.00, 0.10, 0.14, 0.18, 0.20};
        double customerDiscount;
        String strNumOrdered;
        int numOrdered;
        int sub = NUM_RANGES - 1;
        strNumOrdered = JOptionPane.showInputDialog(null,
            "How many items are ordered?");
        numOrdered = Integer.parseInt(strNumOrdered);
        while(sub >= 0 && numOrdered < discountRangeLimits[sub])
            --sub;
        customerDiscount = discountRates[sub];
        JOptionPane.showMessageDialog(null, "Discount rate for " +
            numOrdered + " items is " + customerDiscount);
    }
}
```

Figure 8-13 The `FindDiscount` class

Figure 8-14 Typical execution of the FindDiscount class

In the while loop in the application in Figure 8-13, sub is required to be greater than or equal to 0 before the second half of the statement that compares numOrdered to discountRangeLimits[sub] executes. It is a good programming practice to ensure that a subscript to an array does not fall below zero, causing a runtime error.

Watch the video *Searching an Array.*

TWO TRUTHS & A LIE

Searching an Array and Using Parallel Arrays

1. A parallel array is one with the same number of elements as another and for which the values in corresponding elements are related.

2. When searching an array, it is usually most efficient to abandon the search as soon as the sought-after element is found.

3. In a range match, you commonly compare a value to the midpoint of each of a series of numerical ranges.

The false statement is #3. In a range match, you commonly compare a value to the low or high endpoint of each of a series of numerical ranges but not to the midpoint.

You Do It

Searching an Array

In this section, you modify the `BowlingTeamDemo2` program so that after the bowling team data has been entered, a user can request the roster for a specific team.

1. Open the **BowlingTeamDemo2.java** file, and change the class name to `BowlingTeamDemo3`. Immediately save the file as **BowlingTeamDemo3.java**.

2. At the end of the existing application, just before the two final closing curly braces, insert a prompt asking the user to enter a team name. Then accept the entered value.

    ```
    System.out.print("\n\nEnter a team name to see its roster >> ");
    name = input.nextLine();
    ```

3. Next, insert a nested `for` loop. The outer loop varies `y` from 0 through the highest subscript allowed in the `teams` array. Within this loop, the team name requested by the user is compared to each stored team name; when they are equal, another `for` loop displays the four team member names.

    ```
    for(y = 0; y < teams.length; ++y)
       if(name.equals(teams[y].getTeamName()))
          for(x = 0; x < NUM_TEAM_MEMBERS; ++x)
             System.out.print(teams[y].getMember(x) + " ");
    ```

4. Insert an additional empty `println()` method call.

    ```
    System.out.println();
    ```

5. Save the file, and then compile and execute the program. Figure 8-15 shows the last part of a typical execution.

(continues)

(continued)

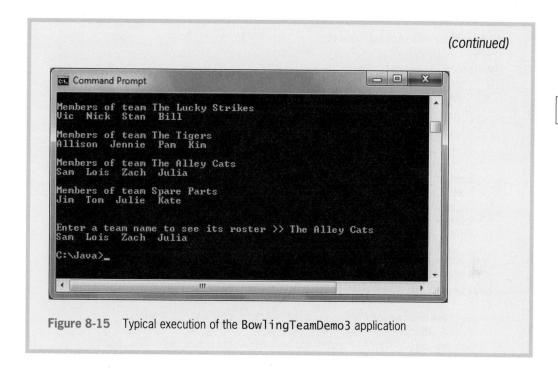

Figure 8-15 Typical execution of the BowlingTeamDemo3 application

Passing Arrays to and Returning Arrays from Methods

You have already seen that you can use any individual array element in the same manner as you use any single variable of the same type. That is, if you declare an integer array as int[] someNums = new int[12];, you can subsequently display someNums[0], or increment someNums[1], or work with any element just as you do for any integer. Similarly, you can pass a single array element to a method in exactly the same manner as you pass a variable.

Examine the PassArrayElement application shown in Figure 8-16 and the output shown in Figure 8-17. The application creates an array of four integers and displays them. Then, the application calls the methodGetsOneInt() method four times, passing each element in turn. The method displays the number, changes the number to 999, and then displays the number again. Finally, back in the main() method, the four numbers are displayed again.

426

```java
public class PassArrayElement
{
    public static void main(String[] args)
    {
        final int NUM_ELEMENTS = 4;
        int[] someNums = {5, 10, 15, 20};
        int x;
        System.out.print("At start of main: ");
        for(x = 0; x < NUM_ELEMENTS; ++x)
            System.out.print(" " + someNums[x] );
        System.out.println();
        for(x = 0; x < NUM_ELEMENTS; ++x)
            methodGetsOneInt(someNums[x]);
        System.out.print("At end of main: ");
        for(x = 0; x < NUM_ELEMENTS; ++x)
            System.out.print(" " + someNums[x]);
        System.out.println();
    }
    public static void methodGetsOneInt(int one)
    {
        System.out.print("At start of method one is: " + one);
        one = 999;
        System.out.println(" and at end of method one is: " + one);
    }
}
```

Figure 8-16   The PassArrayElement class

Figure 8-17   Output of the PassArrayElement application

As you can see in Figure 8-17, the four numbers that were changed in the methodGetsOneInt() method remain unchanged back in main() after the method executes. The variable named one is local to the methodGetsOneInt() method, and any changes to variables passed into the method are not permanent and are not reflected in the array in the main() program. Each variable named one in the methodGetsOneInt() method holds only a copy of the array element passed into the method. The individual array elements are **passed by value**;

that is, a copy of the value is made and used within the receiving method. When any primitive type (boolean, char, byte, short, int, long, float, or double) is passed to a method, the value is passed.

Arrays, like all nonprimitive objects, are **reference types**; this means that the object actually holds a memory address where the values are stored. Because an array name is a reference, you cannot assign another array to it using the = operator, nor can you compare two arrays using the == operator. Additionally, when you pass an array (that is, pass its name) to a method, the receiving method gets a copy of the array's actual memory address. This means that the receiving method has access to, and the ability to alter, the original values in the array elements in the calling method.

The class shown in Figure 8-18 creates an array of four integers. After the integers are displayed, the array name (its address) is passed to a method named methodGetsArray(). Within the method, the numbers are displayed, which shows that they retain their values from main(), but then the value 888 is assigned to each number. Even though methodGetsArray() is a void method—meaning nothing is returned to the main() method—when the main() method displays the array for the second time, all of the values have been changed to 888, as you can see in the output in Figure 8-19. Because the method receives a reference to the array, the methodGetsArray() method "knows" the address of the array declared in main() and makes its changes directly to the original array.

 In some languages, arrays are **passed by reference**, meaning that a receiving method gets the memory address. It is a subtle distinction, but in Java, the receiving method gets a copy of the original address. In other words, in Java, an array is not passed by reference, but a reference to an array is passed by value.

```
public class PassArray
{
    public static void main(String[] args)
    {
        final int NUM_ELEMENTS = 4;
        int[] someNums = {5, 10, 15, 20};
        int x;
        System.out.print("At start of main: ");
        for(x = 0; x < NUM_ELEMENTS; ++x)
            System.out.print(" " + someNums[x] );
        System.out.println();
        methodGetsArray(someNums);
        System.out.print("At end of main: ");
        for(x = 0; x < NUM_ELEMENTS; ++x)
            System.out.print(" " + someNums[x]);
        System.out.println();
    }
```

Figure 8-18 The PassArray class (continues)

(continued)

```java
public static void methodGetsArray(int[] arr)
{
    int x;
    System.out.print("At start of method arr holds: ");
    for(x = 0; x < arr.length; ++x)
        System.out.print(" " + arr[x] );
    System.out.println();
    for(x = 0; x < arr.length; ++x)
        arr[x] = 888;
    System.out.print(" and at end of method arr holds: ");
    for(x = 0; x < arr.length; ++x)
        System.out.print(" " + arr[x] );
    System.out.println();
}
}
```

Figure 8-18   The PassArray class

Notice that in the first shaded statement in Figure 8-18, the array name is passed to the method and no brackets are used. In the method header, brackets are used to show that the parameter is an array of integers (a reference) and not a simple int.

Figure 8-19   Output of the PassArray application

In some other languages, notably C, C++, and C#, you can choose to pass variables to methods by value or reference. In Java, you cannot make this choice. Primitive type variables are always passed by value. When you pass an object, a copy of the reference to the object is always passed.

Returning an Array from a Method

A method can return an array reference. When a method returns an array reference, you include square brackets with the return type in the method header. For example, Figure 8-20 shows a getArray() method that returns a locally declared array of ints. Square brackets are used as part of the return type; the return statement returns the array name without any brackets.

```
public static int[] getArray()
{
    int[] scores = {90, 80, 70, 60};
    return scores;
}
```

Figure 8-20   The getArray() method

When you call the getArray() method in Figure 8-20, you can store its returned value in any integer array reference. For example, you might declare an array and make the method call in the following statement:

```
int[] scoresFromMethod = getArray();
```

 Watch the video *Arrays and Methods.*

TWO TRUTHS & A LIE

Passing Arrays to and Returning Arrays from Methods

1. You pass a single array element to a method using its name, and the method must be prepared to receive the appropriate data type.

2. You pass an array to a method using its name followed by a pair of brackets; arrays are passed by value.

3. When a method returns an array reference, you include square brackets with the return type in the method header.

The false statement is #2. You pass an array to a method using its name; a copy of the array's address is passed to the method.

You Do It

Passing an Array to a Method

Next, you add a method to the `BowlingTeamDemo3` application. The improvement allows you to remove the data entry process from the main program and encapsulate the process in its own method.

1. In your text editor, open the **BowlingTeamDemo3.java** file if it is not already open. Immediately save the file as **BowlingTeamDemo4.java**. Change the class name to match the filename.

2. Just before the closing curly brace for the class, add the following shell for a method that accepts a `BowlingTeam` array argument.

    ```java
    public static void getTeamData(BowlingTeam[] teams)
    {
    }
    ```

3. Within the `getTeamData()` method, add the following six declarations (or copy them from the `main()` method):

    ```java
    String name;
    final int NUM_TEAMS = 4;
    int x;
    int y;
    final int NUM_TEAM_MEMBERS = 4;
    Scanner input = new Scanner(System.in);
    ```

4. Cut the 13 lines of code that assign memory to the `BowlingTeam` array and obtain all the data values. Place these 13 lines within the `getTeamData()` method following the declarations.

    ```java
    for(y = 0; y < NUM_TEAMS; ++y)
    {
        teams[y] = new BowlingTeam();
        System.out.print("Enter team name >> ");
        name = input.nextLine();
        teams[y].setTeamName(name);
        for(x = 0; x < NUM_TEAM_MEMBERS; ++x)
        {
            System.out.print("Enter team member's name >> ");
            name = input.nextLine();
            teams[y].setMember(x, name);
        }
    }
    ```

(continues)

(continued)

5. In place of the 13 cut lines, insert a method call. This call passes a copy of the array reference to the method. Notice that this call does not assign a return value. The method is a `void` method and returns nothing. Nevertheless, the array in the `main()` method will be updated because the method is receiving access to the array's memory address.

```
getTeamData(teams);
```

6. Save the file (as **BowlingTeamDemo4.java**), and then compile and execute the program. Confirm that the program works exactly as it did before the new method was added.

Don't Do It

- Don't forget that the lowest array subscript is 0.

- Don't forget that the highest array subscript is one less than the length of the array.

- Don't forget the semicolon following the closing curly brace in an array initialization list.

- Don't forget that `length` is an array property and not a method. Conversely, `length()` is a `String` method and not a property.

- Don't place a subscript after an object's field or method name when accessing an array of objects. Instead, the subscript for an object follows the object and comes before the dot and the field or method name.

- Don't assume that an array of characters is a string. Although an array of characters can be treated like a string in languages like C++, you can't do this in Java. For example, if you display the name of a character array, you will see its address, not its contents.

- Don't forget that array names are references. Therefore, you cannot assign one array to another using the = operator, nor can you compare array contents using the == operator.

- Don't use brackets with an array name when you pass it to a method. Do use brackets in the method header that accepts the array.

Key Terms

An **array** is a named list of data items that all have the same type.

An **element** is one variable or object in an array.

A **subscript** is an integer contained within square brackets that indicates one of an array's elements.

An **index** is a subscript.

Out of bounds describes a subscript that is not within the allowed range for an array.

An **initialization list** is a series of values provided for an array when it is declared.

Populating an array is the act of providing values for all the elements.

The `length field` contains the number of elements in an array.

An object's instance variable or field is also called a **property** of the object.

The `enhanced for loop` allows you to cycle through an array without specifying the starting and ending points for the loop control variable.

A `foreach loop` is an enhanced `for` loop.

Searching an array is the process of comparing a value to a list of values in an array, looking for a match.

A **parallel array** is one with the same number of elements as another and for which the values in corresponding elements are related.

A **range match** is the process of comparing a value to the endpoints of numerical ranges to find a category in which the value belongs.

When a variable is **passed by value** to a method, a copy is made in the receiving method.

Arrays are **reference types**, meaning that the object actually holds a memory address where the values are stored.

When a value is **passed by reference** to a method, the address is passed to the method.

Chapter Summary

- An array is a named list of data items that all have the same type. You declare an array variable by inserting a pair of square brackets after the type. To reserve memory space for an array, you use the keyword new. You use a subscript contained within square brackets to refer to one of an array's variables, or elements. In Java, any array's elements are numbered beginning with zero.

- Array names represent computer memory addresses. When you declare an array name, no computer memory address is assigned to it. Instead, the array variable name has the special value null. When you use the keyword new or supply an initialization list, then an array acquires an actual memory address. When an initialization list is not provided, each data type has a default value for its array elements.

- You can shorten many array-based tasks by using a variable as a subscript. When an application contains an array, it is common to perform loops that execute from 0 to one less than the size of the array. The `length` field is an automatically created field that is assigned to every array; it contains the number of elements in the array.

- Just as you can declare arrays of integers or `doubles`, you can declare arrays that hold elements of any type, including `Strings` and other objects. To use a method that belongs to an object that is part of an array, you insert the appropriate subscript notation after the array name and before the dot that precedes the method name.

- By looping through an array and making comparisons, you can search an array to find a match to a value. You can use a parallel array with the same number of elements to hold related elements. You perform a range match by placing end values of a numeric range in an array and making greater-than or less-than comparisons.

- You can pass a single array element to a method in exactly the same manner as you would pass a simple variable, and the array receives a copy of the passed value. However, arrays, like all objects, are reference types; this means that when an array name is passed to a method, the method receives a copy of the array's memory address and has access to the values in the original array.

Review Questions

1. An array is a list of data items that _____.

    a. all have the same type
    b. all have different names

    c. all are integers
    d. all are `null`

2. When you declare an array, _____.

    a. you always reserve memory for it in the same statement
    b. you might reserve memory for it in the same statement
    c. you cannot reserve memory for it in the same statement
    d. the ability to reserve memory for it in the same statement depends on the type of the array

3. You reserve memory locations for an array when you _____.

    a. declare the array name
    b. use the keyword `new`
    c. use the keyword `mem`
    d. explicitly store values within the array elements

4. For how many integers does the following statement reserve room?

   `int[] value = new int[34];`

   a. 0

   c. 34

   b. 33

   d. 35

5. Which of the following can be used as an array subscript?

   a. character

   c. `int`

   b. `double`

   d. `String`

6. If you declare an array as follows, how do you indicate the final element of the array?

   `int[] num = new int[6];`

   a. `num[0]`

   c. `num[6]`

   b. `num[5]`

   d. impossible to tell

7. If you declare an integer array as follows, what is the value of `num[2]`?

   `int[] num = {101, 202, 303, 404, 505, 606};`

   a. 101

   c. 303

   b. 202

   d. impossible to tell

8. Array names represent _____.

   a. values

   c. references

   b. functions

   d. allusions

9. Unicode value '\u0000' is also known as _____.

   a. `nil`

   c. `nada`

   b. `void`

   d. `null`

10. When you initialize an array by giving it values upon creation, you _____.

    a. do not explicitly give the array a size

    b. also must give the array a size explicitly

    c. must make all the values zero, blank, or `false`

    d. must make certain each value is different from the others

11. In Java, you can declare an array of 12 elements and initialize _____.

    a. only the first one

    c. Both of these are true.

    b. all of them

    d. Neither of these is true.

12. Assume an array is declared as follows. Which of the following statements correctly assigns the value 100 to each of the array elements?

    ```
    int[] num = new int[4];
    ```

    a. `for(x = 0; x < 3; ++x) num[x] = 100;`

    b. `for(x = 0; x < 4; ++x) num[x] = 100;`

    c. `for(x = 1; x < 4; ++x) num[x] = 100;`

    d. `for(x = 1; x < 5; ++x) num[x] = 100;`

13. Suppose you have declared an array as follows:

    ```
    int[] creditScores = {670, 720, 815};
    ```

    What is the value of `creditScores.length`?

    a. 0   c. 2

    b. 1   d. 3

14. If a class named Student contains a method setID() that takes an int argument, and you write an application in which you create an array of 20 Student objects named scholar, which of the following statements correctly assigns an ID number to the first Student scholar?

    a. `Student[0].setID(1234);`   c. `Student.setID[0](1234);`

    b. `scholar[0].setID(1234);`   d. `scholar.setID[0](1234);`

15. A parallel array is one that _____.

    a. holds values that correspond to those in another array

    b. holds an even number of values

    c. is placed adjacent to another array in code

    d. is placed adjacent to another array in memory

16. In which of the following situations would setting up parallel arrays be most useful?

    a. You need to look up an employee's ID number to find the employee's last name.

    b. You need to calculate interest earned on a savings account balance.

    c. You need to store a list of 20 commonly misspelled words.

    d. You need to determine the shortest distance between two points on a map.

17. When you pass an array element to a method, the method receives _____.

    a. a copy of the array   c. a copy of the value in the element

    b. the address of the array   d. the address of the element

18.   A single array element of a primitive type is passed to a method by _____.

    a.   value   c.   address

    b.   reference   d.   osmosis

19.   When you pass an array to a method, the method receives _____.

    a.   a copy of the array

    b.   a copy of the first element in the array

    c.   the address of the array

    d.   nothing

20.   If a method should return an array to its calling method, _____.

    a.   the method's return type must match its parameter type

    b.   the return type in the method header is preceded by an ampersand

    c.   the return type in the method header is followed by square brackets

    d.   A Java method cannot return an array.

Exercises

 Programming Exercises

1.   Write an application that can hold eight integers in an array. Display the integers from first to last, and then display the integers from last to first. Save the file as **EightInts.java**.

2.   Allow a user to enter any number of `double` values up to 10. The user should enter 99999 to quit entering numbers. Display an error message if the user quits without entering any numbers; otherwise, display each entered value and its distance from the average. Save the file as **DistanceFromAverage.java**.

3.   a. Write an application for Carl's Carpentry that shows a user a list of available items: table, desk, dresser, or entertainment center. Allow the user to enter a string that corresponds to one of the options, and display the price as $250, $325, $420, or $600, accordingly. Display an error message if the user enters an invalid item. Save the file as **CarpentryChoice.java**.

     b. It might not be reasonable to expect users to type long entries such as "entertainment center" accurately. Modify the `CarpentryChoice` class so that as long as the user enters the first three characters of a furniture item, the choice is considered valid. Save the file as **CarpentryChoice2.java**.

4. Create an application containing an array that stores eight integers. The application should (1) display all the integers, (2) display all the integers in reverse order, (3) display the sum of the eight integers, (4) display all values less than 5, (5) display the lowest value, (6) display the highest value, (7) calculate and display the average, and (8) display all values that are higher than the calculated average value. Save the file as **NumberListDemo.java**.

5. Write an application that accepts up to 20 Strings. Divide them into two lists—one for short Strings that are five characters or fewer, and the other for long Strings. After data entry is complete, prompt the user to enter which type of String to display, and then output the correct list. If there are no Strings in a requested list, then output an appropriate message. Save the file as **DivideStrings.java**.

6. a. Create a class named Salesperson. Data fields for Salesperson include an integer ID number and a double annual sales amount. Methods include a constructor that requires values for both data fields, as well as get and set methods for each of the data fields. Write an application named DemoSalesperson that declares an array of 10 Salesperson objects. Set each ID number to 9999 and each sales value to zero. Display the 10 Salesperson objects. Save the files as **Salesperson.java** and **DemoSalesperson.java**.

   b. Modify the DemoSalesperson application so each Salesperson has a successive ID number from 111 through 120 and a sales value that ranges from $25,000 to $70,000, increasing by $5,000 for each successive Salesperson. Save the file as **DemoSalesperson2.java**.

7. a. Create a CollegeCourse class. The class contains fields for the course ID (for example, "CIS 210"), credit hours (for example, 3), and a letter grade (for example, 'A'). Include get and set methods for each field. Create a Student class containing an ID number and an array of five CollegeCourse objects. Create a get() and set() method for the Student ID number. Also create a get() method that returns one of the Student's CollegeCourses; the method takes an integer argument and returns the CollegeCourse in that position (0 through 4). Next, create a set() method that sets the value of one of the Student's CollegeCourses; the method takes two arguments—a CollegeCourse and an integer representing the CollegeCourse's position (0 through 4). Save the files as **CollegeCourse.java** and **Student.java**.

   b. Write an application that prompts a professor to enter grades for five different courses each for 10 students. Prompt the professor to enter data for one student at a time, including student ID and course data for five courses. Use prompts containing the number of the student whose data is being entered and the course number—for example, "Enter ID for student #s", where s is an integer from 1 through 10, indicating the student, and "Enter course ID #n", where n is an integer from 1 through 5, indicating the course number. Verify that the professor enters only A, B, C, D, or F for the grade value for each course. Save the file as **InputGrades.java**.

438

8. Write an application in which the user can enter a date using digits and slashes (for example, "6/24/2014"), and receive output that displays the date with the month shown as a word (such as "June 24, 2014"). Allow for the fact that the user might or might not precede a month or day number with a zero (for example, the user might type "06/24/2014" or "6/24/2014"). Do not allow the user to enter an invalid date, defined as one for which the month is less than 1 or more than 12, or one for which the day number is less than 1 or greater than the number of days in the specified month. Also display the date's ordinal position in the year; for example, 6/24/14 is the 175th day of the year. In this application, use your knowledge of arrays to store the month names, as well as values for the number of days in each month so that you can calculate the number of days that have passed. Save the application as **ConvertDate.java**.

 When determining whether a date is valid and when calculating the number of days that have passed, remember that some years are leap years. In a leap year, February 29th is added to the calendar. A leap year is any year that is evenly divisible by 4, unless the year is also evenly divisible by 100. So 1908 and 2008 were both leap years, but 1900 was not a leap year. Another exception occurs when a year is evenly divisible by 400—the year is a leap year. Therefore, 2000 was a leap year, but 2100 will not be one.

9. Write an application that allows a user to enter the names and phone numbers of up to 20 friends. Continue to prompt the user for names and phone numbers until the user enters "zzz" or has entered 20 names, whichever comes first. When the user is finished entering names, produce a count of how many names were entered, but make certain not to count the application-ending dummy "zzz" entry. Then display the names. Ask the user to type one of the names and display the corresponding phone number. Save the application as **PhoneBook.java**.

10. Write an application containing three parallel arrays that hold 10 elements each. The first array holds four-digit student ID numbers, the second holds first names, and the third holds the students' grade point averages. Use dialog boxes to accept a student ID number and display the student's first name and grade point average. If a match is not found, display an error message that includes the invalid ID number and allow the user to search for a new ID number. Save the file as **StudentIDArray.java**.

11. A personal phone directory contains room for first names and phone numbers for 30 people. Assign names and phone numbers for the first 10 people. Prompt the user for a name, and if the name is found in the list, display the corresponding phone number. If the name is not found in the list, prompt the user for a phone number, and add the new name and phone number to the list. Continue to prompt the user for names until the user enters "quit". After the arrays are full (containing 30 names), do not allow the user to add new entries. Save the file as **PhoneNumbers.java**.

12. In the Exercises in Chapter 4, you created a `CertificateOfDeposit` class and a `TestCertificateOfDeposit` application that instantiated two `CertificateOfDeposit` objects. Now, modify the application to accept data for an array of five `CertificateOfDeposit` objects, and then display the data. Save the application as **TestCertificateOfDepositArray.java**.

13. In the Exercises in Chapter 5, you created a DigitalCamera class and a TestDigitalCamera application that accepted and displayed data for four DigitalCamera objects. Now, modify the TestDigitalCamera application to use an array of four DigitalCamera objects instead of four individual ones. Save the application as **TestDigitalCameraArray.java**.

Debugging Exercises

1. Each of the following files in the Chapter08 folder of your downloadable student files has syntax and/or logic errors. In each case, determine the problem and fix the program. After you correct the errors, save each file using the same filename preceded with *Fix*. For example, DebugEight1.java will become FixDebugEight1.java.

   a. DebugEight1.java   c. DebugEight3.java
   b. DebugEight2.java   d. DebugEight4.java

Game Zone

1. Write an application that contains an array of 10 multiple-choice quiz questions related to your favorite hobby. Each question contains three answer choices. Also create an array that holds the correct answer to each question—A, B, or C. Display each question and verify that the user enters only A, B, or C as the answer—if not, keep prompting the user until a valid response is entered. If the user responds to a question correctly, display "Correct!"; otherwise, display "The correct answer is" and the letter of the correct answer. After the user answers all the questions, display the number of correct and incorrect answers. Save the file as **Quiz.java**.

2. a. In Chapter 4, you created a Die application that randomly "throws" five dice for the computer and five dice for the player. The application displays the values. Modify the application to decide the winner based on the following hierarchy of Die values. Any higher combination beats a lower one; for example, five of a kind beats four of a kind.

   - Five of a kind
   - Four of a kind
   - Three of a kind
   - A pair

   For this game, the dice values do not count; for example, if both players have three of a kind, it's a tie, no matter what the values of the three dice are. Additionally, the game does not recognize a full house (three of a kind plus two of a kind). Figure 8-21 shows a sample execution. Save the application as **FiveDice2.java**.

Figure 8-21   Typical execution of the FiveDice2 application

b. Improve the FiveDice2 game so that when both players have the same combination of dice, the higher value wins. For example, two 6s beats two 5s. Figure 8-22 shows an example execution. Save the application as **FiveDice3.java**.

Figure 8-22   Typical execution of the FiveDice3 application

3. a. In Chapter 7, you modified a previously created Card class so that each Card would hold the name of a suit ("Spades", "Hearts", "Diamonds", or "Clubs") as well as a value ("Ace", "King", "Queen", "Jack", or a number value). Now, create an array of 52 Card objects, assigning a different value to each Card, and display each Card. Save the application as **FullDeck.java**.

   b. In Chapter 7, you created a War2 card game that randomly selects two Card objects (one for the player and one for the computer) and declares a winner or a tie based on the card values. Now create a game that plays 26 rounds of War, dealing a full deck with no repeated cards. Some hints:

   • Start by creating an array of all 52 playing cards, as in Part a of this exercise.

   • Select a random number for the deck position of the player's first card, and assign the card at that array position to the player.

- Move every higher-positioned card in the deck "down" one to fill in the gap. In other words, if the player's first random number is 49, select the card at position 49, move the card that was in position 50 to position 49, and move the card that was in position 51 to position 50. Only 51 cards remain in the deck after the player's first card is dealt, so the available-card array is smaller by one.

- In the same way, randomly select a card for the computer and "remove" the card from the deck.

- Display the values of the player's and computer's cards, compare their values, and determine the winner.

- When all the cards in the deck are exhausted, display a count of the number of times the player wins, the number of times the computer wins, and the number of ties.

Save the game as **War3.java**.

4. In Chapter 7, you created a Secret Phrase game similar to Hangman, in which the user guesses letters in a partially hidden phrase in an attempt to determine the complete phrase. Modify the program so that:

- The phrase to be guessed is selected randomly from a list of at least 10 phrases.

- The clue is presented to the user with asterisks replacing letters to be guessed but with spaces in the appropriate locations. For example, if the phrase to be guessed is "No man is an island," then the user sees the following as a first clue:

** *** ** ** ******

The spaces provide valuable clues as to where individual words start and end.

- Make sure that when a user makes a correct guess, all the matching letters are filled in, regardless of case.

Save the game as **SecretPhrase2.java**.

Case Problems

1. In previous chapters, you developed classes that work with catering event information for Carly's Catering. Now modify the Event and EventDemo classes as follows:

- Modify the Event class to include an integer field that holds an event type. Add a final String array that holds names of the types of events that Carly's caters—wedding, baptism, birthday, corporate, and other. Include get and set methods for the integer event type field. If the argument passed to the method that sets the event type is larger than the size of the array of String event types, then set the integer to the element number occupied by "other". Include a get method that returns an event's String event type based on the numeric event type.

- To keep the EventDemo class simple, remove all the statements that compare event sizes and that display the invitation Strings.

- Modify the EventDemo class so that instead of creating three single Event objects, it uses an array of three Event objects. Get data for each of the objects, and then display all the details for each object.

442

Save the files as **Event.java** and **EventDemo.java**.

2. In previous chapters, you developed classes that hold rental contract information for Sammy's Seashore Supplies. Now modify the Rental and RentalDemo classes as follows:

- Modify the Rental class to include an integer field that holds an equipment type. Add a final String array that holds names of the types of equipment that Sammy's rents—jet ski, pontoon boat, rowboat, canoe, kayak, beach chair, umbrella, and other. Include get and set methods for the integer equipment type field. If the argument passed to the method that sets the equipment type is larger than the size of the array of String equipment types, then set the integer to the element number occupied by "other". Include a get method that returns a rental's String equipment type based on the numeric equipment type.

- To keep the RentalDemo class simple, remove all the statements that compare rental times and that display the coupon Strings.

- Modify the RentalDemo class so that instead of creating three single Rental objects, it uses an array of three Rental objects. Get data for each of the objects, and then display all the details for each object.

Save the files as **Rental.java** and **RentalDemo.java**.

CHAPTER 9

Advanced Array Concepts

In this chapter, you will:

◎ Sort array elements using the bubble sort algorithm

◎ Sort array elements using the insertion sort algorithm

◎ Use two-dimensional and other multidimensional arrays

◎ Use the `Arrays` class

◎ Use the `ArrayList` class

◎ Create enumerations

Sorting Array Elements Using the Bubble Sort Algorithm

Sorting is the process of arranging a series of objects in some logical order. When you place objects in order, beginning with the object that has the lowest value, you are sorting in **ascending order**; conversely, when you start with the object that has the largest value, you are sorting in **descending order**.

The simplest possible sort involves two values that are out of order. To place the values in order, you must swap the two values. Suppose that you have two variables—valA and valB—and further suppose that valA = 16 and valB = 2. To exchange the values of the two variables, you cannot simply use the following code:

```
valA = valB; // 2 goes to valA
valB = valA; // 2 goes to valB
```

If valB is 2, after you execute valA = valB;, both variables hold the value 2. The value 16 that was held in valA is lost. When you execute the second assignment statement, valB = valA;, each variable still holds the value 2.

The solution that allows you to retain both values is to employ a variable to hold valA's value temporarily during the swap:

```
temp = valA; // 16 goes to temp
valA = valB; // 2 goes to valA
valB = temp; // 16 goes to valB
```

Using this technique, valA's value (16) is assigned to the temp variable. The value of valB (2) is then assigned to valA, so valA and valB are equivalent. Then, the temp value (16) is assigned to valB, so the values of the two variables finally are swapped.

If you want to sort any two values, valA and valB, in ascending order so that valA is always the lower value, you use the following if statement to make the decision whether to swap. If valA is more than valB, you want to swap the values. If valA is not more than valB, you do not want to swap the values.

```
if(valA > valB)
{
    temp = valA;
    valA = valB;
    valB = temp;
}
```

Sorting two values is a fairly simple task; sorting more values (valC, valD, valE, and so on) is more complicated. The task becomes manageable when you know how to use an array.

Using the Bubble Sort Algorithm

As an example, you might have a list of five numbers that you want to place in ascending order. Multiple sorting algorithms have been developed; an **algorithm** is a process or set of steps that solve a problem. In the **bubble sort** algorithm, you continue to compare pairs of items, swapping them if they are out of order, so that the smallest items "bubble" to the top of the list, eventually creating a sorted list. The bubble sort is neither the fastest nor most efficient sorting technique, but it is one of the simplest to comprehend and provides deeper understanding of array element manipulation.

To use a bubble sort, you place the original, unsorted values in an array, such as the following:

```
int[] someNums = {88, 33, 99, 22, 54};
```

You compare the first two numbers; if they are not in ascending order, you swap them. You compare the second and third numbers; if they are not in ascending order, you swap them. You continue down the list. Generically, for any someNums[x], if the value of someNums[x] is larger than someNums[x + 1], you want to swap the two values.

With the numbers 88, 33, 99, 22, and 54, the process proceeds as follows:

- Compare 88 and 33. They are out of order. Swap them. The list becomes 33, 88, 99, 22, 54.

- Compare the second and third numbers in the list—88 and 99. They are in order. Do nothing.

- Compare the third and fourth numbers in the list—99 and 22. They are out of order. Swap them. The list becomes 33, 88, 22, 99, 54.

- Compare the fourth and fifth numbers—99 and 54. They are out of order. Swap them. The list becomes 33, 88, 22, 54, 99.

When you reach the bottom of the list, the numbers are not in ascending order, but the largest number, 99, has moved to the bottom of the list. This feature gives the bubble sort its name—the "heaviest" value has sunk to the bottom of the list as the "lighter" values have bubbled to the top.

Assuming b and temp both have been declared as integer variables, the code so far is as follows:

```
for(b = 0; b < someNums.length - 1; ++b)
   if(someNums[b] > someNums[b + 1])
   {
      temp = someNums[b];
      someNums[b] = someNums[b + 1];
      someNums[b + 1] = temp;
   }
```

Instead of comparing b to someNums.length – 1 on every pass through the loop, it would be more efficient to declare a variable to which you assign someNums.length – 1 and use that variable in the comparison. That way, the arithmetic is performed just once. That step is omitted here to reduce the number of steps in the example.

446

Notice that the for statement tests every value of b from 0 through 3. The array someNums contains five integers, so the subscripts in the array range in value from 0 through 4. Within the for loop, each someNums[b] is compared to someNums[b + 1], so the highest legal value for b is 3. For a sort on any size array, the value of b must remain less than the array's length minus 1.

The list of numbers that began as 88, 33, 99, 22, 54 is currently 33, 88, 22, 54, 99. To continue to sort the list, you must perform the entire comparison-swap procedure again.

- Compare the first two values—33 and 88. They are in order; do nothing.

- Compare the second and third values—88 and 22. They are out of order. Swap them so the list becomes 33, 22, 88, 54, 99.

- Compare the third and fourth values—88 and 54. They are out of order. Swap them so the list becomes 33, 22, 54, 88, 99.

- Compare the fourth and fifth values—88 and 99. They are in order; do nothing.

After this second pass through the list, the numbers are 33, 22, 54, 88, and 99—close to ascending order, but not quite. You can see that with one more pass through the list, the values 22 and 33 will swap, and the list is finally placed in order. To fully sort the worst-case list, one in which the original numbers are descending (as out-of-ascending order as they could possibly be), you need to go through the list four times, making comparisons and swaps. At most, you always need to pass through the list as many times as its length minus one. Figure 9-1 shows the entire procedure.

```
for(a = 0; a < someNums.length - 1; ++a)
    for(b = 0; b < someNums.length - 1; ++b)
        if(someNums[b] > someNums[b + 1])
        {
            temp = someNums[b];
            someNums[b] = someNums[b + 1];
            someNums[b + 1] = temp;
        }
```

Figure 9-1   Ascending bubble sort of the someNums array elements

To place the list in descending order, you need to make only one change in the code in Figure 9-1: You change the greater-than sign (>) in if(someNums[b] > someNums[b + 1]) to a less-than sign (<).

When you use a bubble sort to sort any array into ascending order, the largest value "falls" to the bottom of the array after you have compared each pair of values in the array one time. The second time you go through the array making comparisons, there is no need to check the last pair of values. The largest value is guaranteed to already be at the bottom of the array. You can make the sort process even more efficient by using a new variable for the inner for loop and reducing the value by one on each cycle through the array. Figure 9-2 shows how you can use a new variable named comparisonsToMake to control how many comparisons are made in the inner loop during each pass through the list of values to be sorted. In the shaded statement, the comparisonsToMake value is decremented by 1 on each pass through the list.

```
int comparisonsToMake = someNums.length - 1;
for(a = 0; a < someNums.length - 1; ++a)
{
    for(b = 0; b < comparisonsToMake; ++b)
    {
        if(someNums[b] > someNums[b + 1])
        {
            temp = someNums[b];
            someNums[b] = someNums[b + 1];
            someNums[b + 1] = temp;
        }
    }
    --comparisonsToMake;
}
```

Figure 9-2   More efficient ascending bubble sort of the someNums array elements

 Watch the video *Sorting*.

Sorting Arrays of Objects

You can sort arrays of objects in much the same way that you sort arrays of primitive types. The major difference occurs when you make the comparison that determines whether you want to swap two array elements. When you construct an array of the primitive element type, you compare the two array elements to determine whether they are out of order. When array elements are objects, you usually want to sort based on a particular object field.

Assume that you have created a simple Employee class, as shown in Figure 9-3. The class holds four data fields and get and set methods for the fields.

448

```
public class Employee
{
    private int empNum;
    private String lastName;
    private String firstName;
    private double salary;
    public int getEmpNum()
    {
        return empNum;
    }
    public void setEmpNum(int emp)
    {
        empNum = emp;
    }
    public String getLastName()
    {
        return lastName;
    }
    public void setLastName(String name)
    {
        lastName = name;
    }
    public String getFirstName()
    {
        return firstName;
    }
    public void setFirstName(String name)
    {
        firstName = name;
    }
    public double getSalary()
    {
        return salary;
    }
    public void setSalary(double sal)
    {
        salary = sal;
    }
}
```

Figure 9-3   The Employee class

You can write a program that contains an array of five Employee objects using the following statement:

```
Employee[] someEmps = new Employee[5];
```

Assume that after you assign employee numbers and salaries to the `Employee` objects, you want to sort the `Employees` in `salary` order. You can pass the array to a `bubbleSort()` method that is prepared to receive `Employee` objects. Figure 9-4 shows the method.

```
public static void bubbleSort(Employee[] array)
{
    int a, b;
    Employee temp;
    int highSubscript = array.length - 1;
    for(a = 0; a < highSubscript; ++a)
     for(b = 0; b < highSubscript; ++b)
       if(array[b].getSalary() > array[b + 1].getSalary())
       {
           temp = array[b];
           array[b] = array[b + 1];
           array[b + 1] = temp;
       }
}
```

Figure 9-4   The `bubbleSort()` method that sorts `Employee` objects by their salaries

Examine Figure 9-4 carefully, and notice that the `bubbleSort()` method is very similar to the `bubbleSort()` method you use for an array of any primitive type, but there are three major differences:

- The `bubbleSort()` method header shows that it receives an array of type `Employee`.

- The `temp` variable created for swapping is type `Employee`. The `temp` variable will hold an `Employee` object, not just one number or one field. It is important to note that even though only employee salaries are compared, you do not just swap employee salaries. You do not want to substitute one employee's salary for another's. Instead, you swap each `Employee` object's `empNum` and `salary` as a unit.

- The comparison for determining whether a swap should occur uses method calls to the `getSalary()` method to compare the returned salary for each `Employee` object in the array with the salary of the adjacent `Employee` object.

450

TWO TRUTHS & A LIE

Sorting Array Elements Using the Bubble Sort Algorithm

1. In an ascending bubble sort, you compare pairs of items, swapping them if they are out of order, so that the largest items "bubble" to the top of the list, eventually creating a sorted list.

2. When you sort objects, you usually want to sort based on a particular object field.

3. When you make a swap while sorting an array of objects, you typically swap entire objects and not just the field on which the comparison is made.

The false statement is #1. In an ascending bubble sort, you compare pairs of items, swapping them if they are out of order, so that the smallest items "bubble" to the top of the list, eventually creating a sorted list.

 You Do It

Using a Bubble Sort

In this section, you create a program in which you enter values that you sort using the bubble sort algorithm. You display the values during each iteration of the outer sorting loop so that you can track the values as they are repositioned in the array.

1. Open a new file in your text editor, and create the shell for a `BubbleSortDemo` program as follows:

```
import java.util.*;
class BubbleSortDemo
{
    public static void main(String[] args)
    {
    }
}
```

2. Make some declarations between the curly braces of the `main()` method. Declare an array of five integers and a variable to control the number of comparisons to make during the sort. Declare a `Scanner` object, two integers to use as subscripts for handling the array, and a temporary integer value to use during the sort.

(continues)

```
int[] someNums = new int[5];
int comparisonsToMake = someNums.length - 1;
Scanner keyboard = new Scanner(System.in);
int a, b, temp;
```

3. Write a `for` loop that prompts the user for a value for each array element and accepts them.

```
for(a = 0; a < someNums.length; ++a)
{
    System.out.print("Enter number " + (a + 1) + " >> ");
    someNums[a] = keyboard.nextInt();
}
```

4. Next, call a method that accepts the array and the number of sort iterations performed so far, which is 0. The purpose of the method is to display the current status of the array as it is being sorted.

```
display(someNums, 0);
```

5. Add the nested loops that perform the sort. The outer loop controls the number of passes through the list, and the inner loop controls the comparisons on each pass through the list. When any two adjacent elements are out of order, they are swapped. At the end of the nested loop, the current list is output and the number of comparisons to be made on the next pass is reduced by one.

```
for(a = 0; a < someNums.length - 1; ++a)
{
    for(b = 0; b < comparisonsToMake; ++b)
    {
        if(someNums[b] > someNums[b + 1])
        {
            temp = someNums[b];
            someNums[b] = someNums[b + 1];
            someNums[b + 1] = temp;
        }
    }
    display(someNums, (a + 1));
    --comparisonsToMake;
}
```

6. After the closing brace for the `main()` method, but before the closing brace for the class, insert the `display()` method. It accepts the array and the current outer loop index, and it displays the array contents.

(continued)

```java
public static void display(int[] someNums, int a)
{
   System.out.print("Iteration " + a + ": ");
   for(int x = 0; x < someNums.length; ++x)
      System.out.print(someNums[x] + " ");
   System.out.println();
}
```

7. Save the file as **BubbleSortDemo.java**, and then compile and execute it. Figure 9-5 shows a typical execution. Notice that after the first iteration, the largest value has sunk to the bottom of the list. After the second iteration, the two largest values are at the bottom of the list, and so on.

Figure 9-5   Typical execution of the BubbleSortDemo application

8. Modify the BubbleSortDemo application to any size array you choose. Confirm that no matter how many array elements you specify, the sorting algorithm works correctly and ends with a completely sorted list, regardless of the order of your entered values.

Sorting Array Elements Using the Insertion Sort Algorithm

The bubble sort works well and is relatively easy to understand and manipulate, but many other sorting algorithms have been developed. For example, when you use an **insertion sort**, you look at each list element one at a time. If an element is out of order relative to any of the items earlier in the list, you move each earlier item down one position and then insert the tested element. The insertion sort is similar to the technique you would most likely use to sort a group of objects manually. For example, if a list contains the values 2, 3, 1, and 4, and you want to place them in ascending order using an insertion sort, you test the values 2 and 3, but you do not move them because they are in order. However, when you test the third value in the list, 1, you move both 2 and 3 to later positions and insert 1 at the first position.

Figure 9-6 shows the logic that performs an ascending insertion sort using a five-element integer array named someNums. The logic assumes that a, b, and temp have all been declared as integers.

```
int[] someNums = {90, 85, 65, 95, 75};
a = 1;
while(a < someNums.length)
{
    temp = someNums[a];
    b = a - 1;
    while(b >= 0 && someNums[b] > temp)
    {
        someNums[b + 1] = someNums[b];
        --b;
    }
    someNums[b + 1] = temp;
    ++a;
}
```

Figure 9-6   The insertion sort

The outer loop in Figure 9-6 varies a loop control variable a from 1 through one less than the size of the array. The logic proceeds as follows:

First a is set to 1, and then the while loop begins.

1. The value of temp is set to someNums[1], which is 85, and b is set to 0.

2. Because b is greater than or equal to 0 and someNums[b] (90) is greater than temp, the inner loop is entered. (If you were performing a descending sort, then you would ask whether someNums[b] was less than temp.)

3. The value of someNums[1] becomes 90 and b is decremented, making it −1, so b is no longer greater than or equal to 0, and the inner loop ends.

4. Then someNums[0] is set to temp, which is 85.

After these steps, 90 was moved down one position and 85 was inserted in the first position, so the array values are in slightly better order than they were originally. The values are as follows: 85, 90, 65, 95, 75.

Now, in the outer loop, a becomes 2. The logic in Figure 9-6 proceeds as follows:

1. The value of temp becomes 65, and b is set to 1.

2. The value of b is greater than or equal to 0, and someNums[b] (90) is greater than temp, so the inner loop is entered.

3. The value of someNums[2] becomes 90 and b is decremented, making it 0, so the loop executes again.

4. The value of someNums[1] becomes 85 and b is decremented, making it −1, so the loop ends.

5. Then someNums[0] becomes 65.

After these steps, the array values are in better order than they were originally, because 65 and 85 now both come before 90. The values are: 65, 85, 90, 95, 75. Now, a becomes 3. The logic in Figure 9-6 proceeds to work on the new list as follows:

1. The value of temp becomes 95, and b is set to 2.

2. For the loop to execute, b must be greater than or equal to 0, which it is, and someNums[b] (90) must be greater than temp, which it is *not*. So, the inner loop does not execute.

3. Therefore, someNums[2] is set to 90, which it already was. In other words, no changes are made.

Now, a is increased to 4. The logic in Figure 9-6 proceeds as follows:

1. The value of temp becomes 75, and b is set to 3.

2. The value of b is greater than or equal to 0, and someNums[b] (95) is greater than temp, so the inner loop is entered.

3. The value of someNums[4] becomes 95 and b is decremented, making it 2, so the loop executes again.

4. The value of someNums[3] becomes 90 and b is decremented, making it 1, so the loop executes again.

5. The value of someNums[2] becomes 85 and b is decremented, making it 0; someNums[b] (65) is no longer greater than temp (75), so the inner loop ends. In other words, the values 85, 90, and 95 are each moved down one position, but 65 is left in place.

6. Then someNums[1] becomes 75.

    After these steps, all the array values have been rearranged in ascending order as follows: 65, 75, 85, 90, 95.

 Watch the video *The Insertion Sort.*

Many sorting algorithms exist in addition to the bubble sort and insertion sort. You might want to investigate the logic used by the *selection sort*, *cocktail sort*, *gnome sort*, and *quick sort*.

TWO TRUTHS & A LIE

Sorting Array Elements Using the Insertion Sort Algorithm

1. When you use an insertion sort, you look at each list element one at a time and move items down if the tested element should be inserted before them.

2. You can create an ascending list using an insertion sort, but not a descending one.

3. The insertion sort is similar to the technique you would most likely use to sort a group of objects manually.

The false statement is #2. You can create both ascending and descending lists using an insertion sort.

 You Do It

Using an Insertion Sort

In this section, you modify the BubbleSortDemo program so it performs an insertion sort.

1. Open the **BubbleSortDemo.java** file. Change the class name to **InsertionSortDemo**, and immediately save the file as **InsertionSortDemo.java**.

2. Remove the declaration for comparisonsToMake.

3. Remove the 14 lines of code that constitute the nested loops that perform the bubble sort. In other words, remove all the lines from the start of the second for loop through the closing curly brace following the statement that decrements comparisonsToMake.

4. Replace the removed lines with the statements that perform the insertion sort. These are the same statements you saw in Figure 9-6 with the addition of a call to the display() method so that you can track the progress of the sort:

(continues)

(continued)

```
a = 1;
while(a < someNums.length)
{
    temp = someNums[a];
    b = a - 1;
    while(b >= 0 && someNums[b] > temp)
    {
        someNums[b + 1] = someNums[b];
        --b;
    }
    someNums[b + 1] = temp;
    display(someNums, a);
    ++a;
}
```

5. Save the file as **InsertionSortDemo.java**, and then compile and execute it. Figure 9-7 shows a typical execution. During the first loop, 77 is compared with 88 and inserted at the beginning of the array. In the second loop, 66 is compared with both 77 and 88 and inserted at the beginning of the array. Then the same thing happens with 55 and 44 until all the values are sorted.

Figure 9-7   Typical execution of the InsertionSortDemo program

6. Try the program with other input values, and examine the output so that you understand how the insertion sort algorithm works.

Using Two-Dimensional and Other Multidimensional Arrays

When you declare an array such as `int[] someNumbers = new int[3];`, you can envision the three declared integers as a column of numbers in memory, as shown in Figure 9-8. In other words, you can picture the three declared numbers stacked one on top of the next. An array that you can picture as a column of values, and whose elements you can access using a single subscript, is a **one-dimensional** or **single-dimensional array**. You can think of the size of the array as its height.

Java also supports two-dimensional arrays. **Two-dimensional arrays** have two or more columns of values, as shown in Figure 9-9. The two dimensions represent the height and width of the array. Another way to picture a two-dimensional array is as an array of arrays. It is easiest to picture two-dimensional arrays as having both rows and columns. You must use two subscripts when you access an element in a two-dimensional array. When mathematicians use a two-dimensional array, they often call it a **matrix** or a **table**; you might have used a two-dimensional array called a spreadsheet.

| someNumbers[0] |
| someNumbers[1] |
| someNumbers[2] |

Figure 9-8 View of a single-dimensional array in memory

someNumbers[0][0]	someNumbers[0][1]	someNumbers[0][2]	someNumbers[0][3]
someNumbers[1][0]	someNumbers[1][1]	someNumbers[1][2]	someNumbers[1][3]
someNumbers[2][0]	someNumbers[2][1]	someNumbers[2][2]	someNumbers[2][3]

Figure 9-9 View of a two-dimensional array in memory

When you declare a one-dimensional array, you type a set of square brackets after the array's data type. To declare a two-dimensional array in Java, you type two sets of brackets after the array type. For example, the array in Figure 9-9 can be declared as follows, creating an array named `someNumbers` that holds three rows and four columns:

```
int[][] someNumbers = new int[3][4];
```

Just as with a one-dimensional array, if you do not provide values for the elements in a two-dimensional numeric array, the values default to zero. You can assign other values to the array elements later. For example, `someNumbers[0][0] = 14;` assigns the value 14 to the element of the `someNumbers` array that is in the first column of the first row.

Alternatively, you can initialize a two-dimensional array with values when it is created. For example, the following code assigns values to `someNumbers` when it is created:

```
int[][] someNumbers = {{8, 9, 10, 11},
                       {1, 3, 12, 15},
                       {5, 9, 44, 99} };
```

The someNumbers array contains three rows and four columns. You do not *need* to place each row of values for a two-dimensional array on its own line. However, doing so makes the positions of values easier to understand. You contain the entire set of values within an outer pair of curly braces. The first row of the array holds the four integers 8, 9, 10, and 11. Notice that these four integers are placed within their own inner set of curly braces to indicate that they constitute one row, or the first row, which is row 0. Similarly, 1, 3, 12, and 15 make up the second row (row 1), which you reference with the subscript 1. Next, 5, 9, 44, and 99 are the values in the third row (row 2), which you reference with the subscript 2. The value of someNumbers[0][0] is 8. The value of someNumbers[0][1] is 9. The value of someNumbers[2][3] is 99. The value within the first set of brackets following the array name always refers to the row; the value within the second brackets refers to the column.

As an example of how useful two-dimensional arrays can be, assume that you own an apartment building with four floors—a basement, which you refer to as floor zero, and three other floors numbered one, two, and three. In addition, each of the floors has studio (with no bedroom) and one- and two-bedroom apartments. The monthly rent for each type of apartment is different—the higher the floor, the higher the rent (the view is better), and the rent is higher for apartments with more bedrooms. Table 9-1 shows the rental amounts.

Floor	Zero Bedrooms	One Bedroom	Two Bedrooms
0	400	450	510
1	500	560	630
2	625	676	740
3	1000	1250	1600

Table 9-1   Rents charged (in dollars)

To determine a tenant's rent, you need to know two pieces of information: the floor on which the tenant rents an apartment and the number of bedrooms in the apartment. Within a Java program, you can declare an array of rents using the following code:

```
int[][] rents = { {400, 450, 510},
                  {500, 560, 630},
                  {625, 676, 740},
                  {1000, 1250, 1600} };
```

If you declare two integers named floor and bedrooms, then any tenant's rent can be referred to as rents[floor][bedrooms]. Figure 9-10 shows an application that prompts a user for a floor number and number of bedrooms. Figure 9-11 shows a typical execution.

```
import javax.swing.*;
class FindRent
{
    public static void main(String[] args)
    {
        int[][] rents = { {400, 450, 510},
                          {500, 560, 630},
                          {625, 676, 740},
                          {1000, 1250, 1600} };
        String entry;
        int floor;
        int bedrooms;
        entry = JOptionPane.showInputDialog(null,
            "Enter a floor number ");
        floor = Integer.parseInt(entry);
        entry = JOptionPane.showInputDialog(null,
            "Enter number of bedrooms ");
        bedrooms = Integer.parseInt(entry);
        JOptionPane.showMessageDialog(null,
            "The rent for a " + bedrooms +
            " bedroom apartment on floor " + floor +
            " is $" + rents[floor][bedrooms]);
    }
}
```

Figure 9-10   The FindRent class

Figure 9-11   Typical execution of the FindRent program

Passing a Two-Dimensional Array to a Method

When you pass a two-dimensional array to a method, you pass the array name just as you do with a one-dimensional array. A method that receives a two-dimensional array uses two bracket pairs following the data type in the parameter list of the method header. For example, the following method headers accept two-dimensional arrays of ints, doubles, and Employees, respectively:

```
public static void displayScores(int[][]scoresArray)
public static boolean areAllPricesHigh(double[][] prices)
public static double computePayrollForAllEmployees(Employee[][] staff)
```

In each case, notice that the brackets indicating the array in the method header are empty. There is no need to insert numbers into the brackets because each passed array name is a starting memory address. The way you manipulate subscripts within the method determines how rows and columns are accessed.

Using the length Field with a Two-Dimensional Array

In Chapter 8, you learned that a one-dimensional array has a length field that holds the number of elements in the array. With a two-dimensional array, the length field holds the number of rows in the array. Each row, in turn, has a length field that holds the number of columns in the row. For example, suppose you declare a rents array as follows:

```
int[][] rents = { {400, 450, 510},
                  {500, 560, 630},
                  {625, 676, 740},
                  {1000, 1250, 1600} };
```

The value of rents.length is 4 because there are four rows in the array. The value of rents[0].length is 3 because there are three columns in the first row of the rents array. Similarly, the value of rents[1].length also is 3 because there are three columns in the second row.

Figure 9-12 shows an application that uses the length fields associated with the rents array to display all the rents. The floor variable varies from 0 through one less than 4 in the outer loop, and the bdrms variable varies from 0 through one less than 3 in the inner loop. Figure 9-13 shows the output.

```
class DisplayRents
{
   public static void main(String[] args)
   {
      int[][] rents = { {400, 450, 510},
                        {500, 560, 630},
                        {625, 676, 740},
                        {1000, 1250, 1600} };
      int floor;
      int bdrms;
      for(floor = 0; floor < rents.length; ++floor)
         for(bdrms = 0; bdrms < rents[floor].length; ++bdrms)
            System.out.println("Floor " + floor +
               " Bedrooms " + bdrms + "   Rent is $" +
               rents[floor][bdrms]);
   }
}
```

Figure 9-12   The DisplayRents class

Figure 9-13   Output of the DisplayRents program

 Watch the video *Two-Dimensional Arrays*.

Understanding Ragged Arrays

In a two-dimensional array, each row also is an array. In Java, you can declare each row to have a different length. When a two-dimensional array has rows of different lengths, it is a **ragged array** because you can picture the ends of each row as uneven. You create a ragged array by defining the number of rows for a two-dimensional array, but not defining the number of columns in the rows. For example, suppose that you have four sales representatives, each of whom covers a different number of states as their sales territory. Further suppose that you want an array to store total sales for each state for each sales representative. You would define the array as follows:

```
double[][] sales = new double[4][];
```

This statement declares an array with four rows, but the rows are not yet created. Then, you can declare the individual rows, based on the number of states covered by each salesperson as follows:

```
sales[0] = new double[12];
sales[1] = new double[18];
sales[2] = new double[9];
sales[3] = new double[11];
```

Using Other Multidimensional Arrays

Besides one- and two-dimensional arrays, Java also supports arrays with three, four, and more dimensions. The general term for arrays with more than one dimension is **multidimensional arrays**. For example, if you own an apartment building with a number of floors and different numbers of bedrooms available in apartments on each floor, you can use a two-dimensional array to store the rental fees. If you own several apartment buildings, you might want to employ a third dimension to store the building number. An expression such as rents[building][floor][bedrooms] refers to a specific rent figure for a building whose building number is stored in the building variable and whose floor and bedroom numbers are stored in the floor and bedrooms variables. Specifically, rents[5][1][2] refers to a two-bedroom apartment on the first floor of building 5. When you are programming in Java, you can use four, five, or more dimensions in an array. As long as you can keep track of the order of the variables needed as subscripts, and as long as you don't exhaust your computer's memory, Java lets you create arrays of any size.

TWO TRUTHS & A LIE

Using Two-Dimensional and Other Multidimensional Arrays

1. Two-dimensional arrays have both rows and columns, so you must use two subscripts when you access an element in a two-dimensional array.

2. The following array contains two columns and three rows:

```
int[][] myArray = {{12, 14, 19},
                   {33, 45, 88}};
```

3. With a two-dimensional array, the length field holds the number of rows in the array; each row has a length field that holds the number of columns in the row.

The false statement is #2. The array shown has two rows and three columns.

 You Do It

Using a Two-Dimensional Array

In this section, you create an application that demonstrates using a two-dimensional array.

1. Open a new file in your text editor, and start a class that will demonstrate a working two-dimensional array:

```
import java.util.Scanner;
class TwoDimensionalArrayDemo
{
    public static void main(String[] args)
    {
```

2. Declare a three-by-three array of integers. By default, the elements will all be initialized to 0.

```
int[][] count = new int[3][3];
```

3. Declare a Scanner object for input, variables to hold a row and column, and a constant that can be used to indicate when the user wants to quit the application.

```
Scanner input = new Scanner(System.in);
int row, column;
final int QUIT = 99;
```

(continues)

(continued)

4. Prompt the user to enter a row or the QUIT value to quit, then accept the user's input.

```
System.out.print("Enter a row or " + QUIT +
    " to quit > ");
row = input.nextInt();
```

5. In a loop that continues if the user has not entered the QUIT value, prompt the user for a column. If the row and column are both within appropriate ranges, add 1 to the element in the selected position.

```
while(row != QUIT)
{
    System.out.print("Enter a column > ");
    column = input.nextInt();
    if(row < count.length && column < count[row].length)
    {
        count[row][column]++;
```

6. Still within the if statement that checks for a valid row and column, add a nested loop that displays each row and column of the newly incremented array. The elements in each row are displayed on the same line, and a new line is started at the end of each row. Add a closing curly brace for the if statement.

```
        for(int r = 0; r < count.length; ++r)
        {
            for(int c = 0; c < count[r].length; ++c)
                System.out.print(count[r][c] + "  ");
            System.out.println();
        }
    }
```

7. Add an else clause to the if statement to display an error message when the row or column value is too high.

```
else
    System.out.println("Invalid position selected");
```

8. At the end of the loop, prompt the user for and accept the next row number. Add closing curly braces for the loop, the main() method, and the class.

```
        System.out.print("Enter a row or " + QUIT +
            " to quit > ");
        row = input.nextInt();
    }
  }
}
```

(continues)

(continued)

9. Save the file as **TwoDimensionalArrayDemo.java**. Compile and execute the program. Figure 9-14 shows a typical execution. As the user continues to enter row and column values, the appropriate elements in the array are incremented.

```
C:\Java>java TwoDimensionalArrayDemo
Enter a row or 99 to quit > 0
Enter a column > 0
1    0    0
0    0    0
0    0    0
Enter a row or 99 to quit > 2
Enter a column > 1
1    0    0
0    0    0
0    1    0
Enter a row or 99 to quit > 0
Enter a column > 0
2    0    0
0    0    0
0    1    0
Enter a row or 99 to quit > 5
Enter a column > 5
Invalid position selected
Enter a row or 99 to quit > 99

C:\Java>_
```

Figure 9-14   Typical execution of the `TwoDimensionalArrayDemo` program

Using the Arrays Class

When you fully understand the power of arrays, you will want to use them to store all kinds of objects. Frequently, you will want to perform similar tasks with different arrays—for example, filling them with values and sorting their elements. Java provides an **Arrays class**, which contains many useful methods for manipulating arrays. Table 9-2 shows some of the useful methods of the `Arrays` class. For each method listed in the left column of the table, `type` stands for a data type; an overloaded version of each method exists for each appropriate data type. For example, there is a version of the `sort()` method to sort `int`, `double`, `char`, `byte`, `float`, `long`, `short`, and `Object` arrays.

You will learn about the Object class in the chapter *Advanced Inheritance Concepts*.

466

Method	Purpose
static int binarySearch(type [] a, type key)	Searches the specified array for the specified key value using the binary search algorithm
static boolean equals(type[] a, type[] a2)	Returns true if the two specified arrays of the same type are equal to one another
static void fill(type[] a, type val)	Assigns the specified value to each element of the specified array
static void sort(type[] a)	Sorts the specified array into ascending order
static void sort(type[] a, int fromIndex, int toIndex)	Sorts the specified range of the specified array into ascending order

Table 9-2   Useful methods of the Arrays class

The methods in the Arrays class are static methods, which means you use them with the class name without instantiating an Arrays object. The Arrays class is located in the java.util package, so you can use the statement import java.util.*; to access it. The ArraysDemo application in Figure 9-15 demonstrates how you can use some of the methods in the Arrays class. In the ArraysDemo class, the myScores array is created to hold five integers. Then, a message and the array reference are passed to a display() method. The first line of the output in Figure 9-16 shows that the original array is filled with 0s at creation. After the first display, the Arrays.fill() method is called in the first shaded statement in Figure 9-15. Because the arguments are the name of the array and the number 8, when the array is displayed a second time the output is all 8s. In the application, two of the array elements are changed to 6 and 3, and the array is displayed again. Finally, in the second shaded statement, the Arrays.sort() method is called. The output in Figure 9-16 shows that when the display() method executes the fourth time, the array elements have been sorted in ascending order.

```
import java.util.*;
public class ArraysDemo
{
    public static void main(String[] args)
    {
        int[] myScores = new int [5];
        display("Original array:              ", myScores);
        Arrays.fill(myScores, 8);
        display("After filling with 8s:       ", myScores);
        myScores[2] = 6;
        myScores[4] = 3;
        display("After changing two values:   ", myScores);
        Arrays.sort(myScores);
        display("After sorting:               ", myScores);
    }

    public static void display(String message, int array[])
    {
        int sz = array.length;
        System.out.print(message);
        for(int x = 0; x < sz; ++x)
            System.out.print(array[x] + " ");
        System.out.println();
    }
}
```

Figure 9-15   The ArraysDemo application

Figure 9-16   Output of the ArraysDemo application

The Arrays class binarySearch() methods provide convenient ways to search through sorted lists of values of various data types. It is important that the list be in order before you use it in a call to binarySearch(); otherwise, the results are unpredictable. You do not have to understand how a binary search works to use the binarySearch() method, but basically the operation takes place as follows:

- You have a sorted array and an item for which you are searching within the array. Based on the array size, you determine the middle position. (In an array with an even number of elements, this can be either of the two middle positions.)

- You compare the item you are looking for with the element in the middle position of the array and decide whether your item is above that point in the array—that is, whether your item's value is less than the middle-point value.

- If it is above that point in the array, you next find the middle position of the top half of the array; if it is not above that point, you find the middle position of the bottom half. Either way, you compare your item with that of the new middle position and divide the search area in half again.

- Ultimately, you find the element or determine that it is not in the array.

Programmers often refer to a binary search as a "divide and conquer" procedure. If you have ever played a game in which you tried to guess what number someone was thinking, you might have used a similar technique.

Suppose your organization uses six single-character product codes. Figure 9-17 contains a VerifyCode application that verifies a product code entered by the user. The array codes holds six values in ascending order. The user enters a code that is extracted from the first String position using the String class charAt() method. Next, the array of valid characters and the user-entered character are passed to the Arrays.binarySearch() method. If the character is found in the array, its position is returned. If the character is not found in the array, a negative integer is returned and the application displays an error message. Figure 9-18 shows the program's execution when the user enters *K*; the character is found in position 2 (the third position) in the array.

The negative integer returned by the binarySearch() method when the value is not found is the negative equivalent of the array size. In most applications, you do not care about the exact value returned when there is no match; you care only whether it is negative.

```
import java.util.*;
import javax.swing.*;
public class VerifyCode
{
    public static void main(String[] args)
    {
        char[] codes = {'B', 'E', 'K', 'M', 'P', 'T'};
        String entry;
        char usersCode;
        int position;
        entry = JOptionPane.showInputDialog(null,
            "Enter a product code");
        usersCode = entry.charAt(0);
        position = Arrays.binarySearch(codes, usersCode);
        if(position >= 0)
            JOptionPane.showMessageDialog(null, "Position of " +
                usersCode + " is " + position);
        else
            JOptionPane.showMessageDialog(null, usersCode +
                " is an invalid code");
    }
}
```

Figure 9-17   The VerifyCode application

Figure 9-18   Typical execution of the VerifyCode application

 The sort() and binarySearch() methods in the Arrays class are very useful and allow you to achieve results by writing many fewer instructions than if you had to write the methods yourself. This does not mean you wasted your time reading about sorting and searching methods earlier in this chapter. The more completely you understand how arrays can be manipulated, the more useful, efficient, and creative your future applications will be.

TWO TRUTHS & A LIE

Using the Arrays Class

1. The Arrays class contains methods for manipulating arrays, such as binarySearch(), fill(), and sort().

2. You can use the Arrays class binarySearch() method successfully on any array as soon as you have assigned values to the array elements.

3. The binarySearch() method works by continuously deciding whether the element sought is above or below the halfway point in sublists of the original list.

The false statement is #2. Before you can use the Arrays class binarySearch() method successfully, the array elements must be in order.

You Do It

Using Arrays Class Methods

In this section, you create an application that demonstrates several Arrays class methods. The application will allow the user to enter a menu of entrees that are available for the day at a restaurant. Then, the application will present the menu to the user, allow a request, and indicate whether the requested item is on the menu.

1. Open a new file in your text editor, and type the import statements you need to create an application that will use the JOptionPane and the Arrays classes:

    ```
    import java.util.*;
    import javax.swing.*;
    ```

2. Add the first few lines of the MenuSearch application class:

    ```
    public class MenuSearch
    {
        public static void main(String[] args)
        {
    ```

(continues)

(continued)

3. Declare an array to hold the day's menu choices; the user is allowed to enter up to 10 entrees. Also declare two Strings—one to hold the user's current entry and the other to accumulate the entire menu list as it is entered. The two String variables are initialized to empty Strings using quotation marks; if you do not initialize these Strings, you receive a compiler error because you might attempt to display them without having entered a legitimate value. Also, declare an integer to use as a subscript for the array, another to hold the number of menu items entered, and a third to hold the highest allowable subscript, which is 1 less than the array size:

```
String[] menuChoices = new String[10];
String entry= "", menuString = "";
int x = 0;
int numEntered;
int highestSub = menuChoices.length - 1;
```

4. Use the Arrays.fill() method to fill the menu array with z characters, as shown in the following line of code. You use this method so that when you perform a search later, actual values will be stored in any unused menu positions. If you ignore this step and fill less than half the array, your search method might generate an error.

```
Arrays.fill(menuChoices, "zzzzzzz");
```

Lowercase zs were purposely chosen as the array fill characters because they have a higher value than any other letter. Therefore, when the user's entries are sorted, the zzzzzzz entries will be at the bottom of the list.

5. Display an input dialog box into which the user can enter a menu item. Allow the user to quit before entering 10 items by typing "zzz". (Using a value such as "zzz" is a common programming technique to check for the user's desire to stop entering data. If the data items are numeric instead of text, you might use a value such as 999. Values the user enters that are not "real" data, but just signals to stop, are often called **dummy values**.) After the user enters the first menu item, the application enters a loop that continues to add the entered item to the menu list, increase the subscript, and prompt for a new menu item. The loop continues while the user has not entered "zzz" and the subscript has not exceeded the allowable limit. When the loop ends, save the number of menu items entered:

(continues)

(continued)

```
menuChoices[x] = JOptionPane.showInputDialog(null,
    "Enter an item for today's menu, or zzz to quit:");
while(!menuChoices[x].equals("zzz") && x < highestSub)
{
    menuString = menuString + menuChoices[x] + "\n";
    ++x;
    if(x < highestSub)
        menuChoices[x] = JOptionPane.showInputDialog(null,
            "Enter an item for today's menu, or zzz to quit");
}
numEntered = x;
```

6. When the menu is complete, display it for the user and allow the user to make a request:

```
entry = JOptionPane.showInputDialog(null,
    "Today's menu is:\n" + menuString +
    "Please make a selection:");
```

7. Sort the array from index position 0 to `numEntered` so that it is in ascending order prior to using the `binarySearch()` method. If you do not sort the array, the result of the `binarySearch()` method is unpredictable. You could sort the entire array, but it is more efficient to sort only the elements that hold actual menu items:

```
Arrays.sort(menuChoices, 0, numEntered);
```

8. Use the `Arrays.binarySearch()` method to search for the requested entry in the previously sorted array. If the method returns a nonnegative value that is less than the `numEntered` value, display the message "Excellent choice"; otherwise, display an error message:

```
x = Arrays.binarySearch(menuChoices, entry);
if(x >= 0 && x < numEntered)
    JOptionPane.showMessageDialog(null, "Excellent choice");
else
    JOptionPane.showMessageDialog(null,
        "Sorry - that item is not on tonight's menu");
```

9. Add the closing curly braces for the `main()` method and the class, and save the file as **MenuSearch.java**. Compile and execute the application. When prompted, enter as many menu choices as you want, and enter "zzz" when you want to quit data entry. When prompted again, enter a menu choice and observe the results. (A choice you enter must match the spelling in the menu exactly.) Figure 9-19 shows a typical menu as it is presented to the user, and the results after the user makes a valid choice.

(continues)

(continued)

Figure 9-19 Typical execution of the MenuSearch application

Using the ArrayList class

In addition to the Arrays class, Java provides an **ArrayList class** that can be used to create containers that store lists of objects. The ArrayList class provides some advantages over the Arrays class. Specifically, an ArrayList is **dynamically resizable**, meaning that its size can change during program execution. This means that:

- You can add an item at any point in an ArrayList container, and the array size expands automatically to accommodate the new item.
- You can remove an item at any point in an ArrayList container, and the array size contracts automatically.

To use the ArrayList class, you must use one of the following import statements:

```
import java.util.ArrayList;
import java.util.*;
```

Then, to declare an ArrayList, you can use the default constructor, as in the following example:

```
ArrayList names = new ArrayList();
```

The default constructor creates an ArrayList with a capacity of 10 items. An ArrayList's **capacity** is the number of items it can hold without having to increase its size. By definition, an ArrayList's capacity is greater than or equal to its size. You can also specify a capacity if you like. For example, the following statement declares an ArrayList that can hold 20 names:

```
ArrayList names = new ArrayList(20);
```

If you know you will need more than 10 items at the outset, it is more efficient to create an `ArrayList` with a larger capacity.

Table 9-3 summarizes some useful `ArrayList` methods.

Method	Purpose
`public void add(Object)` `public void add(int, Object)`	Adds an item to an `ArrayList`; the default version adds an item at the next available location; an overloaded version allows you to specify a position at which to add the item
`public void remove(int)`	Removes an item from an `ArrayList` at a specified location
`public void set(int, Object)`	Alters an item at a specified `ArrayList` location
`Object get(int)`	Retrieves an item from a specified location in an `ArrayList`
`public int size()`	Returns the current `ArrayList` size

Table 9-3   Useful methods of the `ArrayList` class

In the chapter *Advanced Inheritance Concepts*, you will learn that the `Object` class is the most generic Java class.

To add an item to the end of an `ArrayList`, you can use the `add()` method. For example, to add the name *Abigail* to an `ArrayList` named `names`, you can make the following statement:

```
names.add("Abigail");
```

You can insert an item into a specific position in an `ArrayList` by using an overloaded version of the `add()` method that includes the position. For example, to insert the name *Bob* in the first position of the `names` `ArrayList`, you use the following statement:

```
names.add(0, "Bob");
```

With each of the methods described in this section, you receive an error message if the position number is invalid for the `ArrayList`.

As you can see from Table 9-3, you also can alter and remove items from an `ArrayList`. The `ArrayList` class contains a `size()` method that returns the current size of the `ArrayList`. Figure 9-20 contains a program that demonstrates each of these methods.

```java
import java.util.ArrayList;
public class ArrayListDemo
{
    public static void main(String[] args)
    {
        ArrayList names = new ArrayList();
        names.add("Abigail");
        display(names);
        names.add("Brian");
        display(names);
        names.add("Zachary");
        display(names);
        names.add(2, "Christy");
        display(names);
        names.remove(1);
        display(names);
        names.set(0, "Annette");
        display(names);
    }
    public static void display(ArrayList names)
    {
        System.out.println("\nThe size of the list is " + names.size());
        for(int x = 0; x < names.size(); ++x)
            System.out.println("position " + x + " Name: " +
                names.get(x));
    }
}
```

Figure 9-20 The ArrayListDemo program

 When you compile the ArrayListDemo program, you receive a compiler warning indicating that the program uses unchecked or unsafe operations. You will learn how to eliminate this message in the next section.

In the application in Figure 9-20, an ArrayList is created and *Abigail* is added to the list. The ArrayList is passed to a display() method that displays the current list size and all the names in the list. You can see from the output in Figure 9-21 that at this point, the ArrayList size is 1, and the array contains just one name. Examine the program in Figure 9-20 along with the output in Figure 9-21 so that you understand how the ArrayList is altered as names are added, removed, and replaced.

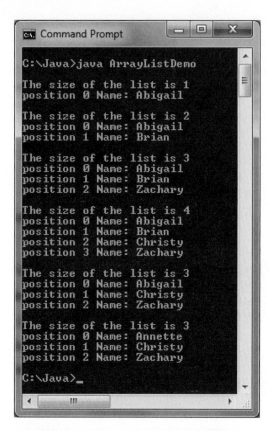

Figure 9-21   Output of the ArrayListDemo program

You can display the contents of an ArrayList of Strings without looping through the values. For example, Figure 9-22 shows an ArrayList named students that the user populates interactively. Displaying the array name as shown in the shaded statement produces a comma-separated list between square brackets. Figure 9-23 shows a typical execution.

```
import javax.swing.*;
import java.util.ArrayList;
public class ArrayListDemo2
{
   public static void main(String[] args)
   {
      ArrayList students = new ArrayList();
      String name;
      final int LIMIT = 4;
      for(int x = 0; x < LIMIT; ++x)
      {
          name = JOptionPane.showInputDialog(null,
            "Enter a student's name");
          students.add(name);
      }
      System.out.println("The names are " + students);
   }
}
```

Figure 9-22   The ArrayListDemo2 class

Figure 9-23   Typical execution of the ArrayListDemo2 application

You can achieve similar results using the name for ArrayLists of any class type. In Chapter 7, you learned that every class contains a toString() method that converts its objects to Strings; this method is used when you display an ArrayList's name. However, unless you have overridden the toString() method within a class, the String that is returned by toString() is not very useful. You will learn more about writing this method in the chapter *Advanced Inheritance Concepts*.

You can sort an ArrayList using the Collections.sort() method and providing the ArrayList as the argument—for example:

Collections.sort(students);

To use this method, you must import the java.util.Collections package at the top of the file.

Understanding the Limitations of the ArrayList Class

An ArrayList can be used to store any type of object reference. In fact, one ArrayList can store multiple types. However, this creates two drawbacks:

- You cannot use an ArrayList to store primitive types such as int, double, or char because those types are not references. If you want to work with primitive types, you can create an array or use the Arrays class, but you cannot use the ArrayList class.

- When you want to store ArrayList elements, you must cast them to the appropriate reference type before you can do so, or you must declare a reference type in the ArrayList declaration.

For example, if you want to declare a String to hold the first name in the names ArrayList, you must make statements such as the following:

```
String firstName;
firstName = (String)names.get(0);
```

The cast operator (String) converts the generic returned object from the get() method to a String. If you do not perform this cast, you receive an error message indicating that you are using incompatible types. (You first learned about the cast operator in Chapter 2.)

You can eliminate the need to perform a cast with ArrayList objects by specifying the type that an ArrayList can hold. For example, you can declare an ArrayList of names as follows:

```
ArrayList<String> names = new ArrayList<String>();
```

Creating an ArrayList declaration with a specified type provides several advantages:

- You no longer have to use the cast operator when retrieving an item from the ArrayList.

- Java checks to make sure that only items of the appropriate type are added to the list.

- The compiler warning that indicates your program uses an unchecked or unsafe operation is eliminated.

TWO TRUTHS & A LIE

Using the `ArrayList` Class

1. An advantage of the `ArrayList` class over the `Arrays` class is that an `ArrayList` is dynamically resizable.

2. An advantage of the `ArrayList` class over the `Arrays` class is that it can hold multiple object types.

3. An advantage of the `ArrayList` class over the `Arrays` class is that it can hold primitive data types such as `int` and `double`.

The false statement is #3. A disadvantage of the `ArrayList` class is that it cannot hold primitive types.

Creating Enumerations

Data types have a specific set of values. For example, in Chapter 2 you learned that a `byte` cannot hold a value larger than 127 and an `int` cannot hold a value larger than 2,147,483,647. You can also create your own data types that have a finite set of legal values. A programmer-created data type with a fixed set of values is an **enumerated data type**.

In Java, you create an enumerated data type in a statement that uses the keyword `enum`, an identifier for the type, and a pair of curly braces that contain a list of the **enum constants**, which are the allowed values for the type. For example, the following code creates an enumerated type named `Month` that contains 12 values:

```
enum Month {JAN, FEB, MAR, APR, MAY, JUN,
    JUL, AUG, SEP, OCT, NOV, DEC};
```

By convention, the identifier for an enumerated type begins with an uppercase letter. This convention makes sense because an enumerated type is a class. Also, by convention, the `enum` constants, like other constants, appear in all uppercase letters. The constants are not strings and they are not enclosed in quotes; they are Java identifiers.

After you create an enumerated data type, you can declare variables of that type. For example, you might declare the following:

```
Month birthMonth;
```

You can assign any of the `enum` constants to the variable. Therefore, you can code a statement such as the following:

```
birthMonth = Month.MAY;
```

An enumeration type like Month is a class, and its enum constants act like objects instantiated from the class, including having access to the methods of the class. These built-in methods include the ones shown in Table 9-4. Each of these methods is nonstatic; that is, each is used with an enum object.

Method	Description	Example if birthMonth = Month.MAY
toString()	The toString() method returns the name of the calling constant object.	birthMonth.toString() has the value "MAY" You can pass birthMonth to print() or println(), and it is automatically converted to its string equivalent.
ordinal()	The ordinal() method returns an integer that represents the constant's position in the list of constants. As with arrays, the first position is 0.	birthMonth.ordinal() is 4
equals()	The equals() method returns true if its argument is equal to the calling object's value.	birthMonth.equals(Month.MAY) is true birthMonth.equals(Month.NOV) is false
compareTo()	The compareTo() method returns a negative integer if the calling object's ordinal value is less than that of the argument, 0 if they are the same, and a positive integer if the calling object's ordinal value is greater than that of the argument.	birthMonth.compareTo(Month.JUL) is negative birthMonth.compareTo(Month.FEB) is positive birthMonth.compareTo(Month.MAY) is 0

Table 9-4   Some useful nonstatic enum methods

Several static methods are also available to use with enumerations. These are used with the type and not with the individual constants. Table 9-5 describes two useful static methods.

Method	Description	Example with Month Enumeration
valueOf()	The valueOf() method accepts a string parameter and returns an enumeration constant.	Month.valueOf("DEC") returns the DEC enum constant.
values()	The values() method returns an array of the enumerated constants.	Month.values() returns an array with 12 elements that contain the enum constants.

Table 9-5   Some static enum methods

You can declare an enumerated type in its own file, in which case the filename matches the type name and has a .java extension. You will use this approach in a "You Do It" exercise later in this chapter. Alternatively, you can declare an enumerated type within a class but not within a method. Figure 9-24 is an application that declares a Month enumeration and demonstrates its use. Figure 9-25 shows two typical executions.

```java
import java.util.Scanner;
public class EnumDemo
{
    enum Month {JAN, FEB, MAR, APR, MAY, JUN,
        JUL, AUG, SEP, OCT, NOV, DEC};

    public static void main(String[] args)
    {
        Month birthMonth;
        String userEntry;
        int position;
        int comparison;
        Scanner input = new Scanner(System.in);
        System.out.println("The months are:");
        for(Month mon : Month.values())
            System.out.print(mon + " ");
        System.out.print("\n\nEnter the first three letters of " +
            "your birth month >> ");
        userEntry = input.nextLine().toUpperCase();
        birthMonth = Month.valueOf(userEntry);
        System.out.println("You entered " + birthMonth);
        position =   birthMonth.ordinal();
        System.out.println(birthMonth + " is in position " + position);
        System.out.println("So its month number is " + (position + 1));
        comparison = birthMonth.compareTo(Month.JUN);
        if(comparison < 0)
            System.out.println(birthMonth +
                " is earlier in the year than " + Month.JUN);
        else
            if(comparison > 0)
                System.out.println(birthMonth +
                    " is later in the year than " + Month.JUN);
            else
                System.out.println(birthMonth + " is " + Month.JUN);
    }
}
```

Figure 9-24   The EnumDemo class

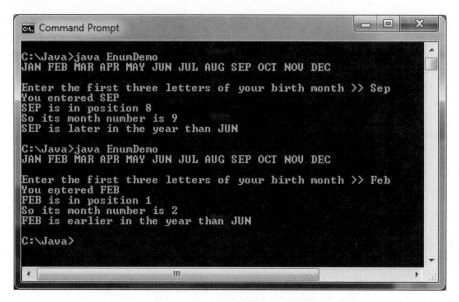

Figure 9-25   Two typical executions of the `EnumDemo` application

In the application in Figure 9-24, a `Month` enumeration is declared; in the `main()` method, a `Month` variable is declared in the first shaded statement. The second shaded statement uses the enhanced `for` loop, which you first learned to use with arrays in Chapter 8. The enhanced `for` loop declares a local `Month` variable named `mon` that takes on the value of each element in the `Month.value()` array in turn so it can be displayed.

In the program in Figure 9-24, the user then is prompted to enter the first three letters for a month, which are converted to their uppercase equivalents. The third shaded statement in the figure uses the `valueOf()` method to convert the user's string to an enumeration value. The fourth shaded statement gets the position of the month in the enumeration list. The last shaded statement compares the entered month to the `JUN` constant. This is followed by an `if` statement that displays whether the user's entered month comes before or after `JUN` in the list or is equivalent to it.

Starting with Java 7, you can use comparison operators with enumeration constants instead of using the `compareTo()` method to return a number. For example, you can write the following:

```
if(birthMonth < Month.JUN)
    System.out.println(birthMonth +
    " is earlier in the year than " + Month.JUN);
```

You can use enumerations to control a switch structure. Figure 9-26 contains a class that declares a `Property` enumeration for a real estate company. The program assigns one of the values to a `Property` variable and then uses a switch structure to display an appropriate message. Figure 9-27 shows the result.

```java
import java.util.Scanner;
public class EnumDemo2
{
   enum Property {SINGLE_FAMILY, MULTIPLE_FAMILY,
      CONDOMINIUM, LAND, BUSINESS};
   public static void main(String[] args)
   {
      Property propForSale = Property.MULTIPLE_FAMILY;
      switch(propForSale)
      {
         case SINGLE_FAMILY:
         case MULTIPLE_FAMILY:
            System.out.println("Listing fee is 5%");
            break;
         case CONDOMINIUM:
            System.out.println("Listing fee is 6%");
            break;
         case LAND:
         case BUSINESS:
            System.out.println
               ("We do not handle this type of property");
      }
   }
}
```

Figure 9-26 The EnumDemo2 class

Figure 9-27 Output of the EnumDemo2 application

Creating an enumeration type provides you with several advantages. For example, the Month enumeration improves your programs in the following ways:

- If you did not create an enumerated type for month values, you could use another type—for example, ints or Strings. The problem is that any value could be assigned to an int or String variable, but only the 12 allowed values can be assigned to a Month.

- If you did not create an enumerated type for month values, you could create another type to represent months, but invalid behavior could be applied to the values. For example, if you used integers to represent months, you could add, subtract, multiply, or divide two months, which is not logical. Programmers say using enums makes the values type-safe. **Type-safe** describes a data type for which only appropriate behaviors are allowed.

- The enum constants provide a form of self-documentation. Someone reading your program might misinterpret what 9 means as a month value, but there is less confusion when you use the identifier OCT.

- As with other classes, you can also add methods and other fields to an enum type.

 Watch the video *Enumerations*.

TWO TRUTHS & A LIE

Creating Enumerations

Assume that you have coded the following:

```
enum Color {RED, WHITE, BLUE};
Color myColor = Color.RED;
```

1. The value of myColor.ordinal() is 1.

2. The value of myColor.compareTo(Color.RED) is 0.

3. The value of myColor < Color.WHITE is true.

The false statement is #1. As the first enum constant, the value of myColor.ordinal() is 0.

 You Do It

Creating Enumerations

In this section, you create two enumerations that hold colors and car model types. You will use them as field types in a Car class and write a demonstration program that shows how the enumerations are used.

1. Open a new file in your text editor, and type the following Color enumeration:

    ```
    enum Color {BLACK, BLUE, GREEN, RED, WHITE, YELLOW};
    ```

2. Save the file as **Color.java**.

(continues)

(continued)

3. Open a new file in your text editor, and create the following Model enumeration:

    ```
    enum Model {SEDAN, CONVERTIBLE, MINIVAN};
    ```

4. Save the file as **Model.java**. Next, open a new file in your text editor, and start to define a Car class that holds three fields: a year, a model, and a color.

    ```
    public class Car
    {
        private int year;
        private Model model;
        private Color color;
    ```

5. Add a constructor for the Car class that accepts parameters that hold the values for year, model, and color as follows:

    ```
    public Car(int yr, Model m, Color c)
    {
        year = yr;
        model = m;
        color = c;
    }
    ```

6. Add a display() method that displays a Car object's data, then add a closing curly brace for the class.

    ```
    public void display()
    {
        System.out.println("Car is a " + year +
            " " + color + " " + model);
    }
    }
    ```

7. Save the file as **Car.java**.

8. Open a new file in your text editor, and write a short demonstration program that instantiates two Car objects and assigns values to them using enumeration values for the models and colors.

    ```
    public class CarDemo
    {
        public static void main(String[] args)
        {
            Car firstCar = new Car(2009, Model.MINIVAN, Color.BLUE);
            Car secondcar = new Car(2011, Model.CONVERTIBLE,
                Color.RED);
            firstCar.display();
            secondcar.display();
        }
    }
    ```

(continues)

(continued)

9. Save the file as **CarDemo.java**, and then compile and execute it. Figure 9-28 shows that the values are assigned correctly.

Figure 9-28 Output of the `CarDemo` program

Don't Do It

- Don't forget that the first subscript used with a two-dimensional array represents the row and that the second subscript represents the column.
- Don't try to store primitive data types in an `ArrayList` structure.
- Don't think `enum` constants are strings; they are not enclosed in quotes.

Key Terms

Sorting is the process of arranging a series of objects in some logical order.

Ascending order describes the order of objects arranged from lowest to highest value.

Descending order describes the order of objects arranged from highest to lowest value.

An **algorithm** is a process or set of steps that solve a problem.

A **bubble sort** is a type of sort in which you continue to compare pairs of items, swapping them if they are out of order, so that the smallest items "bubble" to the top of the list, eventually creating a sorted list.

With an **insertion sort**, you look at each list element one at a time, and if an element is out of order relative to any of the items earlier in the list, you move each earlier item down one position and then insert the tested element.

A **one-dimensional array** or **single-dimensional array** contains one column of values; you access its elements using a single subscript.

Two-dimensional arrays have two or more columns of values, and you must use two subscripts to access an element.

Matrix and **table** are names used for two-dimensional arrays.

A **ragged array** is a two-dimensional array that has rows of different lengths.

Multidimensional arrays contain two or more dimensions.

The Java **Arrays class** is a built-in class that contains many useful methods for manipulating arrays, such as methods to search, fill, compare, and sort arrays.

Dummy values are values the user enters that are not "real" data; they are just signals to stop data entry.

The **ArrayList class** provides a dynamically resizable container that stores lists of objects.

Dynamically resizable describes an object whose size can change during program execution.

An **ArrayList**'s **capacity** is the number of items it can hold without having to increase its size.

An **enumerated data type** is a programmer-created data type with a fixed set of values.

The **enum constants** are the allowed values for an enumerated data type.

Type-safe describes a data type for which only appropriate behaviors are allowed.

Chapter Summary

- Sorting is the process of arranging a series of objects in ascending or descending order. With a bubble sort, you continue to compare pairs of items, swapping them if they are out of order, so that the smallest items "bubble" to the top of the list, eventually creating a sorted list.

- With an insertion sort, you look at each list element one at a time, and if an element is out of order relative to any of the items earlier in the list, you move each earlier item down one position and then insert the tested element.

- You can sort arrays of objects in much the same way that you sort arrays of primitive types. The major difference occurs when you make the comparison that determines whether you want to swap two array elements. When array elements are objects, you usually want to sort based on a particular object field.

- An array that you can picture as a column of values, and whose elements you can access using a single subscript, is a one-dimensional or single-dimensional array. Two-dimensional arrays have both rows and columns. You must use two subscripts when you access an element in a two-dimensional array. To declare a two-dimensional array, you type two sets of brackets after the array type.

- The Java `Arrays` class contains many useful methods for manipulating arrays. These methods provide ways to easily search, compare, fill, and sort arrays.

- The Java `ArrayList` class contains useful methods for manipulating dynamically sized arrays. You can add objects to, remove objects from, and replace objects in `ArrayList` containers.

- A programmer-created data type with a fixed set of values is an enumerated data type. In Java, you create an enumerated data type in a statement that uses the keyword `enum`, an identifier for the type, and a pair of curly braces that contain a list of the `enum` constants, which are the allowed values for the type.

Review Questions

1. When you place objects in order beginning with the object with the highest value, you are sorting in _____ order.

   a. acquiescing   c. demeaning

   b. ascending   d. descending

2. Using a bubble sort involves _____.

   a. comparing parallel arrays

   b. comparing each array element to the average

   c. comparing each array element to the adjacent array element

   d. swapping every array element with its adjacent element

3. When you use a bubble sort to perform an ascending sort, after the first pass through an array the largest value is _____.

   a. at the beginning of the list

   b. in the middle of the list

   c. at the end of the list

   d. It is impossible to determine the answer without more information.

4. When you use a bubble sort to perform an ascending sort, after the first pass through an array the smallest value is _____.

    a. at the beginning of the list
    b. in the middle of the list
    c. at the end of the list
    d. It is impossible to determine the answer without more information.

5. When array elements are objects, you usually want to sort based on a particular _____ of the object.

    a. field   c. name
    b. method   d. type

6. The following defines a _____ array:

    ```
    int[][]nums={{1, 2}, {3, 4}, {5, 6}};
    ```

    a. one-dimensional   c. three-dimensional
    b. two-dimensional   d. six-dimensional

7. How many rows are contained in the following array?

    ```
    double[][] prices = {{2.56, 3.57, 4.58, 5.59},
                         {12.35, 13.35, 14.35, 15.00}};
    ```

    a. 1   c. 4
    b. 2   d. 8

8. How many columns are contained in the following array?

    ```
    double[][] prices = {{2.56, 3.57, 4.58, 5.59},
                         {12.35, 13.35, 14.35, 15.00}};
    ```

    a. 1   c. 4
    b. 2   d. 8

9. In the following array, what is the value of code[2][1]?

    ```
    char[][] code = {{ 'A ', 'D ', 'M '},
                     { 'P ', 'R ', 'S '},
                     { 'U ', 'V ', 'Z '}};
    ```

    a. 'P'   c. 'U'
    b. 'R'   d. 'V'

10. In the following array, what is the value of `address[1][1]`?

```
String address = {{ "123 Oak ", "345 Elm "},
                   { "87 Maple ", "901 Linden "}};
```

a. "123 Oak "   c. "87 Maple "

b. "345 Elm "   d. "901 Linden "

11. In the following array, what is the value of `fees.length`?

```
double[][] fees = {{3.00, 3.50, 4.00, 5.00},
                   {6.35, 7.35, 8.35, 9.00}};
```

a. 2   c. 8

b. 4   d. none of the above

12. In the following array, what is the value of `fees[1].length`?

```
double[][] fees = {{3.00, 3.50, 4.00, 5.00},
                   {6.35, 7.35, 8.35, 9.00}};
```

a. 2   c. 8

b. 4   d. none of the above

13. You place _____ after the data type in the parameter list of a method that receives a two-dimensional array.

a. a pair of empty brackets

b. two pairs of empty brackets

c. a pair of brackets that contain the number of rows followed by a pair of empty brackets

d. a pair of empty brackets followed by brackets that contain the number of columns

14. A _____ array has rows of different lengths.

a. ragged   c. haggard

b. jagged   d. tattered

15. If the value of `credits[0].length` is not equal to `credits[1].length`, you know `credits` is _____.

a. a three-dimensional array   c. a partially populated array

b. an uninitialized array   d. a jagged array

16. Which of the following is true if a successfully running program contains the following statement:

    `Arrays.fill(tax, 10);`

    a. `tax` is a two-dimensional array.
    c. `tax` is an array with 10 elements.
    b. `fill()` is a nonstatic method.
    d. none of the above

17. Which of the following is a requirement when you use a binary search method with an array?

    a. The array must be numeric.
    b. The array must have been sorted in ascending order.
    c. The array must have at least three elements.
    d. none of the above

18. The chief advantage to using the `ArrayList` class instead of the `Arrays` class is that an `ArrayList` _____.

    a. can be much larger
    b. is easier to search
    c. is dynamically resizable
    d. can be used as an argument to a `static` method

19. The chief disadvantage to using the `ArrayList` class instead of the `Arrays` class is that an `ArrayList` _____.

    a. cannot be sorted
    b. cannot store primitive data types
    c. cannot be accessed using subscripts
    d. All of the above are disadvantages to using an `ArrayList`.

20. An advantage to using an enumerated data type is _____.

    a. errors are reduced because only a limited set of values can be used with the type
    b. time is saved because programs with enumerated types compile faster
    c. coding time is reduced because enumerated types are created automatically by the compiler
    d. All of the above are true.

Exercises

Programming Exercises

1. Write an application containing an array of 10 `String` values, and display them in ascending order. Save the file as **SortStrings.java**.

2. a. The mean of a list of numbers is its arithmetic average. The median of a list is its middle value when the values are placed in order. For example, if a list contains 1, 4, 7, 8, and 10, then the mean is 6 and the median is 7. Write an application that allows you to enter five integers and displays the values, their mean, and their median. Save the file as **MeanMedian.java**.

   b. Revise the `MeanMedian` class so that the user can enter any number of values up to 20. If the list has an even number of values, the median is the numeric average of the values in the two middle positions. Save the file as **MeanMedian2.java**.

3. a. Radio station JAVA wants a class to keep track of recordings it plays. Create a class named `Recording` that contains fields to hold methods for setting and getting a `Recording`'s title, artist, and playing time in seconds. Save the file as **Recording.java**.

   b. Write an application that instantiates five `Recording` objects and prompts the user for values for the data fields. Then prompt the user to enter which field the `Recordings` should be sorted by—song title, artist, or playing time. Perform the requested sort procedure, and display the `Recording` objects. Save the file as **RecordingSort.java**.

4. In Chapter 8, you created a `Salesperson` class with fields for an ID number and sales values. Now, create an application that allows a user to enter values for an array of seven `Salesperson` objects. Offer the user the choice of displaying the objects in order by either ID number or sales value. Save the application as **SalespersonSort.java**.

5. In Chapter 8, you created a `Salesperson` class with fields for an ID number and sales values. Now, create an application that allows you to store an array that acts as a database of any number of `Salesperson` objects up to 20. While the user decides to continue, offer three options: to add a record to the database, to delete a record from the database, or to change a record in the database. Then proceed as follows:

   • If the user selects the add option, issue an error message if the database is full. Otherwise, prompt the user for an ID number. If the ID number already exists in the database, issue an error message. Otherwise, prompt the user for a sales value, and add the new record to the database.

- If the user selects the delete option, issue an error message if the database is empty. Otherwise, prompt the user for an ID number. If the ID number does not exist, issue an error message. Otherwise, do not access the record for any future processing.

- If the user selects the change option, issue an error message if the database is empty. Otherwise, prompt the user for an ID number. If the requested record does not exist, issue an error message. Otherwise, prompt the user for a new sales value, and change the sales value for the record.

After each option executes, display the updated database in ascending order by Salesperson ID number, and prompt the user to select the next action. Save the application as **SalespersonDatabase.java**.

6. Write an application that stores at least four different course names and meeting days and times in a two-dimensional array. Allow the user to enter a course name (such as "CIS 110"), and display the day of the week and time that the course is held (such as "Th 3:30"). If the course does not exist, display an error message. Save the file as **Schedule.java**.

7. a. Table 9-6 shows the various services offered by a hair salon, including its prices and times required:

Service Description	Price ($)	Time (Minutes)
Cut	8.00	15
Shampoo	4.00	10
Manicure	18.00	30
Style	48.00	55
Permanent	18.00	35
Trim	6.00	5

Table 9-6   Salon services, prices, and times

Create a class that holds the service description, price, and number of minutes it takes to perform the service. Include a constructor that requires arguments for all three data fields and three get methods that each return one of the data field's values. Save the class as **Service.java**.

b. Write an application named SalonReport that contains an array to hold six Service objects, and fill it with the data from Table 9-6. Include methods to sort the array in ascending order by each of the data fields. Prompt the user for the preferred sort order, and display the list of services in the requested order. Save the program as **SalonReport.java**.

8. Create an application that contains an enumeration that represents the days of the week. Display a list of the days, then prompt the user for a day. Display business hours for the chosen day. Assume that the business is open from 11 to 5 on Sunday, 9 to 9 on weekdays, and 10 to 6 on Saturday. Save the file as **DayOfWeek.java**.

9. Create a class named Majors that includes an enumeration for the six majors offered by a college as follows: ACC, CHEM, CIS, ENG, HIS, PHYS. Display the enumeration values for the user, then prompt the user to enter a major. Display the college division in which the major falls. ACC and CIS are in the Business Division, CHEM and PHYS are in the Science Division, and ENG and HIS are in the Humanities Division. Save the file as **Majors.java**.

10. Create a class named AppointmentKeeper that stores a two-dimensional String array with 31 rows and 24 columns. The program allows a user to choose a day and an hour continuously and then to enter a String value that describes an appointment. After the user finishes entering data, prompt the user continuously to enter a day, and show the 24 appointment slots for the day. Save the file as **AppointmentKeeper.java**. Figure 9-29 shows part of a typical execution.

Figure 9-29   Part of a typical execution of the AppointmentKeeper program

Debugging Exercises

1. Each of the following files in the Chapter09 folder in your downloadable student files has syntax and/or logic errors. In each case, determine the problem and fix the program. After you correct the errors, save each file using the same filename preceded with *Fix*. For example, DebugNine1.java will become FixDebugNine1.java.

   a. DebugNine1.java

   b. DebugNine2.java

   c. DebugNine3.java

   d. DebugNine4.java

   e. Movie.java, which is used by DebugNine2.java.

 Game Zone

1. Create a guessing game called "Does It Have Legs?", in which you think of an animal and the computer tries to guess what it is. The game continually becomes "smarter" as you play because you teach it how to become more specific with its questions. For example, a typical game session might proceed as follows:

Computer: Does the animal you are thinking of have legs?

Player: Yes.

Computer: Is it a dog?

Player: Yes.

Computer: Yay! I win. Do you want to play again?

Player: Yes.

Computer: Does the animal you are thinking of have legs?

Player: Yes.

Computer: Is it a dog?

Player: No.

Computer: I give up. What was your animal?

Player: Horse.

Computer: Type a question for which the answer is Yes for Dog but No for Horse.

Player: Does it live in the house?

Computer: Do you want to play again?

Player: Yes.

Computer: Does the animal you are thinking of have legs?

Player: Yes.

Computer: Does it live in the house?

 Player: No.

Computer: Is it a Horse?

Player: No.

Computer: I give up. What was your animal?

Player: Cow.

Computer: Type a question for which the answer is Yes for Horse but No for Cow.

Player: Do people ride it?

Computer: Do you want to play again?

Player: Yes.

Computer: Does the animal you are thinking of have legs?

Player: Yes.

Computer: Does it live in the house?

Player: No.

Computer: Do people ride it?

Player: No.

Computer: Is it a Cow?

Player: Yes.

Computer: Yay! I win. Do you want to play again?

Player: No.

(*Hint*: You might want to look up "binary trees" on the Internet as a method to organize this application.)

Save the application as **DoesItHaveLegs.java**.

2.   a.   Create a Tic-Tac-Toe game. In this game, two players alternate placing *X*s and *O*s into a grid until one player has three matching symbols in a row, either horizontally, vertically, or diagonally. Create a game in which the user is presented with a three-by-three grid containing the digits 1 through 9. When the user chooses a position by typing a number, place an *X* in the appropriate spot. Generate a random number for the position where the computer will place an *O*. Do not allow the player or the computer to place a symbol where one has already been placed. Figure 9-30 shows the first four windows in a typical game. When either the player or computer has three symbols in a row, declare a winner; if all positions have been exhausted and no one has three symbols in a row, declare a tie. Save the game as **TicTacToe.java**.

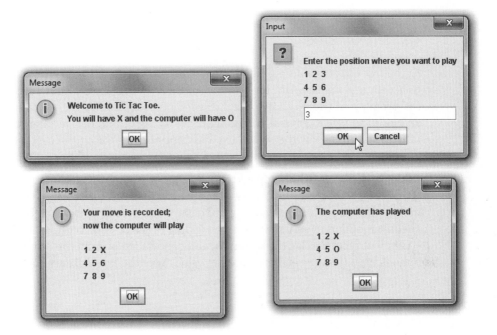

Figure 9-30 Typical game of TicTacToe in progress

    b. In the TicTacToe application, the computer's selection is chosen randomly. Improve the TicTacToe game so that when the computer has two *O*s in any row, column, or diagonal, it selects the winning position for its next move rather than selecting a position randomly. Save the improved game as **TicTacToe2.java**.

3.   In Chapter 8, you created an application class named FullDeck that implemented a 52-element array that represented each card in a standard deck of playing cards. Now, create an enumeration that holds the four suits: SPADES, HEARTS, DIAMONDS, and CLUBS. Save the enumeration in a file named **Suit.java**. Modify the Card class from Chapter 8 to use the enumeration, and save the class as **Card2.java**. Modify the FullDeck application to use the new Card class, and save the application as **FullDeck2.java**.

4.   In Chapter 7, you improved a Rock Paper Scissors game played between a user and the computer. Add an enumeration that holds three values that represent ROCK, PAPER, and SCISSORS, and use it for all comparisons in the program. Save the file as **RockPaperScissors3.java**.

Case Problems

1. In the last chapter, you modified the EventDemo program for Carly's Catering to accept and display data for an array of three Event objects. Now, modify the program to use an array of eight Event objects. Prompt the user to choose an option to sort Events in ascending order by event number, number of guests, or event type. Display the sorted list and continue to prompt the user for sorting options until the user enters a sentinel value. Save the file as **EventDemo.java**.

2. In the last chapter, you modified the RentalDemo program for Sammy's Seashore Supplies to accept and display data for an array of three Rental objects. Now, modify the program to use an array of eight Rental objects. Prompt the user to choose an option to sort Rentals in ascending order by contract number, price, or equipment type. Display the sorted list and continue to prompt the user for sorting options until the user enters a sentinel value. Save the file as **RentalDemo.java**.

Introduction to Inheritance

In this chapter, you will:

◎ Learn about the concept of inheritance

◎ Extend classes

◎ Override superclass methods

◎ Call constructors during inheritance

◎ Access superclass methods

◎ Employ information hiding

◎ Learn which methods you cannot override

Learning About the Concept of Inheritance

In Java and all object-oriented languages, **inheritance** is a mechanism that enables one class to acquire all the behaviors and attributes of another class and then to expand on those features. Inheritance is the principle that allows you to apply your knowledge of a general category to more specific objects. A class can inherit all the attributes of an existing class, meaning that you can create a new class simply by indicating the ways in which it differs from a class that has already been developed and tested.

You are familiar with the concept of inheritance from all sorts of nonprogramming situations. When you use the term *inheritance*, you might think of genetic inheritance. You know from biology that your blood type and eye color are the product of inherited genes; you can say that many facts about you—your attributes, or "data fields"—are inherited. Similarly, you often can credit your behavior to inheritance. For example, your attitude toward saving money might be the same as your grandmother's, and the odd way that you pull on your ear when you are tired might match what your Uncle Steve does—thus, your methods are inherited, too.

You also might choose plants and animals based on inheritance. You plant impatiens next to your house because of your shady street location; you adopt a Doberman Pinscher because you need a watchdog. Every individual plant and pet has slightly different characteristics, but within a species, you can count on many consistent inherited attributes and behaviors. Similarly, the classes you create in object-oriented programming languages can inherit data and methods from existing classes. When you create a class by making it inherit from another class, you are provided with data fields and methods automatically.

Diagramming Inheritance Using the UML

Beginning with the first chapter of this book, you have been creating classes and instantiating objects that are members of those classes. Programmers and analysts sometimes use a graphical language to describe classes and object-oriented processes; this **Unified Modeling Language (UML)** consists of many types of diagrams. UML diagrams can help illustrate inheritance.

For example, consider the simple `Employee` class shown in Figure 10-1. The class contains two data fields, `empNum` and `empSal`, and four methods: a get and set method for each field. Figure 10-2 shows a UML class diagram for the `Employee` class. A **class diagram** is a visual tool that provides you with an overview of a class. It consists of a rectangle divided into three sections—the top section contains the name of the class, the middle section contains the names and data types of the attributes, and the bottom section contains the methods. Only the method return type, name, and arguments are provided in the diagram—the instructions that make up the method body are omitted.

```
public class Employee
{
    private int empNum;
    private double empSal;
    public int getEmpNum()
    {
        return empNum;
    }
    public double getEmpSal()
    {
        return empSal;
    }
    public void setEmpNum(int num)
    {
        empNum = num;
    }
    public void setEmpSal(double sal)
    {
        empSal = sal;
    }
}
```

Figure 10-1   The Employee class

Employee
-empNum : int
-empSal : double
+getEmpNum : int
+getEmpSal : double
+setEmpNum(int num) : void
+setEmpSal(double sal) : void

Figure 10-2   The Employee class diagram

By convention, a class diagram contains the data type following each attribute or method, as shown in Figure 10-2. A minus sign (–) is inserted in front of each private field or method, and a plus sign (+) is inserted in front of each public field or method.

Commonly, UML diagram creators refrain from using Java terminology such as int in a class diagram. Instead, they might use a more general term, such as integer. The Employee class is designed in natural language (English) and might be implemented in any programming language, and languages other than Java might use a different keyword to designate integer variables. Because you are studying Java, this book uses the Java keywords in diagrams. For more information on UML, you can go to the Object Management Group's Web site at *www.omg.org*. OMG is an international, nonprofit computer industry consortium.

After you create the Employee class, you can create specific Employee objects, such as the following:

```
Employee receptionist = new Employee();
Employee deliveryPerson = new Employee();
```

These Employee objects can eventually possess different numbers and salaries, but because they are Employee objects, you know that each Employee has *some* number and salary.

Suppose that you hire a new type of `Employee` named `serviceRep`, and that a `serviceRep` object requires not only an employee number and a salary but also a data field to indicate territory served. You can create a class with a name such as `EmployeeWithTerritory` and provide the class three fields (`empNum`, `empSal`, and `empTerritory`) and six methods (get and set methods for each of the three fields). However, when you do this, you are duplicating much of the work that you have already done for the `Employee` class. The wise, efficient alternative is to create the class `EmployeeWithTerritory` so it inherits all the attributes and methods of `Employee`. Then, you can add just the one field and two methods that are new within `EmployeeWithTerritory` objects. Figure 10-3 shows a class diagram of this relationship. In a UML diagram, an inheritance relationship is indicated with an arrow that points from the descendant class to the original class.

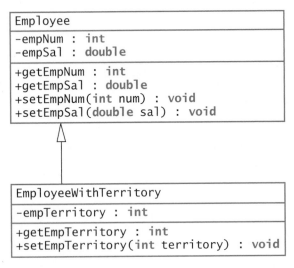

Figure 10-3 Class diagram showing the relationship between `Employee` and `EmployeeWithTerritory`

When you use inheritance to create the `EmployeeWithTerritory` class, you:

- Save time because the `Employee` fields and methods already exist
- Reduce errors because the `Employee` methods already have been used and tested
- Reduce the amount of new learning required to use the new class, because you have used the `Employee` methods on simpler objects and already understand how they work

The ability to use inheritance in Java makes programs easier to write, less error prone, and more quickly understood. Besides creating `EmployeeWithTerritory`, you also can create several other specific `Employee` classes (perhaps `EmployeeEarningCommission`, including a commission rate, or `DismissedEmployee`, including a reason for dismissal). By using inheritance, you can develop each new class correctly and more quickly. The concept of inheritance is useful because it makes a class's code more easily reusable. Each defined data field and each method already written and tested in the original class becomes part of the new class that inherits it.

 In Chapter 4, you learned about the `GregorianCalendar` class. It descends from a more general class named `Calendar`.

Inheritance Terminology

A class that is used as a basis for inheritance, such as `Employee`, is a **base class**. When you create a class that inherits from a base class (such as `EmployeeWithTerritory`), it is a **derived class**. When considering two classes that inherit from each other, you can tell which is the base class and which is the derived class by using the two classes in a sentence with the phrase "is a(n)." A derived class always "is a" case or example of the more general base class. For example, a `Tree` class can be a base class to an `Evergreen` class. An `Evergreen` "is a" `Tree`, so `Tree` is the base class; however, it is not true for all `Trees` that "a `Tree` is an `Evergreen`." Similarly, an `EmployeeWithTerritory` "is an" `Employee`—but not the other way around—so `Employee` is the base class.

 Because a derived class object "is an" instance of the base class, too, you can assign a derived class object's reference to a base class reference. Similarly, if a method accepts a base class object reference, it also will accept references to its derived classes. The next chapter describes these concepts in greater detail.

Do not confuse "is a" situations with "has a" situations. For example, you might create a `Business` class that contains an array of `Department` objects; in turn, each `Department` object might contain an array of `Employee` objects. You would not say "A department is a business" but that "a business has departments." Therefore, this relationship is not inheritance; it is **composition**—the relationship in which a class contains one or more members of another class, when those members would not continue to exist without the object that contains them. (For example, if a `Business` closes, its `Departments` do, too.) Similarly, you would not say "an employee is a department" but that "a department has employees." This relationship is not inheritance either; it is a specific type of composition known as **aggregation**—the relationship in which a class contains one or more members of another class, when those members would continue to exist without the object that contains them. (For example, if a business or department closed, the employees would continue to exist.)

You can use the terms **superclass** and **subclass** as synonyms for base class and derived class, respectively. Thus, `Evergreen` can be called a subclass of the `Tree` superclass. You can also use the terms **parent class** and **child class**. An `EmployeeWithTerritory` is a child to the `Employee` parent. Use the pair of terms with which you are most comfortable; all of these terms are used interchangeably throughout this book.

As an alternative way to discover which of two classes is the base class or subclass, you can try saying the two class names together. When people say their names together, they state the more specific name before the all-encompassing family name, as in "Ginny Kroening." Similarly, with classes, the order that "makes more sense" is the child-parent order. "Evergreen Tree" makes more sense than "Tree Evergreen," so Evergreen is the child class.

Finally, you usually can distinguish superclasses from their subclasses by size. Although it is not required, in general a subclass is larger than a superclass because it usually has additional fields and methods. A subclass description might look small, but any subclass contains all the fields and methods of its superclass, as well as the new, more specific fields and methods you add to that subclass.

 Watch the video *Inheritance*.

TWO TRUTHS & A LIE

Learning About the Concept of Inheritance

1. When you use inheritance in Java, you can create a new class that contains all the data and methods of an existing class.

2. When you use inheritance, you save time and reduce errors.

3. A class that is used as a basis for inheritance is called a subclass.

The false statement is #3. A class that is used as a basis for inheritance is called a superclass, base class, or parent class. A subclass is a class that inherits from a superclass.

Extending Classes

You use the keyword **extends** to achieve inheritance in Java. For example, the following class header creates a superclass-subclass relationship between Employee and EmployeeWithTerritory:

```
public class EmployeeWithTerritory extends Employee
```

Each EmployeeWithTerritory automatically receives the data fields and methods of the superclass Employee; you then add new fields and methods to the newly created subclass. Figure 10-4 shows an EmployeeWithTerritory class.

```
public class EmployeeWithTerritory extends Employee
{
    private int empTerritory;
    public int getEmpTerritory()
    {
        return empTerritory;
    }
    public void setEmpTerritory(int num)
    {
        empTerritory = num;
    }
}
```

Figure 10-4   The EmployeeWithTerritory class

You can write a statement that instantiates a derived class object, such as the following:

EmployeeWithTerritory northernRep = new EmployeeWithTerritory();

Then you can use any of the next statements to get field values for the northernRep object:

```
northernRep.getEmpNum();
northernRep.getEmpSal();
northernRep.getEmpTerritory();
```

The northernRep object has access to all three get methods—two methods that it inherits from Employee and one method that belongs to EmployeeWithTerritory.

Similarly, after the northernRep object is declared, any of the following statements are legal:

```
northernRep.setEmpNum(915);
northernRep.setEmpSal(210.00);
northernRep.setEmpTerritory(5);
```

The northernRep object has access to all the parent Employee class set methods, as well as its own class's new set method.

Inheritance is a one-way proposition; a child inherits from a parent, not the other way around. When you instantiate an Employee object, it does not have access to the EmployeeWithTerritory methods. It makes sense that a parent class object does not have access to its child's data and methods. When you create the parent class, you do not know how many future subclasses it might have or what their data or methods might look like.

In addition, subclasses are more specific than the superclass they extend. An Orthodontist class and Periodontist class are children of the Dentist parent class. You do not expect all members of the general parent class Dentist to have the Orthodontist's applyBraces() method or the Periodontist's deepClean() method. However, Orthodontist objects and Periodontist objects have access to the more general Dentist methods conductExam() and billPatients().

You can use the **instanceof operator** to determine whether an object is a member or descendant of a class. For example, if northernRep is an EmployeeWithTerritory object, then the value of each of the following expressions is true:

```
northernRep instanceof EmployeeWithTerritory
northernRep instanceof Employee
```

If aClerk is an Employee object, then the following is true:

```
aClerk instanceof Employee
```

However, the following is false:

```
aClerk instanceof EmployeeWithTerritory
```

Programmers say that instanceof yields true if the operand on the left can be **upcast** to the operand on the right.

TWO TRUTHS & A LIE

Extending Classes

1. You use the keyword inherits to achieve inheritance in Java.

2. A derived class has access to all its parents' nonprivate methods.

3. Subclasses are more specific than the superclass they extend.

The false statement is #1. You use the keyword extends to achieve inheritance in Java.

 You Do It

Demonstrating Inheritance

In this section, you create a working example of inheritance. To see the effects of inheritance, you create this example in four stages:

- First, you create a Party class that holds just one data field and three methods.

- After you create the general Party class, you write an application to demonstrate its use.

- Then, you create a more specific DinnerParty subclass that inherits the fields and methods of the Party class.

- Finally, you modify the demonstration application to add an example using the DinnerParty class.

(continues)

(continued)

Creating a Superclass and an Application to Use It

1. Open a new file in your text editor, and enter the following first few lines for a simple Party class. The class hosts one integer data field—the number of guests expected at the party:

```
public class Party
{
   private int guests;
```

2. Add the following methods that get and set the number of guests:

```
public int getGuests()
{
   return guests;
}
public void setGuests(int numGuests)
{
   guests = numGuests;
}
```

3. Add a method that displays a party invitation:

```
public void displayInvitation()
{
   System.out.println("Please come to my party!");
}
```

4. Add the closing curly brace for the class, and then save the file as **Party.java**. Compile the class; if necessary, correct any errors and compile again.

Writing an Application That Uses the Party Class

Now that you have created a class, you can use it in an application. A very simple application creates a Party object, prompts the user for the number of guests at the party, sets the data field, and displays the results.

1. Open a new file in your text editor.

2. Write a UseParty application that has one method—a main() method. Enter the beginning of the class, including the start of the main() method, which declares a variable for guests, a Party object, and a Scanner object to use for input:

(continues)

508

(continued)

```
import java.util.*;
public class UseParty
{
    public static void main(String[] args)
    {
        int guests;
        Party aParty = new Party();
        Scanner keyboard = new Scanner(System.in);
```

3. Continue the `main()` method by prompting the user for a number of guests and accepting the value from the keyboard. Set the number of guests in the `Party` object, and then display the value:

```
System.out.print("Enter number of guests for the party >> ");
guests = keyboard.nextInt();
aParty.setGuests(guests);
System.out.println("The party has " + aParty.getGuests() + " guests");
```

4. Add a statement to display the party invitation, and then add the closing curly braces for the `main()` method and for the class:

```
        aParty.displayInvitation();
    }
}
```

5. Save the file as **UseParty.java**, then compile and run the application. Figure 10-5 shows a typical execution.

Figure 10-5   Execution of the `UseParty` application

Creating a Subclass from the Party Class

Next, you create a class named `DinnerParty`. A `DinnerParty` "is a" type of `Party` at which dinner is served, so `DinnerParty` is a child class of `Party`.

(continues)

(continued)

1. Open a new file in your text editor, and type the first few lines for the `DinnerParty` class:

   ```
   public class DinnerParty extends Party
   {
   ```

2. A `DinnerParty` contains a number of guests, but you do not have to define the variable here. The variable is already defined in `Party`, which is the superclass of this class. You need to add only any variables that are particular to a `DinnerParty`. Enter the following code to add an integer code for the dinner menu choice:

   ```
   private int dinnerChoice;
   ```

3. The `Party` class already contains methods to get and set the number of guests, so `DinnerParty` needs methods only to get and set the `dinnerChoice` variable as follows:

   ```
   public int getDinnerChoice()
   {
      return dinnerChoice;
   }
   public void setDinnerChoice(int choice)
   {
      dinnerChoice = choice;
   }
   ```

4. Save the file as **DinnerParty.java**, and then compile it.

Creating an Application That Uses the `DinnerParty` Class

Now you can modify the `UseParty` application so that it creates a `DinnerParty` as well as a plain `Party`.

1. Open the **UseParty.java** file in your text editor. Change the class name to **UseDinnerParty**. Immediately save the file as **UseDinnerParty.java**.

2. Include a new variable that holds the dinner choice for a `DinnerParty`:

   ```
   int choice;
   ```

3. After the statement that constructs the `Party` object, type the following `DinnerParty` object declaration:

   ```
   DinnerParty aDinnerParty = new DinnerParty();
   ```

(continues)

(continued)

4. At the end of the `main()` method, after the `Party` object data and invitation are displayed, add a prompt for the number of guests for the `DinnerParty`. Accept the value the user enters and assign it to the object. Even though the `DinnerParty` class does not contain a `setGuests()` method, its parent class does, so `aDinnerParty` can use the method.

```
System.out.print("Enter number of guests for the dinner party >> ");
guests = keyboard.nextInt();
aDinnerParty.setGuests(guests);
```

5. Next, prompt the user for a dinner choice. To keep this example simple, the program provides only two choices and does not provide range checking. Accept a response from the user, assign it to the object, and then display all the data for the `DinnerParty`. Even though the `DinnerParty` class does not contain a `getGuests()` method, its parent class does, so `aDinnerParty` can use the method. The `DinnerParty` class uses its own `setDinnerChoice()` and `getDinnerChoice()` methods.

```
System.out.print
    ("Enter the menu option -- 1 for chicken or 2 for beef >> ");
choice = keyboard.nextInt();
aDinnerParty.setDinnerChoice(choice);
System.out.println("The dinner party has " +
    aDinnerParty.getGuests() + " guests");
System.out.println("Menu option " +
    aDinnerParty.getDinnerChoice () + " will be served");
```

6. Add a statement to call the `displayInvitation()` method with the `DinnerParty` object. Even though the `DinnerParty` class does not contain a `displayInvitation()` method, its parent class does, so `aDinnerParty` can use the method.

```
aDinnerParty.displayInvitation();
```

7. Save the file, compile it, and run it using values of your choice. Figure 10-6 shows a typical execution. The `DinnerParty` object successfully uses the data field and methods of its superclass, as well as its own data field and methods.

(continues)

(continued)

C:\Java>java UseDinnerParty
Enter number of guests for the party >> 20
The party has 20 guests
Please come to my party!
Enter number of guests for the dinner party >> 8
Enter the menu option -- 1 for chicken or 2 for beef >> 1
The dinner party has 8 guests
Menu option 1 will be served
Please come to my party!

C:\Java>

Figure 10-6 Execution of the `UseDinnerParty` application

Overriding Superclass Methods

When you create a subclass by extending an existing class, the new subclass contains data and methods that were defined in the original superclass. In other words, any child class object has all the attributes of its parent. Sometimes, however, the superclass data fields and methods are not entirely appropriate for the subclass objects; in these cases, you want to override the parent class members.

When you use the English language, you often use the same method name to indicate diverse meanings. For example, if you think of `MusicalInstrument` as a class, you can think of `play()` as a method of that class. If you think of various subclasses such as `Guitar` and `Drum`, you know that you carry out the `play()` method quite differently for each subclass. Using the same method name to indicate different implementations is called **polymorphism**, a term meaning "many forms"—many different forms of action take place, even though you use the same word to describe the action. In other words, many forms of the same word exist, depending on the object associated with the word.

You first learned the term *polymorphism* in Chapter 1. Polymorphism is one of the basic principles of object-oriented programming. If a programming language does not support polymorphism, the language is not considered object oriented.

For example, suppose that you create an `Employee` superclass containing data fields such as `firstName`, `lastName`, `socialSecurityNumber`, `dateOfHire`, `rateOfPay`, and so on, and the methods contained in the `Employee` class include the usual collection of get and set methods. If your usual time period for payment to each Employee object is weekly, your displayRateOfPay() method might include a statement such as:

```
System.out.println("Pay is " + rateOfPay + " per week ");
```

Imagine your company has a few Employees who are not paid weekly. Maybe some are paid by the hour, and others are Employees whose work is contracted on a job-to-job basis. Because each Employee type requires different paycheck-calculating procedures, you might want to create subclasses of Employee, such as HourlyEmployee and ContractEmployee.

When you call the displayRateOfPay() method for an HourlyEmployee object, you want the display to include the phrase "per hour", as in "Pay is $8.75 per hour." When you call the displayRateOfPay() method for a ContractEmployee, you want to include "per contract", as in "Pay is $2000 per contract." Each class—the Employee superclass and the two subclasses—requires its own displayRateOfPay() method. Fortunately, if you create separate displayRateOfPay() methods for each class, the objects of each class use the appropriate method for that class. When you create a method in a child class that has the same name and parameter list as a method in its parent class, you **override the method** in the parent class. When you use the method name with a child object, the child's version of the method is used.

It is important to note that each subclass method overrides any method in the parent class that has both the same name and parameter list. If the parent class method has the same name but a different parameter list, the subclass method does not over*ride* the parent class version; instead, the subclass method over*loads* the parent class method, and any subclass object has access to both versions. You learned about overloading methods in Chapter 4. You first saw the term *override* in Chapter 4, when you learned that a variable declared within a block overrides another variable with the same name declared outside the block.

If you could not override superclass methods, you could always create a unique name for each subclass method, such as displayRateOfPayForHourly(), but the classes you create are easier to write and understand if you use one reasonable name for methods that do essentially the same thing. Because you are attempting to display the rate of pay for each object, displayRateOfPay() is a clear and appropriate method name for all the object types.

A child class object can use an overridden parent's method by using the keyword super. You will learn about this word later in this chapter.

Object-oriented programmers use the term *polymorphism* when discussing any operation that has multiple meanings. For example, the plus sign (+) is polymorphic because it operates differently depending on its operands. You can use the plus sign to add integers or doubles, to concatenate strings, or to indicate a positive value. As another example, methods with the same name but different parameter lists are polymorphic because the method call operates differently depending on its arguments. When Java developers refer to polymorphism, they most often mean **subtype polymorphism**—the ability of one method name to work appropriately for different subclass objects of the same parent class.

Watch the video *Handling Methods and Inheritance*.

TWO TRUTHS & A LIE

Overriding Superclass Methods

1. Any child class object has all the attributes of its parent, but all of those attributes might not be directly accessible.

2. You override a parent class method by creating a child class method with the same identifier but a different parameter list or return type.

3. When a child class method overrides a parent class method, and you use the method name with a child class object, the child class method version executes.

The false statement is #2. You override a parent class method by creating a child class method with the same identifier and parameter list. The return type is not a factor in overloading.

You Do It

Overriding a Superclass Method

In the previous "You Do It" section, you created `Party` and `DinnerParty` classes. The `DinnerParty` class extends `Party` and so can use its `displayInvitation()` method. Suppose that you want a `DinnerParty` object to use a specialized invitation. In this section, you override the parent class method so that the same method name acts uniquely for the child class object.

1. Open the **DinnerParty.java** class in your text editor. Change the class name to **DinnerParty2**, and save the file as **DinnerParty2.java**.

2. Create a `displayInvitation()` method that overrides the parent class method with the same name as follows:

```
public void displayInvitation()
{
    System.out.println("Please come to my dinner party!");
}
```

3. Save the class and compile it.

(continues)

(continued)

4. Open the **UseDinnerParty.java** file. Change the class name to UseDinnerParty2, and immediately save the file as **UseDinnerParty2.java**.

5. Change the declaration of the aDinnerParty object so that it uses the DinnerParty2 class as a data type and DinnerParty2 as the constructor name.

6. Save the class, compile it, and execute it. Figure 10-7 shows a typical execution. Each type of object uses its own version of the displayInvitation() method.

Figure 10-7 Typical execution of the UseDinnerParty2 program

Calling Constructors During Inheritance

When you create any object, as in the following statement, you are calling a class constructor method that has the same name as the class itself:

```
SomeClass anObject = new SomeClass();
```

When you instantiate an object that is a member of a subclass, you are actually calling at least two constructors: the constructor for the base class and the constructor for the extended, derived class. When you create any subclass object, the superclass constructor must execute first, and *then* the subclass constructor executes.

In the chapter *Advanced Inheritance Concepts*, you will learn that every Java object automatically is a child of a class named Object. So, when you instantiate any object, you call its constructor and Object's constructor, and when you create parent and child classes of your own, the child classes use three constructors.

When a superclass contains a default constructor and you instantiate a subclass object, the execution of the superclass constructor is transparent—that is, nothing calls attention to the fact that the superclass constructor is executing. However, you should realize that when you create an object such as the following (where HourlyEmployee is a subclass of Employee), *both* the Employee() and HourlyEmployee() constructors execute:

```
HourlyEmployee clerk = new HourlyEmployee();
```

For example, Figure 10-8 shows three classes. The class named ASuperClass has a constructor that displays a message. The class named ASubClass descends from ASuperClass, and its constructor displays a different message. The DemoConstructors class contains just one statement that instantiates one object of type ASubClass.

```
public class ASuperClass
{
    public ASuperClass()
    {
        System.out.println("In superclass constructor");
    }
}
public class ASubClass extends ASuperClass
{
    public ASubClass()
    {
        System.out.println("In subclass constructor");
    }
}
public class DemoConstructors
{
    public static void main(String[] args)
    {
        ASubClass child = new ASubClass();
    }
}
```

Figure 10-8 Three classes that demonstrate constructor calling when a subclass object is instantiated

Figure 10-9 shows the output when DemoConstructors executes. You can see that when DemoConstructors instantiates the ASubClass object, the parent class constructor executes first, displaying its message, and then the child class constructor executes. Even though only one object is created, two constructors execute.

Figure 10-9   Output of the DemoConstructors application

Of course, most constructors perform many more tasks than displaying a message to inform you that they exist. When constructors initialize variables, you usually want the superclass constructor to take care of initializing the data fields that originate in the superclass. Usually, the subclass constructor only needs to initialize the data fields that are specific to the subclass.

Using Superclass Constructors That Require Arguments

When you create a class and do not provide a constructor, Java automatically supplies you with a default constructor—one that never requires arguments. When you write your own constructor, you replace the automatically supplied version. Depending on your needs, a constructor you create for a class might be a default constructor or might require arguments. When you use a class as a superclass and the class has only constructors that require arguments, you must be certain that any subclasses provide the superclass constructor with the arguments it needs.

 Don't forget that a class can have many constructors. As soon as you create at least one constructor for a class, you can no longer use the automatically supplied version.

When a superclass has a default constructor, you can create a subclass with or without its own constructor. This is true whether the default superclass constructor is the automatically supplied one or one you have written. However, when a superclass contains only constructors that require arguments, you must include at least one constructor for each subclass you create. Your subclass constructors can contain any number of statements, but if all superclass constructors require arguments, then the first statement within each subclass constructor must call one of the superclass constructors. When a superclass requires constructor arguments upon object instantiation, even if you have no other reason to create a subclass constructor, you must write the subclass constructor so it can call its superclass's constructor.

If a superclass has multiple constructors but one is a default constructor, you do not have to create a subclass constructor unless you want to. If the subclass contains no constructor, all subclass objects use the superclass default constructor when they are instantiated.

The format of the statement that calls a superclass constructor from the subclass constructor is:

```
super(list of arguments);
```

The keyword **super** always refers to the superclass of the class in which you use it.

If a superclass contains only constructors that require arguments, you must create a subclass constructor, but the subclass constructor does not necessarily have to have parameters of its own. For example, suppose that you create an Employee class with a constructor that requires three arguments—a character, a double, and an integer—and you create an HourlyEmployee class that is a subclass of Employee. The following code shows a valid constructor for HourlyEmployee:

```
public HourlyEmployee()
{
    super('P', 12.35, 40);
    // Other statements can go here
}
```

This version of the HourlyEmployee constructor requires no arguments, but it passes three constant arguments to its superclass constructor. A different, overloaded version of the HourlyEmployee constructor can require arguments. It could then pass the appropriate arguments to the superclass constructor. For example:

```
public HourlyEmployee(char dept, double rate, int hours)
{
    super(dept, rate, hours);
    // Other statements can go here
}
```

Except for any comments, the super() statement must be the first statement in any subclass constructor that uses it. Not even data field definitions can precede it. Although it seems that you should be able to use the superclass constructor name to call the superclass constructor—for example, Employee()—Java does not allow this. You must use the keyword super.

In Chapter 4, you learned that you can call one constructor from another using this(). In this chapter, you learned that you can call a base class constructor from a derived class using super(). However, you cannot use both this() and super() in the same constructor because each is required to be the first statement in any constructor in which it appears.

Watch the video *Constructors and Inheritance*.

518

TWO TRUTHS & A LIE

Calling Constructors During Inheritance

1. When you create any subclass object, the subclass constructor executes first, and then the superclass constructor executes.

2. When constructors initialize variables, you usually want the superclass constructor to initialize the data fields that originate in the superclass and the subclass constructor to initialize the data fields that are specific to the subclass.

3. When a superclass contains only nondefault constructors, you must include at least one constructor for each subclass you create.

The false statement is #1. When you create any subclass object, the superclass constructor must execute first, and *then* the subclass constructor executes.

 You Do It

Understanding the Role of Constructors in Inheritance

Next, you add a constructor to the Party class. When you instantiate a subclass object, the superclass constructor executes before the subclass constructor executes.

1. Open the **Party.java** file in your text editor, and save it as **PartyWithConstructor.java**. Change the class name to `PartyWithConstructor`.

2. Following the statement that declares the `guests` data field, type a constructor that does nothing other than display a message indicating it is working:

    ```
    public PartyWithConstructor()
    {
        System.out.println("Creating a Party");
    }
    ```

3. Save the file and compile it.

(continues)

(continued)

4. In your text editor, open the **DinnerParty2.java** file, and change the class name to `DinnerPartyWithConstructor`. Change the class in the `extends` clause to `PartyWithConstructor`. Save the file as **DinnerPartyWithConstructor.java**, and compile it.

5. In your text editor, open a new file so you can write an application to demonstrate the use of the base class constructor with an extended class object. This application creates only one child class object:

```
public class UseDinnerPartyWithConstructor
{
    public static void main(String[] args)
    {
        DinnerPartyWithConstructor aDinnerParty =
            new DinnerPartyWithConstructor();
    }
}
```

6. Save the application as **UseDinnerPartyWithConstructor.java**, then compile and run it. The output is shown in Figure 10-10. Even though the application creates only one subclass object (and no superclass objects) and the subclass contains no constructor of its own, the superclass constructor executes.

Figure 10-10 Output of the `UseDinnerPartyWithConstructor` application

Inheritance When the Superclass Requires Constructor Arguments

Next, you modify the `PartyWithConstructor` class so that its constructor requires an argument. Then, you observe that a subclass without a constructor cannot compile.

1. Open the **PartyWithConstructor.java** file in your text editor, and then change the class name to **PartyWithConstructor2**.

(continues)

(continued)

2. Replace the existing constructor with a new version using the new class name. This constructor requires an argument, which it uses to set the number of guests who will attend a party:

```
public PartyWithConstructor2(int numGuests)
{
   guests = numGuests;
}
```

3. Save the file as **PartyWithConstructor2.java**, and then compile it.

4. Open the **DinnerPartyWithConstructor.java** file in your text editor.

5. Change the class header as follows so that the name of the class is `DinnerPartyWithConstructor2` and it inherits from `PartyWithConstructor2`:

```
public class DinnerPartyWithConstructor2 extends
   PartyWithConstructor2
```

6. Save the file as **DinnerPartyWithConstructor2.java**, and then compile it. An error message appears, as shown in Figure 10-11. When you attempt to compile the subclass, no parameterless constructor can be found in the superclass, so the compile fails.

Figure 10-11 Error message generated when compiling the `DinnerPartyWithConstructor2` class

7. To correct the error, open the **DinnerPartyWithConstructor2.java** file in your text editor. Following the `dinnerChoice` field declaration, insert a constructor for the class as follows:

```
public DinnerPartyWithConstructor2(int numGuests)
{
   super(numGuests);
}
```

(continues)

(continued)

8. Save the file and compile it. This time, the compile is successful because the subclass calls its parent's constructor, passing along an integer value. Note that the DinnerPartyWithConstructor2 subclass constructor is not required to receive an integer argument, although in this example it does. For example, it would be acceptable to create a subclass constructor that required no arguments but passed a constant (for example, 0) to its parent. Similarly, the subclass constructor could require several arguments and pass one of them to its parent. The requirement is not that the subclass constructor must have the same number or types of parameters as its parent; the only requirement is that the subclass constructor calls super() and passes to the parent what it needs to execute.

Accessing Superclass Methods

Earlier in this chapter, you learned that a subclass can contain a method with the same name and arguments (the same signature) as a method in its parent class. When this happens, using the subclass method overrides the superclass method. However, instead of overriding the superclass method, you might want to use it within a subclass. If so, you can use the keyword super to access the parent class method.

For example, examine the Customer class in Figure 10-12 and the PreferredCustomer class in Figure 10-13. A Customer has an idNumber and balanceOwed. In addition to these fields, a PreferredCustomer receives a discountRate. In the PreferredCustomer display() method, you want to display all three fields—idNumber, balanceOwed, and discountRate. Because two-thirds of the code to accomplish the display has already been written for the Customer class, it is convenient to have the PreferredCustomer display() method use its parent's version of the display() method before displaying its own discount rate. Figure 10-14 shows a brief application that displays one object of each class, and Figure 10-15 shows the output.

```
public class Customer
{
    private int idNumber;
    private double balanceOwed;
    public Customer(int id, double bal)
    {
        idNumber = id;
        balanceOwed = bal;
    }
    public void display()
    {
        System.out.println("Customer #" + idNumber +
            " Balance $" + balanceOwed);
    }
}
```

Figure 10-12   The Customer class

```
public class PreferredCustomer extends Customer
{
    double discountRate;
    public PreferredCustomer(int id, double bal, double rate)
    {
        super(id, bal);
        discountRate = rate;
    }
    public void display()
    {
        super.display();
        System.out.println("    Discount rate is " + discountRate);
    }
}
```

Figure 10-13   The PreferredCustomer class

```
public class TestCustomers
{
    public static void main(String[] args)
    {
        Customer oneCust = new Customer(124, 123.45);
        PreferredCustomer onePCust = new
            PreferredCustomer(125, 3456.78, 0.15);
        oneCust.display();
        onePCust.display();
    }
}
```

Figure 10-14   The TestCustomers application

Figure 10-15 Output of the `TestCustomers` application

When you call a superclass constructor from a subclass constructor, the call must be the first statement in the constructor. However, when you call an ordinary superclass method within a subclass method, the call is not required to be the first statement in the method, although it can be, as shown in the `display()` method in Figure 10-13.

Comparing `this` and `super`

In a subclass, the keywords `this` and `super` sometimes refer to the same method, but sometimes they do not.

For example, if a subclass has overridden a superclass method named `someMethod()`, then within the subclass, `super.someMethod()` refers to the superclass version of the method, and both `someMethod()` and `this.someMethod()` refer to the subclass version.

On the other hand, if a subclass has *not* overridden a superclass method named `someMethod()`, the child can use the method name with `super` (because the method is a member of the superclass), with `this` (because the method is a member of the subclass by virtue of inheritance), or alone (again, because the method is a member of the subclass).

TWO TRUTHS & A LIE

Accessing Superclass Methods

1. You can use the keyword `this` from within a derived class method to access an overridden base class method.

2. You can use the keyword `super` from within a derived class method to access an overridden base class method.

3. You can use the keyword `super` from within a derived class method to access a base class method that has not been overridden.

The false statement is #1. You can use the keyword super from within a derived class method to access an overridden base class method; if you use the keyword this, then you will access the overriding subclass method.

Employing Information Hiding

The Student class shown in Figure 10-16 is an example of a typical Java class. Within the Student class, as with most Java classes, the keyword private precedes each data field, and the keyword public precedes each method. In fact, the four get and set methods are public within the Student class specifically because the data fields are private. Without the public get and set methods, there would be no way to access the private data fields.

```java
public class Student
{
    private int idNum;
    private double gpa;
    public int getIdNum()
    {
        return idNum;
    }
    public double getGpa()
    {
        return gpa;
    }
    public void setIdNum(int num)
    {
        idNum = num;
    }
    public void setGpa(double gradePoint)
    {
        gpa = gradePoint;
    }
}
```

Figure 10-16   The Student class

When an application is a client of the Student class (that is, it instantiates a Student object), the client cannot directly alter the data in any private field. For example, suppose that you write a main() method that creates a Student as:

Student someStudent = new Student();

Then you cannot change the Student's idNum with a statement such as:

someStudent.idNum = 812; ◄——— **Don't Do It**
You cannot access a private data member of an object.

The idNum of the someStudent object is not accessible in the main() method that uses the Student object because idNum is private. Only methods that are part of the Student class itself are allowed to alter private Student data. To alter a Student's idNum, you must use a public method, as in the following:

someStudent.setIdNum(812);

The concept of keeping data private is known as **information hiding**. When you employ information hiding, your data can be altered only by the methods you choose and only in ways that you can control. For example, you might want the setIdNum() method to check to make certain the idNum is within a specific range of values. If a class other than the Student class could alter idNum, idNum could be assigned a value that the Student class couldn't control.

You first learned about information hiding and using the public and private keywords in Chapter 3. You might want to review these concepts.

When a class serves as a superclass to other classes you create, your subclasses inherit all the data and methods of the superclass. The methods in a subclass can use all of the data fields and methods that belong to its parent, with one exception: private members of the parent class are not accessible within a child class's methods. If a new class could simply extend your Student class and get to its data fields without going through the proper channels, information hiding would not be operating.

If the members of a base class don't have an explicit access specifier, their access is package by default. Such base class members cannot be accessed within a child class unless the two classes are in the same package. You will learn about packages in the next chapter.

Sometimes, you want to access parent class data from within a subclass. For example, suppose that you create two child classes—PartTimeStudent and FullTimeStudent—that extend the Student class. If you want the subclass methods to be able to directly access idNum and gpa, these data fields cannot be private. However, if you don't want other, nonchild classes to access these data fields, they cannot be public. To solve this problem, you can create the fields using the specifier protected. Using the keyword **protected** provides you with an intermediate level of security between public and private access. If you create a protected data field or method, it can be used within its own class or in any classes extended from that class, but it cannot be used by "outside" classes. In other words, protected members are those that can be used by a class and its descendants.

You seldom are required to make parent class fields protected. A child class can access its parent's private data fields by using public methods defined in the parent class, just as any other class can. You need to make parent class fields protected only if you want child classes to be able to access private data directly. (For example, perhaps you do not want a parent class to have a get method for a field, but you do want a child class to be able to access the field. As another example, perhaps a parent class set method enforces limits on a field's value, but a child class object should not have such limits.) Using the protected access specifier for a field can be convenient, and it also improves program performance because a child class can use an inherited field directly instead of "going through" methods to access the data. However, protected data members should be used sparingly. Whenever possible, the principle of information hiding should be observed, so even child classes should have to go through public methods to "get to" their parent's private data. When child classes are allowed direct access to a parent's fields, the likelihood of future errors increases. Classes that directly use fields from parent classes are said to be **fragile** because they are prone to errors—that is, they are easy to "break."

TWO TRUTHS & A LIE

Employing Information Hiding

1. Information hiding describes the concept of keeping data private.

2. A subclass inherits all the data and methods of its superclass, except the `private` ones.

3. If a data field is defined as protected, then a method in a child class can use it directly.

The false statement is #2. A subclass inherits all the data and methods of its superclass, but it cannot access the `private` ones directly.

Methods You Cannot Override

Sometimes when you create a class, you might choose not to allow subclasses to override some of the superclass methods. For example, an `Employee` class might contain a method that calculates each `Employee`'s ID number based on specific `Employee` attributes, and you might not want any derived classes to be able to provide their own versions of this method. As another example, perhaps a class contains a statement that displays legal restrictions to using the class. You might decide that no derived class should be able to display a different version of the statement.

The three types of methods that you cannot override in a subclass are:

- `static` methods
- `final` methods
- Methods within `final` classes

A Subclass Cannot Override `static` Methods in Its Superclass

A subclass cannot override methods that are declared `static` in the superclass. In other words, a subclass cannot override a class method—a method you use without instantiating an object. A subclass can *hide* a `static` method in the superclass by declaring a `static` method in the subclass with the same signature as the `static` method in the superclass;

then, you can call the new static method from within the subclass or in another class by using a subclass object. However, this static method that hides the superclass static method cannot access the parent method using the super object.

Figure 10-17 shows a BaseballPlayer class that contains a single static method named showOrigins(). Figure 10-18 shows a ProfessionalBaseballPlayer class that extends the BaseballPlayer class to provide a salary. Within the ProfessionalBaseballPlayer class, an attempt is made to create a nonstatic method that overrides the static showOrigins() method to display the general Abner Doubleday message about baseball from the parent class as well as the more specific message about professional baseball. However, the compiler returns the error message shown in Figure 10-19—you cannot override a static method with a nonstatic method.

```
public class BaseballPlayer
{
    private int jerseyNumber;
    private double battingAvg;
    public static void showOrigins()
    {
        System.out.println("Abner Doubleday is often " +
            "credited with inventing baseball");
    }
}
```

Figure 10-17 The BaseballPlayer class

```
public class ProfessionalBaseballPlayer extends BaseballPlayer
{
    double salary;
    public void showOrigins()
    {
        super.showOrigins();
        System.out.println("The first professional " +
            "major league baseball game was played in 1871");
    }
}
```

Don't Do It
A nonstatic method cannot override a static member of a parent class.

Figure 10-18 The ProfessionalBaseballPlayer class attempting to override the parent's static method

Figure 10-19   Error message when compiling the `ProfessionalBaseballPlayer` class in Figure 10-18

Figure 10-20 shows a second version of the `ProfessionalBaseballPlayer` class. In this version, the `showOrigins()` method has been changed to `static` in an attempt to fix the problem in Figure 10-19. Figure 10-21 shows the error message that appears when this class is compiled. Because this method version is `static`, the method is not used with an object and does not receive a `this` reference. The keyword `super` can be used in child class, nonstatic, and instance methods and constructors, but not in child class `static` methods.

```
public class ProfessionalBaseballPlayer extends BaseballPlayer
{
   double salary;
   public static void showOrigins()
   {
      super.showOrigins();
      System.out.println("The first professional " +
         "major league baseball game was played in 1871");
   }
}
```

> **Don't Do It**
> You cannot refer to super in a static method.

Figure 10-20   The `ProfessionalBaseballPlayer` class with a static method that attempts to reference `super`

Figure 10-21   Error message when compiling the `ProfessionalBaseballPlayer` class in Figure 10-20

Finally, Figure 10-22 shows a ProfessionalBaseballPlayer class that compiles without error. The class extends BaseballPlayer, and its showOrigins() method is static. Because this method has the same name as the parent class method, when you use the name with a child class object, this method hides the original. However, it cannot use the super keyword to access the Abner Doubleday method. If you want the ProfessionalBaseballPlayer class to display information about baseball in general as well as professional baseball in particular, you can do either of the following:

- You can repeat the parent class message within the child class using a println() statement.

- You can use the parent class name, a dot, and the method name. Although a child class cannot inherit its parent's static methods, it can access its parent's static methods the same way any other class can. The shaded statement in Figure 10-22 uses this approach.

Figure 10-23 shows a class that creates a ProfessionalBaseballPlayer and tests the method; Figure 10-24 shows the output.

```
public class ProfessionalBaseballPlayer extends BaseballPlayer
{
   double salary;
   public static void showOrigins()
   {
      BaseballPlayer.showOrigins();
      System.out.println("The first professional " +
         "major league baseball game was played in 1871");
   }
}
```

Figure 10-22 The ProfessionalBaseballPlayer class

```
public class TestProPlayer
{
   public static void main(String[] args)
   {
      ProfessionalBaseballPlayer aYankee =
         new ProfessionalBaseballPlayer();
      aYankee.showOrigins();
   }
}
```

Figure 10-23 The TestProPlayer class

Figure 10-24 Output of the TestProPlayer application

A Subclass Cannot Override final Methods in Its Superclass

A subclass cannot override methods that are declared final in the superclass. For example, consider the BasketballPlayer and ProfessionalBasketballPlayer classes in Figures 10-25 and 10-26, respectively. When you attempt to compile the ProfessionalBasketballPlayer class, you receive the error message in Figure 10-27, because the class cannot override the final displayMessage() method in the parent class.

```java
public class BasketballPlayer
{
    private int jerseyNumber;
    public final void displayMessage()
    {
        System.out.println("Michael Jordan is the " +
            "greatest basketball player - and that is final");
    }
}
```

Figure 10-25 The BasketballPlayer class

```java
public class ProfessionalBasketballPlayer extends BasketballPlayer
{
    double salary;
    public void displayMessage()
    {
        System.out.println("I have nothing to say");
    }
}
```

Don't Do It
A child class method cannot override a final parent class method.

Figure 10-26 The ProfessionalBasketballPlayer class that attempts to override a final method

```
Command Prompt                                            [ - ][ □ ][ X ]

C:\Java>javac ProfessionalBasketballPlayer.java
ProfessionalBasketballPlayer.java:4: error: displayMessage() in ProfessionalBask
etballPlayer cannot override displayMessage() in BasketballPlayer
   public void displayMessage()
               ^
   overridden method is final
1 error

C:\Java>
```

Figure 10-27 Error message when compiling the `ProfessionalBasketballPlayer` class in Figure 10-26

If you make the `displayMessage()` method `final` in the `ProfessionalBasketballPlayer` class in Figure 10-26, you receive the same compiler error message as shown in Figure 10-27. If you make the `displayMessage()` method `static` in the `ProfessionalBasketballPlayer` class, the class does not compile, but you do receive an additional error message.

In Chapter 2, you learned that you can use the keyword `final` when you want to create a constant, as in `final double TAXRATE = 0.065;`. You can also use the `final` modifier with methods when you don't want the method to be overridden—that is, when you want every child class to use the original parent class version of a method.

In Java, all instance method calls are **virtual method calls** by default—that is, the method used is determined when the program runs because the type of the object used might not be known until the method executes. For example, with the following method you can pass in a `BasketballPlayer` object, or any object that is a child of `BasketballPlayer`, so the "actual" type of the argument `bbplayer`, and which version of `displayMessage()` to use, is not known until the method executes.

```
public void display(BasketballPlayer bbplayer)
{
    bbplayer.displayMessage();
}
```

In other words, the version of the method used is not determined when the program is compiled; it is determined when the method call is made. Determining the correct method takes a small amount of time. An advantage to making a method `final` is that the compiler knows there is only one version of the method—the parent class version. Therefore, the compiler *does* know which method version to use—the only version—and the program is more efficient.

Because a `final` method's definition can never change—that is, can never be overridden with a modified version—the compiler can optimize a program's performance by removing the calls to `final` methods and replacing them with the expanded code of their definitions at each method call location. This process is called **inlining** the code. When a program executes, you are never aware that inlining is taking place; the compiler chooses to use this procedure to save the overhead of calling a method, and the program runs faster. The compiler chooses to inline a `final` method only if it is a small method that contains just one or two lines of code.

A Subclass Cannot Override Methods in a `final` Superclass

You can declare a class to be `final`. When you do, all of its methods are `final`, regardless of which access specifier precedes the method name. A `final` class cannot be a parent. Figure 10-28 shows two classes: a `HideAndGoSeekPlayer` class that is a `final` class because of the word `final` in the class header, and a `ProfessionalHideAndGoSeekPlayer` class that attempts to extend the `final` class, adding a salary field. Figure 10-29 shows the error message generated when you try to compile the `ProfessionalHideAndGoSeekPlayer` class.

```
public final class HideAndGoSeekPlayer
{
   private int count;
   public void displayRules()
   {
      System.out.println("You have to count to " + count +
         " before you start looking for hiders");
   }
}
public final class ProfessionalHideAndGoSeekPlayer
   extends HideAndGoSeekPlayer
{
   private double salary;
}
```

Don't Do It
You cannot extend a final class.

Figure 10-28   The `HideAndGoSeekPlayer` and `ProfessionalHideAndGoSeekPlayer` classes

Figure 10-29   Error message when compiling the `ProfessionalHideAndGoSeekPlayer` class in Figure 10-28

Java's `Math` class, which you learned about in Chapter 4, is an example of a `final` class.

TWO TRUTHS & A LIE

Methods You Cannot Override

1. A subclass cannot override methods that are declared `static` in the superclass.

2. A subclass cannot override methods that are declared `final` in the superclass.

3. A subclass cannot override methods that are declared `private` in the superclass.

The false statement is #3. A subclass can override private methods as well as public or protected ones.

Don't Do It

- Don't capitalize the *o* in the `instanceof` operator. Although the second word in an identifier frequently is capitalized in Java, `instanceof` is an exception.

- Don't try to directly access private superclass members from a subclass.

- Don't forget to call a superclass constructor from within a subclass constructor if the superclass does not contain a default constructor.

- Don't try to override a `final` method in an extended class.

- Don't try to extend a `final` class.

Key Terms

Inheritance is a mechanism that enables one class to inherit, or assume, both the behavior and the attributes of another class.

The **Unified Modeling Language (UML)** is a graphical language used by programmers and analysts to describe classes and object-oriented processes.

A **class diagram** is a visual tool that provides you with an overview of a class. It consists of a rectangle divided into three sections—the top section contains the name of the class, the middle section contains the names and data types of the attributes, and the bottom section contains the methods.

A **base class** is a class that is used as a basis for inheritance.

A **derived class** is a class that inherits from a base class.

Composition is the relationship in which one class contains one or more members of another class that would not continue to exist without the object that contains them.

Aggregation is a type of composition in which a class contains one or more members of another class that would continue to exist without the object that contains them.

Superclass and **subclass** are synonyms for base class and derived class.

Parent class and **child class** are synonyms for base class and derived class.

The keyword **extends** is used to achieve inheritance in Java.

The **instanceof operator** determines whether an object that is the operand on the left is a member or descendant of the class that is the operand on the right.

To **upcast** an object is to change it to an object of a class higher in the object's inheritance hierarchy.

Polymorphism is the technique of using the same method name to indicate different implementations.

To **override a method** in a parent class is to create a method in a child class that has the same name and parameter list as a method in its parent class.

Subtype polymorphism is the ability of one method name to work appropriately for different subclasses of a parent class.

The keyword **super** refers to the parent or superclass of the class in which you use it.

Information hiding is the concept of keeping data private.

The keyword **protected** provides you with an intermediate level of security between `public` and `private` access. `Protected` members are those that can be used by a class and its descendants.

Fragile classes are those that are prone to errors.

Virtual method calls are those in which the method used is determined when the program runs, because the type of the object used might not be known until the method executes. In Java, all instance method calls are virtual calls by default.

Inlining the code is an automatic process that optimizes performance. Because a `final` method's definition can never be overridden, the compiler can optimize a program's performance by removing the calls to `final` methods and replacing them with the expanded code of their definitions at each method call location.

Chapter Summary

- In Java, inheritance is a mechanism that enables one class to inherit both the behavior and the attributes of another class. Using inheritance saves time because the original fields and methods already exist, have been tested, and are familiar to users. A class that is used as a basis for inheritance is a base class. A class you create that inherits from a base class is called a derived class. You can use the terms *superclass* and *subclass* as synonyms for base class and derived class; you can also use the terms *parent class* and *child class*.

- You use the keyword `extends` to achieve inheritance in Java. A parent class object does not have access to its child's data and methods, but when you create a subclass by extending an existing class, the new subclass contains data and methods that were defined in the original superclass.

- Sometimes, superclass data fields and methods are not entirely appropriate for the subclass objects. Polymorphism is the act of using the same method name to indicate different implementations. You use polymorphism when you override a superclass method in a subclass by creating a method with the same name and parameter list.

- When you create any subclass object, the superclass constructor must execute first, and *then* the subclass constructor executes. When a superclass contains only constructors that require arguments, you must include at least one constructor for each subclass you create. Your subclass constructors can contain any number of statements, but the first statement within each constructor must call the superclass constructor. When a superclass requires parameters upon instantiation, even if you have no other reason to create a subclass constructor, you must write the subclass constructor so it can call its superclass's constructor. The format of the statement that calls a superclass constructor is `super(list of arguments);`.

- If you want to use a superclass method within a subclass, you can use the keyword `super` to access the parent class method.

- Subclasses inherit all the data and methods of their superclasses, but `private` members of the parent class are not accessible with a child class's methods. However, if you create a `protected` data field or method, it can be used within its own class or in any classes extended from that class, but it cannot be used by "outside" classes. A subclass cannot override methods that are declared `static` in the superclass. A subclass can *hide* a `static` method in the superclass by declaring a `static` method in the subclass with the same signature as the `static` method in the superclass. A subclass cannot override methods that are declared `final` in the superclass or methods declared within a `final` class.

Review Questions

1. A way to discover which of two classes is the base class and which is the subclass is to _____.

    a. look at the class size
    b. try saying the two class names together
    c. use polymorphism
    d. Both a and b are correct.

2. Employing inheritance reduces errors because _____.

    a. the new classes have access to fewer data fields
    b. the new classes have access to fewer methods
    c. you can copy methods that you already created
    d. many of the methods you need have already been used and tested

3. A base class can also be called a _____.

    a. child class   c. derived class
    b. subclass   d. superclass

4. Which of the following choices is the best example of a parent class/child class relationship?

    a. Rose/Flower   c. Dog/Poodle
    b. Present/Gift   d. Sparrow/Bird

5. The Java keyword that creates inheritance is _____.

    a. static   c. extends
    b. enlarge   d. inherits

6. A class named `Building` has a `public`, nonstatic method named `getFloors()`. If `School` is a child class of `Building`, and `modelHigh` is an object of type `School`, which of the following statements is valid?

    a. `Building.getFloors();`
    b. `School.getFloors();`
    c. `modelHigh.getFloors();`
    d. All of the previous statements are valid.

7. Which of the following statements is true?

    a. A child class inherits from a parent class.
    b. A parent class inherits from a child class.
    c. Both of the preceding statements are true.
    d. Neither a nor b is true.

8. When a subclass method has the same name and argument types as a superclass method, the subclass method _____ the superclass method.

    a. overrides
    b. overuses
    c. overloads
    d. overcompensates

9. When you instantiate an object that is a member of a subclass, the _____ constructor executes first.

    a. subclass
    b. child class
    c. extended class
    d. parent class

10. The keyword **super** always refers to the _____ of the class in which you use it.

    a. child class
    b. derived class
    c. subclass
    d. parent class

11. If the only constructor in a superclass requires arguments, its subclass _____.

    a. must contain a constructor
    b. must not contain a constructor
    c. must contain a constructor that requires arguments
    d. must not contain a constructor that requires arguments

12. If a superclass constructor requires arguments, any constructor of its subclasses must call the superclass constructor _____.

    a. as the first statement
    b. as the last statement
    c. at some time
    d. multiple times if multiple arguments are involved

13. A child class `Motorcycle` extends a parent class `Vehicle`. Each class constructor requires one `String` argument. The `Motorcycle` class constructor can call the `Vehicle` class constructor with the statement _____.

    a. `Vehicle("Honda");`
    b. `Motorcycle("Harley");`
    c. `super("Suzuki");`
    d. none of the above

14. In Java, the concept of keeping data private is known as _____.

    a. polymorphism   c. data deception
    b. information hiding   d. concealing fields

15. If you create a data field or method that is _____, it can be used within its own class or in any classes extended from that class.

    a. public   c. private
    b. protected   d. both a and b

16. Within a subclass, you cannot override _____ methods.

    a. public   c. static
    b. private   d. constructor

17. You call a static method using _____.

    a. the name of its class, a dot, and the method name
    b. the name of the class's superclass, a dot, and the method name
    c. the name of an object in the same class, a dot, and the method name
    d. either a or b

18. You use a _____ method access specifier when you create methods for which you want to prevent overriding in extended classes.

    a. public   c. final
    b. protected   d. subclass

19. A compiler can decide to _____ a final method—that is, determine the code of the method call when the program is compiled.

    a. duplicate   c. redline
    b. inline   d. beeline

20. When a parent class contains a static method, child classes _____ override it.

    a. frequently   c. must
    b. seldom   d. cannot

Exercises

Programming Exercises

1. Create a class named Horse that contains data fields for the name, color, and birth year. Include get and set methods for these fields. Next, create a subclass named RaceHorse, which contains an additional field that holds the number of races in which the horse has competed and additional methods to get and set the new field. Write an application that demonstrates using objects of each class. Save the files as **Horse.java**, **RaceHorse.java**, and **DemoHorses.java**.

2. Mick's Wicks makes candles in various sizes. Create a class for the business named Candle that contains data fields for color, height, and price. Create get methods for all three fields. Create set methods for color and height, but not for price. Instead, when height is set, determine the price as $2 per inch. Create a child class named ScentedCandle that contains an additional data field named scent and methods to get and set it. In the child class, override the parent's setHeight() method to set the price of a ScentedCandle object at $3 per inch. Write an application that instantiates an object of each type and displays the details. Save the files as **Candle.java**, **ScentedCandle.java**, and **DemoCandles.java**.

3. Create a class named TennisGame that holds data about a single tennis game. The class has six fields: the names of the two players, the integer final scores for the players, and the String values of the final scores. Include a get method for each of the six fields. Also include a set method that accepts two players' names, and another set method that accepts the two integer final score values. The integer final score for a player is the number of points the player won during the game; this value should be in the range of 0 through 4. If either of the set method parameters for a score is not in the range of 0 through 4, assign 0 to both scores and assign "error" to the String scores. If both players' score parameters are 4, assign 0 to both scores and "error" to the String scores. The String score values are set by the method that sets the integer score values. The String final score for each player contains the traditional names for points in tennis: *love*, *15*, *30*, *40*, or *game*, respectively, for the values 0 through 4. Create a subclass named DoublesTennisGame that includes two additional fields for the names of the first two players' partners. Include get methods for the names. Override the parent class setNames() method to accept the names of all four players. Write an application named DemoTennisGames that instantiates several objects of each of these classes. Demonstrate that all the methods assign correct values. Save the files as **TennisGame.java**, **DoublesTennisGame.java**, and **DemoTennisGames.java**.

4. a. Create a class named Year that contains a data field that holds the number of days in a year. Include a get method that displays the number of days and a constructor that sets the number of days to 365. Create a subclass named LeapYear. LeapYear's constructor overrides Year's constructor and sets the number of days

to 366. Write an application named `UseYear` that instantiates one object of each class and displays their data. Save the files as **Year.java**, **LeapYear.java**, and **UseYear.java**.

b. Add a method named `daysElapsed()` to the `Year` class you created in Exercise 4a. The `daysElapsed()` method accepts two arguments representing a month and a day; it returns an integer indicating the number of days that have elapsed since January 1 of that year. For example, on March 3 in nonleap years, 61 days have elapsed (31 in January, 28 in February, and 2 in March). Create a `daysElapsed()` method for the `LeapYear` class that overrides the method in the `Year` class. For example, on March 3 in a `LeapYear`, 62 days have elapsed (31 in January, 29 in February, and 2 in March). Write an application named `UseYear2` that prompts the user for a month and day, and calculates the days elapsed in a `Year` and in a `LeapYear`. Save the files as **Year2.java**, **LeapYear2.java**, and **UseYear2.java**.

5. Every summer, Leeland Lakeside resort rents cabins by the week. Create a class named `CabinRental` that includes an integer field for the cabin number and a `double` field for the weekly rental rate. Include get methods for these fields and a constructor that requires an integer argument representing the cabin number. The constructor sets the weekly rate based on the cabin number; cabins numbered 1, 2, and 3 are $950 per week, and others are $1,100 per week. Create an extended class named `HolidayCabinRental` that is used for rentals during weeks that include summer holiday weekends. The constructor for this class requires a room number and adds a $150 surcharge to the regular rental rate. Write an application named `DemoCabinRental` that creates an object of each class, and demonstrate that all the methods work correctly. Save the files as **CabinRental.java**, **HolidayCabinRental.java**, and **DemoCabinRental.java**.

6. Create a class named `Package` with data fields for weight in ounces, shipping method, and shipping cost. The shipping method is a character: *A* for air, *T* for truck, or *M* for mail. The `Package` class contains a constructor that requires arguments for weight and shipping method. The constructor calls a `calculateCost()` method that determines the shipping cost, based on the following table:

Weight (oz.)	Air ($)	Truck ($)	Mail ($)
1 to 8	2.00	1.50	.50
9 to 16	3.00	2.35	1.50
17 and over	4.50	3.25	2.15

The `Package` class also contains a `display()` method that displays the values in all four fields. Create a subclass named `InsuredPackage` that adds an insurance cost to the shipping cost, based on the following table:

Shipping Cost Before Insurance ($)	Additional Cost ($)
0 to 1.00	2.45
1.01 to 3.00	3.95
3.01 and over	5.55

Write an application named UsePackage that instantiates at least three objects of each type (Package and InsuredPackage) using a variety of weights and shipping method codes. Display the results for each Package and InsuredPackage. Save the files as **Package.java**, **InsuredPackage.java**, and **UsePackage.java**.

7. Create a class named CarRental that contains fields that hold a renter's name, zip code, size of the car rented, daily rental fee, length of rental in days, and total rental fee. The class contains a constructor that requires all the rental data except the daily rate and total fee, which are calculated based on the size of the car: economy at $29.99 per day, midsize at $38.99 per day, or full size at $43.50 per day. The class also includes a display() method that displays all the rental data. Create a subclass named LuxuryCarRental. This class sets the rental fee at $79.99 per day and prompts the user to respond to the option of including a chauffeur at $200 more per day. Override the parent class display() method to include chauffeur fee information. Write an application named UseCarRental that prompts the user for the data needed for a rental and creates an object of the correct type. Display the total rental fee. Save the files as **CarRental.java**, **LuxuryCarRental.java**, and **UseCarRental.java**.

8. Create a class named CollegeCourse that includes data fields that hold the department (for example, ENG), the course number (for example, 101), the credits (for example, 3), and the fee for the course (for example, $360). All of the fields are required as arguments to the constructor, except for the fee, which is calculated at $120 per credit hour. Include a display() method that displays the course data. Create a subclass named LabCourse that adds $50 to the course fee. Override the parent class display() method to indicate that the course is a lab course and to display all the data. Write an application named UseCourse that prompts the user for course information. If the user enters a class in any of the following departments, create a LabCourse: BIO, CHM, CIS, or PHY. If the user enters any other department, create a CollegeCourse that does not include the lab fee. Then display the course data. Save the files as **CollegeCourse.java**, **LabCourse.java**, and **UseCourse.java**.

9. Create a class named Vehicle that acts as a superclass for vehicle types. The Vehicle class contains private variables for the number of wheels and the average number of miles per gallon. The Vehicle class also contains a constructor with integer arguments for the number of wheels and average miles per gallon, and a

toString() method that returns a String containing these values. Create two subclasses, Car and MotorCycle, that extend the Vehicle class. Each subclass contains a constructor that accepts the miles-per-gallon value as an argument and forces the number of wheels to the appropriate value—2 for a MotorCycle and 4 for a Car. Write a UseVehicle class to instantiate the two Vehicle objects and display the objects' values. Save the files as **Vehicle.java**, **Car.java**, **MotorCycle.java**, and **UseVehicle.java**.

10. Develop a set of classes for a college to use in various student service and personnel applications. Classes you need to design include the following:

- Person—A Person contains a first name, last name, street address, zip code, and phone number. The class also includes a method that sets each data field, using a series of dialog boxes and a display method that displays all of a Person's information on a single line at the command line on the screen.

- CollegeEmployee—CollegeEmployee descends from Person. A CollegeEmployee also includes a Social Security number, an annual salary, and a department name, as well as methods that override the Person methods to accept and display all CollegeEmployee data.

- Faculty—Faculty descends from CollegeEmployee. This class also includes a Boolean field that indicates whether the Faculty member is tenured, as well as methods that override the CollegeEmployee methods to accept and display this additional piece of information.

- Student—Student descends from Person. In addition to the fields available in Person, a Student contains a major field of study and a grade point average as well as methods that override the Person methods to accept and display these additional facts.

Write an application named CollegeList that declares an array of four "regular" CollegeEmployees, three Faculty, and seven Students. Prompt the user to specify which type of person's data will be entered (C, F, or S), or allow the user to quit (Q). While the user chooses to continue (that is, does not quit), accept data entry for the appropriate type of Person. If the user attempts to enter data for more than four CollegeEmployees, three Faculty, or seven Students, display an error message. When the user quits, display a report on the screen listing each group of Persons under the appropriate heading of College Employees, Faculty, or Students. If the user has not entered data for one or more types of Persons during a session, display an appropriate message under the appropriate heading.

Save the files as **Person.java**, **CollegeEmployee.java**, **Faculty.java**, **Student.java**, and **CollegeList.java**.

Debugging Exercises

1. Each of the following files in the Chapter10 folder of your downloadable student files has syntax and/or logic errors. In each case, determine the problem and fix the program. After you correct the errors, save each file using the same filename preceded with *Fix*. For example, DebugTen1.java will become FixDebugTen1.java.

   a. DebugTen1.java

   b. DebugTen2.java

   c. DebugTen3.java

   d. DebugTen4.java

   e. Eight other Debug files in the Chapter10 folder; these files are used by the DebugTen exercises

 Game Zone

1. a. Create an Alien class. Include at least three protected data members of your choice, such as the number of eyes the Alien has. Include a constructor that requires a value for each data field and a toString() method that returns a String containing a complete description of the Alien. Save the file as **Alien.java**.

   b. Create two classes—Martian and Jupiterian—that descend from Alien. Supply each with a constructor that sets the Alien data fields with values you choose. For example, you can decide that a Martian has four eyes but a Jupiterian has only two. Save the files as **Martian.java** and **Jupiterian.java**.

   c. Create an application that instantiates one Martian and one Jupiterian. Call the toString() method with each object and display the results. Save the application as **CreateAliens.java**.

2. a. In Chapter 4, you created a Die class that you can use to instantiate objects that hold one of six randomly selected values. Modify this class so its value field is protected instead of private. This will allow a child class to access the value. Save the file as **Die.java**.

   b. Create a LoadedDie class that can be used to give a player a slight advantage over the computer. A LoadedDie never rolls a 1; it only rolls values 2 through 6. Save the file as **LoadedDie.java**.

   c. Create a program that rolls two Die objects against each other 1,000 times and counts the number of times the first Die has a higher value than the other Die. Then roll a Die object against a LoadedDie object 1,000 times, and count the number of times the Die wins. Display the results. Save the application as **TestLoadedDie.java**. Figure 10-30 shows two typical executions.

Figure 10-30   Two typical executions of the `TestLoadedDie` application

Case Problems

1. a. In Chapter 8, you created an `Event` class for Carly's Catering. Now extend the class to create a `DinnerEvent` class. In the extended class, include four new integer fields that represent numeric choices for an entrée, two side dishes, and a dessert for each `DinnerEvent` object. Also include three `final` arrays that contain `String` menu options for entrées, side dishes, and desserts, and store at least three choices in each array. Create a `DinnerEvent` constructor that requires arguments for an event number and number of guests, and integer menu choices for one entrée, two side dishes, and one dessert. Pass the first two parameters to the `Event` constructor, and assign the last four parameters to the appropriate local fields. Also include a `getMenu()` method that builds and returns a `String` including the `Strings` for the four menu choices. Save the file as **DinnerEvent.java**.

   b. In Chapter 9, you created an `EventDemo` program for Carly's Catering. The program uses an array of `Event` objects and allows the user to sort `Events` in ascending order by event number, number of guests, or event type. Now modify the program to use an array of four `DinnerEvent` objects. Prompt the user for all values for each object, and then allow the user to continuously sort the `DinnerEvent` descriptions by event number, number of guests, or event type. Save the file as **DinnerEventDemo.java**.

2. a. In Chapter 8, you created a `Rental` class for Sammy's Seashore Supplies. Now extend the class to create a `LessonWithRental` class. In the extended class, include a new Boolean field that indicates whether a lesson is required or optional for the type of equipment rented. Also include a `final` array that contains `Strings` representing the names of the instructors for each of the eight equipment types, and store names that you choose in the array. Create a `LessonWithRental` constructor that requires arguments for an event number, minutes for the rental, and an integer equipment type. Pass the first two parameters to the `Rental` constructor, and assign the last parameter to the equipment type. For the first two equipment types (jet ski and pontoon boat),

set the Boolean lesson required field to true; otherwise, set it to false. Also include a `getInstructor()` method that builds and returns a `String` including the `String` for the equipment type, a message that indicates whether a lesson is required, and the instructor's name. Save the file as **LessonWithRental.java**.

b. In Chapter 9, you created a `RentalDemo` program for Sammy's Seashore Supplies. The program uses an array of `Rental` objects and allows the user to sort `Rentals` in ascending order by contract number, equipment type, or price. Now modify the program to use an array of four `LessonWithRental` objects. Prompt the user for all values for each object, and then allow the user to continuously sort the `LessonWithRental` descriptions by contract number, equipment type, or price. Save the file as **LessonWithRentalDemo.java**.

Advanced Inheritance Concepts

In this chapter, you will:

- ◎ Create and use abstract classes
- ◎ Use dynamic method binding
- ◎ Create arrays of subclass objects
- ◎ Use the `Object` class and its methods
- ◎ Use inheritance to achieve good software design
- ◎ Create and use interfaces
- ◎ Create and use packages

Creating and Using Abstract Classes

Developing new classes is easier after you understand the concept of inheritance. When you use a class as a basis from which to create extended child classes, the child classes are more specific than their parent. When you create a child class, it inherits all the general attributes you need; thus, you must create only the new, more specific attributes. For example, a `SalariedEmployee` and an `HourlyEmployee` are more specific than an `Employee`. They can inherit general `Employee` attributes, such as an employee number, but they add specific attributes, such as pay-calculating methods.

Notice that a superclass contains the features that are shared by its subclasses. For example, the attributes of the `Dog` class are shared by every `Poodle` and `Spaniel`. The subclasses are more specific examples of the superclass type; they add more features to the shared, general features. Conversely, when you examine a subclass, you see that its parent is more general and less specific; for example, `Animal` is more general than `Dog`.

 Recall from Chapter 10 that the terms *base class*, *superclass*, and *parent* are equivalent. Similarly, the terms *derived class*, *subclass*, and *child* are equivalent. Also recall that a child class contains all the members of its parent, whether those members are `public`, `protected`, or `private`. However, a child object cannot directly access a `private` member inherited from a parent.

A **concrete class** is one from which you can instantiate objects. Sometimes, a class is so general that you never intend to create any specific instances of the class. For example, you might never create an object that is "just" an `Employee`; each `Employee` is more specifically a `SalariedEmployee`, `HourlyEmployee`, or `ContractEmployee`. A class such as `Employee` that you create only to extend from is not a concrete class; it is an **abstract class**. In the last chapter, you learned that you can create `final` classes if you do not want other classes to be able to extend them. Classes that you declare to be `abstract` are the opposite; your only purpose in creating them is to enable other classes to extend them. If you attempt to instantiate an object from an abstract class, you receive an error message from the compiler that you have committed an `InstantiationError`. You use the keyword `abstract` when you declare an abstract class. (In other programming languages, such as C++, abstract classes are known as **virtual classes**.)

 In the last chapter, you learned to create class diagrams. By convention, when you show abstract classes and methods in class diagrams, their names appear in italics.

 In Chapter 4, you worked with the `GregorianCalendar` class. `GregorianCalendar` is a concrete class that extends the abstract class `Calendar`. In other words, there are no "plain" `Calendar` objects.

Programmers of an abstract class can include two method types:

- Nonabstract methods, like those you can create in any class, are implemented in the [covered] ... simply inherited by its children.

... ly and must be implemented in child classes.

... least one abstract method. When you create an abstract
... abstract and the rest of the method header, including the
... s. However, the declaration ends there: you do not provide
... hin the method—just a semicolon at the end of the
... method within an abstract class, the method is an abstract
... tly use the keyword abstract when defining the method,
... e keyword for clarity. If you declare a class to be abstract, its
... ut if you declare a method to be abstract, you must also

... nherits an abstract method, you write a method with the
... o code a subclass method to override every empty, abstract
... d. Either the child class method must itself be abstract, or
... ementation, for the inherited method.

... classes to represent different animals, such as Dog and
... stract class named Animal so you can provide generic
... name, only once. An Animal is generic, but all specific
... l sound differs from Animal to Animal. If you code an
... stract Animal class, you require all future Animal
... thod that is specific to the subclass. Figure 11-1 shows
... ing a data field for the name, getName() and setName()
... () method.

```
al

eak();

ing animalName)

}
```

Figure 11-1 The abstract Animal class

The Animal class in Figure 11-1 is declared as abstract; the keyword is shaded. You cannot create a class in which you declare an Animal object with a statement such as Animal myPet = new Animal("Murphy");, because a class that attempts to instantiate an Animal object does not compile. Animal is an abstract class, so no Animal objects can exist.

You create an abstract class such as Animal only so you can extend it. For example, because a dog is an animal, you can create a Dog class as a child class of Animal. Figure 11-2 shows a Dog class that extends Animal.

```
public class Dog extends Animal
{
    public void speak()
    {
        System.out.println("Woof!");
    }
}
```

Figure 11-2   The Dog class

The speak() method within the Dog class is required because you want to create Dog objects and the abstract, parent Animal class contains an abstract speak() method (shaded in Figure 11-1). You can code any statements you want within the Dog speak() method, but the speak() method must exist. If you do not want to create Dog objects but want the Dog class to be a parent to further subclasses, then the Dog class must also be abstract. In that case, you can write code for the speak() method within the subclasses of Dog.

If Animal is an abstract class, you cannot instantiate an Animal object; however, if Dog is a concrete class, instantiating a Dog object is perfectly legal. When you code the following, you create a Dog object:

Dog myPet = new Dog("Murphy");

Then, when you code myPet.speak();, the correct Dog speak() method executes.

The classes in Figures 11-3 and 11-4 also inherit from the Animal class and implement speak() methods. Figure 11-5 contains a UseAnimals application.

```
public class Cow extends Animal
{
    public void speak()
    {
        System.out.println("Moo!");
    }
}
```

Figure 11-3   The Cow class

```
public class Snake extends Animal
{
    public void speak()
    {
        System.out.println("Ssss!");
    }
}
```

Figure 11-4   The Snake class

```
public class UseAnimals
{
    public static void main(String[] args)
    {
        Dog myDog = new Dog();
        Cow myCow = new Cow();
        Snake mySnake = new Snake();
        myDog.setName("My dog Murphy");
        myCow.setName("My cow Elsie");
        mySnake.setName("My snake Sammy");
        System.out.print(myDog.getName() + " says ");
        myDog.speak();
        System.out.print(myCow.getName() + " says ");
        myCow.speak();
        System.out.print(mySnake.getName() + " says ");
        mySnake.speak();
    }
}
```

Figure 11-5   The UseAnimals application

The output in Figure 11-6 shows that when you create Dog, Cow, and Snake objects, each is an Animal with access to the Animal class getName() and setName() methods, and each uses its own speak() method appropriately.

In Figure 11-6, notice how the myDog. getName() and myDog.speak() method calls produce different output from when the same method names are used with myCow and mySnake.

Recall that using the same method name to indicate different implementations is *polymorphism*. Using polymorphism, one method name causes different and appropriate actions for diverse types of objects.

Figure 11-6   Output of the UseAnimals application

Watch the video *Abstract Classes.*

TWO TRUTHS & A LIE

Creating and Using Abstract Classes

1. An abstract class is one from which you cannot inherit, but from which you can create concrete objects.

2. Abstract classes usually have one or more empty abstract methods.

3. An abstract method has no body, curly braces, or statements.

The false statement is #1. An abstract class is one from which you cannot create any concrete objects, but from which you can inherit.

 You Do It

Creating an Abstract Class

In this section, you create an abstract `Vehicle` class. The class includes fields for the power source, the number of wheels, and the price. `Vehicle` is an abstract class; there will never be a "plain" `Vehicle` object. Later, you will create two subclasses, `Sailboat` and `Bicycle`; these more specific classes include price limits for the vehicle type, as well as different methods for displaying data.

1. Open a new file in your text editor, and enter the following first few lines to begin creating an abstract `Vehicle` class:

   ```
   public abstract class Vehicle
   {
   ```

2. Declare the data fields that hold the power source, number of wheels, and price. Declare `price` as `protected` rather than `private`, because you want child classes to be able to access the field.

   ```
   private String powerSource;
   private int wheels;
   protected int price;
   ```

3. The `Vehicle` constructor accepts three parameters and calls three methods. The first method accepts the `powerSource` parameter, the second

(continues)

(continued)

accepts the `wheels` parameter, and the third method prompts the user for a vehicle price.

```
public Vehicle(String powerSource, int wheels)
{
    setPowerSource(powerSource);
    setWheels(wheels);
    setPrice();
}
```

4. Include the following three get methods that return the values for the data fields:

```
public String getPowerSource()
{
    return powerSource;
}
public int getWheels()
{
    return wheels;
}
public int getPrice()
{
    return price;
}
```

5. Enter the following set methods, which assign values to the `powerSource` and `wheels` fields.

```
public void setPowerSource(String source)
{
    powerSource = source;
}
public void setWheels(int wls)
{
    wheels = wls;
}
```

6. The `setPrice()` method is an abstract method. Each subclass you eventually create that represents different vehicle types will have a unique prompt for the price and a different maximum allowed price. Type the abstract method definition and the closing curly brace for the class:

```
public abstract void setPrice();
}
```

7. Save the file as **Vehicle.java**. At the command prompt, compile the file using the **javac** command.

(continues)

(continued)

Extending an Abstract Class

You just created an abstract class, but you cannot instantiate any objects from this class. Rather, you must extend this class to be able to create any `Vehicle`-related objects. Next, you create a `Sailboat` class that extends the `Vehicle` class. This new class is concrete; that is, you can create actual `Sailboat` class objects.

1. Open a new file in your text editor, and then type the following, including a header for a `Sailboat` class that extends the `Vehicle` class:

```
import javax.swing.*;
public class Sailboat extends Vehicle
{
```

2. Add the declaration of a length field that is specific to a `Sailboat` by typing the following code:

```
private int length;
```

3. The `Sailboat` constructor must call its parent's constructor and send two arguments to provide values for the `powerSource` and `wheels` values. It also calls the `setLength()` method that prompts the user for and sets the length of the `Sailboat` objects:

```
public Sailboat()
{
    super("wind", 0);
    setLength();
}
```

4. Enter the following `setLength()` and `getLength()` methods, which respectively ask for and return the `Sailboat`'s length:

```
public void setLength()
{
    String entry;
    entry = JOptionPane.showInputDialog
       (null, "Enter sailboat length in feet ");
    length = Integer.parseInt(entry);
}
public int getLength()
{
    return length;
}
```

5. The concrete `Sailboat` class must contain a `setPrice()` method because the method is abstract in the parent class. Assume that a `Sailboat` has a maximum price of $100,000. Add the following `setPrice()` method that

(continues)

prompts the user for the price and forces it to the maximum value if the entered value is too high:

```
public void setPrice()
{
    String entry;
    final int MAX = 100000;
    entry = JOptionPane.showInputDialog
      (null, "Enter sailboat price ");
    price = Integer.parseInt(entry);
    if(price > MAX)
        price = MAX;
}
```

6. In Chapter 7, you first used the automatically included Object class toString() method that converts any object to a String. Now, you can override that method for this class by writing your own version as follows. When you finish, add a closing curly brace for the class.

```
public String toString()
{
    return("The " + getLength() +
        " foot sailboat is powered by " +
        getPowerSource() + "; it has " + getWheels() +
        " wheels and costs $" + getPrice());
}
}
```

7. Save the file as **Sailboat.java**, and then compile the class.

Extending an Abstract Class with a Second Subclass

The Bicycle class inherits from Vehicle, just as the Sailboat class does. Whereas the Sailboat class requires a data field to hold the length of the boat, the Bicycle class does not. Other differences lie in the content of the setPrice() and toString() methods.

1. Open a new file in your text editor, and then type the following first lines of the Bicycle class:

```
import javax.swing.*;
public class Bicycle extends Vehicle
{
```

2. Enter the following Bicycle class constructor, which calls the parent constructor, sending it power source and wheel values:

```
public Bicycle()
{
    super("a person", 2);
}
```

556

(continued)

3. Enter the following `setPrice()` method that forces a `Bicycle`'s price to be no greater than $4,000:

```
public void setPrice()
{
    String entry;
    final int MAX = 4000;
    entry = JOptionPane.showInputDialog
        (null, "Enter bicycle price ");
    price = Integer.parseInt(entry);
    if(price > MAX)
        price = MAX;
}
```

4. Enter the following `toString()` method, and add the closing curly brace for the class:

```
public String toString()
{
    return("The bicycle is powered by " + getPowerSource() +
        "; it has " + getWheels() + " wheels and costs $" +
        getPrice());
}
}
```

5. Save the file as **Bicycle.java**, and then compile the class.

Instantiating Objects from Subclasses

Next, you create a program that instantiates concrete objects from each of the two child classes you just created.

1. Open a new file in your text editor, and then enter the start of the `DemoVehicles` class as follows:

```
import javax.swing.*;
public class DemoVehicles
{
    public static void main(String[] args)
    {
```

2. Enter the following statements that declare an object of each subclass type.

```
Sailboat aBoat = new Sailboat();
Bicycle aBike = new Bicycle();
```

3. Enter the following statement to display the contents of the two objects. Add the closing curly braces for the `main()` method and the class:

```
        JOptionPane.showMessageDialog(null,
            "\nVehicle descriptions:\n" +
            aBoat.toString() + "\n" + aBike.toString());
    }
}
```

(continues)

(continued)

4. Save the file as **DemoVehicles.java**, and then compile it. After you compile the class with no errors, run this application using the **java DemoVehicles** command. When the application prompts you, enter the length and price for a sailboat, and the price for a bicycle. Figure 11-7 shows output after typical user input.

557

Message

Vehicle descriptions:

The 26 foot sailboat is powered by wind; it has 0 wheels and costs $45000

The bicycle is powered by a person; it has 2 wheels and costs $1985

OK

Figure 11-7 Typical output of the DemoVehicles application

Using Dynamic Method Binding

When you create a superclass and one or more subclasses, each object of each subclass "is a" superclass object. Every SalariedEmployee "is an" Employee; every Dog "is an" Animal. (The opposite is not true. Superclass objects are not members of any of their subclasses. An Employee is not a SalariedEmployee. An Animal is not a Dog.) Because every subclass object "is a" superclass member, you can convert subclass objects to superclass objects.

As you are aware, when a superclass is abstract, you cannot instantiate objects of the superclass; however, you can indirectly create a reference to a superclass abstract object. A reference is not an object, but it points to a memory address. When you create a reference, you do not use the keyword new to create a concrete object; instead, you create a variable name in which you can hold the memory address of a concrete object. So, although a reference to an abstract superclass object is not concrete, you can store a concrete subclass object reference there.

You learned how to create a reference in Chapter 4. When you code SomeClass someObject;, you are creating a reference. If you later code the following statement, including the keyword new and the constructor name, then you actually set aside memory for someObject:

```
someObject = new SomeClass();
```

For example, if you create an `Animal` class, as shown previously in Figure 11-1, and various subclasses, such as `Dog`, `Cow`, and `Snake`, as shown in Figures 11-2 through 11-4, you can create an application containing a generic `Animal` reference variable into which you can assign any of the concrete `Animal` child objects. Figure 11-8 shows an `AnimalReference` application, and Figure 11-9 shows its output. The variable `animalRef` is a type of `Animal`. No superclass `Animal` object is created (none can be); instead, `Dog` and `Cow` objects are created using the `new` keyword. When the `Cow` object is assigned to the `Animal` reference, the `animalRef.speak()` method call results in "Moo!"; when the `Dog` object is assigned to the `Animal` reference, the method call results in "Woof!" Recall that assigning a variable or constant of one type to a variable of another type is called *promotion, implicit conversion,* or *upcasting.*

```java
public class AnimalReference
{
    public static void main(String[] args)
    {
        Animal animalRef;
        animalRef = new Cow();
        animalRef.speak();
        animalRef = new Dog();
        animalRef.speak();
    }
}
```

Figure 11-8   The `AnimalReference` application

Figure 11-9   Output of the `AnimalReference` application

The application in Figure 11-8 shows that using a reference polymorphically allows you to extend a base class and use extended objects when a base class type is expected. For example, you could pass a `Dog` or a `Cow` to a method that expects an `Animal`. This means that all methods written to accept a superclass argument can also be used with its children—a feature that saves child-class creators a lot of work.

Recall from Chapter 10 that you can use the `instanceof` keyword to determine whether an object is an instance of any class in its hierarchy. For example, both of the following expressions are true if `myPoodle` is a `Dog` object and `Dog` is an `Animal` subclass:

```
myPoodle instanceof Animal
myPoodle instanceof Dog
```

The application in Figure 11-8 demonstrates polymorphic behavior. The same statement, `animalRef.speak();`, repeats after `animalRef` is assigned each new animal type. Each call to the `speak()` method results in different output. Each reference "chooses" the correct `speak()` method, based on the type of animal referenced. This flexible behavior is most useful when you pass references to methods; you will learn more about this in the next section. In the last chapter, you learned that in Java all instance method calls are virtual method calls by default—the method that is used is determined when the program runs, because the type of the object used might not be known until the method executes. An application's ability to select the correct subclass method depending on the argument type is known as **dynamic method binding**. When the application executes, the correct method is attached (or bound) to the application based on the current, changing (dynamic) context. Dynamic method binding is also called **late method binding**. The opposite of dynamic method binding is **static (fixed) method binding**. In Java, instance methods (those that receive a `this` reference) use dynamic binding; class methods use static method binding. Dynamic binding makes programs flexible; however, static binding operates more quickly.

In the example in this section, the objects using `speak()` happen to be related (`Cow` and `Dog` are both `Animals`). Be aware that polymorphic behavior can apply to nonrelated classes as well. For example, a `DebateStudent` and a `VentriloquistsDummy` might also `speak()`. When polymorphic behavior depends on method overloading, it is called **ad-hoc polymorphism**; when it depends on using a superclass as a method parameter, it is called **pure polymorphism** or **inclusion polymorphism**.

Using a Superclass as a Method Parameter Type

Dynamic method binding is most useful when you want to create a method that has one or more parameters that might be one of several types. For example, the shaded header for the `talkingAnimal()` method in Figure 11-10 accepts any type of `Animal` argument. The method can be used in programs that contain `Dog` objects, `Cow` objects, or objects of any other class that descends from `Animal`. The application passes first a `Dog` and then a `Cow` to the method. The output in Figure 11-11 shows that the method works correctly no matter which type of `Animal` descendant it receives.

```
public class TalkingAnimalDemo
{
   public static void main(String[] args)
   {
      Dog dog = new Dog();
      Cow cow = new Cow();
      dog.setName("Ginger");
      cow.setName("Molly");
      talkingAnimal(dog);
      talkingAnimal(cow);
   }
   public static void talkingAnimal(Animal animal)
   {
      System.out.println("Come one. Come all.");
      System.out.println
         ("See the amazing talking animal!");
      System.out.println(animal.getName() +
         " says");
      animal.speak();
      System.out.println("****************");
   }
}
```

Figure 11-10 The TalkingAnimalDemo class

Figure 11-11 Output of the TalkingAnimalDemo application

TWO TRUTHS & A LIE

Using Dynamic Method Binding

1. If `Parent` is a parent class and `Child` is its child, then you can assign a `Child` object to a `Parent` reference.

2. If `Parent` is a parent class and `Child` is its child, then you can assign a `Parent` object to a `Child` reference.

3. Dynamic method binding refers to a program's ability to select the correct subclass method for a superclass reference while a program is running.

The false statement is #2. If `Parent` is a parent class and `Child` is its child, then you cannot assign a `Parent` object to a `Child` reference; you can assign a `Child` object only to a `Child` reference. However, you can assign a `Parent` object or a `Child` object to a `Parent` reference.

Creating Arrays of Subclass Objects

Recall that every array element must be the same data type, which can be a primitive, built-in type or a type based on a more complex class. When you create an array in Java, you are not constructing objects. Instead, you are creating space for references to objects. In other words, although it is convenient to refer to "an array of objects," every array of objects is really an array of object references. When you create an array of superclass references, it can hold subclass references. This is true whether the superclass in question is abstract or concrete.

For example, even though `Employee` is an abstract class, and every `Employee` object is either a `SalariedEmployee` or an `HourlyEmployee` subclass object, it can be convenient to create an array of generic `Employee` references. Likewise, an `Animal` array might contain individual elements that are `Dog`, `Cow`, or `Snake` objects. As long as every `Employee` subclass has access to a `calculatePay()` method, and every `Animal` subclass has access to a `speak()` method, you can manipulate an array of superclass objects and invoke the appropriate method for each subclass member.

The following statement creates an array of three `Animal` references:

```
Animal[] animalRef = new Animal[3];
```

The statement reserves enough computer memory for three `Animal` objects named `animalRef[0]`, `animalRef[1]`, and `animalRef[2]`. The statement does not actually instantiate `Animals`; `Animal` is an abstract class and cannot be instantiated. The `Animal` array declaration simply reserves memory for three object references. If you instantiate objects from `Animal` subclasses, you can place references to those objects in the `Animal` array, as Figure 11-12 illustrates. Figure 11-13 shows the output of the `AnimalArrayDemo` application. The array of three references is used to access each appropriate `speak()` method.

```java
public class AnimalArrayDemo
{
    public static void main(String[] args)
    {
        Animal[] animalRef = new Animal[3];
        animalRef[0] = new Dog();
        animalRef[1] = new Cow();
        animalRef[2] = new Snake();
        for(int x = 0; x < 3; ++x)
            animalRef[x].speak();
    }
}
```

Figure 11-12   The `AnimalArrayDemo` application

Figure 11-13   Output of the `AnimalArrayDemo` application

In the `AnimalArrayDemo` application in Figure 11-12, a reference to an instance of the `Dog` class is assigned to the first `Animal` reference, and then references to `Cow` and `Snake` objects are assigned to the second and third array elements. After the object references are in the array, you can manipulate them like any other array elements. The application in Figure 11-12 uses a `for` loop and a subscript to get each individual reference to `speak()`.

TWO TRUTHS & A LIE

Creating Arrays of Subclass Objects

1. You can assign a superclass reference to an array of its subclass type.

2. The following statement creates an array of 10 `Table` references:

   ```
   Table[] table = new Table[10];
   ```

3. You can assign subclass objects to an array that is their superclass type.

The false statement is #1. You can assign a subclass reference to an array of its superclass type, but not the other way around.

You Do It

Using Object References

Next, you write an application in which you create an array of `Vehicle` references. Within the application, you assign `Sailboat` objects and `Bicycle` objects to the same array. Then, because the different object types are stored in the same array, you can easily manipulate them by using a `for` loop.

1. Open a new file in your text editor, and then enter the following first few lines of the `VehicleDatabase` program:

   ```
   import javax.swing.*;
   public class VehicleDatabase
   {
       public static void main(String[] args)
       {
   ```

2. Create the following array of five `Vehicle` references and an integer subscript to use with the array:

   ```
   Vehicle[] vehicles = new Vehicle[5];
   int x;
   ```

3. Enter the following `for` loop that prompts you to select whether to enter a sailboat or a bicycle in the array. Based on user input, instantiate the appropriate object type.

(continues)

```
for(x = 0; x < vehicles.length; ++x)
{
    String userEntry;
    int vehicleType;
    userEntry = JOptionPane.showInputDialog(null,
        "Please select the type of\n " +
        "vehicle you want to enter: \n1 - Sailboat\n" +
        " 2 - Bicycle");
    vehicleType = Integer.parseInt(userEntry);
    if(vehicleType == 1)
        vehicles[x] = new Sailboat();
    else
        vehicles[x] = new Bicycle();
}
```

4. After entering the information for each vehicle, display the array contents by typing the following code. First create a StringBuffer to hold the list of vehicles. Then, in a for loop, build an output String by repeatedly adding a newline character, a counter, and a vehicle from the array to the StringBuffer object. Display the constructed StringBuffer in a dialog box. Then type the closing curly braces for the main() method and the class:

```
StringBuffer outString = new StringBuffer();
for(x = 0; x < vehicles.length; ++x)
{
    outString.append("\n#" + (x + 1) + " ");
    outString.append(vehicles[x].toString());
}
JOptionPane.showMessageDialog(null,
    "Our available Vehicles include:\n" +
    outString);
    }
}
```

5. Save the file as **VehicleDatabase.java**, and then compile it. Run the application, entering five objects of your choice. Figure 11-14 shows typical output after the user has entered data.

Figure 11-14   Output of the VehicleDatabase application

Using the Object Class and Its Methods

Every class in Java is actually a subclass, except one. When you define a class, if you do not explicitly extend another class, your class implicitly is an extension of the Object class. The **Object class** is defined in the java.lang package, which is imported automatically every time you write a program; in other words, the following two class declarations have identical outcomes:

```
public class Animal
{
}
public class Animal extends Object
{
}
```

When you declare a class that does not extend any other class, you always are extending the Object class. The Object class includes methods that descendant classes can use or override as you see fit. Table 11-1 describes the methods built into the Object class; every Object you create has access to these methods.

Method	Description
Object clone()	Creates and returns a copy of this object
boolean equals (Object obj)	Indicates whether some object is equal to the parameter object (this method is described in detail below)
void finalize()	Called by the garbage collector on an object when there are no more references to the object
Class<?> getClass()	Returns the class to which this object belongs at run time
int hashCode()	Returns a hash code value for the object (this method is described briefly below)
void notify()	Wakes up a single thread that is waiting on this object's monitor
void notifyAll()	Wakes up all threads that are waiting on this object's monitor
String toString()	Returns a string representation of the object (this method is described in detail below)
void wait (long timeout)	Causes the current thread to wait until either another thread invokes the notify() method or the notifyAll() method for this object, or a specified amount of time has elapsed
void wait (long timeout, int nanos)	Causes the current thread to wait until another thread invokes the notify() or notifyAll() method for this object, or some other thread interrupts the current thread, or a certain amount of real time has elapsed

Table 11-1   Object class methods

Table 11-1 refers to *threads* in several locations. In Chapter 7, you learned about threads in reference to the `StringBuffer` class. Threads of execution are units of processing that are scheduled by an operating system and that can be used to create multiple paths of control during program execution.

566

Using the `toString()` Method

The `Object` class **`toString()` method** converts an `Object` into a `String` that contains information about the `Object`. Within a class, if you do not create a `toString()` method that overrides the version in the `Object` class, you can use the superclass version of the `toString()` method. For example, examine the `Dog` class originally shown in Figure 11-2 and repeated in Figure 11-15. Notice that it does not contain a `toString()` method and that it extends the `Animal` class.

```
public abstract class Animal
{
    private String name;
    public abstract void speak();
    public String getName()
    {
        return name;
    }
    public void setName(String animalName)
    {
        name = animalName;
    }
}

public class Dog extends Animal
{
    public void speak()
    {
        System.out.println("Woof!");
    }
}

public class DisplayDog
{
    public static void main(String[] args)
    {
        Dog myDog = new Dog();
        String dogString = myDog.toString();
        System.out.println(dogString);
    }
}
```

Figure 11-15   The `Animal` and `Dog` classes and the `DisplayDog` application

Notice that neither the Animal class nor the Dog class in Figure 11-15 defines a toString() method. Yet, when you write the DisplayDog application in Figure 11-15, it uses a toString() method with a Dog object in the shaded statement. The class compiles correctly, converts the Dog object to a String, and produces the output shown in Figure 11-16 because Dog inherits toString() from Object.

```
C:\Java>java DisplayDog
Dog@addbf1

C:\Java>
```

Figure 11-16   Output of the DisplayDog application

The output of the DisplayDog application in Figure 11-16 is not very useful. It consists of the class name of which the object is an instance (Dog), the at sign (@), and a hexadecimal (base 16) number that represents a unique identifier for every object in the current application. The hexadecimal number that is part of the String returned by the toString() method (*addbf1* in Figure 11-16) is an example of a **hash code**—a calculated number used to identify an object. Later in this chapter, you learn about the equals() method, which also uses a hash code.

Instead of using the automatic toString() method with your classes, it is usually more useful to write your own overloaded version that displays some or all of the data field values for the object with which you use it. A good toString() method can be very useful in debugging a program; if you do not understand why a class is behaving as it is, you can display the toString() value and examine its contents. For example, Figure 11-17 shows a BankAccount class that contains a mistake in the shaded line—the BankAccount balance value is set to the account number instead of the balance amount. Of course, if you made such a mistake within one of your own classes, there would be no shading or comment to help you find the mistake. In addition, a useful BankAccount class would be much larger, so the mistake would be more difficult to locate. However, when you ran programs containing BankAccount objects, you would notice that the balances of your BankAccounts were incorrect. To help you discover why, you could create a short application like the TestBankAccount class in Figure 11-18. This application uses the BankAccount class toString() method to display the relevant details of a BankAccount object. The output of the TestBankAccount application appears in Figure 11-19.

568

```
public class BankAccount
{
    private int acctNum;
    private double balance;
    public BankAccount(int num, double bal)
    {
        acctNum = num;
        balance = num;
    }
    public String toString()
    {
        String info = "BankAccount acctNum = " + acctNum +
            "    Balance = $" + balance;
        return info;
    }
}
```

Don't Do It
The bal parameter should be assigned to balance, not the num parameter.

Figure 11-17   The BankAccount class

```
public class TestBankAccount
{
    public static void main(String[] args)
    {
        BankAccount myAccount = new BankAccount(123, 4567.89);
        System.out.println(myAccount.toString());
    }
}
```

Figure 11-18   The TestBankAccount application

Figure 11-19   Output of the TestBankAccount application

From the output in Figure 11-19, you can see that the account number and balance have
the same value, and this knowledge might help you to pin down the location of the
incorrect statement in the BankAccount class. Of course, you do not have to use a method
named toString() to discover a BankAccount's attributes. If the class had methods such

as `getAcctNum()` and `getBalance()`, you could use them to create a similar application. The advantage of creating a `toString()` method for your classes is that `toString()` is Java's conventional name for a method that converts an object's relevant details into `String` format. Because `toString()` originates in the `Object` class, you can be assured that `toString()` compiles with any object whose details you want to see, even if the method has not been rewritten for the subclass in question. In addition, as you write your own applications and use classes written by others, you can hope that those programmers have overridden `toString()` to provide useful information. You don't have to search documentation to discover a useful method—instead you can rely on the likely usefulness of `toString()`. In Chapter 7, you learned that you can use the `toString()` method to convert any object to a `String`. Now you understand why this works—the `String` class overloads the `Object` class `toString()` method.

Using the `equals()` Method

The `Object` class also contains an **`equals()` method** that takes a single argument, which must be the same type as the type of the invoking object, as in the following example:

```
if(someObject.equals(someOtherObjectOfTheSameType))
   System.out.println("The objects are equal");
```

Other classes, such as the `String` class, also have their own `equals()` methods that overload the `Object` class method. You first used the `equals()` method to compare `String` objects in Chapter 7. Two `String` objects are considered equal only if their `String` contents are identical.

The `Object` class `equals()` method returns a `boolean` value indicating whether the objects are equal. This `equals()` method considers two objects of the same class to be equal only if they have the same hash code; in other words, they are equal only if one is a reference to the other. For example, two `BankAccount` objects named `myAccount` and `yourAccount` are not automatically equal, even if they have the same account numbers and balances; they are equal only if they have the same memory address. If you want to consider two objects to be equal only when one is a reference to the other, you can use the built-in `Object` class `equals()` method. However, if you want to consider objects to be equal based on their contents, you must write your own `equals()` method for your classes.

Java's `Object` class contains a `public` method named `hashCode()` that returns an integer representing the hash code. (Discovering this number is of little use to you. The default hash code is the internal JVM memory address of the object.) However, whenever you override the `equals()` method in a professional class, you generally want to override the `hashCode()` method as well, because equal objects should have equal hash codes, particularly if the objects will be used in hash-based methods. See the documentation at the Java Web site for more details.

The application shown in Figure 11-20 instantiates two BankAccount objects using the BankAccount class in Figure 11-17. The BankAccount class does not include its own equals() method, so it does not override the Object equals() method. Thus, the application in Figure 11-20 produces the output in Figure 11-21. Even though the two BankAccount objects have the same account numbers and balances, the BankAccounts are not considered equal because they do not have the same memory address.

```
public class CompareAccounts
{
   public static void main(String[] args)
   {
      BankAccount acct1 = new BankAccount(1234, 500.00);
      BankAccount acct2 = new BankAccount(1234, 500.00);
      if(acct1.equals(acct2))
         System.out.println("Accounts are equal");
      else
         System.out.println("Accounts are not equal");
   }
}
```

Figure 11-20   The CompareAccounts application

Figure 11-21   Output of the CompareAccounts application

If your intention is that within applications, two BankAccount objects with the same account number and balance are equal, and you want to use the equals() method to make the comparison, you must write your own equals() method within the BankAccount class. For example, Figure 11-22 shows a new version of the BankAccount class containing a shaded equals() method. When you reexecute the CompareAccounts application in Figure 11-20, the result appears as in Figure 11-23.

```
public class BankAccount
{
    private int acctNum;
    private double balance;
    public BankAccount(int num, double bal)
    {
        acctNum = num;
        balance = bal;
    }
    public String toString()
    {
        String info = "BankAccount acctNum = " + acctNum +
            "    Balance = $" + balance;
        return info;
    }
    public boolean equals(BankAccount secondAcct)
    {
        boolean result;
        if(acctNum == secondAcct.acctNum && balance == secondAcct.balance)
            result = true;
        else
            result = false;
        return result;
    }
}
```

Figure 11-22   The BankAccount class containing its own equals() method

Figure 11-23   Output of the CompareAccounts application after adding an overloaded equals() method to the BankAccount class

The two BankAccount objects described in the output in Figure 11-23 are equal because their account numbers and balances match. Because the equals() method in Figure 11-22 is part of the BankAccount class, and because equals() is a nonstatic method, the object that calls the method is held by the this reference within the method. That is, in the application in Figure 11-22, acct1 becomes the this reference in the equals() method, so the fields acctNum and balance refer to acct1 object values. In the CompareAccounts application, acct2 is the argument to the equals() method, so within the equals() method, acct2 becomes secondAcct, and secondAcct.acctNum and secondAcct.balance refer to acct2's values.

571

Your organization might consider two BankAccount objects equal if their account numbers match, disregarding their balances. If so, you simply change the if clause in the equals() method. Or, you might decide accounts are equal based on some other criteria. You can implement the equals() method in any way that suits your needs. When you want to compare the contents of two objects, you do not have to overload the Object class equals() method. Instead, you could write a method with a unique name, such as areTheyEqual() or areContentsSame(). However, as with the toString() method, users of your classes will appreciate that you use the expected, usual, and conventional identifiers for your methods.

If you change a class (such as changing BankAccount by adding a new method), not only must you recompile the class, you must also recompile any client applications (such as CompareAccounts) so the newly updated class can be relinked to the application and so the clients include the new features of the altered class. If you execute the CompareAccounts application but do not recompile BankAccount, the application continues to use the previously compiled version of the class.

Watch the video *The Object Class*.

TWO TRUTHS & A LIE

Using the Object Class and Its Methods

1. When you define a class, if you do not explicitly extend another class, your class is an extension of the Object class.

2. The Object class is defined in the java.lang package that is imported automatically every time you write a program.

3. The Object class toString() and equals() methods are abstract.

The false statement is #3. The toString() and equals() methods are not abstract—you are not required to override them in a subclass.

Using Inheritance to Achieve Good Software Design

When an automobile company designs a new car model, the company does not build every component of the new car from scratch. The company might design a new feature completely from scratch; for example, at some point someone designed the first air bag. However, many of a new car's features are simply modifications of existing features. The manufacturer might create a larger gas tank or more comfortable seats, but even these new features still possess many properties of their predecessors in the older models. Most features of new car models are not even modified; instead, existing components, such as air filters and windshield wipers, are included on the new model without any changes.

Similarly, you can create powerful computer programs more easily if many of their components are used either "as is" or with slight modifications. Inheritance does not give you the ability to write programs that you could not write otherwise. If Java did not allow you to extend classes, you *could* create every part of a program from scratch. Inheritance simply makes your job easier. Professional programmers constantly create new class libraries for use with Java programs. Having these classes available makes programming large systems more manageable.

You have already used many "as is" classes, such as System and String. In these cases, your programs were easier to write than if you had to write these classes yourself. Now that you have learned about inheritance, you have gained the ability to modify existing classes. When you create a useful, extendable superclass, you and other future programmers gain several advantages:

- Subclass creators save development time because much of the code needed for the class has already been written.

- Subclass creators save testing time because the superclass code has already been tested and probably used in a variety of situations. In other words, the superclass code is reliable.

- Programmers who create or use new subclasses already understand how the superclass works, so the time it takes to learn the new class features is reduced.

- When you create a new subclass in Java, neither the superclass source code nor the superclass bytecode is changed. The superclass maintains its integrity.

When you consider classes, you must think about the commonalities among them; then you can create superclasses from which to inherit. You might be rewarded professionally when you see your own superclasses extended by others in the future.

TWO TRUTHS & A LIE

Using Inheritance to Achieve Good Software Design

1. If object-oriented programs did not support inheritance, programs could still be written, but they would be harder to write.

2. When you create a useful, extendable superclass, you save development and testing time.

3. When you create a new subclass in Java, you must remember to revise and recompile the superclass code.

The false statement is #3. When you create a new subclass in Java, neither the superclass source code nor the superclass bytecode is changed.

Creating and Using Interfaces

Some object-oriented programming languages, such as C++, allow a subclass to inherit from more than one parent class. For example, you might create an InsuredItem class that contains data fields pertaining to each possession for which you have insurance. Data fields might include the name of the item, its value, the insurance policy type, and so on. You might also create an Automobile class that contains data fields such as vehicle identification number, make, model, and year. When you create an InsuredAutomobile class for a car rental agency, you might want to include InsuredItem information and methods, as well as Automobile information and methods. It would be convenient to inherit from both the InsuredItem and Automobile classes. The capability to inherit from more than one class is called **multiple inheritance**.

Many programmers consider multiple inheritance to be a difficult concept, and when inexperienced programmers use it they encounter many problems. Programmers have to deal with the possibility that variables and methods in the parent classes might have identical names, which creates conflict when the child class uses one of the names. Also, you have already learned that a child class constructor must call its parent class constructor. When there are two or more parents, this task becomes more complicated—to which class should super() refer when a child class has multiple parents? For all of these reasons, multiple inheritance is prohibited in Java. A class can inherit from a superclass that has inherited from another superclass—this represents single inheritance with multiple generations. However, Java does not allow a class to inherit directly from two or more parents.

Java, however, does provide an alternative to multiple inheritance—an interface. An **interface** looks much like a class, except that all of its methods (if any) are implicitly public and abstract, and all of its data items (if any) are implicitly public, static, and final. An interface is a description of what a class does but not how it is done; it declares method headers but not the instructions within those methods. When you create a class that uses an interface, you include the keyword implements and the interface name in the class header. This notation requires class objects to include code for every method in the interface that has been implemented. Whereas using extends allows a subclass to use nonprivate, nonoverridden members of its parent's class, implements requires the subclass to implement its own version of each method.

In English, an interface is a device or a system that unrelated entities use to interact. Within Java, an interface provides a way for unrelated objects to interact with each other. An interface is analogous to a protocol, which is an agreed-on behavior. In some respects, an Automobile can behave like an InsuredItem, and so can a House, a TelevisionSet, and a JewelryPiece.

As an example, recall the Animal and Dog classes from earlier in this chapter. Figure 11-24 shows these classes, with Dog inheriting from Animal.

```
public abstract class Animal
{
    private String name;
    public abstract void speak();
    public String getName()
    {
        return name;
    }
    public void setName(String animalName)
    {
        name = animalName;
    }
}
public class Dog extends Animal
{
    public void speak()
    {
        System.out.println("Woof!");
    }
}
```

Figure 11-24 The Animal and Dog classes

You can create a Worker interface, as shown in Figure 11-25. For simplicity, this example gives the Worker interface a single method named work(). When any class implements Worker, it must either include a work() method or the new class must be declared abstract, and then its descendants must implement the method.

```
public interface Worker
{
    public void work();
}
```

Figure 11-25 The Worker interface

The WorkingDog class in Figure 11-26 extends Dog and implements Worker. A WorkingDog contains a data field that a "regular" Dog does not—an integer that holds hours of training received. The WorkingDog class also contains get and set methods for this field. Because the WorkingDog class implements the Worker interface, it also must contain a work() method that calls the Dog speak() method, and then produces two more lines of output—a statement about working and the number of training hours.

```
public class WorkingDog extends Dog implements Worker
{
    private int hoursOfTraining;
    public void setHoursOfTraining(int hrs)
    {
        hoursOfTraining = hrs;
    }
    public int getHoursOfTraining()
    {
        return hoursOfTraining;
    }
    public void work()
    {
        speak();
        System.out.println("I am a dog who works");
        System.out.println("I have " + hoursOfTraining +
            " hours of professional training!");
    }
}
```

Figure 11-26   The `WorkingDog` class

As you know from other classes you have seen, a class can extend another class without implementing any interfaces. A class can also implement an interface even though it does not extend any other class. When a class both extends and implements, like the `WorkingDog` class, by convention the `implements` clause follows the `extends` clause in the class header.

The `DemoWorkingDogs` application in Figure 11-27 instantiates two `WorkingDog` objects. Each object can use the following methods:

- The `setName()` and `getName()` methods that `WorkingDog` inherits from the `Animal` class

- The `speak()` method that `WorkingDog` inherits from the `Dog` class

- The `setHoursOfTraining()` and `getHoursOfTraining()` methods contained within the `WorkingDog` class

- The `work()` method that the `WorkingDog` class was required to contain when it used the phrase `implements Worker`; the `work()` method also calls the `speak()` method contained in the `Dog` class.

```
public class DemoWorkingDogs
{
    public static void main(String[] args)
    {
        WorkingDog aSheepHerder = new WorkingDog();
        WorkingDog aSeeingEyeDog = new WorkingDog();
        aSheepHerder.setName("Simon, the Border Collie");
        aSeeingEyeDog.setName("Sophie, the German Shepherd");
        aSheepHerder.setHoursOfTraining(40);
        aSeeingEyeDog.setHoursOfTraining(300);

        System.out.println(aSheepHerder.getName() + " says ");
        aSheepHerder.speak();
        aSheepHerder.work();
        System.out.println(); // outputs a blank line for readability

        System.out.println(aSeeingEyeDog.getName() + " says ");
        aSeeingEyeDog.speak();
        aSeeingEyeDog.work();
    }
}
```

Figure 11-27 The `DemoWorkingDogs` application

Figure 11-28 shows the output when the `DemoWorkingDogs` application executes. Each animal is introduced, then it "speaks," and then each animal "works," which includes speaking a second time. Each `Animal` can execute the `speak()` method implemented in its own class, and each can execute the `work()` method contained in the implemented interface. Of course, the `WorkingDog` class was not required to implement the `Worker` interface; instead, it could have just contained a `work()` method that all `WorkingDog` objects could use. If `WorkingDog` was the only class that would ever use `work()`, such an approach would probably be the best course of action. However, if many classes will be `Workers`—that is, require a `work()` method—they all can implement `work()`. If you are already familiar with the `Worker` interface and its method, when you glance at a class definition for a `WorkingHorse`, `WorkingBird`, or `Employee` and see that it implements `Worker`, you do not have to guess at the name of the method that shows the work the class objects perform. Notice that when a class implements an interface, it represents a situation similar to inheritance. Just as a `WorkingDog` "is a" Dog and "is an" Animal, so too it "is a" `Worker`.

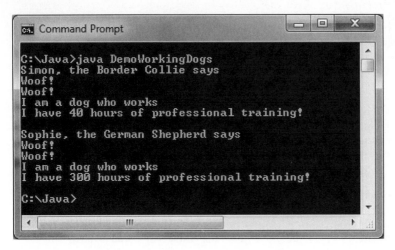

Figure 11-28   Output of the `DemoWorkingDogs` application

You can compare abstract classes and interfaces as follows:

- Abstract classes and interfaces are similar in that you cannot instantiate concrete objects from either one.

- Abstract classes differ from interfaces because abstract classes can contain nonabstract methods, but all methods within an interface must be abstract.

- A class can inherit from only one abstract superclass, but it can implement any number of interfaces.

Beginning programmers sometimes find it difficult to decide when to create an abstract superclass and when to create an interface. Remember, you create an abstract class when you want to provide data or methods that subclasses can inherit, but at the same time these subclasses maintain the ability to override the inherited methods.

Suppose that you create a `CardGame` class to use as a base class for different card games. It contains four methods named `shuffle()`, `deal()`, `displayRules()`, and `keepScore()`. The `shuffle()` method works the same way for every `CardGame`, so you write the statements for `shuffle()` within the superclass, and any `CardGame` objects you create later inherit `shuffle()`. The methods `deal()`, `displayRules()`, and `keepScore()` operate differently for every subclass (for example, for `TwoPlayerCardGames`, `FourPlayerCardGames`, `BettingCardGames`, and so on), so you force `CardGame` children to contain instructions for those methods by leaving them empty in the superclass. The `CardGame` class, therefore, should be an abstract superclass. When you write classes that extend the `CardGame` parent class, you inherit the `shuffle()` method, and write code within the `deal()`, `displayRules()`, and `keepScore()` methods for each specific child.

You create an interface when you know what actions you want to include, but you also want every user to separately define the behavior that must occur when the method executes. Suppose that you create a `MusicalInstrument` class to use as a base for different musical instrument object classes such as `Piano`, `Violin`, and `Drum`. The parent `MusicalInstrument` class contains methods such as `playNote()` and `outputSound()` that apply to every instrument, but you want to implement these methods differently for each type of instrument. By making `MusicalInstrument` an interface, you require every nonabstract subclass to code all the methods.

An interface specifies only the messages to which an object can respond; an abstract class can include methods that contain the actual behavior the object performs when those messages are received.

You also create an interface when you want a class to implement behavior from more than one parent. For example, suppose that you want to create an interactive `NameThatInstrument` card game in which you play an instrument sound from the computer speaker, and ask players to identify the instrument they hear by clicking one of several cards that display instrument images. This game class could not extend from two classes, but it could extend from `CardGame` and implement `MusicalInstrument`.

When you create a class and use the `implements` clause to implement an interface but fail to code one of the interface's methods, the compiler error generated indicates that you must declare your class to be `abstract`. If you want your class to be used only for extending, you can make it `abstract`. However, if your intention is to create a class from which you can instantiate objects, do not make it `abstract`. Instead, find out which methods from the interface you have failed to implement within your class and code those methods.

Java has many built-in interfaces with names such as `Serializable`, `Runnable`, `Externalizable`, and `Cloneable`. See the documentation at the Java Web site for more details.

Creating Interfaces to Store Related Constants

Interfaces can contain data fields, but they must be `public`, `static`, and `final`. It makes sense that interface data must not be `private` because interface methods cannot contain method bodies; without public method bodies, you have no way to retrieve `private` data. It also makes sense that the data fields in an interface are `static` because you cannot create interface objects. Finally, it makes sense that interface data fields are `final` because, without methods containing bodies, you have no way, other than at declaration, to set the data fields' values, and you have no way to change them.

Your purpose in creating an interface containing constants is to provide a set of data that a number of classes can use without having to redeclare the values. For example, the interface class in Figure 11-29 provides a number of constants for a pizzeria. Any class written for the pizzeria can implement this interface and use the permanent values. Figure 11-30 shows an example of one application that uses each value, and Figure 11-31 shows the output. The application in Figure 11-30 only needs a declaration for the current special price; all the constants, such as the name of the pizzeria, are retrieved from the interface.

```
public interface PizzaConstants
{
   public static final int SMALL_DIAMETER = 12;
   public static final int LARGE_DIAMETER = 16;
   public static final double TAX_RATE = 0.07;
   public static final String COMPANY = "Antonio's Pizzeria";
}
```

Figure 11-29   The PizzaConstants interface

```
public class PizzaDemo implements PizzaConstants
{
   public static void main(String[] args)
   {
      double specialPrice = 11.25;
      System.out.println("Welcome to " + COMPANY);
      System.out.println("We are having a special offer:\na " +
         SMALL_DIAMETER + " inch pizza with four toppings\nor a " +
         LARGE_DIAMETER +
         " inch pizza with one topping\nfor only $" + specialPrice);
      System.out.println("With tax, that is only $" +
         (specialPrice + specialPrice * TAX_RATE));
   }
}
```

Figure 11-30   The PizzaDemo application

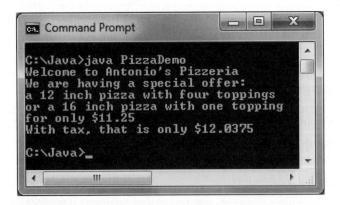

Figure 11-31   Output of the PizzaDemo application

  Watch the video *Interfaces*.

TWO TRUTHS & A LIE

Creating and Using Interfaces

1. Java's capability to inherit from more than one class is called multiple inheritance.

2. All of the methods in an interface are implicitly `public` and `abstract`, and all of its data items (if any) are implicitly `public`, `static`, and `final`.

3. When a class inherits from another, the child class can use the nonprivate, nonoverridden members of its parent's class, but when a class uses an interface, it must implement its own version of each method.

The false statement is #1. The ability to inherit from more than one class is called multiple inheritance, but Java does not have that ability.

 You Do It

Using an Interface

In this section, you create an `Insured` interface for use with classes that represent objects that can be insured. For example, you might use this interface with classes such as `Jewelry` or `House`. Also in this section, you extend `Vehicle` to create an `InsuredCar` class that implements the `Insured` interface, and then you write a short program that instantiates an `InsuredCar` object.

1. Open a new file in your text editor, and type the following `Insured` interface. A concrete class that implements `Insured` will be required to contain `setCoverage()` and `getCoverage()` methods.

```
public interface Insured
{
    public void setCoverage();
    public int getCoverage();
}
```

2. Save the file as **Insured.java** and compile it.

3. Open a new file in your text editor, and start the `InsuredCar` class that extends `Vehicle` and implements `Insured`:

```
import javax.swing.*;
public class InsuredCar extends Vehicle implements Insured
{
```

(continues)

(continued)

4. Add a variable to hold the amount covered by the insurance:

```
private int coverage;
```

5. Add a constructor that calls the `Vehicle` superclass constructor, passing arguments for the `InsuredCar`'s power source and number of wheels.

```
public InsuredCar()
{
    super("gas", 4);
    setCoverage();
}
```

6. Implement the `setPrice()` method required by the `Vehicle` class. The method accepts the car's price from the user and enforces a maximum value of $60,000.

```
public void setPrice()
{
    String entry;
    final int MAX = 60000;
    entry = JOptionPane.showInputDialog
        (null, "Enter car price ");
    price = Integer.parseInt(entry);
    if(price > MAX)
        price = MAX;
}
```

7. Implement the `setCoverage()` and `getCoverage()` methods required by the `Insured` class. The `setCoverage()` method sets the coverage value for an insured car to 90 percent of the car's price:

```
public void setCoverage()
{
    coverage = (int)(price * 0.9);
}
public int getCoverage()
{
    return coverage;
}
```

8. Create a `toString()` method, followed by a closing brace for the class:

```
public String toString()
{
    return("The insured car is powered by " + getPowerSource() +
        "; it has " + getWheels() + " wheels, costs $" +
        getPrice() + " and is insured for $" + getCoverage());
}
}
```

(continues)

(continued)

9. Save the file as **InsuredCar.java** and compile it.

10. Create a demonstration program that instantiates an InsuredCar object and displays its values as follows:

```java
import javax.swing.*;
public class InsuredCarDemo
{
    public static void main(String[] args)
    {
        InsuredCar myCar = new InsuredCar();
        JOptionPane.showMessageDialog(null,
            myCar.toString());
    }
}
```

11. Save the file as **InsuredCarDemo.java**. Compile and execute it. You will be prompted to enter the car's price. Figure 11-32 shows the output during a typical execution.

Figure 11-32 Output of the InsuredCarDemo program

Creating and Using Packages

Throughout most of this book, you have imported packages into your programs. As you learned in Chapter 4, a package is a named collection of classes; for example, the java.lang package contains fundamental classes and is automatically imported into every program you write. You also have created classes into which you explicitly imported optional packages such as java.util and javax.swing. When you create classes, you can place them in packages so that you or other programmers can easily import your related classes into new programs. Placing classes in packages for other programmers increases the classes' reusability. When you create a number of classes that inherit from each other, as well as multiple interfaces that you want to implement with these classes, you often will find it convenient to place these related classes in a package.

Creating packages encourages others to reuse software because it makes it convenient to import many related classes at once. In Chapter 3, you learned that if you do not use one of the three access specifiers `public`, `private`, or `protected` for a class, then it has default access, which means that the unmodified class is accessible to any other class in the same package.

When you create professional classes for others to use, you most often do not want to provide the users with your source code in the files that have .java extensions. You expend significant effort developing workable code for your programs, and you do not want other programmers to be able to copy your programs, make minor changes, and market the new product themselves. Rather, you want to provide users with the compiled files that have .class extensions. These are the files the user needs to run the program you have developed. Likewise, when other programmers use the classes you have developed, they need only the completed compiled code to import into their programs. The .class files are the files you place in a package so other programmers can import them.

In the Java programming language, a package or class library is often delivered to users as a **Java ARchive (JAR) file**. JAR files compress the data they store, which reduces the size of archived class files. The JAR format is based on the popular Zip file format.

If you do not specify a package for a class, it is placed in an unnamed **default package**. A class that will be placed in a nondefault package for others to use must be `public`. If a class is not `public`, it can be used only by other classes within the same package. To place a class in a package, you include a `package` declaration at the beginning of the source code file that indicates the folder into which the compiled code will be placed. When a file contains a `package` declaration, it must be the first statement in the file (excluding comments). If there are import declarations, they follow the `package` declaration. Within the file, the `package` statement must appear outside the class definition. The `package` statement, `import` statements, and comments are the only statements that appear outside class definitions in Java program files.

For example, the following statement indicates that the compiled file should be placed in a folder named com.course.animals:

```
package com.course.animals;
```

That is, the compiled file should be stored in the animals subfolder inside the course subfolder inside the com subfolder (or com\course\animals). The pathname can contain as many levels as you want.

When you compile a file that you want to place in a package, you can copy or move the compiled .class file to the appropriate folder. Alternatively, you can use a compiler option with the `javac` command. The -d (for *directory*) option indicates that you want to place the generated .class file in a folder. For example, the following command indicates that the compiled Animal.java file should be placed in the directory indicated by the `import` statement within the Animal.java file:

```
javac -d . Animal.java
```

The dot (period) in the compiler command indicates that the path shown in the package statement in the file should be created within the current directory.

If the `Animal` class file contains the statement `package com.course.animals;`, the Animal. class file is placed in C:\com\course\animals. If any of these subfolders do not exist, Java creates them. Similarly, if you package the compiled files for Dog.java, Cow.java, and so on, future programs need only use the following statements to be able to use all the related classes:

```
import com.course.animals.Dog;
import com.course.animals.Cow;
```

Because Java is used extensively on the Internet, it is important to give every package a unique name. The creators of Java have defined a package-naming convention that uses your Internet domain name in reverse order. For example, if your domain name is course.com, you begin all of your package names with com.course. Subsequently, you organize your packages into reasonable subfolders.

Creating packages using Java's naming convention helps avoid naming conflicts—different programmers might create classes with the same name, but they are contained in different packages. Class-naming conflicts are sometimes called **collisions**. Because of packages, you can create a class without worrying that its name already exists in Java or in packages distributed by another organization. For example, if your domain name is course.com, then you might want to create a class named `Scanner` and place it in a package named `com.course.input`. The fully qualified name of your `Scanner` class is `com.course.input.Scanner`, and the fully qualified name of the built-in `Scanner` class is `java.util.Scanner`.

TWO TRUTHS & A LIE

Creating and Using Packages

1. Typically, you place .class files in a package so other programmers can import them into their programs.

2. A class that will be placed in a package for others to use must be `protected` so that others cannot read your source code.

3. Java's creators have defined a package-naming convention in which you use your Internet domain name in reverse order.

The false statement is #2. A class that will be placed in a package for others to use must be `public`. If a class is not `public`, it can be used only by other classes within the same package. To prevent others from viewing your source code, you place compiled .class files in distributed packages.

586

 You Do It

Creating a Package

Next, you place the `Vehicle` family of classes into a package. Assume you work for an organization that sponsors a Web site at *vehicleswesell.com*, so you name the package `com.vehicleswesell`. First, you must create a folder named VehiclePackage in which to store your project. You can use any technique that is familiar to you. For example, in Windows, you can double-click Computer, navigate to the device or folder where you want to store the package, right-click, click New, click Folder, replace "New Folder" with the new folder name (VehiclePackage), and press Enter. Alternatively, from the command prompt, you can navigate to the drive and folder where you want the new folder to reside by using the following commands:

- If the command prompt does not indicate the storage device you want, type the name of the drive and a colon to change the command prompt to a different device. For example, to change the command prompt to the F drive on your system, type `F:`.

- If the directory is not the one you want, type `cd\` to navigate to the root directory. The `cd` command stands for "change directory," and the backslash indicates the root directory. Then type `cd` followed by the name of the subdirectory you want. You can repeat this command as many times as necessary to get to the correct subdirectory if it resides many levels down the directory hierarchy.

Next, you can place three classes into a package.

1. Open the **Vehicle.java** file in your text editor.

2. As the first line in the file, insert the following statement:

   `package com.vehicleswesell.vehicle;`

3. Save the file as **Vehicle.java** in the **VehiclePackage** folder.

4. At the command line, at the prompt for the VehiclePackage folder, compile the file using the following command:

   `javac -d . Vehicle.java`

   Be certain that you type a space between each element in the command, including surrounding the dot. Java creates a folder named com\vehicleswesell\vehicle within the directory from which you compiled the program, and the compiled **Vehicle.class** file is placed in this folder.

(continues)

(continued)

If you see a list of compile options when you try to compile the file, you did not type the spaces within the command correctly. Repeat Step 4 to compile again.

The development tool GRASP generates software visualizations to make programs easier to understand. A copy of this tool is included with your downloadable student files. If you are using jGRASP to compile your Java programs, you also can use it to set compiler options. To set a compiler option to –d, do the following:

- Open a jGRASP project workspace. Click the **Settings** menu, point to **Compiler Settings**, and then click **Workspace**. The Settings for workspace dialog box appears.

- Under the FLAGS or ARGS section of the dialog box, click the dot inside the square next to the Compile option and enter the compiler option (**-d**). Then click the **Apply** button.

- Click the **OK** button to close the dialog box, and then compile your program as usual.

5. Examine the folders on your storage device, using any operating system program with which you are familiar. For example, if you are compiling at the DOS command line, type **dir** at the command-line prompt to view the folders stored in the current directory. You can see that Java created a folder named com. (If you have too many files and folders stored, it might be difficult to locate the com folder. If so, type **dir com*.*** to see all files and folders in the current folder that begin with "com".) Figure 11-33 shows the command to compile the Vehicle class and the results of the dir command, including the com folder.

```
C:\Java\VehiclePackage>javac -d . Vehicle.java

C:\Java\VehiclePackage>dir
 Volume in drive C is OS
 Volume Serial Number is 9277-CEAD

 Directory of C:\Java\VehiclePackage

08/18/2013  05:00 PM    <DIR>          .
08/18/2013  05:00 PM    <DIR>          ..
08/18/2013  05:00 PM    <DIR>          com
08/18/2013  04:59 PM               688 Vehicle.java
               1 File(s)            688 bytes
               3 Dir(s)  74,116,796,416 bytes free

C:\Java\VehiclePackage>
```

Figure 11-33 Compiling the Vehicle.java file in a package and viewing the results

(continues)

(continued)

Alternatively, to view the created folders in a Windows operating system, you can double-click **Computer**, double-click the appropriate storage device, and locate the com folder. Within the com folder is a vehicleswesell folder, and within vehicleswesell is a vehicle folder. The **Vehicle.class** file is within the vehicle subfolder and not in the same folder as the .java source file where it ordinarily would be placed.

If you cannot find the com folder on your storage device, you probably are not looking in the same folder where you compiled the class. Repeat Steps 4 and 5, but be certain that you first change to the command prompt for the directory where your source code file resides.

6. You could now delete the copy of the **Vehicle.java** file from the VehiclePackage folder (although you most likely want to retain a copy elsewhere). There is no further need for this source file in the folder you will distribute to users because the compiled .class file is stored in the com\vehicleswesell\vehicle folder. Don't delete the copy of your code from its original storage location; you might want to retain a copy of the code for modification later.

7. Open the **Sailboat.java** file in your text editor. For the first line in the file, insert the following statement:

```
package com.vehicleswesell.vehicle;
```

8. Save the file in the same directory as you saved **Vehicle.java**. At the command line, compile the file using the following command:

```
javac -d . Sailboat.java
```

Then you can delete the **Sailboat.java** source file from the VehiclePackage folder (not from its original location—you want to retain a copy of your original code).

9. Repeat Steps 7 and 8 to perform the same operations using the **Bicycle.java** file.

10. Open the **VehicleDatabase.java** file in your text editor. Insert the following statements at the top of the file:

```
import com.vehicleswesell.vehicle.Vehicle;
import com.vehicleswesell.vehicle.Sailboat;
import com.vehicleswesell.vehicle.Bicycle;
```

11. Save the file as **VehiclePackage\VehicleDatabase.java**. Compile the file, and then run the program. The program's output should be the same as it was before you added the import statements. Placing the Vehicle-related class files in a package is not required for the VehicleDatabase program to execute correctly; you ran it in exactly the same manner before you learned about creating packages.

Placing classes in packages gives you the ability to more easily isolate and distribute files.

Don't Do It

- Don't write a body for an abstract method.

- Don't forget to end an abstract method header with a semicolon.

- Don't forget to override any abstract methods in any subclasses you derive.

- Don't mistakenly overload an abstract method instead of overriding it; the subclass method must have the same parameter list as the parent's abstract method.

- Don't try to instantiate an abstract class object.

- Don't forget to override all the methods in an interface that you implement.

- When you create your own packages, don't try to use the wildcard format to import multiple classes. This technique works only with built-in packages.

Key Terms

Concrete classes are nonabstract classes from which objects can be instantiated.

An **abstract class** is one from which you cannot create any concrete objects but from which you can inherit.

Virtual classes is the name given to abstract classes in other programming languages, such as C++.

An **abstract method** is declared with the keyword abstract. It is a method with no body—no curly braces and no method statements—just a return type, a method name, an optional argument list, and a semicolon. You are required to code a subclass method to override the empty superclass method that is inherited.

Dynamic method binding is the ability of an application to select the correct method during program execution.

Late method binding is another term for dynamic method binding.

Static or **fixed method binding** is the opposite of dynamic method binding; it occurs when a method is selected when the program compiles rather than while it is running.

Ad-hoc polymorphism occurs when a single method name can be used with a variety of data types because various implementations exist; it is another name for method overloading.

Pure polymorphism or **inclusion polymorphism** occurs when a single method implementation can be used with a variety of related objects because they are objects of subclasses of the parameter type.

The **Object class** is defined in the java.lang package that is imported automatically every time you write a program; it includes methods that you can use or override. When you define a class, if you do not explicitly extend another class, your class is an extension of the Object class.

The Object class **toString() method** converts an Object into a String that contains information about the Object.

A **hash code** is a calculated number used to identify an object.

The Object class **equals() method** takes a single argument, which must be the same type as the type of the invoking object, and returns a Boolean value indicating whether two object references are equal.

Multiple inheritance is the capability to inherit from more than one class.

An **interface** looks much like a class, except that all of its methods must be abstract and all of its data (if any) must be static final; it declares method headers but not the instructions within those methods.

A **Java ARchive (JAR) file** compresses the stored data.

A **default package** is the unnamed one in which a class is placed if you do not specify a package for the class.

Collision is a term that describes a class-naming conflict.

Chapter Summary

- A class that you create only to extend from, but not to instantiate from, is an abstract class. Usually, abstract classes contain one or more abstract methods—methods with no method statements. You must code a subclass method to override any inherited abstract superclass method.

- When you create a superclass and one or more subclasses, each object of the subclass "is a" superclass object, so you can convert subclass objects to superclass objects. The ability of a program to select the correct method during execution based on argument type is known as dynamic method binding. You can create an array of superclass object references but store subclass instances in it.

- Every class in Java is an extension of the Object class, whether or not you explicitly extend it. Every class inherits several methods from Object, including toString(), which converts an Object into a String, and equals(), which returns a boolean value indicating whether one object is a reference to another. You can override these methods to make them more useful for your classes.

- When you create a useful, extendable superclass, you save development time because much of the code needed for the class has already been written. In addition, you save testing time and, because the superclass code is reliable, you reduce the time it takes to learn the new class features. You also maintain superclass integrity.

- An interface is similar to a class, but all of its methods are implicitly `public` and `abstract`, and all of its data (if any) is implicitly `public`, `static`, and `final`. When you create a class that uses an interface, you include the keyword `implements` and the interface name in the class header. This notation serves to require class objects to include code for all the methods in the interface.

- Abstract classes and interfaces are similar in that you cannot instantiate concrete objects from either. Abstract classes differ from interfaces because abstract classes can contain nonabstract methods, but all methods within an interface must be abstract. A class can inherit from only one abstract superclass, but it can implement any number of interfaces.

- You can place classes in packages so you or other programmers can easily import related classes into new classes. The convention for naming packages uses Internet domain names in reverse order to ensure that your package names do not conflict with those of any other Internet users.

Review Questions

1. Parent classes are _____ than their child classes.

   a. less specific
   b. more specific

   c. easier to understand
   d. more cryptic

2. Abstract classes differ from other classes in that you _____.

   a. must not code any methods within them
   b. must instantiate objects from them
   c. cannot instantiate objects from them
   d. cannot have data fields within them

3. Abstract classes can contain _____.

   a. abstract methods
   b. nonabstract methods

   c. both of the above
   d. none of the above

4. An abstract class `Product` has two subclasses, `Perishable` and `NonPerishable`. None of the constructors for these classes requires any arguments. Which of the following statements is legal?

   a. `Product myProduct = new Product();`
   b. `Perishable myProduct = new Product();`
   c. `NonPerishable myProduct = new NonPerishable();`
   d. none of the above

5. An abstract class Employee has two subclasses, Permanent and Temporary. The Employee class contains an abstract method named setType(). Before you can instantiate Permanent and Temporary objects, which of the following statements must be true?

a. You must code statements for the setType() method within the Permanent class.

b. You must code statements for the setType() method within both the Permanent and Temporary classes.

c. You must not code statements for the setType() method within either the Permanent or Temporary class.

d. You can code statements for the setType() method within the Permanent class or the Temporary class, but not both.

6. When you create a superclass and one or more subclasses, each object of the subclass _____ superclass object.

a. overrides the   c. "is not a"

b. "is a"   d. is a new

7. Which of the following statements is true?

a. Superclass objects are members of their subclass.

b. Superclasses can contain abstract methods.

c. You can create an abstract class object using the new operator.

d. An abstract class cannot contain an abstract method.

8. When you create a _____ in Java, you create a variable name in which you can hold the memory address of an object.

a. field   c. recommendation

b. pointer   d. reference

9. An application's ability to select the correct subclass method to execute is known as _____ method binding.

a. polymorphic   c. early

b. dynamic   d. intelligent

10. Which statement creates an array of five references to an abstract class named Currency?

a. `Currency[] = new Currency[5];`

b. `Currency[] currencyref = new Currency[5];`

c. `Currency[5] currencyref = new Currency[5];`

d. `Currency[5] = new Currency[5];`

11. You _____ override the `toString()` method in any class you create.

    a. cannot
    c. must

    b. can
    d. must implement `StringListener` to

12. The `Object` class `equals()` method takes _____.

    a. no arguments

    b. one argument

    c. two arguments

    d. as many arguments as you need

13. Assume the following statement appears in a working Java program:

    `if(thing.equals(anotherThing)) x = 1;`

    You know that _____.

    a. `thing` is an object of the `Object` class

    b. `anotherThing` is the same type as `thing`

    c. Both of the above are correct.

    d. None of the above are correct.

14. The `Object` class `equals()` method considers two object references to be equal if they have the same _____.

    a. value in all data fields

    b. value in any data field

    c. data type

    d. memory address

15. Java subclasses have the ability to inherit from _____ parent class(es).

    a. one
    c. multiple

    b. two
    d. no

16. The alternative to multiple inheritance in Java is known as a(n) _____.

    a. superobject
    c. interface

    b. abstract class
    d. none of the above

17. When you create a class that uses an interface, you include the keyword _____ and the interface's name in the class header.

    a. `interface`
    c. `accouterments`

    b. `implements`
    d. `listener`

18. You can instantiate concrete objects from a(n) ——————.

   a. abstract class   c. either a or b

   b. interface   (d.) neither a nor b

19. In Java, a class can ——————.

   (a.) inherit from one abstract superclass at most

   b. implement one interface at most

   c. both a and b

   d. neither a nor b

20. When you want to provide some data or methods that subclasses can inherit, but you want the subclasses to override some specific methods, you should write a(n) ——————.

   (a.) abstract class   c. final superclass

   b. interface   d. concrete object

Exercises

Programming Exercises

1. a. Create an abstract class named Book. Include a String field for the book's title and a double field for the book's price. Within the class, include a constructor that requires the book title, and add two get methods—one that returns the title and one that returns the price. Include an abstract method named setPrice(). Create two child classes of Book: Fiction and NonFiction. Each must include a setPrice() method that sets the price for all Fiction Books to $24.99 and for all NonFiction Books to $37.99. Write a constructor for each subclass, and include a call to setPrice() within each. Write an application demonstrating that you can create both a Fiction and a NonFiction Book and display their fields. Save the files as **Book.java**, **Fiction.java**, **NonFiction.java**, and **UseBook.java**.

   b. Write an application named BookArray in which you create an array that holds 10 Books, some Fiction and some NonFiction. Using a for loop, display details about all 10 books. Save the file as **BookArray.java**.

2. a. The Talk-A-Lot Cell Phone Company provides phone services for its customers. Create an abstract class named PhoneCall that includes a String field for a phone number and a double field for the price of the call. Also include a constructor that requires a phone number parameter and that sets the price to 0.0. Include a set method for the price. Also include three abstract get methods—one that returns the phone number, another that returns the price of the call, and a third that displays information about the call. Create two child classes of PhoneCall: IncomingPhoneCall and OutgoingPhoneCall. The IncomingPhoneCall constructor passes its phone number parameter to its parent's constructor and sets the price of the call to 0.02. The method that displays the phone call information displays the phone number, the rate, and the price of the call (which is the same as the rate). The OutgoingPhoneCall class includes an additional field that holds the time of the call in minutes. The constructor requires both a phone number and the time. The price is 0.04 per minute, and the display method shows the details of the call, including the phone number, the rate per minute, the number of minutes, and the total price. Write an application that demonstrates you can instantiate and display both IncomingPhoneCall and OutgoingPhoneCall objects. Save the files as **PhoneCall.java**, **IncomingPhoneCall.java**, **OutgoingPhoneCall.java**, and **DemoPhoneCalls.java**.

   b. Write an application in which you assign data to a mix of 10 IncomingPhoneCall and OutgoingPhoneCall objects into an array. Use a for loop to display the data. Save the file as **PhoneCallArray.java**.

3. Create an abstract Auto class with fields for the car make and price. Include get and set methods for these fields; the setPrice() method is abstract. Create two subclasses for individual automobile makers (for example, Ford or Chevy), and include appropriate setPrice() methods in each subclass (for example, $20,000 or $22,000). Finally, write an application that uses the Auto class and subclasses to display information about different cars. Save the files as **Auto.java**, **Ford.java**, **Chevy.java**, and **UseAuto.java**.

4. Create an abstract Division class with fields for a company's division name and account number, and an abstract display() method. Use a constructor in the superclass that requires values for both fields. Create two subclasses named InternationalDivision and DomesticDivision. The InternationalDivision includes a field for the country in which the division is located and a field for the language spoken; its constructor requires both. The DomesticDivision includes a field for the state in which the division is located; a value for this field is required by the constructor. Write an application named UseDivision that creates InternationalDivision and DomesticDivision objects for two different companies and displays information about them. Save the files as **Division.java**, **InternationalDivision.java**, **DomesticDivision.java**, and **UseDivision.java**.

5. Create an abstract class named `Element` that holds properties of elements, including their symbol, atomic number, and atomic weight. Include a constructor that requires values for all three properties and a get method for each value. (For example, the symbol for carbon is C, its atomic number is 6, and its atomic weight is 12.01. You can find these values by reading a periodic table in a chemistry reference or by searching the Web.) Also include an abstract method named `describeElement()`.

Create two extended classes named `MetalElement` and `NonMetalElement`. Each contains a `describeElement()` method that displays the details of the element and a brief explanation of the properties of the element type. For example, metals are good conductors of electricity, while nonmetals are poor conductors. Write an application named `ElementArray` that creates and displays an array that holds at least two elements of each type. Save the files as **Element.java**, **MetalElement.java**, **NonMetalElement.java**, and **ElementArray.java**.

6. Create a class named `NewspaperSubscriber` with fields for a subscriber's street address and the subscription rate. Include get and set methods for the subscriber's street address, and include get and set methods for the subscription rate. The set method for the rate is abstract. Include an `equals()` method that indicates two `Subscribers` are equal if they have the same street address. Create child classes named `SevenDaySubscriber`, `WeekdaySubscriber`, and `WeekendSubscriber`. Each child class constructor sets the rate as follows: `SevenDaySubscribers` pay $4.50 per week, `WeekdaySubscribers` pay $3.50 per week, and `WeekendSubscribers` pay $2.00 per week. Each child class should include a `toString()` method that returns the street address, rate, and service type. Write an application named `Subscribers` that prompts the user for the subscriber's street address and requested service, and then creates the appropriate object based on the service type. Do not let the user enter more than one subscription type for any given street address. Save the files as **NewspaperSubscriber.java**, **WeekdaySubscriber.java**, **WeekendSubscriber. java**, **SevenDaySubscriber.java**, and **Subscribers.java**.

7. Picky Publishing House publishes stories in three categories and has strict requirements for page counts in each category. Create an abstract class named `Story` that includes a story title, an author name, a number of pages, and a `String` message. Include get and set methods for each field. The method that sets the number of pages is abstract. Also include constants for the page limits in each category. Create three `Story` subclasses named `Novel`, `Novella`, and `ShortStory`, each with a unique `setPages()` method. A `Novel` must have more than 100 pages, a `Novella` must have between 50 and 100 pages inclusive, and a `ShortStory` must have fewer than 50 pages. If the parameter passed to any of the set methods in the child class is out of range, set the page value but also create and store a message that indicates how many pages must be added or cut to satisfy the rules for the story type. Write an application named `StoryDemo` that creates an array of at least six objects to demonstrate how the methods work for objects created both with valid and invalid page counts for each story type. For each story, display the title, author, page count, and message if any was generated. Figure 11-34 shows a sample execution. Save the files as **Story.java**, **Novel.java**, **Novella.java**, **ShortStory.java**, and **StoryDemo.java**.

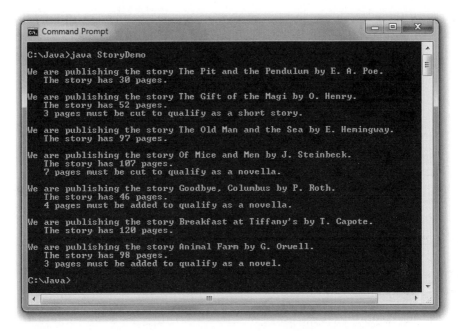

Figure 11-34 Typical execution of the StoryDemo application

8. a. Create an interface named Turner, with a single method named turn(). Create a class named Leaf that implements turn() to display "Changing colors". Create a class named Page that implements turn() to display "Going to the next page". Create a class named Pancake that implements turn() to display "Flipping". Write an application named DemoTurners that creates one object of each of these class types and demonstrates the turn() method for each class. Save the files as **Turner.java**, **Leaf.java**, **Page.java**, **Pancake.java**, and **DemoTurners.java**.

    b. Think of two more objects that use turn(), create classes for them, and then add objects to the DemoTurners application, renaming it **DemoTurners2.java**. Save the files, using the names of new objects that use turn().

9. Write an application named UseInsurance that uses an abstract Insurance class and Health and Life subclasses to display different types of insurance policies and the cost per month. The Insurance class contains a String representing the type of insurance and a double that holds the monthly price. The Insurance class constructor requires a String argument indicating the type of insurance, but the Life and Health class constructors require no arguments. The Insurance class contains a get method for each field; it also contains two abstract methods named setCost() and display(). The Life class setCost() method sets the monthly fee to $36, and the Health class sets the monthly fee to $196. Write an application named UseInsurance that prompts the user for the type of insurance to be

displayed, and then create the appropriate object. Save the files as **Life.java**, **Health.java**, **Insurance.java**, and **UseInsurance.java**.

10. Create an abstract class called `GeometricFigure`. Each figure includes a height, a width, a figure type, and an area. Include an abstract method to determine the area of the figure. Create two subclasses called `Square` and `Triangle`. Create an application that demonstrates creating objects of both subclasses, and store them in an array. Save the files as **GeometricFigure.java**, **Square.java**, **Triangle.java**, and **UseGeometric.java**.

11. Modify Exercise 10, adding an interface called `SidedObject` that contains a method called `displaySides()`; this method displays the number of sides the object possesses. Modify the `GeometricFigure` subclasses to include the use of the interface to display the number of sides of the figure. Create an application that demonstrates the use of both subclasses. Save the files as **GeometricFigure2.java**, **Square2.java**, **Triangle2. java**, **SidedObject.java**, and **UseGeometric2.java**.

12. Create an interface called `Player`. The interface has an abstract method called `play()` that displays a message describing the meaning of "play" to the class. Create classes called `Child`, `Musician`, and `Actor` that all implement `Player`. Create an application that demonstrates the use of the classes. Save the files as **Player.java**, **Child.java**, **Actor.java**, **Musician.java**, and **UsePlayer.java**.

13. Create an abstract class called `Student`. The `Student` class includes a name and a Boolean value representing full-time status. Include an abstract method to determine the tuition, with full-time students paying a flat fee of $2,000 and part-time students paying $200 per credit hour. Create two subclasses called `FullTime` and `PartTime`. Create an application that demonstrates how to create objects of both subclasses. Save the files as **Student.java**, **FullTime.java**, **PartTime.java**, and **UseStudent.java**.

14. Create a `Building` class and two subclasses, `House` and `School`. The `Building` class contains fields for square footage and stories. The `House` class contains additional fields for number of bedrooms and baths. The `School` class contains additional fields for number of classrooms and grade level (for example, elementary or junior high). All the classes contain appropriate get and set methods. Place the `Building`, `House`, and `School` classes in a package named com.course.buildings. Create an application that declares objects of each type and uses the package. Save the necessary files as **Building.java**, **House.java**, **School.java**, and **CreateBuildings.java**.

15. Sanchez Construction Loan Co. makes loans of up to $100,000 for construction projects. There are two categories of `Loans`—those to businesses and those to individual applicants.

    Write an application that tracks all new construction loans. The application must also calculate the total amount owed at the due date (original loan amount + loan fee). The application should include the following classes:

- Loan—A public abstract class that implements the LoanConstants interface. A Loan includes a loan number, customer last name, amount of loan, interest rate, and term. The constructor requires data for each of the fields except interest rate. Do not allow loan amounts over $100,000. Force any loan term that is not one of the three defined in the LoanConstants class to a short-term, one-year loan. Create a toString() method that displays all the loan data.

- LoanConstants—A public interface class. LoanConstants includes constant values for short-term (one year), medium-term (three years), and long-term (five years) loans. It also contains constants for the company name and the maximum loan amount.

- BusinessLoan—A public class that extends Loan. The BusinessLoan constructor sets the interest rate to 1 percent over the current prime interest rate.

- PersonalLoan—A public class that extends Loan. The PersonalLoan constructor sets the interest rate to 2 percent over the current prime interest rate.

- CreateLoans—An application that creates an array of five Loans. Prompt the user for the current prime interest rate. Then, in a loop, prompt the user for a loan type and all relevant information for that loan. Store the created Loan objects in the array. When data entry is complete, display all the loans.

Save the files as **Loan.java**, **LoanConstants.java**, **BusinessLoan.java**, **PersonalLoan. java**, and **CreateLoans.java**.

Debugging Exercises

1. Each of the following files in the Chapter11 folder of your downloadable student files has syntax and/or logic errors. In each case, determine the problem and fix the program. After you correct the errors, save each file using the same filename preceded with *Fix*. For example, DebugEleven1.java will become FixDebugEleven1.java.

    a. DebugEleven1.java
    b. DebugEleven2.java
    c. DebugEleven3.java
    d. DebugEleven4.java
    e. Three other Debug files in the Chapter11 folder

Game Zone

1. In Chapter 10, you created an Alien class as well as two descendant classes, Martian and Jupiterian. Because you never create any "plain" Alien objects, alter the Alien class so it is abstract. Verify that the Martian and Jupiterian classes can still inherit from Alien and that the CreateAliens program still works correctly. Save the altered Alien file as **Alien.java**.

600

2. a. Create an abstract `CardGame` class similar to the one described in this chapter. The class contains a "deck" of 52 playing cards that uses a `Card` class to hold a suit and value for each `Card` object. It also contains an integer field that holds the number of cards dealt to a player in a particular game. The class contains a constructor that initializes the deck of cards with appropriate values (e.g., "King of Hearts"), and a `shuffle()` method that randomly arranges the positions of the `Card`s in the array. The class also contains two abstract methods: `displayDescription()`, which displays a brief description of the game in each of the child classes, and `deal()`, which deals the appropriate number of `Card` objects to one player of a game. Save the file as **CardGame.java**.

    b. Create two child classes that extend `CardGame`. You can choose any games you prefer. For example, you might create a `Poker` class or a `Bridge` class. Create a constructor for each child class that initializes the field that holds the number of cards dealt to the correct value. (For example, in standard poker, a player receives five cards, but in bridge, a player receives 13.) Create an appropriate `displayDescription()` and `deal()` method for each child class. Save each file using an appropriate name—for example, **Poker.java** or **Bridge.java**.

    c. Create an application that instantiates one object of each game type and demonstrates that the methods work correctly. Save the application as **PlayCardGames.java**.

 ## Case Problems

1. a. In previous chapters, you have created several classes for Carly's Catering. Now, create a new abstract class named `Employee`. The class contains data fields for an employee's ID number, last name, first name, pay rate, and job title. The class contains get and set methods for each field; the set methods for pay rate and job title are abstract. Save the file as **Employee.java**.

    b. Create three classes that extend `Employee` named `Waitstaff`, `Bartender`, and `Coordinator`. The method that sets the pay rate in each class accepts a parameter and assigns it to the pay rate, but no `Waitstaff` employee can have a rate higher than 10.00, no `Bartender` can have a rate higher than 14.00, and no `Coordinator` can have a rate higher than 20.00. The method that sets the job title accepts no parameters—it simply assigns the string "waitstaff", "bartender", or "coordinator" to the object appropriately. Save the files as **Waitstaff.java**, **Bartender.java**, and **Coordinator.java**.

    c. In Chapter 10, you created a `DinnerEvent` class that holds event information, including menu choices. Modify the class to include an array of 15 `Employee` objects representing employees who might be assigned to work at a `DinnerEvent`. Include a method that accepts an `Employee` array parameter and assigns it to the `Employee` array field, and include a method that returns the `Employee` array. The filename is **DinnerEvent.java**.

d. Write an application that declares a `DinnerEvent` object, prompts the user for an event number, number of guests, menu options, and contact phone number, and then assigns them to the object. Also prompt the user to enter data for as many `Employees` as needed based on the number of guests. A `DinnerEvent` needs one `Waitstaff Employee` for every event, two if an event has 10 guests or more, three if an event has 20 guests or more, and so on. A `DinnerEvent` also needs one `Bartender` for every 25 guests and one `Coordinator` no matter how many guests attend. All of these `Employees` should be stored in the `Employee` array in the `DinnerEvent` object. (For many events, you will have empty `Employee` array positions.) After all the data values are entered, pass the `DinnerEvent` object to a method that displays all of the details for the event, including all the details about the `Employees` assigned to work. Save the program as **StaffDinnerEvent.java**.

2. a. In previous chapters, you have created several classes for Sammy's Seashore Supplies. Now, Sammy has decided to restructure his rates to include different fees for equipment types in addition to the fees based on rental length and to charge for required lessons for using certain equipment. Create an abstract class named `Equipment` that holds fields for a numeric equipment type, a `String` equipment name, and a fee for renting the equipment. Include a `final` array that holds the equipment names—jet ski, pontoon boat, rowboat, canoe, kayak, beach chair, umbrella, and other. Also include a `final` array that includes the surcharges for each equipment type—$50, $40, $15, $12, $10, $2, $1, and $0, respectively. Include a constructor that requires an equipment type and sets the field to the type unless it is out of range, in which case the type is set to the "other" code. Include get and set methods for each field, and include an abstract method that returns a `String` explaining the lesson policy for the type of equipment. Save the file as **Equipment.java**.

b. Create two classes that extend `Equipment`—`EquipmentWithoutLesson` and `EquipmentWithLesson`. The constructor for each class requires that the equipment type be in range—that is, jet skis, pontoon boats, rowboats, canoes, and kayaks are `EquipmentWithLesson` objects, but other equipment types are not. In both subclasses, the constructors set the equipment type to "other" if it is not in range. The constructors also set the equipment fee, as described in part 2a. Each subclass also includes a method that returns a message indicating whether a lesson is required, and the cost ($27) if it is. Save the files as **EquipmentWithoutLesson.java** and **EquipmentWithLesson.java**.

c. In Chapter 8, you created a `Rental` class. Now, modify it to contain an `Equipment` data field and an additional price field that holds a base price before equipment fees are added. Remove the array of equipment `Strings` from the `Rental` class as well as the method that returns an equipment string. Modify the `Rental` constructor so that it requires three parameters: contract number, minutes for the rental, and an equipment type. The method that sets the hours and minutes now sets a base price before equipment fees are included. Within the constructor, set the contract number and time as before, but add statements to create either an `EquipmentWithLesson` object or an `EquipmentWithoutLesson` object, and assign it to the `Equipment` data field. Assign the sum of the base price (based on time) and the equipment fee (based on the type of equipment) to the price field. Save the file as **Rental.java**.

d. In Chapter 8, you created a `RentalDemo` class that displays details for four `Rental` objects. Modify the class as necessary to use the revised `Rental` class that contains an `Equipment` field. Be sure to modify the method that displays details for the `Rental` to include all the pertinent data for the equipment. Figure 11-35 shows the output from a typical execution. Save the file as **RentalDemo.java**.

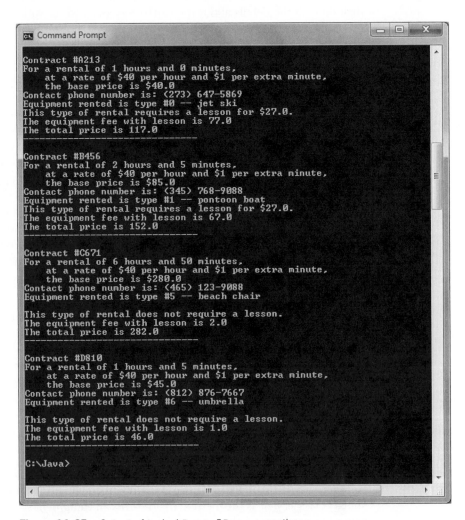

Figure 11-35   Output of typical `RentalDemo` execution

Exception Handling

In this chapter, you will:

◎ Learn about exceptions

◎ Try code and catch exceptions

◎ Throw and catch multiple exceptions

◎ Use the `finally` block

◎ Understand the advantages of exception handling

◎ Specify the exceptions that a method can throw

◎ Trace exceptions through the call stack

◎ Create your own `Exception` classes

◎ Use an assertion

Learning About Exceptions

An **exception** is an unexpected or error condition. The programs you write can generate many types of potential exceptions:

- A program might issue a command to read a file from a disk, but the file does not exist there.

- A program might attempt to write data to a disk, but the disk is full or unformatted.

- A program might ask for user input, but the user enters an invalid data type.

- A program might attempt to divide a value by 0.

- A program might try to access an array with a subscript that is too large or too small.

These errors are called exceptions because, presumably, they are not usual occurrences; they are "exceptional." **Exception handling** is the name for the object-oriented techniques that manage such errors. Unplanned exceptions that occur during a program's execution are also called **runtime exceptions**, in contrast with syntax errors that are discovered during program compilation.

Java includes two basic classes of errors: `Error` and `Exception`. Both of these classes descend from the `Throwable` class, as shown in Figure 12-1. Like all other classes in Java, `Error` and `Exception` originally descend from `Object`.

```
java.lang.Object
|
+--java.lang.Throwable
   |
   +--java.lang.Exception
   |  |
   |  +--java.io.IOException
   |  |
   |  +--java.lang.RuntimeException
   |  |  |
   |  |  +--java.lang.ArithmeticException
   |  |  |
   |  |  +-- java.lang.IndexOutOfBoundsException
   |  |  |  |
   |  |  |  +--java.lang.ArrayIndexOutOfBoundsException
   |  |  |
   |  |  +-- java.util.NoSuchElementException
   |  |  |  |
   |  |  |  +--java.util.InputMismatchException
   |  |  |
   |  |  +--Others..
   |  |
   |  +--Others..
```

Figure 12-1   The `Exception` and `Error` class inheritance hierarchy *(continues)*

(continued)

```
|   |
    +--java.lang.Error
    |
    +-- java.lang.VirtualMachineError
        |
        +--java.lang.OutOfMemoryError
        |
        +--java.lang.InternalError
        |
        +--Others...
```

Figure 12-1   The Exception and Error class inheritance hierarchy

The **Error class** represents more serious errors from which your program usually cannot recover. For example, there might be insufficient memory to execute a program. Usually, you do not use or implement Error objects in your programs. A program cannot recover from Error conditions on its own.

The **Exception class** comprises less serious errors representing unusual conditions that arise while a program is running and from which the program *can* recover. Some examples of Exception class errors include using an invalid array subscript or performing certain illegal arithmetic operations.

Java displays an Exception message when the program code could have prevented an error. For example, Figure 12-2 shows a class named Division that contains a single, small main() method. The method declares three integers, prompts the user for values for two of them, and calculates the value of the third integer by dividing the first two values.

```java
import java.util.Scanner;
public class Division
{
   public static void main(String[] args)
   {
      Scanner input = new Scanner(System.in);
      int numerator, denominator, result;
      System.out.print("Enter numerator >> ");
      numerator = input.nextInt();
      System.out.print("Enter denominator >> ");
      denominator = input.nextInt();
      result = numerator / denominator;
      System.out.println(numerator + " / " + denominator +
         " = " + result);
   }
}
```

Figure 12-2   The Division class

Figure 12-3 shows two typical executions of the Division program. In the first execution, the user enters two usable values and the program executes normally. In the second execution, the user enters 0 as the value for the denominator and an Exception message is displayed. (Java does not allow integer division by 0, but floating-point division by 0 is allowed—the result is displayed as Infinity.) In the second execution in Figure 12-3, most programmers would say that the program experienced a **crash**, meaning that it ended prematurely with an error. The term *crash* probably evolved from the hardware error that occurs when a read/write head abruptly comes into contact with a hard disk, but the term has evolved to include software errors that cause program failure.

Figure 12-3   Two typical executions of the Division application

In Figure 12-3, the Exception is a java.lang.ArithmeticException. ArithmeticException is one of many subclasses of Exception. Java acknowledges more than 75 categories of Exceptions with unusual names such as ActivationException, AlreadyBoundException, AWTException, CloneNotSupportedException, PropertyVetoException, and UnsupportedFlavorException.

Besides the type of Exception, Figure 12-3 also shows some information about the error ("/ by zero"), the method that generated the error (Division.main), and the file and line number for the error (Division.java, line 12).

Figure 12-4 shows two more executions of the Division class. In each execution, the user has entered noninteger data for the denominator—first a string of characters, and second, a floating-point value. In each case, a different type of Exception occurs. You can see from both sets of error messages that the Exception is an InputMismatchException. The last line of the messages indicates that the problem occurred in line 11 of the Division program, and the second-to-last error message shows that the problem occurred within the call to nextInt(). Because the user did not enter an integer, the nextInt() method failed. The second-to-last message also shows that the error occurred in line 2050 of the nextInt() method, but clearly you do not want to alter the nextInt() method that resides in the Scanner class—you either want to rerun the program and enter an integer, or alter the program so that these errors cannot occur in subsequent executions.

```
Command Prompt                                              _  □  X

C:\Java>java Division
Enter numerator >> 12
Enter denominator >> three
Exception in thread "main" java.util.InputMismatchException
        at java.util.Scanner.throwFor(Scanner.java:840)
        at java.util.Scanner.next(Scanner.java:1461)
        at java.util.Scanner.nextInt(Scanner.java:2091)
        at java.util.Scanner.nextInt(Scanner.java:2050)
        at Division.main(Division.java:11)

C:\Java>java Division
Enter numerator >> 12
Enter denominator >> 3.0
Exception in thread "main" java.util.InputMismatchException
        at java.util.Scanner.throwFor(Scanner.java:840)
        at java.util.Scanner.next(Scanner.java:1461)
        at java.util.Scanner.nextInt(Scanner.java:2091)
        at java.util.Scanner.nextInt(Scanner.java:2050)
        at Division.main(Division.java:11)

C:\Java>
```

Figure 12-4 Two executions of the `Division` application in which the user entered noninteger values

The list of error messages after each attempted execution in Figure 12-4 is called a **stack trace history list**, or more simply, a **stack trace**. (You might also hear the terms *stack backtrace* or *stack traceback*.) The list shows each method that was called as the program ran. You will learn more about tracing the stack later in this chapter.

Just because an exception occurs, you don't necessarily have to deal with it. In the `Division` class, you can simply let the offending program terminate as it did in Figure 12-4. However, the program termination is abrupt and unforgiving. When a program divides two numbers (or performs a less trivial task such as balancing a checkbook), the user might be annoyed if the program ends abruptly. However, if the program is used for a mission critical task such as air-traffic control or to monitor a patient's vital statistics during surgery, an abrupt conclusion could be disastrous. (The term **mission critical** refers to any process that is crucial to an organization.) Object-oriented error-handling techniques provide more elegant and safer solutions for errors.

Of course, you can write programs without using exception-handling techniques—you have already written many such programs as you have worked through this book. Programmers had to deal with error conditions long before object-oriented methods were conceived. Probably the most common error-handling solution has been to use a decision to avoid an error. For example, you can change the `main()` method of the `Division` class to avoid dividing by 0 by adding the decision shown in the shaded portion of Figure 12-5:

```java
import java.util.Scanner;
public class Division2
{
    public static void main(String[] args)
    {
        Scanner input = new Scanner(System.in);
        int numerator, denominator, result;
        System.out.print("Enter numerator >> ");
        numerator = input.nextInt();
        System.out.print("Enter denominator >> ");
        denominator = input.nextInt();
        if(denominator == 0)
           System.out.println("Cannot divide by 0");
        else
        {
           result = numerator / denominator;
           System.out.println(numerator + " / " + denominator +
              " = " + result);
        }
    }
}
```

Figure 12-5   The `Division2` application using a traditional error-handling technique

The application in Figure 12-5 displays a message to the user when 0 is entered for a denominator value, but it is not able to recover when noninteger data such as a string or floating-point value is entered. Object-oriented exception handling provides a more elegant solution for handling error conditions.

Programs that can handle exceptions appropriately are said to be more fault tolerant and robust. **Fault-tolerant** applications are designed so that they continue to operate, possibly at a reduced level, when some part of the system fails. **Robustness** represents the degree to which a system is resilient to stress, maintaining correct functioning.

Even if you choose never to use exception-handling techniques in your own programs, you must understand them because built-in Java methods will throw exceptions to your programs.

TWO TRUTHS & A LIE

Learning About Exceptions

1. Exception handling is the name for the object-oriented techniques used to manage runtime errors.

2. The Error class represents serious errors from which your program usually cannot recover; the Exception class comprises less serious errors representing unusual conditions that occur while a program is running and from which the program *can* recover.

3. When an exception occurs, your program must handle it using object-oriented exception-handling techniques.

The false statement is #3. Just because an exception occurs, you don't necessarily have to deal with it. You have already written many programs that do not handle exceptions that arise.

Trying Code and Catching Exceptions

In object-oriented terminology, you "try" a procedure that might cause an error. A method that detects an error condition "throws an exception," and the block of code that processes the error "catches the exception."

When you create a segment of code in which something might go wrong, you place the code in a **try block**, which is a block of code you attempt to execute while acknowledging that an exception might occur. A try block consists of the following elements:

- The keyword try
- An opening curly brace
- Executable statements, including some that might cause exceptions
- A closing curly brace

To handle a thrown exception, you can code one or more catch blocks immediately following a try block. A **catch block** is a segment of code that can handle an exception that might be thrown by the try block that precedes it. The exception might be one that is thrown automatically, or you might explicitly write a throw statement. A **throw statement** is one that sends an Exception object out of a block or a method so that it can be handled elsewhere. A thrown Exception can be caught by a catch block. Each catch block can "catch" one type of exception—that is, one object that is an object of type Exception or one of its child classes. You create a catch block by typing the following elements:

- The keyword catch

- An opening parenthesis

- An Exception type

- A name for an instance of the Exception type

- A closing parenthesis

- An opening curly brace

- The statements that take the action you want to use to handle the error condition

- A closing curly brace

Figure 12-6 shows the general format of a method that includes a shaded try...catch pair. A catch block looks a lot like a method named catch() that takes an argument that is some type of Exception. However, it is not a method; it has no return type, and you can't call it directly. Some programmers refer to a catch block as a *catch clause*.

```
returnType methodName(optional arguments)
{
    // optional statements prior to code that is tried
    try
    {
        // statement or statements that might generate an exception
    }
    catch(Exception someException)
    {
        // actions to take if exception occurs
    }
    // optional statements that occur after try,
    // whether or not catch block executes
}
```

Figure 12-6   Format of try...catch pair

In Figure 12-6, someException represents an object of the Exception class or any of its subclasses. If an exception occurs during the execution of the try block, the statements in the catch block execute. If no exception occurs within the try block, the catch block does not execute. Either way, the statements following the catch block execute normally.

Figure 12-7 shows an application named DivisionMistakeCaught that improves on the Division class. The main() method in the class contains a try block with code that attempts division. When illegal integer division is attempted, an ArithmeticException is automatically created and the catch block executes. Figure 12-8 shows two typical executions, one with a generated Exception and one without.

```java
import java.util.Scanner;
public class DivisionMistakeCaught
{
    public static void main(String[] args)
    {
        Scanner input = new Scanner(System.in);
        int numerator, denominator, result;
        System.out.print("Enter numerator >> ");
        numerator = input.nextInt();
        System.out.print("Enter denominator >> ");
        denominator = input.nextInt();
        try
        {
            result = numerator / denominator;
            System.out.println(numerator + " / " + denominator +
                " = " + result);
        }
        catch(ArithmeticException mistake)
        {
            System.out.println("Attempt to divide by zero");
        }
    }
}
```

Figure 12-7 The DivisionMistakeCaught application

```
C:\Java>java DivisionMistakeCaught
Enter numerator >> 20
Enter denominator >> 5
20 / 5 = 4

C:\Java>java DivisionMistakeCaught
Enter numerator >> 20
Enter denominator >> 0
Attempt to divide by zero

C:\Java>
```

Figure 12-8 Two executions of the DivisionMistakeCaught application

 In the application in Figure 12-7, the throw and catch operations reside in the same method. Later in this chapter, you will learn that throws and their corresponding catch blocks frequently reside in separate methods.

 If you want to send error messages to a location other than "normal" output, you can use System.err instead of System.out. For example, if an application writes a report to a specific disk file, you might want errors to write to a different location—perhaps to a different disk file or to the screen.

611

Although the DivisionMistakeCaught application displays the error message ("Attempt to divide by zero"), you cannot be sure that division by 0 was the source of the error. In reality, *any* ArithmeticException generated within the try block in the program would be caught by the catch block in the method. Instead of writing your own message, you can use the getMessage() method that ArithmeticException inherits from the Throwable class. To retrieve Java's message about any ThrowableException named someException, you code someException.getMessage().

As an example of another condition that could generate an ArithmeticException, if you create an object using Java's BigDecimal class and then perform a division that results in a nonterminating decimal division such as 1/3 but specify that an exact result is needed, an ArithmeticException is thrown. As another example, you could create your own class containing a method that creates a new instance of the ArithmeticException class and throws it under any conditions you specify.

For example, Figure 12-9 shows a DivisionMistakeCaught2 class that uses the getMessage() method (see the shaded statement) to generate the message that "comes with" the caught ArithmeticException argument to the catch block. Figure 12-10 shows the output; the message is "/ by zero".

```
import java.util.Scanner;
public class DivisionMistakeCaught2
{
   public static void main(String[] args)
   {
      Scanner input = new Scanner(System.in);
      int numerator, denominator, result;
      System.out.print("Enter numerator >> ");
      numerator = input.nextInt();
      System.out.print("Enter denominator >> ");
      denominator = input.nextInt();
      try
      {
         result = numerator / denominator;
         System.out.println(numerator + " / " + denominator +
            " = " + result);
      }
      catch (ArithmeticException mistake)
      {
         System.out.println(mistake.getMessage());
      }
   }
}
```

Figure 12-9   The DivisionMistakeCaught2 application

Figure 12-10　Output of the `DivisionMistakeCaught2` application

It should be no surprise that the automatically generated error message in Figure 12-10 is "/ by zero"; you saw the same message in Figure 12-3 when the programmer provided no exception handling, the exception was automatically thrown, and its message was automatically supplied.

Of course, you might want to do more in a `catch` block than display an error message; after all, Java did that for you without requiring you to write the code to catch any exceptions. You also might want to add code to correct the error; for example, such code could force the arithmetic to divide by 1 rather than by 0. Figure 12-11 shows `try...catch` code in which the `catch` block computes the result by dividing by 1 instead of by the `denominator` value. After the `catch` block, the application could continue with a guarantee that `result` holds a valid value—either the division worked in the `try` block and the `catch` block did not execute, or the `catch` block remedied the error.

```
try
{
    result = numerator / denominator;
}
catch(ArithmeticException mistake)
{
    result = numerator / 1;
}
// program continues here; result is guaranteed to have a valid value
```

Figure 12-11　A `try...catch` block in which the `catch` block corrects the error

 In the code in Figure 12-11, you can achieve the same result in the `catch` block by coding `result = numerator;` instead of `result = numerator / 1;`. Explicitly dividing by 1 simply makes the code's intention clearer, but it does require a small amount of time to execute the instruction. As an alternative, you could make the program more efficient by omitting the division by 1 and adding clarity with a comment.

Using a `try` Block to Make Programs "Foolproof"

One of the most common uses for a `try` block is to circumvent user data entry errors. When testing your own programs throughout this book, you might have entered the wrong data type accidentally in response to a prompt. For example, if the user enters a character or floating-point number in response to a `nextInt()` method call, the program crashes. Using a `try` block can allow you to handle potential data conversion exceptions caused by careless users. You can place conversion attempts, such as calling `nextInt()` or `nextDouble()`, in a `try` block and then handle any generated errors.

In Chapter 2, you learned to add a `nextLine()` call after any `next()`, `nextInt()`, or `nextDouble()` call to absorb the Enter key remaining in the input buffer before subsequent `nextLine()` calls. When you attempt to convert numeric data in a `try` block and the effort is followed by another attempted conversion, you also must remember to account for the potential remaining characters left in the input buffer. For example, Figure 12-12 shows a program that accepts and displays an array of six integers. The shaded and commented line is not part of the program when it is executed twice in Figure 12-13.

```java
import java.util.Scanner;
public class EnteringIntegers
{
   public static void main(String[] args)
   {
      int[] numberList = {0, 0, 0, 0, 0, 0};
      int x;
      Scanner input = new Scanner(System.in);
      for(x = 0; x < numberList.length; ++x)
      {
         try
         {
            System.out.print("Enter an integer >> ");
            numberList[x] = input.nextInt();
         }
         catch(Exception e)
         {
            System.out.println("Exception occurred");
         }
         // input.nextLine();
      }
      System.out.print("The numbers are: ");
      for(x = 0; x < numberList.length; ++x)
         System.out.print(numberList[x] + " ");
      System.out.println();
   }
}
```

Figure 12-12 The `EnteringIntegers` program

Figure 12-13 Two typical executions of the `EnteringIntegers` program without the extra `nextLine()` call

In Figure 12-13, you can see that when a user enters valid data in the first execution, the program runs smoothly. However, in the second execution, the user enters some letters instead of numbers. The program correctly displays *Exception occurred*, but the user is not allowed to enter data for any of the remaining numbers. The problem can be corrected by uncommenting the shaded `nextLine()` call in the program in Figure 12-12. After the program is recompiled, it executes as shown in Figure 12-14. Now, the data entry exception is noted, but the user can continue entering data for the remaining array elements.

Figure 12-14 A typical execution of the `EnteringIntegers` program with the extra `nextLine()` call

Declaring and Initializing Variables in `try...catch` Blocks

You can include any legal Java statements within a `try` block or `catch` block, including declaring variables. However, you must remember that a variable declared within a block is local to that block. In other words, the variable goes out of scope when the `try` or `catch` block ends, so any variable declared within one of the blocks should serve only a temporary purpose.

If you want to use a variable both with a `try` or `catch` block and afterward, then you must declare the variable before the `try` block begins. However, if you declare a variable before a `try` block but wait to assign its initial usable value within the `try...catch` block, you must be careful that the variable receives a useful value; otherwise, when you use the variable after the `try...catch` pair ends, the program will not compile.

Figure 12-15 illustrates this scenario. In the `UninitializedVariableTest` program, x is declared and its value is received from the user in a `try` block. Because the user might not enter an integer, the conversion to an integer might fail, and an exception might be thrown. In this example, the `catch` block only displays a message and does not assign a useful value to x. When the program attempts to display x after the `catch` block, an error message is generated, as shown in Figure 12-16. You have three easy options for fixing this error:

- You can assign a value to x before the `try` block starts. That way, even if an exception is thrown, x will have a usable value to display in the last statement.

- You can assign a usable value to x within the `catch` block. That way, if an exception is thrown, x will again hold a usable value.

- You can move the output statement within the `try` block. If the conversion of the user's entry to an integer is successful, the `try` block finishes execution and the value of x is displayed. However, if the conversion fails, the `try` block is abandoned, the `catch` block executes, the error message is displayed, and x is not used.

```java
import java.util.Scanner;
public class UninitializedVariableTest
{
    public static void main(String[] args)
    {
        int x;
        Scanner input = new Scanner(System.in);
        try
        {
            System.out.print("Enter an integer >> ");
            x = input.nextInt();
        }
        catch(Exception e)
        {
            System.out.println("Exception occurred");
        }
        System.out.println("x is " + x);
    }
}
```

Figure 12-15   The `UninitializedVariableTest` program

C:\Java>javac UninitializedVariableTest.java
UninitializedVariableTest.java:17: error: variable x might not have been initialized
        System.out.println("x is " + x);
                                      ^
1 error

C:\Java>

Figure 12-16   The error message generated when compiling the `UninitializedVariableTest` program

  Watch the video *Exceptions*.

TWO TRUTHS & A LIE

Trying Code and Catching Exceptions

1. A `try` block is a block of code you attempt to execute while acknowledging that an exception might occur.

2. You usually code at least one `catch` block immediately following a `try` block to handle an exception that might be thrown by the `try` block.

3. A `throw` statement is one that sends an `Exception` object to a `try` block so it can be handled.

The false statement is #3. A `throw` statement sends an `Exception` object to a catch block.

You Do It

Throwing and Catching an Exception

In this section, you create an application in which the user enters two values to be divided. The application catches an exception if either of the entered values is not an integer.

(continues)

(continued)

1. Open a new file in your text editor, and type the first few lines of an interactive application named **ExceptionDemo**.

```
import javax.swing.*;
public class ExceptionDemo
{
    public static void main(String[] args)
    {
```

2. Declare three integers—two to be input by the user and a third to hold the result after dividing the first two. The numerator and denominator variables must be assigned starting values because their values will be entered within a `try` block. The compiler understands that a `try` block might not complete; that is, it might throw an exception before it is through. Also declare an input `String` to hold the return value of the `JOptionPane showInputDialog()` method.

```
int numerator = 0, denominator = 0, result;
String inputString;
```

3. Add a `try` block that prompts the user for two values, converts each entered `String` to an integer, and divides the values, producing `result`.

```
try
{
    inputString = JOptionPane.showInputDialog(null,
        "Enter a number to be divided");
    numerator = Integer.parseInt(inputString);
    inputString = JOptionPane.showInputDialog(null,
        "Enter a number to divide into the first number");
    denominator = Integer.parseInt(inputString);
    result = numerator / denominator;
}
```

4. Add a `catch` block that catches an `ArithmeticException` object if division by 0 is attempted. If this block executes, display an error message, and force `result` to 0.

```
catch(ArithmeticException exception)
{
    JOptionPane.showMessageDialog(null, exception.getMessage());
    result = 0;
}
```

5. Whether or not the `try` block succeeds, display the result (which might have been set to 0). Include closing curly braces for the `main()` method and for the class.

(continues)

(continued)

```
        JOptionPane.showMessageDialog(null, numerator + " / " +
            denominator + "\nResult is " + result);
    }
}
```

6. Save the file as **ExceptionDemo.java**, and then compile and execute the application. Enter two nonzero integer values. For example, the first execution in Figure 12-17 shows the output when the user enters *12* and *3* as the two input values. The application completes successfully. Click **OK** to end the application, and execute the ExceptionDemo application again. This time, enter **0** for the second value; the output looks like the second part of Figure 12-17. Click **OK** to end the application.

Figure 12-17   Output of two executions of the ExceptionDemo application

Throwing and Catching Multiple Exceptions

You can place as many statements as you need within a try block, and you can catch as many exceptions as you want. If you try more than one statement, only the first error-generating statement throws an exception. As soon as the exception occurs, the logic transfers to the catch block, which leaves the rest of the statements in the try block unexecuted.

When a program contains multiple catch blocks, they are examined in sequence until a match is found for the type of exception that occurred. Then, the matching catch block executes, and each remaining catch block is bypassed.

For example, consider the application in Figure 12-18. The main() method in the DivisionMistakeCaught3 class throws two types of Exception objects: an ArithmeticException and an InputMismatchException. The try block in the application surrounds all the statements in which the exceptions might occur.

```
import java.util.*;
public class DivisionMistakeCaught3
{
    public static void main(String[] args)
    {
        Scanner input = new Scanner(System.in);
        int numerator, denominator, result;
        try
        {
            System.out.print("Enter numerator >> ");
            numerator = input.nextInt();
            System.out.print("Enter denominator >> ");
            denominator = input.nextInt();
            result = numerator / denominator;
            System.out.println(numerator + " / " + denominator +
                " = " + result);
        }
        catch(ArithmeticException mistake)
        {
            System.out.println(mistake.getMessage());
        }
        catch(InputMismatchException mistake)
        {
            System.out.println("Wrong data type");
        }
    }
}
```

Figure 12-18   The DivisionMistakeCaught3 class

The program in Figure 12-18 must import the java.util.InputMismatchException class to be able to use an InputMismatchException object. The java.util package is also needed for the Scanner class, so it's easiest to import the whole package.

If you use the getMessage() method with the InputMismatchException object, you see that the message is null, because null is the default message value for an InputMismatchException object.

In the main() method of the program in Figure 12-18, the try block executes. Several outcomes are possible:

- If the user enters two usable integers, result is calculated, normal output is displayed, and neither catch block executes.

- If the user enters an invalid (noninteger) value at either the first or second shaded statement, an InputMismatchException object is created and thrown. When the program encounters the first catch block (that catches an ArithmeticException), the block is bypassed because the Exception types do not match. When the program encounters the second catch block, the types match, and the "Wrong data type" message is displayed.

● If the user enters 0 for denominator, the division statement throws an ArithmeticException, and the try block is abandoned. When the program encounters the first catch block, the Exception types match, the value of the getMessage() method is displayed, and then the second catch block is bypassed.

Figure 12-19 shows the output of four typical program executions.

Figure 12-19 Four executions of the DivisionMistakeCaught3 application

When you list multiple catch blocks following a try block, you must be careful that some catch blocks don't become unreachable. Unreachable statements are program statements that can never execute under any circumstances. For example, if two successive catch blocks catch an ArithmeticException and an ordinary Exception, respectively, the ArithmeticException errors cause the first catch to execute and other types that derive from Exception "fall through" to the more general Exception catch block. However, if you reverse the sequence of the catch blocks so the one that catches general Exception objects is first, even ArithmeticExceptions would be caught by the Exception catch. The ArithmeticException catch block therefore is unreachable because the Exception catch block is in its way, and the class does not compile. Think of arranging your catch blocks so that the "bigger basket" is always below a smaller one. That is, each Exception should "fall through" as many catch blocks as necessary to reach the one that will hold it.

You first learned about unreachable statements in Chapter 3. For example, statements that follow a method's return statement are unreachable. Creating an unreachable catch block causes a compiler error that generates a message indicating that the exception "has already been caught."

Sometimes, you want to execute the same code no matter which Exception type occurs. For example, within the DivisionMistakeCaught3 application in Figure 12-18, each of the two catch blocks displays a unique message. Instead, you might want both catch blocks to display the same message. Because ArithmeticExceptions and InputMismatchExceptions are both subclasses of Exception, you can rewrite the program as shown in Figure 12-20, using a single generic catch block (shaded) that can catch any type of Exception object.

```java
import java.util.*;
public class DivisionMistakeCaught4
{
    public static void main(String[] args)
    {
        Scanner input = new Scanner(System.in);
        int numerator, denominator, result;
        try
        {
            System.out.print("Enter numerator >> ");
            numerator = input.nextInt();
            System.out.print("Enter denominator >> ");
            denominator = input.nextInt();
            result = numerator / denominator;
            System.out.println(numerator + " / " + denominator +
                " = " + result);
        }
        catch(Exception mistake)
        {
            System.out.println("Operation unsuccessful");
        }
    }
}
```

Figure 12-20   The DivisionMistakeCaught4 application

The catch block in Figure 12-20 accepts a more generic Exception argument type than that thrown by either of the potentially error-causing try statements, so the generic catch block can act as a "catch-all" block. When either an arithmetic error or incorrect input type error occurs, the thrown exception is "promoted" to an Exception error in the catch block. Figure 12-21 shows several executions of the DivisionMistakeCaught4 application. Notice that no matter which type of mistake occurs during execution, the general "Operation unsuccessful" message is displayed by the generic catch block.

Figure 12-21 Several executions of the `DivisionMistakeCaught4` application

As a new feature in Java 7, a `catch` block can also be written to catch specific multiple exception types. For example, the following `catch` block catches two `Exception` types. When either is caught, its local identifier is **e**.

```
catch(ArithmeticException, InputMismatchException e)
{
}
```

Although a method can throw any number of `Exception` types, many developers believe that it is poor style for a method to throw and catch more than three or four types. If it does, one of the following conditions might be true:

- Perhaps the method is trying to accomplish too many diverse tasks and should be broken up into smaller methods.

- Perhaps the `Exception` types thrown are too specific and should be generalized, as they are in the `DivisionMistakeCaught4` application in Figure 12-20.

  Watch the video *Catching Multiple Exceptions*.

624

TWO TRUTHS & A LIE

Throwing and Catching Multiple Exceptions

1. When multiple try block statements throw exceptions, multiple catch blocks might execute.

2. As soon as an exception occurs, the try block that contains it is abandoned and the rest of its statements are unexecuted.

3. When a program contains multiple catch blocks, the first one that matches the thrown Exception type is the one that executes.

The false statement is #1. If you try more than one statement, only the first error-generating statement throws an exception, and then the rest of the try block is abandoned.

 You Do It

Using Multiple catch Blocks

In this section, you add a second catch block to the ExceptionDemo application.

1. Open the **ExceptionDemo.java** file. Change the class name to ExceptionDemo2, and save the file as **ExceptionDemo2.java**.

2. Execute the program, and enter a noninteger value at one of the prompts. Program execution fails. For example, Figure 12-22 shows the error generated when the user types the string "four hundred and seventeen" at the first prompt.

Figure 12-22   Error message generated by the current version of the ExceptionDemo2 application when a user enters a noninteger value

(continues)

(continued)

3. After the existing `catch` block that catches an `ArithmeticException` object, add a `catch` block that catches a `NumberFormatException` object if neither user entry can be converted to an integer. If this block executes, display an error message, set `numerator` and `denominator` to a default value of 999, and force `result` to 1.

```
catch(NumberFormatException exception)
{
    JOptionPane.showMessageDialog(null,
        "This application accepts digits only!");
    numerator = 999;
    denominator = 999;
    result = 1;
}
```

4. Save, compile, and execute the program. This time, if you enter a noninteger value, the output appears as shown in Figure 12-23. Click **OK** to end the application.

Figure 12-23 Error message generated by the improved version of the `ExceptionDemo2` application when a user enters a noninteger value

5. Execute the application a few more times by entering a variety of valid and invalid data. Confirm that the program works appropriately whether you type two usable integers, an unusable 0 for the second integer, or noninteger data such as strings containing alphabetic characters or punctuation.

Using the `finally` Block

When you have actions you must perform at the end of a `try...catch` sequence, you can use a **`finally` block**. The code within a `finally` block executes regardless of whether the preceding `try` block identifies an exception. Usually, you use a `finally` block to perform cleanup tasks that must happen whether or not any exceptions occurred, and whether or not any exceptions that occurred were caught. Figure 12-24 shows the format of a `try...catch` sequence that uses a `finally` block.

```
try
{
    // statements to try
}
catch (Exception e)
{
    // actions that occur if exception was thrown
}
finally
{
    // actions that occur whether catch block executed or not
}
```

Figure 12-24   Format of `try...catch...finally` sequence

Compare Figure 12-24 to Figure 12-6 shown earlier in this chapter. When the `try` code works without error in Figure 12-6, control passes to the statements at the end of the method. Also, when the `try` code fails and throws an exception, and the `Exception` object is caught, the `catch` block executes, and control again passes to the statements at the end of the method. At first glance, it seems as though the statements at the end of the method in Figure 12-6 always execute. However, the final set of statements might never execute for at least two reasons:

- Any `try` block might throw an `Exception` object for which you did not provide a `catch` block. After all, exceptions occur all the time without your handling them, as one did in the first `Division` application in Figure 12-2 earlier in this chapter. In the case of an unhandled exception, program execution stops immediately, the exception is sent to the operating system for handling, and the current method is abandoned.

- The `try` or `catch` block might contain a `System.exit();` statement, which stops execution immediately.

When you include a `finally` block, you are assured that the `finally` statements will execute before the method is abandoned, even if the method concludes prematurely. For example, programmers often use a `finally` block when the program uses data files that must be closed. You will learn more about writing to and reading from data files in the next chapter. For now, however, consider the format shown in Figure 12-25, which represents part of the logic for a typical file-handling program:

```
try
{
    // Open the file
    // Read the file
    // Place the file data in an array
    // Calculate an average from the data
    // Display the average
}
catch (IOException e)
{
    // Issue an error message
    // System exit
}
finally
{
    // If the file is open, close it
}
```

Figure 12-25   Pseudocode that tries reading a file and handles an `IOException`

The pseudocode in Figure 12-25 represents an application that opens a file; in Java, if a file does not exist when you open it, an input/output exception, or `IOException`, is thrown and a `catch` block can handle the error. However, because the application in Figure 12-25 uses an array, an uncaught `IndexOutOfBoundsException` might occur even though the file opened successfully. (An `IndexOutOfBoundsException` occurs, as its name implies, when a subscript is not in the range of valid subscripts for an array.) The `IndexOutOfBoundsException` would not be caught by the existing `catch` block. Also, because the application calculates an average, it might divide by 0 and an `ArithmeticException` might occur; it also would not be caught. In any of these events, you might want to close the file before proceeding. By using the `finally` block, you ensure that the file is closed because the code in the `finally` block executes before control returns to the operating system. The code in the `finally` block executes no matter which of the following outcomes of the `try` block occurs:

- The `try` ends normally.

- The `catch` executes.

- An uncaught exception causes the method to abandon prematurely. An uncaught exception does not allow the `try` block to finish, nor does it cause the `catch` block to execute.

If an application might throw several types of exceptions, you can try some code, catch the possible exception, try some more code and catch the possible exception, and so on. Usually, however, the superior approach is to try all the statements that might throw exceptions, and then include all the needed `catch` blocks and an optional `finally` block. This is the approach shown in Figure 12-25, and it usually results in logic that is easier to follow.

You can avoid using a `finally` block, but you would need repetitious code. For example, instead of using the `finally` block in the pseudocode in Figure 12-25, you could insert the statement "If the file is open, close it" as both the last statement in the `try` block and the second-to-last statement in the `catch` block, just before `System exit`. However, writing code just once in a `finally` block is clearer and less prone to error.

If a `try` block calls the `System.exit()` method and the `finally` block calls the same method, the `exit()` method in the `finally` block executes. The `try` block's `exit()` method call is abandoned.

C++ programmers are familiar with `try` and `catch` blocks, but C++ does not provide a `finally` block. C# and Visual Basic contain the keywords `try`, `catch`, and `finally`.

TWO TRUTHS & A LIE

Using the `finally` Block

1. The code within a `finally` block executes when a `try` block identifies an exception that is not caught.

2. Usually, you use a `finally` block to perform cleanup tasks that must happen whether or not any exceptions occurred, and whether or not any exceptions that occurred were caught.

3. It's possible that the code that follows a `try...catch...finally` sequence might never execute—for example, if a `try` block throws an unhandled exception.

The false statement is #1. The code within a `finally` block executes whether or not the preceding `try` block identifies an exception, and whether or not an exception is caught.

Understanding the Advantages of Exception Handling

Before the inception of object-oriented programming languages, potential program errors were handled using somewhat confusing, error-prone methods. For example, a traditional, non-object-oriented procedural program might perform three methods that depend on each other using code that provides error checking similar to the pseudocode in Figure 12-26.

```
call methodA()
if methodA() worked
{
    call methodB()
    if methodB() worked
    {
        call methodC()
        if methodC() worked
            everything's okay, so display finalResult
        else
            set errorCode to 'C'
    }
    else
        set errorCode to 'B'
}
else
    set errorCode to 'A'
```

Figure 12-26   Pseudocode representing traditional error checking

The pseudocode in Figure 12-26 represents an application in which the logic must pass three tests before finalResult can be displayed. The program executes methodA(); it then calls methodB() only if methodA() is successful. Similarly, methodC() executes only when methodA() and methodB() are both successful. When any method fails, the program sets an appropriate errorCode to 'A', 'B', or 'C'. (Presumably, the errorCode is used later in the application.) The logic is difficult to follow, and the application's purpose and intended usual outcome—to display finalResult—is lost in the maze of if statements. Also, you can easily make coding mistakes within such a program because of the complicated nesting, indenting, and opening and closing of curly braces.

Compare the same program logic using Java's object-oriented, error-handling technique shown in Figure 12-27. Using the try…catch object-oriented technique provides the same results as the traditional method, but the statements of the program that do the "real" work (calling methods A, B, and C and displaying finalResult) are placed together, where their logic is easy to follow. The try steps should usually work without generating errors; after all, the errors are "exceptions." It is convenient to see these business-as-usual steps in one location. The unusual, exceptional events are grouped and moved out of the way of the primary action.

```
try
{
    call methodA() and maybe throw an exception
    call methodB() and maybe throw an exception
    call methodC() and maybe throw an exception
    everything's okay, so display finalResult
}
catch(methodA()'s error)
{
    set errorCode to "A"
}
catch(methodB()'s error)
{
    set errorCode to "B"
}
catch(methodC()'s error)
{
    set errorCode to "C"
}
```

Figure 12-27   Pseudocode representing object-oriented exception handling

Besides clarity, an advantage to object-oriented exception handling is the flexibility it allows in the handling of error situations. When a method you write throws an exception, the same method can catch the exception, although it is not required to do so, and in most object-oriented programs it does not. Often, you don't want a method to handle its own exception. In many cases, you want the method to check for errors, but you do not want to require a method to handle an error if it finds one. Another advantage to object-oriented exception handling is that you gain the ability to appropriately deal with exceptions as you decide how to handle them. When you write a method, it can call another, catch a thrown exception, and you can decide what you want to do. Just as a police officer has leeway to deal with a speeding driver differently depending on circumstances, programs can react to exceptions specifically for their current purposes.

Methods are flexible partly because they are reusable—that is, a well-written method might be used by any number of applications. Each calling application might need to handle a thrown error differently, depending on its purpose. For example, an application that uses a method that divides values might need to terminate if division by 0 occurs. A different program simply might want the user to reenter the data to be used, and a third program might want to force division by 1. The method that contains the division statement can throw the error, but each calling program can assume responsibility for handling the error detected by the method in an appropriate way.

TWO TRUTHS & A LIE

Understanding the Advantages of Exception Handling

1. An advantage to using object-oriented error-handling techniques is that programs are clearer and more flexible.

2. An advantage to using object-oriented error-handling techniques is that when a method throws an exception, it will always be handled in the same, consistent way.

3. In many cases, you want a method to check for errors, but you do not want to require the method to handle an error if it finds one.

The false statement is #2. A well-written method might be used by any number of applications. An advantage of object-oriented exception-handling techniques is that each calling application can handle thrown errors differently, depending on its purpose.

Specifying the Exceptions That a Method Can Throw

If a method throws an exception that it will not catch but will be caught by a different method, you must use the keyword throws followed by an Exception type in the method header. This practice is known as **exception specification**.

For example, Figure 12-28 shows a PriceList class used by a company to hold a list of prices for items it sells. For simplicity, there are only four prices and a single method that displays the price of a single item. The displayPrice() method accepts a parameter to use as the array subscript, but because the subscript could be out of bounds, the method contains a shaded throws clause, acknowledging it could throw an exception.

```
public class PriceList
{
    private static final double[] price = {15.99, 27.88, 34.56, 45.89};
    public static void displayPrice(int item) throws IndexOutOfBoundsException
    {
        System.out.println("The price is $" + price[item]);
    }
}
```

Figure 12-28   The PriceList class

Figures 12-29 and 12-30 show two applications in which programmers have chosen to handle the potential exception differently. In the first class, `PriceListApplication1`, the programmer has chosen to handle the exception in the shaded `catch` block by displaying a price of $0. In the second class, `PriceListApplication2`, the programmer has chosen to handle the exception by using the highest price in the array. Figure 12-31 shows several executions of each program. Other programmers writing other applications that use the `PriceList` class could choose still different actions, but they all can use the flexible `displayPrice()` method because it doesn't limit the calling method's choice of recourse.

```java
import java.util.*;
public class PriceListApplication1
{
    public static void main(String[] args)
    {
        int item;
        Scanner input = new Scanner(System.in);
        System.out.print("Enter item number >> ");
        item = input.nextInt();
        try
        {
            PriceList.displayPrice(item);
        }
        catch(IndexOutOfBoundsException e)
        {
            System.out.println("Price is $0");
        }
    }
}
```

Figure 12-29   The `PriceListApplication1` class

```
import java.util.*;
public class PriceListApplication2
{
    public static void main(String[] args)
    {
        int item;
        Scanner input = new Scanner(System.in);
        final int MAXITEM = 3;
        System.out.print("Enter item number >> ");
        item = input.nextInt();
        try
        {
            PriceList.displayPrice(item);
        }
        catch(IndexOutOfBoundsException e)
        {
            PriceList.displayPrice(MAXITEM);
        }
    }
}
```

Figure 12-30 The `PriceListApplication2` class

Figure 12-31 Several executions of `PriceListApplication1` and `PriceListApplication2`

For most Java methods that you write, you do not use a `throws` clause. For example, you have not needed to use a `throws` clause in any of the many programs you have written while working through this book; however, in those methods, if you divided by 0 or went beyond an array's bounds, an exception was thrown nevertheless. Most of the time, you let Java handle any exception by shutting down the program. Imagine how unwieldy your programs would become if you were required to provide instructions for handling every possible error, including equipment failures and memory problems. Most exceptions never have to be explicitly thrown or caught, nor do you have to include a `throws` clause in the headers of methods that automatically throw these exceptions. The only exceptions that must be caught or named in a `throws` clause are the type known as *checked* exceptions.

Java's exceptions can be categorized into two types:

- **Unchecked exceptions**—These exceptions inherit from the `Error` class or the `RuntimeException` class. Although you *can* handle these exceptions in your programs, you are not required to do so. For example, dividing by zero is a type of `RuntimeException`, and you are not required to handle this exception—you can simply let the program terminate.

- **Checked exceptions**—These exceptions are the type that programmers should anticipate and from which programs should be able to recover. All exceptions that you explicitly throw and that descend from the `Exception` class are checked exceptions.

Java programmers say that checked exceptions are subject to the **catch or specify requirement**, which means if you throw a checked exception from a method, you must do one of the following:

- Catch it within the method.
- Specify the exception in your method header's `throws` clause.

Code that uses a checked exception will not compile if the catch or specify rule is not followed.

If you write a method with a `throws` clause in the header, then any method that uses your method must do one of the following:

- Catch and handle the possible exception.
- Declare the exception in its `throws` clause. The called method can then rethrow the exception to yet another method that might either catch it or throw it yet again.

In other words, when an exception is a checked exception, client programmers are forced to deal with the possibility that an exception will be thrown.

Some programmers feel that using checked exceptions is an example of "syntactic salt." **Syntactic sugar** is a term coined by Peter J. Landin to describe aspects of a computer language that make it "sweeter," or easier, for programmers to use. For example, you learned in Chapter 1 that you do not have to write `import java.lang;` at the top of every Java program file because the package is automatically imported for you. The metaphor has been extended by the term **syntactic salt**, which is a language feature designed to make it harder to write bad code.

If you write a method that explicitly throws a checked exception that is not caught within the method, Java requires that you use the throws clause in the header of the method. Using the throws clause does not mean that the method *will* throw an exception—everything might go smoothly. Instead, it means the method *might* throw an exception. You include the throws clause in the method header so applications that use your methods are notified of the potential for an exception.

In Chapter 3, you learned that a method's signature is the combination of the method name and the number, types, and order of arguments. Some programmers argue that any throws clause is also part of the signature, but most authorities disagree. You cannot create a class that contains multiple methods that differ only in their return types; such methods are not overloaded. The same is true for methods with the same signatures that differ only in their throws clauses; the compiler considers the methods to have an identical signature. Instead of saying that the throws clause is part of the method's signature, you might prefer to say that it is part of the method's interface.

A method that overrides another cannot throw an exception unless it throws the same type as its parent or a subclass of its parent's thrown type. These rules do not apply to overloaded methods. Any exceptions may (or may not) be thrown from one version of an overloaded method without considering what exceptions are thrown by other versions of an overloaded method.

To be able to use a method to its full potential, you must know the method's name and three additional pieces of information:

- The method's return type
- The type and number of arguments the method requires
- The type and number of exceptions the method throws

To use a method, you must know what types of arguments are required. You can call a method without knowing its return type, but if you do, you can't benefit from any value that the method returns. (Also, if you use a method without knowing its return type, you probably don't understand the purpose of the method.) Likewise, you can't make sound decisions about what to do in case of an error if you don't know what types of exceptions a method might throw.

When a method might throw more than one exception type, you can specify a list of potential exceptions in the method header by separating them with commas. As an alternative, if all the exceptions descend from the same parent, you can specify the more general parent class. For example, if your method might throw either an ArithmeticException or an ArrayIndexOutOfBoundsException, you can just specify that your method throws a RuntimeException. One advantage to this technique is that when your method is modified to include more specific RuntimeExceptions in the future, the method header will not change. This saves time and money for users of your methods, who will not have to modify their own methods to accommodate new RuntimeException types.

An extreme alternative is simply to specify that your method throws a general Exception object, so that all exceptions are included in one clause. Doing this simplifies the exception specification you write. However, using this technique disguises information about the specific types of exceptions that might occur, and such information usually has value to users of your methods.

636

Usually, you declare only checked exceptions. Remember that runtime exceptions can occur anywhere in a program, and they can be numerous. Programs would be less clear and more cumbersome if you had to account for runtime exceptions in every method declaration. Therefore, the Java compiler does not require that you catch or specify runtime exceptions.

Watch the video *Specifying Exceptions*.

TWO TRUTHS & A LIE

Specifying the Exceptions That a Method Can Throw

1. Exception specification is the practice of listing possible exceptions in a throws clause in a method header.

2. Many exceptions never have to be explicitly thrown or caught, nor do you have to include a throws clause in the headers of methods that automatically throw these exceptions.

3. If you write a method with a throws clause for a checked exception in the header, then any method that uses your method must catch and handle the possible exception.

The false statement is #3. If you write a method with a throws clause for a checked exception in the header, then any method that uses your method must catch and handle the possible exception or declare the exception in its throws clause so the exception can be rethrown.

Tracing Exceptions Through the Call Stack

When one method calls another, the computer's operating system must keep track of where the method call came from, and program control must return to the calling method when the called method is completed. For example, if methodA() calls methodB(), the operating system has to "remember" to return to methodA() when methodB() ends. Likewise, if methodB() calls methodC(), the computer must "remember" while methodC() executes to return to methodB() and eventually to methodA(). The memory location known as the **call stack** is where the computer stores the list of method locations to which the system must return.

When a method throws an exception and the method does not catch it, the exception is thrown to the next method up the call stack, or in other words, to the method that called the offending method. Figure 12-32 shows how the call stack works. If methodA() calls methodB(), and methodB() calls methodC(), and methodC() throws an exception, Java first looks for a catch block in methodC(). If none exists, Java looks for the same thing in methodB(). If methodB() does not have a catch block, Java looks to methodA(). If methodA() cannot catch the exception, it is thrown to the Java Virtual Machine, which displays a message at the command prompt.

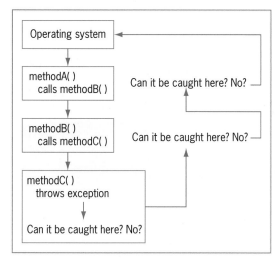

Figure 12-32   Cycling through the call stack

For example, examine the application in Figure 12-33. The main() method of the application calls methodA(), which displays a message and calls methodB(). Within methodB(), another message is displayed and methodC() is called. In methodC(), yet another message is displayed. Then, a three-integer array is declared, and the program attempts to display the fourth element in the array. This program compiles correctly—no error is detected until methodC() attempts to access the out-of-range array element. In Figure 12-33, the comments indicate line numbers so you can more easily follow the sequence of generated error messages. You probably would not add such comments to a working application. Figure 12-34 shows the output when the application executes.

638

```
public class DemoStackTrace
{
    public static void main(String[] args)
    {
        methodA();   // line 5
    }
    public static void methodA()
    {
        System.out.println("In methodA()");
        methodB();   // line 10
    }
    public static void methodB()
    {
        System.out.println("In methodB()");
        methodC();   // line 15
    }
    public static void methodC()
    {
        System.out.println("In methodC()");
        int [] array = {0, 1, 2};
        System.out.println(array[3]);   // line 21
    }
}
```

Don't Do It
You never would purposely use an out-of-range subscript in a professional program.

Figure 12-33   The DemoStackTrace class

Figure 12-34   Error messages generated by the DemoStackTrace application

As you can see in Figure 12-34, three messages are displayed, indicating that methodA(), methodB(), and methodC() were called in order. However, when methodC() attempts to access the out-of-range element in the array, an ArrayIndexOutOfBoundsException is automatically thrown. The error message generated shows that the exception occurred at line 21 of the file in methodC(), which was called in line 15 of the file by methodB(), which was called in line 10 of the file by methodA(), which was called by the main() method in line 5 of the file. Using this list of error messages, you could track down the location where the error was generated. Of course, in a larger application that contains thousands of lines of code, the stack trace history list would be even more useful.

The technique of cycling through the methods in the stack has great advantages because it allows methods to handle exceptions wherever the programmer has decided it is most appropriate—including allowing the operating system to handle the error. However, when a program uses several classes, the disadvantage is that the programmer finds it difficult to locate the original source of an exception.

You have already used the Throwable method getMessage() to obtain information about an Exception object. Another useful Exception method is the printStackTrace() method. When you catch an Exception object, you can call printStackTrace() to display a list of methods in the call stack and determine the location of the statement that caused the exception.

For example, Figure 12-35 shows a DemoStackTrace2 application in which the printStackTrace() method produces a trace of the trail taken by a thrown exception. The differences in the executable statements from the DemoStackTrace application are shaded. The call to methodB() has been placed in a try block so that the exception can be caught. Instead of throwing the exception to the operating system, this application catches the exception, displays a stack trace history list, and continues to execute. The output of the list of methods in Figure 12-36 is similar to the one shown in Figure 12-34, but the application does not end abruptly.

```
public class DemoStackTrace2
{
    public static void main(String[] args)
    {
        methodA();  // line 5
    }
    public static void methodA()
    {
        System.out.println("In methodA()");
        try
        {
            methodB();  // line 12
        }
        catch(ArrayIndexOutOfBoundsException error)
        {
            System.out.println("In methodA() - The stack trace:");
            error.printStackTrace();
        }
        System.out.println("methodA() ends normally.");
        System.out.println("Application could continue " +
            "from this point.");
    }
}
```

Figure 12-35 The DemoStackTrace2 class (continues)

(continued)

```java
   public static void methodB()
   {
      System.out.println("In methodB()");
      methodC();   // line 26
   }
   public static void methodC()
   {
      System.out.println("In methodC()");
      int[] array = {0, 1, 2};
      System.out.println(array[3]);   // line 32
   }
}
```

Figure 12-35   The DemoStackTrace2 class

Figure 12-36   Output of the DemoStackTrace2 application

Usually, you do not want to place a `printStackTrace()` method call in a finished program. The typical application user has no interest in the cryptic messages that are displayed. However, while you are developing an application, `printStackTrace()` can be a useful tool for diagnosing your class's problems.

TWO TRUTHS & A LIE

Tracing Exceptions Through the Call Stack

1. The memory location known as the call stack is where the computer stores the list of locations to which the system must return after each method call.

2. When a method throws an exception and the method does not catch it, the exception is thrown to the next method down the call stack, or in other words, to the next method that the offending method calls.

3. When you catch an exception, you can call printStackTrace() to display a list of methods in the call stack and determine the location of the statement that caused the exception. However, usually you do not want to place a printStackTrace() method call in a finished program.

The false statement is #2. When a method throws an exception and the method does not catch it, the exception is thrown to the next method up the call stack, or in other words, to the method that called the offending method.

Creating Your Own Exception Classes

Java provides over 40 categories of Exceptions that you can use in your programs. However, Java's creators could not predict every condition that might be an exception in your applications. For example, you might want to declare an Exception when your bank balance is negative or when an outside party attempts to access your e-mail account. Most organizations have specific rules for exceptional data; for example, an employee number must not exceed three digits, or an hourly salary must not be less than the legal minimum wage. Of course, you can handle these potential error situations with if statements, but Java also allows you to create your own Exception classes.

To create your own throwable Exception class, you must extend a subclass of Throwable. Recall from Figure 12-1 that Throwable has two subclasses, Exception and Error, which are used to distinguish between recoverable and nonrecoverable errors. Because you always want to create your own exceptions for recoverable errors, your classes should extend the Exception class. You can extend any existing Exception subclass, such as ArithmeticException or NullPointerException, but usually you want to inherit directly from Exception. When you create an Exception subclass, it's conventional to end the name with *Exception*.

The Exception class contains four constructors as follows:

- Exception()—Constructs a new Exception object with null as its detail message

- Exception(String message)—Constructs a new Exception object with the specified detail message

- Exception(String message, Throwable cause)—Constructs a new Exception object with the specified detail message and cause

- Exception(Throwable cause)—Constructs a new Exception object with the specified cause and a detail message of cause.toString(), which typically contains the class and the detail message of cause, or null if the cause argument is null

For example, Figure 12-37 shows a HighBalanceException class. Its constructor contains a single statement that passes a description of an error to the parent Exception constructor. This String would be retrieved if you called the getMessage() method with a HighBalanceException object.

```
public class HighBalanceException extends Exception
{
    public HighBalanceException()
    {
        super("Customer balance is high");
    }
}
```

Figure 12-37   The HighBalanceException class

Figure 12-38 shows a CustomerAccount class that uses a HighBalanceException. The CustomerAccount constructor header indicates that it might throw a HighBalanceException (see the first shaded statement); if the balance used as an argument to the constructor exceeds a set limit, a new, unnamed instance of the HighBalanceException class is thrown (see the second shaded statement).

```
public class CustomerAccount
{
    private int acctNum;
    private double balance;
    public static double HIGH_CREDIT_LIMIT = 20000.00;
    public CustomerAccount(int num, double bal) throws HighBalanceException
    {
        acctNum = num;
        balance = bal;
        if(balance > HIGH_CREDIT_LIMIT)
            throw(new HighBalanceException());
    }
}
```

Figure 12-38   The CustomerAccount class

In the CustomerAccount class in Figure 12-38, you could choose to instantiate a named HighBalanceException and throw it when the balance exceeds the credit limit. By waiting and instantiating an unnamed object only when it is needed, you improve program performance.

Figure 12-39 shows an application that instantiates a CustomerAccount. In this application, a user is prompted for an account number and balance. After the values are entered, an attempt is made to construct a CustomerAccount in a try block (as shown in the first shaded section). If the attempt is successful—that is, if the CustomerAccount constructor does not throw an Exception—the CustomerAccount information is displayed in a dialog box. However, if the CustomerAccount constructor does throw a HighBalanceException, the catch block receives it (as shown in the second shaded section) and displays a message. A different application could take any number of different actions; for example, it could display the return value of the getMessage() method, construct a CustomerAccount object with a lower balance, or construct a different type of object—perhaps a child of CustomerAccount called PreferredCustomerAccount that allows a higher balance. Figure 12-40 shows typical output of the application in a case in which a customer's balance is too high.

643

```java
import javax.swing.*;
public class UseCustomerAccount
{
    public static void main(String[] args)
    {
        int num;
        double balance;
        String input;
        input = JOptionPane.showInputDialog(null,
            "Enter account number");
        num = Integer.parseInt(input);
        input = JOptionPane.showInputDialog(null, "Enter balance due");
        balance = Double.parseDouble(input);
        try
        {
            CustomerAccount ca = new CustomerAccount(num, balance);
            JOptionPane.showMessageDialog(null, "Customer #" +
                num + " has a balance of $" + balance);
        }
        catch( HighBalanceException hbe)
        {
            JOptionPane.showMessageDialog(null, "Customer #" +
                num + " has a balance of $" + balance +
                " which is higher than the credit limit");
        }
    }
}
```

Figure 12-39   The UseCustomerAccount class

Figure 12-40   Typical output of the UseCustomerAccount application

Instead of hard coding error messages into your exception classes, as shown in Figure 12-39, you might consider creating a catalog of possible messages to use. This approach provides several advantages:

- All the messages are stored in one location instead of being scattered throughout the program, making them easier to see and modify.

- The list of possible errors serves as a source of documentation, listing potential problems when running the application.

- Other applications might want to use the same catalog of messages.

- If your application will be used internationally, you can provide messages in multiple languages, and other programmers can use the version that is appropriate for their country.

 You can throw any type of exception at any time, not just exceptions of your own creation. For example, within any program you can code throw(new RuntimeException());. Of course, you would want to do so only with good reason because Java handles RuntimeExceptions for you by stopping the program. Because you cannot anticipate every possible error, Java's automatic response is often the best course of action.

You should not create an excessive number of special Exception types for your classes, especially if the Java development environment already contains an Exception class that will catch the error. Extra Exception types add complexity for other programmers who use your classes. However, when appropriate, specialized Exception classes provide an elegant way for you to handle error situations. They enable you to separate your error code from the usual, nonexceptional sequence of events; they allow errors to be passed up the stack and traced; and they allow clients of your classes to handle exceptional situations in the manner most suitable for their application.

TWO TRUTHS & A LIE

Creating Your Own Exception Classes

1. You must create your own Exception classes for your programs to be considered truly object oriented.

2. To create your own throwable Exception class, you should extend the Exception class.

3. The Exception class contains four constructors, including a default constructor and one that requires a String that contains the message that can be returned by the getMessage() method.

The false statement is #1. You are not required to throw exceptions in object-oriented programs. However, Java does provide many built-in categories of Exceptions that you can use, and you also can create your own Exception classes.

Using Assertions

In Chapter 1, you learned that you might inadvertently create syntax or logical errors when you write a program. Syntax errors are mistakes using the Java language; they are compile-time errors that prevent a program from compiling and creating an executable file with a .class extension.

In Chapter 1, you also learned that a program might contain logical errors even though it is free from syntax errors. Some logical errors cause runtime errors, or errors that cause a program to terminate. In this chapter, you learned how to use exceptions to handle many of these kinds of errors.

Some logical errors do not cause a program to terminate but nevertheless produce incorrect results. For example, if a payroll program should determine gross pay by multiplying hours worked by hourly pay rate, but you inadvertently divide the numbers, no runtime error occurs and no exception is thrown, but the output is wrong. An **assertion** is a Java language feature that can help you detect such logic errors and debug a program. You use an **assert statement** to create an assertion; when you use an assert statement, you state a condition that should be true, and Java throws an AssertionError when it is not.

The syntax of an assert statement is:

```
assert booleanExpression : optionalErrorMessage
```

The Boolean expression in the assert statement should always be true if the program is working correctly. The optionalErrorMessage is displayed if the booleanExpression is false.

Figure 12-41 contains an application that prompts a user for a number and passes it to a method that determines whether a value is even. Within the isEven() method, the remainder is taken when the passed parameter is divided by 2. If the remainder after dividing by 2 is 1, result is set to false. For example, 1, 3, and 5 all are odd, and all result in a value of 1 when % 2 is applied to them. If the remainder after dividing by 2 is not 1, result is set to true. For example, 2, 4, and 6 all are even, and all have a 0 remainder when % 2 is applied to them.

```java
import java.util.Scanner;
public class EvenOdd
{
    public static void main(String[] args)
    {
        Scanner input = new Scanner(System.in);
        int number;
        System.out.print("Enter a number >> ");
        number = input.nextInt();
        if(isEven(number))
            System.out.println(number + " is even");
        else
            System.out.println(number + " is odd");
    }
    public static boolean isEven(int number)
    {
        boolean result;
        if(number % 2 == 1)
            result = false;
        else
            result = true;
        return result;
    }
}
```

Figure 12-41   The flawed EvenOdd program without an assertion

Figure 12-42 shows several executions of the application in Figure 12-41. The output seems correct until the last two executions. The values −5 and −7 are classified as even although they are odd. An assertion might help you to debug this application.

Figure 12-42 Typical executions of the EvenOdd application

Figure 12-43 contains a new version of the isEven() method to which the shaded assert statement has been added. The statement asserts that when the remainder of a number divided by 2 is not 1, it must be 0. If the expression is not true, a message is created using the values of both number and its remainder after dividing by 2.

```java
public static boolean isEven(int number)
{
    boolean result;
    if(number % 2 == 1)
        result = false;
    else
    {
        result = true;
        assert number % 2 == 0 : number + " % 2 is " + number % 2;
    }
    return result;
}
```

Figure 12-43 The flawed isEven() method with an assertion

If you add the assertion shown in Figure 12-43 and then compile and execute the program in the usual way, you get the same incorrect output as in Figure 12-42. To enable the assertion, you must use the -ea option when you execute the program; *ea* stands for *enable assertion*. Figure 12-44 shows the command prompt with an execution that uses the -ea option.

Figure 12-44　Executing an application using the enable assertion option

When the EvenOdd program executes and the user enters −5, the program displays the messages in Figure 12-44 instead of displaying incorrect output. You can see from the message that an AssertionError was thrown and that the value of −5 % 2 is −1, not 1 as you had assumed. The remainder operator results in a negative value when one of its operands is negative, making the output in this program incorrect.

When the programmer sees that −5 % 2 is −1, the reasonable course of action is to return to the source code and change the logic.

Several adjustments are possible:

- The programmer might decide to convert the parameter to the isEven() method to its absolute value before using the remainder operator, as in the following:

```
number = Math.abs(number);
```

- Another option would be to change the if statement to test for even values by comparing number % 2 to 0 first, as follows:

```
if(number % 2 == 0)
    result = true;
else
    result = false;
```

Then values of both 1 and −1 would be classified as not even.

- Other options might include displaying an error message when negative values are encountered, reversing the result values of **true** and **false** when the parameter is negative, or throwing an exception.

An experienced programmer might have found the error in the original EvenOdd application without using an assertion. For example, the programmer might have previously used the remainder operator with a negative operand, remembered that the result might be negative, and changed the code accordingly. Alternatively, the programmer could have inserted statements to display values at strategic points in the program. However, after the mistake is found and fixed, any extra display statements should be removed when the final product is ready for distribution to users. In contrast, any **assert** statements can be left in place, and if the user does not use the **-ea** option when running the program, the user will see no evidence that the `assert` statements exist. Placing `assert` statements in key program locations can reduce development and debugging time.

You do not want to use assertions to check for every type of error that could occur in a program. For example, if you want to ensure that a user enters numeric data, you should use exception-handling techniques that provide the means for your program to recover from the mistake. If you want to ensure that the data falls within a specific range, you should use a decision or a loop. Assertions are meant to be helpful in the development stage of a program, not when it is in production and in the hands of users.

TWO TRUTHS & A LIE

Using Assertions

1. All logical errors cause a program to terminate, and they should be handled by throwing and catching exceptions.

2. The Boolean expression in an `assert` statement should always be `true` if the program is working correctly.

3. To enable an assertion, you must use the `-ea` option when you execute the program.

The false statement is #1. Many logical errors do not cause program termination—they simply produce incorrect results.

 You Do It

Creating a Class That Automatically Throws Exceptions

Next, you create a class that contains two methods that throw exceptions but don't catch them. The `PickMenu` class allows restaurant customers to choose from a dinner menu. Before you create `PickMenu`, you will create the `Menu` class, which lists dinner choices and allows a user to make a selection.

1. Open a new file in your text editor, and then enter the following import statement, class header, and opening curly brace for the `Menu` class:

```
import javax.swing.*;
public class Menu
{
```

(continues)

(continued)

2. Type the following `String` array for three entree choices. Also include a `String` to build the menu that you will display and an integer to hold the numeric equivalent of the selection.

```
private String[] entreeChoice = {"Rosemary Chicken",
    "Beef Wellington", "Maine Lobster"};
private String menu = "";
private int choice;
```

3. Add the `displayMenu()` method, which lists each entree option with a corresponding number the customer can type to make a selection. Even though the allowable `entreeChoice` array subscripts are 0, 1, and 2, most users would expect to type 1, 2, or 3. So, you code x + 1 rather than x as the number in the prompt. After the user enters a selection, convert it to an integer. Return the `String` that corresponds to the user's menu selection—the one with the subscript that is 1 less than the entered value. After the closing curly brace for the `displayMenu()` method, add the closing curly brace for the class.

```
public String displayMenu()
{
    for(int x = 0; x < entreeChoice.length; ++x)
    {
        menu = menu + "\n" + (x + 1) + " for " +
            entreeChoice[x];
    }
    String input = JOptionPane.showInputDialog(null,
        "Type your selection, then press Enter." + menu);
    choice = Integer.parseInt(input);
    return(entreeChoice[choice - 1]);
}
}
```

The curly braces are not necessary in the `for` loop of the `displayMenu()` method because the loop contains only one statement. However, in a later exercise, you will add another statement within this block.

4. Examine the code within the `displayMenu()` method. Consider the exceptions that might occur. The user might not type an integer, so the `parseInt()` method can fail, and even if the user does type an integer, it might not be in the range allowed to access the `entreeChoice` array. Therefore, the `displayMenu()` method, like most methods in which you rely on the user to enter data, might throw exceptions that you can anticipate. (Of course, any method might throw an unanticipated exception.)

5. Save the file as **Menu.java**, and compile the class using the **javac** command.

(continues)

(continued)

Creating a Class That Passes on an Exception *Object*

Next, you create the PickMenu class, which lets a customer choose from the available dinner entree options. The PickMenu class declares a Menu and a String named guestChoice that holds the name of the entree the customer selects.

To enable the PickMenu class to operate with different kinds of Menus in the future, you will pass a Menu to PickMenu's constructor. This technique provides two advantages: First, when the menu options change, you can alter the contents of the Menu.java file without changing any of the code in programs that use Menu. Second, you can extend Menu, perhaps to VegetarianMenu, LowSaltMenu, or KosherMenu, and still use the existing PickMenu class. When you pass any Menu or Menu subclass into the PickMenu constructor, the correct customer options appear.

The PickMenu class is unlikely to directly generate any exceptions because it does not request user input. (Keep in mind that any class might generate an exception for such uncontrollable events as the system not having enough memory available.) However, PickMenu declares a Menu object; the Menu class, because it relies on user input, is likely to generate an exception.

1. Open a new file in your text editor, and then add the following first few lines of the PickMenu class with its data fields (a Menu and a String that reflect the customer's choice):

```java
import javax.swing.*;
public class PickMenu
{
    private Menu briefMenu;
    private String guestChoice = new String();
```

2. Enter the following PickMenu constructor, which receives an argument representing a Menu. The constructor assigns the Menu that is the argument to the local Menu and then calls the setGuestChoice() method, which prompts the user to select from the available menu. The PickMenu() constructor might throw an exception because it calls setGuestChoice(), which calls displayMenu(), a method that uses keyboard input and might throw an exception.

```java
public PickMenu(Menu theMenu)
{
    briefMenu = theMenu;
    setGuestChoice();
}
```

(continues)

(continued)

3. The following `setGuestChoice()` method displays the menu and reads keyboard data entry (so the method throws an exception). It also displays instructions and then retrieves the user's selection.

```
public void setGuestChoice()
{
  JOptionPane.showMessageDialog(null,
    "Choose from the following menu:");
  guestChoice = briefMenu.displayMenu();
}
```

4. Add the following `getGuestChoice()` method that returns a guest's `String` selection from the `PickMenu` class. Also, add a closing curly brace for the class.

```
public String getGuestChoice()
{
    return(guestChoice);
}
}
```

5. Save the file as **PickMenu.java**, and compile it using the **javac** command.

Creating an Application That Can Catch Exceptions

You have created a `Menu` class that simply holds a list of food items, displays itself, and allows the user to make a selection. You also created a `PickMenu` class with fields that hold a user's specific selection from a given menu and methods to get and set values for those fields. The `PickMenu` class might throw exceptions, but it contains no methods that catch those exceptions. Next, you write an application that uses the `PickMenu` class. This application can catch exceptions that `PickMenu` throws.

1. Open a new file in your text editor, and start entering the following `PlanMenu` class, which has just one method—a `main()` method:

```
import javax.swing.*;
public class PlanMenu
{
  public static void main(String[] args)
  {
```

2. Construct the following `Menu` named `briefMenu`, and declare a `PickMenu` object that you name `entree`. You do not want to construct a `PickMenu` object yet because you want to be able to catch the exception that the `PickMenu` constructor might throw. Therefore, you want to wait and construct the `PickMenu` object within a `try` block. For now, you just declare `entree` and assign it `null`. Also, you declare a `String` that holds the customer's menu selection.

(continues)

(continued)

```
Menu briefMenu = new Menu();
PickMenu entree = null;
String guestChoice = new String();
```

3. Write the following `try` block that constructs a `PickMenu` item. If the construction is successful, the next statement assigns a selection to the `entree` object. Because `entree` is a `PickMenu` object, it has access to the `getGuestChoice()` method in the `PickMenu` class, and you can assign the method's returned value to the `guestChoice` String.

```
try
{
   PickMenu selection = new PickMenu(briefMenu);
   entree = selection;
   guestChoice = entree.getGuestChoice();
}
```

4. The `catch` block must immediately follow the `try` block. When the `try` block fails, `guestChoice` will not have a valid value, so recover from the exception by assigning a value to `guestChoice` within the following `catch` block:

```
catch(Exception error)
{
   guestChoice = "an invalid selection";
}
```

5. After the `catch` block, the application continues. Use the following code to display the customer's choice at the end of the `PlanMenu` application, and then add closing curly braces for the `main()` method and the class:

```
        JOptionPane.showMessageDialog(null,
            "You chose " + guestChoice);
    }
}
```

6. Save the file as **PlanMenu.java**, and then compile and execute it. Read the instructions, click **OK**, choose an entree by typing its number from the menu, and click **OK** again. Confirm that the menu selection displayed is the one you chose, and click **OK** to dismiss the last dialog box. Figure 12-45 shows the first dialog box of instructions, the menu that appears, and the output when the user selects option 3.

(continues)

654

(continued)

Figure 12-45   Typical execution of the PlanMenu application

7. The PlanMenu application works well when you enter a valid menu selection. One way that you can force an exception is to enter an invalid menu selection at the prompt. Run the PlanMenu application again, and type **4**, **A**, or any invalid value at the prompt. Entering 4 produces an ArrayIndexOutOfBoundsException, and entering A produces a NumberFormatException. If the program lacked the try...catch pair, either entry would halt the program. However, because the setGuestChoice() method in the PickMenu class throws the exception and the PlanMenu application catches it, guestChoice takes on the value "an invalid selection" and the application ends smoothly, as shown in Figure 12-46.

Figure 12-46   Exceptional execution of the PlanMenu application

(continues)

(continued)

Extending a Class That Throws Exceptions

An advantage to using object-oriented exception handling techniques is that you gain the ability to handle error conditions differently within each program you write. Next, you extend the Menu class to create a class named VegetarianMenu. Subsequently, when you write an application that uses PickMenu with a VegetarianMenu object, you can deal with any thrown exception differently than when you wrote the PlanMenu application.

1. Open the **Menu.java** file in your text editor, and change the access specifier for the entreeChoice array from private to protected. That way, when you extend the class, the derived class will have access to the array. Save the file, and recompile it using the **javac** command.

2. Open a new file in your text editor, and then type the following class header for the VegetarianMenu class that extends Menu:

```
public class VegetarianMenu extends Menu
{
```

3. Provide new menu choices for the VegetarianMenu as follows:

```
String[] vegEntreeChoice = {"Spinach Lasagna",
   "Cheese Enchiladas", "Fruit Plate"};
```

4. Add the following constructor that calls the superclass constructor and assigns each vegetarian selection to the Menu superclass entreeChoice array, and then add the closing curly brace for the class:

```
public VegetarianMenu()
{
   super();
   for(int x = 0; x < vegEntreeChoice.length; ++x)
      entreeChoice[x] = vegEntreeChoice[x];
}
}
```

5. Save the class as **VegetarianMenu.java**, and then compile it.

6. Now write an application that uses VegetarianMenu. You could write any program, but for demonstration purposes, you can simply modify PlanMenu.java. Open the **PlanMenu.java** file in your text editor, then immediately save it as **PlanVegetarianMenu.java**.

7. Change the class name in the header to PlanVegetarianMenu.

(continues)

(continued)

8. Change the first statement within the `main()` method as follows so it declares a `VegetarianMenu` instead of a `Menu`:

   ```
   VegetarianMenu briefMenu = new VegetarianMenu();
   ```

9. Change the `guestChoice` assignment statement in the `catch` block as follows so it is specific to the program that uses the `VegetarianMenu`:

   ```
   guestChoice = "an invalid vegetarian selection";
   ```

10. Save the file, compile it, and run the application. When you see the vegetarian menu, enter a valid selection and confirm that the program works correctly. Run the application again, and enter an invalid selection. The error message shown in Figure 12-47 identifies your invalid entry as "an invalid vegetarian selection". Remember that you did not change the `PickMenu` class. Your new `PlanVegetarianMenu` application uses the `PickMenu` class that you wrote and compiled before a `VegetarianMenu` ever existed. However, because `PickMenu` throws uncaught exceptions, you can handle those exceptions as you see fit in any new applications in which you catch them. Click **OK** to end the application.

Figure 12-47 Output of the `PlanVegetarianMenu` application when the user makes an invalid selection

Creating an Exception Class

Besides using built-in classes that derive from `Exception`, such as `NumberFormatException` and `IndexOutOfBoundsException`, you can create your own `Exception` classes. For example, suppose that although you have asked a user to type a number representing a menu selection, you realize that some users might mistakenly type the initial letter of an option, such as *R* for *Rosemary Chicken*. Although the user has made an error, you want to treat this type of error more leniently than other errors, such as typing a letter that has no discernable connection to the presented menu. In the next section, you create a `MenuException` class that you can use with the `Menu` class to represent a specific type of error.

(continues)

(continued)

1. Open a new file in your text editor, and enter the MenuException class. The class extends Exception. Its constructor requires a String argument, which is passed to the parent class to be used as a return value for the getMessage() method.

```
public class MenuException extends Exception
{
  public MenuException(String choice)
  {
    super(choice);
  }
}
```

2. Save the file as **MenuException.java**, and compile it.

Using an Exception You Created

Next, you modify the Menu, PickMenu, and PlanMenu classes to demonstrate how to use a MenuException object.

1. Open the **Menu** class in your text editor, and immediately save the file as **Menu2.java**.

2. Change the class name to **Menu2**.

3. At the end of the list of class data fields, add an array of characters that can hold the first letter of each of the entrees in the menu.

```
protected char initial[] = new char[entreeChoice.length];
```

4. At the end of the method header for the displayMenu() class, add the following clause:

```
throws MenuException
```

You add this clause because you are going to add code that throws such an exception.

5. Within the displayMenu() method, just before the closing curly brace of the for loop that builds the menu String, add a statement that takes the first character of each entreeChoice and stores it in a corresponding element of the initial array. At the end of the for loop, the initial array holds the first character of each available entree.

```
initial[x] = entreeChoice[x].charAt(0);
```

6. After displaying the JOptionPane dialog box that displays the menu and receives the user's input, add a loop that compares the first letter of the user's choice to each of the initials of valid menu options. If a match is found, throw a new

(continues)

(continued)

instance of the MenuException class that uses the corresponding entree as its String argument. In other words, when this thrown MenuException is caught by another method, the assumed entree is the String returned by the getMessage() method. By placing this test before the call to parseInt(), you cause entries of *R*, *B*, or *M* to throw a MenuException before they can cause a NumberFormatException.

```
for(int y = 0; y < entreeChoice.length; ++y)
   if(input.charAt(0) == initial[y])
      throw (new MenuException(entreeChoice[y]));
```

7. Compare your new class with Figure 12-48, in which all of the changes to the Menu class are shaded.

```java
import javax.swing.*;
public class Menu2
{
    protected String[] entreeChoice = {"Rosemary Chicken",
        "Beef Wellington", "Maine Lobster"};
    private String menu = "";
    private int choice;
    protected char initial[] = new char[entreeChoice.length];
    public String displayMenu() throws MenuException
    {
        for(int x = 0; x < entreeChoice.length; ++x)
        {
            menu = menu + "\n" + (x + 1) + " for " +
                entreeChoice[x];
            initial[x] = entreeChoice[x].charAt(0);
        }
        String input = JOptionPane.showInputDialog(null,
            "Type your selection, then press Enter." + menu);
        for(int y = 0; y < entreeChoice.length; ++y)
            if(input.charAt(0) == initial[y])
                throw(new MenuException(entreeChoice[y]));
        choice = Integer.parseInt(input);
        return(entreeChoice[choice - 1]);
    }
}
```

Figure 12-48   The Menu2 class

8. Save the class, and compile it.

9. Open the **PickMenu** file in your text editor, and immediately save it as **PickMenu2.java**.

(continues)

(continued)

10. Change the class name to **PickMenu2**, and change the declaration of the Menu object to a **Menu2** object. Change the constructor name to **PickMenu2** and its argument to type **Menu2**. Also add a throws clause to the PickMenu2 constructor header so that it throws a MenuException. This constructor does not throw an exception directly, but it calls the setGuestChoice() method, which calls the displayMenu() method, which throws a MenuException.

11. Add the following throws clause to the setGuestChoice() method header:

throws MenuException

12. Compare your modifications to the PickMenu2 class in Figure 12-49, in which the changes from the PickMenu class are shaded. Save your file, and compile it.

```java
import javax.swing.*;
public class PickMenu2
{
    private Menu2 briefMenu;
    private String guestChoice = new String();
    public PickMenu2(Menu2 theMenu) throws MenuException
    {
        briefMenu = theMenu;
        setGuestChoice();
    }
    public void setGuestChoice() throws MenuException
    {
        JOptionPane.showMessageDialog(null,
            "Choose from the following menu:");
        guestChoice = briefMenu.displayMenu();
    }
    public String getGuestChoice()
    {
        return(guestChoice);
    }
}
```

Figure 12-49   The PickMenu2 class

13. Open the **PlanMenu.java** file in your text editor, and immediately save it as **PlanMenu2.java**.

(continues)

(continued)

14. Change the class name to **PlanMenu2**. Within the `main()` method, declare a **Menu2** object and a **PickMenu2** reference instead of the current `Menu` object and `PickMenu` reference.

15. Within the `try` block, change both references of `PickMenu` to **PickMenu2**.

Using Figure 12-50 as a reference, add a `catch` block after the `try` block and before the existing `catch` block. This `catch` block will catch any thrown `MenuExceptions` and display their messages. The message will be the name of a menu item, based on the initial the user entered. All other `Exception` objects, including `NumberFormatExceptions` and `IndexOutOfBoundsExceptions`, will fall through to the second `catch` block and be handled as before.

```java
import javax.swing.*;
public class PlanMenu2
{
    public static void main(String[] args)
    {
        Menu2 briefMenu = new Menu2();
        PickMenu2 entree = null;
        String guestChoice = new String();
        try
        {
            PickMenu2 selection = new PickMenu2(briefMenu);
            entree = selection;
            guestChoice = entree.getGuestChoice();
        }
        catch(MenuException error)
        {
            guestChoice = error.getMessage();
        }
        catch(Exception error)
        {
            guestChoice = "an invalid selection";
        }
        JOptionPane.showMessageDialog(null,
            "You chose " + guestChoice);
    }
}
```

Figure 12-50   The PlanMenu2 class

(continues)

(continued)

16. Save the file, then compile and execute it several times. When you are asked to make a selection, try entering a valid number, an invalid number, an initial letter that is part of the menu, and a letter that is not one of the initial menu letters, and observe the results each time. Whether or not you enter a valid number, the application works as expected. Entering an invalid number still results in an error message. When you enter a letter or a string of letters, the application assumes your selection is valid if you enter the same initial letter, using the same case, as one of the menu options.

Don't Do It

- Don't forget that all the statements in a `try` block might not execute. If an exception is thrown, no statements after that point in the `try` block will execute.

- Don't forget that you might need a `nextLine()` method call after an attempt to read numeric data from the keyboard throws an exception.

- Don't forget that a variable declared in a `try` block goes out of scope at the end of the block.

- Don't forget that when a variable gets its usable value within a `try` block, you must ensure that it has a valid value before attempting to use it.

- Don't forget to place more specific `catch` blocks before more general ones.

- Don't forget to write a `throws` clause for a method that throws a checked exception but does not handle it.

- Don't forget to handle any checked exception thrown to your method either by writing a `catch` block or by listing it in your method's `throws` clause.

Key Terms

An **exception** is an unexpected or error condition.

Exception handling is an object-oriented technique for managing errors.

Runtime exceptions are unplanned exceptions that occur during a program's execution. The term is also used more specifically to describe members of the `RuntimeException` class.

The **Error class** represents more serious errors than the Exception class—those from which your program usually cannot recover.

The **Exception class** comprises less serious errors than those from the Error class; the Exception class represents unusual conditions that arise while a program is running and from which the program can recover.

A **crash** is a premature, unexpected, and inelegant end to a program.

A **stack trace history list**, or more simply a **stack trace**, displays all the methods that were called during program execution.

The term **mission critical** refers to any process that is crucial to an organization.

Fault-tolerant applications are designed so that they continue to operate, possibly at a reduced level, when some part of the system fails.

Robustness represents the degree to which a system is resilient to stress, maintaining correct functioning.

A **try block** is a block of code that might throw an exception that can be handled by a subsequent catch block.

A **catch block** is a segment of code that can handle an exception that might be thrown by the try block that precedes it.

A **throw statement** is one that sends an exception out of a block or a method so it can be handled elsewhere.

A **finally block** is a block of code that holds statements that must execute at the end of a try...catch sequence, whether or not an exception was thrown.

Exception specification is the practice of using the keyword throws followed by an Exception type in the method header. If a method throws a checked Exception object that it will not catch but will be caught by a different method, you must use an exception specification.

Unchecked exceptions are those from which an executing program cannot reasonably be expected to recover.

Checked exceptions are those that a programmer should plan for and from which a program should be able to recover.

The **catch or specify requirement** is the Java rule that checked exceptions require catching or declaration.

Syntactic sugar is a term to describe aspects of a computer language that make it "sweeter," or easier, for programmers to use.

Syntactic salt describes a language feature designed to make it harder to write bad code.

The memory location known as the **call stack** is where the computer stores the list of method locations to which the system must return.

An **assertion** is a Java language feature that can help you detect logic errors and debug a program.

An **assert statement** creates an assertion.

Chapter Summary

- An exception is an unexpected or error condition. Exception handling is the name for the object-oriented techniques that manage such errors. In Java, the two basic classes of errors are Error and Exception; both descend from the Throwable class.

- In object-oriented terminology, a try block holds code that might cause an error and throw an exception, and a catch block processes the error.

- You can place as many statements as you need within a try block, and you can catch as many exceptions as you want. If you try more than one statement, only the first error-generating statement throws an exception. As soon as the exception occurs, the logic transfers to the catch block, which leaves the rest of the statements in the try block unexecuted. When a program contains multiple catch blocks, the first matching catch block executes, and each remaining catch block is bypassed.

- When you have actions you must perform at the end of a try...catch sequence, you can use a finally block that executes regardless of whether the preceding try block identifies an exception. Usually, you use a finally block to perform cleanup tasks.

- Besides clarity, an advantage to object-oriented exception handling is the flexibility it allows in the handling of error situations. Each calling application might need to handle the same error differently, depending on its purpose.

- When you write a method that might throw a checked exception that is not caught within the method, you must type the clause throws <name>Exception after the method header to indicate the type of Exception that might be thrown. Methods in which you explicitly throw a checked exception require a catch or a declaration.

- The memory location known as the call stack is where the computer stores the list of method locations to which the system must return. When you catch an exception, you can call printStackTrace() to display a list of methods in the call stack so you can determine the location of the exception.

- Java provides over 40 categories of Exceptions that you can use in your programs. However, Java's creators could not predict every condition that might be an Exception in your applications, so Java also allows you to create your own Exceptions. To create your own throwable Exception class, you must extend a subclass of Throwable.

- An assertion is a Java language feature that can help you detect logic errors and debug a program. When you use an assertion, you state a condition that should be true, and Java throws an AssertionError when it is not.

Review Questions

1. In object-oriented programming terminology, an unexpected or error condition is a(n) _____ .

   a. anomaly

   b. aberration

   c. deviation

   d. exception

2. All Java Exceptions are _____ .

   a. Errors

   b. RuntimeExceptions

   c. Throwables

   d. Omissions

3. Which of the following statements is true?

   a. Exceptions are more serious than Errors.

   b. Errors are more serious than Exceptions.

   c. Errors and Exceptions are equally serious.

   d. Exceptions and Errors are the same thing.

4. The method that ends the current application and returns control to the operating system is _____ .

   a. System.end()

   b. System.done()

   c. System.exit()

   d. System.abort()

5. In object-oriented terminology, you _____ a procedure that might not complete correctly.

   a. try

   b. catch

   c. handle

   d. encapsulate

6. A method that detects an error condition or Exception _____ an Exception.

   a. throws

   b. catches

   c. handles

   d. encapsulates

7. A try block includes all of the following elements except _____ .

   a. the keyword try

   b. the keyword catch

   c. curly braces

   d. statements that might cause Exceptions

8. The segment of code that handles or takes appropriate action following an exception is a _____ block.

    a. `try`
    b. `catch`
    c. `throws`
    d. `handles`

9. You _____ within a `try` block.

    a. must place only a single statement
    b. can place any number of statements
    c. must place at least two statements
    d. must place a `catch` block

10. If you include three statements in a `try` block and follow the block with three `catch` blocks, and the second statement in the `try` block throws an `Exception`, then _____ .

    a. the first `catch` block executes
    b. the first two `catch` blocks execute
    c. only the second `catch` block executes
    d. the first matching `catch` block executes

11. When a `try` block does not generate an `Exception` and you have included multiple `catch` blocks, _____ .

    a. they all execute
    b. only the first one executes
    c. only the first matching one executes
    d. no `catch` blocks execute

12. The `catch` block that begins `catch(Exception e)` can catch `Exceptions` of type _____ .

    a. `IOException`
    b. `ArithmeticException`
    c. both of the above
    d. none of the above

13. The code within a `finally` block executes when the `try` block _____ .

    a. identifies one or more `Exceptions`
    b. does not identify any `Exceptions`
    c. either a or b
    d. neither a nor b

14. An advantage to using a try...catch block is that exceptional events are _____ .

    a. eliminated

    b. reduced

    c. integrated with regular events

    d. isolated from regular events

15. Which methods can throw an Exception?

    a. methods with a throws clause

    b. methods with a catch block

    c. methods with both a throws clause and a catch block

    d. any method

16. A method can _____ .

    a. check for errors but not handle them

    b. handle errors but not check for them

    c. either of the above

    d. neither of the above

17. Which of the following is least important to know if you want to be able to use a method to its full potential?

    a. the method's return type

    b. the type of arguments the method requires

    c. the number of statements within the method

    d. the type of Exceptions the method throws

18. The memory location where the computer stores the list of method locations to which the system must return is known as the _____ .

    a. registry

    b. call stack

    c. chronicle

    d. archive

19. You can get a list of the methods through which an Exception has traveled by using the _____ method.

    a. getMessage()

    b. callStack()

    c. getPath()

    d. printStackTrace()

20. A(n) _____ is a statement used in testing programs that should be true; if it is not true, an Exception is thrown.

    a. assertion

    b. throwable

    c. verification

    d. declaration

Exercises

Programming Exercises

1. Write an application named BadSubscriptCaught in which you declare an array of 10 first names. Write a try block in which you prompt the user for an integer and display the name in the requested position. Create a catch block that catches the potential ArrayIndexOutOfBoundsException thrown when the user enters a number that is out of range. The catch block should also display an error message. Save the file as **BadSubscriptCaught.java**.

2. The Double.parseDouble() method requires a String argument, but it fails if the String cannot be converted to a floating-point number. Write an application in which you try accepting a double input from a user and catch a NumberFormatException if one is thrown. The catch block forces the number to 0 and displays an appropriate error message. Following the catch block, display the number. Save the file as **TryToParseDouble.java**.

3. In Chapter 9, you wrote a program named MeanMedian that allows a user to enter five integers and then displays the values, their mean, and their median. Now, modify the program to throw an exception if an entered value is not an integer. If an exception is thrown, display an appropriate message and allow the user to reenter the value. Save the file as **MeanMedianHandleException.java**.

4. Write an application that prompts the user to enter a number to use as an array size, and then attempt to declare an array using the entered size. If the array is created successfully, display an appropriate message. Java generates a NegativeArraySizeException if you attempt to create an array with a negative size, and it creates a NumberFormatException if you attempt to create an array using a nonnumeric value for the size. Use a catch block that executes if the array size is nonnumeric or negative, displaying a message that indicates the array was not created. Save the file as **NegativeArray.java**.

5. Write an application that throws and catches an ArithmeticException when you attempt to take the square root of a negative value. Prompt the user for an input value and try the Math.sqrt() method on it. The application either displays the square root or catches the thrown Exception and displays an appropriate message. Save the file as **SqrtException.java**.

6. Create a ProductException class whose constructor receives a String that consists of a product number and price. Save the file as **ProductException.java**. Create a Product class with two fields, productNum and price. The Product constructor requires values for both fields. Upon construction, throw a ProductException if the product number does not consist of three digits, if the price is less than $0.01, or if the price is over $1,000. Save the class as **Product.java**. Write an application that establishes at least four Product objects with valid and

invalid values. Display an appropriate message when a Product object is created successfully and when one is not. Save the file as **ThrowProductException.java**.

7. a. Create an IceCreamConeException class whose constructor receives a String that consists of an ice cream cone's flavor and an integer representing the number of scoops in the IceCreamCone. Pass this String to the IceCreamConeException's parent so it can be used in a getMessage() call. Save the class as **IceCreamConeException.java**. Create an IceCreamCone class with two fields—flavor and scoops. The IceCreamCone constructor calls two data-entry methods—setFlavor() and setScoops(). The setScoops() method throws an IceCreamConeException when the scoop quantity exceeds three. Save the class as **IceCreamCone.java**. Write an application that establishes several IceCreamCone objects and handles the Exceptions. Save the file as **ThrowIceCream.java**.

    b. Create an IceCreamCone2 class in which you modify the IceCreamCone setFlavor() method to ensure that the user enters a valid flavor. Allow at least four flavors of your choice. If the user's entry does not match a valid flavor, throw an IceCreamConeException. Write an application that establishes several IceCreamCone objects and demonstrates the handling of the new Exception. Save the new class file as **IceCreamCone2.java**, and save the new application file as **ThrowIceCream2.java**.

8. Write an application that displays a series of at least five student ID numbers (that you have stored in an array) and asks the user to enter a numeric test score for the student. Create a ScoreException class, and throw a ScoreException for the class if the user does not enter a valid score (less than or equal to 100). Catch the ScoreException, and then display an appropriate message. In addition, store a *0* for the student's score. At the end of the application, display all the student IDs and scores. Save the files as **ScoreException.java** and **TestScore.java**.

9. Write an application that displays a series of at least 10 student ID numbers (that you have stored in an array) and asks the user to enter a test letter grade for the student. Create an Exception class named GradeException that contains a static public array of valid grade letters ('A', 'B', 'C', 'D', 'F', and 'I') you can use to determine whether a grade entered from the application is valid. In your application, throw a GradeException if the user does not enter a valid letter grade. Catch the GradeException, and then display an appropriate message. In addition, store an 'I' (for Incomplete) for any student for whom an exception is caught. At the end of the application, display all the student IDs and grades. Save the files as **GradeException.java** and **TestGrade.java**.

10. Create a DataEntryException class whose getMessage() method returns information about invalid integer data. Write a program named GetIDAndAge that continually prompts the user for an ID number and an age until a terminal *0* is entered for both. Throw a DataEntryException if the ID is not in the range of

valid ID numbers (0 through 999), or if the age is not in the range of valid ages (0 through 119). Catch any `DataEntryException` or `InputMismatchException` that is thrown, and display an appropriate message. Save the files as **DataEntryException.java** and **GetIDAndAge.java**.

11. A company accepts user orders by part numbers interactively. Users might make the following errors as they enter data:

   - The part number is not numeric.

   - The quantity is not numeric.

   - The part number is too low (less than 0).

   - The part number is too high (more than 999).

   - The quantity ordered is too low (less than 1).

   - The quantity ordered is too high (more than 5,000).

   Create a class that stores an array of usable error messages; save the file as **DataMessages.java**. Create a `DataException` class; each object of this class will store one of the messages. Save the file as **DataException.java**. Create an application that prompts the user for a part number and quantity. Allow for the possibility of nonnumeric entries as well as out-of-range entries, and display the appropriate message when an error occurs. If no error occurs, display the message "Valid entry". Save the program as **PartAndQuantityEntry.java**.

12. A company accepts user orders for its products interactively. Users might make the following errors as they enter data:

   - The item number ordered is not numeric.

   - The quantity is not numeric.

   - The item number is too low (less than 0).

   - The item number is too high (more than 9999).

   - The quantity ordered is too low (less than 1).

   - The quantity ordered is too high (more than 12).

   - The item number is not a currently valid item.

   Although the company might expand in the future, its current inventory consists of the items listed in Table 12-1.

Item Number	Price ($)
111	0.89
222	1.47
333	2.43
444	5.99

Table 12-1   Item numbers and prices

Create a class that stores an array of usable error messages; save the file as **OrderMessages.java**. Create an OrderException class that stores one of the messages; save the file as **OrderException.java**. Create an application that contains prompts for an item number and quantity. Allow for the possibility of nonnumeric entries as well as out-of-range entries and entries that do not match any of the currently available item numbers. The program should display an appropriate message if an error has occurred. If no errors exist in the entered data, compute the user's total amount due (quantity times price each) and display it. Save the program as **PlaceAnOrder.java**.

13. a. Gadgets by Mail sells many interesting items through its catalogs. Write an application that prompts the user for order details, including item numbers and quantity of each item ordered, based on the available items shown in Table 12-2.

Item #	Description	Price ($)
101	Electric hand warmer	12.99
124	Battery-operated plant waterer	7.55
256	Gerbil trimmer	9.99
512	Talking bookmark	6.89

Table 12-2   Items offered by Gadgets by Mail

The shipping and handling fee for an order is based on the total order price, as shown in Table 12-3.

Price of Order ($)	Shipping and Handling ($)
0–24.99	5.55
25.00–49.99	8.55
50.00 or more	11.55

Table 12-3   Shipping and handling fees charged by Gadgets by Mail

Create the following classes:

- Gadget, which contains an item number, description, and price for a gadget; a constructor that sets all the fields; and get methods to retrieve the field values.

- Order, which contains an order number, customer name, and address (assume you need just a street address, not city, state, and zip code); a list of item numbers ordered (up to four); the total price of all items ordered; and a shipping and handling fee for the order. Include a constructor to set the field values and get methods to retrieve the field values.

- GadgetOrderTaker, which is an interactive application that takes four customer orders. The class contains an array of the four Gadget objects offered (from Table 12-2). The application prompts each user for a name and street address and assigns a unique order number to each customer, starting with 101. The application asks each user to enter an item number and quantity wanted. When the user enters 999 for the item number, the order is complete, and the next customer can enter data. Each customer can order up to four item numbers. When a customer's order is complete (the customer has entered 999 for an item number, or has ordered four different items), calculate the shipping and handling charges. After four customers have placed Orders, display each Order's data, including the order number, the name and address of the customer, and the list of items ordered, including the item number, description, and price of each Order, the total price for the order, and the shipping and handling charge. The GadgetOrderTaker class handles all thrown Exceptions by displaying an explanatory message and ending the application.

- OrderException, which is an Exception that is created and thrown under any of the following conditions:

  - A customer attempts to order more than four different items.

  - A customer orders more than 100 of any item.

  - A customer enters an invalid item number.

- Also, catch the Exception generated by either of these conditions:

  - A customer enters a nonnumeric character as the item number.

  - A customer enters a nonnumeric character as the quantity.

  Save the files as **Gadget.java**, **Order.java**, **GadgetOrderTaker.java**, and **OrderException.java**.

  b. The GadgetOrderTaker class handles all thrown Exceptions by displaying an explanatory message and ending the application. Create a new application that handles all Exceptions by requiring the user to reenter the offending data. Save the file as **GadgetOrderTaker2.java**.

Debugging Exercises

1. Each of the following files in the Chapter12 folder of your downloadable student files has syntax and/or logic errors. In each case, determine the problem and fix the program. After you correct the errors, save each file using the same filename preceded with *Fix*. For example, DebugTwelve1.java will become FixDebugTwelve1.java. You will also use a file named DebugEmployeeIDException.java with the DebugTwelve4.java file.

    a. DebugTwelve1.java

    b. DebugTwelve2.java

    c. DebugTwelve3.java

    d. DebugTwelve4.java

Game Zone

1. In Chapter 1, you created a class called RandomGuess. In this game, the application generates a random number for a player to guess. In Chapter 5, you improved the application to display a message indicating whether the player's guess was correct, too high, or too low. In Chapter 6, you further improved the game by adding a loop that continually prompts the user to enter the correct value, if necessary. As written, the game should work as long as the player enters numeric guesses. However, if the player enters a letter or other nonnumeric character, the game throws an exception. Discover the type of Exception thrown, then improve the game by handling the exception so that the user is informed of the error and allowed to attempt to enter the correct data again. Save the file as **RandomGuess4.java**.

2. In Chapter 8, you created a Quiz class that contains an array of 10 multiple-choice questions to which the user was required to respond with an *A*, *B*, or *C*. At the time, you knew how to handle the user's response if an invalid character was entered. Rerun the program now to determine whether an exception is thrown if the user enters nothing—that is, the user just presses the Enter key without making an entry. If so, improve the program by catching the exception, displaying an appropriate error message, and presenting the same question to the user again. Save the file as **QuizWithExceptionsCaught.java**.

Case Problems

1. In Chapter 11, you created an interactive StaffDinnerEvent class that obtains all the data for a dinner event for Carly's Catering, including details about the staff members required to work at the event. Now, modify the class so that it becomes immune to user data entry errors by handling exceptions for each numeric entry. Each time the program requires numeric data—for example, for the number of guests, selected menu options, and staff members' salaries—continuously prompt

the user until the data entered is the correct type. Save the revised program as **StaffDinnerEvent.java**.

2. In Chapter 11, you created an interactive `RentalDemo` class that obtains all the data for four rentals from Sammy's Seashore Rentals, including details about the contract number, length of the rental, and equipment type. Now, modify the class so that it becomes immune to user data entry errors by handling exceptions for each numeric entry. Each time the program requires numeric data—for example, for the rental period—continuously prompt the user until the data entered is the correct type. Save the revised program as **RentalDemo.java**.

File Input and Output

In this chapter, you will:

◎ Learn about computer files

◎ Use the `Path` and `Files` classes

◎ Learn about file organization, streams, and buffers

◎ Use Java's IO classes to write to and read from a file

◎ Create and use sequential data files

◎ Learn about random access files

◎ Write records to a random access data file

◎ Read records from a random access data file

Understanding Computer Files

Data items can be stored on two broad types of storage devices in a computer system:

- **Volatile storage** is temporary; values that are volatile, such as those stored in variables, are lost when a computer loses power. **Random access memory (RAM)** is the temporary storage within a computer. When you write a Java program that stores a value in a variable, you are using RAM. Most computer professionals simply call volatile storage *memory*.

- **Nonvolatile storage** is permanent storage; it is not lost when a computer loses power. When you write a Java program and save it to a disk, you are using permanent storage.

> When discussing computer storage, *temporary* and *permanent* refer to volatility, not length of time. For example, a *temporary* variable might exist for several hours in a large program or one that the user forgets to close, but a *permanent* piece of data might be saved and then deleted within a few seconds. In recent years, the distinction between memory and storage has blurred because many systems automatically save data to a nonvolatile device and retrieve it after a power interruption. Because you can erase data from files, some programmers prefer the term "persistent storage" to permanent storage. In other words, you can remove data from a file stored on a device such as a disk drive, so it is not technically permanent. However, the data remains in the file even when the computer loses power; so, unlike with RAM, the data persists, or perseveres.

A **computer file** is a collection of data stored on a nonvolatile device. Files exist on **permanent storage devices**, such as hard disks, Zip disks, USB drives, reels or cassettes of magnetic tape, and compact discs.

You can categorize files by the way they store data:

- **Text files** contain data that can be read in a text editor because the data has been encoded using a scheme such as ASCII or Unicode. (See Appendix B for more information on Unicode.) Some text files are **data files** that contain facts and figures, such as a payroll file that contains employee numbers, names, and salaries; some files are **program files** or **application files** that store software instructions. You have created many such files throughout this book.

- **Binary files** contain data that has not been encoded as text. Their contents are in binary format, which means that you cannot understand them by viewing them in a text editor. Examples include images, music, and the compiled program files with a .class extension that you have created using this book.

Although their contents vary, files have many common characteristics—each file has a size that specifies the space it occupies on a section of disk or other storage device, and each file has a name and a specific time of creation.

Computer files are the electronic equivalent of paper files stored in office file cabinets. When you store a permanent file, you can place it in the main or **root directory** of your storage device. If you compare computer storage to using a file cabinet drawer, saving to the root directory is equivalent to tossing a loose document into the drawer. However, for better organization, most office clerks place documents in folders, and most computer users organize their files into **folders** or **directories**. Users also can create folders within folders to form a hierarchy. A complete list of the disk drive plus the hierarchy of directories in which a file resides is its **path**. For example, the following is the complete path for a Windows file named Data.txt, which is saved on the C drive in a folder named Chapter.13 within a folder named Java:

```
C:\Java\Chapter.13\Data.txt
```

In the Windows operating system, the backslash (\ ) is the **path delimiter**—the character used to separate path components. In the Solaris (UNIX) operating system, a slash (/) is used as the delimiter.

When you work with stored files in an application, you typically perform the following tasks:

- Determining whether and where a path or file exists

- Opening a file

- Writing to a file

- Reading from a file

- Closing a file

- Deleting a file

Java provides built-in classes that contain methods to help you with these tasks.

TWO TRUTHS & A LIE

Understanding Computer Files

1. An advantage of modern computer systems is that both internal computer memory and disk storage are nonvolatile.

2. Data files contain facts and figures; program files store software instructions that might use data files.

3. A complete list of the disk drive plus the hierarchy of directories in which a file resides is the file's path.

The false statement is #1. Internal computer memory (RAM) is volatile storage; disk storage is nonvolatile.

Using the `Path` and `Files` Classes

You can use Java's **Path class** to create objects that contain information about files and directories, such as their locations, sizes, creation dates, and whether they even exist. You use the **Files class** to perform operations on files and directories, such as deleting them, determining their attributes, and creating input and output streams.

You can include the following statement in a Java program to use both the `Path` and `Files` classes:

```
import java.nio.file.*;
```

The *nio* in java.nio stands for *new input/output* because its classes are "new" in that they were developed long after the first Java versions. The `Path` and `Files` classes are new in Java 7; they replace the functionality of the `File` class used in older Java versions. If you search the Web for Java file-handling programs, you will find many that use the older `File` class.

Creating a Path

To create a `Path`, you first determine the default file system on the host computer by using a statement such as the following:

```
FileSystem fs = FileSystems.getDefault();
```

Notice that this statement creates a `FileSystem` object using the `getDefault()` method in the `FileSystems` class. The statement uses two different classes. The `FileSystem` class, without an ending *s*, is used to instantiate the object. `FileSystems`, with an ending *s*, is a class that contains **factory methods**, which assist in object creation.

After you create a `FileSystem` object, you can define a `Path` using the `getPath()` method with it:

```
Path path = fs.getPath("C:\\Java\\Chapter.13\\Data.txt");
```

Recall that the backslash is used as part of an escape sequence in Java. (For example, `'\n'` represents a newline character.) So, to enter a backslash as a path delimiter within a string, you must type two backslashes to indicate a single backslash. An alternative is to use the `FileSystem` method `getSeparator()`. This method returns the correct separator for the current operating system. For example, you can create a `Path` that is identical to the previous one using a statement such as the following:

```
Path filePath = fs.getPath("C:" + fs.getSeparator() + "Java" +
    fs.getSeparator() + "Chapter.13" + fs.getSeparator()  +
    "Data.txt");
```

Another way to create a `Path` is to use the `Paths` class (notice the name ends with *s*). The `Paths` class is a helper class that eliminates the need to create a `FileSystem` object. The `Paths` class `get()` method calls the `getPath()` method of the default file system without requiring you to instantiate a `FileSystem` object. You can create a `Path` object by using the following statement:

```
Path filePath = Paths.get("C:\\Java\\Chapter.13\\SampleFile.txt");
```

After the `Path` is created, you use its identifier (in this case, `filePath`) to refer to the file and perform operations on it. C:\Java\Chapter.13\SampleFile.txt is the full name of a stored file when the operating system refers to it, but the path is known as `filePath` within the application. The idea of a file having one name when referenced by the operating system and a different name within an application is similar to the way a student known as "Arthur" in school might be "Junior" at home. When an application declares a path and you want to use the application with a different file, you would change only the String passed to the instantiating method.

Every Path is either absolute or relative. An **absolute path** is a complete path; it does not need any other information to locate a file on a system. A **relative path** depends on other path information. A full path such as C:\Java\Chapter.13\SampleFile.txt is an absolute path. A simple path such as SampleFile.txt is relative. When you work with a path that contains only a filename, the file is assumed to be in the same folder as the program using it. Similarly, when you refer to a relative path such as Chapter.13\SampleFile.txt (without the drive letter or the top-level Java folder), the Chapter.13 folder is assumed to be a subfolder of the current directory, and SampleFile.txt is assumed to be within the folder.

For Microsoft Windows platforms, the prefix of an absolute pathname that contains a disk-drive specifier consists of the drive letter followed by a colon. For UNIX platforms, the prefix of an absolute pathname is always a forward slash.

Retrieving Information About a Path

Table 13-1 summarizes several useful Path methods. As you have learned with other classes, the toString() method is overridden from the Object class; it returns a String representation of the Path. Basically, this is the list of path elements separated by copies of the default separator for the operating system. The getFileName() method returns the last element in a list of pathnames; frequently this is a filename, but it might be a folder name.

Method	Description
String toString()	Returns the String representation of the Path, eliminating double backslashes
Path getFileName()	Returns the file or directory denoted by this Path; this is the last item in the sequence of name elements
int getNameCount()	Returns the number of name elements in the Path
Path getName(int)	Returns the name in the position of the Path specified by the integer parameter

Table 13-1   Selected Path class methods

A Path's elements are accessed using an index. The top-level element in the directory structure is located at index 0; the lowest element in the structure is accessed by the getName() method and has an index that is one less than the number of items on the list. You can use the getNameCount() method to retrieve the number of names in the list and the getName(int) method to retrieve the name in the position specified by the argument.

Figure 13-1 shows a demonstration program that creates a Path and uses some of the methods in Table 13-1. Figure 13-2 shows the output.

```
import java.nio.file.*;
public class PathDemo
{
    public static void main(String[] args)
    {
        Path filePath =
            Paths.get("C:\\Java\\Chapter.13\\Data.txt");
        int count = filePath.getNameCount();
        System.out.println("Path is " + filePath.toString());
        System.out.println("File name is " + filePath.getFileName());
        System.out.println("There are " + count +
            " elements in the file path");
        for(int x = 0; x < count; ++x)
          System.out.println("Element " + x + " is " +
              filePath.getName(x));
    }
}
```

Figure 13-1   The PathDemo class

Figure 13-2   Output of the PathDemo application

Converting a Relative Path to an Absolute One

The toAbsolutePath() method converts a relative path to an absolute path. For example, Figure 13-3 shows a program that asks a user for a filename and converts it to an absolute path, if necessary.

```
import java.util.Scanner;
import java.nio.file.*;
public class PathDemo2
{
    public static void main(String[] args)
    {
        String name;
        Scanner keyboard = new Scanner(System.in);
        System.out.print("Enter a file name >> ");
        name = keyboard.nextLine();
        Path inputPath = Paths.get(name);
        Path fullPath = inputPath.toAbsolutePath();
        System.out.println("Full path is " + fullPath.toString());
    }
}
```

Figure 13-3   The PathDemo2 class

When the PathDemo2 program executes, the entered filename might represent only a relative path. If the input represents an absolute Path, the program does not modify the input, but if the input represents a relative Path, this program then creates an absolute path by assigning the file to the current directory. Figure 13-4 shows a typical program execution.

Figure 13-4   Output of the PathDemo2 program

Checking File Accessibility

To verify that a file exists and that the program can access it as needed, you can use the checkAccess() method. The following import statement allows you to access constants that can be used as arguments to the method:

```
import static java.nio.file.AccessMode.*;
```

Assuming that you have declared a Path named filePath, the syntax you use with checkAccess() is as follows:

```
filePath.getFileSystem().provider().checkAccess();
```

You can use any of the following as arguments to the checkAccess() method:

- No argument—Checks that the file exists; as an alternative, you can substitute the Files.exists() method and pass it a Path argument.

- READ—Checks that the file exists and that the program has permission to read the file

- WRITE—Checks that the file exists and that the program has permission to write to the file

- EXECUTE—Checks that the file exists and that the program has permission to execute the file

Java's **static import feature** takes effect when you place the keyword static between import and the name of the package being imported. This feature allows you to use static constants without their class name. For example, if you remove static from the import statement for java.nio.file.AccessMode, you must refer to the READ constant by its full name as AccessMode.READ; when you use static, you can refer to it just as READ.

You can use multiple arguments to the checkAccess() method, separated by commas. If the file cannot be accessed as indicated in the method call, an IOException is thrown. (Notice in Figure 13-5 that the java.io.IOException package must be imported because an IOException might be instantiated and thrown.) Figure 13-5 shows an application that declares a Path and checks whether the file can both be read and executed. Figure 13-6 shows the output.

```java
import java.nio.file.*;
import static java.nio.file.AccessMode.*;
import java.io.IOException;
public class PathDemo3
{
    public static void main(String[] args)
    {
        Path filePath =
            Paths.get("C:\\Java\\Chapter.13\\Data.txt");
        System.out.println("Path is " + filePath.toString());
        try
        {
            filePath.getFileSystem().provider().checkAccess(filePath, READ, EXECUTE);
            System.out.println("File can be read and executed");
        }
        catch(IOException e)
        {
            System.out.println
                ("File cannot be used for this application");
        }
    }
}
```

Figure 13-5 The PathDemo3 class

Figure 13-6   Output of the PathDemo3 application

 A program might find a file usable, but then the file might become unusable before it is actually used in a later statement. This type of program bug is called a **TOCTTOU bug** (pronounced *tock too*)—it happens when changes occur from Time Of Check To Time Of Use.

Deleting a Path

The Files class delete() method accepts a Path parameter and deletes the last element (file or directory) in a path or throws an exception if the deletion fails. For example:

- If you try to delete a file that does not exist, a NoSuchFileException is thrown.

- A directory cannot be deleted unless it is empty. If you attempt to delete a directory that contains files, a DirectoryNotEmptyException is thrown.

- If you try to delete a file but you don't have permission, a SecurityException is thrown.

- Other input/output errors cause an IOException.

Figure 13-7 shows a program that displays an appropriate message in each of the preceding scenarios after attempting to delete a file.

```java
import java.nio.file.*;
import java.io.IOException;
public class PathDemo4
{
    public static void main(String[] args)
    {
        Path filePath =
            Paths.get("C:\\Java\\Chapter.13\\Data.txt");
        try
        {
            Files.delete(filePath)
            System.out.println("File or directory is deleted");
        }
```

Figure 13-7   The PathDemo4 class *(continues)*

(continued)

```
        catch (NoSuchFileException e)
        {
           System.out.println("No such file or directory");
        }
        catch (DirectoryNotEmptyException e)
        {
           System.out.println("Directory is not empty");
        }
        catch (SecurityException e)
        {
           System.out.println("No permission to delete");
        }
        catch (IOException e)
        {
           System.out.println("IO exception");
        }
     }
  }
```

Figure 13-7   The `PathDemo4` class

The `Files` class `deleteIfExists()` method also can be used to delete a file, but if the file does not exist, no exception is thrown.

Determining File Attributes

You can use the `readAttributes()` method of the `Files` class to retrieve useful information about a file. The method takes two arguments—a `Path` object and `BasicFileAttributes.class`—and returns an instance of the `BasicFileAttributes` class. You might create an instance with a statement such as the following:

```
BasicFileAttributes attr =
   Files.readAttributes(filePath, BasicFileAttributes.class);
```

After you have created a `BasicFileAttributes` object, you can use a number of methods for retrieving information about a file. For example, the `size()` method returns the size of a file in bytes. Methods such as `creationTime()` and `lastModifiedTime()` return important file times. Figure 13-8 contains a program that uses these methods.

```
import java.nio.file.*;
import java.nio.file.attribute.*;
import java.io.IOException;
public class PathDemo5
{
    public static void main(String[] args)
    {
        Path filePath =
            Paths.get("C:\\Java\\Chapter.13\\Data.txt");
        try
        {
            BasicFileAttributes attr =
                Files.readAttributes(filePath, BasicFileAttributes.class);
            System.out.println("Creation time " + attr.creationTime());
            System.out.println("Last modified time " +
                attr.lastModifiedTime());
            System.out.println("Size " + attr.size());
        }
        catch(IOException e)
        {
            System.out.println("IO Exception");
        }
    }
}
```

Figure 13-8 The PathDemo5 class

The time methods in the PathDemo5 program each return a FileTime object that is converted to a String in the println() method calls. FileTime objects are represented in the following format:

yyyy-mm-ddThh:mm:ss

In a FileTime object, the four-digit year is followed by the two-digit month and two-digit day. Following a T for *Time*, the hour, minute, and seconds (including fractions of a second) are separated by colons. You can see from the output in Figure 13-9 that the file was created in August 2010 and last modified in March 2012.

Figure 13-9 Output of the PathDemo5 program

Frequently, you don't care about a file's exact `FileTime` value, but you are interested in comparing two files. You can use the `compareTo()` method to determine the time relationships between files. For example, Figure 13-10 shows how you might compare the creation times of two files. As shown in the shaded statement, the `compareTo()` method returns a value of less than 0 if the first `FileTime` comes before the argument's `FileTime`. The method returns a value of greater than 0 if the first `FileTime` is later than the argument's, and it returns 0 if the `FileTime` values are the same.

```java
import java.nio.file.*;
import java.nio.file.attribute.*;
import java.io.IOException;
public class PathDemo6
{
    public static void main(String[] args)
    {
        Path file1 =
            Paths.get("C:\\Java\\Chapter.13\\Data.txt");
        Path file2 =
            Paths.get("C:\\Java\\Chapter.13\\Data2.txt");
        try
        {
            BasicFileAttributes attr1 =
                Files.readAttributes(file1, BasicFileAttributes.class);
            BasicFileAttributes attr2 =
                Files.readAttributes(file2, BasicFileAttributes.class);
            FileTime time1 = attr1.creationTime();
            FileTime time2 = attr2.creationTime();
            System.out.println("file1's creation time is: " + time1);
            System.out.println("file2's creation time is: " + time2);
            if(time1.compareTo(time2) < 0)
                System.out.println("file1 was created before file2");
            else
                if(time1.compareTo(time2) > 0)
                    System.out.println("file1 was created after file2");
                else
                    System.out.println
                        ("file1 and file2 were created at the same time");
        }
        catch(IOException e)
        {
            System.out.println("IO Exception");
        }
    }
}
```

Figure 13-10   The `PathDemo6` class

Figure 13-11 shows the output of the application in Figure 13-10. The file named file1 was created in August 2010, and file2 was created in October 2011, so the program correctly determines that file1 was created first.

```
C:\Java>java PathDemo6
file1's creation time is: 2010-08-17T22:55:51.33567Z
file2's creation time is: 2011-10-25T20:30:48.421483Z
file1 was created before file2

C:\Java>_
```

Figure 13-11 Output of the PathDemo6 program

Besides BasicFileAttributes, Java supports specialized classes for DOS file attributes used on DOS systems and POSIX file attributes used on systems such as UNIX. For example, DOS files might be *hidden* or *read only* and UNIX files might have a group owner. For more details on specialized file attributes, visit the Java Web site.

Watch the video *Paths and Attributes*.

TWO TRUTHS & A LIE

Using the Path and Files Classes

1. Java's Path class is used to create objects that contain information to specify the location of files or directories.

2. A relative path is a complete path; it does not need any other information to locate a file on a system.

3. You can use the readAttributes() method of the Files class to retrieve information about a file, such as its size and when it was created.

The false statement is #2. A relative path depends on other path information. An absolute path is a complete path; it does not need any other information to locate a file on a system.

File Organization, Streams, and Buffers

Most businesses generate and use large quantities of data every day. You can store data in variables within a program, but such storage is temporary. When the application ends, the variables no longer exist and the data values are lost. Variables are stored in the computer's main or primary memory (RAM). When you need to retain data for any significant amount of time, you must save the data on a permanent, secondary storage device, such as a disk.

Businesses organize data in a hierarchy, as shown in Figure 13-12. The smallest useful piece of data to most users is the character. A **character** can be any letter, number, or other special symbol (such as a punctuation mark) that makes up data. Characters are made up of bits (the zeros and ones that represent computer circuitry), but people who use data typically do not care whether the internal representation for an *A* is 01000001 or 10111110. Rather, they are concerned with the meaning of *A*—for example, it might represent a grade in a course, a person's initial, or a company code. In computer terminology, a character can be any group of bits, and it does not necessarily represent a letter or number; for example, some "characters" produce a sound or control the display. Also, characters are not necessarily created with a single keystroke; for example, escape sequences are used to create the '\n' character, which starts a new line, and '\\', which represents a single backslash. Sometimes, you can think of a character as a unit of information instead of data with a particular appearance. For example, the mathematical character pi (π) and the Greek letter pi look the same, but have two different Unicode values.

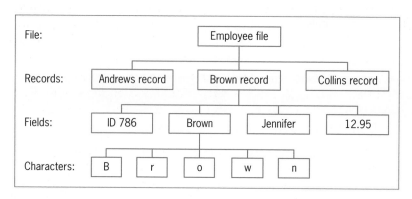

Figure 13-12   Data hierarchy

When businesses use data, they group characters into fields. A **field** is a group of characters that has some meaning. For example, the characters *T*, *o*, and *m* might represent your first name. Other data fields might represent items such as last name, Social Security number, zip code, and salary.

Fields are grouped together to form records. A **record** is a collection of fields that contain data about an entity. For example, a person's first and last names, Social Security number, zip code, and salary represent that person's record. When programming in Java, you have created many classes, such as an Employee class or a Student class. You can think of the data typically stored in each of these classes as a record. These classes contain individual variables that represent data fields. A business's data records usually represent a person, item, sales transaction, or some other concrete object or event.

Records are grouped to create files. Data files consist of related records, such as a company's personnel file that contains one record for each company employee. Some files have only a few records; perhaps your professor maintains a file for your class with 25 records—one record for each student. Other files contain thousands or even millions of records. For example, a large insurance company maintains a file of policyholders, and a mail-order catalog company maintains a file of available items. A data file can be used as a **sequential access file** when each record is accessed one after another in the order in which it was stored. Most frequently, each record is stored in order based on the value in some field; for example, employees might be stored in Social Security number order, or inventory items might be stored in item number order. When records are not used in sequence, the file is used as a random access file. You will learn more about random access files later in this chapter.

When records are stored in a data file, their fields can be organized one to a line, or a character can be used to separate them. A file of **comma-separated values (CSV)** is one in which each value in a record is separated from the next by a comma; CSV is a widely used format for files used in all sorts of applications, including databases and spreadsheets. Later in this chapter, you will see examples of CSV files.

Before an application can use a data file, it must open the file. A Java application **opens a file** by creating an object and associating a stream of bytes with it. Similarly, when you finish using a file, the program should **close the file**—that is, make it no longer available to your application. If you fail to close an input file—a file from which you are reading data—there usually are no serious consequences; the data still exists in the file. However, if you fail to close an output file—a file to which you are writing data—the data might become inaccessible. You should always close every file you open, and usually you should close the file as soon as you no longer need it. When you leave a file open for no reason, you use computer resources, and your computer's performance suffers. Also, particularly within a network, another program might be waiting to use the file.

Whereas people view a file as a series of records, with each record containing data fields, Java does not automatically attribute such meaning to a file's contents. Instead, Java simply views a file as a series of bytes. When you perform an input operation in an application, you can picture bytes flowing into your program from an input device through a **stream**, which functions as a pipeline or channel. When you perform output, some bytes flow out of your application through another stream to an output device, as shown in Figure 13-13. A stream is an object, and like all objects, streams have data and methods. The methods allow you to perform actions such as opening, closing, reading, and writing.

Figure 13-13   File streams

Most streams flow in only one direction; each stream is either an input or output stream. (Random access files use streams that flow in two directions. You will use a random access file later in this chapter.) You might open several streams at once within an application. For example, an application that reads a data disk and separates valid records from invalid ones might require three streams. The data arrives via an input stream; one output stream writes some records to a file of valid records, and another output stream writes other records to a file of invalid records.

Input and output operations are usually the slowest in any computerized system because of limitations imposed by the hardware. For that reason, professional programs often employ buffers. A **buffer** is a memory location where bytes are held after they are logically output but before they are sent to the output device. Using a buffer to accumulate input or output before issuing the actual IO command improves program performance. When you use an output buffer, you sometimes flush it before closing it. **Flushing** clears any bytes that have been sent to a buffer for output but have not yet been output to a hardware device.

 Watch the video *File Organization, Streams, and Buffers*.

TWO TRUTHS & A LIE

File Organization, Streams, and Buffers

1. A field is a group of characters that has some meaning; a record is a collection of fields.

2. A data file is used as a sequential access file when the first field for each record is stored first in a file, the second field for each record is stored next, and so on.

3. Java views files as a series of bytes that flow into and out of your applications through a stream.

The false statement is #2. A data file is used as a sequential access file when each record is stored in order based on the value in some field.

Using Java's IO Classes

Figure 13-14 shows a partial hierarchical relationship of some of the classes Java uses for input and output (IO) operations; it shows that `InputStream`, `OutputStream`, and `Reader` are subclasses of the `Object` class. All three of these classes are abstract. As you learned in Chapter 11, abstract classes contain methods that must be overridden in their child classes. The figure also shows the major IO child classes that you will study in this chapter. The capabilities of these classes are summarized in Table 13-2.

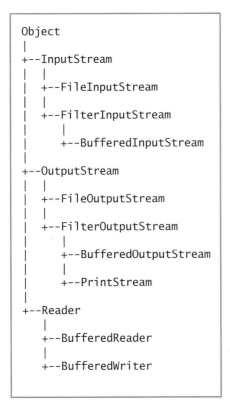

```
Object
|
+--InputStream
|   |
|   +--FileInputStream
|   |
|   +--FilterInputStream
|       |
|       +--BufferedInputStream
|
+--OutputStream
|   |
|   +--FileOutputStream
|   |
|   +--FilterOutputStream
|       |
|       +--BufferedOutputStream
|       |
|       +--PrintStream
|
+--Reader
    |
    +--BufferedReader
    |
    +--BufferedWriter
```

Figure 13-14 Relationship of selected IO classes

Class	Description
InputStream	Abstract class that contains methods for performing input
FileInputStream	Child of InputStream that provides the capability to read from disk files
BufferedInputStream	Child of FilterInputStream, which is a child of InputStream; BufferedInputStream handles input from a system's standard (or default) input device, usually the keyboard
OutputStream	Abstract class that contains methods for performing output
FileOutputStream	Child of OutputStream that allows you to write to disk files
BufferedOutputStream	Child of FilterOutputStream, which is a child of OutputStream; BufferedOutputStream handles input from a system's standard (or default) output device, usually the monitor
PrintStream	Child of FilterOutputStream, which is a child of OutputStream; System.out is a PrintStream object

Table 13-2 Description of selected classes used for input and output *(continues)*

(continued)

Class	Description
Reader	Abstract class for reading character streams; the only methods that a subclass must implement are read(char[], int, int) and close()
BufferedReader	Reads text from a character-input stream, buffering characters to provide for efficient reading of characters, arrays, and lines
BufferedWriter	Writes text to a character-output stream, buffering characters to provide for the efficient writing of characters, arrays, and lines

Table 13-2   Description of selected classes used for input and output

As its name implies, the OutputStream class can be used to produce output. Table 13-3 shows some of the class's common methods. You can use OutputStream to write all or part of an array of bytes. When you finish using an OutputStream, you usually want to flush and close it.

OutputStream Method	Description
void close()	Closes the output stream and releases any system resources associated with the stream
void flush()	Flushes the output stream; if any bytes are buffered, they will be written
void write(byte[] b)	Writes all the bytes to the output stream from the specified byte array
void write(byte[] b, int off, int len)	Writes bytes to the output stream from the specified byte array starting at offset position off for a length of len characters

Table 13-3   Selected OutputStream methods

Java's System class contains a PrintStream object named System.out; you have used this object extensively in the book, along with its print() and println() methods. Besides System.out, the System class defines a PrintStream object named System.err. The output from System.err and System.out can go to the same device; in fact, System.err and System.out are both directed by default to the command line on the monitor. The difference is that System.err is usually reserved for error messages, and System.out is reserved for valid output. You can direct either System.err or System.out to a new location, such as a disk file or printer. For example, you might want to keep a hard copy (printed) log of the error messages generated by a program but direct the standard output to a disk file.

Although you usually have no need to do so, you can create your own OutputStream object and assign System.out to it. Figure 13-15 shows how this works. The application declares a String of letter grades allowed in a course. Then, the getBytes() method converts the String to an array of bytes. An OutputStream object is declared, and System.out is assigned to the OutputStream reference in a try block. The write() method accepts the byte array and sends it to the output device, and then the output stream is flushed and closed. Figure 13-16 shows the execution.

```
import java.io.*;
public class ScreenOut
{
    public static void main(String[] args)
    {
        String s = "ABCDF";
        byte[] data = s.getBytes();
        OutputStream output = null;
        try
        {
            output = System.out;
            output.write(data);
            output.flush();
            output.close();
        }
        catch(Exception e)
        {
            System.out.println("Message: " + e);
        }
    }
}
```

Figure 13-15   The ScreenOut class

Figure 13-16   Output of the ScreenOut program

Writing to a File

The output in Figure 13-16 is not very impressive. Before you knew about streams, you wrote applications that displayed a string on the monitor by using the automatically created System.out object, so the application in Figure 13-15 might seem to contain a lot of unnecessary work at first. However, other output devices can be assigned to OutputStream references, allowing your applications to save data to them.

Instead of assigning the standard output device to OutputStream, you can assign a file. To accomplish this, you can construct a BufferedOutputStream object and assign it to the OutputStream. If you want to change an application's output device, you don't have to modify the application except to assign a new object to the OutputStream; the rest of the logic remains the same. Java lets you assign a file to a Stream object so that screen output and file output work in exactly the same manner.

You can create a writeable file by using the `Files` class `newOutputStream()` method. You pass a `Path` and a `StandardOpenOption` argument to this method. The method creates a file if it does not already exist, opens the file for writing, and returns an `OutputStream` that can be used to write bytes to the file. Table 13-4 shows the `StandardOpenOption` arguments you can use as the second argument to the `newOutputStream()` method. If you do not specify any options and the file does not exist, a new file is created. If the file exists, it is truncated. In other words, specifying no option is the same as specifying both `CREATE` and `TRUNCATE_EXISTING`.

StandardOpenOption	Description
WRITE	Opens the file for writing
APPEND	Appends new data to the end of the file; use this option with WRITE or CREATE
TRUNCATE_EXISTING	Truncates the existing file to 0 bytes so the file contents are replaced; use this option with the WRITE option
CREATE_NEW	Creates a new file only if it does not exist; throws an exception if the file already exists
CREATE	Opens the file if it exists or creates a new file if it does not
DELETE_ON_CLOSE	Deletes the file when the stream is closed; used most often for temporary files that exist only for the duration of the program

Table 13-4   Selected `StandardOpenOption` constants

Figure 13-17 shows an application that writes a `String` of bytes to a file. The only differences from the preceding `ScreenOut` class are shaded in the figure and summarized here:

- Additional `import` statements are used.

- The class name is changed.

- A `Path` is declared for a Grades.txt file.

- Instead of assigning `System.out` to the `OutputStream` reference, a `BufferedOutputStream` object is assigned.

```
import java.nio.file.*;
import java.io.*;
import static java.nio.file.StandardOpenOption.*;

public class FileOut
{
    public static void main(String[] args)
    {
        Path file =
            Paths.get("C:\\Java\\Chapter.13\\Grades.txt");
        String s = "ABCDF";
```

Figure 13-17   The `FileOut` class *(continues)*

(continued)

```
        byte[] data = s.getBytes();
        OutputStream output = null;
        try
        {
            output = new
                BufferedOutputStream(Files.newOutputStream(file, CREATE));
            output.write(data);
            output.flush();
            output.close();
        }
        catch(Exception e)
        {
            System.out.println("Message: " + e);
        }
    }
}
```

Figure 13-17   The FileOut class

When the FileOut program executes, no output appears on the monitor, but a file is created. Figure 13-18 shows the file when it is opened in Notepad.

Figure 13-18   Contents of the Grades.txt file created by the FileOut program

Reading from a File

You use an InputStream like you use an OutputStream. If you want, you can create an InputStream, assign System.in to it, and use the class's read() method with the created object to retrieve keyboard input. Usually, however, it is more efficient to use the Scanner class for keyboard input and to use the InputStream class to input data that has been stored in a file.

To open a file for reading, you can use the Files class newInputStream() method. This method accepts a Path parameter and returns a stream that can read bytes from a file. Figure 13-19 shows a ReadFile class that reads from the Grades.txt file created earlier. The Path is declared, an InputStream is declared using the Path, and, in the first shaded statement in the figure, a stream is assigned to the InputStream reference.

```
import java.nio.file.*;
import java.io.*;
public class ReadFile
{
    public static void main(String[] args)
    {
        Path file = Paths.get("C:\\Java\\Chapter.13\\Grades.txt");
        InputStream input = null;
        try
        {
            input = Files.newInputStream(file);
            BufferedReader reader = new
              BufferedReader(new InputStreamReader(input));
            String s = null;
            s = reader.readLine();
            System.out.println(s);
            input.close();
        }
        catch (IOException e)
        {
            System.out.println(e);
        }
    }
}
```

Figure 13-19   The ReadFile class

If you needed to read multiple lines from the file in the program in Figure 13-19, you could use a loop such as the following:

```
while(s = reader.readLine() != null)
    System.out.println(s);
```

This loop continuously reads and displays lines from the file until the readLine() method returns null, indicating that no more data is available.

In the second shaded statement in the ReadFile class, a BufferedReader is declared. A BufferedReader reads a line of text from a character-input stream, buffering characters so that reading is more efficient. Figure 13-20 shows the ReadFile program's execution. The readLine() method gets the single line of text from the Grades.txt file, and then the line is displayed.

Figure 13-20   Execution of the ReadFile program

When you use the `BufferedReader` class, you must import the `java.io` package into your program. Table 13-5 shows some useful `BufferedReader` methods.

BufferedReader Method	Description
close()	Closes the stream and any resources associated with it
read()	Reads a single character
read(char[] buffer, int off, int len)	Reads characters into a portion of an array from position off for len characters
readLine()	Reads a line of text
skip(long n)	Skips the specified number of characters

Table 13-5   Selected `BufferedReader` methods

TWO TRUTHS & A LIE

Using Java's IO Classes

1. Java's `InputStream`, `OutputStream`, and `Reader` classes are used for handling input and output.

2. You can create your own `OutputStream` object, assign `System.out` to it, and use it for writing output to the screen, or you can use the `Files` class `newOutputStream()` method to create a file and open it for writing.

3. To open a file for reading, you can use the `newOutputStream()` method to get a stream that can read bytes from a file.

The false statement is #3. To open a file for reading, you can use the `newInputStream()` method to get a stream that can read bytes from a file.

Creating and Using Sequential Data Files

Frequently, you want to save more than a single `String` to a file. For example, you might have a data file of personnel records that includes an ID number, name, and pay rate for each employee in your organization. Figure 13-21 shows a program that reads employee ID numbers, names, and pay rates from the keyboard and sends them to a comma-separated file.

```java
import java.nio.file.*;
import java.io.*;
import static java.nio.file.StandardOpenOption.*;
import java.util.Scanner;
public class WriteEmployeeFile
{
    public static void main(String[] args)
    {
        Scanner input = new Scanner(System.in);
        Path file =
            Paths.get("C:\\Java\\Chapter.13\\Employees.txt");
        String s = "";
        String delimiter = ",";
        int id;
        String name;
        double payRate;
        final int QUIT = 999;
        try
        {
            OutputStream output = new
                BufferedOutputStream(Files.newOutputStream(file, CREATE));
            BufferedWriter writer = new
                BufferedWriter(new OutputStreamWriter(output));
            System.out.print("Enter employee ID number >> ");
            id = input.nextInt();
            while(id != QUIT)
            {
                System.out.print("Enter name for employee #" +
                    id + " >> ");
                input.nextLine();
                name = input.nextLine();
                System.out.print("Enter pay rate >> ");
                payRate = input.nextDouble();
                s = id + delimiter + name + delimiter + payRate;
                writer.write(s, 0, s.length());
                writer.newLine();
                System.out.print("Enter next ID number or " +
                    QUIT + " to quit >> ");
                id = input.nextInt();
            }
            writer.close();
        }
        catch(Exception e)
        {
            System.out.println("Message: " + e);
        }
    }
}
```

Figure 13-21 The WriteEmployeeFile class

In Figure 13-21, notice the extra nextLine() call after the employee's ID number is entered. Recall from Chapter 2 that this extra call is necessary to consume the newline character that remains in the input buffer after the ID number is accepted.

The first shaded statement in the WriteEmployeeFile program creates a BufferedWriter named writer. The BufferedWriter class is the counterpart to BufferedReader. It writes text to an output stream, buffering the characters. The class has three overloaded write() methods that provide for efficient writing of characters, arrays, and strings, respectively. Table 13-6 contains all the methods defined in the BufferedWriter class.

BufferedWriter Method	Description
close()	Closes the stream, flushing it first
flush()	Flushes the stream
newline()	Writes a line separator
write(String s, int off, int len)	Writes a String from position off for length len
write(char[] array, int off, int len)	Writes a character array from position off for length len
write(int c)	Writes a single character

Table 13-6 BufferedWriter methods

In the WriteEmployeeFile program, Strings of employee data are constructed within a loop that executes while the user does not enter the QUIT value. When a String is complete—that is, when it contains an ID number, name, and pay rate separated with commas—the String is sent to writer in the second shaded statement in the class. The write() method accepts the String from position 0 for its entire length.

After the String is written, the system's newline character is also written. Although a data file would not require a newline character after each record (each new record could be separated with a comma or any other unique character that was not needed as part of the data), placing each record on a new line makes the output file easier for a person to read and interpret. Because not all platforms use '\n' to separate lines, the BufferedWriter class contains a newLine() method that uses the current platform's line separator. Alternatively, you could write the value of System.getProperty("line.separator "). This method call returns the default line separator for a system; the same separator is supplied either way because the newLine() method actually calls the System.getProperty() method for you.

Any of the input or output methods in the WriteEmployeeFile program might throw an exception, so all the relevant code in the class is placed in a try block. Figure 13-22 shows a typical program execution, and Figure 13-23 shows the output file when it is opened in Notepad.

Figure 13-22   Typical execution of the WriteEmployeeFile program

Figure 13-23   Output file following the program execution in Figure 13-22

Figure 13-24 shows a program that reads the Employees.txt file created by the
WriteEmployeeFile program. The program declares an InputStream for the file, then creates a
BufferedReader using the InputStream. The first line is read into a String; as long as the
readLine() method does not return null, the String is displayed and a new line is read.

```java
import java.nio.file.*;
import java.io.*;
public class ReadEmployeeFile
{
    public static void main(String[] args)
    {
        Path file =
            Paths.get("C:\\Java\\Chapter.13\\Employees.txt");
        String s = "";
        try
```

Figure 13-24   The ReadEmployeeFile class (continues)

(continued)

```
        {
            InputStream input = new
                BufferedInputStream(Files.newInputStream(file));
            BufferedReader reader = new
                BufferedReader(new InputStreamReader(input));
            s = reader.readLine();
            while(s != null)
            {
                System.out.println(s);
                s = reader.readLine();
            }
            reader.close();
        }
        catch(Exception e)
        {
            System.out.println("Message: " + e);
        }
    }
}
```

Figure 13-24   The ReadEmployeeFile class

Figure 13-25 shows the output of the ReadEmployeeFile program when it uses the file that was created during the execution in Figure 13-22. Each comma-separated String is displayed on its own line.

Figure 13-25   Output of the ReadEmployeeFile program

Many applications would not want to use the file data only as a String like the ReadEmployeeFile program does. Figure 13-26 shows a more useful program in which the retrieved file Strings are split into usable fields. The String class split() method accepts an argument that identifies the field delimiter (in this case, a comma) and returns an array of Strings. Each array element holds one field. Then methods such as parseInt() and parseDouble() can be used to reformat the split Strings into their respective data types.

```
import java.nio.file.*;
import java.io.*;
public class ReadEmployeeFile2
{
    public static void main(String[] args)
    {
        Path file =
            Paths.get("C:\\Java\\Chapter.13\\Employees.txt");
        String[] array = new String[3];
        String s = "";
        String delimiter = ",";
        int id;
        String name;
        double payRate;
        double gross;
        final double HRS_IN_WEEK = 40;
        double total = 0;
        try
        {
            InputStream input = new
                BufferedInputStream(Files.newInputStream(file));
            BufferedReader reader = new
                BufferedReader(new InputStreamReader(input));
            System.out.println();
            s = reader.readLine();
            while(s != null)
            {
                array = s.split(delimiter);
                id = Integer.parseInt(array[0]);
                name = array[1];
                payRate = Double.parseDouble(array[2]);
                gross = payRate * HRS_IN_WEEK;
                System.out.println("ID#" + id + "   " + name +
                    "   $" + payRate + "   $" + gross);
                total += gross;
                s = reader.readLine();
            }
            reader.close();
        }
        catch(Exception e)
        {
            System.out.println("Message: " + e);
        }
        System.out.println("  Total gross payroll is $" + total);
    }
}
```

Figure 13-26   The ReadEmployeeFile2 class

As each record is read and split in the `ReadEmployeeFile2` class, its pay rate field is used to calculate gross pay for the employee based on a 40-hour workweek. Then the gross is accumulated to produce a total gross payroll that is displayed after all the data has been processed. Figure 13-27 shows the program's execution.

```
Command Prompt

C:\Java>java ReadEmployeeFile2

ID#145   Harris    $12.55    $502.0
ID#289   Gorman    $15.65    $626.0
ID#364   Parker    $19.95    $798.0
 Total gross payroll is $1926.0

C:\Java>
```

Figure 13-27   Execution of the `ReadEmployeeFile2` program

TWO TRUTHS & A LIE

Creating and Using Sequential Data Files

1. A `BufferedWriter` writes text to an output stream, buffering the characters.

2. A data file does not require a newline character after each record, but adding a newline makes the output file easier for a person to read and interpret.

3. The `String` class `split()` method converts parts of a `String` to `int`s, `double`s, and other data types.

The false statement is #3. The `String` class `split()` method accepts an argument that identifies a field delimiter and returns an array of `String`s in which each array element holds one field. Then you can use methods such as `parseInt()` and `parseDouble()` to convert the split `String`s to other data types.

Learning About Random Access Files

The file examples in the first part of this chapter have been sequential access files, which means that you work with the records in sequential order from beginning to end. For example, in the `ReadEmployeeFile` programs, if you write an employee record with an ID number of 145, and then write a second record with an ID number of 289, the records remain in the original data-entry order when you retrieve them. Businesses store data in sequential order when they use the records for **batch processing**, which involves performing the same tasks with many records, one after the other. For example, when a company produces customer bills, the records for the billing period are gathered in a batch and the bills are calculated and printed in sequence. It really doesn't matter whose bill is produced first because none are distributed to customers until all bills in a group have been printed and mailed.

Besides indicating a system that works with many records, the term *batch processing* can refer to a system in which you issue many operating-system commands as a group.

For many applications, sequential access is inefficient. These applications, known as **real-time** applications, require that a record be accessed immediately while a client is waiting.

A program in which the user makes direct requests is an **interactive program**. For example, if a customer telephones a department store with a question about a monthly bill, the customer service representative does not want to access every customer account in sequence. Suppose that the store's database contains tens of thousands of account records to read and that the customer record in question is near the end of the list. It would take too long to access the customer's record if all the records had to be read sequentially. Instead, customer service representatives require **random access files**—files in which records can be retrieved directly in any order. Random files are also called **direct access files** or **instant access files**.

You can use Java's FileChannel class to create your own random access files. A **file channel** object is an avenue for reading and writing a file. A file channel is **seekable**, meaning you can search for a specific file location and operations can start at any specified position. Table 13-7 describes some FileChannel methods.

FileChannel method	Description
FileChannel open(Path file, OpenOption... options)	Opens or creates a file, returning a file channel to access the file
long position()	Returns the channel's file position
FileChannel position(long newPosition)	Sets the channel's file position
int read(ByteBuffer buffer)	Reads a sequence of bytes from the channel into the buffer
long size()	Returns the size of the channel's file
int write(ByteBuffer buffer)	Writes a sequence of bytes to the channel from the buffer

Table 13-7 Selected FileChannel methods

Several methods in Table 13-7 use a ByteBuffer object. As its name describes, a ByteBuffer is simply a holding place for bytes waiting to be read or written. An array of bytes can be **wrapped**, or encompassed, into a ByteBuffer using the ByteBuffer wrap() method. Wrapping a byte array into a buffer causes changes made to the buffer to change the array as well, and causes changes made to the array to change the buffer. Creating a usable FileChannel for randomly writing data requires creating a ByteBuffer and several other steps:

- You can use the Files class newByteChannel() method to get a ByteChannel for a Path. The newByteChannel() method accepts Path and StandardOpenOption arguments that specify how the file will be opened.

- The ByteChannel returned by the newByteChannel() method can then be cast to a FileChannel using a statement similar to the following:

```
FileChannel fc = (FileChannel)Files.newByteChannel(file, READ, WRITE);
```

- You can create a byte array. For example, a byte array can be built from a String using the getBytes() method as follows:

```
String s = "XYZ";
byte[] data = s.getBytes();
```

- The byte array can be wrapped into a ByteBuffer as follows:

```
ByteBuffer out = ByteBuffer.wrap(data);
```

- Then the filled ByteBuffer can be written to the declared FileChannel with a statement such as the following:

```
fc.write(out);
```

- You can test whether a ByteBuffer's contents have been used up by checking the hasRemaining() method.

- After you have written the contents of a ByteBuffer, you can write the same ByteBuffer contents again by using the rewind() method to reposition the ByteBuffer to the beginning of the buffer.

Figure 13-28 employs all these steps to declare a file and write some bytes in it randomly at positions 0, 22, and 12, in that order.

```
import java.nio.file.*;
import java.io.*;
import java.nio.channels.FileChannel;
import java.nio.ByteBuffer;
import static java.nio.file.StandardOpenOption.*;
public class RandomAccessTest
{
    public static void main(String[] args)
    {
        Path file =
            Paths.get("C:\\Java\\Chapter.13\\Numbers.txt");
        String s = "XYZ";
        byte[] data = s.getBytes();
        ByteBuffer out = ByteBuffer.wrap(data);
        FileChannel fc = null;
        try
```

Figure 13-28   The RandomAccessTest class (continues)

(continued)

```
    {
        fc = (FileChannel)Files.newByteChannel(file, READ, WRITE);
        fc.position(0);
        while(out.hasRemaining())
            fc.write(out);
        out.rewind();
        fc.position(22);
        while(out.hasRemaining())
            fc.write(out);
        out.rewind();
        fc.position(12);
        while(out.hasRemaining())
            fc.write(out);
        fc.close();
    }
    catch (Exception e)
    {
        System.out.println("Error message: " + e);
    }
  }
}
```

Figure 13-28   The RandomAccessTest class

Figure 13-29 shows the Numbers.txt text file before and after executing the RandomAccessTest program in Figure 13-28. The String "XYZ" has been written at positions 0, 8, and 12.

Figure 13-29   The Numbers.txt file before and after execution of RandomAccessTest

---

TWO TRUTHS & A LIE

Learning About Random Access Files

1. Businesses store data in random order when they use the records for batch processing.

2. Real-time applications are interactive and require using random access data files.

3. A `FileChannel` object is a seekable channel for reading and writing a file.

The false statement is #1. Businesses store data in sequential order when they use the records for batch processing.

Writing Records to a Random Access Data File

Writing characters at random text file locations, as in the `RandomAccessTest` program, is of limited value. When you store records in a file, it is often more useful to be able to access the eighth or 12th record rather than the eighth or 12th byte. In such a case, you multiply each record's size by the position you want to access. For example, if you store records that are 50 bytes long, the first record is at position 0, the second record is at position 50, the third record is at position 100, and so on. In other words, you can access the *n*th record in a `FileChannel` named `fc` using the following statement:

```
fc.position((n - 1) * 50);
```

One approach to writing a random access file is to place records into the file based on a key field. A **key field** is the field in a record that makes the record unique from all others. For example, suppose you want to store employee ID numbers, last names, and pay rates in a random access file. In a file of employees, many records might have the same last name or pay rate, but each record has a unique employee ID number, so that field can act as the key field.

The first step in creating the random access employee file is to create a file that holds default records—for example, using zeroes for the ID numbers and pay rates and blanks for the names. For this example, assume that each employee ID number is three digits; in other words, you cannot have more than 1,000 employees because the ID number cannot surpass 999. Figure 13-30 contains a program that creates 1,000 such records.

```java
import java.nio.file.*;
import java.io.*;
import java.nio.ByteBuffer;
import static java.nio.file.StandardOpenOption.*;
public class CreateEmptyEmployeesFile
{
    public static void main(String[] args)
    {
        Path file =
            Paths.get("C:\\Java\\Chapter.13\\RandomEmployees.txt");
        String s = "000,         ,00.00" +
            System.getProperty("line.separator");
        byte[] data = s.getBytes();
        ByteBuffer buffer = ByteBuffer.wrap(data);
        final int NUMRECS = 1000;
        try
        {
            OutputStream output = new
                BufferedOutputStream(Files.newOutputStream(file, CREATE));
            BufferedWriter writer = new
                BufferedWriter(new OutputStreamWriter(output));
            for(int count = 0; count < NUMRECS; ++count)
                writer.write(s, 0, s.length());
            writer.close();
        }
        catch(Exception e)
        {
            System.out.println("Error message: " + e);
        }
    }
}
```

Figure 13-30   The CreateEmptyEmployeesFile class

In the first shaded statement in Figure 13-30, a String that represents a default record is declared. The three-digit employee number is set to zeros, the name consists of seven blanks, the pay rate is 00.00, and the String ends with the system's line separator value. A byte array is constructed from the String and wrapped into a buffer. Then a file is opened in CREATE mode and a BufferedWriter is established.

In the last shaded statement in Figure 13-30, a loop executes 1,000 times. Within the loop, the default employee string is passed to the BufferedWriter object's write() method. Figure 13-31 shows a few records from the created file when it is opened in Notepad.

Figure 13-31 The RandomEmployees.txt file created by the CreateEmptyEmployeesFile program

The default fields in the base random access file don't have to be zeros and blanks. For example, if you wanted 000 to be a legitimate employee ID number or you wanted blanks to represent a correct name, you could use different default values such as 999 and "XXXXXXX". The only requirement is that the default records be recognizable as such.

After you create the base default file, you can replace any of its records with data for an actual employee. You can locate the correct position for the new record by performing arithmetic with the record's key field.

For example, the application in Figure 13-32 creates a single employee record defined in the first shaded statement. The record is for employee 002 with a last name of Newmann and a pay rate of 12.25. In the second shaded statement, the length of this string is assigned to RECSIZE. (In this case, RECSIZE is 19, which includes one character for each character in the sample record string, including the delimiting commas, plus two bytes for the line separator value returned by the System.getProperty() method.) After the FileChannel is established, the record is written to the file at the position that begins at two times the record size. The value 2 is hard-coded in this demonstration program because the employee's ID number is 002.

```
import java.nio.file.*;
import java.io.*;
import java.nio.channels.FileChannel;
import java.nio.ByteBuffer;
import static java.nio.file.StandardOpenOption.*;
public class CreateOneRandomAccessRecord
{
    public static void main(String[] args)
    {
        Path file =
            Paths.get("C:\\Java\\Chapter.13\\RandomEmployees.txt");
        String s = "002,Newmann,12.25" +
            System.getProperty("line.separator");
```

Figure 13-32 The CreateOneRandomAccessRecord class *(continues)*

(continued)

```
        final int RECSIZE = s.length();
        byte[] data = s.getBytes();
        ByteBuffer buffer = ByteBuffer.wrap(data);
        FileChannel fc = null;
        try
        {
            fc = (FileChannel)Files.newByteChannel(file, READ, WRITE);
            fc.position(2 * RECSIZE);
            fc.write(buffer);
            fc.close();
        }
        catch (Exception e)
        {
            System.out.println("Error message: " + e);
        }
    }
}
```

Figure 13-32   The CreateOneRandomAccessRecord class

Figure 13-33 shows the RandomEmployees.txt file contents after the
CreateOneRandomAccessRecord program runs. The employee's data record is correctly
placed in the third position in the file. Later, if employees are added that have ID
numbers 000 and 001, they can be inserted as the first two records in the file.

Figure 13-33   The RandomEmployees.txt file after running the
CreateOneRandomAccessRecord program

A program that inserts one hard-coded employee record into a data file is not very
useful. The program in Figure 13-34 accepts any number of records as user input and
writes records to a file in a loop. As shown in the first shaded line in the figure, each
employee's data value is accepted from the keyboard as a String and converted to an
integer using the parseInt() method. Then, as shown in the second shaded statement,
the record's desired position is computed by multiplying the ID number value by the
record size.

```java
import java.nio.file.*;
import java.io.*;
import java.nio.channels.FileChannel;
import java.nio.ByteBuffer;
import static java.nio.file.StandardOpenOption.*;
import java.util.Scanner;
public class CreateEmployeesRandomFile
{
    public static void main(String[] args)
    {
        Scanner input = new Scanner(System.in);
        Path file =
            Paths.get("C:\\Java\\Chapter.13\\RandomEmployees.txt");
        String s = "000,        ,00.00" +
            System.getProperty("line.separator");
        final int RECSIZE = s.length();
        FileChannel fc = null;
        String delimiter = ",";
        String idString;
        int id;
        String name;
        String payRate;
        final String QUIT = "999";
        try
        {
            fc = (FileChannel)Files.newByteChannel(file, READ, WRITE);
            System.out.print("Enter employee ID number >> ");
            idString = input.nextLine();
            while(!(idString.equals(QUIT)))
            {
                id = Integer.parseInt(idString);
                System.out.print("Enter name for employee #" +
                    id + " >> ");
                name = input.nextLine();
                System.out.print("Enter pay rate >> ");
                payRate = input.nextLine();
                s = idString + delimiter + name + delimiter +
                    payRate + System.getProperty("line.separator");
                byte[] data = s.getBytes();
                ByteBuffer buffer = ByteBuffer.wrap(data);
                fc.position(id * RECSIZE);
                fc.write(buffer);
                System.out.print("Enter next ID number or " +
                    QUIT + " to quit >> ");
                idString = input.nextLine();
            }
            fc.close();
        }
        catch (Exception e)
        {
            System.out.println("Error message: " + e);
        }
    }
}
```

Figure 13-34   The CreateEmployeesRandomFile class

Figure 13-35 shows a typical execution of the program, and Figure 13-36 shows the resulting file. (This program was executed after rerunning the CreateEmptyEmployeesFile program, so all records started with default values, and the record created by the program shown in Figure 13-33 is not part of the file.) In Figure 13-36, you can see that each employee record is not stored based on the order in which it was entered but is located in the correct spot based on its key field.

```
C:\Java>java CreateEmployeesRandomFile
Enter employee ID number >> 004
Enter name for employee #4 >> Lincoln
Enter pay rate >> 11.65
Enter next ID number or 999 to quit >> 014
Enter name for employee #14 >> Greeley
Enter pay rate >> 21.15
Enter next ID number or 999 to quit >> 003
Enter name for employee #3 >> Calhoon
Enter pay rate >> 21.45
Enter next ID number or 999 to quit >> 012
Enter name for employee #12 >> Winters
Enter pay rate >> 17.25
Enter next ID number or 999 to quit >> 999

C:\Java>
```

Figure 13-35   Typical execution of the CreateEmployeesRandomFile program

```
000,          ,00.00
000,          ,00.00
000,          ,00.00
003,Calhoon,21.45
004,Lincoln,11.65
000,          ,00.00
000.          ,00.00
000,          ,00.00
000.          ,00.00
000,          ,00.00
000,          ,00.00
012,Winters,17.25
000,          ,00.00
014,Greeley,21.15
000,          ,00.00
000,          ,00.00
000,          ,00.00
000,          ,00.00
```

Figure 13-36   File created during the execution in Figure 13-35

To keep this example brief and focused on the random access file writing, the `CreateEmployeesFile` application makes several assumptions:

- An employee record contains only an ID number, name, and pay rate. In a real application, each employee would require many more data fields, such as address, phone number, date of hire, and so on.

- Each employee ID number is three digits. In many real applications, ID numbers would be longer to ensure unique values. (Three-digit numbers provide only 1,000 unique combinations.)

- The user will enter valid ID numbers and pay rates. In a real application, this would be a foolhardy assumption because users might type too many digits or type nonnumeric characters. However, to streamline the code and concentrate on the writing of a random access file, error checking for valid ID numbers and pay rates is eliminated from this example.

- The user will not duplicate employee ID numbers. In a real application, a key field should be checked against all existing key fields to ensure that a record is unique before adding it to a file.

- The names entered are all seven characters. This permits each record to be the same size. Only when record sizes are uniform can they be used to arithmetically calculate offset positions. In a real application, you would have to pad shorter names with spaces and truncate longer names to achieve a uniform size.

- Each employee's record is placed in the random access file position that is one less than the employee's ID number. In many real applications, the mathematical computations performed on a key field to determine file placement are more complicated.

TWO TRUTHS & A LIE

Writing Records to a Random Access Data File

1. You can set a `FileChannel`'s reading position based on a key field in a record and the record size.

2. A key field is the field in a record that holds the most sensitive information.

3. A useful technique for creating random access files involves first setting up a file with default records in each position.

The false statement is #2. A key field is the field in a record that makes the record unique from all others.

Reading Records from a Random Access Data File

Just because a file is created as a random access file does not mean it has to be used as one. You can process a random access file either sequentially or randomly.

Accessing a Random Access File Sequentially

The RandomEmployees.txt file created in the previous section contains 1,000 records. However, only four of them contain valuable data. Displaying every record in the file would result in many irrelevant lines of output. It makes more sense to display only those records for which an ID number has been inserted. The application in Figure 13-37 reads through the 1,000-record file sequentially in a `while` loop. The shaded statements check for valid ID numbers. This example assumes that no employee has a valid ID number of 000, so the program displays a record only when the ID is not 000. If 000 could be a valid ID number, then you would want to check for a name that was blank, a pay rate that was 0, or both. Figure 13-38 shows the application's output—a list of the entered records, conveniently in ID number order, which reflects their relative positions within the file.

```
import java.nio.file.*;
import java.io.*;
import static java.nio.file.AccessMode.*;
public class ReadEmployeesSequentially
{
    public static void main(String[] args)
    {
        Path file =
            Paths.get("C:\\Java\\Chapter.13\\RandomEmployees.txt");
        String[] array = new String[3];
        String s = "";
        String delimiter = ",";
        int id;
        String stringId;
        String name;
        double payRate;
        double gross;
        final double HRS_IN_WEEK = 40;
        double total = 0;
        try
        {
            InputStream input = new
                BufferedInputStream(Files.newInputStream(file));
            BufferedReader reader = new
                BufferedReader(new InputStreamReader(input));
            System.out.println();
            s = reader.readLine();
```

Figure 13-37   The ReadEmployeesSequentially class *(continues)*

(continued)

```
            while(s != null)
            {
                array = s.split(delimiter);
                stringId = array[0];
                id = Integer.parseInt(array[0]);
                if(id != 0)
                {
                    name = array[1];
                    payRate = Double.parseDouble(array[2]);
                    gross = payRate * HRS_IN_WEEK;
                    System.out.println("ID#" + stringId + "   " +
                        name + "    $" + payRate + "    $" + gross);
                    total += gross;
                }
                s = reader.readLine();
            }
            reader.close();
        }
        catch(Exception e)
        {
            System.out.println("Message: " + e);
        }
        System.out.println("  Total gross payroll is $" + total);
    }
}
```

Figure 13-37   The ReadEmployeesSequentially class

Figure 13-38   Output of the ReadEmployeesSequentially application

Accessing a Random Access File Randomly

If you simply want to display records in order based on their key field, you do not need to create a random access file and waste unneeded storage. Instead, you could sort the records using one of the techniques you learned in Chapter 9. The benefit of using a random access file is the ability to retrieve a specific record from a file directly, without reading through other records to locate the desired one.

The ReadEmployeesRandomly application in Figure 13-39 allows the user to enter an employee's ID number. The application calculates the correct record position in the data file (one less than the ID number) and positions the file pointer at the correct location to begin reading. The user is then prompted for an ID number, which is converted to an integer with the parseInt() method. (To keep this example brief, the application does not check for a valid ID number, so the parseInt() method might throw an exception to the operating system, ending the execution of the application.) In the shaded portion of the application in Figure 13-39, while the user does not enter 999 to quit, the position of the sought-after record is calculated by multiplying the ID number by the record size and then positioning the file pointer at the desired location. (Again, to keep the example short, the ID number is not checked to ensure that it is 999 or less.) The employee record is retrieved from the data file and displayed, and then the user is prompted for the next desired ID number. Figure 13-40 shows a typical execution.

```java
import java.nio.file.*;
import java.io.*;
import java.nio.channels.FileChannel;
import java.nio.ByteBuffer;
import static java.nio.file.StandardOpenOption.*;
import java.util.Scanner;
public class ReadEmployeesRandomly
{
    public static void main(String[] args)
    {
        Scanner keyBoard = new Scanner(System.in);
        Path file =
            Paths.get("C:\\Java\\Chapter.13\\RandomEmployees.txt");
        String s = "000,          ,00.00" +
            System.getProperty("line.separator");
        final int RECSIZE = s.length();
        byte[] data = s.getBytes();
        ByteBuffer buffer = ByteBuffer.wrap(data);
        FileChannel fc = null;
        String idString;
        int id;
        final String QUIT = "999";
        try
        {
            fc = (FileChannel)Files.newByteChannel(file, READ, WRITE);
            System.out.print("Enter employee ID number or " +
                QUIT + " to quit >> ");
            idString = keyBoard.nextLine();
```

Figure 13-39　The ReadEmployeesRandomly class *(continues)*

(continued)

```java
        while(!idString.equals(QUIT))
        {
            id = Integer.parseInt(idString);
            buffer= ByteBuffer.wrap(data);
            fc.position(id * RECSIZE);
            fc.read(buffer);
            s = new String(data);
            System.out.println("ID #" + id + "  " + s);
            System.out.print("Enter employee ID number or " +
                QUIT + " to quit >> ");
            idString = keyBoard.nextLine();
        }
        fc.close();
    }
    catch (Exception e)
    {
        System.out.println("Error message: " + e);
    }
    }
}
```

Figure 13-39   The ReadEmployeesRandomly class

Figure 13-40   Typical execution of the ReadEmployeesRandomly program

  Watch the video *Random Access Data Files.*

TWO TRUTHS & A LIE

Reading Records from a Random Access Data File

1. When a file is created as a random access file, you also must read it randomly.

2. The benefit of using a random access file is the ability to retrieve a specific record from a file directly, without reading through other records to locate the desired one.

3. When you access a record from a random access file, you usually calculate its position based on a key.

The false statement is #1. Just because a file is created as a random access file does not mean it has to be used as one. You can process the file sequentially or randomly.

 You Do It

Creating Multiple Random Access Files

In this section, you write a class that prompts the user for customer data and assigns the data to one of two files depending on the customer's state of residence. This program assumes that Wisconsin (WI) records are assigned to an in-state file and that all other records are assigned to an out-of-state file. First you will create empty files to store the records, and then you will write the code that places each record in the correct file.

1. Open a new file in your text editor, and type the following required `import` statements:

```
import java.nio.file.*;
import java.io.*;
import java.nio.channels.FileChannel;
import java.nio.ByteBuffer;
import static java.nio.file.StandardOpenOption.*;
import java.util.Scanner;
import java.text.*;
```

2. Enter the beginning lines of the program, which include a `Scanner` class object to accept user input:

```
public class CreateFilesBasedOnState
{
    public static void main(String[] args)
    {
        Scanner input = new Scanner(System.in);
```

(continues)

(continued)

3. This program uses two `Path` objects to hold records for in-state and out-of-state customers. You can use a different `String` value for your `Paths` based on your `System` and the location where you want to save your files.

```
Path inStateFile =
    Paths.get("C:\\Java\\Chapter.13\\InStateCusts.txt");
Path outOfStateFile =
    Paths.get("C:\\Java\\Chapter.13\\OutOfStateCusts.txt");
```

4. Build a `String` that can be used to format the empty files that are created before any actual customer data is written. Include constants for the format of the account number (three digits), the customer name (10 spaces), the customer's state, and the customer's balance (up to 9999.99). After defining the field delimiter (a comma), you can build a generic customer string by assembling the pieces. The record size is then calculated from the dummy record. A consistent record size is important so it can be used to calculate a record's position when the files are accessed randomly.

```
final String ID_FORMAT = "000";
final String NAME_FORMAT = "          ";
final int NAME_LENGTH = NAME_FORMAT.length();
final String HOME_STATE = "WI";
final String BALANCE_FORMAT = "0000.00";
String delimiter = ",";
String s = ID_FORMAT + delimiter + NAME_FORMAT +
    delimiter + HOME_STATE + delimiter + BALANCE_FORMAT +
    System.getProperty("line.separator");
final int RECSIZE = s.length();
```

5. The last declarations are for two `FileChannel` references; `String` and integer representations of the customer's account number; the customer's `name`, `state`, and `balance` fields; and a `QUIT` constant that identifies the end of data entry.

```
FileChannel fcIn = null;
FileChannel fcOut = null;
String idString;
int id;
String name;
String state;
double balance;
final String QUIT = "999";
```

6. Next, you call a method that creates the empty files into which the randomly placed data records can eventually be written. The method accepts the `Path` for a file and the `String` that defines the record format.

```
createEmptyFile(inStateFile, s);
createEmptyFile(outOfStateFile, s);
```

(continues)

(continued)

7. Add closing curly braces for the main() method and the class. Then save the file as **CreateFilesBasedOnState.java** and compile it. Correct any errors before proceeding.

Writing a Method to Create an Empty File

In this section, you write the method that creates empty files using the default record format string. The method will create 1,000 records with an account number of 000.

1. Just before the closing curly brace of the CreateFilesBasedOnState class, insert the header and opening brace for a method that will create an empty file to hold random access records. The method accepts a Path argument and the default record String.

    ```
    public static void createEmptyFile(Path file, String s)
    {
    ```

2. Define a constant for the number of records to be written:

    ```
    final int NUMRECS = 1000;
    ```

3. In a try block, declare a new OutputStream using the method's Path parameter. Then create a BufferedWriter using the OutputStream.

    ```
    try
    {
        OutputStream outputStr = new
            BufferedOutputStream(Files.newOutputStream(file,CREATE));
        BufferedWriter writer = new BufferedWriter(new
            OutputStreamWriter(outputStr));
    ```

4. Use a for loop to write 1,000 default records using the parameter String. Then close the BufferedWriter, and add a closing brace for the try block.

    ```
    for(int count = 0; count < NUMRECS; ++count)
        writer.write(s, 0, s.length());
    writer.close();
    }
    ```

5. Add a catch block to handle any Exception thrown from the try block, and add a closing curly brace for the method.

    ```
    catch(Exception e)
    {
        System.out.println("Error message: " + e);
    }
    }
    ```

6. Save the file and compile it. Correct any errors.

(continues)

(continued)

Adding Data Entry Capability to the Program

In these steps, you add the code that accepts data from the keyboard and writes it to the correct location (based on the customer's account number) within the correct file (based on the customer's state).

1. After the calls to the `createEmptyFile()` method, but before the method header, start a `try` block that will handle all the data entry and file writing for customer records:

   ```
   try
   {
   ```

2. Set up the `FileChannel` references for both the in-state and out-of-state files.

   ```
   fcIn = (FileChannel)Files.newByteChannel(inStateFile, CREATE, WRITE);
   fcOut = (FileChannel)Files.newByteChannel(outOfStateFile, CREATE, WRITE);
   ```

3. Prompt the user for a customer account number, and accept it from the keyboard. Then start a loop that will continue as long as the user does not enter the QUIT value. Next, convert the entered account number to an integer so it can be used to calculate the file position for the entered record. In a full-blown application, you would add code to ensure that the account number is three digits, but to keep this example shorter, this program assumes that the user will enter valid account numbers.

   ```
   System.out.print("Enter customer account number >> ");
   idString = input.nextLine();
   while(!(idString.equals(QUIT)))
   {
       id = Integer.parseInt(idString);
   ```

4. Prompt the user for and accept the customer's name. To ensure that entered names are stored using a uniform length, assign the name to a `StringBuilder` object, and set the length to the standard length. Then assign the newly sized `StringBuilder` back to the `String`.

   ```
   System.out.print("Enter name for customer >> ");
   name = input.nextLine();
   StringBuilder sb = new StringBuilder(name);
   sb.setLength(NAME_LENGTH);
   name = sb.toString();
   ```

5. Prompt the user for and accept the customer's state of residence. (In a fully developed program, you would check the entered state against a list of valid states, but this step is omitted to keep the program shorter.)

   ```
   System.out.print("Enter state >> ");
   state = input.nextLine();
   ```

(continues)

(continued)

6. Prompt the user for and accept the customer's balance. Because you use the `nextDouble()` method to retrieve the balance, you follow it with a call to `nextLine()` to absorb the Enter key value left in the input stream. Then you can use the `DecimalFormat` class to ensure that the balance meets the format requirements of the file. Because the `BALANCE_FORMAT` `String`'s value is 0000.00, zeros will be added to the front or back of any `double` that would not otherwise meet the standard. For example, 200.99 will be stored as 0200.99 and 0.1 will be stored as 0001.00. Appendix C contains more information on the `DecimalFormat` class and describes other potential formats.

```
System.out.print("Enter balance >> ");
balance = input.nextDouble();
input.nextLine();
DecimalFormat df = new DecimalFormat(BALANCE_FORMAT);
```

7. Construct the `String` to be written to the file by concatenating the entered fields with the comma delimiter and the line separator.

```
s = idString + delimiter + name + delimiter +
    state + delimiter + df.format(balance)  +
    System.getProperty("line.separator");
```

8. Convert the constructed `String` to an array of bytes, and wrap the array into a `ByteBuffer`.

```
byte data[] = s.getBytes();
ByteBuffer buffer = ByteBuffer.wrap(data);
```

9. Depending on the customer's state, use the in-state or out-of-state `FileChannel`. Position the file pointer to start writing a record in the correct position based on the account number, and write the data `String`.

```
if(state.equals(HOME_STATE))
{
    fcIn.position(id * RECSIZE);
    fcIn.write(buffer);
}
else
{
    fcOut.position(id * RECSIZE);
    fcOut.write(buffer);
}
```

10. Prompt the user for the next customer account number, and add a closing curly brace for the `while` loop.

```
    System.out.print("Enter next customer account number or " +
        QUIT + " to quit >> ");
    idString = input.nextLine();
}
```

(continues)

(continued)

11. Close the `FileChannels`, and add a closing curly brace for the class.

    ```
    fcIn.close();
    fcOut.close();
    }
    ```

12. Save the file and compile it. Execute the program, and enter several records. Make sure to include names that are longer and shorter than 10 characters and to include a variety of balance values. Figure 13-41 shows a typical execution.

```
C:\Java>java CreateFilesBasedOnState
Enter customer account number >> 213
Enter name for customer >> Morris
Enter state >> KY
Enter balance >> 200.00
Enter next customer account number or 999 to quit >> 215
Enter name for customer >> Johnsonville
Enter state >> AZ
Enter balance >> 44.44
Enter next customer account number or 999 to quit >> 104
Enter name for customer >> Samuels
Enter state >> WI
Enter balance >> 100.99
Enter next customer account number or 999 to quit >> 212
Enter name for customer >> Davis
Enter state >> FL
Enter balance >> 2
Enter next customer account number or 999 to quit >> 101
Enter name for customer >> Franklin
Enter state >> WI
Enter balance >> 1034.38
Enter next customer account number or 999 to quit >> 999

C:\Java>
```

Figure 13-41   Typical execution of the CreateFilesBasedOnState program

13. Locate and open the **InStateCusts.txt** and **OutOfStateCusts.txt** files. Scroll through the files until you find the records you created. Figure 13-42 shows part of both files that contains the records added using the execution in Figure 13-41. Confirm that each record is placed in the correct file location, that each name and balance is in the correct format, and that the records with a state value of "WI" are placed in one file while all the other records are placed in the other file.

(continues)

(continued)

Figure 13-42   Contents of the files created by the program execution in Figure 13-41

Setting Up a Program to Read the Created Files

Now, you can write a program that can use either of the files you just created. The program has four parts:

- The program will prompt the user to enter the filename to be used and set up all necessary variables and constants.
- A few statistics about the file will be displayed.
- The nondefault contents of the file will be displayed sequentially.
- A selected record from the file will be accessed directly.

1. Open a new file in your text editor. Enter all the required import statements and the class header for the `ReadStateFile` application.

```
import java.nio.file.*;
import java.io.*;
import java.nio.file.attribute.*;
import static java.nio.file.StandardOpenOption.*;
import java.nio.ByteBuffer;
import java.nio.channels.FileChannel;
import java.util.Scanner;
public class ReadStateFile
{
```

2. Declare a `Scanner` object to handle keyboard input. Then declare a `String` that will hold the name of the file the program will use. Prompt the user for the filename, concatenate it with the correct path, and create a `Path` object.

(continues)

(continued)

```
Scanner kb = new Scanner(System.in);
String fileName;
System.out.print("Enter name of file to use >> ");
fileName = kb.nextLine();
fileName = "C:\\Java\\Chapter.13\\" + fileName;
Path file = Paths.get(fileName);
```

3. Add the `String` formatting constants and build a sample record `String` so that you can determine the record size. To save time, you can copy these declarations from the `CreateFilesBasedOnState` program.

```
final String ID_FORMAT = "000";
final String NAME_FORMAT = "              ";
final int NAME_LENGTH = NAME_FORMAT.length();
final String HOME_STATE = "WI";
final String BALANCE_FORMAT = "0000.00";
String delimiter = ",";
String s = ID_FORMAT + delimiter + NAME_FORMAT + delimiter +
   HOME_STATE + delimiter + BALANCE_FORMAT +
   System.getProperty("line.separator");
final int RECSIZE = s.length();
```

4. The last set of declarations includes a byte array that you will use with a `ByteBuffer` later in the program, a `String` that represents the account number in an empty account, and an array of strings that can hold the pieces of a split record after it is read from the input file. Add a variable for the numeric customer balance, which will be converted from the `String` stored in the file. Also, declare a total and initialize it to 0 so the total customer balance due value can be accumulated.

```
byte data[] = s.getBytes();
final String EMPTY_ACCT = "000";
String[] array = new String[4];
double balance;
double total = 0;
```

5. Add two closing curly braces for the method and the class. Save the file as **ReadStateFile.java**. Compile the file and correct any errors.

Displaying File Statistics

In the next section of the program, you display the creation time and size of the file.

1. Just before the two closing curly braces you just added to the program, insert a `try` block in which you declare a `BasicFileAttributes` object. Then add statements to display the file's creation time and size. Include a `catch` block to handle any thrown exceptions.

(continues)

(continued)

```
try
{
    BasicFileAttributes attr =
        Files.readAttributes(file, BasicFileAttributes.class);
    System.out.println("\nAttributes of the file:");
    System.out.println("Creation time " + attr.creationTime());
    System.out.println("Size " + attr.size());
}
catch(IOException e)
{
    System.out.println("IO Exception");
}
```

2. Save the file, then compile and execute it. When prompted, you can type the name of either the **InStateCusts.txt** file or the **OutOfStateCusts.txt** file. Figure 13-43 shows a typical execution.

Figure 13-43   Typical execution of the ReadStateFile program

Reading a File Sequentially

In these steps, you display all the entered records in the file of the user's choice.

1. Start a new try...catch pair after the first one ends but before the two closing curly braces in the program. Declare an InputStream and BufferedReader to handle reading the file.

```
try
{
    InputStream iStream = new
        BufferedInputStream(Files.newInputStream(file));
    BufferedReader reader = new
        BufferedReader(new InputStreamReader(iStream));
```

(continues)

(continued)

2. Display a heading, and then read the first record from the file into a `String`.

```
System.out.println("\nAll non-default records:\n");
s = reader.readLine();
```

3. In a loop that continues while there is more data to read, split the `String` using the comma delimiter. Test the first split element, the account number, and proceed only if it is not "000". If the record was entered in the previous program, display the split `String` elements. Add the balance to a running total. As the last action in the loop, read the next record.

```
while(s != null)
{
    array = s.split(delimiter);
    if(!array[0].equals(EMPTY_ACCT))
    {
        balance = Double.parseDouble(array[3]);
        System.out.println("ID #" + array[0] + " " +
            array[1] + array[2] + " $" + array[3]);
        total += balance;
    }
    s = reader.readLine();
}
```

4. After all the records have been processed, display the total and close the reader. Add a closing curly brace for the `try` block.

```
System.out.println("Total of all balances is $" + total);
reader.close();
}
```

5. Create a `catch` block to handle any thrown exceptions.

```
catch(Exception e)
{
    System.out.println("Message: " + e);
}
```

6. Save the file, and then compile and execute it. Enter the name of either data file. Figure 13-44 shows a typical execution. After the file statistics are displayed, the records added earlier are also displayed, and the balances are accumulated.

(continues)

(continued)

Figure 13-44 Typical execution of the ReadStateFile program after code has been added to display records

Reading a File Randomly

In the last part of the program, you ask the user to enter an account number and then display the record directly by repositioning the file pointer.

1. After the closing brace of the last catch block, but before the two final closing braces in the class, add a new try block that declares a FileChannel and ByteBuffer and then prompts the user for and accepts an account to search for in the file.

```
try
{
    FileChannel fc = (FileChannel)Files.newByteChannel(file, READ);
    ByteBuffer buffer = ByteBuffer.wrap(data);
    int findAcct;
    System.out.print("\nEnter account to seek >> ");
    findAcct = kb.nextInt();
```

2. Calculate the position of the sought-after record in the file by multiplying the record number by the file size. Read the selected record into the ByteBuffer, and convert the associated byte array to a String that you can display. Add a closing curly brace for the try block.

```
    fc.position(findAcct * RECSIZE);
    fc.read(buffer);
    s = new String(data);
    System.out.println("Desired record: " + s);
}
```

(continues)

(continued)

3. Add a catch block to handle any exceptions.

```
catch(Exception e)
{
    System.out.println("Message: " + e);
}
```

4. Save the file, and then compile and execute it. Figure 13-45 shows a typical execution. First, the file attributes are displayed, then all the records are displayed, and then a record selected by the user is displayed.

```
Command Prompt                                    _  □  X

C:\Java>java ReadStateFile
Enter name of file to use >> OutOfStateCusts.txt

Attributes of the file:
Creation time 2010-08-30T00:35:17.20445Z
Size 27000

All non-default records:

ID #212  Davis      FL  $0002.00
ID #213  Morris     KY  $0200.00
ID #215  JohnsonvilAZ  $0044.44
Total of all balances is 246.44

Enter account to seek >> 213
Desired record: 213,Morris    ,KY,0200.00

C:\Java>
```

Figure 13-45 Typical execution of the ReadStateFile program after code has been completed

Don't Do It

- Don't forget that a Path name might be relative and that you might need to make the Path absolute before accessing it.

- Don't forget that the backslash character starts the escape sequence in Java, so you must use two backslashes in a string that describes a Path in the DOS operating system.

Key Terms

Volatile storage is temporary storage that is lost when a computer loses power.

Random access memory (RAM) is the temporary storage within a computer.

Nonvolatile storage is permanent storage; it is not lost when a computer loses power.

A **computer file** is a collection of data stored on a nonvolatile device in a computer system.

Permanent storage devices, such as hard disks, Zip disks, USB drives, reels or cassettes of magnetic tape, and compact discs, are nonvolatile and hold files.

Text files contain data that can be read in a text editor because the data has been encoded using a scheme such as ASCII or Unicode.

Data files contain facts and figures, such as a payroll file that contains employee numbers, names, and salaries.

Program files or **application files** store software instructions.

Binary files contain data that has not been encoded as text; their contents are in binary format.

The **root directory** of a storage device is the main directory.

Folders or **directories** are used to organize stored files.

A **path** is the complete list of the disk drive plus the hierarchy of directories in which a file resides.

A **path delimiter** is the character used to separate path components.

You can use Java's **Path class** to create objects that contain information about files and directories, such as their locations, sizes, creation dates, and whether they even exist.

You use the **Files class** to perform operations on files and directories, such as deleting them, determining their attributes, and creating input and output streams.

Factory methods are methods that assist in object creation.

An **absolute path** is a complete path; it does not need any other information to locate a file on a system.

A **relative path** is one that depends on other path information.

Java's **static import feature** allows you to use static constants without their class name.

A **TOCTTOU bug** is an error that occurs when changes take place from Time Of Check To Time Of Use.

A **character** can be any letter, number, or other special symbol (such as a punctuation mark) that constitutes data.

A **field** is a group of characters that has some meaning.

A **record** is a collection of fields that contain data about an entity.

In a **sequential access file**, each record is accessed one after another in the order in which it was stored.

Comma-separated values (CSV) are fields that are separated by a comma.

To **open a file** is to create an object and associate a stream of bytes with it.

To **close the file** is to make it no longer available to an application.

A **stream** is a data pipeline or channel.

A **buffer** is a memory location where bytes are held after they are logically output but before they are sent to the output device.

Flushing clears any bytes that have been sent to a buffer for output but that have not yet been output to a hardware device.

Batch processing involves performing the same tasks with many records, one after the other.

Real-time applications require that a record be accessed immediately while a client is waiting.

In an **interactive program**, a user makes direct requests to a system.

Random access files are files in which records can be retrieved directly in any order.

Direct access files and **instant access files** are alternate names for *random access files*.

A **file channel** object is an avenue for reading and writing a file.

Seekable describes a file channel in which you can search for a specific file location and in which operations can start at any specified position.

To be **wrapped** is to be encompassed in another type.

A **key field** is the field in a record that makes the record unique from all others.

Chapter Summary

- Data items can be stored on two broad types of storage devices—temporary, volatile storage, or permanent, nonvolatile storage. A computer file is a collection of data stored on a nonvolatile device. Files can be text files or binary files, but all files share characteristics, such as a size, name, and time of creation.

- Java's Path class is used to gather file information, such as its location, size, and creation date. You can use the Files class to perform operations on files and directories, such as deleting them, determining their attributes, and creating input and output streams.

732

- Businesses organize data in a hierarchy of character, field, record, and file. When a program performs input and output operations, bytes flow into a program stream, which functions as a pipeline or channel. A buffer is a memory location where bytes are held after they are logically output but before they are sent to the output device. Using a buffer to accumulate input or output improves program performance. Flushing clears any bytes that have been sent to a buffer for output but that have not yet been output to a hardware device.

- `InputStream`, `OutputStream`, and `Reader` are subclasses of the `Object` class that are used for input and output. Output devices can be assigned to `OutputStream` references, allowing applications to save data to them. You can create a file and write to it by using the `Files` class `newOutputStream()` method. To open a file for reading, you can use the `newInputStream()` method.

- The `BufferedWriter` class contains `write()` methods that are used to create data files. Files can be read using the `BufferedReader` class. The `String` class `split()` method accepts an argument that identifies a field delimiter and returns an array of `Strings` in which each array element holds one field.

- Businesses store data in sequential order when they use the records for batch processing. Real-time applications require interactive processing with random access files. Java's `FileChannel` class creates random access files. A file channel is seekable, meaning you can search for a specific file location and operations can start at any specified position.

- One approach to writing a random file is to place records into the file based on a key field that makes a record unique from all others. The first step in creating the random access file is to create a file that holds default records. Then you can replace any default record with actual data by setting the file channel position.

- You can process a random access file either sequentially or randomly. The benefit of using a random access file is the ability to retrieve a specific record from a file directly, without reading through other records to locate the desired one.

Review Questions

1. Which of the following statements is true?

   a. Volatile storage lasts only a few seconds.

   b. Volatile storage is lost when a computer loses power.

   c. Computer disks are volatile storage devices.

   d. All of the above are true.

2. A collection of data stored on a nonvolatile device in a computer system is _____ .

   a. a file   c. volatile

   b. an application   d. a type of binary file

3. A complete list of the disk drive plus the hierarchy of directories in which a file resides is its _____ .

   a. directory   c. delimiter

   b. folder   d. path

4. Which of the following statements creates a `Path` named p to a `FileStream` named f?

   a. `Path p = new Path("C:\\Java\\MyFile.txt");`

   b. `Path p = f("C:\\Java\\MyFile.txt");`

   c. `Path p = f.getPath("C:\\Java\\MyFile.txt");`

   d. `Path p = getPath(new f("C:\\Java\\MyFile.txt"));`

5. A path that needs no other information to locate a file on a system is _____ .

   a. an absolute path   c. a final path

   b. a relative path   d. a constant path

6. The `Path` class `getFileName()` method returns _____ .

   a. the `String` representation of a `Path`

   b. an absolute `Path`

   c. the first item in a `Path`'s list of name elements

   d. the last item in a `Path`'s list of name elements

7. Which of the following statements always returns the same value as `Files.exists(file)`?

   a. `file.checkAccess()`   c. `file.checkAccess(READ, WRITE)`

   b. `file.checkAccess(EXISTS)`   d. `file.checkAccess(file.exists())`

8. You cannot delete a `Path` _____ .

   a. under any circumstances

   b. if it represents a directory

   c. if it represents a directory that is not empty

   d. if it represents more than five levels

9. The data hierarchy occurs in the following order from the smallest to largest piece of data: _____ .

   a. character, field, record, file   c. character, record, field, file

   b. character, file, record, field   d. record, character, field, file

10. When records are accessed one after the other in the order in which they were stored, their file is being used as a _____ access file.

   a. random   c. chronological

   b. binary   d. sequential

11. If you fail to close an output file, _____ .

    a. there are usually no serious consequences

    b. you might lose access to the written data

    c. Java will close it for you automatically

    d. Two of the above are correct.

12. Which of the following is true of streams?

    a. Streams are channels through which bytes flow.

    b. Streams always flow in two directions.

    c. Only one stream can be open in a program at a time.

    d. All of the above are true.

13. A buffer _____ .

    a. holds bytes that are scheduled for input or output

    b. deteriorates program performance

    c. cannot be flushed in Java

    d. All of the above are true.

14. `InputStream` is _____ .

    a. a child of `OutputStream`

    b. an abstract class

    c. used for screen output as opposed to file output

    d. All of the above are true.

15. Java's `print()` and `println()` methods are defined in the _____ class.

    a. `BufferedOutputStream`   c. `PrintStream`

    b. `System`   d. `Print`

16. The `newOutputStream()` method _____ .

    a. is defined in the `Files` class

    b. creates a file if it does not already exist

    c. opens a file for writing

    d. All of the above are true.

17. Which of the following does the same thing as the `BufferedWriter` class `newLine()` method?

    a. `System.getProperty("line.separator ")`

    b. `Path.getProperty("line.separator ")`

    c. `System.out.println()`

    d. `System.out.print("\n")`

18. Which of the following systems is most likely to use batch processing?

    a. an airline reservation system

    (b.) payroll

    c. point-of-sale credit checking

    d. an e-mail application

19. Real-time applications _____ .

    a. use sequential access files

    b. use batch processing

    (c.) use random access files

    d. seldom are interactive

20. A file channel _____ .

    a. can be read from

    b. can be written to

    (c.) is seekable

    d. All of the above are true.

Exercises

 Programming Exercises

1. Create a file using any word-processing program or text editor. Write an application that displays the file's name, containing folder, size, and time of last modification. Save the file as **FileStatistics.java**.

2. Create two files using any word-processing program or text editor. Write an application that determines whether the two files are located in the same folder. Save the file as **SameFolder.java**.

3. Create a file that contains your favorite movie quote. Use a text editor such as Notepad, and save the file as **quote.txt**. Copy the file contents, and paste them into a word-processing program such as Word. Save the file as **quote.docx**. Write an application that displays the sizes of the two files as well as the ratio of their sizes to each other. Save the file as **FileStatistics2.java**.

4. Write an application that determines which, if any, of the following files are stored in the folder where you have saved the exercises created in this chapter: autoexec.bat, SameFolder.java, FileStatistics.class, and Hello.doc. Save the file as **FindSelectedFiles.java**.

5. a. Create a program that accepts a series of employee ID numbers, first names, and last names from the keyboard and saves the data to a file. Save the program as **WriteEmployeeList.java**. When you execute the program, be sure to enter multiple records that have the same first name because you will search for repeated first names in part d of this exercise.

    b. Write an application that reads the file created by the `WriteEmployeeList` application and displays the records. Save the file as **DisplaySavedEmployeeList.java**.

c. Write an application that allows you to enter any ID number and displays the first and last name for the record stored in the employee file with the given ID number. Display an appropriate message if the ID number cannot be found in the input file. Save the file as **DisplaySelectedIDNumbers.java**.

d. Write an application that allows you to enter any first name and displays all the ID numbers and last names for any records stored in the employee file with the given first name. Display an appropriate message if the first name cannot be found in the input file. Save the file as **DisplaySelectedFirstNames.java**.

6. Using a text editor, create a file that contains a list of at least 10 six-digit account numbers. Read in each account number and display whether it is valid. An account number is valid only if the last digit is equal to the sum of the first five digits divided by 10. For example, the number 223355 is valid because the sum of the first five digits is 15, the remainder when 15 is divided by 10 is 5, and the last digit is 5. Write only valid account numbers to an output file, each on its own line. Save the application as **ValidateCheckDigits.java**.

7. a. Write an application that allows a user to enter a filename and an integer representing a file position. Assume that the file is in the same folder as your executing program. Access the requested position within the file, and display the next 20 characters there. Save the file as **SeekPosition.java**.

   b. Modify the SeekPosition application so that instead of displaying 20 characters, the user enters the number of characters to display, beginning with the requested position. Save the file as **SeekPosition2.java**.

8. a. Create an application that allows you to enter salesperson data that consists of an ID number, first name, last name, and current month sales in whole dollars. Depending on whether the salesperson's sales value exceeds $1,000, output each record either to a high-performers file or a low-performers file. Save the program as **HighAndLowSales.java**.

   b. Create an application that displays each record in the two files created in the HighAndLowSales application in Exercise 8a. Display a heading to introduce the list produced from each file. For each record, display the ID number, first name, last name, sales value, and the amount by which the sales value exceeds or falls short of the $1,000 cutoff. Save the program as **HighAndLowSalesDisplay.java**.

9. a. The Rochester Bank maintains customer records in a random access file. Write an application that creates 10,000 blank records and then allows the user to enter customer account information, including an account number that is 9999 or less, a last name, and a balance. Insert each new record into a data file at a location that is equal to the account number. Assume that the user will not enter invalid account numbers. Force each name to eight characters, padding

it with spaces or truncating it if necessary. Also assume that the user will not enter a bank balance greater than 99,000.00. Save the file as **CreateBankFile.java**.

b. Create an application that uses the file created by the user in Exercise 9a and displays all existing accounts in account-number order. Save the file as **ReadBankAccountsSequentially.java**.

c. Create an application that uses the file created by the user in Exercise 9a and allows the user to enter an account number to view the account balance. Allow the user to view additional account balances until entering an application-terminating value. Save the file as **ReadBankAccountsRandomly.java**.

10. a. Write a program that allows you to create a file of customers for a company. The first part of the program should create an empty file suitable for writing a three-digit ID number, six-character last name, and five-digit zip code for each customer. The second half of the program accepts user input to populate the file. For this exercise, assume that the user will correctly enter ID numbers and zip codes, but force the customer name to seven characters if it is too long or too short. Issue an error message, and do not save the records if the user tries to save a record with an ID number that has already been used. Save the program as **CreateCustomerFile.java**.

b. Write a program that creates a file of items carried by the company. Include a three-digit item number and up to a 20-character description for each item. Issue an error message if the user tries to store an item number that has already been used. Save the program as **CreateItemFile.java**.

c. Write an application that takes customer orders. Allow a user to enter a customer number and item ordered. Display an error message if the customer number does not exist in the customer file or the item does not exist in the item file; otherwise, display all the customer information and item information. Save the program as **CustomerItemOrder.java**.

 Debugging Exercises

1. Each of the following files in the Chapter13 folder of your downloadable student files has syntax and/or logic errors. In each case, determine the problem and fix the program. After you correct the errors, save each file using the same filename preceded with *Fix*. For example, DebugThirteen1.java will become FixDebugThirteen1.java.

a. DebugThirteen1.java   c. DebugThirteen3.java

b. DebugThirteen2.java   d. DebugThirteen4.java

The Chapter13 folder contains four additional data files named DebugData1.txt, DebugData2.txt, DebugData3.txt, and DebugData4.txt. These files are used by the Debug programs.

Game Zone

1. In several Game Zone assignments earlier in this book, you created games similar to Hangman in which the user guesses a secret phrase by selecting a series of letters. These versions had limited appeal because each contained only a few possible phrases to guess; after playing the games a few times, the user would have memorized all the phrases. Now create a version in which any number of secret phrases can be saved to a file before the game is played. Use a text editor such as Notepad to type any number of phrases into a file, one per line. Save the file as **Phrases.txt**. Then, create a game that randomly selects a phrase from the file and allows a user to guess the phrase letter by letter. Save the game as **SecretPhraseUsingFile.java**.

2. In Chapter 8, you created a game named Quiz in which the user could respond to multiple-choice questions. Modify the game so that it stores the player's highest score from any previous game in a file and displays the high score at the start of each new game. (The first time you play the game, the high score is 0.) Save the game as **QuizUsingFile.java**.

3. Use a text editor to create a comma-delimited file of user IDs and passwords. Revise any one of the games you have created throughout this book so the user must first enter a correct ID and its associated password before playing. Save the program as **GameWithPassword.java**.

Case Problems

1. a. In Chapter 12, you created an interactive StaffDinnerEvent class that obtains all the data for a dinner event for Carly's Catering, including details about the event and all the staff members required to work at the event. Now, modify the program to prompt the user for data for three dinner events and to create a data file that contains each event number, event type code, number of guests, and price. Save the program as **StaffDinnerEventAndCreateFile.java**.

    b. Write a program that displays the data saved in the file created in part 1a. Save the program as **DisplayDinnerEventFile.java**.

2. a. In Chapter 12, you created an interactive RentalDemo class that obtains all the data for four rentals from Sammy's Seashore Rentals, including details about the contract number, length of the rental, and equipment type. Now, modify the program to create a data file that contains each contract number, rental time in hours and minutes, equipment type code and name, and price. Save the program as **RentalDemoAndCreateFile.java**.

    b. Write a program that displays the data saved in the file created in part 2a. Save the program as **DisplayRentalFile.java**.

Introduction to Swing Components

In this chapter, you will:

◎ Understand Swing components

◎ Use the JFrame class

◎ Use the JLabel class

◎ Use a layout manager

◎ Extend the JFrame class

◎ Add JTextFields, JButtons, and tool tips to a JFrame

◎ Learn about event-driven programming

◎ Understand Swing event listeners

◎ Use the JCheckBox, ButtonGroup, and JComboBox classes

Understanding Swing Components

Computer programs usually are more user friendly (and more fun to use) when they contain user interface (UI) components. **UI components** are buttons, text fields, and other components with which the user can interact. Java's creators have packaged a number of prewritten components in the Swing package. **Swing components** are UI elements such as dialog boxes and buttons; you can usually recognize their names because they begin with *J*.

Swing components were named after a musical style that was popular in the 1940s. The name is meant to imply that the components have style and pizzazz. You have already used the JOptionPane component that is part of the Swing class. The Swing classes are part of a more general set of UI programming capabilities that are collectively called the **Java Foundation Classes**, or **JFC**. JFC includes Swing component classes and selected classes from the java.awt package.

In early versions of Java, components had simple names, such as Frame and Button. The components created from these original classes did not have a consistent appearance when used with different browsers and operating systems. When Java's creators designed new, improved classes, they needed new names for the classes, so they used a J in front of each new class name. Hence, Swing components have names like JFrame, JButton, JScrollbar, JOptionPane, and so on.

UI components are also called *controls* or *widgets*. Each Swing component is a descendant of a JComponent, which in turn inherits from the java.awt.Container class. You can insert the statement import javax.swing.*; at the beginning of your Java program files so you can take advantage of the Swing UI components and their methods. When you import Swing classes, you use the javax.swing package instead of java.swing. The *x* originally stood for *extension*, so named because the Swing classes were an extension of the original Java language specifications.

Almost all Swing components are said to be **lightweight components** because they are written completely in Java and do not have to rely on the local operating system code. This means the components are not "weighed down" by having to interact with the operating system (for example, Windows or Macintosh) in which the application is running. Some Swing components, such as JFrames, are known as **heavyweight components** because they do require interaction with the local operating system. A lightweight component reuses the native (original) window of its closest heavyweight ancestor; a heavyweight component has its own opaque native window. The only heavyweight components used in Swing are swing.JFrame, swing.JDialog, swing.JWindow, swing.JApplet, awt.Component, awt.Container, and awt.JComponent.

When you use Swing components, you usually place them in containers. A **container** is a type of component that holds other components so you can treat a group of them as a single entity. Containers are defined in the Container class. Often, a container takes the form of a window that you can drag, resize, minimize, restore, and close.

As you know from reading about inheritance in Chapters 10 and 11, all Java classes descend from the Object class. The Component class is a child of the Object class, and the Container class is a child of the Component class. Therefore, every Container object "is a" Component, and every Component object (including every Container) "is an" Object. The Container class is also a parent class, and the Window class is a child of Container. However, Java programmers rarely use Window objects because the Window subclass Frame and its child, the Swing component **JFrame**, both allow you to create more useful objects. Window objects do not have title bars or borders, but JFrame objects do.

TWO TRUTHS & A LIE

Understanding Swing Components

1. Swing components are elements such as buttons; you can usually recognize their names because they contain the word *Swing*.

2. Each Swing component is a descendant of a JComponent, which in turn inherits from the java.awt.Container class.

3. You insert the import statement import javax.swing.*; at the beginning of your Java program files so you can use Swing components.

The false statement is #1. You can usually recognize Swing component names because they begin with J.

Using the JFrame Class

You usually create a JFrame so that you can place other objects within it for display. Figure 14-1 shows the JFrame's inheritance tree. Recall that the Object class is defined in the java.lang package, which is imported automatically every time you write a Java program. However, Object's descendants (shown in Figure 14-1) are not automatically imported.

```
java.lang.Object
   !--java.awt.Component
          !--java.awt.Container
                 !--java.awt.Window
                        !--java.awt.Frame
                               !--javax.swing.JFrame
```

Figure 14-1   Relationship of the JFrame class to its ancestors

The JFrame class has four constructors:

- JFrame() constructs a new frame that initially is invisible and has no title.

- JFrame(String title) creates a new, initially invisible JFrame with the specified title.

- JFrame(GraphicsConfiguration gc) creates a JFrame in the specified GraphicsConfiguration of a screen device with a blank title. (You will learn about the GraphicsConfiguration class as you continue to study Java.)

- JFrame(String title, GraphicsConfiguration gc) creates a JFrame with the specified title and the specified GraphicsConfiguration of a screen.

You can construct a JFrame as you do other objects, using the class name, an identifier, the assignment operator, the new operator, and a constructor call. For example, the following two statements construct two JFrames: one with the title "Hello" and another with no title:

```
JFrame firstFrame = new JFrame("Hello");
JFrame secondFrame = new JFrame();
```

After you create a JFrame object, you can use the now-familiar object-dot-method format you have used with other objects to call methods that manipulate a JFrame's features. Table 14-1 describes some useful JFrame class methods.

The methods in Table 14-1 represent only a small portion of the available methods you can use with a JFrame. Each of the methods listed in Table 14-1 is inherited from either JFrame's Component or Frame parent class. These classes contain many useful methods in addition to the few listed here. You can read the documentation for all the methods at *www.oracle.com/technetwork/java/index.html*.

Method	Purpose
void setTitle(String)	Sets a JFrame's title using the String argument
void setSize(int, int)	Sets a JFrame's size in pixels with the width and height as arguments
void setSize(Dimension)	Sets a JFrame's size using a Dimension class object; the Dimension(int, int) constructor creates an object that represents both a width and a height
String getTitle()	Returns a JFrame's title
void setResizable(boolean)	Sets the JFrame to be resizable by passing true to the method, or sets the JFrame not to be resizable by passing false to the method
boolean isResizable()	Returns true or false to indicate whether the JFrame is resizable
void setVisible(boolean)	Sets a JFrame to be visible using the boolean argument true and invisible using the boolean argument false
void setBounds(int, int, int, int)	Overrides the default behavior for the JFrame to be positioned in the upper-left corner of the computer screen's desktop. The first two arguments are the horizontal and vertical positions of the JFrame's upper-left corner on the desktop. The final two arguments set the width and height.

Table 14-1　Useful methods inherited by the JFrame class

Assuming you have declared a JFrame named firstFrame, you can use the following statements to set the firstFrame object's size to 250 pixels horizontally by 100 pixels vertically and set the JFrame's title to display a String argument. **Pixels** are the picture elements, or tiny dots of light, that make up the image on your computer monitor.

```
firstFrame.setSize(250, 100);
firstFrame.setTitle("My frame");
```

When you set a JFrame's size, you do not have the full area available to use because part of the area is consumed by the JFrame's title bar and borders.

Figure 14-2 shows an application that creates a small, empty JFrame.

```
import javax.swing.*;
public class JFrame1
{
    public static void main(String[] args)
    {
        JFrame aFrame = new JFrame("First frame");
        aFrame.setSize(250, 100);
        aFrame.setVisible(true);
    }
}
```

Figure 14-2   The JFrame1 application

The application in Figure 14-2 produces the JFrame shown in Figure 14-3. It resembles frames that you have probably seen when using different UI programs you have downloaded or purchased. One reason to use similar frame objects in your own programs is that users are already familiar with the frame environment. When users see frames on their computer screens, they expect to see a title bar at the top containing text information (such as "First frame"). Users also expect to see Minimize, Maximize or Restore, and Close buttons in the frame's upper-right corner. Most users assume that they can change a frame's size by dragging its border or reposition the frame on their screen by dragging the frame's title bar to a new location. The JFrame in Figure 14-3 has all of these capabilities.

Figure 14-3   Output of the JFrame1 application

In the application in Figure 14-2, all three statements in the main() method are important. After you instantiate aFrame, if you do not use setVisible(true), you do not see the JFrame, and if you do not set its size, you see only the title bar of the JFrame because the JFrame size is 0 × 0 by default. It might seem unusual that the default state for a JFrame is invisible. However, consider that you might want to construct a JFrame in the background while other actions are occurring and that you might want to make it visible later, when appropriate (for example, after the user has taken an action such as selecting an option). To make a frame visible, some Java programmers use the show() method instead of the setVisible() method.

When a user closes a JFrame by clicking the Close button in the upper-right corner, the default behavior is for the JFrame to become hidden and for the application to keep running. This makes sense when there are other tasks for the program to complete after the main frame is closed—for example, displaying additional frames, closing open data files, or printing an activity report. However, when a JFrame serves as a Swing application's main user interface (as happens frequently in interactive programs), you usually want the program to exit when the user clicks the Close button. To change this behavior, you can call a JFrame's setDefaultCloseOperation() method and use one of the following four values as an argument:

- JFrame.EXIT_ON_CLOSE exits the program when the JFrame is closed.

- WindowConstants.DISPOSE_ON_CLOSE closes the frame, disposes of the JFrame object, and keeps running the application.

- WindowConstants.DO_NOTHING_ON_CLOSE keeps the JFrame open and continues running. In other words, it disables the Close button.

- WindowConstants.HIDE_ON_CLOSE closes the JFrame and continues running; this is the default operation that you frequently want to override.

When you execute an application in which you have forgotten to exit when the JFrame is closed, you can end the program by typing Ctrl+C.

Each of the four usable setDefaultCloseOperation() arguments represents an integer; for example, the value of JFrame.EXIT_ON_CLOSE is 3. However, it is easier to remember the constant names than the numeric values they represent, and other programmers more easily understand your intentions if you use the named constant identifier.

Customizing a JFrame's Appearance

The appearance of the JFrame in Figure 14-3 is provided by the operating system in which the program is running (in this case, Windows). For example, the coffee-cup icon in the frame's title bar and the Minimize, Restore, and Close buttons look and act as they do in other Windows applications. The icon and buttons are known as **window decorations**; by default, window decorations are supplied by the operating system. However, you can request that Java's look and feel provide the decorations for a frame. A **look and feel** is the default appearance and behavior of any user interface.

Optionally, you can set a JFrame's look and feel using the setDefaultLookAndFeelDecorated() method. For example, Figure 14-4 shows an application that calls this method.

```
import javax.swing.*;
public class JFrame2
{
    public static void main(String[] args)
    {
        JFrame.setDefaultLookAndFeelDecorated(true);
        JFrame aFrame = new JFrame("Second frame");
        aFrame.setSize(250, 100);
        aFrame.setVisible(true);
    }
}
```

Figure 14-4   The JFrame2 class

 You can provide a custom icon for a frame instead of using your operating system's default icon or the Java look-and-feel icon. For details, go to the Java Web site and search for "How to Make Frames."

The program in Figure 14-4 differs from Figure 14-2 only in the shaded areas, which show the class name, the text in the title bar, and the look-and-feel statement. Figure 14-5 shows the output. If you compare the frame in Figure 14-5 with the one in Figure 14-3, you can see that Java's look and feel has similar features to that of Windows, but their appearance is different. Java's look and feel is also known by the name *Metal*.

Figure 14-5   Output of the JFrame2 application

 Look and feel is a legal issue because some software companies claim that competitors are infringing on their copyright protection by copying the look and feel of their products.

 Watch the video *Using the JFrame class*.

TWO TRUTHS & A LIE

Using the JFrame Class

1. The JFrame class contains overloaded constructors; for example, you can specify a title or not.

2. An advantage of using a JFrame is that it resembles traditional frames that people are accustomed to using.

3. When a user closes a JFrame by clicking the Close button in the upper-right corner, the default behavior is for the application to end.

The false statement is #3. When a user closes a JFrame by clicking the Close button in the upper-right corner, the default behavior is for the JFrame to become hidden and for the application to keep running.

You Do It

Creating a JFrame

In this section, you create a JFrame object that appears on the screen.

1. Open a new file in your text editor, and type the following statement to import the javax.swing classes:

```
import javax.swing.*;
```

2. On the next lines, type the following class header for the JDemoFrame class, its opening curly brace, the main() method header, and its opening curly brace:

```
public class JDemoFrame
{
    public static void main(String[] args)
    {
```

3. Within the body of the main() method, enter the following code to declare a JFrame with a title, set its size, and make it visible. If you neglect to set a JFrame's size, you see only the title bar of the JFrame (because the size is 0 × 0 by default); if you neglect to make the JFrame visible, you do not see anything. Add two closing curly braces—one for the main() method and one for the JDemoFrame class.

(continues)

(continued)

```
        JFrame aFrame = new JFrame("This is a frame");
        final int WIDTH = 250;
        final int HEIGHT = 250;
        aFrame.setSize(WIDTH, HEIGHT);
        aFrame.setVisible(true);
    }
}
```

4. Save the file as **JDemoFrame.java**. Compile and then run the program. The output looks like Figure 14-6—an empty JFrame with a title bar, a little taller than it is wide. The JFrame has all the properties of frames you have seen in applications you have used. For example, click the JFrame's **Minimize** button, and the JFrame minimizes to an icon on the Windows taskbar.

Figure 14-6 Output of the JDemoFrame application

5. Click the JFrame's **icon** on the taskbar. The JFrame returns to its previous size.

6. Click the JFrame's **Maximize** button. The JFrame fills the screen.

7. Click the JFrame's **Restore** button. The JFrame returns to its original size.

8. Position your mouse pointer on the JFrame's title bar, and then drag the JFrame to a new position on your screen.

9. Click the JFrame's **Close** button. The JFrame disappears or hides. The default behavior of a JFrame is simply to hide when the user clicks the Close button—not to end the program.

(continues)

747

(continued)

10. To end the program and return control to the command line, click the Command Prompt window, and then press **Ctrl+C**. In Chapter 6, you learned to press Ctrl+C to stop a program that contains an infinite loop. This situation is similar—you want to stop a program that does not have a way to end automatically.

Ending an Application When a JFrame Closes

Next, you modify the JDemoFrame program so that the application ends when the user clicks the JDemoFrame Close button.

1. Within the JDemoFrame class file, change the class name to **JDemoFrameThatCloses**.

2. Add a new line of code as the final executable statement within the main() method, as follows:

   ```
   aFrame.setDefaultCloseOperation(JFrame.EXIT_ON_CLOSE);
   ```

3. Save the file as **JDemoFrameThatCloses.java**, and compile and execute the application.

4. When the JFrame appears on your screen, confirm that it still has Minimize, Maximize, and Restore capabilities. Then click the JFrame's **Close** button. The JFrame closes, and the command prompt returns as the program relinquishes control to the operating system.

Using the JLabel Class

One of the components you might want to place on a JFrame is a JLabel. **JLabel** is a built-in Java Swing class that holds text you can display. The inheritance hierarchy of the JLabel class is shown in Figure 14-7.

```
java.lang.Object
    |
  +--java.awt.Component
        |
        +--java.awt.Container
              |
              +--javax.swing.JComponent
                    |
                    +--javax.swing.JLabel
```

Figure 14-7   The JLabel class inheritance hierarchy

Available constructors for the JLabel class include the following:

- JLabel() creates a JLabel instance with no image and with an empty string for the title.
- JLabel(Icon image) creates a JLabel instance with the specified image.
- JLabel(Icon image, int horizontalAlignment) creates a JLabel instance with the specified image and horizontal alignment.

- JLabel(String text) creates a JLabel instance with the specified text.
- JLabel(String text, Icon icon, int horizontalAlignment) creates a JLabel instance with the specified text, image, and horizontal alignment.
- JLabel(String text, int horizontalAlignment) creates a JLabel instance with the specified text and horizontal alignment.

For example, you can create a JLabel named greeting that holds the words "Good day" by writing the following statement:

```
JLabel greeting = new JLabel("Good day");
```

You then can add the greeting object to the JFrame object named aFrame using the **add() method** as follows:

```
aFrame.add(greeting);
```

Figure 14-8 shows an application in which a JFrame is created and its size, visibility, and close operation are set. Then a JLabel is created and added to the JFrame. Figure 14-9 shows the output.

```java
import javax.swing.*;
public class JFrame3
{
    public static void main(String[] args)
    {
        final int FRAME_WIDTH = 250;
        final int FRAME_HEIGHT = 100;
        JFrame aFrame = new JFrame("Third frame");
        aFrame.setSize(FRAME_WIDTH, FRAME_HEIGHT);
        aFrame.setVisible(true);
        aFrame.setDefaultCloseOperation(JFrame.EXIT_ON_CLOSE);
        JLabel greeting = new JLabel("Good day");
        aFrame.add(greeting);
    }
}
```

Figure 14-8   The JFrame3 class

Figure 14-9 Output of the JFrame3 application

The counterpart to the add() method is the **remove() method**. The following statement removes greeting from aFrame:

```
aFrame.remove(greeting);
```

If you add or remove a component from a container after it has been made visible, you should also call the invalidate(), validate(), and repaint() methods, or else you will not see the results of your actions. Each performs slightly different functions, but all three together guarantee that the results of changes in your layout will take effect. The invalidate() and validate() methods are part of the Container class, and the repaint() method is part of the Component class.

> If you add or remove a component in a JFrame during construction, you do not have to call repaint() if you later alter the component—for example, by changing its text. You only need to call repaint() if you add or remove a component after construction. You will learn more about the repaint() method in the Graphics chapter.

You can change the text in a JLabel by using the Component class **setText() method** with the JLabel object and passing a String to it. For example, the following code changes the value displayed in the greeting JLabel:

```
greeting.setText("Howdy");
```

You can retrieve the text in a JLabel (or other Component) by using the **getText() method**, which returns the currently stored String.

Changing a JLabel's Font

If you use the Internet and a Web browser to visit Web sites, you probably are not very impressed with the simple application displayed in Figure 14-9. You might think that the string "Good day" is plain and lackluster. Fortunately, Java provides you with a **Font class** from which you can create an object that holds typeface and size information. The **setFont() method** requires a Font object argument. To construct a Font object, you need three arguments: typeface, style, and point size.

- The **typeface argument** to the Font constructor is a String representing a font. Common fonts have names such as Arial, Century, Monospaced, and Times New Roman. The typeface argument in the Font constructor is only a request; the system on which your program runs might not have access to the requested font, and if necessary, it substitutes a default font.

- The **style argument** applies an attribute to displayed text and is one of three values: Font.PLAIN, Font.BOLD, or Font.ITALIC.

- The **point size argument** is an integer that represents about 1/72 of an inch. Printed text is commonly 12 points; a headline might be 30 points.

In printing, point size defines a measurement between lines of text in a single-spaced text document. The point size is based on typographic points, which are approximately 1/72 of an inch. Java adopts the convention that one point on a display is equivalent to one unit in user coordinates. For more information, see the Font documentation at the Java Web site.

To give a JLabel object a new font, you can create a Font object, as in the following:

Font headlineFont = new Font("Monospaced", Font.BOLD, 36);

The typeface name is a String, so you must enclose it in double quotation marks.

You can use the setFont() method to assign the Font to a JLabel with a statement such as:

greeting.setFont(headlineFont);

Figure 14-10 shows a class named JFrame4. All the changes from JFrame3 are shaded.

```
import javax.swing.*;
import java.awt.*;
public class JFrame4
{
    public static void main(String[] args)
    {
        final int FRAME_WIDTH = 250;
        final int FRAME_HEIGHT = 100;
        Font headlineFont = new Font("Arial", Font.BOLD, 36);
        JFrame aFrame = new JFrame("Fourth frame");
        aFrame.setSize(FRAME_WIDTH, FRAME_HEIGHT);
        aFrame.setVisible(true);
        aFrame.setDefaultCloseOperation(JFrame.EXIT_ON_CLOSE);
        JLabel greeting = new JLabel("Good day");
        greeting.setFont(headlineFont);
        aFrame.add(greeting);
    }
}
```

Figure 14-10   The JFrame4 program

The program in Figure 14-10 includes a new import statement for the package that contains the Font class. The program contains a Font object named headlineFont that is applied to the greeting. Figure 14-11 shows the execution of the JFrame4 program; the greeting appears in a 36-point, bold, Arial font.

Figure 14-11　Output of the JFrame4 program

You are not required to provide an identifier for a Font. For example, you could omit the shaded statement that declares headlineFont in Figure 14-10 and set the greeting Font with the following statement that uses an anonymous Font object:

```
greeting.setFont(new Font("Arial", Font.BOLD, 36));
```

After you create a Font object, you can create a new object with a different type and size using the deriveFont() method with appropriate arguments. For example, the following two statements create a headlineFont object and a textBodyFont object that is based on the first object:

```
Font headlineFont = new Font("Arial", Font.BOLD, 36);
Font textBodyFont = headlineFont.deriveFont(Font.PLAIN, 14);
```

TWO TRUTHS & A LIE

Using the JLabel Class

1. JLabel is a built-in Java Swing class that holds text you can display.

2. You can change a JLabel's text by using its JFrame's name, a dot, and the add() method, and then using the desired text as the argument to the method.

3. If you add or remove a component from a container after it has been made visible, you should also call the validate() and repaint() methods, or else you will not see the results of your actions.

The false statement is #2. You change a JLabel's text using the setText() method, including the new text as the argument. You add a JLabel to a JFrame by using the JFrame's name, a dot, and the add() method, and then by using the JLabel's name as an argument to the method.

Using a Layout Manager

When you want to add multiple components to a JFrame or other container, you usually need to provide instructions for the layout of the components. For example, Figure 14-12 shows an application in which two JLabels are created and added to a JFrame in the final shaded statements.

```java
import javax.swing.*;
import java.awt.*;
public class JFrame5
{
    public static void main(String[] args)
    {
        final int FRAME_WIDTH = 250;
        final int FRAME_HEIGHT = 100;
        JFrame aFrame = new JFrame("Fifth frame");
        aFrame.setSize(FRAME_WIDTH, FRAME_HEIGHT);
        aFrame.setVisible(true);
        aFrame.setDefaultCloseOperation(JFrame.EXIT_ON_CLOSE);
        JLabel greeting = new JLabel("Hello");
        JLabel greeting2 = new JLabel("Who are you?");
        aFrame.add(greeting);
        aFrame.add(greeting2);
    }
}
```

Figure 14-12   The JFrame5 program

Figure 14-13 shows the output of the application in Figure 14-12. Although two JLabels are added to the frame, only the last one added is visible. The second JLabel has been placed on top of the first one, totally obscuring it. If you continued to add more JLabels to the program, only the last one added to the JFrame would be visible.

Figure 14-13   Output of the JFrame5 program

To place multiple components at specified positions in a container so they do not hide each other, you must explicitly use a **layout manager**—a class that controls component positioning. The normal (default) behavior of a JFrame is to use a layout format named BorderLayout. A **BorderLayout**, created by using the BorderLayout class, divides a container into regions. When you do not specify a region in which to place a component (as the

JFrame5 program fails to do), all the components are placed in the same region, and they obscure each other.

When you use a FlowLayout instead of a BorderLayout, components do not lie on top of each other. Instead, the **flow layout manager** places components in a row, and when a row is filled, components automatically spill into the next row.

Three constants are defined in the FlowLayout class that specify how components are positioned in each row of their container. These constants are FlowLayout.LEFT, FlowLayout.RIGHT, and FlowLayout.CENTER. For example, to create a layout manager named flow that positions components to the right, you can use the following statement:

```
FlowLayout flow = new FlowLayout(FlowLayout.RIGHT);
```

If you do not specify how components are laid out, by default they are centered in each row.

Suppose that you create a FlowLayout object named flow as follows:

```
FlowLayout flow = new FlowLayout();
```

Then the layout of a JFrame named aFrame can be set to the newly created FlowLayout using the statement:

```
aFrame.setLayout(flow);
```

A more compact syntax that uses an anonymous FlowLayout object is:

```
aFrame.setLayout(new FlowLayout());
```

Figure 14-14 shows an application in which the JFrame's layout manager has been set so that multiple components are visible.

```
import javax.swing.*;
import java.awt.*;
public class JFrame6
{
    public static void main(String[] args)
    {
        final int FRAME_WIDTH = 250;
        final int FRAME_HEIGHT = 100;
        JFrame aFrame = new JFrame("Sixth frame");
        aFrame.setSize(FRAME_WIDTH, FRAME_HEIGHT);
        aFrame.setVisible(true);
        aFrame.setDefaultCloseOperation(JFrame.EXIT_ON_CLOSE);
        JLabel greeting = new JLabel("Hello");
        JLabel greeting2 = new JLabel("Who are you?");
        aFrame.setLayout(new FlowLayout());
        aFrame.add(greeting);
        aFrame.add(greeting2);
    }
}
```

Figure 14-14   The JFrame6 program

Figure 14-15 shows the execution of the JFrame6 program. Because a FlowLayout is used, the two JLabels appear side by side. If there were more JLabels or other components, they would continue to be placed side by side across the JFrame until there was no more room. Then, the additional components would be placed in a new row beneath the first row of components.

```
Sixth frame                    —  □  X

        Hello  Who are you?
```

Figure 14-15   Output of the JFrame6 program

 Other layout managers allow you to position components in a container more precisely. You will learn about these in the *Graphics* chapter. The examples in this chapter will use FlowLayout because it is the easiest of the layout managers to use.

 Watch the video *Using a Layout Manager.*

TWO TRUTHS & A LIE
Using a Layout Manager

1. If you do not provide a layout manager for a JFrame, you cannot add multiple components to it.

2. The normal (default) behavior of a JFrame is to use a layout format named BorderLayout.

3. The flow layout manager places components in a row, and when a row is filled, it automatically spills components into the next row.

The false statement is #1. If you do not provide a layout manager for a JFrame, you can add multiple components to it, but only the most recently added one is visible.

Extending the `JFrame` Class

You can instantiate a simple `JFrame` object within an application's `main()` method or with any other method of any class you write. Alternatively, you can create your own class that descends from the `JFrame` class. The advantage of creating a child class of `JFrame` is that you can set the `JFrame`'s properties within your object's constructor; then, when you create your `JFrame` child object, it is automatically endowed with the features you have specified, such as title, size, and default close operation.

You already know that you create a child class by using the keyword `extends` in the class header, followed by the parent class name. You also know that you can call the parent class's constructor using the keyword `super`, and that when you call `super()`, the call must be the first statement in the constructor. For example, the JMyFrame class in Figure 14-16 extends `JFrame`. Within the JMyFrame constructor, the `super()` `JFrame` constructor is called; it accepts a `String` argument to use as the `JFrame`'s title. (Alternatively, the `setTitle()` method could have been used.) The JMyFrame constructor also sets the size, visibility, and default close operation for every JMyFrame. Each of the methods—`setSize()`, `setVisible()`, and `setDefaultCloseOperation()`—appears in the constructor in Figure 14-16 without an object, because the object is the current JMyFrame being constructed. Each of the three methods could be preceded with a `this` reference with exactly the same meaning. That is, within the JMyFrame constructor, the following two statements have identical meanings:

```
setSize(WIDTH, HEIGHT);
this.setSize(WIDTH, HEIGHT);
```

Each statement sets the size of "this" current JMyFrame instance.

```
import javax.swing.*;
public class JMyFrame extends JFrame
{
    final int WIDTH = 200;
    final int HEIGHT = 120;
    public JMyFrame()
    {
        super("My frame");
        setSize(WIDTH, HEIGHT);
        setVisible(true);
        setDefaultCloseOperation(JFrame.EXIT_ON_CLOSE);
    }
}
```

Figure 14-16   The JMyFrame class

Figure 14-17 shows an application that declares two JMyFrame objects. Each has the same set of attributes, determined by the JMyFrame constructor.

```
public class CreateTwoJMyFrameObjects
{
    public static void main(String[] args)
    {
        JMyFrame myFrame = new JMyFrame();
        JMyFrame mySecondFrame = new JMyFrame();
    }
}
```

Figure 14-17   The CreateTwoJMyFrameObjects application

When you execute the application in Figure 14-17, the two JMyFrame objects are displayed with the second one on top of, or obscuring, the first. Figure 14-18 shows the output of the CreateTwoJMyFrameObjects application after the top JMyFrame has been dragged to partially expose the bottom one.

Figure 14-18   Output of the CreateTwoJMyFrameObjects application after dragging the top frame

 You could use the setBounds() method with one of the JMyFrame objects that produces the output in Figure 14-18 so that you don't have to move one JMyFrame object to view the other. See Table 14-1 for details. The Object class also includes a setLocation() method you can use with a JFrame. To use this method, you provide horizontal and vertical position values as method arguments. You will learn more about the setLocation() method in the chapter *Applets, Images, and Sound*.

 You exit the application when you click the Close button on either of the two JMyFrame objects shown in Figure 14-18. Each object has the same default close operation because each uses the same constructor that specifies this operation. To allow only one JMyFrame to control the program's exit, you could use the setDefaultCloseOperation() method with one or both of the objects in the application to change its close behavior. For example, you could use DISPOSE_ON_CLOSE to dismiss one of the frames but keep the application running.

When you extend a JFrame to create a new custom class, you must remember to make decisions as to which attributes you want to set within the class and which you want to leave to the applications that will use the class. For example, you can place the setVisible()

statement within the JFrame child class constructor (using either an explicit or implied this reference), or you can allow the application to use a setVisible() statement (using the name of an instantiated object followed by a dot and the method name). Either one works, but if you fail to do either, the frame will not be visible.

Programmers frequently place a main() method within a class such as JMyFrame. Then the class provides the option to be used to instantiate objects, as in the CreateTwoJMyFrameObjects application, or to be used to execute as a program that creates an object.

TWO TRUTHS & A LIE

Extending the JFrame Class

1. The advantage of creating a child class of JFrame is that you can set the JFrame's properties within your object's constructor so it is automatically endowed with the features that you have specified.

2. When a class descends from JFrame, you can use super() or setTitle() to set the title within any of the child's methods.

3. When you extend a JFrame to create a new custom class, you can decide which attributes you want to set within the class and which you want to leave to the applications that will use the class.

The false statement is #2. When a class descends from JFrame, you can use super() or setTitle() to set the title within the child's constructor. However, super() does not work in other methods.

Adding JTextFields, JButtons, and Tool Tips to a JFrame

In addition to including JLabel objects, JFrames often contain other window features, such as JTextFields, JButtons, and tool tips.

Adding JTextFields

A **JTextField** is a component into which a user can type a single line of text data. (Text data comprises any characters you can enter from the keyboard, including numbers and punctuation.) Figure 14-19 shows the inheritance hierarchy of the JTextField class.

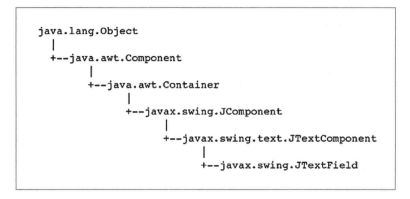

```
java.lang.Object
   |
   +--java.awt.Component
          |
          +--java.awt.Container
                 |
                 +--javax.swing.JComponent
                        |
                        +--javax.swing.text.JTextComponent
                               |
                               +--javax.swing.JTextField
```

Figure 14-19 The JTextField class inheritance hierarchy

Typically, a user types a line into a JTextField and then presses Enter on the keyboard or clicks a button with the mouse to enter the data. You can construct a JTextField object using one of several constructors:

- public JTextField() constructs a new JTextField.
- public JTextField(int columns) constructs a new, empty JTextField with a specified number of columns.
- public JTextField(String text) constructs a new JTextField initialized with the specified text.
- public JTextField(String text, int columns) constructs a new JTextField initialized with the specified text and columns.

For example, to provide a JTextField that allows enough room for a user to enter approximately 10 characters, you can code the following:

```
JTextField response = new JTextField(10);
```

To add the JTextField named response to a JFrame named frame, you write:

```
frame.add(response);
```

The number of characters a JTextField can display depends on the font being used and the actual characters typed. For example, in most fonts, w is wider than i, so a JTextField of size 10 using the Arial font can display 24 i characters, but only eight w characters.

Try to anticipate how many characters your users might enter when you create a JTextField. The user can enter more characters than those that display, but the extra characters scroll out of view. It can be disconcerting to try to enter data into a field that is not large enough. It is usually better to overestimate than underestimate the size of a text field.

Several other methods are available for use with JTextFields. The setText() method allows you to change the text in a JTextField (or other Component) that has already been created, as in the following:

```
response.setText("Thank you");
```

After a user has entered text in a JTextField, you can clear it out with a statement such as the following, which assigns an empty string to the text:

```
response.setText("");
```

The getText() method allows you to retrieve the String of text in a JTextField (or other Component), as in:

```
String whatUserTyped = response.getText();
```

When a JTextField has the capability of accepting keystrokes, the JTextField is **editable**. A JTextField is editable by default. If you do not want the user to be able to enter data in a JTextField, you can send a boolean value to the **setEditable() method** to change the JTextField's editable status. For example, if you want to give a user a limited number of chances to answer a question correctly, you can count data entry attempts and then prevent the user from replacing or editing the characters in the JTextField by using a statement similar to the following:

```
if(attempts > LIMIT)
    response.setEditable(false);
```

Adding JButtons

A **JButton** is a Component the user can click with a mouse to make a selection. A JButton is even easier to create than a JTextField. There are five JButton constructors:

- public JButton() creates a button with no set text.

- public JButton(Icon icon) creates a button with an icon of type Icon or ImageIcon.

- public JButton(String text) creates a button with text.

- public JButton(String text, Icon icon) creates a button with initial text and an icon of type Icon or ImageIcon.

- public JButton(Action a) creates a button in which properties are taken from the Action supplied. (Action is a Java class.)

The inheritance hierarchy of the JButton class is shown in Figure 14-20.

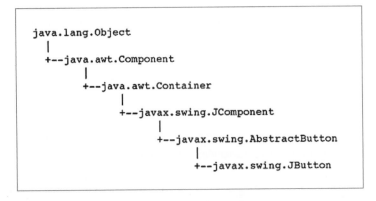

```
java.lang.Object
    |
    +--java.awt.Component
            |
            +--java.awt.Container
                    |
                    +--javax.swing.JComponent
                            |
                            +--javax.swing.AbstractButton
                                    |
                                    +--javax.swing.JButton
```

Figure 14-20   The JButton class inheritance hierarchy

To create a JButton with the label "Press when ready", you can write the following:

```
JButton readyJButton = new JButton("Press when ready");
```

You can add a JButton to a JFrame (or other container) using the add() method. You can change a JButton's label with the setText() method, as in:

```
readyJButton.setText("Don't press me again!");
```

You can retrieve the text from a JButton and assign it to a String object with the getText() method, as in:

```
String whatsOnJButton = readyJButton.getText();
```

Figure 14-21 shows a class that extends JFrame and holds several components. As the components (two JLabels, a JTextField, and a JButton) are added to the JFrame, they are placed from left to right in horizontal rows across the JFrame's surface. Figure 14-22 shows the program that instantiates an instance of the JFrame.

```
import javax.swing.*;
import java.awt.*;
public class JFrameWithManyComponents extends JFrame
{
    final int FRAME_WIDTH = 300;
    final int FRAME_HEIGHT = 150;
    public JFrameWithManyComponents()
    {
        super("Demonstrating many components");
        setSize(FRAME_WIDTH, FRAME_HEIGHT);
        setDefaultCloseOperation(JFrame.EXIT_ON_CLOSE);
        JLabel heading = new JLabel("This frame has many components");
        heading.setFont(new Font("Arial", Font.BOLD, 16));
        JLabel namePrompt = new JLabel("Enter your name:");
        JTextField nameField = new JTextField(12);
        JButton button = new JButton("Click to continue");
        setLayout(new FlowLayout());
        add(heading);
        add(namePrompt);
        add(nameField);
        add(button);
    }
}
```

Figure 14-21   The JFrameWithManyComponents class

```
public class ComponentDemo
{
   public static void main(String[] args)
   {
      JFrameWithManyComponents frame =
         new JFrameWithManyComponents();
      frame.setVisible(true);
   }
}
```

Figure 14-22 A ComponentDemo application that instantiates a JFrameWithManyComponents

When you execute the ComponentDemo program, the JFrame contains all the components that were added in the frame's constructor, as shown in Figure 14-23. A user can minimize or restore the frame and can alter its size by dragging the frame borders. The user can type characters in the JTextField and click the JButton. When the button is clicked, it appears to be pressed just like buttons you have used in professional applications. However, when the user types characters or clicks the button, no resulting actions occur because code has not yet been written to handle those user-initiated events.

Figure 14-23 Execution of the ComponentDemo program

Using Tool Tips

Tool tips are popup windows that can help a user understand the purpose of components in an application; the tool tip appears when a user hovers the mouse pointer over the component. You define the text to be displayed in a tool tip by using the **setToolTipText() method** and passing an appropriate String to it. For example, in the JFrameWithManyComponents program in Figure 14-21, you can add a tool tip to the button component by using the following statement in the JFrame constructor:

```
button.setToolTipText("Click this button");
```

Figure 14-24 shows the result when the JFrame is displayed and the user's mouse pointer is placed over the button.

Figure 14-24   JFrame with added tool tip

 The JFrameWithToolTip.java file in your downloadable student files contains a revised version of JFrameWithManyComponents with the tool tip added. The ToolTipDemo.java file contains an application that instantiates a JFrameWithToolTip object.

TWO TRUTHS & A LIE

Adding JTextFields, JButtons, and Tool Tips to a JFrame

1. A JTextField is a component into which a user can type a single line of text data; typically, a user types a line into a JTextField and then presses Enter on the keyboard or clicks a button with the mouse to enter the data.

2. A JButton is a Component the user can click with a mouse to make a selection.

3. Tool tips are the different symbols you can select to display as a cursor in your applications.

The false statement is #3. Tool tips are popup windows that can help a user understand the purpose of components in an application; the tool tip appears when a user hovers the mouse pointer over the component.

You Do It

Adding Components to a JFrame

Next, you create a Swing application that displays a JFrame that holds a JLabel, JTextField, and JButton.

1. Open a new file in your text editor, then type the following first few lines of an application. The import statements make the Swing and AWT components available, and the class header indicates that the class is a JFrame. The class contains several components: a label, field, and button.

```
import javax.swing.*;
import java.awt.*;
public class JFrameWithComponents extends JFrame
{
    JLabel label = new JLabel("Enter your name");
    JTextField field = new JTextField(12);
    JButton button = new JButton("OK");
```

2. In the JFrameWithComponents constructor, set the JFrame title to "Frame with Components" and the default close operation to exit the program when the JFrame is closed. Set the layout manager. Add the label, field, and button to the JFrame.

```
public JFrameWithComponents()
{
    super("Frame with Components");
    setDefaultCloseOperation(JFrame.EXIT_ON_CLOSE);
    setLayout(new FlowLayout());
    add(label);
    add(field);
    add(button);
}
```

3. Add a closing curly brace for the class, and then save the file as **JFrameWithComponents.java**.

4. Compile the class and correct any errors.

5. Next, write an application that creates a new JFrameWithComponents named aFrame, sizes it using the setSize() method, and then sets its visible property to true.

(continues)

(continued)

```java
import javax.swing.*;
public class CreateJFrameWithComponents
{
    public static void main(String[] args)
    {
        JFrameWithComponents aFrame =
            new JFrameWithComponents();
        final int WIDTH = 350;
        final int HEIGHT = 100;
        aFrame.setSize(WIDTH, HEIGHT);
        aFrame.setVisible(true);
    }
}
```

6. Save the file as **CreateJFrameWithComponents.java**. Compile and then execute the application. The output is shown in Figure 14-25.

Figure 14-25　Output of the CreateJFrameWithComponents application

7. Click the JButton. It acts like a button should—that is, it appears to be pressed when you click it, but nothing happens because you have not yet written instructions for the button clicks to execute.

8. Close the application.

Learning About Event-Driven Programming

An **event** occurs when a user takes action on a component, such as clicking the mouse on a JButton object. In an **event-driven program**, the user might initiate any number of events in any order. For example, if you use a word-processing program, you have dozens of choices at your disposal at any time. You can type words, select text with the mouse, click a button to change text to bold, click a button to change text to italic, choose a menu item, and so on. With each word-processing document you create, you choose options in any order that seems appropriate at the time. The word-processing program must be ready to respond to any event you initiate.

Within an event-driven program, a component on which an event is generated is the **source** of the event. A button that a user can click is an example of a source; a text field that a user can use to enter text is another source. An object that is interested in an event is a **listener**. Not all objects listen for all possible events—you probably have used programs in which clicking many areas of the screen has no effect. If you want an object to be a listener for an event, you must register the object as a listener for the source.

Social networking sites maintain lists of people in whom you are interested and notify you each time a person on your list posts a comment or picture. Similarly, a Java component source object (such as a button) maintains a list of registered listeners and notifies all of them when any event occurs. For example, a JFrame might want to be notified of any mouse click on its surface. When the listener "receives the news," an event-handling method contained in the listener object responds to the event.

A source object and a listener object can be the same object. For example, you might program a JButton to change its own label when a user clicks it.

To respond to user events within any class you create, you must do the following:

- Prepare your class to accept event messages.
- Tell your class to expect events to happen.
- Tell your class how to respond to events.

Preparing Your Class to Accept Event Messages

You prepare your class to accept button-press events by importing the java.awt.event package into your program and adding the phrase implements ActionListener to the class header. The java.awt.event package includes event classes with names such as ActionEvent, ComponentEvent, and TextEvent. ActionListener is an interface—a class containing a set of specifications for methods that you can use. Implementing ActionListener provides you with standard event method specifications that allow your listener to work with ActionEvents, which are the types of events that occur when a user clicks a button.

You learned to create and implement interfaces in Chapter 11. You can identify interfaces such as ActionListener because they use the keyword implements. In ordinary language, an item that is implemented is put into service, or used. Implementation has a similar meaning when applied to interfaces. In contrast, packages that are imported are brought into an application, and classes that are added onto are extended.

Telling Your Class to Expect Events to Happen

You tell your class to expect ActionEvents with the **addActionListener() method**. If you have declared a JButton named aButton, and you want to perform an action when a user clicks aButton, aButton is the source of a message, and you can think of your class as a target to which to send a message. You learned in Chapter 4 that the this reference means "this current object," so the code aButton.addActionListener(this); causes any ActionEvent messages (button clicks) that come from aButton to be sent to "this current object."

Not all Events are ActionEvents with an addActionListener() method. For example, KeyListeners have an addKeyListener() method, and FocusListeners have an addFocusListener() method. Additional event types and methods are covered in more detail in the next chapter.

Telling Your Class How to Respond to Events

The ActionListener interface contains the **actionPerformed(ActionEvent e) method** specification. When a class, such as a JFrame, has registered as a listener with a Component such as a JButton, and a user clicks the JButton, the actionPerformed() method executes. You implement the actionPerformed() method, which contains a header and a body, like all methods. You use the following header, in which e represents any name you choose for the Event (the JButton click) that initiated the notification of the ActionListener (which is the JFrame):

```
public void actionPerformed(ActionEvent e)
```

The body of the method contains any statements that you want to execute when the action occurs. You might want to perform mathematical calculations, construct new objects, produce output, or execute any other operation. For example, Figure 14-26 shows a JFrame containing a JLabel that prompts the user for a name, a JTextField into which the user can type a response, a JButton to click, and a second JLabel that displays the name entered by the user. The actionPerformed() method executes when the user clicks the pressMe JButton; within the method, the String that a user has typed into the JTextField is retrieved and stored in the name variable. The name is then used as part of a String that alters the second JLabel on the JFrame. Figure 14-27 shows an application that instantiates a JHelloFrame object and makes it visible.

```
import javax.swing.*;
import java.awt.*;
import java.awt.event.*;
public class JHelloFrame extends JFrame implements ActionListener
{
    JLabel question = new JLabel("What is your name?");
    Font bigFont = new Font("Arial", Font.BOLD, 16);
    JTextField answer = new JTextField(10);
    JButton pressMe = new JButton("Press me");
    JLabel greeting = new JLabel("");
    final int WIDTH = 275;
    final int HEIGHT = 225;
    public JHelloFrame()
    {
        super("Hello Frame");
        setSize(WIDTH, HEIGHT);
        setLayout(new FlowLayout());
        question.setFont(bigFont);
        greeting.setFont(bigFont);
        add(question);
        add(answer);
        add(pressMe);
        add(greeting);
        setDefaultCloseOperation(JFrame.EXIT_ON_CLOSE);
        pressMe.addActionListener(this);
    }
    public void actionPerformed(ActionEvent e)
    {
        String name = answer.getText();
        String greet = "Hello, " + name;
        greeting.setText(greet);
    }
}
```

Figure 14-26   The JHelloFrame class that produces output when the user clicks the JButton

```
public class JHelloDemo
{
    public static void main(String[] args)
    {
        JHelloFrame frame = new JHelloFrame();
        frame.setVisible(true);
    }
}
```

Figure 14-27   An application that instantiates a JHelloFrame object

Figure 14-28 shows a typical execution of the JHelloDemo program. The user enters *Lindsey* into the JTextField, and the greeting with the name is displayed after the user clicks the button.

Figure 14-28 Typical execution of the JHelloDemo program

When more than one component is added and registered to a JFrame, it might be necessary to determine which component was used to initiate an event. For example, in the JHelloFrame class in Figure 14-26, you might want the user to be able to see the message after either clicking the button or pressing Enter in the JTextField. In that case, you would designate both the pressMe button and the answer text field to be message sources by using the addActionListener() method with each, as follows:

```
pressMe.addActionListener(this);
answer.addActionListener(this);
```

These two statements make the JFrame (this) the receiver of messages from either object. The JFrame has only one actionPerformed() method, so it is the method that executes when either the pressMe button or the answer text field sends a message.

If you want different actions to occur depending on whether the user clicks the button or presses Enter, you must determine the source of the event. Within the actionPerformed() method, you can use the getSource() method of the object sent to determine which component generated the event. For example, within a method with the header public void actionPerformed(ActionEvent e), e is an ActionEvent. ActionEvent and other event classes are part of the java.awt.event package and are subclasses of the EventObject class. To determine what object generated the ActionEvent, you can use the following statement:

```
Object source = e.getSource();
```

For example, if a JFrame contains two JButtons named option1 and option2, you can use the decision structure in the method in Figure 14-29 to take different courses of action based on the button that is clicked. Whether an event's source is a JButton, JTextField, or other Component, it can be assigned to an Object because all components descend from Object.

```
public void actionPerformed(ActionEvent e)
{
    Object source = e.getSource();
    if(source == option1)
        //execute these statements when user clicks option1
    else
        //execute these statements when user clicks any other option
}
```

Figure 14-29   An `actionPerformed()` method that takes one of two possible actions

Alternatively, you can also use the `instanceof` keyword to determine the source of the event. The `instanceof` keyword is used when it is necessary to know only the component's type, rather than what component triggered the event. For example, if you want to take some action when a user enters data into any `JTextField`, but not when an event is generated by a different `Component` type, you could use the method format shown in Figure 14-30.

```
void actionPerformed(ActionEvent e)
{
    Object source = e.getSource();
    if(source instanceof JTextField)
    {
        // execute these statements when any JTextField
        // generates the event
        // but not when a JButton or other Component does
    }
}
```

Figure 14-30   An `actionPerformed()` method that executes a block of statements when a user generates an event from any `JTextField`

Using the `setEnabled()` Method

You probably have used computer programs in which a component becomes disabled or unusable. For example, a `JButton` might become dim and unresponsive when the programmer no longer wants you to have access to the `JButton`'s functionality. Components are enabled by default, but you can use the **`setEnabled()` method** to make a component available or unavailable by passing **true** or **false** to it, respectively. For example, Figure 14-31 shows a `JFrame` with two `JButton` objects. The one on top is enabled, but the one on the bottom has been disabled.

Figure 14-31 A JFrame with an enabled JButton and a disabled JButton

Your downloadable student files contain a file named JTwoButtons.java that produces the JFrame shown in Figure 14-31.

TWO TRUTHS & A LIE

Learning About Event-Driven Programming

1. Within an event-driven program, a component on which an event is generated is a listener.

2. You prepare your class to accept button-press events by importing the java.awt.event package into your program and adding the phrase implements ActionListener to the class header.

3. A class that can react to ActionEvents includes an actionPerformed() method.

The false statement is #1. Within an event-driven program, a component on which an event is generated is the source of the event, and an object that is interested in an event is a listener.

You Do It

Adding Functionality to a JButton and a JTextField

Next, you add functionality to the JButton and JTextField that you created in the JFrameWithComponents class.

1. Open the **JFrameWithComponents.java** file. Immediately save the file as **JAction.java**.

2. After the existing import statements at the top of the file, add the following import statement that will allow event handling:

```
import java.awt.event.*;
```

3. Change the class name to **JAction** to match the new filename. Also change the constructor header to match the new class name. Within the constructor, change the string argument to the super() method from "Frame with Components" to "Action".

4. After extends JFrame at the end of the JAction class header, add the following phrase so that the class can respond to ActionEvents:

```
implements ActionListener
```

5. Register the JAction class as a listener for events generated by either the button or the text field by adding the following statements at the end of, but within, the JAction() constructor:

```
button.addActionListener(this);
field.addActionListener(this);
```

6. Just prior to the closing curly brace for the class, add the following actionPerformed() method. The method changes the text on both the label and the button whenever the user clicks the button or presses Enter in the text field.

```
public void actionPerformed(ActionEvent e)
{
    label.setText("Thank you");
    button.setText("Done");
}
```

7. Just after the actionPerformed() method, and just before the closing curly brace for the class, add a main() method to the class so that you can instantiate a JAction object for demonstration purposes.

(continues)

(continued)

```
public static void main(String[] args)
{
    JAction aFrame = new JAction();
    final int WIDTH = 250;
    final int HEIGHT = 100;
    aFrame.setSize(WIDTH, HEIGHT);
    aFrame.setVisible(true);
}
```

8. Save the file, then compile and execute it. The output looks like the frame on the left side of Figure 14-32. Type a name in the text field, and then click the **OK** button. Its text changes to "Done", and its size increases slightly because the label "Done" requires more space than the label "OK". The other label requires less space than it did because "Thank you" is a shorter message than "Enter your name". Therefore, all the components are redistributed because the FlowLayout manager places as many components as will fit horizontally in the top row before adding components to subsequent rows. The output looks like the right side of Figure 14-32.

Figure 14-32   Typical execution of the JAction application after the user clicks the OK button

9. Close the application and then execute it again. This time, enter a name in the text field and press **Enter**. Again, the button text changes, showing that the actionPerformed() method reacts to actions that take place on either the button or the text field.

10. Close the application.

Distinguishing Event Sources

Next, you will modify the actionPerformed() method of the JAction class so that different results occur depending on which action a user takes.

1. Open the **JAction.java** file in your text editor if the file is not still open. Immediately save the file as **JAction2.java**.

(continues)

773

(continued)

2. Change the class name and the constructor name to match the new filename by adding **2** to each name.

3. In the `main()` method, change the statement that instantiates the `JFrame` object to the following:

```
JAction2 aFrame = new JAction2();
```

4. Within the `actionPerformed()` method, you can use the named `ActionEvent` argument and the `getSource()` method to determine the source of the event. Using an `if` statement, you can take different actions when the argument represents different sources. For example, you can change the label in the frame to indicate the event's source. Change the `actionPerformed()` method to:

```
public void actionPerformed(ActionEvent e)
{
    Object source = e.getSource();
    if(source == button)
        label.setText("You clicked the button");
    else
        label.setText("You pressed Enter");
}
```

5. Save the file (as JAction2.java), then compile and execute it. Type a name, press **Enter** or click the button, and notice the varying results in the frame's label. For example, Figure 14-33 shows the application after the user has typed a name and pressed Enter.

Figure 14-33   Typical execution of the `JAction2` application

6. Close the application.

Understanding Swing Event Listeners

Many types of listeners exist in Java, and each of these listeners can handle a specific event type. A class can implement as many event listeners as it needs—for example, a class might need to respond to both a mouse button press and a keyboard key press, so you might implement both ActionListener and KeyListener interfaces. Table 14-2 lists some event listeners and the types of events for which they are used.

Listener	Type of Events	Example
ActionListener	Action events	Button clicks
AdjustmentListener	Adjustment events	Scroll bar moves
ChangeListener	Change events	Slider is repositioned
FocusListener	Keyboard focus events	Text field gains or loses focus
ItemListener	Item events	Check box changes status
KeyListener	Keyboard events	Text is entered
MouseListener	Mouse events	Mouse clicks
MouseMotionListener	Mouse movement events	Mouse rolls
WindowListener	Window events	Window closes

Table 14-2   Alphabetical list of some event listeners

An event occurs every time a user types a character or clicks a mouse button. Any object can be notified of an event as long as it implements the appropriate interface and is registered as an event listener on the appropriate event source. You already know that you establish a relationship between a JButton and a JFrame that contains it by using the addActionListener() method. Similarly, you can create relationships between other Swing components and the classes that react to users' manipulations of them. In Table 14-3, each component listed on the left is associated with a method on the right. For example, when you want a JCheckBox to respond to a user's clicks, you can use the addItemListener() method to register the JCheckBox as the type of object that can create an ItemEvent. The argument you place within the parentheses of the call to the addItemListener() method is the object that should respond to the event—perhaps a JFrame that contains the event-generating JCheckBox. The format is:

```
theSourceOfTheEvent.addListenerMethod(theClassThatShouldRespond);
```

Component(s)	Associated Listener-Registering Method(s)
JButton, JCheckBox, JComboBox, JTextField, and JRadioButton	addActionListener()
JScrollBar	addAdjustmentListener()
All Swing components	addFocusListener(), addKeyListener(), addMouseListener(), and addMouseMotionListener()
JButton, JCheckBox, JComboBox, and JRadioButton	addItemListener()
All JWindow and JFrame components	addWindowListener()
JSlider and JCheckBox	addChangeListener()

Table 14-3   Some Swing components and their associated listener-registering methods

Any event source can have multiple listeners registered on it. Conversely, a single listener can be registered with multiple event sources. In other words, a single instance of JCheckBox might generate ItemEvents and FocusEvents, and a single instance of the JFrame class might respond to ActionEvents generated by a JButton and ItemEvents generated by a JCheckBox.

The class of the object that responds to an event must contain a method that accepts the event object created by the user's action. A method that executes because it is called automatically when an appropriate event occurs is an **event handler**. In other words, when you register a component (such as a JFrame) to be a listener for events generated by another component (such as a JCheckBox), you must write an event handler method. You cannot choose your own name for event handlers—specific method identifiers react to specific event types. Table 14-4 lists just some of the methods that react to events.

Listener	Method
ActionListener	actionPerformed(ActionEvent)
AdjustmentListener	adjustmentValueChanged(AdjustmentEvent)
FocusListener	focusGained(FocusEvent) and focusLost(FocusEvent)
ItemListener	itemStateChanged(ItemEvent)

Table 14-4   Selected methods that respond to events

Each listener in Table 14-4 is associated with only one or two methods. Other listeners, such as KeyListener and MouseListener, are associated with multiple methods. You will learn how to use these more complicated listeners in the chapter *Advanced GUI Topics*.

Until you become familiar with the event-handling model, it can seem quite confusing. For now, remember these tasks you must perform when you declare a class that handles an event:

- The class that handles an event must either implement a listener interface or extend a class that implements a listener interface. For example, if a JFrame named MyFrame needs to respond to a user's clicks on a JCheckBox, you would write the following class header:

```
public class MyFrame extends JFrame
    implements ItemListener
```

If you then declare a class that extends MyFrame, you need not include implements ItemListener in its header. The new class inherits the implementation.

- You must register each instance of the event-handling class as a listener for one or more components. For example, if MyFrame contains a JCheckBox named myCheckBox, then within the MyFrame class you would code:

```
myCheckBox.addItemListener(this);
```

The this reference is to the class in which myCheckBox is declared—in this case, MyFrame.

- You must write an event handler method with an appropriate identifier (as shown in Table 14-4) that accepts the generated event and reacts to it.

 Watch the video *Event-Driven Programming*.

TWO TRUTHS & A LIE

Understanding Swing Event Listeners

1. A class can implement as many event listeners as it needs.

2. Any object can be notified of a mouse click or keyboard press as long as it implements the appropriate interface and is registered as an event listener on the appropriate event source.

3. Every event-handling method accepts a parameter that represents the listener for the event.

The false statement is #3. Every event-handling method accepts a parameter that represents the generated event.

Using the JCheckBox, ButtonGroup, and JComboBox Classes

Besides JButtons and JTextFields, several other Java components allow a user to make selections in a UI environment. These include JCheckBoxes, ButtonGroups, and JComboBoxes.

The JCheckBox Class

A **JCheckBox** consists of a label positioned beside a square; you can click the square to display or remove a check mark. Usually, you use a JCheckBox to allow the user to turn an option on or off. For example, Figure 14-34 shows the code for an application that uses four JCheckBoxes, and Figure 14-35 shows the output.

```java
import java.awt.*;
import javax.swing.*;
import java.awt.event.*;
public class CheckBoxDemonstration
    extends JFrame implements ItemListener
{
    FlowLayout flow = new FlowLayout();
    JLabel label = new JLabel("What would you like to drink?");
    JCheckBox coffee = new JCheckBox("Coffee", false);
    JCheckBox cola = new JCheckBox("Cola", false);
    JCheckBox milk = new JCheckBox("Milk", false);
    JCheckBox water = new JCheckBox("Water", false);
    String output, insChosen;
    public CheckBoxDemonstration()
    {
        super("CheckBox Demonstration");
        setDefaultCloseOperation(JFrame.EXIT_ON_CLOSE);
        setLayout(new FlowLayout());
        label.setFont(new Font("Arial", Font.ITALIC, 22));
        coffee.addItemListener(this);
        cola.addItemListener(this);
        milk.addItemListener(this);
        water.addItemListener(this);
        add(label);
        add(coffee);
        add(cola);
        add(milk);
        add(water);
    }
```

Figure 14-34 The CheckBoxDemonstration class *(continues)*

(continued)

```java
    public void itemStateChanged(ItemEvent check)
    {
        // Actions based on choice go here
    }
    public static void main(String[] arguments)
    {
        final int FRAME_WIDTH = 350;
        final int FRAME_HEIGHT = 120;
        CheckBoxDemonstration frame =
            new CheckBoxDemonstration();
        frame.setSize(FRAME_WIDTH, FRAME_HEIGHT);
        frame.setVisible(true);
    }
}
```

Figure 14-34   The CheckBoxDemonstration class

In the application in Figure 14-34, the CheckBoxDemonstration class and the main() method that instantiates an instance of it are part of the same class. You could also store the two parts in separate classes, as in previous examples.

Figure 14-35   Output of the CheckBoxDemonstration class

The inheritance hierarchy of the JCheckBox class is shown in Figure 14-36; frequently used JCheckBox methods appear in Table 14-5.

```
java.lang.Object
  !--java.awt.Component
        !--java.awt.Container
              !--javax.swing.JComponent
                    !--javax.swing.AbstractButton
                          !--javax.swing.JToggleButton
                                !--javax.swing.JCheckBox
```

Figure 14-36   The inheritance hierarchy of the JCheckBox class

Method	Purpose
void setText(String)	Sets the text for the JCheckBox
String getText()	Returns the JCheckBox text
void setSelected(boolean)	Sets the state of the JCheckBox to true for selected or false for unselected
boolean isSelected()	Gets the current state (checked or unchecked) of the JCheckBox

Table 14-5   Frequently used JCheckBox methods

Several constructors can be used with JCheckBoxes. When you construct a JCheckBox, you can choose whether to assign it a label; you can also decide whether the JCheckBox appears selected (JCheckBoxes start unselected by default). The following statements create four JCheckBox objects—one with no label and unselected, two with labels and unselected, and one with a label and selected.

- JCheckBox box1 = new JCheckBox();
      // No label, unselected

- JCheckBox box2 = new JCheckBox("Check here");
      // Label, unselected

- JCheckBox box3 = new JCheckBox("Check here", false);
      // Label, unselected

- JCheckBox box4 = new JCheckBox("Check here", true);
      // Label, selected

If you do not initialize a JCheckBox with a label and you want to assign one later, or if you want to change an existing label, you can use the setText() method, as in the following example:

box1.setText("Check this box now");

You can set the state of a JCheckBox with the setSelected() method; for example, you can use the following statement to ensure that box1 is unchecked:

box1.setSelected(false);

The isSelected() method is most useful in Boolean expressions, as in the following example, which adds one to a voteCount variable if box2 is currently checked.

if(box2.isSelected())
    ++voteCount;

When the status of a JCheckBox changes from unchecked to checked (or from checked to unchecked), an ItemEvent is generated, and the itemStateChanged() method executes. You can use the getItem() method to determine which object generated the event and the getStateChange() method to determine whether the event was a selection or a deselection.

The getStateChange() method returns an integer that is equal to one of two class variables—ItemEvent.SELECTED or ItemEvent.DESELECTED. For example, in Figure 14-37 the itemStateChanged() method calls the getItem() method, which returns the object named source. Then, the value of source is tested in an if statement to determine if it is equivalent to a JCheckBox object named checkBox. If the two references are to the same object, the code determines whether the checkBox was selected or deselected, and in each case appropriate actions are taken.

```
public void itemStateChanged(ItemEvent e)
{
    Object source = e.getItem();
    if(source == checkBox)
    {
        int select = e.getStateChange();
        if(select == ItemEvent.SELECTED)
            // statements that execute when the box is checked
        else
            // statements that execute when the box is unchecked
    }
    else
    {
        // statements that execute when the source of the event is
        // some component other than the checkBox object
    }
}
```

Figure 14-37   Typical itemStateChanged() method

The ButtonGroup Class

Sometimes, you want options to be mutually exclusive—that is, you want the user to be able to select only one of several choices. When you create a **ButtonGroup**, you can group several components, such as JCheckBoxes, so a user can select only one at a time. When you group JCheckBox objects, all of the other JCheckBoxes are automatically turned off when the user selects any one check box. The inheritance hierarchy for the ButtonGroup class is shown in Figure 14-38. You can see that ButtonGroup descends directly from the Object class. Even though it does not begin with a *J*, the ButtonGroup class is part of the javax.swing package.

```
java.lang.Object
   |--javax.swing.ButtonGroup
```

Figure 14-38   The inheritance hierarchy for the ButtonGroup class

A group of JCheckBoxes in which a user can select only one at a time also acts like a set of radio buttons (for example, those used to select preset radio stations on an automobile radio), which you can create using the JRadioButton class. The JRadioButton class is very similar to the JCheckBox class, and you might prefer to use it when you have a list of mutually exclusive user options. It makes sense to use ButtonGroups with items that can be selected (that is, those that use an isSelected() method). You can find more information about the JRadioButton class at *http://java.sun.com*.

To create a ButtonGroup in a JFrame and then add a JCheckBox, you must perform four steps:

- Create a ButtonGroup, such as ButtonGroup aGroup = new ButtonGroup();.
- Create a JCheckBox, such as JCheckBox aBox = new JCheckBox();.
- Add aBox to aGroup with aGroup.add(aBox);.
- Add aBox to the JFrame with add(aBox);.

You can create a ButtonGroup and then create the individual JCheckBox objects, or you can create the JCheckBoxes and then create the ButtonGroup. If you create a ButtonGroup but forget to add any JCheckBox objects to it, then the JCheckBoxes act as individual, nonexclusive check boxes.

A user can set one of the JCheckBoxes within a group to "on" by clicking it with the mouse, or the programmer can select a JCheckBox within a ButtonGroup with a statement such as the following:

aGroup.setSelected(aBox);

Only one JCheckBox can be selected within a group. If you assign the selected state to a JCheckBox within a group, any previous assignment is negated.

You can determine which, if any, of the JCheckBoxes in a ButtonGroup is selected using the isSelected() method.

After a JCheckBox in a ButtonGroup has been selected, one in the group will always be selected. In other words, you cannot "clear the slate" for all the items that are members of a ButtonGroup. You could cause all the JCheckBoxes in a ButtonGroup to initially *appear* unselected by adding one JCheckBox that is not visible (using the setVisible() method). Then, you could use the setSelected() method to select the invisible JCheckBox, and all the others would appear to be deselected.

The JComboBox Class

A **JComboBox** is a component that combines two features: a display area showing a default option and a list box that contains additional, alternate options. (A list box is also known as a combo box or a drop-down list.) The display area contains either a button that a user can click or an editable field into which the user can type. When a JComboBox appears on the screen, the default option is displayed. When the user clicks the JComboBox, a list of alternative items drops down; if the user selects one, it replaces the box's displayed item. Users often expect to view JComboBox options in alphabetical order. If it makes sense for your application, consider displaying your options this way. Other reasonable approaches are to place choices in logical order, such as "small", "medium", and "large", or to position the most frequently selected options first.

Figure 14-39 shows a JComboBox as it looks when first displayed and as it looks after a user clicks it. The inheritance hierarchy of the JComboBox class is shown in Figure 14-40.

Figure 14-39   A JComboBox before and after the user clicks it

 The code that produces the JComboBox in Figure 14-39 is contained in the file named ComboBoxDemonstration.java in your downloadable student files.

```
java.lang.Object
   !--java.awt.Component
        !--java.awt.Container
             !--javax.swing.JComponent
                  !--javax.swing.JComboBox
```

Figure 14-40   The inheritance hierarchy of the JComboBox class

You can build a JComboBox by using a constructor with no arguments and then adding items (for example, Strings) to the list with the addItem() method. The following statements create a JComboBox named majorChoice that contains three options from which a user can choose:

```
JComboBox<String> majorChoice = new JComboBox<String>();
majorChoice.addItem("English");
majorChoice.addItem("Math");
majorChoice.addItem("Sociology");
```

In the declaration of the JComboBox, notice the use of <String> following the class name. By default, a JComboBox expects items that are added to be Object types. Adding the angle brackets and String notifies the compiler of the expected items in the JComboBox and allows the compiler to check for errors if invalid items are added. If you do not insert a data type for a JComboBox, the program compiles, but a warning message is issued with each addItem() method call. Programmers say that JComboBox uses *generics*. **Generic programming** is a feature of modern languages that allows multiple data types to be used safely with methods.

As an alternative, you can construct a JComboBox using an array of Objects as the constructor argument; the Objects in the array become the listed items within the JComboBox. For example, the following code creates the same majorChoice JComboBox as the preceding code:

```
String[] majorArray = {"English", "Math", "Sociology"};
JComboBox majorChoice = new JComboBox(majorArray);
```

Table 14-6 lists some methods you can use with a JComboBox object. For example, you can use the setSelectedItem() or setSelectedIndex() method to choose one of the items in a JComboBox to be the initially selected item. You also can use the getSelectedItem() or getSelectedIndex() method to discover which item is currently selected.

Method	Purpose
void addItem(Object)	Adds an item to the list
void removeItem(Object)	Removes an item from the list
void removeAllItems()	Removes all items from the list
Object getItemAt(int)	Returns the list item at the index position specified by the integer argument
int getItemCount()	Returns the number of items in the list
int getMaximumRowCount()	Returns the maximum number of items the combo box can display without a scroll bar
int getSelectedIndex()	Returns the position of the currently selected item
Object getSelectedItem()	Returns the currently selected item
Object[] getSelectedObjects()	Returns an array containing selected Objects
void setEditable(boolean)	Sets the field to be editable or not editable
void setMaximumRowCount(int)	Sets the number of rows in the combo box that can be displayed at one time
void setSelectedIndex(int)	Sets the index at the position indicated by the argument
void setSelectedItem(Object)	Sets the selected item in the combo box display area to be the Object argument

Table 14-6   Some JComboBox class methods

You can treat the list of items in a JComboBox object as an array; the first item is at position 0, the second is at position 1, and so on. It is convenient to use the getSelectedIndex() method to determine the list position of the currently selected item; then you can use the index to access corresponding information stored in a parallel array. For example, if a JComboBox named historyChoice has been filled with a list of historical events, such as "Declaration of Independence," "Pearl Harbor," and "Man walks on moon," you can code the following to retrieve the user's choice:

```
int positionOfSelection = historyChoice.getSelectedIndex();
```

The variable positionOfSelection now holds the position of the selected item, and you can use the variable to access an array of dates so you can display the date that corresponds to the selected historical event. For example, if you declare the following, then dates[positionOfSelection] holds the year for the selected historical event:

```
int[] dates = {1776, 1941, 1969};
```

A JComboBox does not have to hold items declared as Strings; it can hold an array of Objects and display the results of the toString() method used with those objects. In other words, instead of using parallel arrays to store historical events and dates, you could design a HistoricalEvent class that encapsulates Strings for the event and ints for the date.

In addition to JComboBoxes for which users click items presented in a list, you can create JComboBoxes into which users type text. To do this, you use the setEditable() method. A drawback to using an editable JComboBox is that the text a user types must exactly match an item in the list box. If the user misspells the selection or uses the wrong case, no valid value is returned from the getSelectedIndex() method. You can use an if statement to test the value returned from getSelectedIndex(); if it is negative, the selection did not match any items in the JComboBox, and you can issue an appropriate error message.

TWO TRUTHS & A LIE

Using the JCheckBox, ButtonGroup, and JComboBox Classes

1. A JCheckBox consists of a label positioned beside a square; you can click the square to display or remove a check mark.

2. When you create a ButtonGroup, you can group several components, such as JCheckBoxes, so a user can select multiple options simultaneously.

3. When a user clicks a JComboBox, a list of alternative items drops down; if the user selects one, it replaces the box's displayed item.

The false statement is #2. When you create a ButtonGroup, you can group several components, such as JCheckBoxes, so a user can select only one at a time.

You Do It

Including JCheckBoxes in an Application

Next, you create an interactive program for a resort. The base price for a room is $200, and a guest can choose from several options. Reserving a room for a weekend night adds $100 to the price, including breakfast adds $20, and including a round of golf adds $75. A guest can select none, some, or all of these premium additions. Each time the user changes the option package, the price is recalculated.

1. Open a new file in your text editor, then type the following first few lines of a Swing application that demonstrates the use of a JCheckBox. Note that the JResortCalculator class implements the ItemListener interface:

```
import javax.swing.*;
import java.awt.*;
import java.awt.event.*;
public class JResortCalculator extends
    JFrame implements ItemListener
{
```

2. Declare the named constants that hold the base price for a resort room and the premium amounts for a weekend stay, including breakfast and a round of golf. Also include a variable that holds the total price for the stay, and initialize it to the value of the base price. Later, depending on the user's selections, premium fees might be added to totalPrice, making it more than BASE_PRICE.

```
final int BASE_PRICE = 200;
final int WEEKEND_PREMIUM = 100;
final int BREAKFAST_PREMIUM = 20;
final int GOLF_PREMIUM = 75;
int totalPrice = BASE_PRICE;
```

3. Declare three JCheckBox objects. Each is labeled with a String that contains a description of the option and the cost of the option. Each JCheckBox starts unchecked or deselected.

```
JCheckBox weekendBox = new JCheckBox
    ("Weekend premium $" + WEEKEND_PREMIUM, false);
JCheckBox breakfastBox = new
    JCheckBox("Breakfast $" + BREAKFAST_PREMIUM, false);
JCheckBox golfBox = new JCheckBox
    ("Golf $" + GOLF_PREMIUM, false);
```

(continues)

(continued)

4. Include `JLabels` to hold user instructions and information and a `JTextField` in which to display the total price:

```
JLabel resortLabel = new JLabel
    ("Resort Price Calculator");
JLabel ePrice = new JLabel("The price for your stay is");
JTextField totPrice = new JTextField(4);
JLabel optionExplainLabel = new JLabel
    ("Base price for a room is $"
    + BASE_PRICE + ".");
JLabel optionExplainLabel2 = new JLabel
    ("Check the options you want.");
```

5. Begin the `JResortCalculator` class constructor. Include instructions to set the title by passing it to the `JFrame` parent class constructor, to set the default close operation, and to set the layout manager. Then add all the necessary components to the `JFrame`.

```
public JResortCalculator()
{
    super("Resort Price Estimator");
    setDefaultCloseOperation(JFrame.EXIT_ON_CLOSE);
    setLayout(new FlowLayout());
    add(resortLabel);
    add(optionExplainLabel);
    add(optionExplainLabel2);
    add(weekendBox);
    add(breakfastBox);
    add(golfBox);
    add(priceLabel);
    add(totPrice);
```

6. Continue the constructor by setting the text of the `totPrice` `JTextField` to display a dollar sign and the `totalPrice` value. Register the class as a listener for events generated by each of the three `JCheckBoxes`. Finally, add a closing curly brace for the constructor.

```
    totPrice.setText("$" + totalPrice);
    weekendBox.addItemListener(this);
    breakfastBox.addItemListener(this);
    golfBox.addItemListener(this);
}
```

(continues)

(continued)

7. Begin the `itemStateChanged()` method that executes when the user selects or deselects a `JCheckBox`. Use the appropriate methods to determine which `JCheckBox` is the source of the current `ItemEvent` and whether the event was generated by selecting a `JCheckBox` or by deselecting one.

```java
public void itemStateChanged(ItemEvent event)
{
   Object source = event.getSource();
   int select = event.getStateChange();
```

8. Write a nested `if` statement that tests whether the source is equivalent to the `weekendBox`, `breakfastBox`, or, by default, the `golfBox`. In each case, depending on whether the item was selected or deselected, add or subtract the corresponding premium fee from the `totalPrice`. Display the total price in the `JTextField`, and add a closing curly brace for the method.

```java
   if(source == weekendBox)
      if(select == ItemEvent.SELECTED)
         totalPrice += WEEKEND_PREMIUM;
      else
         totalPrice -= WEEKEND_PREMIUM;
   else if(source == breakfastBox)
   {
      if(select == ItemEvent.SELECTED)
         totalPrice += BREAKFAST_PREMIUM;
      else
         totalPrice -= BREAKFAST_PREMIUM;
   }
   else      // if(source == golfBox) by default
      if(select == ItemEvent.SELECTED)
         totalPrice += GOLF_PREMIUM;
      else
         totalPrice -= GOLF_PREMIUM;
      totPrice.setText("$" + totalPrice);
}
```

9. Add a `main()` method that creates an instance of the `JFrame` and sets its size and visibility. Then add a closing curly brace for the class.

```java
public static void main(String[] args)
{
   JResortCalculator aFrame =
      new JResortCalculator();
   final int WIDTH = 300;
   final int HEIGHT = 200;
   aFrame.setSize(WIDTH, HEIGHT);
   aFrame.setVisible(true);
}
}
```

(continues)

(continued)

10. Save the file as **JResortCalculator.java**. Compile and execute the application. The output appears in Figure 14-41 with the base price initially set to $200.

Figure 14-41 Initial output of the `JResortCalculator` application

11. Select the **Weekend premium** JCheckBox, and note the change in the total price of the event. Experiment with selecting and deselecting options to ensure that the price changes correctly. For example, Figure 14-42 shows the application with the weekend and golf options selected, adding a total of $175 to the $200 base price. After testing all the option combinations, close the application.

Figure 14-42 Output of the `JResortCalculator` application after the user has made selections

Don't Do It

- Don't forget the *x* in javax when you import Swing components into an application.

- Don't forget to use a JFrame's setVisible() method if you want the JFrame to be visible.

- Don't forget to use setLayout() when you add multiple components to a JFrame.

- Don't forget to call validate() and repaint() after you add or remove a component from a container that has been made visible.

- Don't forget that the ButtonGroup class does not begin with a *J*.

Key Terms

UI components are user interface components, such as buttons and text fields, with which the user can interact.

Swing components are UI elements such as dialog boxes and buttons; you can usually recognize their names because they begin with *J*.

Java Foundation Classes, or **JFC**, include Swing component classes and selected classes from the java.awt package.

Lightweight components are written completely in Java and do not have to rely on the code written to run the local operating system.

Heavyweight components require interaction with the local operating system.

A **container** is a type of component that holds other components so you can treat a group of them as a single entity. Often, a container takes the form of a window that you can drag, resize, minimize, restore, and close.

A **JFrame** is a container with a title bar and border.

Pixels are the picture elements, or tiny dots of light, that make up the image on your computer monitor.

Window decorations are the icons and buttons that are part of a window or frame.

A **look and feel** is the default appearance and behavior of any user interface.

JLabel is a built-in Java Swing class that holds text you can display.

The **add() method** adds components to a container.

The **remove() method** removes components from a container.

The **setText() method** allows you to change the text in a Component that has already been created.

The **getText() method** allows you to retrieve the String of text in a Component.

The **Font class** holds typeface and size information.

The **setFont() method** changes a JLabel's font.

The **typeface argument** to the Font constructor is a String representing a font. Common fonts have names such as Arial, Century, Monospaced, and Times New Roman.

The **style argument** to the Font constructor applies an attribute to displayed text and is one of three values: Font.PLAIN, Font.BOLD, or Font.ITALIC.

The **point size argument** to the Font constructor is an integer that represents about 1/72 of an inch.

A **layout manager** is a class that controls component positioning.

A **BorderLayout** is a layout manager that divides a container into regions.

The **flow layout manager** places components in a row, and when a row is filled, components automatically spill into the next row. By default, the components in each row are centered.

A **JTextField** is a component into which a user can type a single line of text data.

Editable describes a component that can accept keystrokes.

The **setEditable() method** changes the editable status of a JTextField.

A **JButton** is a Component the user can click with a mouse to make a selection.

Tool tips are popup windows that can help a user understand the purpose of components in an application; a tool tip appears when a user hovers the mouse pointer over the component.

The **setToolTipText() method** defines the text to be displayed in a tool tip.

An **event** occurs when a user takes action on a component.

In an **event-driven program**, the user might initiate any number of events in any order.

The **source** of an event is the component on which an event is generated.

A **listener** is an object that is interested in an event.

You tell a class to expect ActionEvents with the **addActionListener() method**.

The **actionPerformed(ActionEvent e) method** specification defines the actions that occur in response to an event.

The **setEnabled() method** makes a component available or dimmed and unavailable.

An **event handler** is a method that executes because it is called automatically when an appropriate event occurs.

A **JCheckBox** consists of a label positioned beside a square; you can click the square to display or remove a check mark. Usually, you use a JCheckBox to allow the user to turn an option on or off.

A **ButtonGroup** groups several components, such as JCheckBoxes, so a user can select only one at a time.

A **JComboBox** is a component that combines two features: a display area showing a default option and a list box containing additional options. The display area contains either a button that a user can click or an editable field into which the user can type.

Generic programming is a feature of languages that allows methods to be used safely with multiple data types.

Chapter Summary

- Swing components are UI elements such as dialog boxes and buttons. Each Swing component is a descendant of a JComponent, which in turn inherits from the java.awt.Container class. Swing components usually are placed in a container—a type of component that holds other components. Containers are defined in the Container class. Often, a container takes the form of a window that you can drag, resize, minimize, restore, and close.

- A JFrame holds and displays other objects. Useful methods include setSize(), setTitle(), setVisible(), setBounds(), and setDefaultCloseOperation(). JFrames include a title bar at the top containing text information, and Minimize, Maximize or Restore, and Close buttons in the frame's upper-right corner. When a user closes a JFrame by clicking the Close button in the upper-right corner, the default behavior is for the JFrame to become hidden and for the application to keep running.

- JLabel is a built-in Java Swing class that holds text you can display. You then can add a JLabel to a JFrame using the add() method. The setFont() method changes the font typeface, style, and point size.

- To place multiple components at specified positions in a container so they do not hide each other, you must use a layout manager—a class that controls component positioning. The normal (default) behavior of a JFrame is to use a layout format named BorderLayout. When you use FlowLayout, components do not lie on top of each other. Instead, components are placed in a row, and when a row is filled, components automatically spill into the next row.

- The advantage of creating a child class of JFrame is that you can set the JFrame's properties within your object's constructor; then, when you create your JFrame child object, it is automatically endowed with the features you have specified, such as title, size, and default close operation.

- A JTextField is a component into which a user can type a single line of text data. A JButton is a Component the user can click with a mouse to make a selection. Tool tips are popup windows that can help a user understand the purpose of components in an application; the tool tip appears when a user hovers the mouse pointer over the component.

- Within an event-driven program, a component on which an event is generated is the source of the event. An object that is interested in an event is a listener. You prepare your class to accept button-press events by importing the java.awt.event package into your program and adding the phrase implements ActionListener to the class header. You tell your class to expect ActionEvents with the addActionListener() method. The ActionListener interface contains the actionPerformed(ActionEvent e) method specification. You implement this method with the actions that should occur in response to the event. Within the actionPerformed() method, you can use the getSource() method of the object sent to determine which component generated the event.

- A class can implement as many event listeners as it needs. Examples of event listeners are ActionListener, ItemListener, KeyListener, and MouseListener. Any object can be notified of an event as long as it implements the appropriate interface and is registered as an event listener on the appropriate event source. To add a listener method to a source, you must use the appropriate designated add() method. Specific methods react to specific event types; they include actionPerformed() and itemStateChanged().

- A JCheckBox consists of a label positioned beside a square; you can click the square to display or remove a check mark. Usually, you use a JCheckBox to allow the user to turn an option on or off. A ButtonGroup groups components so a user can select only one at a time. After a JCheckBox in a ButtonGroup has been selected, one in the group will always be selected. A JComboBox is a component that combines two features: a display area showing a default option and a list box containing additional options. You can treat the list of items in a JComboBox object as an array and use the getSelectedIndex() method to determine the list position of the currently selected item.

Review Questions

1. A JFrame is a descendant of each of the following classes except the _____ class.

   a. Component   c. Container
   b. Jar   d. Window

2. A programmer might prefer using a JFrame instead of a Window because, unlike a window, a JFrame _____ .

   a. can hold other objects   c. can have descendants
   b. can be made visible   d. has a title bar and border

3. The statement JFrame myFrame = new JFrame(); creates a JFrame that
    is _____ .

    a. invisible and has no title   c. visible and has no title
    b. invisible and has a title   d. visible and has a title

4. To create a JFrame named aFrame that is 300 pixels wide by 200 pixels tall, you
    can _____ .

    a. use the declaration JFrame aFrame = new JFrame(300, 200);
    b. declare a JFrame named aFrame and then code aFrame.setSize(300, 200);
    c. declare a JFrame named aFrame and then code aFrame.setBounds(300, 200);
    d. use any of the above

5. When a user closes a JFrame, the default behavior is for _____ .

    a. the JFrame to close and the application to keep running
    b. the JFrame to become hidden and the application to keep running
    c. the JFrame to close and the application to exit
    d. nothing to happen

6. An advantage of extending the JFrame class is _____ .

    a. you can set the child class properties within the class constructor
    b. there is no other way to cause an application to close when the user clicks a
        JFrame's Close button
    c. there is no other way to make a JFrame visible
    d. all of the above

7. Suppose that you create an application in which you instantiate a JFrame named
    frame1 and a JLabel named label1. Which of the following statements within the
    application adds label1 to frame1?

    a. label1.add(frame1);   c. this.add(label1);
    b. frame1.add(label1);   d. two of the above

8. The arguments required by the Font constructor include all of the following
    except _____ .

    a. typeface   c. mode
    b. style   d. point size

9. A class that controls component positioning in a JFrame is a _____.

    a. container   c. formatter

    b. layout manager   d. design supervisor

10. Which of the following is not true of a JTextField?

    a. A user can type text data into it.

    b. Its data can be set in the program instead of by the user.

    c. A program can set its attributes so that a user cannot type in it.

    d. It is a type of Container.

11. _____ are popup windows that can help a user understand the purpose of components in an application and that appear when a user hovers the mouse pointer over the component.

    a. Navigation notes   c. Help icons

    b. Tool tips   d. Graphic suggestions

12. Within an event-driven program, a component on which an event is generated is the _____.

    a. performer   c. source

    b. listener   d. handler

13. A class that will respond to button-press events must use which phrase in its header?

    a. import java.event   c. extends JFrame

    b. extends Action   d. implements ActionListener

14. A JFrame contains a JButton named button1 that should execute an actionPerformed() method when clicked. Which statement is needed in the JFrame class?

    a. addActionListener(this);

    b. addActionListener(button1);

    c. button1.addActionListener(this);

    d. this.addActionListener(button1);

15. When you use the getSource() method with an ActionEvent object, the result is _____.

    a. an Object   c. a Component

    b. an ActionEvent   d. a TextField

16. A class can implement _____.

    a. one listener

    b. two listeners

    c. as many listeners as it needs

    d. any number of listeners as long as they are not conflicting listeners

17. When you write a method that reacts to JCheckBox changes, you name the method _____.

    a. `itemStateChanged()`   c. `checkBoxChanged()`

    b. `actionPerformed()`   d. any legal identifier you choose

18. If a class contains two components that might each generate a specific event type, you can determine which component caused the event by using the _____ method.

    a. `addActionListener()`   c. `whichOne()`

    b. `getSource()`   d. `identifyOrigin()`

19. To group several components such as JCheckBoxes so that a user can select only one at a time, you create a _____.

    a. `JCheckBoxGroup`   c. `JButtonGroup`

    b. `CheckBoxGroup`   d. `ButtonGroup`

20. Suppose that you have declared a `ButtonGroup` named `threeOptions` and added three JCheckBoxes named box1, box2, and box3 to it. If you code `threeOptions.setSelected(box1);`, then `threeOptions.setSelected(box2);`, and then `threeOptions.setSelected(box3);`, the selected box is _____.

    a. box1   c. box3

    b. box2   d. all of the above

Exercises

Programming Exercises

1. Write an application that displays a JFrame containing the first few lines of your favorite song. Save the file as **JLyrics.java**.

2. a. Write an application that instantiates a JFrame that contains a JButton. Disable the JButton after the user clicks it. Save the file as **JFrameDisableButton.java**.

    b. Modify the JFrameDisableButton program so that the JButton is not disabled until the user has clicked at least eight times. At that point, display a JLabel that indicates "That's enough!". Save the file as **JFrameDisableButton2.java**.

3. Create an application with a JFrame and five labels that contain the names of five friends. Every time the user clicks a JButton, remove one of the labels and add a different one. Save the file as **JDisappearingFriends.java**.

4. Write an application for Lambert's Vacation Rentals. Use separate ButtonGroups to allow a client to select one of three locations, the number of bedrooms, and whether meals are included in the rental. Assume that the locations are parkside for $600 per week, poolside for $750 per week, or lakeside for $825 per week. Assume that the rentals have one, two, or three bedrooms and that each bedroom over one adds $75 to the base price. Assume that if meals are added, the price is $200 more per rental. Save the file as **JVacationRental**.

5. a. Write an application that allows a user to select one of at least 12 songs from a combo box. Display the purchase price, which is different for each song. Save the file as **JTunes.java**.

   b. Change the JTunes application to include an editable combo box. Allow the user to type the name of a song to purchase. Display an appropriate error message if the desired song is not available. Save the file as **JTunes2.java**.

6. Design an application for a pizzeria. The user makes pizza order choices from list boxes, and the application displays the price. The user can choose a pizza size of small ($7), medium ($9), large ($11), or extra large ($14), and one of any number of toppings. There is no additional charge for cheese, but any other topping adds $1 to the base price. Offer at least five different topping choices. Save the file as **JPizza.java**.

7. Write an application that allows a user to select a city from a list box that contains at least seven options. Display the population of the city in a text field after the user makes a selection. Save the file as **JPopulation.java**.

8. Write an application that allows the user to choose insurance options in JCheckBoxes. Use a ButtonGroup to allow the user to select only one of two insurance types—HMO (health maintenance organization) or PPO (preferred provider organization). Use regular (single) JCheckBoxes for dental insurance and vision insurance options; the user can select one option, both options, or neither option. As the user selects each option, display its name and price in a text field; the HMO costs $200 per month, the PPO costs $600 per month, the dental coverage adds $75 per month, and the vision care adds $20 per month. When a user deselects an item, make the text field blank. Save the file as **JInsurance.java**.

9. a. Search the Java Web site for information on how to use a JTextArea, its constructors, and its setText() and append() methods. Write an application that allows the user to select options for a dormitory room. Use JCheckBoxes for options such as private room, Internet connection, cable TV connection, microwave, refrigerator, and so on. When the application starts, use a text area to display a message listing the options that are not yet selected. As the user selects and deselects options, add appropriate messages to the common text area so it accumulates a running list that reflects the user's choices. Save the file as **JDorm.java**.

b. Modify the JDorm application so that instead of a running list of the user's choices, the application displays only the current choices. Save the file as **JDorm2.java**.

10. Create an application for Paula's Portraits, a photography studio. Paula's base price is $40 for a photo session with one person. The in-studio fee is $75 for a session with two or more subjects, and $95 for a session with a pet. A $90 fee is added to take photos on location instead of in the studio. The application allows users to compute the price of a photography session. Include a set of mutually exclusive check boxes to select the portrait subject and another set of mutually exclusive check boxes for the session location. Include labels as appropriate to explain the application's functionality. Save the file as **JPhotoFrame.java**.

 Debugging Exercises

1. Each of the following files in the Chapter14 folder of your downloadable student files has syntax and/or logic errors. In each case, determine the problem and fix the program. After you correct the errors, save each file using the same filename preceded with *Fix*. For example, DebugFourteen1.java will become FixDebugFourteen1.java.

   a. DebugFourteen1.java   c. DebugFourteen3.java
   b. DebugFourteen2.java   d. DebugFourteen4.java

 Game Zone

1. a. Create a quiz game that displays, in turn, five questions about any topic of your choice. All five questions should have the same three possible multiple-choice answers. For example, you might ask trivia questions about U.S. states for which the correct response is either California, Florida, or New York. After each question is displayed, allow the user to choose one, two, or all three answers by selecting JCheckBoxes. In other words, if the user is sure of an answer, he will select just one box, but if he is uncertain, he might select two or three boxes. When the user is ready to submit the answer(s), he clicks a button. If the user's answer to the question is correct and he has selected just one box, award 5 points. If the user is correct but has selected two boxes, award 2 points. If the user has selected all three boxes, award 1 point. If the user has selected fewer than three boxes but is incorrect, the user receives 0 points. A total of 25 points is possible. If the user has accumulated more than 21 points at the end of the quiz, display the message "Fantastic!". If the user has accumulated more than 15 points, display the message "Very good", and if the user has accumulated fewer points, display "OK". Save the file as **HedgeYourBet.java**.

b. Modify the HedgeYourBet game so that it stores the player's score from the last game in a file and displays the previous score at the start of each new game. (The first time you play the game, the previous score should be 0.) Save the game as **HedgeYourBetUsingFile.java**.

2. In Chapter 5, you created a lottery game application. Create a similar game using check boxes. For this game, generate six random numbers, each between 0 and 30, inclusive. Allow the user to choose six check boxes to play the game. (Do not allow the user to choose more than six boxes.) After the player has chosen six numbers, display the randomly selected numbers, the player's numbers, and the amount of money the user has won, as follows:

Matching Numbers	Award ($)
Three matches	100
Four matches	10,000
Five matches	50,000
Six matches	1,000,000
Zero, one, or two matches	0

Save the file as **JLottery2.java**.

3. a. Create a game called Last Man Standing in which the objective is to select the last remaining JCheckBox. The game contains 10 JCheckBoxes. The player can choose one, two, or three boxes, and then click a JButton to indicate the turn is complete. The computer then randomly selects one, two, or three JCheckBox objects. When the last JCheckBox is selected, display a message indicating the winner. Save the game as **LastManStanding.java**.

b. In the current version of the Last Man Standing game, the computer might seem to make strategic mistakes because of its random selections. For example, when only two JCheckBox objects are left, the computer might randomly choose to check only one, allowing the player to check the last one and win. Modify the game to make it as smart as possible, using a random value for the number of the computer's selections only when there is no superior alternative. Save the improved game as **SmarterLastManStanding.java**.

 Case Problems

1. In previous chapters, you have created a number of programs for Carly's Catering. Now, create an interactive program that allows the user to enter the number of guests for an event into a text field; if the value entered is not numeric, set the event price to 0. Also allow the user to choose one entree from a group of at least four choices, up to two side dishes from a group of at least four choices, and one

dessert from a group of at least three choices. Display the cost of the event as $35 per person; as the user continues to select and deselect menu items, display a list of the current items chosen. If a user attempts to choose more than two side dishes, remove all the current side dish selections so that the user can start over. Save the program as **JCarlysCatering.java**.

2. In previous chapters, you have created a number of programs for Sammy's Seashore Rentals. Now, create an interactive GUI program that allows the user to enter a rental time in hours into a text field; if the value entered is not numeric, set the rental price to 0. Also allow the user to choose one equipment type to rent from a group of seven choices. The rental fee is $40 per hour for a jet ski or pontoon boat; $20 per hour for a rowboat, canoe, or kayak; and $7 per hour for a beach chair or umbrella. Let the user add an equipment lesson for an extra $5. Display a message that indicates all the details for the rental, including the total price. Save the program as **JSammysSeashore.java**.

Advanced GUI Topics

In this chapter, you will:

- ◎ Use content panes
- ◎ Use color
- ◎ Learn more about layout managers
- ◎ Use `JPanel`s to increase layout options
- ◎ Create `JScrollPane`s
- ◎ Understand events and event handling more thoroughly
- ◎ Use the `AWTEvent` class methods
- ◎ Handle mouse events
- ◎ Use menus

Understanding the Content Pane

The JFrame class is a **top-level container** Java Swing class. (The other two top-level container classes are JDialog and JApplet.) Every GUI component that appears on the screen must be part of a containment hierarchy. A **containment hierarchy** is a tree of components that has a top-level container as its root (that is, at its uppermost level). Every top-level container has a **content pane** that contains all the visible components in the container's user interface. The content pane can directly contain components like JButtons, or it can hold other containers, like JPanels, that in turn contain such components.

A top-level container can contain a menu bar. A **menu bar** is a horizontal strip that conventionally is placed at the top of a container and contains user options. The menu bar, if there is one, is just above (and separate from) the content pane. A **glass pane** resides above the content pane. Figure 15-1 shows the relationship between a JFrame and its root, content, and glass panes.

```
JFrame
   Root pane
      Menu bar
      Content pane
         Glass pane
```

Figure 15-1   Parts of a JFrame

 The glass pane is a powerful container feature. Tool tips, which you learned about in Chapter 14, reside on the glass pane. You also can draw your own graphics on the glass pane "on top of" components on a JFrame or JApplet. (You will learn about drawing in the *Graphics* chapter, and about JApplets in the chapter *Applets, Images, and Sound*.) If you add a MouseListener to the glass pane, it prevents the mouse from triggering events on the components below the glass pane on the JFrame.

An additional layered pane exists above the root pane, but it is not often used explicitly by Java programmers. For more details, see the Java Web site.

Whenever you create a JFrame (or other top-level container), you can get a reference to its content pane using the **getContentPane() method**. In Chapter 14, you added and removed components from JFrames and set their layout managers without understanding you were using the content pane. You had this ability because Java automatically converts add(), remove(), and setLayoutManager() statements to more complete versions. For example, the following three statements are equivalent within a class that descends from JFrame:

```
this.getContentPane().add(aButton);
getContentPane().add(aButton);
add(aButton);
```

In the first statement, this refers to the JFrame class in which the statement appears, and getContentPane() provides a reference to the content pane. In the second statement, the this reference is implied. In the third statement, both the this reference and the getContentPane() call are implied.

Although you do not need to worry about the content pane if you only add components to, remove components from, or set the layout manager of a JFrame, you must refer to the content pane for all other actions, such as setting the background color.

When you write an application that adds multiple components to a content pane, it is more efficient to declare an object that represents the content pane than to keep calling the getContentPane() method. For example, consider the following code in a JFrame class that adds three buttons:

```
getContentPane().add(button1);
getContentPane().add(button2);
getContentPane().add(button3);
```

You might prefer to write the following statements. The call to getContentPane() is made once, its reference is stored in a variable, and the reference name is used repeatedly with the call to the add() method:

```
Container con = getContentPane();
con.add(button1);
con.add(button2);
con.add(button3);
```

As an example, the class in Figure 15-2 creates a JFrame like the ones you created throughout Chapter 14, although to keep the example simple, the default close operation was not set and the button was not assigned any tasks.

```
import java.awt.*;
import javax.swing.*;
public class JFrameWithExplicitContentPane extends JFrame
{
    private final int SIZE = 180;
    private Container con = getContentPane();
    private JButton button = new JButton("Press Me");
```

Figure 15-2   The JFrameWithExplicitContentPane class *(continues)*

(continued)

```
    public JFrameWithExplicitContentPane()
    {
        super("Frame");
        setSize(SIZE, SIZE);
        con.setLayout(new FlowLayout());
        con.add(button);
    }
    public static void main(String[] args)
    {
        JFrameWithExplicitContentPane frame =
            new JFrameWithExplicitContentPane();
        frame.setVisible(true);
    }
}
```

Figure 15-2   The `JFrameWithExplicitContentPane` class

In Figure 15-2, the `getContentPane()` method assigns a reference to a `Container` named con, and the `Container` reference is used later with the `setLayout()` and `add()` methods. Figure 15-3 shows the result. The frame constructed from the class in Figure 15-2 is identical to the one that would be constructed if the shaded parts were omitted.

Figure 15-3   Output of the `JFrameWithExplicitContentPane` application

When you want to use methods other than `add()`, `remove()`, or `setLayout()`, you must use a content pane. In the next sections you will learn about methods such as `setBackground()`, which is used to change a `JFrame`'s background color, and `setLayout()`, which is used to change a `JFrame`'s layout manager. If you use these methods with a `JFrame` instead of its content pane, the user will not see the results.

Using Color

The **Color class** defines colors for you to use in your applications. The Color class can be used with the setBackground() and setForeground() methods of the Component class to make your applications more attractive and interesting. When you use the Color class, you include the statement import java.awt.Color; at the top of your class file.

The statement import java.awt.* uses the wildcard to import all of the types in the java.awt package, but it does not import java.awt.Color, java.awt.Font, or any other packages within awt. If you plan to use the classes from java.awt and from java.awt.Color, you must use both import statements.

The Color class defines named constants that represent 13 colors, as shown in Table 15-1. Java constants are usually written in all uppercase letters, as you learned in Chapter 2. However, Java's creators declared two constants for every color in the Color class—an uppercase version, such as BLUE, and a lowercase version, such as blue. Earlier versions of Java contained only the lowercase Color constants. (The uppercase Color constants use an underscore in DARK_GRAY and LIGHT_GRAY; the lowercase versions are a single word: darkgray and lightgray.)

BLACK	GREEN	RED
BLUE	LIGHT_GRAY	WHITE
CYAN	MAGENTA	YELLOW
DARK_GRAY	ORANGE	
GRAY	PINK	

Table 15-1   Color class constants

You can also create your own Color object with the following statement:

Color someColor = new Color(r, g, b);

In this statement, r, g, and b are numbers representing the intensities of red, green, and blue you want in your color. The numbers can range from 0 to 255. For example, the color black is created using r, g, and b values 0, 0, 0, and white is created by 255, 255, 255. The following statement produces a dark purple color that has red and blue components, but no green.

Color darkPurple = new Color(100, 0, 100);

You can create more than 16 million custom colors using this approach. Some computers cannot display each of the 16 million possible colors; each computer displays the closest color it can to the requested color.

You can discover the red, green, or blue components of any existing color with the methods getRed(), getGreen(), and getBlue(). Each of these methods returns an integer. For example, you can discover the amount of red in MAGENTA by displaying the value of Color.MAGENTA.getRed();.

Figure 15-4 shows a short application that sets the background color of a JFrame's content pane and sets both the foreground and background colors of a JButton. Figure 15-5 shows the output.

```java
import java.awt.*;
import javax.swing.*;
import java.awt.Color;
public class JFrameWithColor extends JFrame
{
    private final int SIZE = 180;
    private Container con = getContentPane();
    private JButton button =
        new JButton("Press Me");
```

Figure 15-4   The JFrameWithColor class *(continues)*

(continued)

```
    public JFrameWithColor()
    {
        super("Frame");
        setSize(SIZE, SIZE);
        con.setLayout(new FlowLayout());
        con.add(button);
        con.setBackground(Color.YELLOW);
        button.setBackground(Color.RED);
        button.setForeground(Color.WHITE);
    }
    public static void main(String[] args)
    {
        JFrameWithColor frame =
            new JFrameWithColor();
        frame.setVisible(true);
    }
}
```

Figure 15-4 The JFrameWithColor class

Figure 15-5 Execution of the JFrameWithColor application

 Because this book is printed in only two colors, you can't see the full effect of setting applications' colors in the figures. However, when you work through the "You Do It" exercises later in this chapter, you can observe the effect of color changes on your own monitor.

TWO TRUTHS & A LIE

Using Color

1. The `Color` class can be used with the `setBackground()` and `setForeground()` methods of the `Component` class to make your applications more attractive and interesting.

2. The `Color` class defines named constants that represent 256 colors.

3. You can create your own `Color` object using values that represent the intensities of red, green, and blue you want in your color.

The false statement is #2. The `Color` class defines named constants that represent 13 colors.

Learning More About Layout Managers

A layout manager is an object that controls the size and position (that is, the layout) of components inside a `Container` object. The layout manager that you assign to a `Container` determines how its components are sized and positioned. Layout managers are interface classes that are part of the JDK; they align your components so the components neither crowd each other nor overlap. For example, you have already learned that the `FlowLayout` layout manager positions components in rows from left to right across their container. Other layout managers arrange components in equally spaced columns and rows or center components within their container. Each component you place within a `Container` can also be a `Container` itself, so you can assign layout managers within layout managers. The Java platform supplies layout managers that range from the very simple (`FlowLayout` and `GridLayout`) to the special purpose (`BorderLayout` and `CardLayout`) to the very flexible (`GridBagLayout` and `BoxLayout`). Table 15-2 lists each layout manager and situations in which each is commonly used.

Layout Manager	When to Use
BorderLayout	Use when you add components to a maximum of five sections arranged in north, south, east, west, and center positions.
FlowLayout	Use when you need to add components from left to right; FlowLayout automatically moves to the next row when needed, and each component takes its preferred size.
GridLayout	Use when you need to add components into a grid of rows and columns; each component is the same size.
CardLayout	Use when you need to add components that are displayed one at a time.
BoxLayout	Use when you need to add components into a single row or a single column.
GridBagLayout	Use when you need to set size, placement, and alignment constraints for every component that you add.

Table 15-2   Java layout managers

Using BorderLayout

The **BorderLayout manager** is the default manager class for all content panes. You can use the BorderLayout class with any container that has five or fewer components. (However, any of the components could be a container that holds even more components.) When you use the BorderLayout manager, the components fill the screen in five regions: north, south, east, west, and center. Figure 15-6 shows a JFrame that uses BorderLayout; each of the five regions in the content pane contains a JButton object with descriptive text.

Figure 15-6   Output of the JDemoBorderLayout application

When you add a component to a container that uses BorderLayout, the add() method uses two arguments: the component and the region to which the component is added. The BorderLayout class provides five named constants for the regions—BorderLayout.NORTH, .SOUTH, .EAST, .WEST, and .CENTER—or you can use the Strings those constants represent:

"North", "South", "East", "West", or "Center". Figure 15-7 shows the class that creates the output in Figure 15-6.

```java
import javax.swing.*;
import java.awt.*;
public class JDemoBorderLayout extends JFrame
{
    private JButton nb = new JButton("North Button");
    private JButton sb = new JButton("South Button");
    private JButton eb = new JButton("East Button");
    private JButton wb = new JButton("West Button");
    private JButton cb = new JButton("Center Button");
    private Container con = getContentPane();
    public JDemoBorderLayout()
    {
        con.setLayout(new BorderLayout());
        con.add(nb, BorderLayout.NORTH);
        con.add(sb, BorderLayout.SOUTH);
        con.add(eb, BorderLayout.EAST);
        con.add(wb, BorderLayout.WEST);
        con.add(cb, BorderLayout.CENTER);
        setSize(400, 150);
    }
    public static void main(String[] args)
    {
        JDemoBorderLayout frame = new JDemoBorderLayout();
        frame.setVisible(true);
    }
}
```

Figure 15-7 The JDemoBorderLayout class

When using BorderLayout, you can use the constants PAGE_START, PAGE_END, LINE_START, LINE_END, and CENTER instead of NORTH, SOUTH, EAST, WEST, and CENTER. Rather than using geographical references, these constants correspond to positions as you might picture them on a printed page. Also, if you add the following import statement at the top of your file, you can simply refer to CENTER instead of BorderLayout.CENTER:

```java
import static java.awt.BorderLayout.*;
```

When you place exactly five components in a container and use BorderLayout, each component fills one entire region, as illustrated in Figure 15-6. When the application runs, Java determines the exact size of each component based on the component's contents. When you resize a Container that uses BorderLayout, the regions also change in size. If you drag the Container's border to make it wider, the north, south, and center regions become wider, but the east and west regions do not change. If you increase the Container's height, the east, west, and center regions become taller, but the north and south regions do not change.

In Figure 15-7, an anonymous BorderLayout object is created when the constructor is called from within the setLayout() method. Instead, you could declare a named BorderLayout object and use its identifier in the setLayout() call. However, it's not necessary to use either technique to specify BorderLayout because it is the default layout manager for all content panes; that's why, in many examples in the last chapter, you had to specify FlowLayout to acquire the easier-to-use manager.

When you use BorderLayout, you are not required to add components into each of the five regions. If you add fewer components, any empty component regions disappear, and the remaining components expand to fill the available space. If any or all of the north, south, east, or west areas are left out, the center area spreads into the missing area or areas. However, if the center area is left out, the north, south, east, or west areas do not change. A common mistake when using BorderLayout is to add a Component to a content pane or frame without naming a region. This can result in some of the components not being visible.

Using FlowLayout

Recall from the last chapter, *Introduction to Swing Components*, that you can use the **FlowLayout manager** class to arrange components in rows across the width of a Container. With FlowLayout, each Component that you add is placed to the right of previously added components in a row; or, if the current row is filled, the Component is placed to start a new row.

When you use BorderLayout, the Components you add fill their regions—that is, each Component expands or contracts based on its region's size. However, when you use FlowLayout, each Component retains its default size, or **preferred size**. For example, a JButton's preferred size is the size that is large enough to hold the JButton's text. When you use BorderLayout and then resize the window, the components change size accordingly because their regions change. When you use FlowLayout and then resize the window, each component retains its size, but it might become partially obscured or change position.

The FlowLayout class contains three constants you can use to align Components with a Container:

- FlowLayout.LEFT
- FlowLayout.CENTER
- FlowLayout.RIGHT

If you do not specify alignment, Components are center-aligned in a FlowLayout Container by default. Figure 15-8 shows an application that uses the FlowLayout.LEFT and FlowLayout.RIGHT constants to reposition JButtons. In this example, a FlowLayout object named layout is used to set the layout of the content pane. When the user clicks a button, the shaded code in the actionPerformed() method changes the alignment to left or right using the FlowLayout class setAlignment() method. Figure 15-9 shows the application when it starts, how the JButton Components are repositioned after the user clicks the "L" button, and how the Components are repositioned after the user clicks the "R" button.

```
import javax.swing.*;
import java.awt.*;
import java.awt.event.*;
public class JDemoFlowLayout extends JFrame implements ActionListener
{
    private JButton lb = new JButton("L Button");
    private JButton rb = new JButton("R Button");
    private Container con = getContentPane();
    private FlowLayout layout = new FlowLayout();
    public JDemoFlowLayout()
    {
        con.setLayout(layout);
        con.add(lb);
        con.add(rb);
        lb.addActionListener(this);
        rb.addActionListener(this);
        setSize(500, 100);
    }
    public void actionPerformed(ActionEvent event)
    {
        Object source = event.getSource();
        if(source == lb)
            layout.setAlignment(FlowLayout.LEFT);
        else
            layout.setAlignment(FlowLayout.RIGHT);
        con.invalidate();
        con.validate();
    }
    public static void main(String[] args)
    {
        JDemoFlowLayout frame = new JDemoFlowLayout();
        frame.setVisible(true);
    }
}
```

Figure 15-8   The JDemoFlowLayout application

The last statements in the JDemoFlowLayout class call invalidate() and validate().
The invalidate() call marks the container (and any of its parents) as needing to be laid out. The
validate() call causes the components to be rearranged based on the newly assigned layout.

Figure 15-9 The `JDemoFlowLayout` application as it first appears on the screen, after the user chooses the "L" Button, and after the user chooses the "R" Button

Using `GridLayout`

If you want to arrange components into equal rows and columns, you can use the **GridLayout manager** class. When you create a `GridLayout` object, you indicate the numbers of rows and columns you want, and then the container surface is divided into a grid, much like the screen you see when using a spreadsheet program. For example, the following statement establishes an anonymous `GridLayout` with four horizontal rows and five vertical columns in a `Container` named con:

```
con.setLayout(new GridLayout(4, 5));
```

Specifying rows and then columns when you use `GridLayout` might seem natural to you, because this is the approach you take when defining two-dimensional arrays.

As you add new `Components` to a `GridLayout`, they are positioned in sequence from left to right across each row. Unfortunately, you can't skip a position or specify an exact position for a component. (However, you can add a blank label to a grid position to give the illusion of skipping a position.) You also can specify a vertical and horizontal gap measured in pixels, using two additional arguments. For example, Figure 15-10 shows a `JDemoGridLayout` program that uses the shaded statement to establish a `GridLayout` with three horizontal rows and two vertical columns, and horizontal and vertical gaps of five pixels each. Five `JButton` `Components` are added to the `JFrame`'s automatically retrieved content pane.

```
import javax.swing.*;
import java.awt.*;
public class JDemoGridLayout extends JFrame
{
    private JButton b1 = new JButton("Button 1");
    private JButton b2 = new JButton("Button 2");
    private JButton b3 = new JButton("Button 3");
    private JButton b4 = new JButton("Button 4");
    private JButton b5 = new JButton("Button 5");
    private GridLayout layout = new GridLayout(3, 2, 5, 5);
    private Container con = getContentPane();
    public JDemoGridLayout()
    {
        con.setLayout(layout);
        con.add(b1);
        con.add(b2);
        con.add(b3);
        con.add(b4);
        con.add(b5);
        setSize(200, 200);
    }
    public static void main(String[] args)
    {
        JDemoGridLayout frame = new JDemoGridLayout();
        frame.setVisible(true);
    }
}
```

Figure 15-10   The JDemoGridLayout class

Figure 15-11 shows the output of the JDemoGridLayout application. The Components are placed into the pane across the three rows. Because there are six positions but only five Components, one spot remains unused.

Figure 15-11 Output of the JDemoGridLayout program

With GridLayout, you can specify the number of rows and use 0 for the number of columns to let the layout manager determine the number of columns, or you can use 0 for the number of rows, specify the number of columns, and let the layout manager calculate the number of rows.

When trying to decide whether to use GridLayout or FlowLayout, remember the following:

- Use GridLayout when you want components in fixed rows and columns and you want the components' size to fill the available space.

- Use FlowLayout if you want Java to determine the rows and columns, do not want a rigid row and column layout, and want components to retain their "natural" size so their contents are fully visible.

Using CardLayout

The **CardLayout manager** generates a stack of containers or components, one on top of another, much like a blackjack dealer reveals playing cards one at a time from the top of a deck. Each component in the group is referred to as a card, and each card can be any component type—for example, a JButton, JLabel, or JPanel. You use a CardLayout when you want multiple components to share the same display space.

A card layout is created from the CardLayout class using one of two constructors:

- CardLayout() creates a card layout without a horizontal or vertical gap.

- CardLayout(int hgap, int vgap) creates a card layout with the specified horizontal and vertical gaps. The horizontal gaps are placed at the left and right edges. The vertical gaps are placed at the top and bottom edges.

For example, Figure 15-12 shows a JDemoCardLayout class that uses a CardLayout manager to create a stack of JButtons that contain the labels "Ace of Hearts", "Three of Spades", and "Queen of Clubs". In the class constructor, you need a slightly different version of the add() method to add a component to a content pane whose layout manager is CardLayout. The format of the method is:

```
add(aString, aContainer);
```

In this statement, aString represents a name you want to use to identify the Component card that is added.

```java
import javax.swing.*;
import java.awt.*;
import java.awt.event.*;
public class JDemoCardLayout extends JFrame
    implements ActionListener
{
    private CardLayout cards = new CardLayout();
    private JButton b1 = new JButton("Ace of Hearts");
    private JButton b2 = new JButton("Three of Spades");
    private JButton b3 = new JButton("Queen of Clubs");
    private Container con = getContentPane();
    public JDemoCardLayout()
    {
        con.setLayout(cards);
        con.add("ace", b1);
        b1.addActionListener(this);
        con.add("three", b2);
        b2.addActionListener(this);
        con.add("queen", b3);
        b3.addActionListener(this);
        setSize(200, 100);
    }
    public void actionPerformed(ActionEvent e)
    {
        cards.next(getContentPane());
    }
    public static void main(String[] args)
    {
        JDemoCardLayout frame = new JDemoCardLayout();
        frame.setVisible(true);
    }
}
```

Figure 15-12   The JDemoCardLayout class

In a program that has a CardLayout manager, a change of cards is usually triggered by a user's action. For example, in the JDemoCardLayout program, each JButton can trigger the actionPerformed() method. Within this method, the statement next(getContentPane()) flips to the next card of the container. (The order of the cards depends on the order in which you add them to the container.) You also can use previous(getContentPane());, first(getContentPane());, and last(getContentPane()); to flip to the previous, first, and last card, respectively. You can go to a specific card by using the String name assigned in the add() method call. For example, in the application in Figure 15-12, the following statement would display "Three of Spades" because "three" is used as the first argument when the b2 object is added to the content pane in the JDemoCardLayout constructor:

```
cards.show(getContentPane(), "three");
```

Figure 15-13 shows the output of the JDemoCardLayout program when it first appears on the screen, after the user clicks the button once, and after the user clicks the button a second time. Because each JButton is a card, each JButton consumes the entire viewing area in the container that uses the CardLayout manager. If the user continued to click the card buttons in Figure 15-13, the cards would continue to cycle in order.

Figure 15-13   Output of JDemoCardLayout when it first appears on the screen, after the user clicks once, and after the user clicks twice

The JTabbedPane class operates like a container with a CardLayout, but folder-type tabs are in place for the user to select the various components. You can find out more about the class at www.oracle.com/technetwork/java/index.html.

Using Advanced Layout Managers

Just as professional Java programmers are constantly creating new Components, they also create new layout managers. You are certain to encounter new and interesting layout managers during your programming career; you might even create your own.

For example, when GridLayout is not sophisticated enough for your purposes, you can use GridBagLayout. The **GridBagLayout manager** allows you to add Components to precise locations within the grid, as well as to indicate that specific Components should span multiple rows or columns within the grid. For example, if you want to create a JPanel with six JButtons, in which two of the JButtons are twice as wide as the others, you can use GridBagLayout. This class is difficult to use because you must set the position and size for each component, and more than 20 methods are associated with the class. Visit the Java Web site for details on how to use this class.

Another layout manager option is the **BoxLayout manager**, which allows multiple components to be laid out either vertically or horizontally. The components do not wrap, so a vertical arrangement of components, for example, stays vertically arranged when the frame is resized. The Java Web site can provide you with details.

 Watch the video *Layout Managers*.

TWO TRUTHS & A LIE

Learning More About Layout Managers

1. The FlowLayout manager is the default manager class for all content panes.

2. The BorderLayout manager can directly hold only up to five components.

3. The GridLayout manager arranges components in rows and columns.

The false statement is #1. The BorderLayout manager is the default manager class for all content panes.

 You Do It

Using *BorderLayout*

Using layout managers in the containers in your applications allows flexibility in arranging the components that users see on the screen. In this section, you create a JFrame that uses a BorderLayout and place components in each region. In the following sections, you will observe how the same components appear when other layout managers are used.

1. Open a new file in your text editor, and then type the following first few lines of a program that demonstrates BorderLayout with five objects:

```
import javax.swing.*;
import java.awt.*;
public class JBorderLayout extends JFrame
{
```

(continues)

(continued)

2. Instantiate five JButton objects, each with a label that is the name of one of the regions used by BorderLayout:

```
private JButton nb = new JButton("North");
private JButton sb = new JButton("South");
private JButton eb = new JButton("East");
private JButton wb = new JButton("West");
private JButton cb = new JButton("Center");
```

3. Write the constructor that sets the JFrame's layout manager and adds each of the five JButtons to the appropriate region. Also set the default close operation for the JFrame.

```
public JBorderLayout()
{
    setLayout(new BorderLayout());
    add(nb, BorderLayout.NORTH);
    add(sb, BorderLayout.SOUTH);
    add(eb, BorderLayout.EAST);
    add(wb, BorderLayout.WEST);
    add(cb, BorderLayout.CENTER);
    setDefaultCloseOperation(JFrame.EXIT_ON_CLOSE);
}
```

4. Add a main() method that instantiates a JBorderLayout object and sets its size and visibility, and include a closing curly brace for the class:

```
public static void main(String[] args)
{
    JBorderLayout jbl = new JBorderLayout();
    jbl.setSize(250, 250);
    jbl.setVisible(true);
}
}
```

5. Save the file as **JBorderLayout.java**, and then compile and execute it. The output looks like Figure 15-14. Each JButton entirely fills its region. (If you click the JButtons, they appear to be pressed, but because you have not implemented ActionListener, no other action is taken.)

(continues)

(continued)

Figure 15-14   Output of the JBorderLayout program

6. So you can observe the effects of changing the size of the viewing area, use your mouse to drag the right border of the JFrame to increase the width to approximately that shown in Figure 15-15. Notice that the center region expands, while the east and west regions retain their original size.

Figure 15-15   Output of the JBorderLayout program after the user drags the right border to increase the width

(continues)

(continued)

7. Experiment with resizing both the width and height of the JFrame. Close the JFrame when you finish.

Using Fewer than Five Components with the BorderLayout Manager

When you use JBorderLayout, you are not required to place components in every region. For example, you might use only four components, leaving the north region empty. Next, you remove one of the objects from the JBorderLayout JFrame to observe the effect.

1. Open the **JBorderLayout.java** file in your text editor. Immediately save it as **JBorderLayoutNoNorth.java**.

2. Change the class name to JBorderLayoutNoNorth. Also change the constructor name and the two instances of the class name in the main() method.

3. Remove the declaration of the "North" button, and within the constructor, remove the statement that adds the "North" button to the JFrame.

4. Save the file, compile it, and then run the program. The output appears as shown in Figure 15-16. The center region occupies the space formerly held by the north region.

Figure 15-16   Output of the JBorderLayoutNoNorth program

5. Experiment with removing some of the other components from the JBorderLayoutNoNorth program.

(continues)

(continued)

Using FlowLayout

Next, you modify the JBorderLayout program to demonstrate how the same components appear when using FlowLayout.

1. Open the **JBorderLayout.java** file in your text editor, and immediately save it as **JFlowLayoutRight.java**.

2. Change the class name from JBorderLayout to **JFlowLayoutRight**. Also change the constructor name and the references to the name in the main() method.

3. Within the constructor, change the setLayout() statement to use FlowLayout and right alignment:

   ```
   setLayout(new FlowLayout(FlowLayout.RIGHT));
   ```

4. Alter each of the five add() statements so that just the button name appears within the parentheses and the region is omitted. For example, add(nb, BorderLayout.NORTH); becomes the following:

   ```
   add(nb);
   ```

5. Save the file, and then compile and execute it. Your output should look like Figure 15-17. The components have their "natural" size (or preferred size)—the minimum size the buttons need to display their labels. The buttons flow across the JFrame surface in a row until no more can fit; in Figure 15-17 the last two buttons added cannot fit in the first row, so they appear in the second row, right-aligned.

Figure 15-17   Output of the JFlowLayoutRight program

(continues)

(continued)

6. Experiment with widening and narrowing the JFrame, and observe how the components realign. Then close the JFrame.

823

Using GridLayout

Next, you modify a JFrame to demonstrate GridLayout.

1. Open the **JFlowLayoutRight.java** file in your text editor, and save the file as **JGridLayout.java**.

2. Change the class name from JFlowLayoutRight to **JGridLayout**. Change the constructor name and the two references to the class in the main() method.

3. Within the constructor, change the setLayout() statement to establish a GridLayout with two rows, three columns, a horizontal space of two pixels, and a vertical space of four pixels:

   ```
   setLayout(new GridLayout(2, 3, 2, 4));
   ```

4. Save the file, and then compile and execute it. The components are arranged in two rows and three columns from left to right across each row, in the order they were added to their container. Because there are only five components, one grid position still is available. See Figure 15-18.

Figure 15-18   Output of the JGridLayout program

5. Close the program.

(continues)

(continued)

Using *CardLayout*

Next, you create a CardLayout with five cards, each holding one of the JButtons used in the previous examples.

1. Open the **JGridLayout.java** file in your text editor, and save the file as **JCardLayout.java**.

2. Change the class name from JGridLayout to **JCardLayout**. Also change the constructor name and the two references in the main() method.

3. Within the constructor, change the setLayout() statement to establish a CardLayout:

   ```
   setLayout(new CardLayout());
   ```

4. Change the five add() statements that add the buttons to the content pane so that each includes a String that names the added component, as follows:

   ```
   add("north", nb);
   add("south", sb);
   add("east", eb);
   add("west", wb);
   add("center", cb);
   ```

5. Save the file, and then compile and execute it. The output looks like Figure 15-19. You see only the "North" JButton because, as the first one added, it is the top card. You can click the button, but no actions take place because you have not implemented ActionListener.

Figure 15-19   Output of the JCardLayout program

(continues)

(continued)

6. Close the program.

Viewing All the Cards in CardLayout

Next, you modify the JCardLayout program so that its buttons can initiate events that allow you to view all five JButtons you add to the content pane.

1. Open the **JCardLayout.java** file in your text editor, and save the file as **JCardLayout2.java**.

2. Change the class name, constructor name, and two main() method references from JCardLayout to **JCardLayout2**.

3. At the top of the file, add the import statement that adds the classes and methods that allow the class to respond to events:

```
import java.awt.event.*;
```

4. At the end of the class header, insert the following phrase so the JFrame can respond to button clicks:

```
implements ActionListener
```

5. Instead of an anonymous layout manager, you need to create a CardLayout manager with an identifier that you can use with the next() method when the user clicks a button. Immediately after the five JButton declaration statements, insert the following statement:

```
CardLayout cardLayout = new CardLayout();
```

6. Within the constructor, change the setLayout() statement so it uses the named layout manager:

```
setLayout(cardLayout);
```

7. At the end of the constructor, add five statements that allow each of the buttons to initiate an ActionEvent:

```
nb.addActionListener(this);
sb.addActionListener(this);
eb.addActionListener(this);
wb.addActionListener(this);
cb.addActionListener(this);
```

(continues)

(continued)

8. After the constructor's closing curly brace, add an `actionPerformed()` method that responds to user clicks. The method uses the `next()` method to display the next card (next button) in the collection.

```java
public void actionPerformed(ActionEvent e)
{
    cardLayout.next(getContentPane());
}
```

9. Save, compile, and run the program. The output looks the same as in Figure 15-19: you see only the "North" `JButton`. However, when you click it, the button changes to "South", "East", "West", and "Center" in succession. Close the `JFrame` when you finish.

Using the `JPanel` Class

Using the `BorderLayout`, `FlowLayout`, `GridLayout`, and `CardLayout` managers would provide a limited number of screen arrangements if you could place only one `Component` in a section of the layout. Fortunately, you can greatly increase the number of possible component arrangements by using the `JPanel` class. A **JPanel** is a plain, borderless surface that can hold lightweight UI components. Figure 15-20 shows the inheritance hierarchy of the `JPanel` class. You can see that every `JPanel` is a `Container`; you use a `JPanel` to hold other UI components, such as `JButtons`, `JCheckBoxes`, or even other `JPanels`. By using `JPanels` within `JPanels`, you can create an infinite variety of screen layouts. The default layout manager for every `JPanel` is `FlowLayout`.

```
java.lang.Object
   !--java.awt.Component
         !--java.awt.Container
               !--javax.swing.JComponent
                     !--javax.swing.JPanel
```

Figure 15-20   The inheritance hierarchy of the `JPanel` class

To add a component to a `JPanel`, you call the container's `add()` method, using the component as the argument. For example, Figure 15-21 shows the code that creates a `JFrameWithPanels` class that extends `JFrame`. A `JButton` is added to a `JPanel` named `panel1`, and two more `JButtons` are added to another `JPanel` named `panel2`. Then `panel1` and `panel2` are added to the `JFrame`'s content pane.

```
import javax.swing.*;
import java.awt.*;
import java.awt.Color;
public class JFrameWithPanels extends JFrame
{
    private final int WIDTH = 250;
    private final int HEIGHT = 120;
    private JButton button1 = new JButton("One");
    private JButton button2 = new JButton("Two");
    private JButton button3 = new JButton("Three");
    public JFrameWithPanels()
    {
        super("JFrame with Panels");
        setDefaultCloseOperation(JFrame.EXIT_ON_CLOSE);
        JPanel panel1 = new JPanel();
        JPanel panel2 = new JPanel();
        Container con = getContentPane();
        con.setLayout(new FlowLayout());
        con.add(panel1);
        con.add(panel2);
        panel1.add(button1);
        panel1.setBackground(Color.BLUE);
        panel2.add(button2);
        panel2.add(button3);
        panel2.setBackground(Color.BLUE);
        setSize(WIDTH, HEIGHT);
    }
    public static void main(String[] args)
    {
        JFrameWithPanels frame = new JFrameWithPanels();
        frame.setVisible(true);
    }
}
```

Figure 15-21 The JFrameWithPanels class

Figure 15-22 shows the output of the JFrameWithPanels program. Two JPanels have been added to the JFrame. Because this application uses the setBackground() method to make each JPanel's background blue, you can see where one panel ends and the other begins. The first JPanel contains a single JButton, and the second one contains two JButtons.

Figure 15-22   Output of the JFrameWithPanels application

When you create a JPanel object, you can use one of four constructors. The different constructors allow you to use default values or to specify a layout manager and whether the JPanel is double buffered. If you indicate **double buffering**, which is the default buffering strategy, you specify that additional memory space will be used to draw the JPanel offscreen when it is updated. With double buffering, a redrawn JPanel is displayed only when it is complete; this provides the viewer with updated screens that do not flicker while being redrawn. The four constructors are as follows:

- JPanel() creates a JPanel with double buffering and a flow layout.
- JPanel(LayoutManager layout) creates a JPanel with the specified layout manager and double buffering.
- JPanel(Boolean isDoubleBuffered) creates a JPanel with a flow layout and the specified double-buffering strategy.
- JPanel(LayoutManager layout, Boolean isDoubleBuffered) creates a JPanel with the specified layout manager and the specified buffering strategy.

When you employ double buffering, the visible screen surface is called the **primary surface**, and the offscreen image is called the **back buffer**. The act of copying the contents from one surface to another is frequently referred to as a **block line transfer**, or **blitting**, because of the acronym *blt*, pronounced *blit*. Double buffering prevents "tearing," the visual effect that occurs when you see parts of different images because the redrawing rate is not fast enough. As with most beneficial features, double buffering has a cost: additional memory requirements.

As with many aspects of Java, there are multiple ways to achieve the same results. For example, each of the following techniques creates a JPanel that uses a BorderLayout manager:

- You can create a named layout and use it as an argument in a JPanel constructor:

```
BorderLayout border = new BorderLayout();
JPanel myPanel = new JPanel(border);
```

- You can use an anonymous layout manager in the JPanel constructor:

```
JPanel myPanel = new JPanel(new BorderLayout());
```

- You can create a `JPanel` and then set its layout manager using the `setLayout()` method:

```
JPanel myPanel = new JPanel();
myPanel.setLayout(new BorderLayout());
```

When a `JPanel` will have a layout other than `FlowLayout`, specifying the layout manager when you create the `JPanel` is preferable for performance reasons. If you create the `JPanel` first and change its layout later, you automatically create an unnecessary `FlowLayout` object for the original instantiation.

You add components to a `JPanel` with the `add()` method. Figure 15-23 shows a `JDemoManyPanels` program in which the `JFrame` contains four `JPanels` and 12 `JButtons` that each display a single spelled-out number so you can better understand their positions. The automatically supplied content pane for the `JFrame` is assigned a `BorderLayout`, and each `JPanel` is assigned either a `GridLayout` or `FlowLayout` and placed in one of the regions (leaving the north region empty). One or more `JButtons` are then placed on each `JPanel`. Figure 15-24 shows the output as the user adjusts the borders of the `JFrame` to change its size. Using the code as a guide, be certain you understand why each `JButton` appears as it does in the `JFrame`.

```java
import javax.swing.*;
import java.awt.*;
public class JDemoManyPanels extends JFrame
{
// Twelve buttons
   private JButton button01 = new JButton("One");
   private JButton button02 = new JButton("Two");
   private JButton button03 = new JButton("Three");
   private JButton button04 = new JButton("Four");
   private JButton button05 = new JButton("Five");
   private JButton button06 = new JButton("Six");
   private JButton button07 = new JButton("Seven");
   private JButton button08 = new JButton("Eight");
   private JButton button09 = new JButton("Nine");
   private JButton button10 = new JButton("Ten");
   private JButton button11 = new JButton("Eleven");
   private JButton button12 = new JButton("Twelve");

// Four panels
   private JPanel panel01 = new JPanel(new GridLayout(2, 0));
   private JPanel panel02 = new JPanel(new FlowLayout());
   private JPanel panel03 = new JPanel(new FlowLayout());
   private JPanel panel04 = new JPanel(new GridLayout(2, 0));
```

Figure 15-23   The `JDemoManyPanels` class *(continues)*

(continued)

```
    public JDemoManyPanels()
    {
      setLayout(new BorderLayout());
      add(panel01, BorderLayout.WEST);
      add(panel02, BorderLayout.CENTER);
      add(panel03, BorderLayout.SOUTH);
      add(panel04, BorderLayout.EAST);

      panel01.add(button01);
      panel01.add(button02);
      panel01.add(button03);

      panel02.add(button04);
      panel02.add(button05);
      panel02.add(button06);

      panel03.add(button07);

      panel04.add(button08);
      panel04.add(button09);
      panel04.add(button10);
      panel04.add(button11);
      panel04.add(button12);

      setSize(400, 250);
    }
    public static void main(String[] args)
    {
      JDemoManyPanels frame = new JDemoManyPanels();
      frame.setVisible(true);
    }
  }
```

Figure 15-23   The JDemoManyPanels class

If you were creating a program with as many buttons and panels as the one in Figure 15-23, you might prefer to create arrays of the components instead of so many individually named ones. This example does not use an array so you can more easily see how each component is placed.

Figure 15-24   Output of the JDemoManyPanels program: three views as the user adjusts the JFrame borders

Swing containers other than JPanel and content panes generally provide Application Program Interface (API) methods that you should use instead of the add() method. See the Java Web site for details.

GridLayout provides you with rows and columns that are similar to a two-dimensional array. Therefore, it particularly lends itself to displaying arrays of objects. For example, Figure 15-25 contains a Checkerboard class that displays a pattern of eight rows and columns in alternating colors. The JPanel placed in the content pane has a GridLayout of eight by eight. Sixty-four JPanels are declared, and in a loop, one by one, they are instantiated and assigned to a section of the grid (see shaded statements). After each set of eight JPanels is assigned to the grid (when x is evenly divisible by 8), the first and second color values are reversed, so that the first row starts with a blue square, the second row starts with a white square, and so on. Within each row, all the even-positioned squares are filled with one color, and the odd-positioned squares are filled with the other. Figure 15-26 shows the output.

```java
import java.awt.*;
import javax.swing.*;
import java.awt.Color;
public class Checkerboard extends JFrame
{
    private final int ROWS = 8;
    private final int COLS = 8;
    private final int GAP = 2;
    private final int NUM = ROWS * COLS;
    private int x;
    private JPanel pane = new JPanel
        (new GridLayout(ROWS, COLS, GAP, GAP));
    private JPanel[] panel = new JPanel[NUM];
    private Color color1 = Color.WHITE;
    private Color color2 = Color.BLUE;
    private Color tempColor;
    public Checkerboard()
    {
        super("Checkerboard");
        setDefaultCloseOperation(JFrame.EXIT_ON_CLOSE);
        add(pane);
        for(x = 0; x < NUM; ++x)
        {
            panel[x] = new JPanel();
            pane.add(panel[x]);
            if(x % COLS == 0)
            {
                tempColor = color1;
                color1 = color2;
                color2 = tempColor;
            }
```

Figure 15-25　The Checkerboard class *(continues)*

(continued)

```
            if(x % 2 == 0)
                panel[x].setBackground(color1);
            else
                panel[x].setBackground(color2);
        }
    }
    public static void main(String[] args)
    {
        Checkerboard frame = new Checkerboard();
        final int SIZE = 300;
        frame.setSize(SIZE, SIZE);
        frame.setVisible(true);
    }
}
```

Figure 15-25   The Checkerboard class

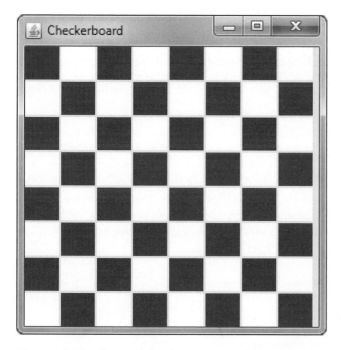

Figure 15-26   Output of the Checkerboard application

When creating the Checkerboard class, you might be tempted to create just two JPanels, one blue and one white, and add them to the content pane multiple times. However, each GUI component can be contained only once. If a component is already in a container and you try to add it to another container, the component will be removed from the first container and then added to the second.

  Watch the video *The JPanel Class*.

TWO TRUTHS & A LIE

Using the JPanel Class

1. A JPanel is a plain, borderless surface that can hold lightweight UI components.

2. To add a component to a JPanel, you call the component's add() method, using the JPanel as the argument.

3. Different JPanel constructors allow you to use default values or to specify a layout manager and whether the JPanel is double buffered.

The false statement is #2. To add a component to a JPanel, you call the container's add() method, using the component as the argument.

Creating JScrollPanes

When components in a Swing UI require more display area than they have been allocated, you can use a JScrollPane container to hold the components in a way that allows a user to scroll initially invisible parts of the pane into view. A **JScrollPane** provides scroll bars along the side or bottom of a pane, or both, with a viewable area called a **viewport**. Figure 15-27 displays the inheritance hierarchy of the JScrollPane class.

```
java.lang.Object
   !--java.awt.Component
         !--java.awt.Container
               !--javax.swing.JComponent
                     !--javax.swing.JScrollPane
```

Figure 15-27   The inheritance hierarchy of the JScrollPane class

The JScrollPane constructor takes one of four forms:

- JScrollPane() creates an empty JScrollPane in which both horizontal and vertical scroll bars appear when needed.

- JScrollPane(Component) creates a JScrollPane that displays the contents of the specified component.

- JScrollPane(Component, int, int) creates a JScrollPane that displays the specified component and includes both vertical and horizontal scroll bar specifications.

- JScrollPane(int, int) creates a JScrollPane with both vertical and horizontal scroll bar specifications.

When you create a simple scroll pane using the constructor that takes no arguments, as in the following example, horizontal and vertical scroll bars appear only if they are needed, that is, if the contents of the pane cannot be fully displayed without them:

```
JScrollPane aScrollPane = new JScrollPane();
```

To force the display of a scroll bar, you can use class variables defined in the ScrollPaneConstants class, as follows:

```
ScrollPaneConstants.HORIZONTAL_SCROLLBAR_AS_NEEDED
ScrollPaneConstants.HORIZONTAL_SCROLLBAR_ALWAYS
ScrollPaneConstants.HORIZONTAL_SCROLLBAR_NEVER
ScrollPaneConstants.VERTICAL_SCROLLBAR_AS_NEEDED
ScrollPaneConstants.VERTICAL_SCROLLBAR_ALWAYS
ScrollPaneConstants.VERTICAL_SCROLLBAR_NEVER
```

For example, the following code creates a scroll pane that displays an image named picture, a vertical scroll bar, and no horizontal scroll bar:

```
JScrollPane scroll = new JScrollPane(picture,
    ScrollPaneConstants.VERTICAL_SCROLLBAR_ALWAYS,
    ScrollPaneConstants.HORIZONTAL_SCROLLBAR_NEVER);
```

Figure 15-28 shows a JScrollDemo class in which a label with a large font is added to a panel. The scroll pane named scroll includes the panel and two scroll bars.

```
import javax.swing.*;
import java.awt.*;
public class JScrollDemo extends JFrame
{
    private JPanel panel = new JPanel();
    private JScrollPane scroll = new JScrollPane(panel,
        ScrollPaneConstants.VERTICAL_SCROLLBAR_ALWAYS,
        ScrollPaneConstants.HORIZONTAL_SCROLLBAR_ALWAYS);
```

Figure 15-28   The JScrollDemo application *(continues)*

(continued)

```
    private JLabel label = new JLabel("Four score and seven");
    private Font bigFont = new Font("Arial", Font.PLAIN, 20);
    private Container con;
    public JScrollDemo()
    {
        super("JScrollDemo");
        setDefaultCloseOperation(JFrame.EXIT_ON_CLOSE);
        con = getContentPane();
        label.setFont(bigFont);
        con.add(scroll);
        panel.add(label);
    }
    public static void main(String[] args)
    {
        final int WIDTH = 180;
        final int HEIGHT = 100;
        JScrollDemo aFrame = new JScrollDemo();
        aFrame.setSize(WIDTH, HEIGHT);
        aFrame.setVisible(true);
    }
}
```

Figure 15-28   The JScrollDemo application

The JScrollDemo object in the program in Figure 15-28 is purposely set small enough (180 × 100) so that only part of the label it contains is visible at a time. A user can slide the scroll bars to view the entire label. Figure 15-29 shows the output with the scroll bar in two positions.

Figure 15-29   Output of the JScrollDemo application

TWO TRUTHS & A LIE

Creating JScrollPanes

1. A `JScrollPane` can provide scroll bars along the side or bottom of a pane, or both.

2. When you create a simple scroll pane using the constructor that takes no arguments, horizontal and vertical scroll bars appear only if they are needed.

3. You cannot force the display of a scroll bar in a `JScrollPane` unless the components it contains require too much room.

The false statement is #3. You can use class variables defined in the ScrollPaneConstants class to force the display of a scroll bar.

A Closer Look at Events and Event Handling

In the chapter *Introduction to Swing Components*, you worked with ActionEvents and ItemEvents that are generated when a user works with a control that is included in one of your programs. The parent class for all events is EventObject, which descends from the Object class. EventObject is the parent of AWTEvent, which in turn is the parent of specific event classes such as ActionEvent and ItemEvent. The abstract class AWTEvent is contained in the package java.awt.event. Although you might think it would have been logical for the developers to name the event base class Event, there is no currently active, built-in Java class named Event (although there was one in Java 1.0). Figure 15-30 illustrates the inheritance hierarchy of these relationships.

```
java.lang.Object
   |--java.util.EventObject
        |--java.awt.AWTEvent
              |--java.awt.event.ActionEvent
              +--java.awt.event.AdjustmentEvent
              +--java.awt.event.ItemEvent
              +--java.awt.event.TextEvent
              +--java.awt.event.ComponentEvent
                    |--java.awt.event.ContainerEvent
                    +--java.awt.event.FocusEvent
                    +--java.awt.event.PaintEvent
                    +--java.awt.event.WindowEvent
                    +--java.awt.event.InputEvent
                          |--java.awt.event.KeyEvent
                          +--java.awt.event.MouseEvent
```

Figure 15-30 The inheritance hierarchy of event classes

You can see in Figure 15-30 that ComponentEvent is a parent to several event classes, including InputEvent, which is a parent of KeyEvent and MouseEvent. The family tree for events has roots that go fairly deep, but the class names are straightforward, and they share basic roles within your programs. For example, ActionEvents are generated by components that users can click, such as JButtons and JCheckBoxes, and TextEvents are generated by components into which the user enters text, such as a JTextField. MouseEvents include determining the location of the mouse pointer and distinguishing between a single- and double-click. Table 15-3 lists some common user actions and the events that are generated from them.

User Action	Resulting Event Type
Click a button	ActionEvent
Click a component	MouseEvent
Click an item in a list box	ItemEvent
Click an item in a check box	ItemEvent
Change text in a text field	TextEvent
Open a window	WindowEvent
Iconify a window	WindowEvent
Press a key	KeyEvent

Table 15-3   Examples of user actions and their resulting event types

Because ActionEvents involve the mouse, it is easy to confuse ActionEvents and MouseEvents. If you are interested in ActionEvents, you focus on changes in a component (for example, a JButton on a JFrame being pressed); if you are interested in MouseEvents, your focus is on what the user does manually with the mouse (for example, clicking the left mouse button).

When you write programs with GUIs, you are always handling events that originate with the mouse or keys on specific Components or Containers. Just as your telephone notifies you when you have a call, the computer's operating system notifies the user when an AWTEvent occurs, for example, when the mouse is clicked. Just as you can ignore your phone when you're not expecting or interested in a call, you can ignore AWTEvents. If you don't care about an event, such as when your program contains a component that produces no effect when clicked, you simply don't look for a message to occur.

When you care about events—that is, when you want to listen for an event—you can implement an appropriate interface for your class. Each event class shown in Table 15-3 has a listener interface associated with it, so that for every event class, <name>Event, there is a similarly named <name>Listener interface. For example, ActionEvent has an ActionListener interface. (The MouseEvent class has an additional listener besides MouseListener: MouseMotionListener.)

Remember that an interface contains only abstract methods, so all interface methods are empty. If you implement a listener, you must provide your own methods for all the methods that are part of the interface. Of course, you can leave the methods empty in your implementation, providing a header and curly braces but no statements.

Every <name>Listener interface method has the return type void, and each takes one argument: an object that is an instance of the corresponding <name>Event class. Thus, the ActionListener interface has an event handler method named actionPerformed(), and its header is void actionPerformed(ActionEvent e). When an action takes place, the actionPerformed() method executes, and e represents an instance of that event. Instead of implementing a listener class, you can extend an adapter class. An **adapter class** implements all the methods in an interface, providing an empty body for each method. For example, the MouseAdapter class provides an empty method for all the methods contained in MouseListener. The advantage to extending an adapter class instead of implementing a listener class is that you need to write only the methods you want to use, and you do not have to bother creating empty methods for all the others. (If a listener has only one method, there is no need for an adapter. For example, the ActionListener class has one method, actionPerformed(), so there is no ActionAdapter class.)

Whether you use a listener or an adapter, you create an event handler when you write code for the listener methods; that is, you tell your class how to handle the event. After you create the handler, you must also register an instance of the class with the component that you want the event to affect. For any <name>Listener, you must use the form object.add<name>Listener(Component) to register an object with the Component that will listen for objects emanating from it. The add<name>Listener() methods, such as addActionListener() and addItemListener(), all work the same way. They register a listener with a Component, return void, and take a <name>Listener object as an argument. For example, if a JFrame is an ActionListener and contains a JButton named pushMe, then the following statement registers this JFrame as a listener for the pushMe JButton:

pushMe.addActionListener(this);

Table 15-4 lists the events with their listeners and handlers.

Event	Listener(s)	Handler(s)
ActionEvent	ActionListener	actionPerformed(ActionEvent)
ItemEvent	ItemListener	itemStateChanged(ItemEvent)
TextEvent	TextListener	textValueChanged(TextEvent)
AdjustmentEvent	AdjustmentListener	adjustmentValueChanged (AdjustmentEvent)
ContainerEvent	ContainerListener	componentAdded(ContainerEvent) componentRemoved(ContainerEvent)
ComponentEvent	ComponentListener	componentMoved(ComponentEvent) componentHidden(ComponentEvent) componentResized(ComponentEvent) componentShown(ComponentEvent)
FocusEvent	FocusListener	focusGained(FocusEvent) focusLost(FocusEvent)
MouseEvent	MouseListener MouseMotionListener	mousePressed(MouseEvent) mouseReleased(MouseEvent) mouseEntered(MouseEvent) mouseExited(MouseEvent) mouseClicked(MouseEvent) mouseDragged(MouseEvent) mouseMoved(MouseEvent)
KeyEvent	KeyListener	keyPressed(KeyEvent) keyTyped(KeyEvent) keyReleased(KeyEvent)
WindowEvent	WindowListener	windowActivated(WindowEvent) windowClosing(WindowEvent) windowClosed(WindowEvent) windowDeiconified(WindowEvent) windowIconified(WindowEvent) windowOpened(WindowEvent)
MouseWheelEvent	MouseWheelListener	mouseWheelMoved(MouseWheelEvent)

Table 15-4   Events with their related listeners and handlers

An Event-Handling Example: KeyListener

You use the **KeyListener interface** when you are interested in actions the user initiates
from the keyboard. The KeyListener interface contains three methods: keyPressed(),
keyTyped(), and keyReleased(). For most keyboard applications in which the user must
press a keyboard key, it is probably not important whether you take resulting action when a

user first presses a key, during the key press, or upon the key's release; most likely, these events occur in quick sequence. However, on those occasions when you don't want to take action while the user holds down the key, you can place the actions in the keyReleased() method. It is best to use the keyTyped() method when you want to discover which character was typed. When the user presses a key that does not generate a character, such as a function key (sometimes called an **action key**), keyTyped() does not execute. The methods keyPressed() and keyReleased() provide the only ways to get information about keys that don't generate characters. The KeyEvent class contains constants known as **virtual key codes** that represent keyboard keys that have been pressed. For example, when you type *A*, two virtual key codes are generated: Shift and "a". The virtual key code constants have names such as VK_SHIFT and VK_ALT. See the Java Web site for a complete list of virtual key codes. Figure 15-31 shows a JDemoKeyFrame class that uses the keyTyped() method to discover which key the user typed last.

 Java programmers call keyTyped() events "higher-level" events because they do not depend on the platform or keyboard layout. (For example, the key that generates VK_Q on a U.S. keyboard layout generates VK_A on a French keyboard layout.) In contrast, keyPressed() and keyReleased() events are "lower-level" events and do depend on the platform and keyboard layout. According to the Java documentation, using keyTyped() is the preferred way to find out about character input.

```java
import javax.swing.*;
import java.awt.*;
import java.awt.event.*;
public class JDemoKeyFrame extends JFrame
    implements KeyListener
{
    private JLabel prompt = new JLabel("Type keys below:");
    private JLabel outputLabel = new JLabel();
    private JTextField textField = new JTextField(10);
    public JDemoKeyFrame()
    {
        setTitle("JKey Frame");
        setDefaultCloseOperation(JFrame.EXIT_ON_CLOSE);
        setLayout(new BorderLayout());
        add(prompt, BorderLayout.NORTH);
        add(textField, BorderLayout.CENTER);
        add(outputLabel, BorderLayout.SOUTH);
        addKeyListener(this);
        textField.addKeyListener(this);
    }
    public void keyTyped(KeyEvent e)
    {
        char c = e.getKeyChar();
        outputLabel.setText("Last key typed: " + c);
    }
```

Figure 15-31   The JDemoKeyFrame class *(continues)*

842

(continued)

```java
    public void keyPressed(KeyEvent e)
    {
    }
    public void keyReleased(KeyEvent e)
    {
    }
    public static void main(String[] args)
    {
        JDemoKeyFrame keyFrame = new JDemoKeyFrame();
        final int WIDTH = 250;
        final int HEIGHT = 100;
        keyFrame.setSize(WIDTH, HEIGHT);
        keyFrame.setVisible(true);
    }
}
```

Figure 15-31   The `JDemoKeyFrame` class

A prompt in the north border area asks the user to type in the text field in the center area. With each key press by the user, the `keyTyped()` method changes the label in the south border area of the frame to display the key that generated the most recent `KeyEvent`. Figure 15-32 shows the output after the user has typed several characters into the text field.

Figure 15-32   Output of the `JDemoKeyFrame` application after the user has typed several characters

  Watch the video *Event Handling*.

TWO TRUTHS & A LIE

A Closer Look at Events and Event Handling

1. ActionEvents are generated by components that users can click, TextEvents are generated by components into which the user enters text, and MouseEvents are generated by mouse actions.

2. Every <name>Listener interface method has a return type that refers to an instance of the corresponding <name>Event class.

3. An adapter class implements all the methods in an interface, providing an empty body for each method.

The false statement is #2. Every <name>Listener interface method has the return type void, and each takes one argument: an object that is an instance of the corresponding <name>Event class.

Using AWTEvent Class Methods

In addition to the handler methods included with the event listener interfaces, the AWTEvent classes themselves contain many other methods that return information about an event. For example, the ComponentEvent class contains a getComponent() method that allows you to determine which of multiple Components generates an event. The WindowEvent class contains a similar method, getWindow(), that returns the Window that is the source of an event. Table 15-5 lists some useful methods for many of the event classes. All Components have these methods:

- addComponentListener()

- addFocusListener()

- addMouseListener()

- addMouseMotionListener()

Class	Method	Purpose
EventObject	Object getSource()	Returns the Object involved in the event
ComponentEvent	Component getComponent()	Returns the Component involved in the event
WindowEvent	Window getWindow()	Returns the Window involved in the event
ItemEvent	Object getItem()	Returns the Object that was selected or deselected
ItemEvent	int getStateChange()	Returns an integer named ItemEvent.SELECTED or ItemEvent.DESELECTED
InputEvent	int getModifiers()	Returns an integer to indicate which mouse button was clicked
InputEvent	int getWhen()	Returns a time indicating when the event occurred
InputEvent	boolean isAltDown()	Returns whether the Alt key was pressed when the event occurred
InputEvent	boolean isControlDown()	Returns whether the Ctrl key was pressed when the event occurred
InputEvent	boolean isShiftDown()	Returns whether the Shift key was pressed when the event occurred
KeyEvent	int getKeyChar()	Returns the Unicode character entered from the keyboard
MouseEvent	int getClickCount()	Returns the number of mouse clicks; lets you identify the user's double-clicks
MouseEvent	int getX()	Returns the x-coordinate of the mouse pointer
MouseEvent	int getY()	Returns the y-coordinate of the mouse pointer
MouseEvent	Point getPoint()	Returns the Point Object that contains the x- and y-coordinates of the mouse location

Table 15-5   Useful event class methods

You can call any of the methods listed in Table 15-5 by using the object-dot-method format that you use with all class methods. For example, if you have a KeyEvent named inputEvent and an integer named unicodeVal, the following statement is valid:

```
unicodeVal = inputEvent.getKeyChar();
```

When you use an event, you can use any of the event's methods, and through the power of inheritance, you can also use methods that belong to any superclass of the event. For example, any KeyEvent has access to the InputEvent, ComponentEvent, AWTEvent, EventObject, and Object methods, as well as to the KeyEvent methods.

Understanding x- and y-Coordinates

Table 15-5 refers to x- and y-coordinates of a mouse pointer. A window or frame consists of a number of horizontal and vertical pixels on the screen. Any component you place on the screen has a horizontal, or **x-axis**, position as well as a vertical, or **y-axis**, position in the window. The upper-left corner of any display is position 0, 0. The first, or **x-coordinate**, value increases as you travel from left to right across the window. The second, or **y-coordinate**, value increases as you travel from top to bottom. Figure 15-33 illustrates some screen coordinate positions.

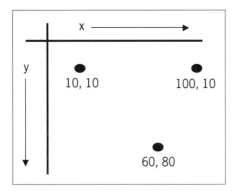

Figure 15-33   Screen coordinate positions

TWO TRUTHS & A LIE

Using AWTEvent Class Methods

1. You use many of the AWTEvent class methods to determine the nature of and facts about an event.

2. The getSource() method returns the Object involved in an event, and the getComponent() method returns the Component involved in an event.

3. The methods isAltDown() and isShiftDown() are ActionEvent methods.

The false statement is #3. The methods isAltDown() and isShiftDown() are KeyEvent methods.

Handling Mouse Events

Even though Java program users sometimes type characters from a keyboard, when you write GUI programs you probably expect users to spend most of their time operating a mouse. The **MouseMotionListener interface** provides you with methods named mouseDragged() and mouseMoved() that detect the mouse being rolled or dragged across a component surface. The **MouseListener interface** provides you with methods named mousePressed(), mouseClicked(), and mouseReleased() that are analogous to the keyboard event methods keyPressed(), keyTyped(), and keyReleased(). With a mouse, however, you are interested in more than its button presses; you sometimes simply want to know where a mouse is pointing. The additional interface methods mouseEntered() and mouseExited() inform you when the user positions the mouse over a component (entered) or moves the mouse off a component (exited). The **MouseInputListener interface** implements all the methods in both the MouseListener and MouseMotionListener interfaces; although it has no methods of its own, it is a convenience when you want to handle many different types of mouse events. Tables 15-6 and 15-7 show the methods of the MouseListener and MouseMotionListener classes, respectively.

Method	Description
void mouseClicked(MouseEvent e)	Invoked when the mouse button has been clicked (pressed and released) on a component
void mouseEntered(MouseEvent e)	Invoked when the mouse pointer enters a component
void mouseExited(MouseEvent e)	Invoked when the mouse pointer exits a component
void mousePressed(MouseEvent e)	Invoked when a mouse button has been pressed on a component
void mouseReleased(MouseEvent e)	Invoked when a mouse button has been released on a component

Table 15-6   MouseListener methods

Many of the methods in Tables 15-6 and 15-7 also appear in tables earlier in this chapter. They are organized by interface here so you can better understand the scope of methods that are available for mouse actions. Don't forget that because MouseListener, MouseMotionListener, and MouseInputListener are interfaces, you must include each method in every program that implements them, even if you choose to place no instructions within some of the methods.

Method	Description
void mouseDragged(MouseEvent e)	Invoked when a mouse button is pressed on a component and then dragged
void mouseMoved(MouseEvent e)	Invoked when the mouse pointer has been moved onto a component but no buttons have been pressed

Table 15-7   MouseMotionListener methods

The MouseWheelListener interface contains just one method named mouseWheelMoved(), and it accepts a MouseWheelEvent argument.

Each of the methods in Tables 15-6 and 15-7 accepts a MouseEvent argument. A **MouseEvent** is the type of event generated by mouse manipulation. Figure 15-34 shows the inheritance hierarchy of the MouseEvent class. From this diagram, you can see that a MouseEvent is a type of InputEvent, which is a type of ComponentEvent. The MouseEvent class contains many instance methods and fields that are useful in describing mouse-generated events. Table 15-8 lists some of the more useful methods of the MouseEvent class, and Table 15-9 lists some fields.

```
java.lang.Object
  └──java.util.EventObject
        └──java.awt.AWTEvent
              └──java.awt.event.ComponentEvent
                    └──java.awt.event.InputEvent
                          └──java.awt.event.MouseEvent
```

Figure 15-34   The inheritance hierarchy of the MouseEvent class

Method	Description
int getButton()	Returns which, if any, of the mouse buttons has changed state; uses fields NOBUTTON, BUTTON1, BUTTON2, and BUTTON3
int getClickCount()	Returns the number of mouse clicks associated with the current event
int getX()	Returns the horizontal x-position of the event relative to the source component
int getY()	Returns the vertical y-position of the event relative to the source component

Table 15-8   Some useful MouseEvent methods

Field	Description
static int BUTTON1	Indicates mouse button #1; used by getButton()
static int BUTTON2	Indicates mouse button #2; used by getButton()
static int BUTTON3	Indicates mouse button #3; used by getButton()
static int NOBUTTON	Indicates no mouse buttons; used by getButton()
static int MOUSE_CLICKED	The "mouse clicked" event
static int MOUSE_DRAGGED	The "mouse dragged" event
static int MOUSE_ENTERED	The "mouse entered" event
static int MOUSE_EXITED	The "mouse exited" event

Table 15-9 Some useful MouseEvent fields

Figure 15-35 shows a JMouseActionFrame application that demonstrates several of the mouse listener and event methods. JMouseActionFrame extends JFrame, and because it implements the MouseListener interface, it must include all five methods—mouseClicked(), mouseEntered(), mouseExited(), mousePressed(), and mouseReleased()—even though no actions are included in the mousePressed() or mouseReleased() methods.

```
import javax.swing.*;
import java.awt.*;
import java.awt.event.*;
public class JMouseActionFrame extends JFrame implements MouseListener
{
    private int x, y;
    private JLabel label= new JLabel("Do something with the mouse");
    String msg = "";

    public JMouseActionFrame()
    {
        setTitle("Mouse Actions");
        setDefaultCloseOperation(JFrame.EXIT_ON_CLOSE);
        setLayout(new FlowLayout());
        addMouseListener(this);
        add(label);
    }
```

Figure 15-35 The JMouseActionFrame application *(continues)*

(continued)

```java
    public void mouseClicked(MouseEvent e)
    {
        int whichButton = e.getButton();
        msg = "You pressed mouse ";
        if(whichButton == MouseEvent.BUTTON1)
            msg += "button 1.";
        else
            if(whichButton == MouseEvent.BUTTON2)
                msg += "button 2.";
            else
                msg += "button 3.";
        msg += " You are at position " +
            e.getX() + ", " + e.getY() + ".";
        if(e.getClickCount() == 2)
            msg += " You double-clicked.";
        else
            msg += " You single-clicked.";
        label.setText(msg);
    }
    public void mouseEntered(MouseEvent e)
    {
        msg = "You entered the frame.";
        label.setText(msg);
    }
    public void mouseExited(MouseEvent e)
    {
        msg = "You exited the frame.";
        label.setText(msg);
    }

    public void mousePressed(MouseEvent e)
    {
    }

    public void mouseReleased(MouseEvent e)
    {
    }
    public static void main(String[] args)
    {
        JMouseActionFrame mFrame = new JMouseActionFrame();
        final int WIDTH = 750;
        final int HEIGHT = 300;
        mFrame.setSize(WIDTH, HEIGHT);
        mFrame.setVisible(true);
    }
}
```

Figure 15-35   The JMouseActionFrame application

The JMouseActionFrame application in Figure 15-35 displays messages as the user generates mouse actions. At the start of the class, two integers are declared to hold the mouse position x- and y-coordinates. A JLabel and a String are also declared to hold messages that inform the user of the mouse actions taken. In the first shaded section of Figure 15-35, the constructor sets a frame title by passing it to the parent of JMouseActionFrame, sets a close operation, sets the layout manager, enables the frame to listen for mouse events, and adds the JLabel to the JFrame.

In Figure 15-35, most of the action occurs in the mouseClicked() method (the second unshaded area in the figure). The method builds a String that is ultimately assigned to the JLabel. The same actions could have been placed in the mousePressed() or mouseReleased() method because the statements could be placed in the frame just as well at either of those times. Within the mouseClicked() method, the MouseEvent object named e is used several times. It is used with the getButton() method to determine which mouse button the user clicked, getX() and getY() are used to retrieve the mouse position, and getClickCount() is used to distinguish between single- and double-clicks.

In Figure 15-35, different messages also are generated in the mouseEntered() and mouseExited() methods, so the user is notified when the mouse pointer has "entered"—that is, passed over the surface area of—the JFrame, the component that is listening for actions.

The main() method at the end of the class creates one instance of the JMouseActionFrame class and sets its size and visibility.

Figure 15-36 shows the JMouseActionFrame application during execution. At this point, the user has just clicked the left mouse button near the upper-right corner of the frame. Of course, in your own applications you might not want only to notify users of their mouse actions; instead, you might want to perform calculations, create files, or generate any other programming tasks.

Figure 15-36   Typical execution of the JMouseActionFrame application

> **TWO TRUTHS & A LIE**
>
> ### Handling Mouse Events
>
> 1. The `MouseMotionListener` interface provides you with methods that detect the mouse being rolled or dragged across a component surface.
>
> 2. The `MouseListener` interface provides you with methods that are analogous to the keyboard event methods `keyPressed()`, `keyTyped()`, and `keyReleased()`.
>
> 3. The `MouseListener` interface implements all the methods in the `MouseInputListener` interface.
>
> The false statement is #3. The `MouseInputListener` interface implements all the methods in both the `MouseListener` and `MouseMotionListener` interfaces.

Using Menus

Menus are lists of user options; they are commonly added features in GUI programs. Application users are used to seeing horizontal menu bars across the tops of frames, and they expect to be able to click those options to produce drop-down lists that display more choices. The horizontal list of `JMenu`s is a `JMenuBar`. Each `JMenu` can contain options, called `JMenuItems`, or can contain submenus that also are `JMenus`. For example, Figure 15-37 shows a `JFrame` that illustrates the use of the following components:

- A `JMenuBar` that contains two `JMenus` named `File` and `Colors`.

- Three items within the `Colors` `JMenu`: `Bright`, `Dark`, and `White`. `Dark` and `White` are `JMenuItems`. `Bright` is a `JMenu` that holds a submenu. You can tell that `Bright` is a submenu because an arrow sits to the right of its name, and when the mouse hovers over `Bright`, two additional `JMenuItems` appear: `Pink` and `Yellow`.

Figure 15-37 A JFrame with a horizontal JMenuBar that holds two JMenus

To create the output shown in Figure 15-37, a series of JMenuBar, JMenu, and JMenuItem objects were created and put together in stages. You can create each of the components you see in the menus in Figure 15-37 as follows:

- You can create a JMenuBar much like other objects—by using the new operator and a call to the constructor, as follows:

  ```
  JMenuBar mainBar = new JMenuBar();
  ```

- You can create the two JMenus that are part of the JMenuBar:

  ```
  JMenu menu1 = new JMenu("File");
  JMenu menu2 = new JMenu("Colors");
  ```

- The three components within the Colors JMenu are created as follows:

  ```
  JMenu bright = new JMenu("Bright");
  JMenuItem dark = new JMenuItem("Dark");
  JMenuItem white = new JMenuItem("White");
  ```

- The two JMenuItems that are part of the Bright JMenu are created as follows:

  ```
  JMenuItem pink = new JMenuItem("Pink");
  JMenuItem yellow = new JMenuItem("Yellow");
  ```

Once all the components are created, you assemble them.

- You add the JMenuBar to a JFrame using the setJMenuBar() method as follows:

  ```
  setJMenuBar(mainBar);
  ```

Using the setJMenuBar() method assures that the menu bar is anchored to the top of the frame and looks like a conventional menu bar. Notice that the JMenuBar is not added to a JFrame's content pane; it is added to the JFrame itself.

- The JMenus are added to the JMenuBar using the add() method. For example:

```
mainBar.add(menu1);
mainBar.add(menu2);
```

- A submenu and two JMenuItems are added to the Colors menu as follows:

```
menu2.add(bright);
menu2.add(dark);
menu2.add(white);
```

- A submenu can contain its own JMenuItems. For example, the Bright JMenu that is part of the Colors menu in Figure 15-37 contains its own two JMenuItem objects:

```
bright.add(pink);
bright.add(yellow);
```

Figure 15-38 shows a complete working program that creates a frame with a greeting and the JMenu shown in Figure 15-37.

```
import javax.swing.*;
import java.awt.*;
import java.awt.event.*;
import java.awt.Color;
public class JMenuFrame extends JFrame implements
    ActionListener
{
    private JMenuBar mainBar = new JMenuBar();
    private JMenu menu1 = new JMenu("File");
    private JMenu menu2 = new JMenu("Colors");
    private JMenuItem exit = new JMenuItem("Exit");
    private JMenu bright = new JMenu("Bright");
    private JMenuItem dark = new JMenuItem("Dark");
    private JMenuItem white = new JMenuItem("White");
    private JMenuItem pink = new JMenuItem("Pink");
    private JMenuItem yellow = new JMenuItem("Yellow");
    private JLabel label = new JLabel("Hello");
```

Figure 15-38   The JMenuFrame class (continues)

(*continued*)

```java
public JMenuFrame()
{
   setTitle("Menu Demonstration");
   setDefaultCloseOperation(JFrame.EXIT_ON_CLOSE);
   setLayout(new FlowLayout());
   setJMenuBar(mainBar);
   mainBar.add(menu1);
   mainBar.add(menu2);
   menu1.add(exit);
   menu2.add(bright);
   menu2.add(dark);
   menu2.add(white);
   bright.add(pink);
   bright.add(yellow);
   exit.addActionListener(this);
   dark.addActionListener(this);
   white.addActionListener(this);
   pink.addActionListener(this);
   yellow.addActionListener(this);
   add(label);
   label.setFont(new Font("Arial", Font.BOLD, 26));
}
public void actionPerformed(ActionEvent e)
{
   Object source = e.getSource();
   Container con = getContentPane();
   if(source == exit)
      System.exit(0);
   else if(source == dark)
      con.setBackground(Color.BLACK);
   else if(source == white)
      con.setBackground(Color.WHITE);
   else if(source == pink)
      con.setBackground(Color.PINK);
   else con.setBackground(Color.YELLOW);
}

public static void main(String[] args)
{
   JMenuFrame mFrame = new JMenuFrame();
   final int WIDTH = 250;
   final int HEIGHT = 200;
   mFrame.setSize(WIDTH, HEIGHT);
   mFrame.setVisible(true);
}
}
```

Figure 15-38   The JMenuFrame class

In the application in Figure 15-38, each JMenuItem becomes a source for an ActionEvent, and the JFrame is assigned the role of listener for each. The actionPerformed() method determines the source of any generated event. If the user selects the Exit option from the File menu, the application ends. If the user selects any of the colors from the Colors menu, the background color of the JFrame is altered accordingly.

Using JCheckBoxMenuItem and JRadioButtonMenuItem Objects

The JCheckBoxMenuItem and JRadioButtonMenuItem classes derive from the JMenuItem class. Each provides more specific menu items as follows:

- JCheckBoxMenuItem objects appear with a check box next to them. An item can be selected (displaying a check mark in the box) or not. Usually, you use check box items to turn options on or off.

- JRadioButtonMenuItem objects appear with a round radio button next to them. Users usually expect radio buttons to be mutually exclusive, so you usually make radio buttons part of a ButtonGroup. Then, when any radio button is selected, the others are all deselected.

The state of a JCheckBoxMenuItem or JRadioButtonMenuItem can be determined with the isSelected() method, and you can alter the state of the check box with the setSelected() method.

Figure 15-39 shows a JMenuFrame2 application in which two JCheckBoxMenuItems and three JRadioButtonMenuItems have been added to a JMenu. The controls have not yet been assigned any tasks, but Figure 15-40 shows how the menu looks when the application executes.

```
import javax.swing.*;
import java.awt.*;
import java.awt.event.*;
public class JMenuFrame2 extends JFrame
{
    private JMenuBar mainBar = new JMenuBar();
    private JMenu menu1 = new JMenu("File");
    private JCheckBoxMenuItem check1 = new
        JCheckBoxMenuItem("Check box A");
    private JCheckBoxMenuItem check2 = new
        JCheckBoxMenuItem("Check box B");
```

Figure 15-39   The JMenuFrame2 application (continues)

(continued)

```java
    private JRadioButtonMenuItem radio1 = new
        JRadioButtonMenuItem("Radio option 1");
    private JRadioButtonMenuItem radio2 = new
        JRadioButtonMenuItem("Radio option 2");
    private JRadioButtonMenuItem radio3 = new
        JRadioButtonMenuItem("Radio option 3");
    private ButtonGroup group = new ButtonGroup();

    public JMenuFrame2()
    {
        setTitle("Menu Demonstration");
        setDefaultCloseOperation(JFrame.EXIT_ON_CLOSE);
        setLayout(new FlowLayout());
        setJMenuBar(mainBar);
        mainBar.add(menu1);
        menu1.add(check1);
        menu1.add(check2);
        menu1.addSeparator();
        menu1.add(radio1);
        menu1.add(radio2);
        menu1.add(radio3);
        group.add(radio1);
        group.add(radio2);
        group.add(radio3);
    }

    public static void main(String[] args)
    {
        JMenuFrame2 frame = new JMenuFrame2();
        final int WIDTH = 150;
        final int HEIGHT = 200;
        frame.setSize(WIDTH, HEIGHT);
        frame.setVisible(true);
    }
}
```

Figure 15-39 The JMenuFrame2 application

Figure 15-40 Execution of the `JMenuFrame2` application

Using `addSeparator()`

The shaded statement in Figure 15-39 calls the `addSeparator()` method. This method adds a horizontal line to menus in order to visually separate groups for your users. In Figure 15-40, you can see that the separator falls between the `JCheckBoxMenuItems` and the `JRadioButtonMenuItems` because that's the order in which the shaded `addSeparator()` method call was made. The separator does not change the functionality of the menu; it simply makes the menu more visually organized for the user.

Using `setMnemonic()`

A **mnemonic** is a key that causes an already visible menu item to be chosen. You can use the `setMnemonic()` method to provide a shortcut menu key for any visible menu item. For example, when you add the following statement to the `JMenuFrame2` constructor in Figure 15-39, the menu appears as in Figure 15-41:

```
menu1.setMnemonic('F');
```

The mnemonic for the File menu is set to *F*, so the *F* in *File* is underlined. When a user presses Alt+F on the keyboard, the result is the same as if the user had clicked File on the menu: the menu list is opened and displayed.

Figure 15-41   The File menu with a mnemonic applied

 Your downloadable student files contain a JMenuFrame3 application that includes the setMnemonic() instruction that produces the output in Figure 15-41.

You should use a different mnemonic for each menu item that has one; if you use the same mnemonic multiple times, only the first assignment works. Usually, you use the first letter of the option—for example, *F* for *File*. If multiple menu items start with the same letter, the convention is to choose the next most prominent letter in the name. For example, *X* is often chosen as the mnemonic for *Exit*.

An **accelerator** is similar to a mnemonic. It is a key combination that causes a menu item to be chosen whether or not it is visible. For example, many word-processing programs allow you to press Ctrl+P to print from anywhere in the program. Only **leaf menu items**—menus that don't bring up other menus—can have accelerators. (They are called "leaves" because they are at the end of a branch with no more branches extending from them.) See the Java Web site for more details.

TWO TRUTHS & A LIE

Using Menus

1. The horizontal list of JMenus at the top of a JFrame is a JMenu.

2. Each JMenu can contain options, called JMenuItems, or it can contain submenus that also are JMenus.

3. You add a JMenuBar to a JFrame using the setJMenuBar() method.

The false statement is #1. The horizontal list of JMenus at the top of a JFrame is a JMenuBar.

 You Do It

Using a Menu Bar and JPanels

Next, you create an application for a party planning company that uses a menu bar with multiple user options, and that uses separate JPanels with different layout managers to organize components.

1. Open a new file in your text editor, and enter the following first few lines of the EventSelector class. The class extends JFrame and implements ActionListener because the JFrame contains potential user mouse selections.

```
import javax.swing.*;
import java.awt.*;
import java.awt.event.*;
import java.awt.Color;
public class EventSelector extends JFrame implements ActionListener
{
```

2. Create a JMenuBar and its two JMenus as follows:

```
private JMenuBar mainBar = new JMenuBar();
private JMenu menu1 = new JMenu("File");
private JMenu menu2 = new JMenu("Event types");
```

(continues)

(continued)

3. Next, create the items that will appear within the menus. The File menu contains an Exit option. The Event types menu contains two submenus: Adult and Child. Each of those submenus contains more options. For example, Figure 15-42 shows the expanded Adult event types menu in the finished program.

```
private JMenuItem exit = new JMenuItem("Exit");
private JMenu adult = new JMenu("Adult");
private JMenu child = new JMenu("Child");
private JMenuItem adultBirthday = new JMenuItem("Birthday");
private JMenuItem anniversary = new JMenuItem("Anniversary");
private JMenuItem retirement = new JMenuItem("Retirement");
private JMenuItem adultOther = new JMenuItem("Other");
private JMenuItem childBirthday = new JMenuItem("Birthday");
private JMenuItem childOther = new JMenuItem("Other");
```

Figure 15-42   The Adult menu

4. Declare several other components that will be used to show how JFrames are composed:

```
private JPanel birthdayPanel = new JPanel();
private JPanel otherPanel = new JPanel();
private JLabel birthdayLabel = new
   JLabel("Birthday events are our specialty");
private JLabel otherLabel = new
   JLabel("We have lots of ideas for memorable events");
private JPanel buttonPanel = new JPanel();
private JRadioButton radButton1 = new
   JRadioButton("Formal events");
private JRadioButton radButton2 = new
   JRadioButton("Casual events");
```

(continues)

(continued)

5. Write the constructor for the `JFrame`. Set the title, the default close operation, and the layout. Call separate methods to compose the menu, to add the necessary action listeners to the menu items, and to lay out the `JFrame`'s components. These tasks could be performed directly within the constructor, but you can place them in separate methods to better organize the application.

```java
public EventSelector()
{
    setTitle("Event Selector");
    setDefaultCloseOperation(JFrame.EXIT_ON_CLOSE);
    setLayout(new FlowLayout());
    composeMenus();
    addActionListeners();
    layoutComponents();
}
```

6. Add the `composeMenus()` method. Set the main menu bar, and add two menus to it. Then add one option to the first menu and two submenus to the second menu. Finally, add four items to the first submenu and two items to the other one.

```java
public void composeMenus()
{
    setJMenuBar(mainBar);
    mainBar.add(menu1);
    mainBar.add(menu2);
    menu1.add(exit);
    menu2.add(adult);
    menu2.add(child);
    adult.add(adultBirthday);
    adult.add(anniversary);
    adult.add(retirement);
    adult.add(adultOther);
    child.add(childBirthday);
    child.add(childOther);
}
```

7. Add the `addActionListeners()` method, which makes the `JFrame` become a listener for each menu item:

```java
public void addActionListeners()
{
    exit.addActionListener(this);
    adultBirthday.addActionListener(this);
    anniversary.addActionListener(this);
    retirement.addActionListener(this);
    adultOther.addActionListener(this);
    childBirthday.addActionListener(this);
    childOther.addActionListener(this);
}
```

(continues)

(continued)

8. The `layoutComponents()` method arranges all the components that appear in the content pane. The `birthdayPanel` object contains a single label. The `otherPanel` object contains a label and another panel (`buttonPanel`) in a grid. The `buttonPanel` contains two radio buttons. For this demonstration, the radio buttons are not functional, but in a more complicated application, an `addActionListener()` method could be applied to them. Also, in a more complicated application, you could continue to place panels within another panel to achieve complex designs.

```
public void layoutComponents()
{
   birthdayPanel.setLayout(new FlowLayout());
   otherPanel.setLayout(new GridLayout(2, 1, 3, 3));
   birthdayPanel.add(birthdayLabel);
   otherPanel.add("other", otherLabel);
   otherPanel.add("buttons", buttonPanel);
   buttonPanel.add(radButton1);
   buttonPanel.add(radButton2);
   add(birthdayPanel);
   add(otherPanel);
}
```

9. Add an `actionPerformed()` method that responds to menu selections. Different background colors are set depending on the user's choices.

```
public void actionPerformed(ActionEvent e)
{
   Object source = e.getSource();
   Container con = getContentPane();
   if(source == exit)
      System.exit(0);
   else if(source == childBirthday || source == childOther)
      con.setBackground(Color.PINK);
   else
      con.setBackground(Color.WHITE);
   if(source == adultBirthday || source == childBirthday)
   {
      birthdayPanel.setBackground(Color.YELLOW);
      otherPanel.setBackground(Color.WHITE);
   }
   else
   {
      birthdayPanel.setBackground(Color.WHITE);
      otherPanel.setBackground(Color.YELLOW);
   }
}
```

(continues)

(continued)

10. Add the `main()` method, which instantiates an `EventSelector` object and sets its size and visibility. Add a closing curly brace for the class.

```
public static void main(String[] args)
{
    EventSelector frame = new EventSelector();
    final int WIDTH = 400;
    final int HEIGHT = 200;
    frame.setSize(WIDTH, HEIGHT);
    frame.setVisible(true);
}
}
```

11. Save the application as **EventSelector.java**, and then compile and run it. Make various selections and observe the effects. Figure 15-43 shows the running application after the user has made some selections. After you experiment with the application, dismiss the frame.

Figure 15-43   The `EventSelector` application

12. Experiment by making changes to the `EventSelector` application. For example, some menu selections could change the `JFrame` background to a different color, and others could add a new `JLabel` to the `JFrame` content pane.

Don't Do It

- Don't forget that the content pane is operating behind the scenes when you use a top-level container and that, depending on the operations you want to perform, you might need to get a reference to it.

- Don't forget that when you create a custom `Color` object, 0 represents the darkest shade and 255 represents the lightest.

- Don't forget to set a layout manager if you do not want to use the default one for a container.

- Don't use add() to place a `JFrame`'s menu bar. You must use the `setMenuBar()` method to place a menu bar correctly.

- Don't use the same mnemonic for multiple menu items.

Key Terms

A **top-level container** is one at the top of a containment hierarchy. The Java top-level containers are `JFrame`, `JDialog`, and `JApplet`.

A **containment hierarchy** is a tree of components that has a top-level container as its root (that is, at its uppermost level).

A **content pane** contains all the visible components in a top-level container's user interface.

A **menu bar** is a horizontal strip that is placed at the top of a container and that contains user options.

A **glass pane** resides above the content pane in a container. It can contain tool tips.

The **getContentPane() method** returns a reference to a container's content pane.

The **Color class** defines colors for you to use in your applications.

The **BorderLayout manager** is the default manager class for all content panes. With the BorderLayout manager, components fill the screen in five regions: north, south, east, west, and center.

The **FlowLayout manager** arranges components in rows across the width of a `Container`; when the current row is filled, additional `Components` are placed in new rows.

The **preferred size** of a `Component` is its default size.

The **GridLayout manager** divides a container surface into a grid.

The **CardLayout manager** generates a stack of containers or components, one on top of another.

The **GridBagLayout manager** allows you to add Components to precise locations within the grid, as well as to indicate that specific Components should span multiple rows or columns within the grid.

The **BoxLayout manager** allows multiple components to be laid out either vertically or horizontally. The components do not wrap, so a vertical arrangement of components, for example, stays vertically arranged when the frame is resized.

A **JPanel** is a plain, borderless surface that can hold lightweight UI components.

Double buffering is the default buffering strategy in which JPanels are drawn offscreen when they are updated and displayed only when complete.

The **primary surface** is the visible screen surface during double buffering.

The **back buffer** is the offscreen image during double buffering.

A **block line transfer**, or **blitting**, is the act of copying the contents from one surface to another.

A **JScrollPane** provides scroll bars along the side or bottom of a pane, or both, so that the user can scroll initially invisible parts of the pane into view.

The **viewport** is the viewable area in a JScrollPane.

An **adapter class** implements all the methods in an interface, providing an empty body for each method.

The **KeyListener interface** contains methods that react to actions the user initiates from the keyboard.

An **action key** is a keyboard key that does not generate a character.

Virtual key codes represent keyboard keys that have been pressed.

The **x-axis** is an imaginary horizontal line that indicates screen position.

The **y-axis** is an imaginary vertical line that indicates screen position.

The **x-coordinate** is a value that increases as you travel from left to right across a window.

The **y-coordinate** is a value that increases as you travel from top to bottom across a window.

The **MouseMotionListener interface** provides you with methods named mouseDragged() and mouseMoved() that detect the mouse being rolled or dragged across a component surface.

The **MouseListener interface** provides you with methods named mousePressed(), mouseClicked(), and mouseReleased() that are analogous to the keyboard event methods keyPressed(), keyTyped(), and keyReleased().

The **MouseInputListener interface** implements all the methods in both the MouseListener and MouseMotionListener interfaces.

A **MouseEvent** is the type of event generated by mouse manipulation.

Menus are lists of user options.

A **mnemonic** is a key that causes an already visible menu item to be chosen.

An **accelerator** is a key combination that causes a menu item to be chosen, whether or not the menu item is visible.

A **leaf menu item** is a menu item that does not bring up another menu.

Chapter Summary

- Every top-level container has a content pane that contains all the visible components in the container's user interface. The content pane can contain components and other containers. Whenever you create a top-level container, you can get a reference to its content pane using the getContentPane() method.

- The Color class defines 13 colors for you to use in your applications. It can be used with the setBackground() and setForeground() methods of the Component class to make your applications more attractive and interesting. You also can create more than 16 million custom colors.

- The layout manager assigned to a Container determines how the components are sized and positioned within it. The BorderLayout manager is the default manager class for all content panes; when you use it, the components fill the screen in five regions: north, south, east, west, and center. The FlowLayout manager arranges components in rows across the width of a Container. When you create a GridLayout object, you indicate the numbers of rows and columns you want, and then the container surface is divided into a grid. The CardLayout manager generates a stack of containers or components, one on top of another.

- A JPanel is a plain, borderless surface that can hold lightweight UI components.

- A JScrollPane provides scroll bars along the side or bottom of a pane, or both, so that the user can scroll initially invisible parts of the pane into view.

- ActionEvents are generated by components that users can click, such as JButtons and JCheckBoxes, and TextEvents are generated by components into which the user enters text, such as a JTextField. MouseEvents include determining the location of the mouse pointer and distinguishing between a single- and double-click. When you want to listen for an event, you implement an appropriate interface for your class. For every event class, such as <name>Event, there is a similarly named <name>Listener interface. Instead of implementing a listener class, you can extend an adapter class.

- In addition to the handler methods included with the event listener interfaces, the AWTEvent classes themselves contain methods that return information about an event.

- The MouseMotionListener interface provides you with methods named mouseDragged() and mouseMoved() that detect the mouse being rolled or dragged across a component surface. The MouseListener interface provides you with methods named mousePressed(), mouseClicked(), and mouseReleased(). The additional interface methods mouseEntered() and mouseExited() inform you when the user positions the mouse over a component (entered) or moves the mouse off a component (exited). The MouseInputListener interface implements all the methods in both the MouseListener and MouseMotionListener interfaces.

- Menus are lists of user options. You use JMenuBar, JMenu, JMenuItem, and other classes in menu creation.

Review Questions

1. If you add fewer than five components to a BorderLayout, _____.

    a. any empty component regions disappear

    b. the remaining components expand to fill the available space

    c. both a and b

    d. none of the above

2. When you resize a Container that uses BorderLayout, _____.

    a. the Container and the regions both change in size

    b. the Container changes in size, but the regions retain their original sizes

    c. the Container retains its size, but the regions change or might disappear

    d. nothing happens

3. When you create a JFrame named myFrame, you can set its layout manager to BorderLayout with the statement _____.

    a. myFrame.setLayout = new BorderLayout();

    b. myFrame.setLayout(new BorderLayout());

    c. setLayout(myFrame = new BorderLayout());

    d. setLayout(BorderLayout(myFrame));

4. Which of the following is the correct syntax for adding a JButton named b1 to a Container named con when using CardLayout?

    a. con.add(b1);   c. con.add("Options", b1);

    b. con.add("b1");   d. none of the above

5. You can use the _____ class to arrange components in a single row or column of a container.

   a. FlowLayout   c. CardLayout

   b. BorderLayout   d. BoxLayout

6. When you use _____ , the components you add fill their region; they do not retain their default size.

   a. FlowLayout   c. FixedLayout

   b. BorderLayout   d. RegionLayout

7. The statement _____ ensures that components are placed from left to right across a JFrame surface until the first row is full, at which point a second row is started at the frame surface's left edge.

   a. setLayout(FlowLayout.LEFT);

   b. setLayout(new FlowLayout(LEFT));

   c. setLayout(new FlowLayout(FlowLayout.LEFT));

   d. setLayout(FlowLayout(FlowLayout.LEFT));

8. The GridBagLayout class allows you to _____ .

   a. add components to precise locations within the grid

   b. indicate that specific components should span multiple rows or columns within the grid

   c. both a and b

   d. none of the above

9. The statement setLayout(new GridLayout(2,7)); establishes a GridLayout with _____ horizontal row(s).

   a. zero   c. two

   b. one   d. seven

10. As you add new components to a GridLayout, _____ .

    a. they are positioned from left to right across each row in sequence

    b. you can specify exact positions by skipping some positions

    c. both of the above

    d. none of the above

11. A JPanel is a _____ .

    a. Window   c. both of the above

    b. Container   d. none of the above

12. The _____ class allows you to arrange components as if they are stacked like index or playing cards.

    a. GameLayout   c. BoxLayout
    b. CardLayout   d. GridBagLayout

13. AWTEvent is the child class of _____.

    a. EventObject   c. ComponentEvent
    b. Event   d. ItemEvent

14. When a user clicks a JPanel or JFrame, the action generates a(n) _____.

    a. ActionEvent   c. PanelEvent
    b. MouseEvent   d. KeyboardEvent

15. Event handlers are _____.

    a. abstract classes   c. listeners
    b. concrete classes   d. methods

16. The return type of getComponent() is _____.

    a. Object   c. int
    b. Component   d. void

17. The KeyEvent method getKeyChar() returns a(n) _____.

    a. int   c. KeyEvent
    b. char   d. AWTEvent

18. The MouseEvent method that allows you to identify double-clicks is _____.

    a. getDouble()   c. getDoubleClick()
    b. isClickDouble()   d. getClickCount()

19. You can use the _____ method to determine the Object in which an ActionEvent originates.

    a. getObject()   c. getOrigin()
    b. getEvent()   d. getSource()

20. Which of the following is true in a standard menu application?

    a. A JMenuItem holds a JMenu.
    b. A JMenuItem holds a JMenuBar.
    c. A JMenuBar holds a JMenu.
    d. A JMenu holds a JMenuBar.

Exercises

 Programming Exercises

1. Create a JFrame, and set the layout to BorderLayout. Place a JButton in each region, and place the name of an appropriate United States landmark on each JButton. For example, New York's Statue of Liberty might be the landmark in the east region. Save the file as **JLandmarkFrame.java**.

2. Create an educational program for children that distinguishes between vowels and consonants as the user clicks buttons. Create 26 JButtons, each labeled with a different letter of the alphabet. Create a JFrame to hold three JPanels in a two-by-two grid. Randomly select eight of the 26 JButtons and place four in each of the first two JPanels. Add a JLabel to the third JPanel. When the user clicks a JButton, the text of the JLabel identifies the button's letter as a vowel or consonant, and then a new randomly selected letter replaces the letter on the JButton. Save the file as **JVowelConsonant.java**.

3. Create a JFrame that holds five buttons with the names of five different fonts. Include a sixth button that the user can click to make a font larger or smaller. Display a demonstration JLabel using the font and size that the user selects. Save the file as **JFontSelector.java**.

4. Create a JFrame that uses BorderLayout. Place a JButton in the center region. Each time the user clicks the JButton, change the background color in one of the other regions. Save the file as **JColorFrame.java**.

5. Create a JFrame with JPanels, a JButton, and a JLabel. When the user clicks the JButton, reposition the JLabel to a new location in a different JPanel. Save the file as **JMovingFrame.java**.

6. Create a class named JPanelOptions that extends JPanel and whose constructor accepts two colors and a String. Use the colors for background and foreground to display the String. Create an application named JTeamColors with GridLayout. Display four JPanelOptions JPanels that show the names, in their team colors, of four of your favorite sports teams. Save the files as **JPanelOptions.java** and **JTeamColors.java**.

7. Write an application that lets you determine the integer value returned by the InputEvent method getModifiers() when you click your left, right, or—if you have one—middle mouse button on a JFrame. Save the file as **JLeftOrRight.java**.

8. a. Search the Java Web site for information on how to use a JTextArea. Write an application for the WebBuy Company that allows a user to compose the three parts of a complete e-mail message: the "To:", "Subject:", and "Message:" text. The "To:" and "Subject:" text areas should provide a single line for data entry. The "Message:" area should allow multiple lines of input and be able to scroll if necessary to accommodate a long message. The user clicks a button to send the e-mail message. When the message is complete and the Send button is clicked, the application should display "Mail has been sent!" on a new line in the message area. Save the file as **JEMail.java**.

   b. Modify the JEMail application to include a Clear button that the user can click at any time to clear the "To:", "Subject:", and "Message:" fields. Save the file as **JEMail2.java**.

9. a. Create an application that uses a graphic interface to capture room assignment data for dormitory residents and writes that data to a random access output file. The data required for each assignment includes a room number from 1 through 99 inclusive and the first and last names of the resident. Allow the user to enter data one record at a time and to click a button to save it. Save the class as **CreateRandomDormFile.java**.

   b. Create an application that allows the user to enter a room number and display the name of the stored resident for the room, if any. Save the file as **ReadRandomDormFile.java**.

10. Create a JFrame for the Summervale Resort. Allow the user to view information about different rooms available, dining options, and activities offered. Include at least two options in each menu, and display appropriate information when the user makes a choice. Save the file as **SummervaleResort.java**.

Debugging Exercises

1. Each of the following files in the Chapter15 folder of your downloadable student files has syntax and/or logic errors. In each case, determine the problem and fix the program. After you correct the errors, save each file using the same filename preceded with *Fix*. For example, DebugFifteen1.java will become FixDebugFifteen1.java.

   a. DebugFifteen1.java
   b. DebugFifteen2.java
   c. DebugFifteen3.java
   d. DebugFifteen4.java

Game Zone

As you create some of the games in this section, you might find it convenient to add or remove components in a container after construction. Recall from Chapter 14 that in order for the user to see your changes, you might need to call the `validate()`, `invalidate()`, and `repaint()` methods. You will learn more about the `repaint()` method in the next chapter, *Graphics*.

1. a. Create a Mine Field game in which the user attempts to click 10 panels of a grid before hitting the "bomb." Set up a `JFrame` using `BorderLayout`, use the `NORTH` region for a congratulatory message, and use the `CENTER` region for the game. In the `CENTER` region, create a four-by-five grid using `GridLayout` and populate the grid with `JPanels`. Set the background color for all the `JPanels` to `Color.BLUE`. Randomly choose one of the panels to be the bomb; the other 19 panels are "safe." Allow the player to click on grids. If the player chooses a safe panel, turn the panel to `Color.WHITE`. If the player chooses the bomb panel, turn the panel to `Color.RED` and turn all the remaining panels white. If the user successfully chooses 10 safe panels before choosing the bomb, display a congratulatory message in the `NORTH` `JFrame` region. Save the game as **MineField.java**.

   b. Improve the Mine Field game by allowing the user to choose a difficulty level before beginning. Place three buttons labeled "Easy", "Intermediate", and "Difficult" in one region of the `JFrame`, and place the game grid and congratulatory message in other regions. Require the user to select a difficulty level before starting the game, and then disable the buttons. If the user chooses "Easy", the user must select only five safe panels to win the game. If the user selects "Intermediate", require 10 safe panels, as in the original game. If the user selects "Difficult", require 15 safe panels. Save the game as **MineField2.java**.

2. a. Create a game that helps new mouse users improve their hand-eye coordination. Within a `JFrame`, display an array of 48 `JPanels` in a `GridLayout` using eight rows and six columns. Randomly display an *X* on one of the panels. When the user clicks the correct panel (the one displaying the *X*), remove the *X* and display it on a different panel. After the user has successfully "hit" the correct panel 10 times, display a congratulatory message that includes the user's percentage (hits divided by clicks). Save the file as **JCatchTheMouse.java**.

   b. Review how to use the `GregorianCalendar` class from Chapter 4, and then revise the `JCatchTheMouse` game to conclude by displaying the number of seconds it took the user to click all 10 *X*s. When the application starts, create a `GregorianCalendar` object and use the `get(Calendar.SECOND)` and `get(Calendar.MINUTE)` methods with it to get the `SECOND` and `MINUTE` values at the start of the game. When the user has clicked all 10 *X*s, create a second `GregorianCalendar` object and get the `SECOND` and `MINUTE` values at the end of the game. If the user starts and ends a game during the same minute, then the playing time is simply the difference between the two SECOND values. Make sure your application times the game correctly even if the start and stop times do not occur during the same MINUTE. Save the file as **JCatchTheMouseTimed.java**.

c. In the JCatchTheMouseTimed game described in Game Zone exercise 2b, the timer does not work correctly if the user happens to play when the hour, day, or year changes. Visit the Java Web site to find out how to use the GregorianCalendar class method getTimeInMillis(), and then modify the game to measure playing time accurately, no matter when the user plays the game. Save the file as **JCatchTheMouseTimed2.java**.

If you were writing a professional timed game, you would test the timer's accuracy regardless of when the user decided to play. For example, if the user played over the midnight hour on New Year's Eve, you would either have to test the game then (which is impractical), or reset your system's clock to simulate New Year's Eve. If you are writing the programs in this book on a school's computer network, you might be blocked by the administrator from changing the date and time. Even if you are working on your own computer, do not attempt to change the date and time unless you understand the impact on other installed applications. For example, your operating system might assume that an installed virus-protection program is expired, or a financial program might indicate that automatically paid bills are overdue.

3. The game Corner the King is played on a checkerboard. To begin, a checker is randomly placed in the bottom row. The player can move one or two squares to the left or upward, and then the computer can move one or two squares left or up. The first to reach the upper-left corner wins. Design a game in which the computer's moves are chosen randomly. When the game ends, display a message that indicates the winner. Save the game as **CornerTheKing.java**.

4. Create a target practice game that allows the user to click moving targets and displays the number of hits in a 10-second period. Create a grid of at least 100 JPanels. Randomly display an *X* on five panels to indicate targets. As the user clicks each *X*, change the label to indicate a hit. When all five *X*s have been hit, randomly display a new set of five targets. Continue with as many sets as the user can hit in 10 seconds. (Use *www.oracle.com/technetwork/java/index.html* to find how to use the GregorianCalendar class method getTimeInMillis() to calculate the time change.) When the time is up, display a count of the number of targets hit. Save the file as **JTargetPractice.java**.

5. You set up the card game Concentration by placing pairs of cards face down in a grid. The player turns up two cards at a time, exposing their values. If the cards match, they are removed from the grid. If the cards do not match, they are turned back over so their values are hidden again, and the player selects two more cards to expose. Using the knowledge gained by the previously exposed cards, the player attempts to remove all the pairs of cards from play. Create a Java version of this game using a GridLayout that is four rows high and five columns wide. Randomly assign two of the numbers 0 through 9 to each of 20 JPanels, and place each of the

20 JPanels in a cell of the grid. Initially, show only "backs" of cards by setting each panel's background to a solid color. When the user clicks a first card, change its color and expose its value. After the user clicks a second card, change its color to the same color as the first exposed card, expose the second card's value, and keep both cards exposed until the user's mouse pointer exits the second card. If the two exposed cards are different, hide the cards again. If the two turned cards match, then "remove" the pair from play by setting their background colors to white. When the user has matched all 20 cards into 10 pairs, display a congratulatory message. Save the game as **JConcentration.java**.

6. Create a Mine Sweeper game by setting up a grid of rows and columns in which "bombs" are randomly hidden. You choose the size and difficulty of the game; for example, you might choose to create a fairly simple game by displaying a four-by-five grid that contains four bombs. If a player clicks a panel in the grid that contains a bomb, then the player loses the game. If the clicked panel is not a bomb, display a number that indicates how many adjacent panels contain a bomb. For example, if a user clicks a panel containing a 0, the user knows it is safe to click any panel above, below, beside, or diagonally adjacent to the cell, because those cells cannot possibly contain a bomb. If the player loses by clicking a bomb, display all the numeric values as well as the bomb positions. If the player succeeds in clicking all the panels except those containing bombs, the player wins and you should display a congratulatory message. Figure 15-44 shows the progression of a typical game. In the first screen, the user has clicked a panel, and the display indicates that two adjacent cells contain a bomb. In the second screen, the user has clicked a second panel, and the display indicates that three adjacent cells contain bombs. In the last screen, the user has clicked a bomb panel, and all the bomb positions are displayed. Save the game as **MineSweeper.java**.

Figure 15-44 Typical progression of MineSweeper game

7. Create the game Lights Out using a `BorderLayout`. Place a five-by-five grid of panels in one region, and reserve another region for a congratulatory message. Randomly set each panel in the grid to a dark color or light color. The object of the game is to force all the panels to be dark, thus turning the "lights out." When the player clicks a panel, turn all the panels in the same row and column, including the clicked panel, to the opposite color. For example, if the user clicks the panel in the second row, third column, then darken all the light-colored panels in the second row and third column, and lighten all the dark-colored panels in that row and column. When all the panels in the grid are dark, all the lights are out, so display a congratulatory message. Save the game as **LightsOut.java**.

8. The game StopGate is played on a checkerboard with a set of dominoes; each domino is large enough to cover two checkerboard squares. One player places a domino horizontally on the checkerboard, covering any two squares. The other player then places a domino vertically to cover any other two squares. When a player has no more moves available, that player loses. Create a computerized version of the game in which the player places the horizontal pieces and the computer randomly selects a position for the vertical pieces. (Game construction will be simpler if you allow the player to select only the left square of a two-square area and assume that the domino covers that position plus the position immediately to the right.) Use a different color for the player's dominoes and the computer's dominoes. Display a message naming the winner when no more moves are possible. Figure 15-45 shows a typical game after the player (blue) and computer (black) have each made one move, and near the end of the game when the player is about to win—the player has two moves remaining, but the computer has none. Save the file as **StopGate.java**.

Figure 15-45   A typical game of StopGate just after play begins and near the end of the game

Case Problems

1. In Chapter 14, you created an interactive GUI application for Carly's Catering that allows the user to enter a number of guests for an event and to choose an entrée, two side dishes, and a dessert from groups of choices. Then, the application displays the cost of the event and a list of the chosen items. Now, modify the interface to include separate panels for the guest number entry, each group of menu choices, and the output. Use at least two different layout managers and at least two different colors in your application. Save the program as **JCarlysCatering.java**.

2. In Chapter 14, you created an interactive GUI application for Sammy's Seashore Rentals that allows the user to enter a rental time in hours, an equipment type, and a lesson option. Then, the application displays the cost of the rental and rental details. Now, modify the interface to include separate panels for the hour entry, each group of menu choices, and the output. Use at least two different layout managers and at least two different colors in your application. Save the program as **JSammysSeashore.java**.

Graphics

In this chapter, you will:

- ◎ Learn about the `paint()` and `repaint()` methods
- ◎ Use the `drawString()` method to draw `String`s using various fonts and colors
- ◎ Draw lines and shapes
- ◎ Learn more about fonts
- ◎ Draw with Java 2D graphics

Learning About the `paint()` and `repaint()` Methods

When you run a Java program that contains graphics, such as the JFrame applications in the previous chapters, the display surface frequently must be redisplayed, or **rerendered**. Redisplaying a surface also is called **painting**. Painting operations fall into two broad categories based on what causes them:

- **System-triggered painting** operations occur when the system asks a component to render its contents. This happens when the component is first made visible, if it is resized, or if it is damaged. For example, a component becomes damaged when another component that previously covered part of it has been moved, revealing a portion that was not visible.

- **Application-triggered painting** operations occur when the internal state of a component has changed. For example, when a user clicks a button, a "pressed" version of the button must be rendered.

Whether a paint request is triggered by the system or by an application, a Component's **`paint()` method** is invoked. The header for the `paint()` method is:

```
public void paint(Graphics g)
```

The parameter to the method is a Graphics object. The **Graphics class** is an abstract class that descends directly from Object and holds data about graphics operations and methods for drawing shapes, text, and images. When AWT invokes the `paint()` method, the Graphics object parameter is preconfigured with the appropriate values for drawing on the component:

- The Graphics object's *color* is set to the component's foreground property.

- The Graphics object's *font* is set to the component's font property.

- The Graphics object's *translation* is set such that the coordinates 0, 0 represent the upper-left corner of the component.

- The Graphics object's *clip rectangle* is set to the area of the component that needs repainting.

Programs must use this Graphics object (or one derived from it) to render graphic output. They can change the values of the Graphics object as necessary.

You override the `paint()` method in your programs when you want specific actions to take place when components must be rendered. You don't usually call the `paint()` method directly. Instead, you call the **`repaint()` method**, which you can use when a window needs to be updated, such as when it contains new images or you have moved a new object onto the screen. The Java system calls the `repaint()` method when it needs to update a window, or you can call it yourself—in either case, `repaint()` creates a Graphics object for you that becomes the `paint()` method parameter. The `repaint()` method calls another method named `update()`, which clears its Component's content pane and calls the `paint()` method. The series of events is best described with an example. Figure 16-1 shows a JDemoPaint class that extends JFrame. The frame contains a JButton. The constructor sets a title, layout manager, and default close operation, and it adds the button to the frame. The button is designated as a source for actions to which the frame can respond.

```java
import javax.swing.*;
import java.awt.*;
import java.awt.event.*;
public class JDemoPaint extends JFrame implements ActionListener
{
    JButton pressButton = new JButton("Press");
    public JDemoPaint()
    {
        setTitle("Paint Demo");
        setLayout(new FlowLayout());
        setDefaultCloseOperation(JFrame.EXIT_ON_CLOSE);
        add(pressButton);
        pressButton.addActionListener(this);
    }
    public void actionPerformed(ActionEvent e)
    {
        System.out.print("Button pressed. ");
        repaint();
    }
    public void paint(Graphics g)
    {
        super.paint(g);
        System.out.println("In paint method.");
    }
    public static void main(String[] args)
    {
        JDemoPaint frame = new JDemoPaint();
        frame.setSize(150, 100);
        frame.setVisible(true);
    }
}
```

Figure 16-1 The JDemoPaint class

In Figure 16-1, the shaded first line of code in the `paint()` method is `super.paint(g);`. This statement is a call to the `paint()` method that is part of JDemoPaint's parent class (JFrame), and it passes the local Graphics object (named g) to this method. Although this program and others in this chapter will work without this statement, omitting it causes errors in more complicated applications. For now, get in the habit of including this method call as the first statement in any JFrame's `paint()` method, using whatever local name you have declared for your `paint()` method's Graphics argument.

In the JDemoPaint class in Figure 16-1, the `actionPerformed()` method executes when the user presses the JButton. The method contains a call to `repaint()`, which is unseen in the class and which automatically calls the `paint()` method.

The `paint()` method in the JDemoPaint class overrides the automatically supplied `paint()` method. The `paint()` method displays a line of output at the command line—it announces that the `paint()` method is executing. Figure 16-2 shows a typical execution of the program. The JFrame is first drawn when it is constructed, and the message "In paint method." appears at the command line. When the user clicks the button on the frame, two messages are displayed: "Button pressed." from the actionPerformed() method, and "In paint method." from the paint() method that is called by repaint(). When the user minimizes and restores the frame, paint() is called automatically, and the "In paint method." message is displayed again.

Figure 16-2 Typical execution of the JDemoPaint program

If you call repaint() alone in a class that is a container, then the entire container is repainted. (The call to repaint() in Figure 16-1 is actually this.repaint();.) Repainting the entire container might be unnecessary and waste time if only part of the container has changed. If you call repaint() with a component, as in pressButton.repaint(), then only that component is repainted.

The repaint() method only requests that Java repaint the screen. If a second request to repaint() occurs before Java can carry out the first request, Java executes only the last repaint() method.

Before the built-in paint() method is called, the entire container is filled with its background color. Then the paint() method redraws the contents. The effect is that components are "erased" before being redrawn.

Using the setLocation() Method

The **setLocation() method** allows you to place a component at a specific location within a JFrame's content pane. In Chapter 15, you learned that a window or frame consists of a number of pixels on the screen, and that any component you place on the screen has a horizontal, or x-axis, position as well as a vertical, or y-axis, position. The horizontal position number increases from left to right across the screen, and the vertical position number increases from top to bottom.

When you allow a layout manager to position components, specific positions are selected automatically for each component. You can change the position of a component by using the setLocation() method and passing it x- and y-coordinate positions. For example, to position a JLabel object named someLabel at the upper-left corner of a JFrame, you write the following within the JFrame class:

```
someLabel.setLocation(0, 0);
```

If a window is 200 pixels wide by 100 pixels tall, you can place a `Button` named `pressMe` in the approximate center of the window with the following statement:

`pressMe.setLocation(100, 50);`

The coordinate arguments can be numeric constants or variables.

When you use `setLocation()`, the upper-left corner of the component is placed at the specified x- and y-coordinates. In other words, if a window is 100 by 100 pixels, `aButton.setLocation(100,100);` places the `JButton` outside the window, where you cannot see the component.

Figure 16-3 shows a `JDemoLocation` class that uses a call to the `setLocation()` method in the `actionPerformed()` method. The values of the x- and y-coordinates passed to `setLocation()` are initialized to 0, and then each is increased by 30 every time the user clicks the `JButton`. The `JButton` moves 30 pixels down and to the right every time it is clicked.

```java
import javax.swing.*;
import java.awt.*;
import java.awt.event.*;
public class JDemoLocation extends JFrame implements ActionListener
{
    JButton pressButton = new JButton("Press");
    int x = 0, y = 0;
    final int GAP = 30;
    public JDemoLocation()
    {
        setTitle("Location Demo");
        setLayout(new FlowLayout());
        setDefaultCloseOperation(JFrame.EXIT_ON_CLOSE);
        add(pressButton);
        pressButton.addActionListener(this);
    }
    public void actionPerformed(ActionEvent e)
    {
        pressButton.setLocation(x, y);
        x += GAP;
        y += GAP;
    }
    public static void main(String[] args)
    {
        JDemoLocation frame = new JDemoLocation();
        frame.setSize(150, 150);
        frame.setVisible(true);
    }
}
```

Figure 16-3 The JDemoLocation class

Figure 16-4 shows the JFrame in four positions: when it starts with the JButton in its default position; after the user clicks the JButton once, moving it to position 0, 0; after the user clicks it a second time, moving it to position 30, 30; and after the user clicks it a third time, moving it to position 60, 60. If the user continues to click the JButton, it moves off the frame surface. You could add a decision to prevent continued progression of the setLocation() coordinates.

Figure 16-4   Execution of the JDemoLocation program

The setLocation() method works correctly only when it is used after the layout manager has finished positioning all the application's components (or in cases where no layout manager is functioning). If you try to use setLocation() on a component within its container's constructor, the component will not be repositioned because the layout manager will not be finished placing components.

Creating Graphics Objects

When you call the paint() method from an application, you can use the automatically created Graphics object that is passed to it, but you can also instantiate your own Graphics objects. For example, you might want to use a Graphics object when some action occurs, such as a mouse event. Because the actionPerformed() method does not supply you with a Graphics object automatically, you can create your own.

To display a string when the user clicks a JButton, you can code an actionPerformed() method such as the following:

```
public void actionPerformed(ActionEvent e)
{
    Graphics draw = getGraphics();
    draw.drawString("You clicked the button!", 50, 100);
}
```

This method instantiates a Graphics object named draw. (You can use any legal Java identifier.) The getGraphics() method provides the draw object with Graphics capabilities. Then the draw object can employ Graphics methods such as setFont(), setColor(), and drawString().

Notice that when you create the draw object, you are not calling the Graphics constructor directly. (The name of the Graphics constructor is Graphics(), not getGraphics().)

This operation is similar to the way you call `getContentPane()`. You are not allowed to call the `Graphics` or `ContentPane` constructors because those classes are **abstract** classes.

If you call `getGraphics()` in a frame that is not visible, you receive a `NullPointerException`, and the program will not execute.

 Watch the video *Using `paint()` and `repaint()`.*

TWO TRUTHS & A LIE

Learning About the `paint()` and `repaint()` Methods

1. Painting can be system triggered (for example, when a component is resized) or application triggered (for example, when a user clicks a button).

2. When the `paint()` method is called, the `Graphics` object parameter is preconfigured with the appropriate state for drawing on the component, including the color and font.

3. You override the `repaint()` method in your programs when you want specific actions to take place when components must be rendered. You usually call the `paint()` method directly, and it calls `repaint()`.

The false statement is #3. You override the `paint()` method in your programs when you want specific actions to take place when components must be rendered. You don't usually call the `paint()` method directly—you call `repaint()`.

Using the `drawString()` Method

The **`drawString()` method** allows you to draw a `String` in a `JFrame` or other component. The `drawString()` method requires three arguments: a `String`, an x-axis coordinate, and a y-axis coordinate.

You are already familiar with x- and y-axis coordinates because you used them with the `setLocation()` method for components. However, there is a minor difference in how you place components using the `setLocation()` method and how you place `Strings` using the `drawString()` method. When you use x- and y-coordinates with components, such as `JButtons` or `JLabels`, the upper-left corner of the component is placed at the coordinate position. When you use x- and y-coordinates with `drawString()`, the lower-left corner of the

String appears at the coordinates. Figure 16-5 shows the positions of a JLabel placed at the coordinates 30, 10 and a String placed at the coordinates 10, 30.

Figure 16-5 Placement of String and JLabel objects on a frame

The drawString() method is a member of the Graphics class, so you need to use a Graphics object to call it. Recall that the paint() method header shows that the method receives a Graphics object from the update() method. If you use drawString() within paint(), the Graphics object you name in the header is available to you. For example, if you write a paint() method with the header public void paint(Graphics brush), you can draw a String within your paint() method by using a statement such as:

```
brush.drawString("Hi", 50, 80);
```

Interestingly, when you use the drawString() method with a negative font size, the string appears upside down. The coordinates then indicate the lower-right corner of the string.

Using the setFont() and setColor() Methods

You can improve the appearance of strings drawn using Graphics objects by using the setFont() method. The setFont() method requires a Font object, which, as you may recall from Chapter 14, you can create with a statement such as:

```
Font someFont = new Font("Arial", Font.BOLD, 16);
```

Then you can instruct a Graphics object to use the font by inserting the font as the argument in a setFont() method. For example, if a Graphics object is named artist and a Font object is named smallFont, the font is set to smallFont with the following:

```
artist.setFont(smallFont);
```

Figure 16-6 shows an application that uses the setFont() method with a Graphics object named brush.

```
import javax.swing.*;
import java.awt.*;
public class JDemoFont extends JFrame
{
    Font bigFont = new Font("Serif", Font.ITALIC, 48);
    String hello = "Hello";
    public void paint(Graphics brush)
    {
        super.paint(brush);
        brush.setFont(bigFont);
        brush.drawString(hello, 10, 100);
    }
    public static void main(String[] args)
    {
        JDemoFont frame = new JDemoFont();
        frame.setSize(180, 150);
        frame.setVisible(true);
    }
}
```

Figure 16-6   The JDemoFont class

When the paint() method executes in the JDemoFont example, bigFont is assigned to the automatically created brush object. Then the brush object is used to draw the hello string at position 10, 100. Figure 16-7 shows the output.

Figure 16-7   Output of the JDemoFont program

Using Color

You can designate a Graphics color with the setColor() method. As you learned in Chapter 15, the Color class contains 13 constants; you can use any of these constants as an argument to the setColor() method. For example, you can instruct a Graphics object named brush to apply green paint by using the following statement:

brush.setColor(Color.GREEN);

Until you change the color, subsequent graphics output appears as green.

TWO TRUTHS & A LIE

Using the drawString() Method

1. The drawString() method requires three arguments: a String, an x-axis coordinate, and a y-axis coordinate.

2. When you use x- and y-coordinates with components such as JButtons or JLabels, the lower-left corner of the component is placed at the coordinate position, but when you use x- and y-coordinates with drawString(), the upper-left corner of the String appears at the coordinates.

3. The drawString() method is a member of the Graphics class, so you need to use a Graphics object to call it.

The false statement is #2. When you use x- and y-coordinates with components, such as JButtons or JLabels, the upper-left corner of the component is placed at the coordinate position, but when you use x- and y-coordinates with drawString(), the lower-left corner of the String appears at the coordinates.

You Do It

Using the drawString() Method

In the next steps, you write a class that extends JFrame and uses the drawString() method.

1. Open a new text file, and begin a class definition for a JDemoGraphics class by typing the following:

```
import javax.swing.*;
import java.awt.*;
public class JDemoGraphics extends JFrame
{
```

2. Declare a String by typing the following:

```
String movieQuote = new String("You talkin' to me?");
```

3. Add a constructor to set the default close operation:

```
public JDemoGraphics()
{
    setDefaultCloseOperation(JFrame.EXIT_ON_CLOSE);
}
```

(continues)

(continued)

4. Type the following paint() method that calls the super() method and uses a Graphics object to draw the movieQuote String.

```
public void paint(Graphics gr)
{
    super.paint(gr);
    gr.drawString(movieQuote, 30, 100);
}
```

5. Add a main() method that instantiates a JDemoGraphics object and sets its size and visibility. Then add the closing curly brace for the class:

```
public static void main(String[] args)
{
    JDemoGraphics frame = new JDemoGraphics();
    frame.setSize(280, 200);
    frame.setVisible(true);
}
}
```

6. Save the file as **JDemoGraphics.java**, and then compile and execute it. The program's output appears in Figure 16-8.

Figure 16-8   Output of the JDemoGraphics program

7. Close the JFrame to end the application.

Using Fonts and Colors

Next, you use your knowledge of fonts and colors to set the color and font style of a drawn String.

(continues)

(continued)

1. Open the **JDemoGraphics.java** text file in your text editor, and immediately save it as **JDemoGraphics2.java**. Change the class name, the constructor name, and the two references in the `main()` method to match.

2. Add a new `import` statement to the current list so that the application can use color:

    ```
    import java.awt.Color;
    ```

3. Just after the `movieQuote` declaration, add a `Font` object by typing the following:

    ```
    Font bigFont = new Font("Boopee", Font.ITALIC, 30);
    ```

4. Within the `paint()` method after the call to `super()`, type the following statements so the `gr` object uses the `bigFont` object and the color magenta:

    ```
    gr.setFont(bigFont);
    gr.setColor(Color.MAGENTA);
    ```

5. Following the existing `drawString()` method call, type the following lines to change the color and add another call to the `drawString()` method:

    ```
    gr.setColor(Color.BLUE);
    gr.drawString(movieQuote, 60, 140);
    ```

6. Save the file, compile it, and execute it. The program's output appears in Figure 16-9. Although the figure is shown in black and white in this book, notice that the `String`s on your screen are displayed as magenta and blue text. The font that appears in your program might be different from the one shown in the figure, depending on your computer's installed fonts. (Later in this chapter, you will learn how to view a list of all the available fonts on your computer.)

Figure 16-9   Output of the JDemoGraphics2 program

(continues)

(continued)

7. Close the `JFrame` to end the application.

Creating Your Own Graphics Object

Next, you create a `Graphics` object named `pen` and use the object to draw a `String` on the screen. The text of the `String` will appear to move each time a `JButton` is clicked.

1. Open a new text file in your text editor, and type the following `import` statements for the program:

```
import javax.swing.*;
import java.awt.*;
import java.awt.event.*;
import java.awt.Color;
```

2. Start typing the following class that extends `JFrame` and uses the mouse. The class defines a `String`, a `JButton`, a `Font`, and four integers: two to hold x- and y-coordinates, one to act as a constant size to measure the gap between lines displayed on the screen, and one to hold the size of the `JFrame`:

```
public class JDemoCreateGraphicsObject extends JFrame
    implements ActionListener
{
    String movieQuote = new String("Here's looking at you, kid");
    JButton moveButton = new JButton("Move It");
    Font broadwayFont = new Font("Broadway", Font.ITALIC, 12);
    int x = 10, y = 50;
    final int GAP = 20;
    final int SIZE = 400;
```

3. Type the following constructor; it changes the background color and sets the layout of the `Container`, adds the `JButton`, prepares the `JFrame` to listen for `JButton` events, sets the close operation, and sets the size of the frame:

```
public JDemoCreateGraphicsObject()
{
    Container con = getContentPane();
    con.setBackground(Color.YELLOW);
    con.setLayout(new FlowLayout() );
    con.add(moveButton);
    moveButton.addActionListener(this);
    setDefaultCloseOperation(JFrame.EXIT_ON_CLOSE);
    setSize(SIZE, SIZE);
}
```

(continues)

(continued)

4. Within the `actionPerformed()` method, you can create a `Graphics` object and use it to draw the `String` on the screen. Each time a user clicks the `JButton`, the x- and y-coordinates both increase, so a copy of the movie quote appears slightly below and to the right of the previous one. Type the following `actionPerformed()` method to accomplish this processing:

```
public void actionPerformed(ActionEvent e)
{
    Graphics pen = getGraphics();
    pen.setFont(broadwayFont);
    pen.setColor(Color.MAGENTA);
    pen.drawString(movieQuote, x += GAP, y += GAP);
}
```

5. Add a `main()` method to instantiate a `JDemoCreateGraphicsObject` object and give it visibility. Add a closing curly brace for the class.

```
public static void main(String[] args)
{
    JDemoCreateGraphicsObject frame = new
        JDemoCreateGraphicsObject();
    frame.setVisible(true);
}
}
```

6. Save the file as **JDemoCreateGraphicsObject.java**, and then compile and run the program. Click the **Move It** button several times to see the `String` message appear and move on the screen.

7. When you finish clicking the button, close the `JFrame` to end the application.

Examining Screen Coordinates

If you run `JDemoCreateGraphicsObject` and click the `JButton` enough times, the movie quote `String` appears to march off the bottom of the `JFrame`. Every time you click the `JButton`, the x- and y-coordinates used by `drawString()` increase, and there is no limit to their value. You can prevent this error by checking the screen coordinates' values to see if they exceed the `JFrame`'s dimensions.

1. Open the **JDemoCreateGraphicsObject** file, and immediately save it as **JDemoCreateGraphicsObject2**. Change the class name, constructor name, and the two references to the class in the `main()` method to match.

(continues)

(continued)

2. Because the screen size is 400 by 400, you can ensure that at least part of the `String` appears in the frame by preventing the y-coordinate from exceeding a value that is slightly less than 400. Create a constant to hold this limit by adding the following just after the declaration of `SIZE`:

```
final int LIMIT = SIZE - 50;
```

3. In the `actionPerformed()` method, replace the stand-alone call to `drawString()` with one that depends on `LIMIT` as follows:

```
if(y < LIMIT)
    pen.drawString(movieQuote, x += GAP, y += GAP);
```

4. Add an `else` clause that disables the `JButton` after the x-coordinate becomes too large:

```
else
    moveButton.setEnabled(false);
```

5. Save the file, compile it, and execute it. Now when you click the **Move It** button, the movie quote moves until the y-coordinate reaches 350. At that point, the `JButton` is disabled, and the movie quote no longer violates the frame's size limits.

6. Close the frame to end the program.

Drawing Lines and Shapes

Just as you can draw `Strings` using a `Graphics` object and the `drawString()` method, Java provides you with several methods for drawing a variety of lines and geometric shapes. Any line or shape is drawn in the current color you set with the `setColor()` method. When you do not set a color, lines are drawn in black by default.

 It is almost impossible to draw a picture of any complexity without sketching it first on a piece of graph paper to help you determine correct coordinates.

Drawing Lines

You can use the **drawLine() method** to draw a straight line between any two points on the screen. The `drawLine()` method takes four arguments: the x- and y-coordinates of the line's starting point and the x- and y-coordinates of the line's ending point. For example, if you create a `Graphics` object named `pen`, then the following statement draws a straight line that slants down and to the right, from position 50, 50 to position 100, 200, as shown in Figure 16-10.

```
pen.drawLine(50, 50, 100, 200);
```

Because you can start at either end when you draw a line, an identical line is created with the following:

```
pen.drawLine(100, 200, 50, 50);
```

Figure 16-10   A line created with `pen.drawLine(50, 50, 100, 200)`

Your downloadable student files contain a JDemoLine.java file with a working program that draws the line shown in Figure 16-10.

Drawing Rectangles

You could draw a rectangle by drawing four lines. Alternatively, you can use the **drawRect()** **method** and **fillRect()** **method**, respectively, to draw the outline of a rectangle or to draw a solid, or filled, rectangle. Each of these methods requires four arguments. The first two arguments represent the x- and y-coordinates of the upper-left corner of the rectangle. The last two arguments represent the width and height of the rectangle. For example, the following statement draws a short, wide rectangle that begins at position 20, 100, and is 200 pixels wide by 10 pixels tall:

```
drawRect(20, 100, 200, 10);
```

The **clearRect()** **method** also requires four arguments and draws a rectangle. The difference between using the `drawRect()` and `fillRect()` methods and the `clearRect()` method is that the first two methods use the current drawing color, whereas the `clearRect()` method draws what appears to be an empty or "clear" rectangle. A rectangle created with the `clearRect()` method is not really "clear"; in other words, it is not transparent. When you create a rectangle, you do not see objects that might be hidden behind it. Instead, the `clearRect()` method clears anything drawn from view, showing the original content pane.

For example, the constructor in the `JDemoRectangles` program shown in Figure 16-11 sets the background color of the content pane to blue and sets the layout manager.

```java
import javax.swing.*;
import java.awt.*;
import java.awt.Color;
public class JDemoRectangles extends JFrame
{
    Container con = getContentPane();
    public JDemoRectangles()
    {
        con.setBackground(Color.BLUE);
        con.setLayout(new FlowLayout());
    }
    public void paint(Graphics gr)
    {
        super.paint(gr);
        gr.setColor(Color.RED);
        gr.fillRect(40, 40, 120, 120);
        gr.setColor(Color.YELLOW);
        gr.fillRect(80, 80, 160, 160);
        gr.clearRect(50, 60, 50, 50);
    }
    public static void main(String[] args)
    {
        JDemoRectangles frame = new JDemoRectangles();
        frame.setSize(200, 200);
        frame.setVisible(true);
    }
}
```

Figure 16-11 The `JDemoRectangles` class

In the `paint()` method in Figure 16-11, the drawing color is set to red, and a filled rectangle is drawn. Then the drawing color is changed to yellow and a second filled rectangle is drawn to overlap the first. Finally, a smaller, "clear" rectangle is drawn that overlaps the other rectangles. As Figure 16-12 shows, you cannot see the boundaries of the original rectangles in the "clear" area—you simply see that portions of the filled rectangles have been removed from the drawing.

Figure 16-12 Output of the JDemoRectangles program

You can create rectangles with rounded corners when you use the **drawRoundRect() method**. The drawRoundRect() method requires six arguments. The first four arguments match the four arguments required to draw a rectangle: the x- and y-coordinates of the upper-left corner, the width, and the height. The two additional arguments represent the arc width and height associated with the rounded corners (an **arc** is a portion of a circle). If you assign zeros to the arc coordinates, the rectangle is not rounded; instead, the corners are square. At the other extreme, if you assign values to the arc coordinates that are at least the width and height of the rectangle, the rectangle is so rounded that it is a circle. The paint() method in Figure 16-13 draws four rectangles with increasingly large corner arcs. The first rectangle is drawn at coordinates 20, 40, and the horizontal coordinate is increased by 100 for each subsequent rectangle. Each rectangle is the same width and height, but each set of arc values becomes larger, producing rectangles that are not rounded, slightly rounded, very rounded, and completely rounded in sequence. Figure 16-14 shows the program's output.

```
import javax.swing.*;
import java.awt.*;
public class JDemoRoundRectangles extends JFrame
{
    public void paint(Graphics gr)
    {
        super.paint(gr);
        int x = 20;
        int y = 40;
        final int WIDTH = 80, HEIGHT = 80;
        final int HORIZONTAL_GAP = 100;
        for(int arcSize = x; arcSize <= HEIGHT; arcSize += 20)
        {
            gr.drawRoundRect(x, y, WIDTH, HEIGHT, arcSize, arcSize);
            x += HORIZONTAL_GAP;
        }
    }
}
```

Figure 16-13 The JDemoRoundRectangles class *(continues)*

(continued)

```
    public static void main(String[] args)
    {
        JDemoRoundRectangles frame = new JDemoRoundRectangles();
        frame.setSize(420, 140);
        frame.setVisible(true);
    }
}
```

Figure 16-13 The JDemoRoundRectangles class

Figure 16-14 Output of the JDemoRoundRectangles program

Java also contains a fillRoundRect() method that creates a filled rounded rectangle and a clearRoundRect() method that creates a clear rounded rectangle.

Creating Shadowed Rectangles

The **draw3DRect() method** is a minor variation on the drawRect() method. You use the draw3DRect() method to draw a rectangle that appears to have "shadowing" on two of its edges—the effect is that of a rectangle that is lit from the upper-left corner and slightly raised or slightly lowered. The draw3DRect() method requires a fifth argument in addition to the x- and y-coordinates and width and height required by the drawRect() method. The fifth argument is a Boolean value, which is true if you want the raised rectangle effect (darker on the right and bottom) and false if you want the lowered rectangle effect (lighter on the right and bottom). There is also a **fill3DRect() method** for creating filled three-dimensional (3D) rectangles; this method is used in the program in Figure 16-15.

```
import javax.swing.*;
import java.awt.*;
import java.awt.Color;
public class JDemo3DRectangles extends JFrame
{
    public void paint(Graphics gr)
    {
        super.paint(gr);
        final int WIDTH = 60, HEIGHT = 80;
        gr.setColor(Color.PINK);
        gr.fill3DRect(20, 40, WIDTH, HEIGHT, true);
        gr.fill3DRect(100, 40, WIDTH, HEIGHT, false);
    }
    public static void main(String[] args)
    {
        JDemo3DRectangles frame = new JDemo3DRectangles();
        frame.setSize(180, 150);
        frame.setVisible(true);
    }
}
```

Figure 16-15   The JDemo3DRectangles class

The program in Figure 16-15 creates two filled 3D rectangles in pink. (The 3D methods work best with lighter drawing colors.) You can see that the shadowing effect on the output in Figure 16-16 is very subtle; the shadowing is only one pixel wide.

Figure 16-16   Output of the JDemo3DRectangles program

Drawing Ovals

You can draw an oval using the drawRoundRect() or fillRoundRect() method, but it is usually easier to use the **drawOval()** and **fillOval() methods**. The drawOval() and fillOval() methods both draw ovals using the same four arguments that rectangles use. When you supply drawOval() or fillOval() with x- and y-coordinates for the upper-left corner and width and height measurements, you can picture an imaginary rectangle that uses the four arguments. The oval is then placed within the rectangle so it touches the rectangle at the center of each of the rectangle's sides. For example, suppose that you create a `Graphics` object named `tool` and draw a rectangle with the following statement:

```
tool.drawRect(50, 50, 100, 60);
```

Suppose that then you create an oval with the same coordinates as follows:

```
tool.drawOval(50, 50, 100, 60);
```

The output appears as shown in Figure 16-17, with the oval edges just skimming the rectangle's sides.

Figure 16-17   Demonstration of the `drawOval()` method

Your downloadable student files contain a JDemoOval.java file that produces the frame in Figure 16-17.

If you draw a rectangle with identical height and width, you draw a square. If you draw an oval with identical height and width, you draw a circle.

Drawing Arcs

In Java, you can draw an arc using the `Graphics` **`drawArc()` method**. To use the `drawArc()` method, you provide six arguments:

- The x- and y-coordinates of the upper-left corner of an imaginary rectangle that represents the bounds of the imaginary circle that contains the arc
- The width and height of the imaginary rectangle that represents the bounds of the imaginary circle that contains the arc
- The beginning arc position and the arc angle

Arc positions and angles are measured in degrees; there are 360 degrees in a circle. The 0° position for any arc is the three o'clock position, as shown in Figure 16-18. The other 359 degree positions increase as you move counterclockwise around an imaginary circle, so 90°

is at the top of the circle in the 12 o'clock position, 180° is opposite the starting position at nine o'clock, and 270° is at the bottom of the circle in the six o'clock position.

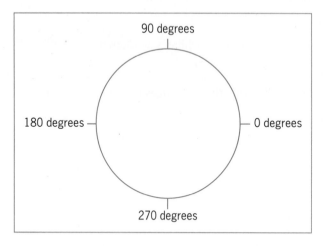

Figure 16-18 Arc positions

The arc angle is the number of degrees over which you want to draw the arc, traveling counterclockwise from the starting position. For example, you can draw a half circle by indicating an arc angle of 180° or a quarter circle by indicating an arc angle of 90°. If you want to travel clockwise from the starting position, you express the degrees as a negative number. Just as when you draw a line, when drawing any arc you can take one of two approaches: either start at point A and travel to point B, or start at point B and travel to point A. For example, to create an arc object using a `Graphics` object named g that looks like the top half of a circle, the following statements produce identical results:

```
g.drawArc(x, y, w, h, 0, 180);
g.drawArc(x, y, w, h, 180, -180);
```

The first statement starts an arc at the three o'clock position and travels 180 degrees counterclockwise to the nine o'clock position. The second statement starts at nine o'clock and travels clockwise to three o'clock.

The **fillArc() method** creates a solid arc. The arc is drawn, and two straight lines are drawn from the arc endpoints to the center of the imaginary circle whose perimeter the arc occupies. For example, assuming you have declared a `Graphics` object named g, the following two statements together produce the output shown in Figure 16-19:

```
g.fillArc(20, 50, 100, 100, 20, 320);
g.fillArc(60, 50, 100, 100, 340, 40);
```

Each of the two arcs is in a circle that has a size of 100 by 100. The first arc almost completes a full circle, starting at position 20 (near two o'clock) and ending 320 degrees around the circle (at position 340, near four o'clock). The second filled arc more closely resembles a pie slice, starting at position 340 and extending 40 degrees to end at position 20.

Figure 16-19   Two filled arcs

   Your downloadable student files contain a program named JDemoFillArc.java that produces Figure 16-19.

Creating Polygons

When you want to create a shape that is more complex than a rectangle, you can use a sequence of calls to the drawLine() method, or you can use the **drawPolygon() method** to draw complex shapes. The drawPolygon() method requires three arguments: two integer arrays and a single integer.

The first integer array holds a series of x-coordinate positions, and the second array holds a series of corresponding y-coordinate positions. These positions represent points that are connected to form the polygon. The third integer argument is the number of pairs of points you want to connect. If you don't want to connect all the points represented by the array values, you can assign this third argument integer a value that is smaller than the number of elements in each array. However, an error occurs if the third argument is a value higher than the available number of coordinate pairs.

For example, examine the code shown in Figure 16-20, which is a JFrame application that has one task: to draw a star-shaped polygon.

```
import javax.swing.*;
import java.awt.*;
public class JStar extends JFrame
{
   public void paint(Graphics gr)
   {
      super.paint(gr);
      int xPoints[] = {42, 52, 72, 52,  60, 40, 15,  28, 9,  32, 42};
      int yPoints[] = {38, 62, 68, 80, 105, 85, 102, 75, 58, 60, 38};
      gr.drawPolygon(xPoints, yPoints, xPoints.length);
   }
   public static void main(String[] args)
   {
      JStar frame = new JStar();
      frame.setSize(80, 150);
      frame.setVisible(true);
   }
}
```

Figure 16-20   The JStar class

In the JStar program, two parallel arrays are assigned x- and y-coordinates. It is almost impossible to create a program like this without sketching the desired shape on a piece of graph paper to discover appropriate coordinate values. The drawPolygon() method uses the two arrays and the length of one of the arrays for the number of points. The program's output appears in Figure 16-21.

Figure 16-21   Output of the JStar program

You can use the **fillPolygon() method** to draw a solid shape. The major difference between the drawPolygon() and fillPolygon() methods is that if the beginning and ending points used with the fillPolygon() method are not identical, the two endpoints are connected by a straight line before the polygon is filled with color.

Rather than providing the `fillPolygon()` method with three arguments, you can also create a `Polygon` object and pass the constructed object as a single argument to the `fillPolygon()` method. The `Polygon` constructor requires an array of x-coordinates, an array of y-coordinates, and a size. For example, you can create a filled polygon using the following statements:

```
Polygon someShape = new Polygon(xPoints, yPoints, xPoints.length);
gr.fillPolygon(someShape);
```

The `Polygon` class also has a default constructor, so you can instantiate an empty `Polygon` object (with no points) using the following statement:

```
Polygon someFutureShape = new Polygon();
```

Whether you use the default constructor or not, you can add points to a polygon after construction. For example, you might want to add points that are determined by user input or mathematical calculations. You use the **addPoint() method** in statements such as the following to add points to the polygon later:

```
someFutureShape.addPoint(100, 100);
someFutureShape.addPoint(150, 200);
someFutureShape.addPoint(50, 250);
```

Points can be added to a polygon indefinitely.

Copying an Area

After you create a graphics image, you might want to create copies of the image. For example, you might want a company logo to appear several times in an application. Of course, you can redraw the picture, but you can also use the **copyArea() method** to copy any rectangular area to a new location. The `copyArea()` method requires six parameters:

- The x- and y-coordinates of the upper-left corner of the area to be copied
- The width and height of the area to be copied
- The horizontal and vertical displacement of the destination of the copy

For example, the following line of code causes a `Graphics` object named gr to copy an area 20 pixels wide by 30 pixels tall from the upper-left corner of your `JFrame` (coordinates 0, 0) to an area that begins 100 pixels to the right and 50 pixels down:

```
gr.copyArea(0, 0, 20, 30, 100, 50);
```

Using the `paintComponent()` Method with `JPanel`s

When you create drawings on a `JPanel` (or other `JComponent`) instead of on a `JFrame`, you should use the `paintComponent()` method rather than the `paint()` method. A `JFrame`'s `paint()` method automatically calls `paintComponent()` for its components, but `JFrame` is not a child of `JComponent`, so it does not have its own `paintComponent()` method.

For example, Figure 16-22 shows a JGraphicsPanel class that overrides JPanel. Its constructor accepts a color to use as a background color. Its only method is a paintComponent() method that overrides the paintComponent() method in the JPanel class. The parameter Graphics object is passed to the parent class constructor, the drawing color is set to yellow, and two small circles are drawn.

```java
import javax.swing.*;
import java.awt.*;
import java.awt.Color;
public class JGraphicsPanel extends JPanel
{
    public JGraphicsPanel(Color color)
    {
        setBackground(color);
    }
    public void paintComponent(Graphics g)
    {
        super.paintComponent(g);
        g.setColor(Color.YELLOW);
        g.fillOval(10, 5, 40, 40);
        g.fillOval(60, 5, 40, 40);
    }
}
```

Figure 16-22   The JGraphicsPanel class

Figure 16-23 contains a program that adds two JGraphicsPanel objects to a JFrame—one with a blue background and the other with a red background. Figure 16-24 shows the output, which displays two JPanels that are placed side by side using a GridLayout.

```java
import javax.swing.*;
import java.awt.*;
import java.awt.Color;
public class JGraphicsPanelFrame extends JFrame
{
    Container con = null;
    JGraphicsPanel p1 = new JGraphicsPanel(Color.BLUE);
    JGraphicsPanel p2 = new JGraphicsPanel(Color.RED);

    public JGraphicsPanelFrame ()
    {
        con = this.getContentPane();
        con.setLayout(new GridLayout(2,1));
        con.add(p1);
        con.add(p2);
```

Figure 16-23   The JGraphicsPanelFrame class (continues)

(*continued*)

```
        setSize(250, 250);
        setVisible(true);
        setDefaultCloseOperation(JFrame.EXIT_ON_CLOSE);
    }
    public static void main(String args[])
    {
        JGraphicsPanelFrame app = new JGraphicsPanelFrame();
        app.setVisible(true);
        app.setSize(140, 140);
    }
}
```

Figure 16-23   The JGraphicsPanelFrame class

Figure 16-24   Output of the JGraphicsPanelFrame program

   Watch the video *Drawing Lines and Shapes.*

TWO TRUTHS & A LIE

Drawing Lines and Shapes

1. You can use the `drawLine()` method to draw a straight line between any two points on the screen.

2. You can use methods named `drawRect()`, `fillRect()`, `clearRect()`, `drawOval()`, and `fillOval()` to create a variety of shapes.

3. When you draw an arc, the zero-degree position is at 12 o'clock on an imaginary clock, and the 90-degree position is at three o'clock.

The false statement is #3. When you draw an arc, the zero-degree position is at three o'clock, and the degree values increase as you move counterclockwise in a 360-degree circle, so the 90-degree position is at 12 o'clock.

 You Do It

Creating a Drawing

Next, you add a simple line drawing to the `JDemoCreateGraphicsObject2` program. The drawing appears after the user clicks the `JButton` enough times to disable the `JButton`.

1. Open the **JDemoCreateGraphicsObject2** file, and immediately save it as **JDemoCreateGraphicsObject3.java**. Change the class name, constructor name, and two references in the `main()` method to match.

2. Replace the current `if…else` structure that tests whether `y` is less than `LIMIT` in the `actionPerformed()` method. Instead, use the following code, which tests the value of `y` and either draws the quote or disables the `JButton` and draws a picture. Set the drawing color to black, and create a simple drawing of a stick person that includes a head, torso, and two legs:

```
if(y < LIMIT)
    pen.drawString(movieQuote, x += GAP, y += GAP);
else
{
    moveButton.setEnabled(false);
    pen.setColor(Color.BLACK);
```

(continues)

(continued)

```
      pen.drawOval(50, 170, 70, 70);
      pen.drawLine(85, 240, 90, 280);
      pen.drawLine(90, 280, 60, 380);
      pen.drawLine(90, 280, 110, 380);
   }
```

3. Save the file, compile it, and execute it. After the movie quote moves to the LIMIT value, the JButton is disabled and the drawing appears, as shown in Figure 16-25.

Figure 16-25   The JDemoCreateGraphicsObject3 program after the JButton is disabled

4. Close the application.

5. Modify the application so the drawing has more details, such as arms, feet, and a simple face. Save the revised application as **JDemoCreateGraphicsObject4.java**.

(continues)

(continued)

Copying an Area

Next, you learn how to copy an area containing a shape that you want to appear several times on a JFrame. By copying, you do not have to re-create the shape each time.

1. Open a new text file in your text editor, and then enter the beginning statements for a JFrame that uses the copyArea() method:

```
import javax.swing.*;
import java.awt.*;
import java.awt.Color;
public class JThreeStars extends JFrame
{
```

2. Add the following statements, which create a polygon in the shape of a star:

```
int xPoints[] = {42, 52, 72, 52,
    60, 40, 15, 28, 9, 32, 42};
int yPoints[] = {38, 62, 68, 80,
    105, 85, 102, 75, 58, 60, 38};
Polygon aStar = new Polygon(xPoints, yPoints, xPoints.length);
```

3. Add a constructor that sets the default close operation:

```
public JThreeStars()
{
    setDefaultCloseOperation(JFrame.EXIT_ON_CLOSE);
}
```

4. Add the following paint() method, which sets a color, draws a star, and then draws two additional identical stars:

```
public void paint(Graphics star)
{
    super.paint(star);
    star.setColor(Color.BLUE);
    star.drawPolygon(aStar);
    star.copyArea(0, 0, 75, 105, 80, 40);
    star.copyArea(0, 0, 75, 105, 40, 150);
}
```

5. Add a main() method that instantiates a JThreeStars object and sets its size and visibility. Add a closing brace to end the class:

```
public static void main(String[] args)
{
    JThreeStars frame = new JThreeStars();
    frame.setSize(200, 300);
    frame.setVisible(true);
}
}
```

(continues)

(continued)

6. Save the file as **JThreeStars.java**, and then compile the program. When you run the program, the output looks like Figure 16-26.

Figure 16-26   Output of the JThreeStars program with one star

7. Close the frame to end the application.

8. Modify the program to add two more stars in any location you choose, save and compile the program, and confirm that the stars are copied to your desired locations.

Learning More About Fonts

As you add more components in your GUI applications, positioning becomes increasingly important. In particular, when you draw Strings using different fonts, it is difficult to place them correctly so they don't overlap, making them difficult or impossible to read. In addition, the number of available fonts varies greatly across operating systems, so even when you define a font using a string argument such as "Arial" or "Courier", you have no guarantee that the font will be available on every computer that runs your application. If a user's computer does not have the requested font loaded, Java chooses a default replacement font, so you can never be completely certain how your output will look. Fortunately, Java provides many useful methods for obtaining information about the fonts you use.

You can discover the fonts that are available on your system by using the **getAvailableFontFamilyNames() method**, which is part of the GraphicsEnvironment class defined in the java.awt package. The GraphicsEnvironment class describes the collection of Font objects and GraphicsDevice objects available to a Java application on a particular platform. The getAvailableFontFamilyNames() method returns an array of String objects that are the names of available fonts. For example, the following statements declare a GraphicsEnvironment object named ge, and then use the object with the getAvailableFontFamilyNames() method to store the font names in a string array:

910

```
GraphicsEnvironment ge =
    GraphicsEnvironment.getLocalGraphicsEnvironment();
String[] fontnames = ge.getAvailableFontFamilyNames();
```

Notice in the preceding example that you can't instantiate the GraphicsEnvironment object directly. Instead, you must get a reference object to the current computer environment by calling the static getLocalGraphicsEnvironment() method. Figure 16-27 shows a JFrame that lists all the available font names on the computer on which the program was executed. After the GraphicsEnvironment object is created and the getAvailableFontFamilyNames() method is used to retrieve the array of font names, the names are displayed on the screen using a for loop in which the horizontal coordinate where each font String is drawn is increased by a fixed value so that five columns are displayed equally spaced across the JFrame surface. After five items are displayed, the horizontal coordinate is set back to 10 and the vertical coordinate is increased so that the next five-column row is displayed below the previous one. Typical output is shown in Figure 16-28.

```
import javax.swing.*;
import java.awt.*;
public class JFontList extends JFrame
{
    public void paint(Graphics gr)
    {
        super.paint(gr);
        int i, x, y = 40;
        final int VERTICAL_SPACE = 10;
        final int HORIZONTAL_SPACE = 160;
        GraphicsEnvironment ge =
            GraphicsEnvironment.getLocalGraphicsEnvironment();
        String[] fontnames = ge.getAvailableFontFamilyNames();
        for(i = 0; i < fontnames.length; i += 5)
        {
            x = 10;
            gr.setFont(new Font("Arial", Font.PLAIN, 10));
            gr.drawString(fontnames[i], x, y);
            if(i + 1 < fontnames.length)
                gr.drawString(fontnames[i + 1], x += HORIZONTAL_SPACE, y);
            if(i + 2 < fontnames.length)
                gr.drawString(fontnames[i + 2], x += HORIZONTAL_SPACE, y);
            if(i + 3 < fontnames.length)
                gr.drawString(fontnames[i + 3], x += HORIZONTAL_SPACE, y);
```

Figure 16-27   The JFontList class *(continues)*

(*continued*)

```
            if(i + 4 < fontnames.length)
                gr.drawString(fontnames[i + 4], x += HORIZONTAL_SPACE, y);
            y = y + VERTICAL_SPACE;
        }
    }
    public static void main(String[] args)
    {
        JFontList frame = new JFontList();
        frame.setSize(820, 620);
        frame.setVisible(true);
    }
}
```

Figure 16-27 The `JFontList` class

Figure 16-28 Typical output of the `JFontList` program

Discovering Screen Statistics Using the `Toolkit` Class

Frequently, before you can determine the best `Font` size to use, it is helpful to know statistics about the screen on which the `Font` will be displayed. For example, you can discover the resolution and screen size on your system by using the `getScreenResolution()` and `getScreenSize()` methods, which are part of the `Toolkit` class.

The **`getDefaultToolkit()` method** provides information about the system in use. The **`getScreenResolution()` method** returns the number of pixels as an integer. You can create a `Toolkit` object and get the screen resolution using the following code:

```
Toolkit tk = Toolkit.getDefaultToolkit();
int resolution = tk.getScreenResolution();
```

The `Dimension` class is useful for representing the width and height of a user interface component, such as a `JFrame` or a `JButton`. The `Dimension` class has three constructors:

- The `Dimension()` method creates an instance of `Dimension` with a width of 0 and a height of 0.

- `Dimension(Dimension d)` creates an instance of `Dimension` whose width and height are the same as for the specified dimension.

- `Dimension(int width, int height)` constructs a `Dimension` and initializes it to the specified width and height.

The **`getScreenSize()` method**, a member of the `Toolkit` object, returns an object of type `Dimension`, which specifies the width and height of the screen in pixels. Knowing the number of pixels for the width and height of your display is useful to set the coordinates for the position, width, and height of a window. For example, the following code stores the width and height of a screen in separate variables:

```
Toolkit tk = Toolkit.getDefaultToolkit();
Dimension screen = tk.getScreenSize();
int width = screen.width;
int height = screen.height;
```

Discovering Font Statistics

Typesetters and desktop publishers measure the height of every font in three parts: ascent, descent, and leading. **Ascent** is the height of an uppercase character from a baseline to the top of the character. **Descent** measures the part of characters that "hang below" the baseline, such as the tails on the lowercase letters *g* and *j*. **Leading** (pronounced *ledding*) is the amount of space between the bottom of the descent of one line and the top of the characters in the successive line of type. The **height of a font** is the sum of the leading, ascent, and descent. Figure 16-29 labels each of these measurements.

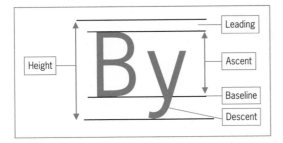

Figure 16-29 Parts of a font's height

You can discover a font's statistics by first using the Graphics class **getFontMetrics() method** to return a FontMetrics object, and then by using one of the following FontMetrics class methods with the object to return one of a Font's statistics:

- `public int getLeading()`

- `public int getAscent()`

- `public int getDescent()`

- `public int getHeight()`

 Another method, getLineMetrics(), is more complicated to use but returns similar font statistics. For more details, see the Java Web site.

Each of these methods returns an integer value representing the font size in points (one point measures 1/72 of an inch) of the requested portion of the Font object. For example, if you define a Font object named myFont and a Graphics object named paintBrush, you can set the current font for the Graphics object by using the following statements:

```
paintBrush.setFont(myFont);
int heightOfFont = paintBrush.getFontMetrics().getHeight();
```

 When you define a Font object, you use point size. However, when you use the FontMetrics get methods, the sizes are returned in pixels.

Then the heightOfFont variable holds the total height of myFont characters.

A practical use for discovering the height of a font is to space Strings correctly as you display them. For example, instead of placing every String in a series vertically equidistant from the previous String with a statement such as the following:

```
pen.drawString("Some string", x, y += INCREASE);
```

(where INCREASE has been defined as a constant), you can make the actual increase in the vertical position dependent on the font. If you code the following, you are assured that each String has enough room, regardless of which font is currently in use by the Graphics pen object:

```
pen.drawString("Some string",
   x, y += pen.getFontMetrics().getHeight());
```

When you create a String, you know how many characters are in the String. However, you cannot be certain which font Java will use or substitute, and because fonts have different measurements, it is difficult to know the exact width of the String that appears in a JFrame. Fortunately, the FontMetrics class contains a **stringWidth() method** that returns the integer width of a String. As an argument, the stringWidth() method requires the name of a String. For example, if you create a String named myString, you can retrieve the width of myString with the following code:

```
int width = gr.getFontMetrics().stringWidth(myString);
```

 Watch the video *Font Methods*.

TWO TRUTHS & A LIE

Learning More About Fonts

1. Java is widely used partly because its fonts are guaranteed to look the same on all computers.

2. You can discover the resolution and screen size on your system by using the getScreenResolution() and getScreenSize() methods, which are part of the Toolkit class.

3. Ascent is the height of an uppercase character from a baseline to the top of the character, and descent measures the part of characters that "hang below" the baseline, such as the tail on the lowercase letter *y*.

The false statement is #1. If a user's computer does not have a font you have requested, Java chooses a default replacement font, so you can never be completely certain how your output will look.

You Do It

Using FontMetrics Methods to Compare Fonts

Next, you write a program to demonstrate FontMetrics methods. You will create three Font objects and display their metrics.

1. Open a new text file in your text editor, and then enter the first few lines of the JDemoFontMetrics program:

```
import javax.swing.*;
import java.awt.*;
public class JDemoFontMetrics extends JFrame
{
```

2. Type the following code to create a String and a few fonts to use for demonstration purposes:

```
String movieQuote =
    new String("Go ahead, make my day");
Font courierItalic = new Font("Courier New", Font.ITALIC, 16),
    timesPlain = new Font("Times New Roman", Font.PLAIN, 16),
    scriptBold = new Font("Freestyle Script", Font.BOLD, 16);
```

3. Add the following code to define four integer variables to hold the four font measurements, and two integer variables to hold the current horizontal and vertical output positions within the JFrame:

```
int ascent, descent, height, leading;
int x = 20, y = 50;
```

4. Within the JFrame, you will draw Strings positioned 40 pixels apart vertically. After each of those Strings, the Strings that hold the statistics will be 15 pixels apart. Type the following statements to create constants to hold these vertical increase values:

```
final int INCREASE_SMALL = 15;
final int INCREASE_LARGE = 40;
```

5. Add a constructor as follows:

```
public JDemoFontMetrics()
{
    setDefaultCloseOperation(JFrame.EXIT_ON_CLOSE);
}
```

6. Add the following statements to start writing a paint() method. Within the method, you set the Font to courierItalic, draw the phrase String to show a working example of the font, and then call a displayMetrics() method

(continues)

(continued)

that you will write in Step 7. Pass the `Graphics` object to the `displayMetrics()` method, so the method can discover the sizes associated with the current font. Perform the same three steps using the `timesPlain` and `scriptBold` fonts.

```
public void paint(Graphics pen)
{
    super.paint(pen);
    pen.setFont(courierItalic);
    pen.drawString(moviequote, x, y);
    displayMetrics(pen);
    pen.setFont(timesPlain);
    pen.drawString(moviequote, x, y += INCREASE_LARGE);
    displayMetrics(pen);
    pen.setFont(scriptBold);
    pen.drawString(moviequote, x, y += INCREASE_LARGE);
    displayMetrics(pen);
}
```

7. Next, add the header and opening curly brace for the `displayMetrics()` method. The method will receive a `Graphics` object from the `paint()` method. Add the following statements to call the four `getFontMetrics()` methods to obtain values for the leading, ascent, descent, and height variables:

```
public void displayMetrics(Graphics metrics)
{
    leading = metrics.getFontMetrics().getLeading();
    ascent = metrics.getFontMetrics().getAscent();
    descent = metrics.getFontMetrics().getDescent();
    height = metrics.getFontMetrics().getHeight();
```

8. Add the following four `drawString()` statements to display the values. Use the expression `y += INCREASE_SMALL` to change the vertical position of each `String` by the constant.

```
    metrics.drawString("Leading is " + leading,
        x, y += INCREASE_SMALL);
    metrics.drawString("Ascent is " + ascent,
        x, y += INCREASE_SMALL);
    metrics.drawString("Descent is " + descent,
        x, y += INCREASE_SMALL);
    metrics.drawString("Height is " + height,
        x, y += INCREASE_SMALL);
}
```

(continues)

(continued)

9. Add a `main()` method, and include a closing curly brace for the class:

```java
public static void main(String[] args)
{
    JDemoFontMetrics frame = new JDemoFontMetrics();
    frame.setSize(250, 350);
    frame.setVisible(true);
}
}
```

10. Save the file as **JDemoFontMetrics.java**, and then compile it. When you run the program, the output should look like Figure 16-30. Notice that even though each Font object was constructed with a size of 16, the individual statistics vary for each Font object.

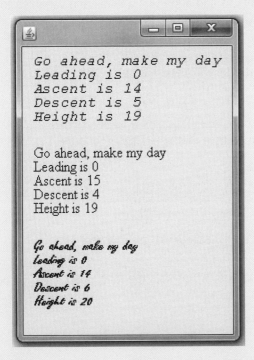

Figure 16-30   Output of the JDemoFontMetrics program

11. Close the frame to end the program.

(continues)

(continued)

Using FontMetrics *Methods to Place a Border Around a* String

Next, you use the FontMetrics methods to draw a rectangle around a String. Instead of guessing at appropriate pixel positions, you can use the height and width of the String to create a box with borders placed symmetrically around the String.

1. Open a new file in your text editor, and enter the first few lines of a JBoxAround JFrame:

```
import javax.swing.*;
import java.awt.*;
public class JBoxAround extends JFrame
{
```

2. Enter the following statements to add a String, a Font, and variables to hold the font metrics and x- and y-coordinates:

```
String movieQuote =
    new String("An offer he can't refuse");
Font serifItalic = new Font("Serif", Font.ITALIC, 20);
int leading, ascent, height, width;
int x = 40, y = 60;
```

3. Create the following named constant that holds a number indicating the dimensions in pixels of the rectangle that you draw around the String:

```
static final int BORDER = 5;
```

4. Add a constructor as follows:

```
public JBoxAround()
{
    setDefaultCloseOperation(JFrame.EXIT_ON_CLOSE);
}
```

5. Add the following paint() method, which sets the font, draws the String, and obtains the font metrics:

```
public void paint(Graphics gr)
{
    super.paint(gr);
    gr.setFont(serifItalic);
    gr.drawString(movieQuote, x, y);
    leading = gr.getFontMetrics().getLeading();
    ascent = gr.getFontMetrics().getAscent();
    height = gr.getFontMetrics().getHeight();
    width = gr.getFontMetrics().stringWidth(movieQuote);
```

(continues)

(continued)

6. Draw a rectangle around the String using the following drawRect() method. In Figure 16-31, the x- and y-coordinates of the upper-left edge are set at x - BORDER, y - (ascent + leading + BORDER). The proper width and height are then determined to draw a uniform rectangle around the string.

   The values of the x- and y-coordinates used in the drawString() method indicate the left side of the baseline of the first character in the String. You want to position the upper-left corner of the rectangle five pixels to the left of the String, so the first argument to drawRect() is five less than x, or x - BORDER. The second argument to drawRect() is the y-coordinate of the String minus the ascent of the String, minus the leading of the String, minus five, or y - (ascent + leading + BORDER). The final two arguments to drawRect() are the width and height of the rectangle. The width is the String's width plus five pixels on the left and five pixels on the right. The height of the rectangle is the String's height, plus five pixels above the String and five pixels below the String.

   ```
   gr.drawRect(x - BORDER, y - (ascent + leading + BORDER),
       width + 2 * BORDER, height + 2 * BORDER);
   }
   ```

7. Add the following main() method and a closing brace for the class:

   ```
   public static void main(String[] args)
   {
       JBoxAround frame = new JBoxAround();
       frame.setSize(330, 100);
       frame.setVisible(true);
   }
   }
   ```

8. Save the file as **JBoxAround.java**. Compile and execute it. Your output should look like Figure 16-31.

Figure 16-31   Output of the JBoxAround program

9. Experiment with changing the contents of the String, the x and y starting coordinates, and the value of the BORDER constant. Confirm that the rectangle is drawn symmetrically around any String object.

Drawing with Java 2D Graphics

Drawing operations earlier in this chapter were called using a `Graphics` object—either an automatically generated one that was passed to the `paint()` method or one the programmer instantiated. In addition, you can call drawing operations using an object of the **Graphics2D class**. The advantage of using Java 2D objects is the higher-quality, two-dimensional (2D) graphics, images, and text they provide.

Features of some of the 2D classes include:

- Fill patterns, such as gradients
- Strokes that define the width and style of a drawing stroke
- Anti-aliasing, a graphics technique for producing smoother screen graphics

`Graphics2D` is found in the `java.awt` package. A `Graphics2D` object is produced by casting, or converting and promoting, a `Graphics` object. For example, in a `paint()` method that automatically receives a `Graphics` object, you can cast the object to a `Graphics2D` object using the following code to start the method:

```
public void paint(Graphics pen)
{
    Graphics2D newpen = (Graphics2D)pen;
```

The process of drawing with Java 2D objects includes:

- Specifying the rendering attributes
- Setting a drawing stroke
- Creating objects to draw

Specifying the Rendering Attributes

The first step in drawing a 2D object is to specify how a drawn object is rendered. Whereas drawings that are not 2D can only use the attribute `Color`, with 2D you can designate other attributes, such as line width and fill patterns. You specify 2D colors by using the `setColor()` method, which works like the `Graphics` method of the same name. Using a `Graphics2D` object, you can set the color to black using the following code:

```
gr2D.setColor(Color.BLACK);
```

Fill patterns control how a drawing object is filled in. In addition to using a solid color, 2D fill patterns can be a gradient fill, a texture, or even a pattern that you devise. A fill pattern is created by using the `setPaint()` method of `Graphics2D` with a fill pattern object as the only argument. Classes from which you can construct a fill pattern include `Color`, `TexturePaint`, and `GradientPaint`.

A **gradient fill** is a gradual shift from one color at one coordinate point to a different color at a second coordinate point. If the color shift occurs once between the points—for example, slowly changing from yellow to red—you are using an **acyclic gradient**, one that does not cycle between the colors. If the shift occurs repeatedly, such as from yellow to red and back to yellow again, you are using a **cyclic gradient**, one that does cycle between the colors.

Figure 16-32 shows an application that demonstrates acyclic and cyclic gradient fills. The first shaded setPaint() method call sets a gradient that begins at coordinates 20, 40 in LIGHT_GRAY and ends at coordinates 180, 100 in DARK_GRAY. The last argument to the GradientPaint() constructor is false, indicating an acyclic gradient. After the Graphics2D object's paint is applied, a filled rectangle is drawn over the same area. These statements produce the rectangle on the left in Figure 16-33, which gradually shifts from light gray to dark gray, moving down and to the right. The second shaded setPaint() statement in Figure 16-32 establishes a new gradient beginning farther to the right. In this statement, the final argument to GradientPaint() is true, creating a cyclic gradient. As you can see on the right side in Figure 16-33, this rectangle's shading changes gradually across its surface.

 Later in this chapter, you will learn about the Rectangle2D.Double class used to create the rectangles in this application.

```java
import javax.swing.*;
import java.awt.*;
import java.awt.geom.*;
import java.awt.Color;
public class JGradient extends JFrame
{
    public void paint(Graphics gr)
    {
        super.paint(gr);
        int x = 20, y = 40, x2 = 180, y2 = 100;
        Graphics2D gr2D = (Graphics2D)gr;
        gr2D.setPaint(new GradientPaint(x, y, Color.LIGHT_GRAY,
            x2, y2, Color.DARK_GRAY, false));
        gr2D.fill(new Rectangle2D.Double(x, y, x2, y2));
        x = 210;
        gr2D.setPaint(new GradientPaint(x, y, Color.LIGHT_GRAY,
            x2, y2, Color.DARK_GRAY, true));
        gr2D.fill(new Rectangle2D.Double(x, y, x2, y2));
    }
    public static void main(String[] args)
    {
        JGradient frame = new JGradient();
        frame.setSize(440, 180);
        frame.setVisible(true);
    }
}
```

Figure 16-32   The JGradient class

Figure 16-33   Output of the JGradient application

Setting a Drawing Stroke

All lines in non-2D graphics operations are drawn as solid, with square ends and a line width of one pixel. With the 2D methods, the drawing line is a **stroke**, which represents a single movement as if you were using a drawing tool, such as a pen or a pencil. In Java 2D, you can change a stroke's width using the **setStroke() method**. Stroke is actually an interface; the class that defines line types and implements the Stroke interface is named **BasicStroke**. A BasicStroke constructor takes three arguments:

- A float value representing the line width

- An int value determining the type of cap decoration at the end of a line

- An int value determining the style of juncture between two line segments

BasicStroke class variables determine the endcap and juncture style arguments. **Endcap styles** apply to the ends of lines that do not join with other lines, and include CAP_BUTT, CAP_ROUND, and CAP_SQUARE. **Juncture styles**, for lines that join, include JOIN_MITER, JOIN_ROUND, and JOIN_BEVEL.

The following statements create a BasicStroke object and make it the current stroke:

```
BasicStroke aLine = new BasicStroke(1.0f,
    BasicStroke.CAP_ROUND, BasicStroke.JOIN_ROUND);
```

Figure 16-34 shows a program that draws a rectangle using a very wide stroke.

```
import javax.swing.*;
import java.awt.*;
import java.awt.geom.*;
public class JStroke extends JFrame
{
    public void paint(Graphics gr)
    {
        super.paint(gr);
        Graphics2D gr2D = (Graphics2D)gr;
        BasicStroke aStroke = new BasicStroke(15.0f,
            BasicStroke.CAP_ROUND, BasicStroke.JOIN_ROUND);
        gr2D.setStroke(aStroke);
        gr2D.draw(new Rectangle2D.Double(40, 40, 100, 100));
    }
    public static void main(String[] args)
    {
        JStroke frame = new JStroke();
        frame.setSize(180, 180);
        frame.setVisible(true);
    }
}
```

Figure 16-34   The JStroke class

The shaded statement in the JStroke class sets the BasicStroke width to 15 pixels using round endcap and juncture parameters. Notice that the line width value is followed by an f, making the value a float instead of a double. Figure 16-35 shows the drawn rectangle.

Figure 16-35   Output of the JStroke program

Creating Objects to Draw

After you have created a Graphics2D object and specified the rendering attributes, you can create different objects to draw. Objects that are drawn in Java 2D are first created by defining them as geometric shapes using the java.awt.geom package classes. You can define the shape of lines, rectangles, ovals, and arcs; after you define the shape, you use it as an argument to the draw() or fill() methods. The Graphics2D class does not have different methods for each shape you can draw.

Lines

Lines are created using the Line2D.Float class or the Line2D.Double class. Each of these classes has a constructor that takes four arguments, which are the x- and y-coordinates of the line endpoints. For example, to create a line from the endpoint 60, 5 to the endpoint 13, 28, you could write the following:

```
Line2D.Float line = new Line2D.Float(60F, 5F, 13F, 28F);
```

It also is possible to create lines based on points. You can use the Point2D.Float or Point2D.Double class to create points that have both x- and y-coordinates. For example, you could create two Point2D.Float points using the following code:

```
Point2D.Float pos1 = new Point2D.Float(60F, 5F);
Point2D.Float pos2 = new Point2D.Float(13F, 28F);
```

Then the code to create a line might be:

```
Line2D.Float line = new Line2D.Float(pos1, pos2);
```

Rectangles

You can create rectangles by using a Rectangle2D.Float or a Rectangle2D.Double class. As with the Line and Point classes, these two classes are distinguished by the type of argument used to call their constructors: float or double. Both Rectangle2D.Float and Rectangle2D.Double can be created using four arguments representing the x-coordinate, y-coordinate, width, and height. For example, the following code creates a Rectangle2D.Float object named rect at 10, 10 with a width of 50 and height of 40:

```
Rectangle2D.Float rect = new Rectangle2D.Float(10F, 10F, 50F, 40F);
```

Ovals

You can create Oval objects with the Ellipse2D.Float or Ellipse2D.Double class. The Ellipse2D.Float constructor requires four arguments representing the x-coordinate, y-coordinate, width, and height. The following code creates an Ellipse2D.Float object named ell at 10, 73 with a width of 40 and height of 20:

```
Ellipse2D.Float ell = new Ellipse2D.Float(10F, 73F, 40F, 20F);
```

Arcs

You can create arcs with the `Arc2D.Float` or `Arc2D.Double` class. The `Arc2D.Float` constructor takes seven arguments. The first four arguments represent the x-coordinate, y-coordinate, width, and height that apply to the ellipse of which the arc is a part. The remaining three arguments are as follows:

- The starting position of the arc
- The number of degrees it travels
- An integer field indicating how it is closed

The starting position is expressed in degrees in the same way as in the `Graphics` class `drawArc()` method; for example, 0 is the three o'clock position. The number of degrees traveled by the arc is specified in a counterclockwise direction using positive numbers. The final argument uses one of the three class fields:

- `Arc2D.PIE` connects the arc to the center of an ellipse and looks like a pie slice.
- `Arc2D.CHORD` connects the arc's endpoints with a straight line.
- `Arc2D.OPEN` is an unclosed arc.

To create an `Arc2D.Float` object named `ac` at 10, 133 with a width of 30 and height of 33, a starting degree of 30, 120 degrees traveled, and using the class variable `Arc2D.PIE`, you use the following statement:

```
Arc2D.Float ac = new Arc2D.Float(10,133,30,33,30,120,Arc2D.PIE);
```

Polygons

You create a `Polygon` object by defining movements from one point to another. The movement that creates a polygon is a `GeneralPath` object; the `GeneralPath` class is found in the `java.awt.geom` package.

- The statement `GeneralPath pol = new GeneralPath();` creates a `GeneralPath` object named `pol`.
- The `moveTo()` method of `GeneralPath` is used to create the beginning point of the polygon. Thus, the statement `pol.moveTo(10F, 193F);` starts the polygon named `pol` at the coordinates 10, 193.
- The `lineTo()` method is used to create a line that ends at a new point. The statement `pol.lineTo(25F, 183F);` creates a second point using the arguments of 25 and 183 as the x- and y-coordinates of the new point.
- The statement `pol.lineTo(100F, 223F);` creates a third point. The `lineTo()` method can be used to connect the current point to the original point. Alternatively, you can use the `closePath()` method without any arguments.

926

TWO TRUTHS & A LIE

Drawing with Java 2D Graphics

1. The advantage of using Java 2D objects is the higher-quality, 2D graphics, images, and text they provide.

2. With Java's 2D graphics, you can designate attributes such as color, line width, and fill patterns.

3. With Java's 2D methods, the drawing line is a brush that represents a single movement as if you were using a drawing tool, such as a pen or a pencil.

The false statement is #3. With Java's 2D methods, the drawing line is a stroke that represents a single movement as if you were using a drawing tool, such as a pen or a pencil.

 You Do It

Using Drawing Strokes

Next, you create a line with a drawing stroke to illustrate how it can have different end types and juncture types where lines intersect.

1. Open a new file in your text editor, and then enter the first few lines of a J2DLine JFrame. (Note that you are importing the `java.awt.geom` package.)

    ```
    import javax.swing.*;
    import java.awt.*;
    import java.awt.geom.*;
    public class J2DLine extends JFrame
    {
    ```

2. Add a constructor:

    ```
    public J2DLine()
    {
        setDefaultCloseOperation(JFrame.EXIT_ON_CLOSE);
    }
    ```

3. Enter the following statements to create a `paint()` method, create a Graphics environment gr, and cast the Graphics environment to a Graphics2D environment gr2D. Create x- and y-points with the Point2D.Float class.

(continues)

(continued)

```java
public void paint(Graphics gr)
{
    super.paint(gr);
    Graphics2D gr2D = (Graphics2D)gr;
    Point2D.Float pos1 = new Point2D.Float(80, 50);
    Point2D.Float pos2 = new Point2D.Float(20, 100);
```

927

4. Create a `BasicStroke` object, and then create a drawing stroke named `aStroke`. Note that the line width is set to 15 pixels, and the endcap style and juncture style are set to `CAP_ROUND` and `JOIN_MITER`, respectively.

```java
BasicStroke aStroke = new BasicStroke(15.0f,
    BasicStroke.CAP_ROUND, BasicStroke.JOIN_MITER);
```

5. Add the following code to create a line between the points `pos1` and `pos2`, and draw the line:

```java
gr2D.setStroke(aStroke);
Line2D.Float line = new Line2D.Float(pos1, pos2);
gr2D.draw(line);
}
```

6. Add a `main()` method and the closing curly brace for the class:

```java
public static void main(String[] args)
{
    J2DLine frame = new J2DLine();
    frame.setSize(100, 120);
    frame.setVisible(true);
}
}
```

7. Save the file as **J2DLine.java**, and then compile and execute it. Your output should look like Figure 16-36.

Figure 16-36   Output of the J2DLine program

(continues)

(continued)

8. Experiment by making the `JFrame` size larger and adding more lines to create an interesting design.

Working with Shapes

Next, you use the Java 2D drawing object types to create a `JFrame` that illustrates sample rectangles, ovals, arcs, and polygons.

1. Open a new file in your text editor, and then enter the first few lines of a JShapes2D `JFrame`:

```
import javax.swing.*;
import java.awt.*;
import java.awt.geom.*;
public class JShapes2D extends JFrame
{
```

2. Add a constructor that sets the default close operation as follows:

```
public JShapes2D()
{
    setDefaultCloseOperation(JFrame.EXIT_ON_CLOSE);
}
```

3. Enter the following statements to create a `paint()` method, create a `Graphics` environment gr, and cast the `Graphics` environment to a `Graphics2D` environment gr2D:

```
public void paint(Graphics gr)
{
    super.paint(gr);
    Graphics2D gr2D = (Graphics2D)gr;
```

4. Create two `Rectangle2D.Float` objects named rect and rect2. Draw the rect object and fill the rect2 object:

```
Rectangle2D.Float rect =
    new Rectangle2D.Float(20F, 40F, 40F, 40F);
Rectangle2D.Float rect2 =
    new Rectangle2D.Float(20F, 90F, 40F, 40F);
gr2D.draw(rect);
gr2D.fill(rect2);
```

(continues)

(continued)

5. Create two `Ellipse2D.Float` objects named `ellipse` and `ellipse2`. Draw the `ellipse` object and fill the `ellipse2` object:

```
Ellipse2D.Float ellipse = new
    Ellipse2D.Float(20F, 140F, 40F, 40F);
Ellipse2D.Float ellipse2 = new
    Ellipse2D.Float(20F, 190F, 40F, 40F);
gr2D.draw(ellipse);
gr2D.fill(ellipse2);
```

6. Create two `Arc2D.Float` objects named `ac` and `ac2`. Draw the `ac` object and fill the `ac2` object:

```
Arc2D.Float ac = new
    Arc2D.Float(20, 240, 50, 50, 30, 120, Arc2D.PIE);
Arc2D.Float ac2 = new
    Arc2D.Float(20, 290, 50, 50, 30, 120, Arc2D.PIE);
gr2D.draw(ac);
gr2D.fill(ac2);
```

7. Create a new `GeneralPath` object named `pol`. Set the starting point of the polygon and create two additional points. Use the `closePath()` method to close the polygon by connecting the current point to the starting point. Draw the `pol` object, and then end the method with a curly brace:

```
GeneralPath pol = new GeneralPath();
pol.moveTo(20F,320F);
pol.lineTo(40F,380F);
pol.lineTo(100F,400F);
pol.closePath();
gr2D.draw(pol);
}
```

8. Add a `main()` method and the final curly brace for the class:

```
public static void main(String[] args)
{
    JShapes2D frame = new JShapes2D();
    frame.setSize(100, 420);
    frame.setVisible(true);
}
}
```

9. Save the file as **JShapes2D.java**, and compile and execute the program. Your output should look like Figure 16-37. When you are ready, close the window, and then experiment with making changes to the program to produce different shapes.

(continues)

(continued)

Figure 16-37   Output of the JShapes2D program

Don't Do It

- Don't forget to call super.paint() as the first statement in the paint() method when you write a class that extends JFrame. Failing to do so can cause odd results, especially when you combine GUI widgets with graphics.

- Don't forget that the setLocation() method works correctly only when it is used after the layout manager has finished positioning all the application's components (or in cases where no layout manager is functioning).

- Don't forget that the lower-left corner of a String is placed at the coordinates used when you call drawString().

- Don't forget to use paintComponent() rather than paint() when creating graphics on a JPanel.

Key Terms

To **rerender** a drawing is to repaint or redisplay it.

Painting is the act of redisplaying a surface.

System-triggered painting operations occur when the system requests a component to render its contents.

Application-triggered painting operations occur when the internal state of a component has changed.

The **paint() method** runs when Java displays a screen; you can write your own paint() method to override the automatically supplied one whenever you want to paint graphics such as shapes on the screen.

The **Graphics class** is an abstract class that descends directly from Object and holds data about graphics operations and methods for drawing shapes, text, and images.

The **repaint() method** updates a window when it contains new images.

The **setLocation() method** allows you to place a component at a specific location within a JFrame's content pane.

The **drawString() method** allows you to draw a String in a JFrame or other component.

The **drawLine() method** draws a straight line between any two points on the screen.

The **drawRect() method** draws the outline of a rectangle.

The **fillRect() method** draws a solid, or filled, rectangle.

The **clearRect() method** draws a rectangle using the background color to create what appears to be an empty or "clear" rectangle.

The **drawRoundRect() method** draws rectangles with rounded corners.

An **arc** is a portion of a circle.

The **draw3DRect() method** draws a rectangle that appears to have "shadowing" on two of its edges—the effect is that of a rectangle that is lit from the upper-left corner and slightly raised or slightly lowered.

The **fill3DRect() method** creates filled, 3D rectangles.

The **drawOval() method** draws an oval.

The **fillOval() method** draws a solid, filled oval.

The **drawArc() method** draws an arc.

The **fillArc() method** creates a solid arc.

The **drawPolygon() method** draws complex shapes.

The **fillPolygon() method** draws a solid complex shape.

The **addPoint() method** adds points to a Polygon object.

The **copyArea() method** copies any rectangular area to a new location.

The **getAvailableFontFamilyNames() method** returns the fonts that are available on your system.

The **getDefaultToolkit() method** provides information about the system in use.

The **getScreenResolution() method** returns the screen resolution on the current system.

The **getScreenSize() method** returns the screen size as a Dimension object.

Ascent is one of three measures of a Font's height; it is the height of an uppercase character from a baseline to the top of the character.

Descent is one of three measures of a Font's height; it measures the part of characters that "hang below" the baseline, such as the tails on the lowercase letters *g* and *j*.

Leading is one of three measures of a Font's height; it is the amount of space between the bottom of the descent of one line and the top of the characters in the successive line of type.

The **height of a font** is the sum of its leading, ascent, and descent.

The **getFontMetrics() method** in the Graphics class returns a FontMetrics object; with it you can discover many characteristics of a Font object.

The **stringWidth() method** in the FontMetrics class contains the integer width of a String.

The **Graphics2D class** provides tools for 2D drawing.

Fill patterns control how a drawing object is filled in.

A **gradient fill** is a gradual shift from one color at one coordinate point to a different color at a second coordinate point.

An **acyclic gradient** is a fill pattern in which a color shift occurs once between two points.

A **cyclic gradient** is a fill pattern in which a shift between colors occurs repeatedly between two points.

A **stroke** is a line-drawing feature in Java 2D that represents a single movement as if you were using a drawing tool, such as a pen or a pencil.

The **setStroke() method** changes a stroke's width in Java 2D.

BasicStroke is the class that defines line types and implements the Stroke interface.

Endcap styles apply to the ends of lines that do not join with other lines, and include CAP_BUTT, CAP_ROUND, and CAP_SQUARE.

Juncture styles, for lines that join, include JOIN_MITER, JOIN_ROUND, and JOIN_BEVEL.

933

Chapter Summary

- Painting operations can be system triggered or application triggered. Painting operations are performed by a Component's paint() method, which takes a Graphics argument that renders output. You override the paint() method in your programs when you want specific actions to take place when components must be rendered. The setLocation() method allows you to place a component at a specific location within a JFrame's content pane.

- The drawString() method allows you to draw a String. The method requires three arguments: a String, an x-axis coordinate, and a y-axis coordinate. The drawString() method is a member of the Graphics class, so you need to use a Graphics object to call it. You can improve the appearance of strings drawn using Graphics objects by using the setFont() and setColor() methods.

- Java provides you with several methods for drawing a variety of lines and geometric shapes, such as drawLine(), drawRect(), drawOval(), drawPolygon(), and others. You can also use the copyArea() method to copy any rectangular area to a new location.

- If a user's computer does not have a requested font, Java chooses a default replacement font. You can discover the fonts that are available on your system by using the getAvailableFontFamilyNames() method, which is part of the GraphicsEnvironment class. This class describes the collection of Font objects and GraphicsDevice objects available to a Java application on a particular platform. You can discover the resolution and screen size on your system by using the getScreenResolution() and getScreenSize() methods, which are part of the Toolkit class. The height of every font is the sum of three parts: ascent, descent, and leading.

- The advantage to using Graphics2D objects is the higher-quality 2D graphics, images, and text they provide. With 2D you can designate attributes such as line width and fill patterns.

Review Questions

1. Repainting of a visible surface is triggered by _____.

   a. the operating system
   b. the application
   c. either of these
   d. none of these

2. The method that calls the `paint()` method for you is _____.

   a. `callPaint()`   c. `requestPaint()`

   b. `repaint()`   d. `draw()`

3. The `paint()` method header requires a(n) _____ argument.

   a. `void`   c. `String`

   b. `integer`   d. `Graphics`

4. The `setLocation()` method _____.

   a. is used to position a `JFrame` on the screen

   b. is used to set regional and national preferences for an application

   c. takes two integer arguments that represent position coordinates

   d. must be used with every component placed on a `JFrame`

5. The statement `g.drawString(someString, 50, 100);` places `someString`'s _____ corner at position 50, 100.

   a. upper-left   c. upper-right

   b. lower-left   d. lower-right

6. If you use the `setColor()` method to change a `Graphics` object's color to yellow, _____.

   a. only the next output from the object appears in yellow

   b. all output from the object for the remainder of the method always appears in yellow

   c. all output from the object for the remainder of the application always appears in yellow

   d. all output from the object appears in yellow until you change the color

7. The correct statement to instantiate a `Graphics` object named `picasso` is _____.

   a. `Graphics picasso;`

   b. `Graphics picasso = new Graphics();`

   c. `Graphics picasso = getGraphics();`

   d. `Graphics picasso = getGraphics(new);`

8. The statement `g.drawRoundRect(100, 100, 100, 100, 0, 0);` draws a shape that looks most like a _____.

   a. square   c. circle

   b. round-edged rectangle   d. straight line

9. If you draw an oval with the same value for width and height, you draw a(n) —————— .

    a. circle   c. rounded square

    b. square   d. ellipsis

10. The zero-degree position for any arc is at the —————— o'clock position.

    a. three   c. nine

    b. six   d. twelve

11. The method you use to create a solid arc is —————— .

    a. `solidArc()`   c. `arcSolid()`

    b. `fillArc()`   d. `arcFill()`

12. You use the —————— method to copy any rectangular area to a new location.

    a. `copyRect()`   c. `repeatRect()`

    b. `copyArea()`   d. `repeatArea()`

13. The measurement of an uppercase character from the baseline to the top of the character is its —————— .

    a. ascent   c. leading

    b. descent   d. height

14. To be certain that a vertical series of `Strings` has enough room to appear in a frame, you use which of the following statements?

    a.
```
g.drawString("Some string",
     x, y += g.getFontMetrics().getHeight());
```

    b.
```
g.drawString("Some string",
     x, y += g.getFontMetrics().getLeading());
```

    c.
```
g.drawString("Some string", x,
     y += g.getFontMetrics().getAscent());
```

    d.
```
g.drawString("Some string",
     x, y += g.getFontMetrics().getDescent());
```

15. You can discover the fonts that are available on your system by using the —————— .

    a. `getAvailableFontFamilyNames()` method of the `GraphicsEnvironment` class

    b. `getFonts()` method of the `Graphics` class

    c. `getMyFonts()` method of the `GraphicsFonts` class

    d. `getAllFonts()` method of the `Fonts` class

16. The getScreenResolution() method and getScreenSize() method _____.

   a. both return the number of pixels as an int type

   b. respectively return the number of pixels as an int type and an object of type Dimension

   c. both return an object of type Dimension

   d. respectively return the number of pixels as a double type and an object of type Dimension

17. A Graphics2D object is produced by _____.

   a. the setGraphics2D() method

   b. the Graphics2D newpen = Graphics2D() statement

   c. the Graphics2D = Graphics(g) statement

   d. casting a Graphics object

18. The process of drawing with Java 2D objects includes _____.

   a. specifying the rendering attributes

   b. setting a drawing stroke

   c. both of the above

   d. none of the above

19. A gradient fill is a gradual change in _____.

   a. color   c. drawing style
   b. font size   d. line thickness

20. With the 2D methods, the drawing line is a _____.

   a. brush   c. belt
   b. stroke   d. draw

Exercises

 Programming Exercises

1. Write an application that extends JFrame and that displays a phrase in every font size from 6 through 20. Save the file as **JFontSizes.java**.

2. a. Write an application that extends JFrame and that displays a phrase in one color the first time the user clicks a JButton. The next time the user clicks the JButton, make the first phrase seem to disappear. (*Hint*: Redraw it using the background color.) At the same time, draw the phrase again in a different color,

size, and horizontal position. The third click should change the color, size, and position of the phrase again. Save the file as **JChangeSizeAndColor.java**.

b. Modify the JChangeSizeAndColor application so that it continuously changes the size, color, and location of a phrase as long as the user continues to click the button. Save the application as **JChangeSizeAndColor2.java**.

3. Write an application that extends JFrame and that displays a phrase upside down when the user clicks a button. The phrase is displayed normally when the user clicks the button again. Save the application as **JUpsideDown.java**.

4. Write an application that extends JFrame and that displays eight nested rectangles, like those in Figure 16-38. You may use only one drawRect() statement in the program. (*Hint*: Use it in a loop.) Save the file as **JNestedBoxes.java**.

Figure 16-38   Output of the JNestedBoxes program

5. Write an application that extends JFrame and that displays 15 nested circles, like those in Figure 16-39. You may use only one drawOval() statement in the program. Save the file as **JNestedCircles.java**.

Figure 16-39   Output of the `JNestedCircles` program

6.   Write an application that extends `JFrame` and that displays diagonal lines in a square, like those in Figure 16-40. Save the file as **JDiagonalLines.java**.

Figure 16-40   Output of the `JDiagonalLines` program

7. a. Write an application that extends JFrame and that displays a yellow smiling face on the screen. Save the file as **JSmileFace.java**.

   b. Add a JButton to the JSmileFace program so the smile changes to a frown when the user clicks the JButton. Save the file as **JSmileFace2.java**.

8. a. Use polygons and lines to create a graphics image that looks like a fireworks display. Write an application that extends JFrame and that displays the fireworks. Save the file as **JFireworks.java**.

   b. Add a JButton to the JFireworks program. Do not show the fireworks until the user clicks the JButton. Save the file as **JFireworks2.java**.

9. a. Write an application that extends JFrame and that displays your name. Place boxes around your name at intervals of 10, 20, 30, and 40 pixels. Save the file as **JBorders.java**.

   b. Modify the JBorders program so that each of the four borders is a different color. Save the file as **JBorders2.java**.

10. Search the Web for the approximate value of the U.S. dollar in other currencies. Write an application that extends JFrame and that prompts the user to enter a value in U.S. dollars. Use Graphics2D methods to display the dollar amount as well as the equivalent values of two other currencies of your choice. Save the file as **JCurrencies.java**.

11. Write an application that extends JFrame and that uses the Graphics2D environment to create a GeneralPath object. Use the GeneralPath object to create the outline of your favorite state. Display the state name at the approximate center of the state boundaries. Save the file as **JFavoriteState.java**.

12. Write an application that extends JFrame and that draws a realistic-looking stop sign. Save the file as **JStopSign.java**.

13. Write an application that displays a JFrame that does the following:

    - Turns yellow when the user's mouse enters the frame
    - Turns black when the user's mouse exits the frame
    - Displays a larger circle at a point near where the user left-clicks
    - Displays a smaller circle at a point near where the user right-clicks

    At most, one circle should appear on the surface of the frame at a time. Save the file as **JMouseFrame.java**.

Debugging Exercises

1. Each of the following files in the Chapter16 folder of your downloadable student files has syntax and/or logic errors. In each case, determine the problem and fix the program. After you correct the errors, save each file using the same filename preceded with *Fix*. For example, DebugSixteen1.java will become FixDebugSixteen1.java.

   a. DebugSixteen1.java   c. DebugSixteen3.java
   b. DebugSixteen2.java   d. DebugSixteen4.java

Game Zone

1. a. In Chapter 9, you created a Tic Tac Toe game in which you used a 2D array of characters to hold *X*s and *O*s for a player and the computer. Now create a JFrame that uses an array of nine JButtons to represent the Tic Tac Toe grid. When the user clicks a JButton that has not already been taken, place an *X* on the button and then allow the computer to place an *O* on a different button. Announce the winner when either the computer or the player achieves three marks in sequence, or announce that the game was a tie. Figure 16-41 shows a typical game in progress and after the player has won. Save the game as **JTicTacToe.java**.

Figure 16-41   Typical execution of the JTicTacToe program

    b. Add a graphic that displays a large letter representing the winning player of the game in Game Zone exercise 1a. Draw a large *X*, *O*, or, in case of a tie, an overlapping *X* and *O* in different colors. Save the game as **JTicTacToe2.java**.

2.   Create an application that plays a card game named Lucky Seven. In real life, the game can be played with seven cards, each containing a number from 1 through 7, that are shuffled and dealt number-side down. To start the game, a player turns over any card. The exposed number on the card determines the position (reading from left to right) of the next card that must be turned over. For example, if the player turns over the first card and its number is 7, the next card turned must be the seventh card (counting from left to right). If the player turns over a card whose number denotes a position that was already turned, the player loses the game. If the player succeeds in turning over all seven cards, the player wins.

    Instead of cards, you will use seven buttons labeled 1 through 7 from left to right. Randomly associate one of the seven values 1 through 7 with each button. (In other words, the associated value might or might not be equivalent to the button's labeled value.) When the player clicks a button, reveal the associated hidden value. If the value represents the position of a button already clicked, the player loses. If the revealed number represents an available button, force the user to click it; that is, do not take any action until the user clicks the correct button. After a player clicks a button, remove the button from play. (After you remove a button, you can call `repaint()` to ensure that the image of the button is removed.)

    For example, a player might click Button 7, revealing a 4. Then the player clicks Button 4, revealing a 2. Then the player clicks Button 2, revealing a 7. The player loses because Button 7 was already used. Save the game as **JLuckySeven.java**.

3.   a. In Chapters 7 and 8, you created a game named Secret Phrase in which the user guesses a randomly selected secret phrase by entering one letter at a time. Now create a GUI application that plays the game, allowing users to choose a letter by selecting one of 26 buttons. (*Hint*: Consider creating an array of buttons rather than 26 individually named buttons.)

        Disable a letter button once it has been guessed, and after the puzzle is complete, disable all the letters. Figure 16-42 shows a typical execution (1) after the user has guessed an *A*, which is in the phrase; (2) after the user has guessed a *D*, which is not in the phrase; and (3) after the user has completed the puzzle. Save the file as **JSecretPhrase.java**.

Figure 16-42 Typical execution of the `JSecretPhrase` program

b. Make the `JSecretPhrase` game more like the traditional letter-guessing game Hangman by drawing a "hanged" person piece by piece with each missed letter. For example, when the user chooses a correct letter, place it in the appropriate position or positions in the phrase, but the first time the user chooses a letter that is not in the target phrase, draw a head for the "hanged" man. The second time the user makes an incorrect guess, add a torso. Continue with arms and legs. If the complete body is drawn before the user has guessed all the letters in the phrase, display a message indicating that the player has lost the game. If the user completes the phrase before all the body parts are drawn, display a message that the player has won. Save the game as **JSecretPhrase2.java**.

Case Problems

1. In Chapters 14 and 15, you developed an interactive GUI application for Carly's Catering. Now, design a `JPanel` that uses graphics to display a logo for the company, and modify the GUI application to include it. Save the `JPanel` class as **JCarlysLogoPanel.java**, and save the GUI application as **JCarlysCatering.java**.

2. In Chapters 14 and 15, you developed an interactive GUI application for Sammy's Seashore Rentals. Now, design a `JPanel` that uses graphics to display a logo for the company, and modify the GUI application to include it. Save the `JPanel` class as **JSammysLogoPanel.java**, and save the GUI application as **JSammysSeashore.java**.

Applets, Images, and Sound

In this chapter, you will:

◎ Learn about applets

◎ Write an HTML document to host an applet

◎ Use the `init()` method

◎ Work with `JApplet` components

◎ Understand the `JApplet` life cycle

◎ Understand multimedia and use images

◎ Add sound to `JApplet`s

Introducing Applets

An **applet** is a program that is called within another application—often a Web browser. It can contain any number of components, such as buttons, text fields, and pictures, and it can respond to user-initiated events, such as mouse clicks or keyboard presses. Many of an applet's behaviors come from methods that reside in a Java class named JApplet—the programmer can create additional behaviors. The name *applet* means "little application." An applet is "little" in that it is not a full-blown program; it relies on other programs to execute it.

A Java applet is like a Java application in several ways:

- You save both applets and applications with a .java file extension.

- You compile both applets and applications into bytecode using the javac command, and the bytecode is stored in a file with a .class file extension.

- Both applets and applications can contain any number of methods you define and any number of variables and constants. Both can contain decisions, loops, arrays, and all the other language elements you have learned about in Java.

- Both can (and applets almost always do) contain GUI elements such as buttons and labels, and event listeners that respond to user-initiated actions.

An applet also is different from an application in several ways:

- Unlike applications, applets descend from the JApplet class.

- Unlike applications, applets run from another application. You do not use the java command to execute an applet.

- Unlike applications, applets do not contain a main() method. In this chapter, you will learn about the methods every applet contains.

- Unlike an application that uses a JFrame, you do not set a default close operation for a JApplet.

- Applets cannot delete, read, or create files on the user's system.

- Applets cannot run any other program on the user's system.

Understanding the JApplet Class

JApplet is a Swing class from which you can inherit. A JApplet is a Component, and it is also a Container. Figure 17-1 shows the relationship of JApplet to its ancestors. When you create a JApplet, you gain access to over 200 methods through inheritance.

```
java.lang.Object
    |
  +--java.awt.Component
          |
        +--java.awt.Container
              |
            +--java.awt.Panel
                  |
                +--java.applet.Applet
                      |
                    +--javax.swing.JApplet
```

Figure 17-1 Inheritance hierarchy of the JApplet class

You can import the JApplet class to a program by using one of the following statements:

```
import javax.swing.JApplet;
import javax.swing.*;
```

Running an Applet

To view an applet, it must be called from another document; frequently the document is written in HTML. **HTML**, or **Hypertext Markup Language**, is a simple language used to create Web pages for the Internet. HTML contains many commands that allow you to format text on a Web page, import graphic images, and link your page to other Web pages. You run applets within a page on the Internet, an intranet, or a local computer.

The current version of HTML is **Extensible Hypertext Markup Language (XHTML)**. The differences are minor, although XHTML is stricter. Most Web developers are continuing to use HTML until XHTML matures and some compatibility issues are resolved. You can find more information and tutorials on both HTML and XHTML at *www.w3schools.com*.

You can run an applet in one of two ways:

- You can run an applet in a Web browser, such as Internet Explorer, Firefox, Opera, or Safari. To do so, you open the applet-hosting HTML document in the browser. For example, in Internet Explorer, you click File on the menu bar, click Open, and type the complete path for the HTML document that you created. After you press Enter, the applet appears on your screen. The applet can be run within a page on the Internet or an intranet, but you do not have to connect to the Internet to run an applet in your browser—you can simply use the browser locally.

- You can also view your applet on a local computer by using the **Applet Viewer**, which is a program that comes with the Java Development Kit (JDK) that provides a convenient environment in which to test your applets. To use the Applet Viewer, type the **appletviewer command** at the command line, followed by the full HTML filename, including the extension. When you press Enter, the Applet Viewer window opens and displays the applet.

When you save an HTML file, you can use .html or .htm as a file extension. In some older versions of DOS and Windows, filename extensions were not allowed to be more than three characters. Current Web browsers and servers accept files with .htm and .html extensions. Examples in this book use the four-character .html extension.

TWO TRUTHS & A LIE

Introducing Applets

1. An applet can contain any number of components, such as buttons, text fields, and pictures, and can respond to user-initiated events, such as mouse clicks or keyboard presses.

2. Applets and applications are similar in that both have .java file extensions and you compile both with the `javac` command.

3. Applets and applications are different in that applets do not use loops and arrays.

The false statement is #3. Applets use all the language constructs in Java.

Writing an HTML Document to Host an Applet

When you create an applet, you do the following:

- Write the applet in Java and save it with a .java file extension, just as when you write a Java application.

- Compile the applet into bytecode using the `javac` command, just as when you write a Java application.

- Write an HTML document that includes a statement to call your compiled Java class.

- Load the HTML document into a Web browser (such as Internet Explorer) or run the Applet Viewer program, which in turn uses the HTML document.

Java in general and applets in particular are popular topics among programmers, partly because users can execute applets using a Web browser on the Internet. A **Web browser** is a program that allows you to display HTML documents on your computer screen. Web documents often contain Java applets.

Because applets are sent over the Internet and run from other applications, applet code is not trusted. A malicious programmer might try to include code that contains a virus, reads data from your files, or performs other unwanted tasks. Therefore, applet code runs in a constrained area called a sandbox. A **sandbox** is a safe area in which a program can run, much like a real sandbox is an area in a yard where children can play safely.

Fortunately, to run a Java applet, you don't need to learn much HTML; you need to learn only two pairs of HTML commands, called **tags**. The tag that begins every HTML document is **<html>**. Like all tags, this opening tag is surrounded by angle brackets. The html within the tag is an HTML keyword that specifies that an HTML document follows the keyword. The tag that ends every HTML document is **</html>**. The preceding slash indicates that the tag is a closing tag. The following is the simplest HTML document you can write:

```
<html>
</html>
```

Unlike Java, HTML is not case sensitive, so you can use <HTML> in place of <html>. However, this book uses the all-lowercase convention when displaying HTML code. With the growing importance of XML and XHTML, many programmers recommend putting all HTML tags in lowercase because XML and XHTML are case sensitive, even though HTML is not.

The simple HTML document, containing just the pair of html tags, begins and ends and does nothing in between; you can create an analogous situation in a Java method by typing an opening curly brace and following it immediately with the closing curly brace. HTML documents generally contain more statements. For example, to run an applet from an HTML document, you add an **<object>** and **</object>** tag pair. Usually, you place three attributes within the <object> tag: code, width, and height. **Tag attributes**, sometimes referred to as arguments, promote activity or describe the features of the tag; with arguments, the HTML tag can do something in a certain way. Note the following example:

```
<object code = "AClass.class" width = 300 height = 200> </object>
```

The three **object** tag attributes in the previous example are described with their corresponding arguments in the following list:

- **code** = is followed by the name of the compiled applet you are calling.

- **width** = is followed by the width of the applet on the screen.

- **height** = is followed by the height of the applet on the screen.

The name of the applet you call must be a compiled Java applet (with a .class file extension). The width and height of an applet are measured in pixels. For monitors that display 1024 pixels horizontally and 768 pixels vertically, a statement such as **width = 512 height = 384** creates an applet that occupies approximately one-fourth of most screens (half the height and half the width).

When you assign a height and width to an applet, keep in mind that a browser's menu bar and screen elements (such as the toolbar and the scroll bars) take up some of the screen viewing area for an applet.

Instead of the <object> and </object> tag pair, you can use <applet> and </applet> in your HTML applet host documents. However, the World Wide Web Consortium recommends using object rather than applet because it is more general, and it includes new and future media types in addition to applets. For more information, including definitions of and recommendations for using all the other HTML tags, visit www.w3.org.

Figure 17-2 shows an HTML file that could be used to run a JApplet named JHello. The applet will be 450 pixels wide by 150 pixels tall.

```
<html>
<object code = "JHello.class" width = 450 height = 150>
</object>
</html>
```

Figure 17-2   The TestJHello.html file

In Figure 17-2, the JHello.class file resides in the same folder as the HTML file, so no path is necessary in the object code statement. Later in this chapter, you will learn how to create the JHello class.

TWO TRUTHS & A LIE

Writing an HTML Document to Host an Applet

1. You must run applets within a Web page.

2. To view an applet, it must be called from another document, such as one written in HTML.

3. All HTML tags are surrounded by angle brackets.

The false statement is #1. You run applets within a page on the Internet or an intranet; you also can run an applet on a local computer from another program called Applet Viewer.

Using the init() Method

The JApplet class uses several methods that are invoked by a Web browser when the browser runs an applet. In a Java application, the main() method calls other methods that you write, but in contrast, an applet does not contain a main() method. With an applet, the browser or

Applet Viewer calls several methods automatically at different times. The following five methods are inherited from JApplet, are called automatically, and constitute the life cycle of an applet:

- public void init()

- public void start()

- public void paint()

- public void stop()

- public void destroy()

You can override any of these methods within a JApplet that you write. If you fail to implement one or more of these methods, your JApplet will use the versions that belong to the parent JApplet class. To create a Java applet that does anything useful, you must code statements within at least one of these methods.

For example, you can create a JApplet using only the init() method. The **init() method** is the first method called in any applet. You use it to perform initialization tasks, such as setting variables to initial values or placing applet components on the screen. In general, tasks that you would place in the constructor for a JFrame in an application are the same types of tasks you place in an init() method in a JApplet.

You must code the init() method's header as follows:

public void init()

Figure 17-3 shows the JApplet that displays "Hello. Who are you?" in a JLabel on the screen. The default layout manager for a JApplet is BorderLayout, so when the JLabel is added to the applet without a specified region, the JLabel occupies the entire JApplet surface.

```
import javax.swing.*;
import java.awt.*;
public class JHello extends JApplet
{
    JLabel greeting = new JLabel("Hello. Who are you?");
    public void init()
    {
        add(greeting);
    }
}
```

Figure 17-3   The JHello JApplet

After you write this JApplet, you do the following:

- Save this file as JHello.java, and compile it.

- Run the Applet Viewer using the command appletviewer TestJHello.html and the saved file shown in Figure 17-2.

Figure 17-4 Output of the `JHello JApplet` when run in the Applet Viewer

Figure 17-4 shows how the applet appears on your screen. After you view a `JApplet`, you can click the close button on the Applet Viewer to end the application. Unlike a `JFrame`, you do not need to set a default close operation with a `JApplet`.

 Watch the video *Writing and Running an Applet.*

TWO TRUTHS & A LIE

Using the `init()` Method

1. In a Java applet, the `main()` method is the first to execute; it calls other methods that you write.

2. The following five methods can automatically be called by every applet: `init()`, `start()`, `paint()`, `stop()`, and `destroy()`.

3. You can create a `JApplet` using only the `init()` method, which is the first method called in any applet.

The false statement is #1. In a Java application, the `main()` method calls other methods that you write, but in contrast, an applet does not contain a `main()` method.

You Do It

Creating an HTML Document to Host an Applet

In this section, you create a simple HTML document that you will use to display the applet you will create in the next section. You will name the applet JGreet, and it will occupy a screen area of 450 by 100 pixels.

1. Open a new file in your text editor. Type the opening HTML tag:

   `<html>`

2. On the next line, type the opening `object` tag that contains the applet's name and dimensions:

   `<object code = "JGreet.class" width = 450 height = 200>`

3. On the next line, type the applet's closing tag:

   `</object>`

4. On the next line, type the closing HTML tag:

   `</html>`

5. Save the file as **TestJGreet.html**. Just as when you create a Java application, be certain that you save the file as text only and use an .html extension. The .html file extension is required and makes the file easy to identify as an HTML file.

Creating and Running a `JApplet`

Next, you create the JGreet applet for which you prepared the HTML document.

1. Open a new text file in your text editor. Enter the following `import` statements you need for the `JApplet`. You need the `javax.swing` package because it defines `JApplet`, and you need the `java.awt` package because it defines `Container`.

   ```
   import javax.swing.*;
   import java.awt.*;
   ```

2. Next, enter the JGreet JApplet. It contains a Container that holds a JLabel. The init() method adds the JLabel to the Container.

(continues)

954

(continued)

```java
public class JGreet extends JApplet
{
   Container con = getContentPane();
   JLabel greeting = new JLabel("Greetings!");
   public void init()
   {
      con.add(greeting);
   }
}
```

3. Save the file as **JGreet.java**. Then compile the class. If necessary, correct any errors and compile again.

4. At the command line, type **appletviewer TestJGreet.html**, and then press **Enter**. The applet appears on your screen, as shown in Figure 17-5.

Figure 17-5   Execution of the `JGreet JApplet`

5. Use the mouse pointer to drag any corner of the Applet Viewer window to resize it. Notice that if you increase or decrease the window's height, the window is redrawn on the screen and the `JLabel` is automatically repositioned to remain centered within the window. If you make the window narrower by dragging its right border to the left, the `JLabel` eventually becomes partially obscured when the window becomes too narrow for the display.

 If your operating system does not allow you to make the window narrow enough to obscure part of the greeting, make the string in the label longer—for example, "Greetings to you and all your family!" Recompile the applet and then use the `appletviewer` command to display the HTML document again. The string displayed will be long enough for you to observe the effects when you narrow the width of the window.

6. Close the Applet Viewer by clicking the **Close button** in the upper-right corner of the window.

(continues)

(continued)

Running a JApplet in Your Web Browser

1. Open any Web browser, such as Internet Explorer. You do not have to connect to the Internet; you will use the browser locally. (If you do not have a Web browser installed on your computer, skip to the end of Step 3.)

2. Click **File** on the menu bar, click **Open**, type the complete path for the HTML document that you created to access JGreet.class (for example, **C:\Java\Chapter17\TestJGreet.html**), and then press **Enter**. Instead of typing the filename, you can click the **Browse** button, browse to the file location, and then click **OK**. You might have to agree to several security messages before you can view the applet. The applet should appear in the browser on your screen. If you receive an error message, verify that the path and spelling of the HTML file are correct.

3. Close the browser.

 Some applets might not work correctly with your browser. Java was designed with a number of security features so that when an applet is displayed on the Internet, the applet cannot perform malicious tasks, such as deleting a file from your hard drive. If an applet does nothing to compromise security, testing it using the Web browser or the `appletviewer` command achieves the same results. For now, you can get your applets to perform better by using the Applet Viewer window because the output does not depend on the browser type or version.

Working with JApplet Components

The output in Figures 17-4 and 17-5 is not very attractive or interesting. Fortunately, all the techniques that you used with JFrames in Chapters 14, 15, and 16 can also be used with JApplets. For example, you can do the following:

- Change the font and color of labels
- Use layout managers
- Add multiple GUI components
- Change the background color
- Add listeners for user events
- Add images and sounds

For example, Figure 17-6 shows how you can write a JApplet that displays a prompt, allows the user to enter text and press a button, and displays output. The JApplet also uses color and interesting fonts. The `init()` method sets up the applet surface and enables both the button and text box to generate events to which the JApplet can respond. The setLayout() method is used to set the content pane's layout manager to FlowLayout; without the setLayout() statement, the content pane would use the default BorderLayout.

```java
import javax.swing.*;
import java.awt.*;
import java.awt.event.*;
import java.awt.Color;
public class JHello2 extends JApplet implements ActionListener
{
    JLabel greeting = new JLabel("Hello. Who are you?");
    Font font1 = new Font("Teen", Font.BOLD, 36);
    Font font2 = new Font("Teen", Font.ITALIC, 48);
    JTextField answer = new JTextField(10);
    JButton pressMe = new JButton("Press me");
    JLabel personalGreeting = new JLabel(" ");
    Container con = getContentPane();
    public void init()
    {
        greeting.setFont(font1);
        personalGreeting.setFont(font2);
        con.add(greeting);
        con.add(answer);
        con.add(pressMe);
        con.setLayout(new FlowLayout());
        con.setBackground(Color.YELLOW);
        pressMe.addActionListener(this);
        answer.addActionListener(this);
    }
    public void actionPerformed(ActionEvent e)
    {
        String name = answer.getText();
        con.remove(greeting);
        con.remove(pressMe);
        con.remove(answer);
        personalGreeting.setText("Hello, " + name + "!  ");
        con.add(personalGreeting);
        con.setBackground(Color.PINK);
        validate();
    }
}
```

Figure 17-6   The JHello2 class that adds a JLabel when the user clicks the JButton

The code in the actionPerformed() method in the JHello2 class shows that after the user clicks the button, the name is retrieved from the text field; the label, button, and text field are removed from the applet surface; and the setText() method sets the JLabel text for personalGreeting to "Hello, " + name + "! ". Then the personal greeting is added to the

JApplet's Container, and the background color is changed. You learned about all of the same methods when you studied JFrames in Chapters 14 and 15. Figure 17-7 shows a typical execution.

Figure 17-7 Typical execution of the JHello2 JApplet

In the actionPerformed() method in Figure 17-6, the final statement following the addition of the JLabel is validate(). As you learned in Chapter 15, invoking the validate() method after adding one or more JComponents to an applet ensures that the Components draw themselves on the screen. It isn't necessary to call the validate() method every time you add a JComponent to a JApplet. For example, when you add components in the init() or start() methods, you do not have to call validate(). When you add components in other methods (frequently event-handling methods), you must call validate().

The validate() method is complex. Even the online Java documentation refers to its performance as "voodoo."

Watch the video *Working with JApplet Components*.

958

TWO TRUTHS & A LIE

Working with `JApplet` Components

1. In an applet, you can change fonts and colors of GUI components just as you can in an application.

2. `JApplets` can contain an `actionPerformed()` method to respond to mouse clicks.

3. Invoking the `validate()` method in an applet allows it to pass security restrictions.

The false statement is #3. Invoking the `validate()` method after adding one or more JComponents to an applet ensures that the Components draw themselves on the screen.

 You Do It

Creating a More Complicated `JApplet`

Next, you change the font of the text in your `JGreet` applet, add components, and make other changes to make a more complicated and useful `JApplet`.

1. Open the **JGreet.java** file in your text editor, and change the class name to **JGreet2**. Immediately save the file using the filename **JGreet2.java**.

2. After the declaration of the `greeting` JLabel, declare a Font object named `bigFont` by typing the following:

    ```
    Font bigFont = new Font("Times Roman", Font.ITALIC, 24);
    ```

3. Within the `init()` method, set the `greeting` font to `bigFont` by typing the following:

    ```
    greeting.setFont(bigFont);
    ```

4. Along with the other declarations, declare two `JLabels`, two empty `JTextFields`, and a `JButton` with the label **View Greeting** by typing the following:

(continues)

959

(continued)

```
JLabel firstLabel = new JLabel("Please enter your first name:");
JLabel lastLabel = new JLabel("Please enter your last name:");
JTextField firstField = new JTextField("",10);
JTextField lastField = new JTextField("",10);
JButton viewButton = new JButton("View Greeting");
```

5. Set the new layout manager to a flow layout with the following statement:

```
FlowLayout flow = new FlowLayout();
```

6. Within the `init()` method, set a layout manager as follows:

```
con.setLayout(flow);
```

7. Add all the newly created components to the applet by typing the following:

```
con.add(firstLabel);
con.add(firstField);
con.add(lastLabel);
con.add(lastField);
con.add(viewButton);
```

8. On the next line, request focus for the first-name text field by typing:

```
firstField.requestFocus();
```

9. Save the file and compile it.

10. Open the **TestJGreet.html** document you created earlier, and change the class name in the `object code` statement to **JGreet2.class**. Save the file as **TestJGreet2.html**. Execute the **appletviewer TestJGreet2.html** command. The output is shown in Figure 17-8. Confirm that you can type characters into the `JTextField`s and that you can click the `JButton` using the mouse. You haven't coded any action to take place as a result of a `JButton` click yet, but the components should function.

Figure 17-8 The JGreet2 JApplet

11. Close the Applet Viewer window.

(continues)

(continued)

Making the `JApplet`'s *Button Respond to Events*

Next, you make your applet an event-driven program by adding functionality to the applet. When the user enters a name and clicks the `JButton`, the `JApplet` displays a personalized greeting.

1. Open the **JGreet2.java** file in your text editor, and change the class name to `JGreet3`. Immediately save the file as **JGreet3.java**.

2. Add a third `import` statement to your program by typing the following:

    ```
    import java.awt.event.*;
    ```

3. Add the following phrase to the class header:

    ```
    implements ActionListener
    ```

4. Prepare your `JApplet` for `JButton`-sourced events by typing the following statement within the `init()` method:

    ```
    viewButton.addActionListener(this);
    ```

5. Following the `init()` method, add the following `actionPerformed()` method. In the method, declare two `String`s—one to hold the user's first name and another for the last name—and then use the `getText()` method on the `JTextField`s to retrieve values for these `String`s. Using the `String`s, display a personalized question for the user.

    ```java
    public void actionPerformed(ActionEvent thisEvent)
    {
        String firstName = firstField.getText();
        String lastName = lastField.getText();
        greeting.setText("How are you, " + firstName + " " +
            lastName + "?");
    }
    ```

6. Save the file and compile the program. Edit the file **TestJGreet2.html** to change the class reference to **JGreet3.class**, and then save the file as **TestJGreet3.html**. Run the applet using the **appletviewer TestJGreet3.html** command.

7. Type your name in the `JTextField`s, and then click the **View Greeting** button. The personalized message should appear, similar to the one in Figure 17-9.

(continues)

(continued)

Figure 17-9   Typical execution of the JGreet3 JApplet

8. Drag the mouse to highlight the first or last name (or both) in the Applet Viewer window, and then type a different name. Click the **View Greeting** button. A greeting that uses the new name appears.

9. Close the Applet Viewer window.

Understanding the JApplet Life Cycle

Applets are popular because they are easy to use in Web pages. Because applets execute in a browser, the JApplet class contains methods that are automatically called by the browser. You already are familiar with the paint() method. In Chapter 16 you learned that the system can request that a component's contents be repainted or that the application can request repainting. The paint() method is always called after the init() and start() methods execute. It is also called if an applet needs repainting—if, for example, the user covers part of an applet with another open window and then uncovers it. The method works the same way with JApplets as with JFrames. The method header is as follows:

```
public void paint(Graphics g)
```

As you learned in Chapter 16, the paint() method provides you with a Graphics object. If you override the paint() method in your applet, you can use the automatically provided Graphics object to draw shapes and strings.

The other four methods that are automatically called in a JApplet are init(), start(), stop(), and destroy().

The init() Method

You have already seen examples of JApplets that contain init() methods. When a Web page containing a JApplet is loaded in the browser, or when you run the appletviewer command within an HTML document that calls a JApplet, the applet's init() method executes. The init() method might be your version (if you have written one to override the version in the parent class) or the automatically provided version. You should write your own init() method when you have any initialization tasks to perform, such as setting up user interface components.

962

The start() Method

The **start() method** executes after the init() method, and it executes again every time the applet becomes active after it has been inactive. For example, if you run a JApplet using the appletviewer command and then minimize the Applet Viewer window, the JApplet becomes inactive. When you restore the window, the JApplet becomes active again. On the Internet, users can leave a Web page, visit another page, and then return to the first site. Again, the JApplet becomes inactive and then active. When you write your own start() method, you must include any actions you want your JApplet to take when a user revisits the JApplet. For example, you might want to resume some animation that you suspended when the user left the applet.

The stop() Method

When a user leaves a Web page (perhaps by minimizing a window or traveling to a different Web page), the **stop() method** is invoked. You override the existing empty stop() method only if you want to take some action when a JApplet is no longer visible. You usually don't need to write your own stop() methods.

The destroy() Method

The **destroy() method** is called when the user closes the browser or Applet Viewer. Closing the browser or Applet Viewer releases any resources the JApplet might have allocated. As with the stop() method, you do not usually have to write your own destroy() methods.

 Advanced Java programmers override the stop() and destroy() methods when they want to add instructions to "suspend a thread," or stop a chain of events that were started by a JApplet but are not yet completed.

Every JApplet has the same life cycle outline, as shown in Figure 17-10. When the applet executes, the init() method runs, followed by the start() method. If the user leaves the JApplet's page, the stop() method executes. When the user returns, the start() method executes. The stop() and start() sequence might continue any number of times until the user closes the browser (or Applet Viewer), which invokes the destroy() method.

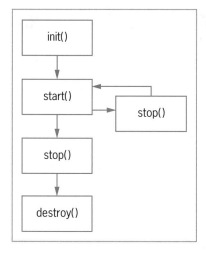

Figure 17-10   The JApplet life cycle

TWO TRUTHS & A LIE

Understanding the JApplet Life Cycle

1. The paint() method is always called after the init() and start() methods execute or if an applet needs repainting.

2. When a Web page containing a JApplet is loaded in the browser, the applet's start() method is the first to execute.

3. When a user leaves a Web page, the stop() method executes.

The false statement is #2. When a Web page containing a JApplet is loaded in the browser, or when you run the appletviewer command within an HTML document that calls a JApplet, the applet's init() method is the first to execute.

 You Do It

Understanding the Applet Life Cycle

To demonstrate the life cycle methods in action, you can write a JApplet that overrides all four methods: init(), start(), stop(), and destroy(). When you run this applet, you can observe the number of times each method executes.

(continues)

(continued)

1. Open a new text file in your text editor, and then type the following `import` statements:

```
import javax.swing.*;
import java.awt.*;
import java.awt.event.*;
```

2. To make the `JApplet` include a `JButton` that the user can click, and to implement an `ActionListener`, type the following header for a `JLifeCycle` applet and include an opening curly brace for the class:

```
public class JLifeCycle extends JApplet implements ActionListener
{
```

3. Declare the following six `JLabel` objects, which display each of the six methods that execute during the lifetime of the applet:

```
JLabel messageInit = new JLabel("init ");
JLabel messageStart = new JLabel("start ");
JLabel messageDisplay = new JLabel("display ");
JLabel messageAction = new JLabel("action ");
JLabel messageStop = new JLabel("stop ");
JLabel messageDestroy = new JLabel("destroy ");
```

4. Declare a `JButton` by typing the following:

```
JButton pressButton = new JButton("Press");
```

5. Declare six integers that hold the number of occurrences of each of the six methods by typing the following code:

```
int countInit, countStart, countDisplay, countAction,
    countStop, countDestroy;
```

6. Start the `init()` method by adding a container and flow layout manager with the following statements:

```
public void init()
{
  Container con = getContentPane();
  con.setLayout (new FlowLayout());
```

7. Add the following statements, which add 1 to `countInit`, place the components within the applet, and then call the `display()` method:

(continues)

(continued)

```
    ++countInit;
    con.add(messageInit);
    con.add(messageStart);
    con.add(messageDisplay);
    con.add(messageAction);
    con.add(messageStop);
    con.add(messageDestroy);
    con.add(pressButton);
    pressButton.addActionListener(this);
    display();
}
```

8. Add the following `start()` method, which adds 1 to `countStart` and calls `display()`:

```
public void start()
{
    ++countStart;
    display();
}
```

9. Add the following `display()` method, which adds 1 to `countDisplay`, displays the name of each of the six methods with the current count, and indicates how many times the method has executed:

```
public void display()
{
    ++countDisplay;
    messageInit.setText("init " + countInit);
    messageStart.setText("start " + countStart);
    messageDisplay.setText("display " + countDisplay);
    messageAction.setText("action " + countAction);
    messageStop.setText("stop " + countStop);
    messageDestroy.setText("destroy " + countDestroy);
}
```

10. Add the following `stop()` and `destroy()` methods. Each adds 1 to the appropriate counter and calls `display()`:

```
public void stop()
{
    ++countStop;
    display();
}
public void destroy()
{
    ++countDestroy;
    display();
}
```

(continues)

(continued)

11. When the user clicks `pressButton`, the following `actionPerformed()` method executes; it adds 1 to `countAction` and displays it:

```
public void actionPerformed(ActionEvent e)
{
   ++countAction;
   display();
}
```

12. Add the closing curly brace for the class. Save the file as **JLifeCycle.java**. Compile the class.

   Take a moment to examine the code you created for the `JLifeCycle` applet. Each method adds 1 to one of the six counters, but you never explicitly call any of the methods except `display()`; each of the other methods is called automatically.

Creating an HTML Document to Host the `JApplet`

Next, you create an HTML document so you can test the `JLifeCycle` applet.

1. Open a new file in your text editor, and then enter the following HTML code:

```
<html>
<object code = "JLifeCycle.class" width = 460 height = 60>
</object>
</html>
```

2. Save the file as **TestJLifeCycle.html**.

3. Run the HTML document using the following command:

```
appletviewer TestJLifeCycle.html
```

   Figure 17-11 shows the output. When the applet begins, the `init()` method is called, so 1 is added to `countInit`. The `init()` method calls `display()`, so 1 is added to `countDisplay`. Immediately after the `init()` method executes, the `start()` method is executed, and 1 is added to `countStart`. The `start()` method calls `display()`, so 1 more is added to `countDisplay`. The first time you see the applet, `countInit` is 1, `countStart` is 1, and `countDisplay` is 2. The methods `actionPerformed()`, `stop()`, and `destroy()` have not yet been executed.

(continues)

(continued)

Figure 17-11   The JLifeCycle JApplet when it first executes

4. Click the **Minimize** button to minimize the Applet Viewer window, and then click the **Taskbar** button to restore it. The applet now looks like Figure 17-12. The init() method still has been called only once, but when you minimized the applet, the stop() method executed, and when you restored it, the start() method executed. Therefore, countStop is now 1 and countStart has increased to 2. In addition, because start() and stop() call display(), countDisplay is increased by 2 and now holds the value 4.

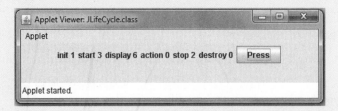

Figure 17-12   The JLifeCycle JApplet after minimizing and restoring

5. Minimize and restore the Applet Viewer window again. Now, the stop() method has executed twice, the start() method has executed three times, and the display() method has executed a total of six times, as shown in Figure 17-13.

Figure 17-13   The JLifeCycle JApplet after minimizing and restoring twice

(continues)

(continued)

6. Click the **Press** button. The count for the `actionPerformed()` method is now 1, and `actionPerformed()` calls `display()`, so `countDisplay` is now 7, as shown in Figure 17-14.

Figure 17-14   The `JLifeCycle` `JApplet` after minimizing and restoring twice, and then pressing the button

7. Continue to minimize, maximize, and click the **Press** button. Note the changes that occur with each activity until you can correctly predict the outcome. Notice that the `destroy()` method is not executed until you close the applet, and then it is too late to observe an increase in `countDestroy`.

8. Close the Applet Viewer.

Understanding Multimedia and Using Images

Multimedia describes the use of sound, images, graphics, and video in computer programs. Most computers that are sold today are "multimedia ready"—that is, they have CD-RW and DVD-RW drives, audio boards, and video capabilities. Java provides extensive multimedia tools, including the following:

- Java programmers can use the Java 2D or the Java 3D Application Programming Interface (API) to create 3D graphics applications.
- The Java Media Framework (JMF) API allows you to add audio and video media to an application.
- Java Sound allows you to play, record, and modify audio files.
- The Java Advanced Imaging API provides image-manipulation capabilities.
- The Java Speech API allows a user to input speech commands and allows an application to produce speech output.

Adding Images to JApplets

An **image** is a likeness of a person or thing. Images abound on the Internet in all shapes, colors, and sizes. Image formats supported by Java include:

- Graphics Interchange Format (GIF), which can contain a maximum of 256 different colors

- Joint Photographic Experts Group (JPEG), which is commonly used to store photographs and is a more sophisticated way to represent a color image

- Portable Network Graphics (PNG), which is more flexible than GIF and stores images in a lossless form. (PNG was originally designed to be a portable image storage form for computer-originated images.) **Lossless data compression** is a set of rules that allows an exact replica of data to be reconstructed from a compressed version. If you have ever worked with a .zip file, you have worked with lossless data compression.

The Image class provides many of Java's image capabilities; this class loads images that have been stored in one of the allowed Image formats. The Image class, which you can find in the java.awt package, is an abstract class. Recall that an abstract class is one from which you cannot create any objects, but which you can use as an interface or from which you can inherit. Because Image is abstract, you must create Image objects indirectly using the getImage() method.

The getImage() method is used to load an Image into the named Image in the applet. One version of the getImage() method can take up to two arguments: a location where the image is stored and its filename. For example, you can create and load an Image named companyLogo with a statement such as the following:

```
companyLogo = getImage(getCodeBase(), "logo.gif");
```

The getCodeBase() call returns the Uniform Resource Locator (URL) where the code is located. That is, it finds the directory from which the code is running.

You can use the applet paint() method to display Image object images. The drawImage() method is a Graphics method that uses the following four arguments:

- The first argument is a reference to the Image object in which the image is stored.

- The second argument is the x-coordinate where the image appears on the applet.

- The third argument is the y-coordinate where the image appears on the applet.

- The fourth argument is a reference to an ImageObserver object.

An ImageObserver object can be any object that implements the ImageObserver interface. Because the Component class implements the ImageObserver interface, all Components, including JApplets, inherit this implementation. Usually, the ImageObserver object is the object on which the image appears—in this case, the JApplet. Recall from Chapter 4 that the this reference refers to the current object using a method. Frequently, with the drawImage() method, you use the this reference to indicate that you want the Image drawn on the current JApplet. For example, the code to display the companyLogo image in the upper-left corner of the JApplet is as follows:

```
g.drawImage(companyLogo, 0, 0, this);
```

You can use an overloaded version of the Graphics method drawImage()to output a scaled image. This method takes six arguments. Notice that the first three arguments are the same as those for the four-argument version of the drawImage() method. In the overloaded version:

- The first argument is a reference to the Image object in which the image is stored.

- The second and third arguments are the x- and y-coordinates where the image appears on the applet.

- The fourth and fifth arguments are the width and height of the scaled object.

- The sixth argument uses the this reference to implement the ImageObserver object.

For example, the following code displays the companyLogo image at coordinates 0, 120 using the full width of the JApplet, but 100 pixels less than the height:

```
g.drawImage(companyLogo, 0, 120, getWidth(), getHeight() - 100, this);
```

Figure 17-15 shows a JApplet that draws an image twice. The JCompanyImage JApplet uses an image file named CompanyLogo.png, which holds a logo that is originally 287 pixels wide by 129 pixels high. Within the paint() method in the JApplet, the image is drawn first in its "natural," or original, size in the upper-left corner. Then it is redrawn lower at twice its original size. Figure 17-16 shows the contents of the HTML document that displays the applet; the output of the JCompanyImage applet is shown in Figure 17-17.

```
import java.awt.*;
import java.applet.*;
import javax.swing.*;
public class JCompanyImage extends JApplet
{
    Image companyLogo;
    final int WIDTH = 287;
    final int HEIGHT = 129;
    final int FACTOR = 2;
    public void init()
    {
        companyLogo = getImage(getCodeBase(), "CompanyLogo.png");
    }
    public void paint(Graphics g)
    {
        super.paint(g);
        // Draw image at its natural size
        g.drawImage(companyLogo, 0, 0, this);
        // Draw the image scaled - twice as large
        g.drawImage(companyLogo, 0, HEIGHT, WIDTH * FACTOR,
            HEIGHT * FACTOR, this);
    }
}
```

Figure 17-15   The JCompanyImage JApplet

```
<html>
<object code = "JCompanyImage.class" width = 600 height = 390>
</object>
</html>
```

Figure 17-16 The TestJCompanyImage HTML document

Figure 17-17 Output of the JCompanyImage JApplet

 You can examine the CompanyLogo.png file in the Chapter 17 folder of your downloadable student files.

Using ImageIcons

You can also use the ImageIcon class to create images in your applications and applets. In general, working with the ImageIcon class is simpler than working with Image. You can use all the Image methods with an ImageIcon, plus many additional methods. Unlike with the Image class, you can create ImageIcon objects directly. Also, unlike with Images, you can place an ImageIcon on a Component, such as a JPanel, JLabel, or JButton, as well as on a JApplet or JFrame. For example, the following statements create a JButton that contains a picture of an arrow:

```
ImageIcon arrowPicture = new ImageIcon("arrow.gif");
JButton arrowButton = new JButton(arrowPicture);
```

Behind the scenes, each ImageIcon object uses an Image object to hold the image data and a MediaTracker object to keep track of the image's loading status. As you are aware if you have visited many Web pages, some images can require a good deal of time to load. To improve performance, the Image get() methods return immediately while the image continues to load, so that your application does not have to wait before performing other operations.

You can also use the paintIcon() method to display ImageIcon images. This method requires four arguments:

- The first argument is a reference to the Component on which the image appears—this in the following example.

- The second argument is a reference to the Graphics object used to render the image—g in the following example.

- The third and fourth arguments are the x- and y-coordinates for the upper-left corner of the image.

The code to display the arrowPicture ImageIcon using the paintIcon() method is:

```
arrowPicture.paintIcon(this, g, 180, 0);
```

You can retrieve an ImageIcon's width and height with methods named getIconWidth() and getIconHeight(); each returns an integer. Figure 17-18 contains a JApplet that manipulates an ImageIcon's width and height to achieve display effects. In the JBear JApplet, an ImageIcon is created using a .gif file. In the init() method, the width and height of the ImageIcon are stored in variables named width and height. In the actionPerformed() method, the width and height of the image are doubled with every button click. Figure 17-19 shows the JApplet when it starts, after the user has clicked the button once, and after the user has clicked the button twice.

```java
import java.awt.*;
import java.awt.event.*;
import javax.swing.*;
public class JBear extends JApplet implements ActionListener
{
    private ImageIcon image = new ImageIcon("bear.gif");
    private JButton closerButton = new JButton("Oh my!");
    private int width, height;
    Container con = getContentPane();
    public void init()
    {
        con.setLayout(new FlowLayout());
        closerButton.addActionListener(this);
        con.add(closerButton);
        width = image.getIconWidth();
        height = image.getIconHeight();
    }
    public void actionPerformed(ActionEvent event)
    {
        width = width * 2;
        height = height * 2;
        repaint();
    }
    public void paint(Graphics g)
    {
        super.paint(g);
        g.drawImage(image.getImage(), 0, 0, width, height, this);
    }
}
```

Figure 17-18   The JBear JApplet

Figure 17-19   Output of the JBear JApplet

The first statement in the paint() method of the JBear applet passes the Graphics object to the JApplet class paint() method so that the applet surface is cleared. If you eliminate the call to super.paint() and then get a series of new bear images, all the previous versions remain on the screen "behind" the newest, larger one.

Notice that the drawImage() method call in the paint() method uses image.getImage() as an argument. An ImageIcon cannot be drawn to scale, but an Image can, so you use the getImage() method to return a scalable Image reference for the ImageIcon object.

TWO TRUTHS & A LIE

Understanding Multimedia and Using Images

1. Multimedia describes the use of sound, images, graphics, and video in computer programs; most computers that are sold today are "multimedia ready."

2. Image formats supported by Java include GIF, JPEG, and PNG.

3. You can use the Picture class to create images in your applications and applets.

The false statement is #3. You can use the Image or ImageIcon class to create images in your applications and applets; you can even place an ImageIcon on a Component, such as a JPanel or JButton.

You Do It

Displaying Images

In the next steps, you add an animated image to an applet.

1. Open a new file in your text editor, and then enter the first few lines of the JMonkey JApplet:

```
import java.awt.*;
import javax.swing.*;
public class JMonkey extends JApplet
{
```

2. Declare an ImageIcon and initialize it with the monkey.gif file that is stored in your downloadable student files. The file contains an animated image of a chimpanzee shaking its head from side to side. Declare variables to hold the width and height of the image, the content pane for the applet, and horizontal and vertical placement positions.

```
private ImageIcon image = new ImageIcon("monkey.gif");
private int width, height;
Container con = getContentPane();
int x = 30;
int y = 30;
```

(continues)

(continued)

3. Write the `init()` method to set the layout manager and get the width and height of the image.

```
public void init()
{
    con.setLayout(new FlowLayout());
    width = image.getIconWidth();
    height = image.getIconHeight();
}
```

4. The `paint()` method calls the parent's method, then draws a string and draws the image 20 pixels lower. Add the method shown below, and then add a closing curly brace for the class.

```
public void paint(Graphics g)
{
    super.paint(g);
    g.drawString("No, no, no", x, y);
    g.drawImage(image.getImage(), x, y + 20,
        width, height, this);
}
}
```

5. Save the file as **JMonkey.java**, and compile it.

6. Write an HTML document to host the applet as follows:

```
<html>
<object code = "JMonkey.class" width = 200 height = 150>
</object>
</html>
```

7. Save the HTML document as **TestJMonkey.html**. Run the applet. The output should look like Figure 17-20. On your screen, you will see the animated monkey move.

Figure 17-20   Execution of the `JMonkey` applet

Adding Sound to JApplets

Java programs can play audio clips on computers that have speakers and a sound card (which includes most computers that are sold today). Java supports sound using methods from the `Applet` class, rather than `JApplet`. You can use these methods to retrieve and play sound files that use various sound formats. These formats include the Windows Wave file format (.wav), Sun Microsystems Audio file format (.au), and Music and Instrument Digital Interface file format (.midi or .mid).

The simplest way to retrieve and play a sound is to use the `play()` method of the `Applet` class. The `play()` method retrieves and plays the sound as soon as possible after it is called. The `play()` method takes one of two forms:

- `play()` with one argument—The argument is a URL object that loads and plays an audio clip when both the URL object and the audio clip are stored at the same URL.

- `play()` with two arguments—The first argument is a URL object, and the second argument is a folder path name that loads and plays the audio file. The first argument is often a call to a `getCodeBase()` method or `getDocumentBase()` method to retrieve the URL object; the second argument is the name of the audio clip within the folder path that is stored at that URL.

Used with the `codebase` attribute, which indicates the filename of the applet's main class file, the `getCodeBase()` and `getDocumentBase()` methods direct the browser to look in a different folder for the applet and other files it uses. This is necessary when the desired files are in a different location than the Web page containing the applet. By calling `getCodeBase()` in an applet, you get a URL object that represents the folder in which the applet's class file is stored. For example, the following statement retrieves and plays the tune.au sound file, which is stored in the same place as the applet:

```
play(getCodeBase(),"tune.au");
```

The `getDocumentBase()` method returns an absolute URL naming the directory of the document in which the applet is stored. It is sometimes used instead of `getCodeBase()` as a matter of preference. An applet is restricted to reading files only from the server that hosts it.

To play a sound more than once, or to start or stop the sound, you must load the sound into an `AudioClip` object using the applet's `newAudioClip()` method. `AudioClip` is part of the `java.awt.Applet` class and must be imported into your program. Like the `play()` method, the `getAudioClip()` method can take one or two arguments. The first argument (or only argument, if there is only one) is a URL argument that identifies the sound file; the second argument is a folder path reference needed for locating the file.

The following statement loads the sound file from the previous example into the clip object:

```
AudioClip aClip = new AudioClip(getCodeBase(), "audio/tune.au");
```

Here, the sound file reference indicates that the tune.au sound file is in the audio folder. After you have created an `AudioClip` object, you can use the `play()` method to call and play the sound, the `stop()` method to halt the playback, and the `loop()` method to play the sound repeatedly. Multiple AudioClip items can play at the same time, and the resulting sound is mixed together to produce a composite.

In the next "You Do It" section, you will create a JApplet that plays a sound.

978

Watch the video *Using Images and Sound in an Applet*.

TWO TRUTHS & A LIE

Adding Sound to JApplets

1. Java programs can play audio clips on computers that have speakers and a sound card.

2. Java supports sound using methods from the JApplet class.

3. Sound formats that applets can use include the Windows Wave file format (.wav), Sun Audio file format (.au), and Music and Instrument Digital Interface file format (.midi or .mid).

The false statement is #2. Java supports sound using methods from the Applet class (rather than JApplet).

You Do It

Playing Sounds

Next, you will use the loop() method and an AudioClip to play a sound continually in an applet. You will also create and add a Graphics2D object.

1. Open a new file in your text editor, and then enter the first few lines of the JSound JApplet:

```
import java.awt.*;
import java.applet.*;
import javax.swing.*;
public class JSound extends JApplet
{
```

(continues)

(continued)

2. Enter the following statement to declare an `AudioClip` object named `sound`:

```
AudioClip sound;
```

3. Create the `init()` method and an `AudioClip` object to play the mysteryTune.au sound file by entering the following code:

```
public void init()
{
    sound = getAudioClip(getCodeBase(),"mysteryTune.au");
}
```

You can find the mysteryTune.au file in the Chapter 17 folder of your downloadable student files.

4. Create the following `start()` method. This method uses the `loop()` method to play the mysteryTune.au sound file continually:

```
public void start()
{
    sound.loop();
}
```

5. Create the following `stop()` method to halt the mysteryTune.au sound file:

```
public void stop()
{
    sound.stop();
}
```

6. Create a `Graphics` object using `paint(Graphics g)`, and then use a cast to change the graphics context to a `Graphics2D` object. Use the `drawString()` method to create a message that appears on the screen while the `JApplet` plays. Add a closing curly brace for the class.

```
public void paint(Graphics g)
{
    super.paint(g);
    Graphics2D g2D = (Graphics2D)g;
    g2D.drawString("Listen to the mystery tune ",
        10, 10);
}
}
```

7. Save the file as **JSound.java**, and then compile it.

8. Open a new file in your text editor, and then enter the following HTML document to test the `JApplet`:

(continues)

(continued)

```
<html>
<object code = "JSound.class" width = 200 height = 50>
</object>
</html>
```

9. Save the HTML document as **TestJSound.html**, and then run it using the **appletviewer TestJSound.html** command. The output should look like Figure 17-21. If speakers are installed on your system and they are on, you should also be able to hear sound playing continually.

Figure 17-21   Output of the `JSound JApplet`

Don't Do It

- Don't forget a matching closing tag for every opening tag in an HTML document.

- Don't forget to use the .class extension with the name of a `JApplet` you want to execute from an HTML document.

- Don't add a `main()` method to a `JApplet`; it will not execute automatically like it does in an application.

- Don't try to execute an applet using the `java` command. An applet doesn't contain a `main()` method and won't execute like an application.

Key Terms

An **applet** is a Java program that is called from another application.

`JApplet` is a `Swing` class from which you can inherit to create your own applet.

HTML, or **Hypertext Markup Language**, is a simple language used to create Web pages for the Internet.

Extensible Hypertext Markup Language (XHTML) is an extension of HTML.

Applet Viewer is a program that comes with the JDK that allows you to view applets without using a Web browser.

The **appletviewer command** allows you to view an applet in a viewing program that comes with the JDK.

A **Web browser** is a program that allows you to display HTML documents on your computer screen.

A **sandbox** is a safe area in which a program can run without causing harm to other areas of a system.

Tags are HTML commands.

<html> is the tag that begins every HTML document.

</html> is the tag that ends every HTML document.

Tag attributes, sometimes referred to as arguments, promote activity or describe the features of an HTML tag.

The **init() method** is the first method called in any applet.

The **start() method** executes after the init() method, and it executes again every time the applet becomes active after it has been inactive.

The **stop() method** is invoked in an applet when a user leaves a Web page (perhaps by minimizing a window or traveling to a different Web page).

The **destroy() method** is called in an applet when the user closes the browser or Applet Viewer.

Multimedia describes the use of sound, images, graphics, and video in computer programs.

An **image** is a likeness of a person or thing.

Lossless data compression is a set of rules that allows an exact replica of data to be reconstructed from a compressed version.

Chapter Summary

- An applet is a program that is called within another application—often a Web browser or a program called the Applet Viewer. Applets descend from the JApplet class and do not contain a main() method.

- To view an applet, it must be called from another document written in Hypertext Markup Language (HTML), which is a simple language used to create Web pages for the Internet. When you create an applet, you write it in Java, save it with a .java file extension, compile it, and write an HTML document that includes a statement to call your compiled Java class. You then load the HTML document into a Web browser or run the Applet Viewer program, which in turn uses the HTML document.

- With an applet, the browser calls several methods automatically at different times. The five methods that are included in every applet are init(), start(), paint(), stop(), and destroy(). You can override any of those methods within a JApplet that you write.

- When you write a JApplet, you can add components, use fonts and colors, change the layout manager, and add event listeners, in much the same way you do in a JFrame.

- An applet's paint() method is always called after the init() and start() methods execute. It is also called if an applet needs repainting. When a Web page containing a JApplet is loaded in the browser, or when you run the appletviewer command within an HTML document that calls a JApplet, the applet's init() method executes. The start() method executes after the init() method, and it executes again every time the applet becomes active after it has been inactive. When a user leaves a Web page, the stop() method is invoked. The destroy() method is called when the user closes the browser or Applet Viewer.

- Multimedia describes the use of sound, images, graphics, and video in computer programs. Image formats supported by Java include Graphics Interchange Format (GIF), Joint Photographic Experts Group (JPEG), and Portable Network Graphics (PNG). The Image class provides many of Java's image capabilities. You can also use the ImageIcon class to create images in your applications and applets.

- Java programs can play audio clips on computers that have speakers and a sound card. Supported sound formats include the Windows Wave file format (.wav), Sun Audio file format (.au), and Music and Instrument Digital Interface file format (.midi or .mid). The simplest way to retrieve and play a sound is to use the play() method of the Applet class.

Review Questions

1. An applet is like a Java application in all of the following ways *except* _____.

   a. you save it with a .java file extension

   b. you compile it into bytecode, creating a file with a .class extension

   c. it can contain decisions, loops, arrays, and all the other language elements of Java

   d. it requires a main() method

2. How is a JApplet different from an application that instantiates a JFrame?

   a. JFrames use graphics.

   b. JApplets run from another program.

   c. JFrames are larger than JApplets.

   d. The user cannot close a JApplet; the program must issue a command to do so.

3. A program that allows you to display HTML documents on your computer screen is a _____.

   a. search engine   c. browser
   b. compiler   d. server

4. HTML contains commands that allow you to do all of the following except _____.

   a. add `JButtons` to `JApplets`
   b. format text on a Web page
   c. import graphic images to a Web page
   d. link your page to other Web pages

5. Pairs of HTML commands are called _____.

   a. tickets   c. tags
   b. labels   d. keywords

6. The name of any applet called using `code` within an HTML document must use the extension _____.

   a. .exe   c. .java
   b. .code   d. .class

7. Which `JApplet` method can you override in your extended version?

   a. `init()`   c. `paint()`
   b. `stop()`   d. all of the above

8. A `JApplet` is a(n) _____.

   a. `Container`   c. `Object`
   b. `Component`   d. all of the above

9. The first method called in any `JApplet` is the _____ method.

   a. `init()`   c. `begin()`
   b. `start()`   d. `main()`

10. A `JApplet`'s `init()` method is closest in purpose to a `JFrame`'s _____.

    a. `main()` method
    b. `actionPerformed()` method
    c. `start()` method
    d. constructor

11. Which of the following `JApplet` methods is likely to execute the greatest number of times?

    a. `init()`
    b. `start()`

    c. `destroy()`
    d. `main()`

12. The `paint()` method is automatically called _____.

    a. before the `init()` method
    b. after the `start()` method
    c. from the `actionPerformed()` method
    d. never

13. The `start()` method called in any `JApplet` is called _____.

    a. as the first method when an applet starts
    b. when the user closes the browser
    c. when a user revisits an applet
    d. when a user leaves a Web page

14. To respond to user events within a `JApplet`, you must _____.

    a. prepare the applet to accept event messages
    b. import the `java.applet.*` package
    c. tell your applet how to respond to events
    d. accomplish both a and c

15. When a user leaves a Web page, the `JApplet` method that executes is _____.

    a. `stop()`
    b. `destroy()`

    c. `kill()`
    d. `exit()`

16. _____ describes the use of sound, images, graphics, and video in computer programs.

    a. Inheritance
    b. Multimedia

    c. Art
    d. Graphics

17. Image formats supported by Java include all of the following except _____.

    a. GIF
    b. JPEG

    c. MIDI
    d. PNG

18. Unlike using the `Image` class, objects of the `ImageIcon` class _____.

    a. are harder to work with

    b. cannot be extended

    c. can be placed on components such as `JButtons`

    d. cannot be created by calling the class constructor

19. The `Applet` class method that retrieves sound is _____.

    a. `sound()`   c. `record()`

    b. `music()`   d. `play()`

20. The method that plays a sound repeatedly is _____.

    a. `play()`   c. `repeat()`

    b. `loop()`   d. `continue()`

Exercises

 Programming Exercises

For each `JApplet` you create in the following exercises, create an HTML host document named **Test** plus the `JApplet` name. For example, the host document for the **JRiddle.java** file is named **TestJRiddle.html**.

1. Create a `JApplet` with a `JLabel` that contains a riddle and a `JButton`. When the user clicks the button, display the answer in a large font on another `JLabel`. Save the file as **JRiddle.java**.

2. a. Create a `JApplet` that asks a user to enter a password into a `JTextField` and to then press Enter. Compare the password to *Rosebud*; if it matches exactly, display "Access Granted". If not, display "Access Denied". Save the file as **JPasswordA.java**.

   b. Modify the password applet in Exercise 2a to ignore differences in case between the typed password and *Rosebud*. Save the file as **JPasswordB.java**.

   c. Modify the password applet in Exercise 2b to compare the password to a list of five valid passwords: *Rosebud, Redrum, Jason, Surrender,* or *Dorothy*. Save the file as **JPasswordC.java**.

3. Create a `JApplet` that contains a `JLabel` and `JButton`. When the user clicks the `JButton`, change the font typeface, style, and size on the `JLabel`. Save the file as **JChangeFont.java**.

4. Create a `JApplet` that contains a `JButton` and a `JTextField`. When the user clicks the `JButton`, display "Today is ", the date, and the time in the `JTextField`. Save the file as **JDateAndTime.java**.

5. Create a `JApplet` that allows a user to type a product number in a `JTextField`. Compare the product number to an array of at least eight valid product numbers. If the typed number is valid, display a product description and price; otherwise, display an appropriate error message. Save the file as **JProductFinder.java**.

6. Create a `JApplet` that contains two parallel arrays with at least five friends' names and phone numbers. Allow the user to enter either a name or phone number and to click a `JButton` to display the other. Include a `JLabel` to describe each `JTextField`. Save the file as **JFriendsPhones.java**.

7. Create a `JApplet` that initially displays a single `JButton`. When the user clicks the `JButton`, display a `JLabel` that prompts the user to enter an integer, a `JTextField` into which the user can type the integer, and a second `JButton` that contains the text *Double Me*. When the user clicks the second button, the integer is doubled and the answer is displayed in the `JTextField`. Save the file as **JDouble.java**.

8. Create a `JApplet` named `JBMICalculator` that allows the user to enter a height in inches and a weight in pounds. When the user clicks a `JButton`, the body mass index (BMI) is displayed. BMI is calculated by dividing weight by height squared and multiplying the result by 703. Save the file as **JBMICalculator.java**.

9. Write a `JApplet` that uses the `ImageIcon` class to place `ImageIcon` objects on four `JButtons`. Download any free JPEG or GIF files from the Internet; if necessary, reduce the size of the images to approximately 30 by 30 pixels. Alternatively, you can use the four files named up.jpg, down.jpg, left.jpg, and right.jpg in your downloadable student files. Each time a `JButton` is clicked, display a different message below the `JButtons`. Save the file as **JButtonIcons.java**.

10. Create a `JApplet` that paints an `ImageIcon` the first time its `paint()` method is called, and then randomly draws small filled ovals in the background color over the image each time a `JButton` is clicked. The resulting effect is that the image seems to be erased by an increasing number of small overlapping ovals. For example, if you place an `ImageIcon` at the coordinates contained in variables named `startPosX` and `startPosY`, you can create a series of 15-by-10 filled ovals placed randomly on the `ImageIcon`'s surface using the following for loop:

```
for(int count = 0; count < 20; ++count)
{
    int x = (int) (Math.random() * imageWidth) + startPosX;
    int y = (int) (Math.random() * imageHeight) + startPosY;
    g.fillOval(x, y, 10, 10);
}
```

Save the file as **JEraseImage.java**.

11. Create a JApplet for Business Associates, a consulting firm whose motto is "Let Business Associates take care of your business." Include two JButtons: clicking one JButton plays the tune "Taking Care of Business" continuously, and clicking the other stops the music. You can find the business.mid file in your downloadable student files. Save the file as **JBusiness.java**.

12. Write an applet that prompts the user for a color name. If it is not red, white, or blue, throw an Exception. Otherwise, change the applet's background color appropriately. Create an HTML document to host the JApplet. Save the file as **RWBApplet.java**.

13. Write a JApplet that uses a JPanel to show the messages "Mouse Entered Applet" and "Mouse Exited Applet" when the mouse enters and exits the applet. Also, when the mouse is clicked on the applet, a message "Mouse Clicked Here" should appear near the clicked location. Save the file as **JMouse.java**.

 Debugging Exercises

1. Each of the following files in the Chapter17 folder of your downloadable student files has syntax and/or logic errors. In each case, determine the problem and fix the program. After you correct the errors, save each file using the same filename preceded with *Fix*. For example, DebugSeventeen1.java will become FixDebugSeventeen1.java. You can test each applet with four downloadable student files named TestFixDebugSeventeen1.html through TestFixDebugSeventeen4.html.

    a. DebugSeventeen1.java
    b. DebugSeventeen2.java

    c. DebugSeventeen3.java
    d. DebugSeventeen4.java

Game Zone

1. In Chapter 2, you created a *Mad Libs* game in which the user entered several words out of context that were then inserted into a rhyme or story, producing humorous effects. Modify the game so it becomes an applet. In turn, prompt the user for each required word. After all the words are entered, display the completed rhyme or story. Figure 17-22 shows the first and last screens displayed during a typical execution. Save the applet as **JMadLib.java**.

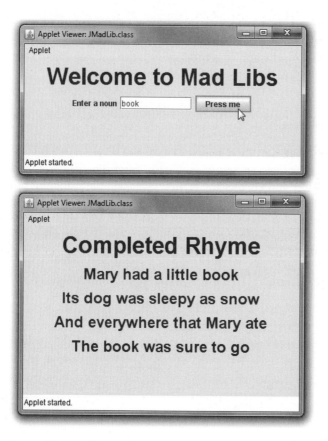

Figure 17-22   First and last screens in a typical execution of the JMadLib applet

2. In Chapter 5, you created a Rock Paper Scissors game. Now create it as a `JApplet` in which the user can click one of three buttons labeled "Rock", "Paper", or "Scissors". The computer's choice is still randomly generated. Figure 17-23 shows a typical execution after the user has played a few games. Save the applet as **JRockPaperScissors.java**.

Figure 17-23 Typical execution of the `JRockPaperScissors` applet

3. In earlier chapters, you created and used a `Card` class in which each object represents a playing `Card`, and in Chapter 8 you constructed a deck of 52 unique `Cards`. Create a `JApplet` that uses such a deck. Start the player with a $10 stake. Randomly deal a card to the computer, and allow the player to make one of four bets:

- $5 that the player's card will be higher than the computer's card
- $10 that the player's card will be higher than the computer's card
- $5 that the player's card will be lower than the computer's card
- $10 that the player's card will be lower than the computer's card

After the player makes a bet, deal the player's card and add or subtract the correct amount from the player's winnings based on the results. When the computer's and player's cards are the same value, the computer wins. The game ends when the first of these events happens:

- The player goes broke (the winnings go to $0 or below).
- The player wins $100.
- All 52 cards are exhausted without a winner.

As shown in the game in progress in Figure 17-24, when the player is making a bet, enable four betting buttons. After the player makes a bet, disable the betting buttons while the player examines the outcome, and enable an OK button. When the player is ready to resume play and clicks OK, disable the OK button and, if the game isn't over, enable the four betting buttons. Save the game as **JCardBet.java**.

Figure 17-24   Typical execution of the `JCardBet` applet

4. a. In Chapters 10 and 11, you created an `Alien` class and `Martian` and `Jupiterian` classes that descend from it. Add a `draw()` method for each child class. The `draw()` method accepts a `Graphics` object and x- and y- starting coordinates. The method draws the `Aliens` in any way you choose, using lines, ovals, rectangles, and so on. Using the `drawString()` method, include a description that names each drawing. Save the files as **Martian.java** and **Jupiterian.java**.

b. Create an applet that instantiates a `Martian` and a `Jupiterian`. In the applet's `paint()` method, draw each type of `Alien`. Save the file as **JDemoAliens.java**. Figure 17-25 shows some sample `Aliens`, but your `Aliens` might look very different.

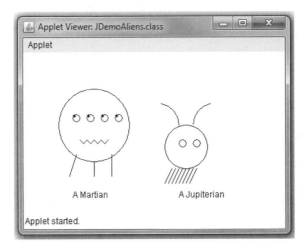

Figure 17-25   Some aliens

c. Create an applet that contains an Alien Hunt game. Place eight numbered buttons in the applet. Randomly assign `Martians` to six of the buttons and `Jupiterians` to two. (*Hint*: You do not need to create an `Alien` array; you can simply create an array that randomly contains *0*s and *1*s, representing `Martians` and `Jupiterians`.) The object of the game is to find all the `Martians` before finding both `Jupiterians`. When a user clicks a button, display the `Alien` represented by the button. If the user clicks two `Jupiterians` before clicking six `Martians`, the player loses the game. When this happens, display two `Jupiterians` and a message telling the user that Earth has been destroyed. Disable any button after it has been selected. Save the game as **JAlienHunt.java**.

5. a. In Chapter 4, you created a `Die` class that you can use to instantiate objects that hold one of six values. Create a `GraphicDie` class that descends from `Die` but adds a `drawDie()` method that draws a representation of the die on the screen. Design the method so it accepts a `Graphics` object as well as x- and y-coordinate positions where the drawing should be placed. Create the drawing of a `Die` based on its value and using the `drawRect()` and `fillOval()` methods. Save the file as **GraphicDie.java**.

b. Create a `JGraphicDie` `JApplet` that instantiates a `GraphicDie` object. In the `JApplet`'s `paint()` method, pass the method's `Graphics` object and two values to the `GraphicDie` object's `drawDie()` method. Save the file as **JGraphicDie.java**.

c. In Chapter 8, you created a FiveDice3 game in which a player's random roll of five dice is compared to the computer's roll and a winner is determined. Now create an applet that plays the game. At each roll, initiated by a player's button click, display the player's five dice and the computer's five dice. Save the file as **JFiveDice.java**. Figure 17-26 shows a typical game.

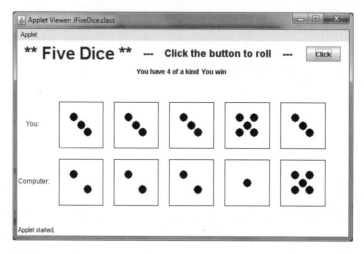

Figure 17-26   The JFiveDice applet

 Case Problems

1. Throughout this book you have created applications for Carly's Catering. Now create a JApplet that advertises the business. Use at least one animation file and one sound file in your JApplet. Save the JApplet as **JCarlys.java**, and save the HTML host file as **TestJCarlys.html**.

2. Throughout this book you have created applications for Sammy's Seashore Rentals. Now create a JApplet that advertises the business. Use at least one animation file and one sound file in your JApplet. Save the JApplet as **JSammys.java**, and save the HTML host file as **TestJSammys.html**.

Working with the Java Platform

In this appendix, you will:

- ◎ Configure Windows to work with the Java SE Development Kit
- ◎ Use Notepad to save and edit source code
- ◎ Use TextPad to work with Java

Configuring Windows to Work with the Java SE Development Kit

Several versions of Java are available for free at the Java Web site (*www.oracle.com/technetwork/java/index.html*). The official name of the most recent version is Java Platform, Standard Edition 7, often called **Java SE 7** for short. Two version numbers (for example, 1.7.0 and 7) are used to identify this release of the Java Platform. Version 7 is the product version, and 1.7.0 is the developer version. The number 7 is used to reflect Java's evolving level of maturity. As updates to existing versions emerge or entirely new versions containing advanced features are released, you can download them. For example, a recent update as this book was being written is Java SE 7u7; *7u7* is short for *version 7, update 7.*

Java's Web site was *http://java.sun.com* before Java was purchased by Oracle. Now the Web site is *http://www.oracle.com/technetwork/java/index.html*. However, the shorter URL redirects you to the longer one, so you can use the shorter address if it is more convenient. Each new version of Java has a code name. The code name for version 7 is Dolphin. The name for version 5 was Tiger, and the name for version 6 was Mustang.

Over the years, Java has been inconsistent in numbering new versions. Before version 6, the standard editions were called JDK 1.0.3, JDK 1.1.2 through 1.1.8, J2SE 1.2.0 through 1.4.2, and J2SE 5.0. With versions 6 and 7, Java is attempting to simplify the name and number changes. Java sometimes adds a "half step" for minor revisions in a version, such as JDK 1.7.0_05.

The different names for Java versions are somewhat confusing and frequently misused. If you download Java to use with this book, you want to acquire the Java Standard Edition (SE) Development Kit, also known as the **JDK**. Java also supports the **Java Enterprise Edition** (EE), which includes all of the classes in the Java SE, plus a number of classes that are more useful to programs running on servers than on workstations. The Java EE Development Kit is known as **SDK**. The names of the development kits have changed frequently; originally, JDK meant "Java Development Kit," but that interpretation was used with the earliest Java versions and is no longer used officially.

The **Java Micro Edition** (ME) is another Java platform, which is used for small devices such as PDAs (personal digital assistants), cell phones, and other consumer appliances.

To configure your Windows operating system with the JDK, you must add the Java bin directory to the command path of your operating system (OS). That way, your OS will know where to look for the Java commands that you use.

One way to update the OS path for Windows is to edit or set the OS path in the autoexec.bat file. This file is automatically executed every time you start your computer. A simpler and less error-prone alternative is to type two commands at the OS prompt when you want to begin a session of working on Java programs. (These two commands are described later in this appendix.)

You do not need to be an operating system expert to issue operating system commands. Learning just a few commands allows you to create and run all the examples in this book.

Finding the Command Prompt

To locate the command prompt on your Windows computer, click Start, point to Programs, point to Accessories, and then click Command Prompt.

 In earlier versions of Windows, the console window was called the *MS-DOS (Microsoft Disk Operating System) prompt*, or more simply, the *DOS prompt*. Many people still use this term instead of *command prompt*.

Command Prompt Anatomy

The Windows command prompt contains at least a disk drive name followed by a colon, a backslash, and a greater-than sign (for example, C:\>). You might also see folder or directory names within the command prompt just before the greater-than sign, as shown in the following examples:

C:\Documents and Settings>

C:\Documents and Settings\Administrator>

Each directory in the path is separated by a backslash.

Changing Directories

You can back up one directory level by typing cd for "change directory," followed by two periods:

cd..

For example, if your OS prompt contains C:\Documents and Settings\Primary> and you type cd.., the command prompt changes to C:\Documents and Settings>. If you type cd.. again, the prompt changes to C:\>, indicating the root directory. Figure A-1 shows this progression.

Figure A-1 Results following two cd.. commands

When you have multiple directories to back through, it is easier to use the following command:

```
cd\
```

This takes you immediately to the root directory instead of backing up one level at a time.

At the command prompt, you can change to another disk drive by typing its name and a colon, then pressing Enter. For example, the following command changes the command prompt to refer to the A drive:

```
A:
```

You can change the directory by typing cd followed by the name of the directory. For example, if you have a folder named Java and it contains a folder named Chapter.01, you can change the command prompt to the Chapter.01 folder by backing up to the root directory and typing the following:

```
cd Java
cd Chapter.01
```

As shown in Figure A-2, the command prompt now reads C:\Java\Chapter.01>. When you compile and execute your Java programs, you should start from the command prompt where the files are stored.

When your command prompt display is filled with commands, it can look confusing. If you want, you can type cls (for Clear Screen) to remove old commands.

Figure A-2 Changing to the Java\Chapter.01 directory from the root directory

Setting the `class` and `classpath` Variables

When you start a Java session, you might need to set the `class` and `classpath` options. These settings tell the operating system where to find the Java compiler and your classes. If you or someone else has altered your autoexec.bat file to contain these commands, you do not need to type them. Otherwise, every time you want to compile and execute Java programs, you need to type statements similar to the following:

```
path = c:\program files\java\jdk1.7.0\bin
set classpath=.
```

After you have typed the `class` and `classpath` statements, you can compile and run as many Java programs as you want without typing these commands again. You must type them again if you close the Command Prompt window or restart your computer.

The first statement sets the path and allows the OS to recognize the `javac` command you use when compiling programs. Consider the following example:

```
path = c:\program files\java\jdk1.7.0\bin
```

This example assumes that you are using JDK 1.7.0 and that it is stored in the java folder in the program files folder. These are the defaults when you download Java from the Java Web site; if you installed Java in a different location, you need to alter the command accordingly.

The command `set classpath=.` tells Java to find your compiled classes in the current directory when you execute your applications and applets. There must be no space between `classpath` and the equal sign, or between the equal sign and the period.

After you set the path correctly, you should be able to use the `javac` command. If you attempt to compile a Java class and see an error message that `javac` is not a recognized command, either Java was not properly installed or the path command was incorrect. If classes compile successfully but do not execute, you might have entered the `classpath` command incorrectly.

Changing a File's Name

When working through the examples in this book, you will often find it convenient to change the name of an existing file—for example, when you want to experiment with altering code without losing the original version, or if you find that when you previously saved a file, you mistyped a filename so that it did not match the class name within the .java file you created. You can take at least three approaches:

- Open the existing file using the appropriate software application (for example, Notepad), click File on the menu bar, and then click Save As. Select the folder you want, then type a new filename for the file. Now you have two versions—one with the old name and one with the new.

- In Windows, open My Computer and locate the misnamed file. Select the file and then click the filename. (Do not double-click the filename unless you want to open the file.) You can then edit the filename by using a combination of the Backspace, Delete, and character keys. Press Enter when the filename is correct.

- At the command prompt, use the `rename` command. You type `rename`, a space, the old filename, another space, and the new filename. For example, to change a file named xyz.java to abc.java, type the following at the command prompt for the directory containing the existing file:

```
rename xyz.java abc.java
```

Compiling and Executing a Java Program

At the command prompt, change from the default drive prompt to the drive where your application is stored. Then change the directory (or folder) to the directory that holds your application.

To compile an application or applet, you type the `javac` command to start the Java compiler, then type a space and the complete name of the .java file—for example, First.java. If the application doesn't compile successfully, the path might not be set correctly to the Java JDK bin directory where the javac.exe file is located. Also, you might have failed to use the same spelling as the Java filename.

When you compile a .java file correctly, the Java compiler creates a .class file that has the same filename as the .java file. Thus, a successful compilation of the First.java file creates a file named First.class. To run a Java application, you use the `java` command and the class name without the .class extension. For example, after an application named First.java is compiled, producing First.class, you execute the program using the following command:

```
java First
```

After the program executes, control is returned to the command prompt. If a program does not end on its own, or you want to end it prematurely, you can press Ctrl+C to return to the command prompt.

After you compile a Java program, you can execute it as many times as you want without recompiling. If you change the source code, you must save and compile again before you can see the changed results in an executed application.

 When you are testing a Java program, you often issue the commands to compile and execute it many times before you are satisfied with the results. If you press the Up Arrow key at the command line, the previous commands appear in reverse succession. When you find the command you want to repeat, just press Enter.

Using Notepad to Save and Edit Source Code

You can use the Windows Notepad text editor to save and edit the source code for Java programs. To start Notepad using Windows, click the Start menu, point to All Programs, point to Accessories, and click Notepad. After you start Notepad, you can enter and edit the code just as you would with any text editor.

Saving source code in Notepad requires that the Java source file be saved with a .java extension. Because Java is case sensitive, you must save a file with the proper capitalization. If the class name of the file and the filename do not match in both spelling and case, you receive an error when you attempt to execute compiled source code. The default extension for Notepad documents is .txt. To create a file with a .java extension, use Save As, locate the folder you want, and type the filename. In Windows 7 or Vista, you can simply type the filename. In older Windows operating systems, type the filename with double quotation marks around it, as in "First.java". This ensures that the file is not saved as "First.java.txt". Then click Save.

Using TextPad to Work with Java

As an alternative to Notepad, you can use TextPad—a text editor that includes many features helpful to Java programmers. You can download a trial version from *www.textpad.com*. Unlike Notepad, TextPad is not included with Windows; to install TextPad, run the setup file after downloading it from the TextPad Web site, and then respond to the dialog box options. Because you download a trial version, you should purchase TextPad if you decide to use it beyond the trial period. Note that TextPad runs only under the Windows operating system. If you are not using Windows, you can use the text editor that comes with your operating system, or you can search the Web to find a text editor that better suits your needs.

To enter and edit source code in TextPad, you can use the same techniques that you use with any other Windows text editor. In short, you can use the standard Windows shortcut keystrokes and menus to enter, edit, and save your code. You can use the File menu to open and close files. You can use the Edit menu to cut, copy, and paste text, and you can use the Search menu to find and replace text. In addition, TextPad color-codes the source files so it is easier to recognize the Java syntax. TextPad also makes it easier to save Java files with the proper capitalization and extension. To compile the current source code, you can select the Compile Java command from the Tools menu. If the source code does not compile cleanly, TextPad displays a Command Results window, including line numbers that identify the source of problems. With TextPad, you can choose to display line numbers in your code.

Key Terms

Java SE 7 is the most recent version of Java. The full, official name is Java Platform, Standard Edition 7.

The **JDK** is the Java Standard Edition Development Kit.

The **Java Enterprise Edition** (EE) includes all of the classes in the Java SE, plus a number of classes that are more useful to programs running on servers.

The **SDK** is the Java EE Development Kit.

The **Java Micro Edition** (ME) is another Java platform, which is used for small devices such as PDAs, cell phones, and other consumer appliances.

Learning About Data Representation

In this appendix, you will:

- ◎ Work with numbering systems
- ◎ Represent numeric values
- ◎ Represent character values

Understanding Numbering Systems

You can use devices such as computers, cell phones, microwave ovens, and automobiles without understanding how they work internally. Likewise, you can write many Java programs without understanding how the data items they use are represented internally. However, once you learn how data items are stored, you gain a deeper understanding of computer programming in general and Java in particular. You also can more easily troubleshoot some types of problems that arise in your programs.

The numbering system you know best is the **decimal numbering system**, which is based on 10 digits, 0 through 9. When you use the decimal system, no other symbols are available; if you want to express a value larger than 9, you must use multiple digits from the same pool of 10, placing them in columns. Decimal numbers are also called base 10 numbers.

When you use the decimal system, you analyze a multicolumn number by mentally assigning place values to each column. The value of the rightmost column is 1, the value of the next column to the left is 10, the next column's value is 100, and so on; you multiply the column value by 10 as you move to the left. There is no limit to the number of columns you can use; you simply add them to the left as you need to express higher values. For example, Figure B-1 shows how the value 305 is represented in the decimal system. You simply multiply the digit in each column by the value of the column, and then add the values together.

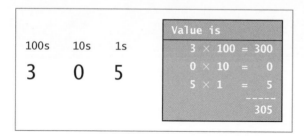

Figure B-1   Representing 305 in the decimal system

The **binary numbering system** works in the same way as the decimal numbering system, except that it uses only two digits, _0_ and _1_. When you use the binary system and you want to express a value greater than 1, you must use multiple columns because no single symbol represents any value other than 0 or 1. Instead of each new column to the left being 10 times greater than the previous column, each new binary column is only two times the value of the previous column. Binary numbers are called base 2 numbers.

For example, Figure B-2 shows how the numbers 9 and 305 are represented in the binary system. Notice that both the binary and decimal systems allow you to create numbers with 0 in one or more columns. As with the decimal system, the binary system has no limit to the number of columns—you can use as many as it takes to express a value.

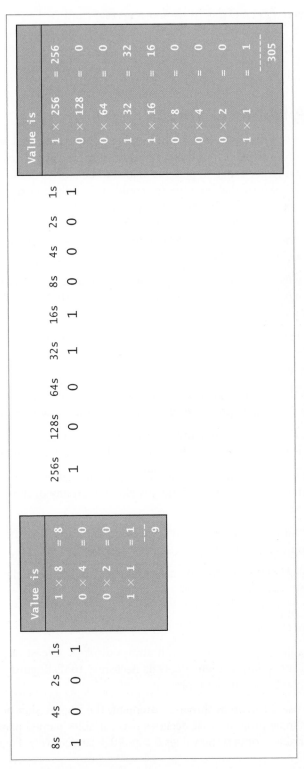

Figure B-2 Representing decimal values 9 and 305 in the binary system

A computer stores every piece of data it uses as a set of *0*s and *1*s. Each *0* or *1* is known as a **bit**, which is short for *binary digit*. Every computer uses *0*s and *1*s because all its values are stored as electronic signals that are either on or off. This two-state system is most easily represented using just two digits.

Representing Numeric Values

In Chapter 2, you learned that a floating-point number contains decimal positions. The term *floating-point* comes from the fact that the decimal point can be at any location in the stored value, allowing a much larger range of possible values to be stored in the same amount of memory. For example, assume that a computer could store only four digits and that the decimal point had to fall after the first two. The positive values that could be stored would then range from 00.00 through 99.99. However, if the decimal point could fall anywhere, the values could range from .0000 through 9999. Computers use more storage for each value, and store negative values as well, but the principle is the same.

Because of the binary nature of computers, representing floating-point numbers is imprecise. For example, suppose you want to represent the value 1/10 (0.10). You could try using each of the following techniques:

- If you use two bits to store the value, only four combinations are available (00, 01, 10, and 11), so they can only represent 0/4, 1/4, 2/4 (or 1/2), and 3/4. None of these is exactly 1/10, but 0/4 is the closest.

- Suppose you use three bits. This allows twice as many combinations, or eight, and the closest to 1/10 is 1/8. The approximation is closer than with two bits, but still not exact.

- Suppose you use four bits, which allows 16 combinations. The closest value to 1/10 is 2/16. This value is no closer to 1/10 than you could achieve with three bits.

- Suppose you use eight bits. Now, there are 256 bit combinations from 0/256 through 255/256. The value of 26/256, at 0.1015625, is closer than any of the other values so far, but it's still not exact.

- No matter how many bits you add to the representation, doubling the number of combinations each time, you can never express 0.1 exactly.

Although you cannot store 0.1 exactly, you can still display it. For example, the following two lines of code display 0.1 as expected:

```
double oneTenth = 0.1;
System.out.println(oneTenth);
```

When Java displays a floating-point number, it always displays at least one digit after the decimal. After that, it uses only as many digits as necessary to distinguish the number from the nearest floating-point value it can represent.

However, when you use 0.1 in an arithmetic statement, the imprecision becomes evident. Figure B-3 shows a simple program that declares two variables named oneTenth and threeTenths; the variables contain the values 0.1 and 0.3, respectively. Figure B-4 shows the result of summing oneTenth three times and of comparing that sum to threeTenths. Because of floating-point imprecision, the first value is calculated to be slightly more than 0.3, so the comparison of oneTenth + oneTenth + oneTenth to threeTenths is false.

```java
import java.util.Scanner;
public class FloatingPointTest
{
    public static void main(String[] args)
    {
        double oneTenth = 0.1;
        double threeTenths = 0.3;
        System.out.println(oneTenth + oneTenth + oneTenth);
        System.out.println(oneTenth + oneTenth + oneTenth ==
            threeTenths);
    }
}
```

Figure B-3   The FloatingPointTest class

Figure B-4   Output of the FloatingPointTest program

For many purposes, you do not care about the small imprecisions generated by floating-point calculations, but sometimes they can make a difference. For example, several popular movies have used the idea that small amounts of extra money can be sliced off bank balances when compounding interest and then siphoned to a criminal's account. Many programmers recommend that you use the Java class BigDecimal when working with monetary or scientific values where precision is important. Additionally, be aware that when you test two floating-point values for equivalency, you might not get the expected results.

When precision is not an issue, but better-looking output is important, you can format the output to eliminate the small imprecisions that occur far to the right of the decimal point. Appendix C teaches you many techniques for formatting output to a desired number of decimal places.

Representing Character Values

The characters used in Java are represented in **Unicode**, which is a 16-bit coding scheme for characters. For example, the letter *A* actually is stored in computer memory as a set of 16 zeros and ones as 0000 0000 0100 0001 (a space is inserted after each set of four digits for readability). Because 16-digit numbers are difficult to read, programmers often use a shorthand notation called the **hexadecimal numbering system**, or base 16. The hexadecimal system uses 16 values, 0 through 9 and A through F, to represent the decimal values 0 through 15. In hexadecimal shorthand, 0000 becomes 0, 0100 becomes 4, and 0001 becomes 1, so the letter *A* is represented in hexadecimal as 0041. You tell the compiler to treat the four-digit hexadecimal 0041 as a single character by preceding it with the \u escape sequence. Therefore, there are two ways to store the character *A*:

```
char letter = 'A';
char letter = '\u0041';
```

 For more information about Unicode, go to *www.unicode.org*.

The second option, using hexadecimal, is obviously more difficult and confusing than the first method, so it is not recommended that you store letters of the alphabet using hexadecimal values. However, you can produce some interesting output using the Unicode format. For example, the sequence '\u0007' produces a bell-like noise if you send it to output. Letters from foreign alphabets that use characters instead of letters (Greek, Hebrew, Chinese, and so on) and other special symbols (foreign currency symbols, mathematical symbols, geometric shapes, and so on) are available using Unicode but not on a standard keyboard, so it may be important that you know how to use Unicode characters.

 Two-digit, base 16 numbers can be converted to base 10 numbers by multiplying the left digit by 16 and adding the right digit. For example, hexadecimal 41 is 4 times 16 plus 1, or 65.

In the United States, the most widely used character set traditionally has been **ASCII** (American Standard Code for Information Interchange). The ASCII character set contains 128 characters. You can create any Unicode character by adding eight *0*s to the beginning of its ASCII character equivalent. This means that the decimal value of any ASCII character is the same as that of the corresponding Unicode character. For example, *B* has the value 66 in both character sets. The decimal values are important because they allow you to show nonprintable characters, such as a carriage return, in decimal codes. Also, the numeric values of the coding schemes are used when a computer sorts numbers and strings. When you sort characters in ascending order, for example, numbers are sorted first (because their Unicode values begin with decimal code 48), followed by capital letters (starting with decimal 65), and then lowercase letters (starting with decimal 97).

Chapter 2 contains a list of Unicode values for some commonly used characters. For a complete list, see *www.unicode.org/charts*. There you will find Greek, Armenian, Hebrew, Tagalog, Cherokee, and a host of other character sets. Unicode also contains characters for mathematical symbols, geometric shapes, and other unusual characters. The ASCII character set is more limited than Unicode because it contains only letters and symbols used in the English language.

Key Terms

The **decimal numbering system** is based on 10 digits, 0 through 9, in which each column represents a value 10 times higher than the column to its right.

The **binary numbering system** is based on two digits, 0 and 1, in which each column represents a value two times higher than the column to its right.

A **bit** is each binary digit, 0 or 1, used to represent computerized values.

Unicode is a 16-bit coding scheme for representing characters.

The **hexadecimal numbering system** is based on 16 digits, 0 through F, in which each column represents a value 16 times higher than the column to its right.

ASCII (American Standard Code for Information Interchange) is a character set widely used to represent computer data.

Formatting Output

In this appendix, you will:

◎ Round numbers

◎ Use the `printf()` method

◎ Use the `DecimalFormat` class

Rounding Numbers

In Chapter 2 and Appendix B, you learned about the imprecision of floating-point numbers. For example, if you write a program that subtracts 2.00 from 2.20, the result is not 0.20—it is 0.20000000000000018. To eliminate odd-looking output and nonintuitive comparisons caused by imprecise calculations in floating-point numbers, you can take the approach shown in the class in Figure C-1. If you want to round a number to two decimal places, note the shaded steps in the figure:

- Multiply the value by 100. So, for example, 0.20000000000000018 becomes 20.000000000000018.

- Add 0.5. This increases a value's whole number part by 1 if the fractional part is 0.5 or greater. For example, 41.6 would become 42.1. In this case, 20.000000000000018 becomes 20.500000000000018.

- Cast the value to an integer. In this case, 20.500000000000018 becomes 20.

- Divide by 100. In this case, the value becomes 0.20.

```java
public class RoundingDemo1
{
    public static void main(String[] args)
    {
        double answer = 2.20 - 2.00;
        boolean isEqual;
        isEqual = answer == 0.20;
        System.out.println("Before conversion");
        System.out.println("answer is " + answer);
        System.out.println("isEqual is " + isEqual);
        answer = answer * 100;
        answer = answer + 0.5;
        answer = (int) answer;
        answer = answer / 100;
        isEqual = answer == 0.20;
        System.out.println("After conversion");
        System.out.println("answer is " + answer);
        System.out.println("isEqual is " + isEqual);
    }
}
```

Figure C-1   The RoundingDemo1 class

Figure C-2 shows the output of the program. Without rounding, the displayed difference between 2.20 and 2.00 is 0.20000000000000018. However, after applying the rounding technique, the result is displayed as 0.2 as expected.

Figure C-2   Output of the `RoundingDemo1` program

As an alternative, you can use the `round()` method that is supplied with Java's `Math` class. The `round()` method returns the nearest `long` value. Figure C-3 shows a program that multiplies the `double` answer by 100, rounds it, and then divides by 100.0. The output is identical to that shown in Figure C-2.

```java
public class RoundingDemo2
{
    public static void main(String[] args)
    {
        double answer = 2.20 - 2.00;
        boolean isEqual;
        isEqual = answer == 0.20;
        System.out.println("Before conversion");
        System.out.println("answer is " + answer);
        System.out.println("isEqual is " + isEqual);
        answer = answer * 100;
        long roundedAnswer = Math.round(answer);
        answer = roundedAnswer / 100.0;
        isEqual = answer == 0.20;
        System.out.println("After conversion");
        System.out.println("answer is " + answer);
        System.out.println("isEqual is " + isEqual);
    }
}
```

Figure C-3   The `RoundingDemo2` class

Using the `printf()` Method

When you display numbers using the `println()` method in Java applications, it sometimes is difficult to make numeric values appear as you want. For example, in the output in Figure C-2, the difference between 2.20 and 2.00 is displayed as 0.2. By default, Java eliminates trailing zeros when floating-point numbers are displayed because they do not add any mathematical information. You might prefer to see 0.20 because the original numbers were both expressed to two decimal places, or, in particular, if the values represent currency.

Additionally, you frequently want to align columns of numeric values. For example, Figure C-4 shows a NumberList application that contains an array of floating-point values. The application displays the values using a for loop, but as the output in Figure C-5 shows, the numbers are not aligned by the decimal point as you usually would want numbers to be aligned. Because the println() method displays values as Strings, the displayed values are left-aligned, just as series of words would be. The numeric values are accurate; they just are not attractively arranged.

```java
public class NumberList
{
    public static void main(String[] args)
    {
        double[] list = {0.20, 2.00, 2.20, 22.22,
            22.20, 222.00, 222.22};
        int x;
        for(x = 0; x < list.length; ++x)
            System.out.println(list[x]);
    }
}
```

Figure C-4   The NumberList application

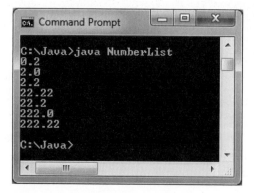

Figure C-5   Output of the NumberList application

The **System.out.printf() method** is used to format numeric values. It is a newer Java feature that was first included in the Formatter class in Java 1.5.0. (This is the internal version number of the Java Development Kit; the external version number is 5.0.) Because this class is contained in the java.util package, you do not need to include any import statements to use it. The printf() method allows you to format numeric values in two useful ways:

- By specifying the number of decimal places to display
- By specifying the field size in which to display values

The `Formatter` class contains many formats that are not covered here. To view the details of formatting data types such as `BigDecimal` and `Calendar`, visit the Java Web site.

C programmers use a `printf()` function that is very similar to Java's `printf()` method. Although the `printf()` method is used in these examples, in Java, you can substitute `System.out.format()` for `System.out.printf()`. There is no difference in the way you use these two methods.

When creating numeric output, you can specify a number of decimal places to display by using the `printf()` method with two types of arguments that represent the following:

- A format string
- A list of arguments

A **format string** is a string of characters; it includes optional text (that is displayed literally) and one or more format specifiers. A **format specifier** is a placeholder for a numeric value. Within a call to `printf()`, you include one argument (either a variable or a constant) for each format specifier.

The format specifiers for general, character, and numeric types contain the following elements, in order:

- A percent sign (%), which indicates the start of every format specifier
- An optional argument index, which is an integer indicating the position of the argument in the argument list. The integer is followed by a dollar sign. You will learn more about this option later in this appendix.
- Optional flags that modify the output format. The set of valid flags depends on the data type you are formatting. You can find more details about this feature at the Java Web site.
- An optional field width, which is an integer indicating the minimum number of characters to be written to the output. You will learn more about this option later in this appendix.
- An optional precision factor, which is a decimal point followed by a number and typically used to control the number of decimal places displayed. You will learn more about this option in the next section.
- The required conversion character, which indicates how its corresponding argument should be formatted. Java supports a variety of conversion characters, but the three you want to use most frequently are d, f, and s, the characters that represent decimal (base 10 integer), floating-point (`float` and `double`), and string values, respectively.

Other conversion characters include those used to display hexadecimal numbers and scientific notation. If you need these display formats, you can find more details at the Java Web site.

For example, you can use the ConversionCharacterExamples class in Figure C-6 to display a declared integer and double. The main() method of the class contains three printf() statements. The three calls to printf() in this class each contain a format string; the first two calls contain a single additional argument, and the last printf() statement contains two arguments after the string. None of the format specifiers in this class use any of the optional parameters—only the required percent sign and conversion character. The first printf() statement uses %d in its format string as a placeholder for the integer argument at the end. The second printf() statement uses %f as a placeholder for the floating-point argument at the end. The last printf() statement uses both a %d and %f to indicate the positions of the integer and floating-point values at the end, respectively. If you attempt to use a conversion character that is invalid for the data type, the program will compile, but it will throw an exception during execution when it encounters the wrong conversion character for the value being displayed.

```
public class ConversionCharacterExamples
{
    public static void main(String[] args)
    {
        int age = 23;
        double money = 123.45;
        System.out.printf("Age is %d\n",age);
        System.out.printf("Money is $%f\n", money);
        System.out.printf
            ("Age is %d and money is $%f\n", age, money);
    }
}
```

Figure C-6   The ConversionCharacterExamples application

Figure C-7 shows the output of the program, in which the values are inserted in the appropriate places in their strings. Note that floating-point values are displayed with six decimal positions by default.

Figure C-7   Output of the ConversionCharacterExamples application

Notice that in the ConversionCharacterExamples class, the output appears on three separate lines only because the newline character ('\n') has been included at the end of each printf() format string. Unlike the println() statement, printf() does not include an automatic new line.

Specifying a Number of Decimal Places to Display with `printf()`

You can control the number of decimal places displayed when you use a floating-point value in a `printf()` statement by adding the optional precision factor to the format specifier. Between the percent sign and the conversion character, you can add a decimal point and the number of decimal positions to display. For example, the following statements produce the output "Money is $123.45", displaying the money value with just two decimal places instead of six, which would occur without the precision factor:

```
double money = 123.45;
System.out.printf("Money is $%.2f\n", money);
```

Similarly, the following statements display 8.10. If you use the `println()` equivalent with amount, only 8.1 is displayed; if you use a `printf()` statement without inserting the .2 precision factor, 8.100000 is displayed.

```
double amount = 8.1;
System.out.printf("%.2f",amount);
```

When you use a precision factor on a value that contains more decimal positions than you want to display, the result is rounded. For example, the following statements produce 100.457 (not 100.456), displaying three decimals because of the precision factor.

```
double value = 100.45678;
System.out.printf("%.3f",value);
```

You cannot use the precision factor with an integer value; if you do, your program will throw an `IllegalFormatConversionException`.

Specifying a Field Size with `printf()`

You can indicate a field size in which to display output by using an optional integer as the field width. For example, the `NumberList2` class in Figure C-8 displays each array element in a field with a size of 6, using two decimal places. Figure C-9 shows the output of the application. Each value is displayed right-aligned in its field; for example, 0.20 is preceded by two blank spaces, and 22.20 is preceded by one blank space. If a numeric value contains more positions than you indicate for its `printf()` field size, the field size is ignored, and the entire value is displayed.

```
public class NumberList2
{
    public static void main(String[] args)
    {
        double[] list = {0.20, 2.00, 2.20, 22.22,
            22.20, 222.00, 222.22};
        int x;
        for(x = 0; x < list.length; ++x)
            System.out.printf("%6.2f\n", list[x]);
    }
}
```

Figure C-8 The `NumberList2` class

Figure C-9   Output of the NumberList2 class

Throughout this book, you have been encouraged to use named constants for numeric values instead of literal constants, so that your programs are clearer. In the program in Figure C-9, you could define constants such as:

```
final int DISPLAY_WIDTH = 6;
final int DISPLAY_DECIMALS = 2;
```

Then the printf() statement would be:

```
System.out.printf("%" + DISPLAY_WIDTH + "." +
    DISPLAY_DECIMALS + "f\n", list[x]);
```

Another, perhaps clearer alternative is to define a format string such as the following:

```
final String FORMAT = "%6.2f\n";
```

Then the printf() statement would be:

```
System.out.printf(FORMAT, list[x]);
```

You can specify that a value be left-aligned in a field instead of right-aligned by inserting a negative sign in front of the width. Although you can do this with numbers, most often you choose to left-align strings. For example, the following code displays five spaces followed by "hello" and then five spaces followed by "there". Each string is left-aligned in a field with a size of 10.

```
String string1 = "hello";
String string2 = "there";
System.out.printf("%-10s%-10s", string1, string2);
```

Using the Optional Argument Index with printf()

The **argument index** is an integer that indicates the position of an argument in the argument list of a printf() statement. To separate it from other formatting options, the argument index is followed by a dollar sign ($). The first argument is referenced by "1$", the second by "2$", and so on.

For example, the `printf()` statement in the following code contains four format specifiers but only two variables in the argument list:

```
int x = 56;
double y = 78.9;
System.out.printf("%1$6d%2$6.2f%1$6d%2$6.2f", x, y);
```

The `printf()` statement displays the value of the first argument, x, in a field with a size of 6, and then it displays the second argument, y, in a field with a size of 6 with two decimal places. Then, the value of x is displayed again, followed by the value of y. The output appears as follows:

```
56 78.90     56 78.90
```

Using the DecimalFormat Class

The **DecimalFormat class** provides ways to easily convert numbers into strings, allowing you to control the display of leading and trailing zeros, prefixes and suffixes, grouping (thousands) separators, and the decimal separator. You specify the formatting properties of DecimalFormat with a pattern String. The **pattern String** is composed of symbols that determine what the formatted number looks like; it is passed to the DecimalFormat class constructor.

The symbols you can use in a pattern String include:

- A pound sign (#), which represents a digit
- A period (.), which represents a decimal point
- A comma (,), which represents a thousands separator
- A zero (0), which represents leading and trailing zeros when it replaces the pound sign

 The pound sign is typed using Shift+3 on standard computer keyboards. It also is called an **octothorpe**, a number sign, a hash sign, square, tic-tac-toe, gate, and crunch.

For example, the following lines of code result in value being displayed as 12,345,678.90.

```
double value = 12345678.9;
DecimalFormat aFormat = new DecimalFormat("#,###,###,###.00");
System.out.printf("%s\n", aFormat.format(value));
```

A DecimalFormat object is created using the pattern #,###,###,###.00. When the object's format() method is used in the printf() statement, the first two pound signs and the comma between them are not used because value is not large enough to require those positions. The value is displayed with commas inserted where needed, and the decimal portion is displayed with a trailing 0 because the 0s at the end of the pattern indicate that they should be used to fill out the number to two places.

When you use the DecimalFormat class, you must use the import statement import java.text.*;. Figure C-10 shows a class that creates a String pattern that it passes to the DecimalFormat constructor to create a moneyFormat object. The class displays an array of values, each in a field that is 10 characters wide. Some of the values require commas, and some do not. Figure C-11 shows the output.

```java
import java.text.*;
public class DecimalFormatTest
{
    public static void main(String[] args)
    {
        String pattern = "###,###.00";
        DecimalFormat moneyFormat = new DecimalFormat(pattern);
        double[] list = {1.1, 23.23, 456.249, 7890.1, 987.5678, 65.0};
        int x;
        for(x = 0; x < list.length; ++x)
            System.out.printf("%10s\n", moneyFormat.format(list[x]));
    }
}
```

Figure C-10   The DecimalFormatTest class

Figure C-11   Output of the DecimalFormatTest program

Key Terms

The **System.out.printf() method** is used to format numeric values.

A **format string** in a printf() statement is a string of characters; it includes optional text (that is displayed literally) and one or more format specifiers.

A **format specifier** in a printf() statement is a placeholder for a numeric value.

The **argument index** in a `printf()` statement is an integer that indicates the position of an argument in the argument list.

The `DecimalFormat` **class** provides ways to easily convert numbers into strings, allowing you to control the display of leading and trailing zeros, prefixes and suffixes, grouping (thousands) separators, and the decimal separator.

A **pattern** `String` is composed of symbols that determine what a formatted number looks like; it is passed to the `DecimalFormat` class constructor.

An **octothorpe** is a pound sign.

Generating Random Numbers

In this appendix, you will:

- ◎ Understand random numbers generated by computers
- ◎ Use the `Math.random()` method
- ◎ Use the `Random` class

Understanding Random Numbers Generated by Computers

A **random number** is a number whose value cannot be predicted. Many types of programs use random numbers. For example, simulations that predict phenomena such as urban traffic patterns, crop production, and weather systems typically use random numbers. You might want to use random numbers to change your screen's appearance; for example, screen savers often use random numbers so that a changing pattern remains interesting.

Random numbers are also used in many computer game applications. When you play games with human opponents, their choices are often unpredictable (and sometimes even irrational). Computers usually are predictable and rational, so when you play a game against a computer opponent, you frequently need to generate random numbers. For example, a guessing game would not be very interesting if you were asked to guess the same number every time you played.

Most computer programming languages, including Java, come with built-in methods that generate random numbers. The random numbers are calculated based on a starting value, called a **seed**. The random numbers generated using these methods are not truly random; they are **pseudorandom** in that they produce the same set of numbers whenever the seed is the same. Therefore, if you seed a random-number generator with a constant, you always receive the same sequence of values. Many computer programs use the time of day as a random number-generating seed. For game applications, this method works well, as a player is unlikely to reset his computer's clock and attempt to replay a game beginning at exactly the same moment in time.

For applications in which randomness is more crucial than in game playing, you can use other methods (such as using the points in time at which a radioactive source decays) to generate truly random starting numbers.

There are two approaches to generating random numbers in Java. Both techniques are explained in this appendix and summarized in Table D-1.

Method/Class	Advantages
`Math.random()` method	You do not need to create an object
	You do not need to understand constructors and multiple methods
`Random` class and its methods	You can generate numbers in the format you need without arithmetic manipulation
	You can create reproducible results if necessary

Table D-1 Generating random numbers in Java

Using the `Math.random()` Method

Java's `Math` class provides a `random()` method that returns a `double` value in the range of 0.0 up to, but not including, 1.0. For example, the application in Figure D-1 generates three random numbers and displays them. Figure D-2 shows three successive executions of the program.

```java
public class SomeRandomNumbers
{
    public static void main (String[] args)
    {
        double ran;
        ran = Math.random();
        System.out.println(ran);
        ran = Math.random();
        System.out.println(ran);
        ran = Math.random();
        System.out.println(ran);
    }
}
```

Figure D-1   The SomeRandomNumbers class

Figure D-2   Three executions of the SomeRandomNumbers program

The values displayed in Figure D-2 appear to be random, but they are not typical of the values you need in a game-playing program. Usually, you need a relatively small number of whole values. For example, a game that involves a coin flip might need only two values to represent heads or tails, and a dice game might need only six values to represent rolls of a single die. Even in a complicated game in which 40 types of space aliens might attack the player, you need only 40 whole numbers generated to satisfy the program requirements.

For example, suppose you need a random number from 1 to 10. To change any value generated by the `Math.random()` method to fall between 0 and 10, you can multiply the generated number by 10. For example, the last three numbers in Figure D-2 would become approximately 2.75, 6.15, and 9.66. Then, you can eliminate the fractional part of each number by casting it to an `int`; after this step, every generated number will be a value from 0 to 9 inclusive. Finally, you can add 1 to a value so it falls in the range from 1 to 10 instead of 0 to 9. In short, the following statement generates a random number from 1 through 10 inclusive, and assigns it to `ran`:

```
int ran = 1 + (int)(Math.random() * 10);
```

Suppose that, instead of 1 through 10, you need random numbers from 1 through 13. (For example, standard decks of playing cards have 13 values from which you might want to select.) When you use the modulus operator (%) to find a remainder, the remainder is always a value from 0 to one less than the number. For example, if you divide any number by 4, the remainder is always a value from 0 through 3. Therefore, to find a number from 1 through 13, you can use a statement like the following:

```
int ranCardValue = ((int)(Math.random() * 100) % 13 + 1);
```

In this statement, a randomly generated value (for example, 0.447) is multiplied by 100 (producing 44.7). The result is converted to an `int` (44). The remainder after dividing by 13 is 5. Finally, 1 is added so the result is 1 through 13 instead of 0 through 12 (giving 6). In short, the general format for assigning a random number to a variable is:

```
int result = ((int)(Math.random() * 100) %
   HIGHEST_VALUE_WANTED + LOWEST_VALUE_WANTED);
```

 Instead of using 100 as the multiplier, you might prefer to use a higher value such as 1,000 or 10,000. For most games, the randomness generated using 100 is sufficient.

Using the Random Class

The `Random` class provides a generator that creates a list of random numbers. To use this class, you must use one of the following import statements:

```
import java.util.*;
import java.util.Random;
```

You also must instantiate a random-number generator object using one of the following constructors:

- `Random()`, in which the seed comes from the operating system. This constructor sets the seed of the random-number generator to a value that is probably distinct from any other invocation of this constructor.

- `Random(long seed)`, in which you provide a starting seed so that your results are reproducible

After you create a random-number generator object, you can use any of the methods in Table D-2 to get the next random number from the generator.

Method	Explanation
nextInt(int n)	Returns a pseudorandom int value between 0 (inclusive) and the specified value n (exclusive), drawn from the random-number generator's sequence
nextInt()	Returns a pseudorandom int value between 0 (inclusive) and 1.0 (exclusive), drawn from the random-number generator's sequence
nextLong()	Returns the next pseudorandom long value from the generator's sequence
nextFloat()	Returns the next pseudorandom float value between 0.0 and 1.0 from the generator's sequence
nextDouble()	Returns the next pseudorandom double value between 0.0 and 1.0 from the generator's sequence
nextBoolean()	Returns the next pseudorandom boolean value from the generator's sequence

Table D-2   Selected Random class methods

For example, Figure D-3 contains an application that declares a Random generator named ran, using the version of the constructor that takes no arguments. This ensures that the results are different each time the application runs. The program then defines LIMIT as 10 and calls ran.nextInt(LIMIT) three times, displaying the results (see Figure D-4).

```
import java.util.*;
public class SomeRandomNumbers2
{
    public static void main(String[] args)
    {
        Random ran = new Random();
        final int LIMIT = 10;
        System.out.print(ran.nextInt(LIMIT) + " ");
        System.out.print(ran.nextInt(LIMIT) + " ");
        System.out.println(ran.nextInt(LIMIT));
    }
}
```

Figure D-3   The SomeRandomNumbers2 class

1026

Figure D-4   Three executions of the SomeRandomNumbers2 program

In Figure D-4, each displayed value falls between 0 and LIMIT. (Of course, to select values between 1 and LIMIT inclusive, you could add 1 to each result.)

Figure D-5 shows a class using the version of the Random constructor that takes an argument (shaded). In this example, a value between 0 and 6 inclusive is generated 15 times. Figure D-6 shows the output when the program is run three times. Although the 15 numbers displayed for each execution constitute a random list, the list is identical in each program execution. You use a seed when you want random but reproducible results. For games, you usually want to use the no-argument version of the Random constructor.

```java
import java.util.*;
public class SomeRandomNumbers3
{
    public static void main(String[] args)
    {
        Random ran = new Random(129867L);
        final int TIMES = 15;
        final int LIMIT = 7;
        for(int x = 0; x < TIMES; ++x)
            System.out.print(ran.nextInt(LIMIT) + " ");
        System.out.println();
    }
}
```

Figure D-5   The SomeRandomNumbers3 class

Figure D-6   Three executions of the SomeRandomNumbers3 program

Key Terms

A **random number** is a number whose value cannot be predicted.

A **seed** is a starting value.

Pseudorandom numbers appear to be random but are the same set of numbers whenever the seed is the same.

Javadoc

In this appendix, you will:

◎ Learn about the Javadoc documentation generator

◎ Understand Javadoc comment types

◎ Generate Javadoc documentation

The Javadoc Documentation Generator

Javadoc is a documentation generator created by Sun Microsystems that allows you to generate Application Programming Interface (API) documentation in Hypertext Markup Language (HTML) format from Java source code. In Chapter 1, you learned that you can place both line and block comments anywhere in a program to provide documentation that can be useful both to yourself and others. A **Javadoc comment** is a special form of block comment that provides a standard way to document Java code. After you write Javadoc comments, they can be interpreted by special utility programs that generate an HTML document. The resulting HTML document provides an attractive format for the documentation when you open it in a browser. Most class libraries, both commercial and open source, provide Javadoc documents. If you have visited the Java Web site to research how to use a class, you most likely have viewed documentation created by the Javadoc utility.

In Chapter 1, you learned that block comments start with /* and end with */ and can span as many lines as necessary, and that Javadoc comments start with /** and end with */. For symmetry, many developers end their Javadoc comments with **/. By convention, asterisks start intermediate lines in a Javadoc comment. This is not required, but it helps you more easily distinguish comments from code.

Javadoc comments can contain tags. A **Javadoc tag** is a keyword within a comment that the Javadoc tool can process. Tags begin with an at-sign (@) and use a limited vocabulary of keywords. Some commonly used Javadoc tags include:

- @author: Describes the author of a document

- @param: Describes a parameter of a method or constructor

- @return: Describes the return type of a method

- @throws: Describes an exception a method may throw

- @exception: Describes an exception

Javadoc Comment Types

There are two types of Javadoc comments:

- Class-level comments that provide a description of a class

- Member-level comments that describe the purposes of class members

Class-level Javadoc comments provide a description of a class; you place class-level comments above the code that declares a class. Class-level comments frequently contain author tags and a description of the class. Figure E-1 shows a shaded class-level comment in a class.

```
/**
 * @author Joyce Farrell.
 * The Employee class contains data about one employee.
 * Fields include an ID number and an hourly pay rate.
 */
public class Employee
{
    private int idNum;
    private double hourlyPay;
    public Employee(int id, double pay)
    {
        idNum = id;
        hourlyPay = pay;
    }
    int getIdNum()
    {
        return idNum;
    }
    void setIdNum(int id)
    {
        idNum = id;
    }
}
```

Figure E-1 An `Employee` class with class-level comments

Member-level Javadoc comments describe the fields, methods, and constructors of a class. Method and constructor comments may contain tags that describe the parameters, and method comments may also contain return tags. Figure E-2 shows a class with some shaded member-level comments.

```
/**
 * @author Joyce Farrell.
 * The Employee2 class contains data about one employee.
 * Fields include an ID number and an hourly pay rate.
 */
public class Employee2
{
    /**
     * Employee ID number
     */
    private int idNum;
    /**
     * Employee hourly pay
     */
```

Figure E-2 An `Employee2` class with class-level and member-level comments *(continues)*

(continued)

```java
    private double hourlyPay;
    /**
     * Sole constructor for Employee2
     */
    public Employee2(int id, double pay)
    {
        idNum = id;
        hourlyPay = pay;
    }
    /**
     * Returns the Employee2 ID number
     *
     * @return int
     */
    int getIdNum()
    {
        return idNum;
    }
    /**
     * Sets the Employee2 ID number
     *
     * @param id employee ID number
     */
    void setIdNum(int id)
    {
        idNum = id;
    }
}
```

Figure E-2   An `Employee2` class with class-level and member-level comments

Like all program comments, Javadoc comments *can* contain anything. However, you should follow the conventions for Javadoc comments. For example, developers expect all Javadoc comments to begin with an uppercase letter, and they recommend that method comments start with a verb such as "Returns" or "Sets." For more information, go to the Java Web site.

Generating Javadoc Documentation

To generate the Javadoc documentation from your class, you should do the following:

1. Create a folder in which to store your class. For example, you might store the Employee2.java file in a folder named Employee2.

2. Within the folder, you can create a Documents subfolder to hold the documentation that you generate. However, if you omit this step and use the syntax described in Step 3, the folder is created for you automatically.

3. Go to the command prompt, and navigate to the directory that holds the Employee2.java file. (See Appendix A for information on finding the command prompt and changing directories.) From the command prompt, run the following command:

```
javadoc -d Documents *.java
```

The –d is the directory option. If you omit it, all the generated files are saved in the current directory. By including this option, you indicate that the files should be saved in the Documents directory.

To see the author's name in the resulting documentation, change the Javadoc command to the following:
```
javadoc -d Documents -author *.java
```

If you are using the jGRASP development environment to create your Java programs, you can execute the Javadoc command with a button click. You can download the jGRASP program from *http://jGRASP.org*.

4. Navigate to the Documents folder. You will see a number of generated files, as shown in Figure E-3. The list includes HTML documents with information about all the constants in your class, all the deprecated methods in your class, and so on. (The Employee2 class has no constants or deprecated methods, but you can open the files and view the format that the contents would take if they existed.)

Figure E-3   Contents of the Employee2 Documents folder in Internet Explorer

The index.html file provides an index of all class interface, constructor, field, and method names; when you double-click it, the file opens in your default browser. Figure E-4 shows how the first part of the index.html file for `Employee2` appears in Internet Explorer. If you have searched the Java Web site for documentation, the format of the page in Figure E-4 is familiar to you. The class name and other information appear in a font and style consistent with other classes in the Java API. You can see information about the class constructor and the notes that you added in your comments. You see inheritance information—`Employee2` descends directly from `Object`. The format of this documentation is familiar to users, making it much easier for them to find what they need than if each developer created documentation formats independently.

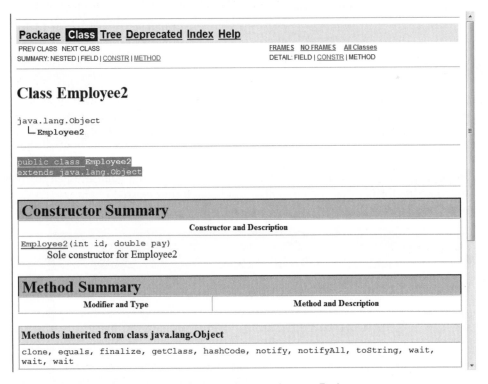

Figure E-4   The `Employee2` class documentation in Internet Explorer

The Javadoc tool will run on .java source files that are stub files with no method bodies. This means you can write documentation comments and run the Javadoc tool when you are first designing classes, before you have written implementations for the class's methods.

Writing acceptable Javadoc comments requires adherence to some style standards. For example, professionals recommend that multiple @author tags should be listed in chronological order, with the creator of the class listed at the top, and that multiple @param tags should be listed in argument-declaration order. Additionally, Javadoc comments can provide hyperlinks that allow navigation from one document to another. For example, when a class contains a field that is an object of another class, you might want to link to the other class's documentation. For more information, see the recommendations from Java developers at the Java Web site.

Specifying Visibility of Javadoc Documentation

By default, Javadoc documents only `public` and `protected` members of an API. In other words, even if you write Javadoc comments for `private` members, the comments do not appear in the generated documentation unless you take special action to make them visible. Although the index.html file contains details about the `Employee2` class's constructor and methods, there is no information about the `private` fields `idNum` and `hourlyPay`. To generate that documentation, you must specify `private` visibility by using the following `javadoc` command:

```
javadoc -d Documents -private *.java
```

Figure E-5 shows the documentation generated by this command. You can see that the newly generated documentation includes a Field Summary section. It lists the fields in alphabetical order preceded by their access specifiers and data types. Each field identifier is followed by the appropriate description that was provided in the Javadoc comment in the source code.

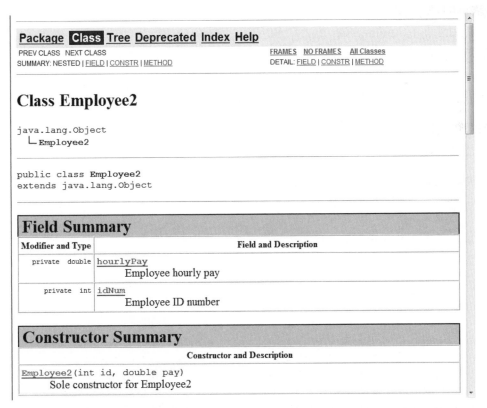

Figure E-5 The `Employee2` class documentation when `private` members are included

You can specify four types of visibility:

- public—Displays public members only

- protected—Displays public and protected members only; this is the default option

- package—Displays package classes and members in addition to public and protected members

- private—Displays all members

Key Terms

Javadoc is a documentation generator created by Sun Microsystems that allows you to generate Application Programming Interface (API) documentation in Hypertext Markup Language (HTML) format from Java source code.

A **Javadoc comment** is a special form of block comment that provides a standard way to document Java code.

A **Javadoc tag** is a keyword within a comment that the Javadoc tool can process.

Class-level Javadoc comments provide a description of a class; you place class-level comments above the code that declares a class.

Member-level Javadoc comments describe the fields, methods, and constructors of a class.

Glossary

A

absolute path—a complete file path that does not require any other information to locate a file on a system.

abstract class—a class from which no concrete objects can be instantiated, but which can serve as a basis for inheritance. Abstract classes usually have one or more empty abstract methods. Contrast with *concrete class*.

abstract data type—a type whose implementation is hidden and accessed through its public methods.

abstract method—a method declared with the keyword `abstract`; it is a method with no body that must be implemented in a subclass.

abstraction—the programming feature that allows a method name to encapsulate multiple statements.

accelerator—a key combination that causes a menu item to be chosen, whether or not the menu item is visible.

access modifier—an access specifier.

access specifier—defines the circumstances under which a class can be accessed and the other classes that have the right to use a class.

accessor methods—methods that return information about an object.

accumulating—the process of repeatedly increasing a value by some amount to produce a total.

action key—a keyboard key that does not generate a character.

actionPerformed(ActionEvent e) method—a method that defines the actions that occur in response to an event.

actual parameters—the arguments in a method call. Contrast with *formal parameters*.

acyclic gradient—a fill pattern in which a color shift occurs once between two points.

adapter class—a class that implements all the methods in an interface, providing an empty body for each method.

add and assign operator—an operator that alters the value of the operand on the left by adding the operand on the right to it; it is composed of a plus sign and an equal sign (+=).

add() method—a method that adds components to a container.

addActionListener() method—a method that tells a class to expect `ActionEvents`.

addPoint() method—a method that adds points to a `Polygon` object.

ad-hoc polymorphism—polymorphism that occurs when a single method name can be used with a variety of data types because various implementations exist; it is another name for method overloading.

aggregation—a type of composition in which a class contains one or more members of another class that would continue to exist without the object that contains them.

algorithm—a process or set of steps that solves a problem.

Allman style—the indent style in which curly braces are aligned and each occupies its own line; it is named for Eric Allman, a programmer who popularized the style. Contrast with *K & R style*.

ambiguous—describes a situation in which the compiler cannot determine which method to use.

anonymous classes—nested, local classes that have no identifier.

anonymous object—an unnamed object.

append() method—a `StringBuilder` class method that adds characters to the end of a `StringBuilder` object.

applet—a Java program that is called from within another application, frequently a Web page.

Applet Viewer—a program that comes with the JDK and displays applets without using a Web browser.

appletviewer command—a command that starts the Applet Viewer.

application software—programs that perform tasks for users. Contrast with *system software*.

application-triggered painting—painting operations that occur when the internal state of a component has changed. Contrast with *system-triggered painting*.

arc—a portion of a circle.

architecturally neutral—describes the feature of Java that allows a program to run on any platform.

argument index—in a `printf()` statement, an integer that indicates the position of an argument in the argument list.

arguments—data items sent to methods in a method call.

arithmetic operators—operators used to perform calculations with values.

array—a named list of data items that all have the same type.

ArrayList class—a Java class that provides a dynamically resizable container that stores lists of objects.

Arrays class—a built-in Java class that contains many useful methods for manipulating arrays, such as methods to search, fill, compare, and sort arrays.

ascending order—the order of objects arranged from lowest to highest value. See also *descending order*.

ascent—one of three measures of a `Font`'s height; it is the height of an uppercase character from a baseline to the top of the character. See also *leading* and *descent*.

ASCII—an acronym for American Standard Code for Information Interchange, a character set widely used to represent computer data.

assert statement—a statement that creates an assertion.

assertion—a Java language feature that can help detect logic errors and debug a program.

assignment—the act of providing a value for a variable.

assignment operator—the equal sign (=); any value to the right of the equal sign is assigned to the variable on the left of the equal sign.

associativity—describes the order in which operands are used with operators.

at run time—describes the period of time during which a program executes.

attributes—the characteristics that define an object as part of a class.

B

back buffer—the offscreen image during double buffering.

base class—a class that is used as a basis for inheritance.

BasicStroke—a class that defines line types and implements the Stroke interface.

batch processing—processing that involves performing the same tasks with many records, one after the other.

binary files—files that contain data that has not been encoded as text; their contents are in binary format.

binary numbering system—a numbering system based on two digits, 0 and 1, in which each column represents a value two times higher than the column to its right.

binary operators—operators that require two operands.

bit—a binary digit, 0 or 1, used to represent computerized values.

black box—a device that can be used solely in terms of input and output without regard to how it works internally.

blank final—a final variable that has not yet been assigned a value.

block—the code between a pair of curly braces.

block comments—comments that start with a forward slash and an asterisk (/*) and end with an asterisk and a forward slash (*/). Block comments can appear on a line by themselves, on a line before executable code, or on a line after executable code. Block comments also can extend across as many lines as needed. Contrast with *line comments*.

block line transfer or **blitting**—the act of copying contents from one surface to another.

Boolean values—true or false values; every computer decision results in a Boolean value.

boolean variable—a variable of the boolean data type that can hold only one of two values—true or false.

BorderLayout—a layout manager that divides a container into five regions.

BorderLayout manager—the default manager class for all content panes.

BoxLayout manager—a layout manager that allows multiple components to be laid out either vertically or horizontally. The components do not wrap, so a vertical arrangement of components, for example, stays vertically arranged when the frame is resized.

bubble sort—a type of sort in which pairs of items are compared and, if necessary, swapped so that the smallest items "bubble" to the top of the list, eventually creating a sorted list.

buffer—a memory location that holds data temporarily—for example, during input and output operations.

ButtonGroup—a UI component that groups several components, such as JCheckBoxes, so a user can select only one at a time.

byte—the data type that holds very small integers, from –128 to 127.

bytecode—programming statements that have been compiled into binary format.

C

call a procedure—to invoke a method.

call stack—the memory location where the computer stores the list of method locations to which the system must return.

called method—a term used to describe the relationship between two methods; a method that is invoked by another.

calling method—a term used to describe the relationship between two methods; a method that invokes another.

camel casing—a naming style in which an identifier begins with a lowercase letter and subsequent words within the identifier are capitalized. Contrast with *Pascal casing*.

capacity—an attribute of an `ArrayList` whose value is the number of items it can hold without having to increase its size. Also, with a `StringBuilder` object, the actual length of the buffer, as opposed to that of the string contained in the buffer.

capacity() method—a `StringBuilder` class method that returns the actual length, or capacity, of the `StringBuilder` object.

CardLayout manager—a layout manager that generates a stack of containers or components, one on top of another.

cast operator—an operator that performs an explicit type conversion; it is created by placing the desired result type in parentheses before the expression to be converted.

catch block—a segment of code that can handle an exception that might be thrown by the `try` block that precedes it.

catch or specify requirement—the Java rule that checked exceptions require catching or declaration.

char—the data type that holds any single character.

character—any letter, number, or special symbol (such as a punctuation mark) that makes up data.

Character class—a class whose instances can hold a single character value. This class also defines methods that can manipulate or inspect single-character data.

charAt() method—a `String` and `StringBuilder` class method that requires an integer argument that indicates the position of the character that the method returns.

checked exceptions—exceptions that a programmer should plan for and from which a program should be able to recover. Contrast with *unchecked exceptions*.

child class—a derived class.

class—a group or collection of objects with common properties.

class body—the set of data items and methods between the curly braces that follow the class header.

class client—an application or class that instantiates objects of another class. See also *class user*.

class definition—a description of attributes and methods of objects instantiated from a class.

class diagram—a visual tool that provides an overview of a class. It consists of a rectangle divided into three sections—the top section contains the name of the class, the middle section contains the names and data types of the attributes, and the bottom section contains the methods.

class methods—static methods that do not have a this reference (because they have no object associated with them).

class user—an application or class that instantiates objects of another prewritten class. See also *class client*.

class variables—static variables that are shared by every instantiation of a class.

class-level Javadoc comments—Javadoc comments that provide a description of a class and that should be placed above the code that declares a class.

clean build—a compilation that is created after deleting all previously compiled versions of a class.

clearRect() method—a method that draws a rectangle using the background color to create what appears to be an empty or "clear" rectangle.

client method—a method that calls another method.

close the file—to make a file no longer available to an application.

closer in scope—a term that describes the status of a local variable over others that it shadows.

collision—describes a class-naming conflict.

Color class—a class that defines built-in colors.

comes into scope—describes what happens to a variable when it is declared. Contrast with *goes out of scope*.

comma-separated values (CSV)—fields that are separated with a comma.

commands—program statements.

comment out—the technique of turning a program statement into a comment so the compiler will not execute its command.

compareTo() method—a String class method used to compare two Strings; the method returns a number that describes the differences between the Strings.

comparison operator—a relational operator.

compiler—a program that translates language statements into machine code. A compiler translates an entire program before executing it. Contrast with *interpreter*.

compile-time error—an error for which the compiler detects a violation of language syntax rules and is unable to translate the source code to machine code.

composition—describes the relationship between classes when an object of one class is a data field within another class. See also *has-a relationship*.

computer file—a collection of stored information in a computer system.

computer program—a set of instructions that tells a computer what to do; software.

computer simulations—programs that attempt to mimic real-world activities so that their processes can be improved or so that users can better understand how the real-world processes operate.

concatenated—describes values that are added onto the end of another value.

concatenation—the process of joining a variable to a string to create a longer string.

concrete class—a nonabstract class from which objects can be instantiated. Contrast with *abstract class*.

conditional operator—an operator that requires three expressions separated with a question mark and a colon; the operator is used as an abbreviated version of the `if . . . else` structure.

confirm dialog box—a window that can be created using the `showConfirmDialog()` method in the `JOptionPane` class and that displays the options Yes, No, and Cancel.

console applications—programs that support character output to a computer screen in a DOS window.

constant—describes values that cannot be changed during the execution of an application.

constructor—a method that establishes an object.

consume—to retrieve and discard an entry without using it.

container—a type of component that holds other components so they can be treated as a single entity.

containment hierarchy—a tree of components that has a top-level container as its root (that is, at its uppermost level).

content pane—a component that contains all the visible components in a top-level container's user interface.

copyArea() method—a method that copies any rectangular area to a new location.

counter-controlled loop—a definite loop. Contrast with *event-controlled loop*.

counting—the process of continually incrementing a variable to keep track of the number of occurrences of some event.

crash—a premature, unexpected, and inelegant end to a program.

cyclic gradient—a fill pattern in which a shift between colors occurs repeatedly between two points.

D

data fields—data variables declared in a class outside of any method.

data files—files that consist of related records that contain facts and figures, such as employee numbers, names, and salaries.

data type—describes the type of data that can be stored in a variable, how much memory the item occupies, and what types of operations can be performed on the data.

dead code—unreachable statements.

debugging—the process of locating and repairing a program's error.

decimal numbering system—the numbering system based on 10 digits, 0 through 9, in which each column value is 10 times the value of the column to its right.

DecimalFormat class—a class that provides ways to easily convert numbers into strings, allowing leading and trailing zeros, prefixes and suffixes, grouping (thousands) separators, and the decimal separator to be used for formatting.

decision structure—a logical structure that involves choosing between alternative courses of action based on some value within a program.

declaration—another name for a method header; also, the statement that assigns a data type and identifier to a variable.

decrementing—the act of subtracting 1 from a variable.

default constructor—a constructor that requires no arguments.

default package—the unnamed package in which a class is placed if no package is specified.

definite loop—a loop that executes a specific number of times; a counted loop. Contrast with *indefinite loop*.

derived class—a class that inherits from a base class.

descending order—the order of objects arranged from highest to lowest value. See also *ascending order*.

descent—one of three measures of a Font's height; it measures the part of characters that "hang below" the baseline, such as the tails on the lowercase letters g and j. See also *ascent* and *leading*.

destroy() method—a method invoked in an applet when the user closes the browser or Applet Viewer.

development environment—a set of tools that helps programmers by providing such features as displaying a language's keywords in color.

dialog box—a GUI object resembling a window that displays messages.

direct access files—random access files.

directories—elements in a storage organization hierarchy. See also *folders*.

divide and assign operator—an operator that alters the value of the operand on the left by dividing the operand on the right into it; it is composed of a slash and an equal sign (/=).

documentation comments—comments that automatically generate well-formatted program documentation.

do-nothing loop—a loop that performs no actions other than looping.

double—a data type that can hold a floating-point value of up to 14 or 15 significant digits of accuracy. Contrast with *float*.

double buffering—the default buffering strategy in which JPanels are drawn offscreen when they are updated and displayed only when complete.

Double class—a wrapper class that contains a simple double and useful methods to manipulate it.

double-precision floating-point number—a type of value that is stored in a double.

do...while loop—a loop that executes a loop body at least one time; it checks the loop control variable at the bottom of the loop after one repetition has occurred.

draw3DRect() method—a method that draws a rectangle that appears to have "shadowing" on two of its edges—the effect is that of a rectangle that is lit from the upper-left corner and slightly raised or slightly lowered.

drawArc() method—a method that draws an arc.

drawLine() method—a method that draws a straight line between two points on the screen.

drawOval() method—a method that draws an oval.

drawPolygon() method—a method that draws complex shapes.

drawRect() method—a method that draws the outline of a rectangle.

drawRoundRect() method—a method that draws rectangles with rounded corners.

drawString() method—a method that draws a String in a JFrame or other component.

dual-alternative if—a decision structure that takes one of two possible courses of action. Contrast with *single-alternative if*.

dummy values—values the user enters that are not "real" data but just signals to stop data entry.

dynamic method binding—the ability of an application to select the correct subclass method when the program executes. See also *late method binding*.

dynamically resizable—describes an object whose size can change during program execution.

E

echoing the input—the act of repeating the user's entry as output so the user can visually confirm the entry's accuracy.

editable—describes a component that can accept keystrokes.

element—one variable or object in an array.

else clause—the part of an if. . .else statement that executes when the evaluated Boolean expression is false.

else. . .if clause—a format used in nested if statements in which each instance of else and its subsequent if are placed on the same line.

empty body—a block with no statements in it.

empty statement—a statement that contains only a semicolon.

encapsulation—the act of hiding data and methods within an object.

endcap styles—styles applied to the ends of lines that do not join with other lines; they include CAP_BUTT, CAP_ROUND, and CAP_SQUARE.

endsWith() method—a String class method that takes a String argument and returns true or false if a String object does or does not end with the specified argument.

enhanced for loop—a language construct that cycles through an array without specifying the starting and ending points for the loop control variable.

enum constants—the allowed values for an enumerated data type.

enumerated data type—a programmer-created data type with a fixed set of values.

equals() method—an Object class method that takes a single argument, which must be the same type as the type of the invoking object, and returns a Boolean value indicating whether two object references are equal. The method is overridden in the String class to evaluate the contents of two String objects to determine if they are equivalent.

equalsIgnoreCase() method—a String class method that ignores case when determining if two Strings are equivalent.

equivalency operator—the operator composed of two equal signs that compares values and returns true if they are equal.

Error class—a class that represents more serious errors than the Exception class—those from which a program usually cannot recover.

escape sequence—a sequence that begins with a backslash followed by a character; the pair frequently represents a nonprinting character.

event—a result when a user takes action on a component.

event-controlled loop—an indefinite loop. Contrast with *counter-controlled loop*.

event-driven program—a program in which the user might initiate any number of events in any order.

event handler—a method that executes because it is called automatically when an appropriate event occurs.

exception—in object-oriented terminology, an unexpected or error condition.

Exception class—a class comprising less serious errors than those from the `Error` class; the `Exception` class represents unusual conditions that arise while a program is running, and from which the program can recover.

exception handling—an object-oriented technique for managing errors.

exception specification—the practice of using the keyword `throws` followed by an `Exception` type in the method header. An exception specification is required when a method throws a checked `Exception` that it will not catch but will be caught by a different method.

executing—the act of carrying out a program statement or program.

explicit conversion—the data type transformation caused by using a cast operator.

extended—describes classes that have descended from another class.

extends—a keyword used to achieve inheritance in Java.

Extensible Hypertext Markup Language (XHTML)—an extension of HTML.

F

factory methods—methods that assist in object creation.

FAQs—frequently asked questions.

fault-tolerant—describes applications that are designed so that they continue to operate, possibly at a reduced level, when some part of the system fails.

field—a data variable declared in a class outside of any method. In reference to storage, a group of characters that has some meaning.

file channel—an object that is an avenue for reading and writing a file.

Files class—a class used to perform operations on files and directories, such as deleting them, determining their attributes, and creating input and output streams.

fill patterns—patterns that describe how drawing objects are filled in.

fill3DRect() method—a method that creates filled, three-dimensional rectangles.

fillArc() method—a method that creates a solid arc.

fillOval() method—a method that draws a solid, filled oval.

fillPolygon() method—a method that draws a solid shape.

fillRect() method—a method that draws a solid, or filled, rectangle.

final—the keyword that precedes named constants, that describes superclass methods that cannot be overridden in a subclass, and that describes classes in which all methods are final.

finally block—a block of code that executes at the end of a `try...catch` sequence.

fixed method binding—the opposite of dynamic method binding; it occurs when a subclass method is selected while the program compiles rather than while it is running. See also *static method binding*.

float—a data type that can hold a floating-point value of up to six or seven significant digits of accuracy. Contrast with *double*.

floating-point—describes a number that contains decimal positions.

floating-point division—the operation in which two values are divided and either or both are floating-point values.

flowchart—a tool that helps programmers plan a program's logic by writing the steps in diagram form, as a series of shapes connected by arrows.

FlowLayout manager—a layout manager that arranges components in rows across the width of a Container; when the current row is filled, additional Components are placed in new rows. By default, the components in each row are centered.

flushing—an operation to clear bytes that have been sent to a buffer for output but that have not yet been output to a hardware device.

folders—elements in a storage organization hierarchy. See also *directories*.

Font class—a Java class that holds typeface and size information.

for loop—a loop that can be used when a definite number of loop iterations is required.

foreach loop—the enhanced for loop.

formal parameters—the variables in a method declaration that accept the values from actual parameters. Contrast with *actual parameters*.

format specifier—in a printf() statement, a placeholder for a numeric value.

format string—in a printf() statement, a string of characters that includes optional text (that is displayed literally) and one or more format specifiers.

fragile—describes classes that are prone to errors.

fully qualified identifier—describes a filename that includes the entire hierarchy in which a class is stored.

fundamental classes—basic classes contained in the java.lang package that are automatically imported into every program. Contrast with *optional classes*.

G

garbage value—the unknown value stored in an uninitialized variable.

generic programming—a feature of languages that allows methods to be used safely with multiple data types.

getAvailableFontFamilyNames() method—a method that returns the names of all available fonts.

getContentPane() method—a method that returns a reference to a container's content pane.

getDefaultToolkit() method—a method that provides information about the system in use.

getFontMetrics() method—a method that returns a FontMetrics object that contains information about the leading, ascent, descent, and height of a font.

getScreenResolution() method—a method that returns the screen resolution on the current system.

getScreenSize() method—a method that returns the screen size as a Dimension object.

getText() method—a method that retrieves the String of text in a Component.

glass pane—a pane that resides above the content pane in a container. It can contain tool tips.

goes out of scope—describes what happens to a variable at the end of the block in which it is declared. Contrast with *comes into scope*.

gradient fill—a gradual shift from one color at one coordinate point to a different color at a second coordinate point.

graphical user interfaces (GUIs)—environments that allow users to interact with a program in a graphical environment.

Graphics class—an abstract class that descends directly from `Object` and holds data about graphics operations and methods for drawing shapes, text, and images.

Graphics2D class—a class that provides tools for two-dimensional drawing.

GridBagLayout manager—a layout manager that allows the addition of `Components` to precise locations within the grid, as well as to indicate that specific `Components` should span multiple rows or columns within the grid.

GridLayout manager—a layout manager that divides a container surface into a grid.

H

hardware—the general term for computer equipment.

has-a relationship—a relationship based on composition.

hash code—a calculated number used to identify an object.

header—the first line of a method; its declaration.

heavyweight components—components that require interaction with the local operating system. Contrast with *lightweight components*.

height of a font—the sum of its leading, ascent, and descent.

hexadecimal numbering system—a numbering system based on 16 digits, 0 through F, in which each column represents a value 16 times higher than the column to its right.

high-level programming language—a language that uses a vocabulary of reasonable terms, such as "read," "write," or "add," instead of referencing the sequences of on and off switches that perform these tasks. Contrast with *low-level programming language*.

</html>—the tag that ends every HTML document.

<html>—the tag that begins every HTML document.

HTML, or Hypertext Markup Language—a simple language used to create Web pages for the Internet.

I

identifier—the name of a program component such as a class, object, or variable.

if clause—the part of an `if...else` statement that executes when the evaluated Boolean expression is true.

if...else statement—the statement that provides the mechanism to perform one action when a Boolean expression evaluates as `true`, and to perform a different action when a Boolean expression evaluates as `false`.

if statement—the single-alternative decision statement.

image—a likeness of a person or thing.

immutable—describes objects that cannot be changed.

implementation—the actions that execute within a method; the method body.

implementation hiding—a principle of object-oriented programming that describes the encapsulation of method details within a class.

implicit conversion—the automatic transformation of one data type to another. Also called *promotion*.

import statement—a Java statement that allows access to a built-in Java class that is contained in a package.

inclusion polymorphism—the situation in which a single method implementation can be used with a variety of related objects because they are objects of subclasses of the parameter type. See also *pure polymorphism*.

incrementing—the act of adding 1 to a variable.

indefinite loop—a loop in which the final number of iterations is unknown. Contrast with *definite loop*.

indexOf() method—a String class method that determines whether a specific character occurs within a String. If it does, the method returns the position of the character; the first position of a String begins with zero. The return value is −1 if the character does not exist in the String.

infinite loop—a loop that never ends.

information hiding—the object-oriented programming principle used when creating private access for data fields; a class's private data can be changed or manipulated only by a class's own methods, and not by methods that belong to other classes.

inheritance—a mechanism that enables one class to inherit, or assume, both the behavior and the attributes of another class.

init() method—the first method called in any applet.

initialization—the act of making an assignment at the time of variable declaration.

inlining—an automatic process that optimizes performance in which calls to final methods are replaced with the expanded code of their definitions at each method call location.

inner block—a block contained in an outer block. See also *inside block*.

inner classes—nested classes that require an instance. See also *nonstatic member classes*.

inner loop—a loop that is contained entirely within another loop.

input dialog box—a GUI object that asks a question and provides a text field in which the user can enter a response.

insert() method—a StringBuilder class method that adds characters at a specific location within a StringBuilder object.

inside block—a block contained in an outside block. See also *inner block*.

instance—an existing object of a class.

instance methods—methods used with object instantiations. See also *nonstatic methods*.

instance variables—the data components of a class.

instanceof operator—an operator that determines whether an object that is the operand on the left is a member or descendant of the class that is the operand on the right.

instantiate—to create an instance; to create an object.

instantiation—an object; one tangible example of a class.

int—the data type used to declare variables and constants that store integers in the range of −2,147,483,648 to +2,147,483,647.

integer—a whole number without decimal places.

Integer class—a wrapper class that contains a simple integer and useful methods to manipulate it.

integer division—the operation in which one integer value is divided by another; the result contains no fractional part.

interactive program—an application in which the user makes direct requests, as opposed to one in which input comes from a file.

interface—a construct similar to a class, except that all of its methods must be abstract and all of its data (if any) must be `static final`; it declares method headers but not the instructions within those methods. Also used to describe the part of a method that a client sees and uses—it includes the method's return type, name, and arguments.

interpreter—a program that translates language statements into machine code. An interpreter translates and executes one statement at a time. Contrast with *compiler*.

invoke—to call or execute a method.

is-a relationship—the relationship between an object and the class of which it is a member.

iteration—one loop execution.

J

JApplet—a `Swing` class that serves as the basis for inheritance for applets.

Java—a programming language developed by Sun Microsystems as an object-oriented language used both for general-purpose business applications and for interactive, World Wide Web–based Internet applications.

Java API—the application programming interface, a collection of information about how to use every prewritten Java class.

Java applications—stand-alone Java programs.

Java ARchive (JAR) file—a file that compresses the stored data.

Java Enterprise Edition (EE)—a Java edition that includes all of the classes in the Java SE, plus a number of classes that are more useful to programs running on servers.

Java Foundation Classes (JFC)—selected classes from the `java.awt` package, including `Swing` component classes.

Java interpreter—the program that checks bytecode and communicates with the operating system, executing the bytecode instructions line by line within the Java virtual machine.

Java Micro Edition (ME)—a Java platform that is used for small devices such as PDAs, cell phones, and other consumer appliances.

Java SE 7—the most recent version of Java. The full, official name is Java Platform, Standard Edition 7.

Java Virtual Machine (JVM)—a hypothetical (software-based) computer on which Java runs.

java.lang—the package that is implicitly imported into every Java program and that contains the fundamental classes.

Javadoc—a documentation generator that creates Application Programming Interface (API) documentation in Hypertext Markup Language (HTML) format from Java source code.

Javadoc comment—a special form of block comment that provides a standard way to document Java code.

Javadoc tag—a keyword within a comment that the Javadoc tool can process.

JButton—a Component the user can click with a mouse to make a selection.

JCheckBox—a UI component that consists of a label positioned beside a square; a user can click the square to display or remove a check mark. Usually, a JCheckBox is used to turn an option on or off.

JComboBox—a UI component that combines two features: a display area showing an option and a list box containing additional options. The display area contains either a button that a user can click or an editable field into which the user can type.

JDK—the Java Standard Edition Development Kit.

JFrame—a container with a title bar and border.

jGRASP—a development environment and source code editor.

JLabel—a built-in Java Swing class that holds displayable text.

JOptionPane—a Java class that produces dialog boxes.

JPanel—a plain, borderless surface that can hold lightweight UI components.

JScrollPane—a pane that provides scroll bars along the side or bottom, or both, so that the user can scroll initially invisible parts of the pane into view.

JTextField—a component into which a user can type a single line of text data.

juncture styles—styles applied to lines that join; they include JOIN_MITER, JOIN_ROUND, and JOIN_BEVEL.

K

K & R style—the indent style in which the opening brace follows the header line; it is named for Kernighan and Ritchie, who wrote the first book on the C programming language. Contrast with *Allman style*.

key field—the field in a record that makes the record unique from all others.

keyboard buffer—a small area of memory where keystrokes are stored before they are retrieved into a program. Also called the *type-ahead buffer*.

KeyListener interface—an interface that provides methods that respond to actions the user initiates from the keyboard. The KeyListener interface contains three methods—keyPressed(), keyTyped(), and keyReleased().

keywords—the words that are part of a programming language.

L

late method binding—the ability of an application to select the correct subclass method when the program executes. See also *dynamic method binding*.

layout manager—a class that controls component positioning in a UI environment.

leading—one of three measures of a Font's height; it is the amount of space between baselines. See also *ascent* and *descent*.

leaf menu item—a menu item that does not bring up another menu.

length field—a field that contains the number of elements in an array.

length() method—a String class method that returns the length of a String.

lexicographical comparison—a comparison based on the integer Unicode values of characters.

library of classes—a folder that provides a convenient grouping for classes. See also *package*.

lightweight components—components written completely in Java that do not have to rely on the code written to run in the local operating system. Contrast with *heavyweight components*.

line comments—comments that start with two forward slashes (//) and continue to the end of the current line. Line comments can appear on a line by themselves or at the end of a line following executable code. Contrast with *block comments*.

listener—an object that is interested in and reacts to an event.

literal constant—a value that is taken literally at each use. See also *unnamed constant*.

literal string—a series of characters that appear exactly as entered. Any literal string in Java appears between double quotation marks.

local classes—nested classes that are local to a block of code.

local variable—a variable known only within the boundaries of a method.

logic—describes the order of program statements that produce correct results.

logic error—an error that occurs when a program compiles successfully but produces an error during execution.

logical AND operator—an operator used between Boolean expressions to determine whether both are `true`. The AND operator is written as two ampersands (&&).

logical OR operator—an operator used between Boolean expressions to determine

whether either expression is `true`. The OR operator is written as two pipes (||).

long—the data type that holds very large integers, from −9,223,372,036,854,775,808 to 9,223,372,036,854,775,807.

look and feel—describes the default appearance and behavior of any user interface.

loop—a structure that allows repeated execution of a block of statements.

loop body—the block of statements that executes when the Boolean expression that controls the loop is `true`.

loop control variable—a variable whose value determines whether loop execution continues.

loop fusion—the technique of combining two loops into one.

lossless data compression—a set of rules that allows an exact replica of data to be reconstructed from a compressed version.

low-level programming language—a language that corresponds closely to a computer processor's circuitry. Contrast with *high-level programming language*. Compare with *machine language*.

lvalue—an expression that can appear on the left side of an assignment statement. Contrast with *rvalue*.

M

machine code—machine language.

machine language—circuitry-level language; a series of on and off switches. Compare with *low-level programming language*.

magic number—a value that does not have immediate, intuitive meaning or a number that cannot be explained without additional knowledge. Unnamed constants are magic numbers.

matrix—a two-dimensional array.

member-level Javadoc comments— Javadoc comments that describe the fields, methods, and constructors of a class.

menu bar—a horizontal strip that is placed at the top of a container and that contains user options.

menus—lists of user options.

method—a program module that contains a series of statements that carry out a task.

method body—the set of statements between curly braces that follow the method header and carry out the method's actions.

method header—the declaration or first line of a method that contains information about how other methods interact with it.

method's type—the method's return type.

mission critical—describes any process that is crucial to an organization.

mnemonic—a key that causes an already visible menu item to be chosen.

modulus operator—the percent sign; when it is used with two integers, the result is an integer with the value of the remainder after division takes place. Also called the *remainder operator*; sometimes called just *mod*.

MouseEvent—the type of event generated by mouse manipulation.

MouseInputListener interface—an interface that implements all the methods in both the MouseListener and MouseMotionListener interfaces.

MouseListener interface—an interface that provides methods named mousePressed(), mouseClicked(), and

mouseReleased() that are analogous to the keyboard event methods keyPressed(), keyTyped(), and keyReleased().

MouseMotionListener interface—an interface that provides methods named mouseDragged() and mouseMoved() that detect the mouse being rolled or dragged across a component surface.

multidimensional arrays—arrays that contain two or more dimensions.

multimedia—describes the use of sound, images, graphics, and video in computer programs.

multiple inheritance—the capability to inherit from more than one class; Java does not support multiple inheritance.

multiply and assign operator—an operator that alters the value of the operand on the left by multiplying the operand on the right by it; it is composed of an asterisk and an equal sign.

mutator methods—methods that set field values.

N

named constant—a named memory location whose value cannot change during program execution; in Java, its declaration includes the keyword final.

NaN—a three-letter abbreviation for "Not a number."

nested—describes the relationship of statements, blocks, or classes when one contains the other.

nested classes—classes contained in other classes.

nested if statements—describes if statements when one is contained within the other.

new operator—an operator that allocates the memory needed to hold an object.

nonstatic member classes—nested classes that require an instance. See also *inner classes*.

nonstatic methods—methods used with object instantiations. See also *instance methods*.

nonvolatile storage—storage that does not require power to retain information. Contrast with *volatile storage*.

NOT operator—the exclamation point (!); it negates the result of any Boolean expression.

null String—an empty `String` created by typing a set of quotes with nothing between them.

numeric constant—a number whose value is taken literally at each use.

O

object—an instance of a class.

Object class—a class defined in the `java.lang` package that is imported automati-cally into every Java program and that is the base class for all other Java classes.

object-oriented programming—a style of programming that involves creating classes, creating objects from those classes, and creating applications that use those objects. Contrast with *procedural programming*.

octothorpe—the pound sign.

one-dimensional array—an array that contains one column of values and whose elements are accessed using a single subscript. See also *single-dimensional array*.

open a file—the action that creates an object and associates a stream of bytes with it.

operand—a value used in an arithmetic statement.

operator precedence—the rules for the order in which parts of a mathematical expression are evaluated.

optional classes—classes that reside in packages that must be explicitly imported into programs. Contrast with *fundamental classes*.

out of bounds—describes a subscript that is not within the allowed range for an array.

outer block—a block that contains a nested block. See also *outside block*.

outer loop—a loop that contains another loop.

outside block—a block that contains a nested block. See also *outer block*.

overloading—describes using one term to indicate diverse meanings, or writing multiple methods with the same name but with different arguments.

override a method—the action in which a child class method takes precedence over one in the parent class that has the same name and argument list.

overrides—describes what a variable or method does to another with the same name when it takes precedence over the other variable.

P

package—a named collection or library of classes. See also *library of classes*.

paint() method—a method that runs when Java displays a screen and that is commonly overridden in programs that use graphics.

painting—the act of displaying or redisplaying a surface.

parallel array—an array with the same number of elements as another, and for which the values in corresponding elements are related.

parameters—data items received by a method.

parent class—a base class.

parse—to break into component parts; the process the compiler uses to divide source code into meaningful portions for analysis.

parseDouble() method—a Double class method that takes a String argument and returns its double value.

parseInt() method—an Integer class method that takes a String argument and returns its integer value.

parsing—the process the compiler uses to divide source code into meaningful portions for analysis.

Pascal casing—the style of using an uppercase letter to begin an identifier and to start each new word in an identifier. Contrast with *camel casing*. Compare to *upper camel casing*.

passed by reference—describes a variable passed to a method when the address is passed to the method. Contrast with *passed by value*.

passed by value—describes a variable passed to a method when a copy is made in the receiving method. Contrast with *passed by reference*.

passing arguments—the act of sending arguments to a method.

path—the complete list of the disk drive plus the hierarchy of directories in which a file resides.

Path class—a Java class used to work with file information, such as location, size, creation date, and whether the file exists.

path delimiter—the character used to separate path components.

pattern String—an argument passed to the DecimalFormat constructor that is composed of symbols that determine what a formatted number looks like.

permanent storage devices—hardware storage devices that retain data even when power is lost.

pixels—the picture elements, or tiny dots of light, that make up the image on a video monitor.

point size argument—an argument to the Font constructor that is an integer that represents about 1/72 of an inch.

polymorphism—the feature of languages that allows the same word to be interpreted correctly in different situations based on the context; the act of using the same method name to indicate different implementations.

populating an array—the act of providing values for all of the elements in an array.

postfix ++ or the **postfix increment operator**—an operator that is composed by placing two plus signs to the right of a variable; it evaluates the variable, then adds 1 to it. Contrast with *prefix ++*.

posttest loop—a loop in which the loop control variable is tested after the loop body executes. Contrast with *pretest loop*.

preferred size—a Component's default size.

prefix ++ or the **prefix increment operator**—an operator that is composed by placing two plus signs to the left of a variable; it adds 1 to the variable, then evaluates it. Contrast with *postfix ++*.

prefix and postfix decrement operators—operators that subtract 1 from a variable before and after evaluating it, respectively.

pretest loop—a loop in which the loop control variable is tested before the loop body executes. Contrast with *posttest loop*.

primary key—a unique identifier for data within a database.

primary surface—the visible screen surface during double buffering.

priming read or **priming input**—the first input statement prior to a loop that will execute subsequent input statements for the same variable.

primitive type—a simple data type. Java's primitive types are `byte`, `short`, `int`, `long`, `float`, `double`, `char`, and `boolean`.

private access—refers to a field that no other classes can access.

procedural programming—a style of programming in which sets of operations are executed one after another in sequence. Contrast with *object-oriented programming*.

procedures—sets of operations performed by a computer program.

program—a set of written computer instructions.

program comments—nonexecuting statements added to a Java file for the purpose of documentation.

program files—files that store software instructions.

program statements—similar to English sentences; they carry out the tasks that programs perform.

programmer-defined data type—a type that is created by a programmer and not built into the language; a class.

promotion—an implicit conversion.

prompt—a message that requests and describes user input.

property—an instance variable, field, or attribute of a class.

protected—a Java keyword that provides an intermediate level of security between `public` and `private` access. Protected members are those that can be used by a class and its descendants.

pseudocode—a tool that helps programmers plan a program's logic by writing plain English statements.

pseudorandom—describes numbers that appear to be random but are the same set of numbers whenever the seed is the same.

pure polymorphism—the situation in which a single method implementation can be used with a variety of related objects because they are objects of subclasses of the parameter type. See also *inclusion polymorphism*.

R

ragged array—a two-dimensional array that has rows of different lengths.

random access files—files in which records can be located in any order.

random access memory (RAM)—temporary, volatile storage.

random number—a number whose value cannot be predicted.

range check—a series of statements that determine within which of a set of ranges a value falls.

range match—the process of comparing a value to the endpoints of numerical ranges to find a category in which the value belongs.

real-time—describes applications that require a record to be accessed immediately while a client is waiting.

record—a collection of fields that contains data about an entity.

redeclare a variable—to attempt to declare a variable twice—an illegal action.

reference—a variable that holds a memory address.

reference to an object—the name for a memory address where the object is held.

reference types—objects that hold memory addresses.

regionMatches() method—a String class method that compares two String regions.

relational operator—an operator that compares two items; an expression that contains a relational operator has a Boolean value.

relative path—a path that depends on other path information to be complete.

remainder and assign operator—an operator that alters the value of the operand on the left by assigning the remainder when the left operand is divided by the right operand; it is composed of a percent sign and an equal sign (%=).

remainder operator—the percent sign; when it is used with two integers, the result is an integer with the value of the remainder after division takes place. Also called the *modulus operator*.

remove() method—a method that removes components from a container.

repaint() method—a method that executes when a window needs to be updated, such as when it contains new images.

replace() method—a String class method that replaces all occurrences of a specified character within a String.

rerender—to repaint or redisplay a drawing.

return a value—to send a data value from a called method back to the calling method.

return statement—a statement that ends a method and frequently sends a value from a called method back to the calling method.

return type—the type of data that, upon completion of a method, is sent back to its calling method.

robustness—describes the degree to which a system is resilient to stress, maintaining correct functioning.

root directory—the main directory of a storage device, outside any folders.

runtime error—an error that occurs when a program compiles successfully but does not execute.

runtime exceptions—unplanned exceptions that occur during a program's execution. The term is also used more specifically to describe members of the RuntimeException class.

rvalue—an expression that can appear only on the right side of an assignment statement. Contrast with *lvalue*.

S

sandbox—a safe area in which a program can run without causing harm to other areas of a system.

scalar—describes simple, primitive variables, such as int, double, or char.

scientific notation—a display format that more conveniently expresses large or small numeric values; a multidigit number is converted to a single-digit number and multiplied by 10 to a power.

scope—in reference to a variable, the portion of a program within which the variable exists and can be referenced.

SDK—a software development kit, or a set of tools useful to programmers; the Java EE Development Kit.

searching an array—the process of comparing a value to a list of values in an array, looking for a match.

seed—a starting value.

seekable—describes a file channel in which operations can start at any specified position.

semantic errors—the type of errors that occur when a correct word is used in the wrong context in program code.

sequence structure—a logical structure in which one step follows another unconditionally.

sequential access file—a data file in which each record is stored in order, based on the value in some field.

setCharAt() method—a `StringBuilder` class method that changes a character at a specified position within a `StringBuilder` object.

setEditable() method—a method that changes the editable status of a `JTextField`.

setEnabled() method—a method that makes a component available or dimmed and unavailable.

setFont() method—a method that changes a `JLabel`'s font.

setLength() method—a `StringBuilder` class method that changes the length of the characters in the `String` in a `StringBuilder` object.

setLocation() method—a method that places a component at a specific location within a `JFrame`'s content pane.

setStroke() method—a Java 2D method that alters a stroke's width.

setText() method—a method that changes the text in a `Component` that has already been created.

setToolTipText() method—a method that defines the text to be displayed in a tool tip.

shadowing—the action that occurs when a local variable hides a variable with the same name that is further away in scope.

short—the data type that holds small integers, from −32,768 to 32,767.

short-circuit evaluation—describes the feature of the AND and OR operators in which evaluation is performed only as far as necessary to make a final decision.

showInputDialog() method—a method that creates an input dialog box.

signature—a method's name and the number, types, and order of arguments.

significant digits—refers to the mathematical accuracy of a value.

single-alternative `if`—a decision structure that performs an action, or not, based on one alternative. Contrast with *dual-alternative `if`*.

single-dimensional array—an array that contains one column of values and whose elements are accessed using a single subscript. See also *one-dimensional array*.

single-precision floating-point number—a type of value that is stored in a `float`.

software—the general term for computer programs.

sorting—the process of arranging a series of objects in some logical order.

source—a component on which an event is generated.

source code—programming statements written in a high-level programming language.

stack trace history list, or more simply **stack trace**—a list that displays all the methods that were called during program execution.

standard arithmetic operators—operators that are used to perform common calculations.

standard input device—normally the keyboard.

standard output device—normally the monitor.

start() method—a method that executes after the init() method in an applet and executes again every time the applet becomes active after it has been inactive.

startsWith() method—a String class method that takes a String argument and returns true or false if a String object does or does not start with the specified argument, respectively.

state—the values of the attributes of an object.

static—a keyword that means a method is accessible and usable even though no objects of the class exist.

static member class—a type of nested class that has access to all static methods of its top-level class.

static method binding—the opposite of dynamic method binding; it occurs when a subclass method is selected while the program compiles rather than while it is running. See also *fixed method binding*.

stop() method—a method invoked in an applet when a user leaves a Web page (perhaps by minimizing a window or traveling to a different Web page).

stream—a pipeline or channel through which bytes flow into and out of an application.

String class—a class used to work with fixed-string data—that is, unchanging data composed of multiple characters.

String variable—a named object of the String class.

StringBuilder and **StringBuffer classes**—classes used to store and manipulate changeable data composed of multiple characters that are used as alternatives to the String class.

stringWidth() method—a FontMetrics class method that returns the integer width of a String.

stroke—a line-drawing feature in Java 2D that represents a single movement using a drawing tool similar to a pen or pencil.

strongly typed language—a language in which all variables must be declared before they can be used.

stub—a method that contains no statements; programmers create stubs as temporary placeholders during the program development process.

style argument—an argument to the Font constructor that applies an attribute to displayed text and is one of three values: Font.PLAIN, Font.BOLD, or Font.ITALIC.

subclass—a derived class.

subscript—an integer contained within square brackets that indicates one of an array's variables, or elements.

substring() method—a String class method that extracts part of a String.

subtract and assign operator—an operator that alters the value of the operand on the left by subtracting the operand on the right from it; it is composed of a minus sign and an equal sign (−=).

subtype polymorphism—the ability of one method name to work appropriately for different subclasses of a parent class.

super—a Java keyword that always refers to a class's immediate superclass.

superclass—a base class.

Swing components—UI elements such as dialog boxes and buttons; their names usually begin with *J*.

switch statement—a statement that uses up to four keywords to test a single variable against a series of exact integer or character values. The keywords are switch, case, break, and default.

symbolic constant—a named constant.

syntactic salt—describes a language feature designed to make it harder to write bad code.

syntactic sugar—describes aspects of a computer language that make it "sweeter," or easier, for programmers to use.

syntax—the rules of a language.

syntax error—a programming error that occurs when a program contains typing errors or incorrect language use. A program containing syntax errors will not compile.

system software—the set of programs that manage the computer. Contrast with *application software*.

System.out.printf() method—a method used to format numeric values.

system-triggered painting—painting operations that occur when the system asks a component to render its contents. Contrast with *application-triggered painting*.

T

table—a two-dimensional array; a matrix.

tag attributes—arguments that promote activity or describe the features of an HTML tag.

tags—HTML commands.

ternary operator—an operator that needs three operands.

text files—files that contain data that can be read in a text editor because the data has been encoded using a scheme such as ASCII or Unicode.

this reference—a reference to an object that is passed to any object's nonstatic class method.

threads of execution—units of processing that are scheduled by an operating system and that can be used to create multiple paths of control during program execution.

throw statement—a statement that sends an Exception out of a block or a method so it can be handled elsewhere.

TOCTTOU bug—an error that occurs when changes take place from Time Of Check To Time Of Use.

token—a unit of data; the Scanner class separates input into tokens.

toLowerCase() method—a String class method that converts any String to its lowercase equivalent.

tool tips—popup windows that can help a user understand the purpose of components in an application; a tool tip appears when a user hovers a mouse pointer over the component.

top-level class—the containing class in nested classes.

top-level container—a container at the top of a containment hierarchy. The Java top-level containers are `JFrame`, `JDialog`, and `JApplet`.

toString() method—an `Object` class method that converts an `Object` into a `String` that contains information about the `Object`. Also, a `String` class method that converts any object to a `String`.

toUpperCase() method—a `String` class method that converts any `String` to its uppercase equivalent.

try block—a block of code that a programmer acknowledges might generate an exception.

two-dimensional array—an array that contains two or more columns of values and whose elements are accessed using multiple subscripts. Contrast with *one-dimensional array*.

type-ahead buffer—the keyboard buffer.

type casting—an action that forces a value of one data type to be used as a value of another type.

type conversion—the process of converting one data type to another.

typeface argument—an argument to the `Font` constructor that is a `String` representing a font. Common fonts have names such as Arial, Century, Monospaced, and Times New Roman.

type-safe—describes a data type for which only appropriate behaviors are allowed.

type-wrapper classes—a method that can process primitive type values.

U

UI components—user interface components, such as buttons and text fields, with which the user can interact.

unary cast operator—a more complete name for the cast operator that performs explicit conversions.

unary operator—an operator that uses only one operand.

unchecked exceptions—exceptions that cannot reasonably be expected to be recovered from while a program is executing. Contrast with *checked exceptions*.

Unicode—an international system of character representation.

Unified Modeling Language (UML)—a graphical language used by programmers and analysts to describe classes and object-oriented processes.

unifying type—a single data type to which all operands in an expression are converted.

uninitialized variable—a variable that has been declared but that has not been assigned a value.

unnamed constant—a constant value that has no identifier associated with it. See also *literal constant*.

unreachable statements—statements that cannot be executed because the logical path can never encounter them; in some languages, including Java, an unreachable statement causes a compiler error. See also *dead code*.

upcast—to change an object to an object of a class higher in its inheritance hierarchy.

upper camel casing—Pascal casing.

V

validating data—the process of ensuring that a value falls within a specified range.

variable—a named memory location whose contents can be altered during program execution.

variable declaration—a statement that reserves a named memory location.

viewport—the viewable area in a JScrollPane.

virtual classes—the name given to abstract classes in some other programming languages, such as C++.

virtual key codes—codes that represent keyboard keys that have been pressed.

virtual method calls—method calls in which the method used is determined when the program runs, because the type of the object used might not be known until the method executes. In Java, all instance method calls are virtual calls by default.

void—a keyword that, when used in a method header, indicates that the method does not return any value when it is called.

volatile storage—memory that requires power to retain information. Contrast with *nonvolatile storage*.

W

Web browser—a program that displays HTML documents on the screen.

while loop—a construct that executes a body of statements continually as long as the Boolean expression that controls entry into the loop continues to be true.

whitespace—any combination of nonprinting characters; for example, spaces, tabs, and carriage returns (blank lines).

wildcard symbol—a symbol used to indicate that it can be replaced by any set of characters. In Java, the wildcard symbol is an asterisk; in an import statement, the wildcard symbol represents all the classes in a package.

window decorations—the icons and buttons that are part of a window or frame.

windowed applications—programs that create a graphical user interface (GUI) with elements such as menus, toolbars, and dialog boxes.

wrapped—to be encompassed in another type.

wrapper—a class or object that is "wrapped around" a simpler element.

"write once, run anywhere" (WORA)—a slogan developed by Sun Microsystems to describe the ability of one Java program version to work correctly on multiple platforms.

X

x-axis—an imaginary horizontal line that indicates screen position.

x-coordinate—a position value that increases from left to right across a window.

XHTML—Extensible Hypertext Markup Language, an extension of HTML.

Y

y-axis—an imaginary vertical line that indicates screen position.

y-coordinate—a position value that increases from top to bottom across a window.

Index

Note: Page numbers in **boldface** refer to definitions of key terms.